Generations of Feeling

Generations of Feeling is the first book to provide a comprehensive history of emotions in pre- and early-modern Western Europe. Charting the varieties, transformations, and constants of human sentiments over the course of eleven centuries, Barbara H. Rosenwein explores the feelings expressed in a wide range of "emotional communities," as well as the theories that served to inform and reflect their times. Focusing particularly on groups within England and France, chapters address communities as diverse as the monastery of Rievaulx in twelfth-century England and the ducal court of fifteenth-century Burgundy, assessing the ways in which emotional norms and modes of expression respond to, and in turn create, their social, religious, ideological, and cultural environments. Contemplating emotions experienced "on the ground" as well as those theorized in the treatises of Alcuin, Thomas Aquinas, Jean Gerson, and Thomas Hobbes, this insightful study offers a profound new narrative of emotional life in the West.

Barbara H. Rosenwein is Professor Emerita, Department of History, Loyola University Chicago.

Generations of Feeling

A History of Emotions, 600–1700

Barbara H. Rosenwein

Loyola University Chicago

CAMBRIDGE
UNIVERSITY PRESS

CAMBRIDGE
UNIVERSITY PRESS

University Printing House, Cambridge CB2 8BS, United Kingdom

Cambridge University Press is part of the University of Cambridge.

It furthers the University's mission by disseminating knowledge in the pursuit of education, learning and research at the highest international levels of excellence.

www.cambridge.org
Information on this title: www.cambridge.org/9781107480841

First published 2016

Printed in the United States of America by Sheridan Books, Inc.

A catalog record for this publication is available from the British Library

Library of Congress Cataloging in Publication data
Rosenwein, Barbara H., author.
Generations of feeling : a history of emotions, 600–1700 / Barbara H. Rosenwein.
   pages   cm
Includes bibliographical references and index.
ISBN 978-1-107-09704-9
1. Emotions – History. 2. Emotions (Philosophy) – History. I. Title.
BF531.R6825   2016
152.409–dc23

                         2015014696

ISBN HB 978-1-107-09704-9
ISBN PB 978-1-107-48084-1

For Tom

The human world provides a spectacle
convulsive with opposing desires and contending wills.

Geoffrey O'Brien, "Balzac on the Brink"

Contents

List of plates   *page* viii
List of figures   ix
List of maps and genealogies   x
List of tables   xi
Prefatory note   xiii
Acknowledgments   xiv
List of abbreviations   xvi

Introduction   1

1 Ancient theories   16

2 Attachment and detachment   35

3 Alcuin's therapy   67

4 Love and treachery   88

5 Thomas' passions   144

6 Theatricality and sobriety   169

7 Gerson's music   227

8 Despair and happiness   248

9 Hobbes' motions   288

   Conclusion   314

   Bibliography   322
   Index   359

Plates

1.1 An early icon of friendship in Christ   *page* 26
3.1 A Carolingian image of wisdom   77
6.1 Wauquelin's "piteous words"   180
6.2 Jean de la Huerta's mourner   188
6.3 and 6.4 Christ's Passion at Norwich   208
7.1 and 7.2 Gerson's *canticordum* as a cross   240
9.1 *Leviathan* title page, sketch for Charles II   296
9.2 *Leviathan* frontispiece (1651)   302

Figures

4.1 Aelred's two forms of *amor*   *page* 96
5.1 Aquinas' body-soul composite   148
5.2 Aquinas' sequence of the concupiscible passions   153
5.3 Aquinas' sequence of the concupiscible and irascible passions   154
7.1 The hexachord system   237
7.2 Gerson's hand of the passions   238
7.3 Gerson's cross of the passions   239

Maps and genealogies

Maps

2.1 Early medieval Francia   *page* 36
4.1 England and France in the twelfth and thirteenth
    centuries   92
6.1 France, England, and Burgundy in the fifteenth
    century   171

Genealogical Tables

2.1 The Merovingians (simplified)   50
6.1 The Pastons   212

Tables

1.1	Cicero's genera of *perturbationes animi*	*page* 18
1.2	Cicero's *constantiae*	18
1.3	Cicero's *aegritudines*	19
1.4	Cicero's *perturbationes* (apart from the *aegritudines*)	20
1.5	Cicero's "good" emotions	23
1.6	Augustine's emotion words	33
3.1	Alcuin's emotion words	82
3.2	Alcuin's emotion words enhanced	84
4.1	Old Occitan words associated with *cor*	121
4.2	Old Occitan emotional vocabulary at the Toulouse court	122
4.3	Emotion words in the *acta*	126
5.1	Aquinas' concupiscible and irascible passions	150
5.2	Aquinas' *passiones animae*	156
5.3	The moral virtues that regulate Aquinas' passions and affections	166
6.1	Emotions associated with the heart in Monstrelet, *Chronique*	176
6.2	Enhanced list of emotions associated with the heart in Monstrelet, *Chronique*	186
6.3	Margery's heart-felt terms and those associated with them	196
6.4	Margery's typical emotional sequence	205
6.5	Paston emotion words	216
7.1	The Stoic emotional grid	230
7.2	Gerson's terms of pain and sorrow	231
7.3	Gerson's list of the passions of animals and men	235
7.4	Names of the voices of Gerson's *canticordum*	244
8.1	Bright's "primitive" and "derivative" emotions	257
8.2	Burton's emotions	262
8.3	General sequence of emotions in *Spirituall Experiences*	268
8.4	Emotions valued and devalued by Walker	274
8.5	A Leveller list of vices	278
9.1	Hobbes' motions in the *Leviathan*	294
9.2	Hobbes' passions in "life's race to get ahead"	305

Prefatory note

I have regularized the use of *i/j* and *u/v* in Latin quotations in accordance with the guidelines of H. A. Kelly, "Uniformity and Sense in Editing and Medieval Texts," in *Medieval Academy News* (Spring 2004), 8: I use the *i* and *u* for the vowel sound and *j* and *v* for the consonant sound. However, I have not regularized other orthography, nor have I changed the punctuation of the editions that I use.

In note citations I normally leave out p. (standing for page number) unless the citation involves a series of numbers (chapter, section, and so on), in which case the p. is used.

I do not ordinarily cite the full original Latin of Latin-language sources in my notes. However, I include relevant Latin terms in my translations. I do give the original texts of Moyen français, Old Occitan, and Middle English in the notes. All translations are my own unless otherwise noted, but I have taken into account (and herewith express my gratitude for) numerous modern translations.

Acknowledgments

I began this project nearly ten years ago. My debts range from chance meetings, emails, and papers as much as they do from solicited advice, invitations, and critical readings. In short, this book owes so much to so many people that it is impossible for me to name and thank them all. Some of those who helped me will find their names in fitting places in chapter footnotes. I hope that others will forgive me if I have left out their names. Although their names are perhaps omitted, their impact remains very real and very much appreciated.

Here I will limit myself to thanking four people who have sustained me in ways more than I can say throughout the long process of writing this book.

My first debt is to Riccardo Cristiani. I first met him when he was a doctoral student at the University of Bologna. He eventually became my research assistant. In the course of our work together, he has become a collaborator. He has an amazing knack for seeing problems in argument and exposition, for doubting (and being right to doubt) the accuracy or the completeness of a point, and for critiquing weak translations and paraphrasing. He identified new and essential bibliography for me to read. Via email and Skype and even more intensely when we got together in person, we discussed the emotional consequences of mankind's Fall from Paradise; hammered out the differences between one theorist and another; disagreed (until we agreed) about the contents of chapter introductions; and worried about the suitability of words, phrases, and formulations. Together we wrote the first half of Chapter 4 on Aelred and all of Chapter 5 on Thomas Aquinas. Together we laughed and anguished over passages of reading and writing. In addition to all of that, Riccardo did the essential "little things" that make or break a book: proofreading, preparing the genealogies, maps, figures, bibliography, and index – even checking to be sure that my commas and periods were in the right places. Rather than thank him separately in each chapter, which might seem merely repetitive, I want here to say that there is nothing in this book that does not bear witness to his incisive input.

Lester K. Little has been my mentor and colleague throughout my career. Indeed, he inspired that career. It was Lester who first made clear to me that one could talk about feelings in history without being anachronistic: as an undergraduate, I sat enthralled in his classroom as he talked about how medieval Christians projected their anxieties onto Jews. We have collaborated often both formally and informally, and the latter is the case for this book, of which Lester read and critiqued a near-final draft. I am deeply indebted to him.

Dominique Iogna-Prat has been my intellectual companion since I began work, years ago, on the monastery of Cluny. He and I subsequently changed our focus almost simultaneously, he looking at social and ecclesial theory across the medieval and early modern divide, I doing much the same for emotions. After reading the entire manuscript of this book in draft, Dominique offered numerous observations and suggestions. Extraordinarily attuned to continuities and transformations, he saw connections and gaps that had never occurred to me. I am very grateful.

Finally, I thank my husband, Tom. For years he has lived with this book in the process of becoming and a wife eternally at her desk. He has been unfailingly supportive in every way. In the interstices of his own busy law practice, he has done the laundry, washed the dishes, and purchased the groceries. He has listened to me complain, gush with enthusiasm, and wallow in misery about theorists, courts, and churchmen. When the manuscript was finished in draft, he read it, offering me both feedback and encouragement. I dedicate the book to him.

Let me end with some institutions and people who helped me continuously with this project: Loyola University Chicago, its library (above all Interlibrary Loan Librarian Jennifer Stegen), and its Department of History (above all chairmen Timothy Gilfoyle and Robert Bucholz); and Cambridge University Press (especially Elizabeth Friend-Smith, Amanda George, Katherine Law, and Rebecca Taylor).

To all, my grateful thanks.

Abbreviations

Aelred,	Aelred of Rievaulx
BS	*De bello standardii*, ed. J.-P. Migne
Gen.	*Genealogia Regis Anglie Henrici iunioris*, ed. J.-P. Migne
Inclus.	*De institutione inclusarum*, in *OO*, 637–682
Lament	*Eulogium Davidis regis Scotorum*, in *Pinkerton's Lives of the Scottish Saints*, ed. William M. Metcalfe
OO	*Aelredi Rievallensis. Opera Omnia*, 1: *Opera ascetica* ed. Anselme Hoste and Charles H. Talbot
SA	*De spiritali amicitia*, in *OO*, 287–350
Spec. car.	*De speculo caritatis*, in *OO*, 3–161
Aimeric de Belenoi	Aimeric de Belenoi, *Le Poesie*, ed. and trans. Andrea Poli
Alcuin,	Alcuin of York
DR	*Disputatio de rhetorica et de virtutibus sapientissimi Regis Caroli et Albini magistri*, in *The Rhetoric of Alcuin and Charlemagne*, ed. and trans. Wilbur Samuel Howell
DVV	*De virtutibus et vitiis liber ad Widonem comitem*, ed. J.-P. Migne
Ep.	*Epistolae*, ed. Ernst Dümmler
Aquinas,	Thomas Aquinas
ST	*Summa theologiae*, in *Corpus Thomisticum*, ed. Enrique Alarcón
Super Sent.	*Scriptum super Sententiis*, in *Corpus Thomisticum*, ed. Enrique Alarcón

Augustine,	Augustine of Hippo
Civ. dei	*De civitate dei*, ed. Bernard Dombart and Alphonse Kalb
Conf.	*Confessions*, ed. and trans. Pierre de Labriolle
Lib. arb.	*De libero arbitrio*, in *Il "De Libero Arbitrio" di S. Agostino*, ed. and trans. Franco De Capitani
Tractatus	*Commentaire de la première épître de S. Jean*, ed. and trans. Paul Agaësse
Bernart	*The Songs of Bernart de Ventadorn*, ed. and trans. Stephen G. Nichols, Jr. et al.
BMK	*The Book of Margery Kempe*, ed. Sanford Brown Meech and Hope Emily Allen
Cadenet	*Les Poésies du troubadour Cadenet*, ed. and trans. Josef Zemp
Cat. Rai.	*Catalogues raimondins (1112–1229). Actes des comtes de Toulouse, ducs de Narbonne et marquis de Provence*, ed. Laurent Macé
CCCM	Corpus Christianorum. Continuatio Mediaevalis
CCSL	Corpus Cristianorum. Series Latina
Chanson	*Chanson de la Croisade albigeoise*, ed. and trans. Eugène Martin-Chabot
Cicero,	Marcus Tullius Cicero
DA	*Laelius: de Amicitia*, trans. William Armistead Falconer
TD	*M. Tulli Ciceronis Tusculanae Disputationes*, ed. Michaelangelus Giusta
CSEL	Corpus Scriptorum Ecclesiasticorum Latinorum
DLFMA	*Dictionnaire des lettres françaises: Le Moyen Age*

DNB   *Oxford Dictionary of National Biography*

EEBO   Early English Books Online

FQ   Edmund Spenser, *The Faerie Queene*, ed.
                                 A. C. Hamilton, 2d rev. ed. Hiroshi
                                 Yamashita and Toshiyuki Suzuki

Gaucelm Faidit   *Les poèmes de Gaucelm Faidit. Troubadour
                                 du XIIe siècle*, ed. and trans. Jean
                                 Mouzat

George, *A Latin Poet*   Judith W. George. *Venantius Fortunatus:
                                 A Latin Poet in Merovingian Gaul*

Gerson,   Jean Gerson
    CP   *Canticordum au pélerin*, in *La doctrine du
                                 chant du Coeur de Jean Gerson*, ed. and
                                 trans. Isabelle Fabre
    DP long   *De passionibus animae*, in OC, 9:1–25
    DP short   *De passionibus animae*, in OC, 9:155–57
    EP   *Enumeratio peccatorum ab Alberto posita*,
                                 in OC, 9:160–66
    OC   *Oeuvres complètes*, ed. Palémon Glorieux
    TC   *Tractatus de canticis*, in *La doctrine du
                                 chant du Coeur de Jean Gerson*, ed.
                                 and trans. Isabelle Fabre

Greg. Tur.,   Gregory of Tours
    Histories   *Historiarum libri X*, ed. Bruno Krusch
                                 and Wilhelm Levison
    VP   *Liber vitae patrum*, ed. Bruno Krusch

Hobbes,   Thomas Hobbes
    Lev.   *Leviathan*, ed. J. C. A. Gaskin
    OL   *Thomas Hobbes Malmesburiensis opera
                                 philosophica quae latine scripsit, omnia
                                 in unum corpus nunc primum collecta*,
                                 ed. William Molesworth

La Marche   Olivier de La Marche, *Mémoires*, ed.
                                 Henri   Beaune   and   Jean
                                 d'Arbaumont

LB   *The Holy Bible … made from the Latin
                                 Vulgate by John Wycliffe and his*

	Followers, ed. Josiah Forshall and Frederic Madden
Lefèvre	Jean Lefèvre, *Chronique*, ed. François Morand
Loeb, "Le relations thesis"	Ariane Loeb, "Les relations entre les troubadours et les comtes de Toulouse (1112–1229)." M.A. Thesis
MGH	Monumenta Germaniae Historica
AA	*Auctores antiquissimi*
SRM	*Scriptores rerum Merovingicarum*
SS	*Scriptores (in Folio)*
Monstrelet	Enguerrand Monstrelet, *Chronique*, ed. L. Douët-D'Arcq
Paston	*Paston Letters and Papers of the Fifteenth Century*, pts. 1 and 2, ed. Norman Davis, pt. 3, ed. Richard Beadle and Colin Richmond
Peire Vidal	Peire Vidal, *Poesie*, ed. Silvio Avalle d'Arco
PL	Patrologia Latina, ed. J.-P. Migne
Raimon de Miraval	*Les poésies du troubadour Raimon de Miraval*, ed. and trans. L. T. Topsfield
RB	*The Rule of Saint Benedict*, ed. and trans. Bruce L. Venarde
SC	Sources chrétiennes
SE	*Spirituall experiences, of sundry beleevers. Held forth by them at severall solemne meetings, and Conferences to that end. With the recommendation of the sound, spiritual, and savoury worth of them, to the sober and spirituall Reader, By Vavasor Powel, Minister of the Gospel*
Staley	*The Book of Margery Kempe*, trans. Lynn Staley

VA

Walter Daniel, *The Life of Ailred of Rievaulx*, ed. and trans. Frederick M. Powicke

WW

The Writings of William Walwyn, ed. Jack R. McMichael and Barbara Taft

Introduction

How can there be a history of emotions? In today's scientific world, psychologists and neuropsychologists generally consider human emotions to be universal and "hard-wired." Thus, for example, fear in all its manifestations today – as a facial grimace, as a bodily reaction, as a product of specific brain systems, or as a chemical process – is assumed to have been the same in the past.[1] Evolutionary psychologists Leda Cosmides and John Tooby claim that the human mind today has not changed since the Stone Age. "Our modern skulls house a stone age mind," is their curt summary.[2] How indeed can there be a history of emotions?

What are emotions?

Although many scientists today think of emotions as universal, biological, and invariable, this is not true of all. For example, some neuroscientists today think that emotions are as much products of top-down processing (in which case they depend on cognitive work) as of bottom-up (in which case they are connected to precognitive, automatic biological responses).[3] That view suggests that socialization affects emotions because it helps

[1] For the facial expression of fear, the classic article, now the basis for thousands of studies, is Paul Ekman and Wallace V. Friesen, "Constants across Cultures in the Face and Emotion," *Journal of Personality and Social Psychology* 17 (1971): 124–29. For bodily reactions in the autonomic nervous system, see Robert W. Levenson, "Blood, Sweat, and Fears: The Autonomic Architecture of Emotion," *Annales of the New York Academy of Sciences* 1000 (2003): 348–66. For the brain's role in fear, see M. C. Carvalho et al., "Participation of NK1 Receptors of the Amygdala on the Processing of Different Types of Fear," *Neurobiology of Learning and Memory* 102 (2013): 20–27, where the amygdala and related brain regions are involved in filtering and expressing fear. To be sure, these sorts of studies only rarely take up the past explicitly, but like all scientific experiments they are meant to describe unchanging laws.

[2] Leda Cosmides and John Tooby, "Evolutionary Psychology: A Primer" (1997), online at www.cep.ucsb.edu/primer.html.

[3] See, for example, Christine L. Larson et al., "The Interplay of Attention and Emotion: Top-Down Attention Modulates Amygdala Activation in Psychopathy," *Cognitive, Affective & Behavioral Neuroscience* 13/4 (2013): 757–70; Benjamin Otto et al.,

1

determine what is – and what is not – relevant to one's goals and values, which are aspects of cognition.[4] On another front, a recent book by evolutionary biologist Marlene Zuk argues that change in whole populations can take place in a very short period of time under the right circumstances.[5] The "Stone Age" mind disappears if this is true. It is thus very unlikely that emotions are invariable.

But what are emotions? In 1981 researchers attempting to make sense of the welter of current definitions of emotions tried (to little effect) to find a common denominator.[6] Many experimental psychologists and neuropsychologists today cling to the series of photographed faces developed by Paul Ekman and said to represent the expression of the six universal basic emotions: anger, disgust, fear, happiness, sadness, and surprise. But many other researchers are unconvinced, emphasizing the experiential nature of emotions, a characteristic entirely lacking in the posed faces of Ekman's photos.[7] Thomas Dixon has shown that the very category of "emotion" is relatively recent, tracing the ways in which a great variety of passions and sentiments were brought together under the practical but limited term "emotion."[8] Ute Frevert and her colleagues have demonstrated that notions about emotions – their location, their importance, their associations with gender, civility, and society – have been in constant flux since the eighteenth century.[9] This book will show that the same was true long before that.

"Functional Overlap of Top-Down Emotion Regulation and Generation: An fMRI Study Identifying Common Neural Substrates between Cognitive Reappraisal and Cognitively Generated Emotions," *Cognitive, Affective & Behavioral Neuroscience* 14/3 (2014): 923–38, "Everyday emotions likely consist of a blend of bottom-up processing of emotional stimuli and the top-down interpretation of self-relevant situations" (924).

[4] See *The Psychological Construction of Emotion*, ed. Lisa Feldman Barrett and James A. Russell (New York, 2015), and Jennifer Greenwood, "Wide Externalism and the Roles of Biology and Culture in Human Emotional Development," *Emotion Review* 4 (2012): 423–31.

[5] Marlene Zuk, *Paleofantasy: What Evolution Really Tells Us about Sex, Diet, and How We Live* (New York, 2013).

[6] Paul R. Kleinginna, Jr. and Anne M. Kleinginna, "A Categorized List of Emotion Definitions, with Suggestions for a Consensual Definition," *Motivation and Emotion* 5 (1981): 345–79.

[7] For the original article introducing the six, see Ekman and Friesen, "Constants across Cultures"; for illustrations of faces posed to show the basic emotions, see, for example, https://writersforensicsblog.wordpress.com/2013/08/19/facial-expressions-and-emotions. For emotions as "a domain of phenomena of feelings, behaviors, and bodily reactions," see Nico H. Frijda, "The Psychologists' Point of View," in *Handbook of Emotions*, ed. Michael Lewis, Jeannette M. Haviland-Jones, and Lisa Feldman Barrett, 3d ed. (New York, 2008), 68–87 at 69.

[8] Thomas Dixon, *From Passions to Emotions: The Creation of a Secular Psychological Category* (Cambridge, 2003).

[9] Ute Frevert et al., *Emotional Lexicons: Continuity and Change in the Vocabulary of Feeling 1700–2000* (Oxford, 2014).

It is only right that I state my own "definition," namely that there is a biological and universal human aptitude for feeling and expressing what we now call "emotions." But what those emotions are, what they are called, how they are evaluated and felt, and how they are expressed (or not) – all these are shaped by "emotional communities."

Emotional communities

Emotional communities are groups – usually but not always social groups – that have their own particular values, modes of feeling, and ways to express those feelings. Like "speech communities," they may be very close in practice to other emotional communities of their time, or they may be quite unique and marginal.[10] They are not "bounded entities." Indeed, the researcher may define them quite broadly – upper-class English society in the nineteenth century, for example – or rather narrowly, as I do in this book. More narrowly delineated communities allow the researcher to characterize in clearer fashion the emotional style of the group. Larger communities will contain variants and counterstyles – "emotional subcommunities" if you will.

Emotional communities are not always "emotional." They simply share important norms concerning the emotions that they value and deplore and the modes of expressing them. Thus the members of an emotional community will not necessarily express love or affection toward one another if that community values hostile, aggressive, or ambivalent interpersonal relations.

Any given society at any period of time will likely contain more than one emotional community. These are rarely entirely separate, and sometimes they overlap in important – even essential – ways. In Chapter 6, for example, one member of the Paston family, John II, member of a very quiet and undemonstrative emotional community, marveled at and enjoyed his stay at the Burgundian court, a far more dramatically expressive community. Nevertheless, I would not say that therefore John "joined" the Burgundian emotional community. Rather, *for him* the

---

[10] For speech communities, see George Yule, *The Study of Language*, 4th ed. (Cambridge, 2010), 253: "A speech community is a group of people who share a set of norms and expectations regarding the use of language." For more on the notion of speech community, its uses and its limitations, see Peter L. Patrick, "The Speech Community," in *The Handbook of Language Variation and Change*, ed. J. K. Chambers, Peter Trudgill, and Natalie Schilling-Estes (Oxford, 2002), 573–98. For the classic exposition, see John Gumperz, "The Speech Community," in *International Encyclopedia of the Social Sciences*, ed. David Sills (Macmillan, 1968), 381–86, rpr. in *Language and Social Context: Selected Readings*, ed. Pier Paolo Giglioli (Harmondsworth, 1972), 219–31. I am grateful to Daniel L. Smail for suggesting this analogy to emotional communities.

court of Burgundy constituted what Mark Seymour has called an "emotional arena."[11] At the same time, because coexisting emotional communities must respond to the same or similar material, technological, and ideational conditions, they are usually recognizably related to one another, whether as variants of one another or as reactions to one another within a wider cultural framework. Thus, we will see in Chapter 4, for example, how a monastic community in England and a courtly one in southern France valued the same emotions even as they expressed their anxieties about those and other emotions very differently. In general, the historian may expect emotional communities from the same period and the same general culture to imitate, borrow from, or distance themselves from one another.

When studying a community's emotions, what should the historian look for? Because emotions are inchoate until they are given names, emotional vocabularies are exceptionally important for the ways in which people understand, express, and indeed "feel" their emotions. Consider that we often call music "emotional"; yet when we ask, "What emotion does it express?" we find we must use words. Often they seem inadequate no matter how nuanced: words cannot quite compass music's full emotional meaning. Neither do our emotion words. That's one of the reasons that William Reddy created the notion of "emotives," for one of its implications is that emotional expressions are only "drafts" of our attempts to express our feelings.[12]

Without question, emotions are made known also through tones of voice, gestures, grimaces, dancing, blanching, blushing, fainting, and bowing. Breaking into song may be a sign of emotion, as may whispering or declaiming. Historians have evidence for some of this. In the Roman world, certain feelings were accompanied by gestures so typical and characteristic as to be essentially codified.[13] Similarly, some gestures had well-known meanings in medieval visual sources, while others are only now being discovered by art historians.[14] Written sources tell us

---

[11] Mark Seymour, "Emotional Arenas: From Provincial Circus to National Courtroom in Late Nineteenth-Century Italy," in *Emotional Styles – Concepts and Challenges*, ed. Benno Gammerl, *Rethinking History: The Journal of Theory and Practice* 16 (2012): 177–97.

[12] William M. Reddy, *The Navigation of Feeling: A Framework for the History of Emotions* (Cambridge, 2001). Yet, at the same time, because emotions are "cognitive habits" (*ibid.*, 32), they are generally expressed in habitual ways.

[13] Anthony Corbeill, *Nature Embodied: Gesture in Ancient Rome* (Princeton, 2004).

[14] The classics are Moshe Barasch, *Gestures of Despair in Medieval and Early Renaissance Art* (New York, 1976), and Jean-Claude Schmitt, *La raison des gestes dans l'Occident médiéval* (Paris, 1990). Johanna Scheel, *Das altniederländische Stifterbild. Emotionsstrategien des Sehens und der Selbsterkenntnis* (Berlin, 2014), takes up the many emotions that viewers

about some of these gestures, describing laughing and weeping for example. Such descriptions bring us right back to words.

Thus, words are mainly what researchers must work with. When neuroscientists say that parts of our brain "light up" in fMRIs under the influence of a particular emotion, they should explain that the subject already knows which emotion is being tested (thus has the "word") and that the researcher has set the criteria for the colors of their results (which in fact signify degrees of oxygenation). Emotions have communicative functions, whether with ourselves alone or with others. Such communications do not rely on oxygenated brain cells. They must depend on social signals, chief among them words. It is true that many psychologists see facial expressions as the chief conveyers of emotional expression.[15] This view remains salient today even though it has been powerfully challenged.[16] Even (against my own view) were it true, it still relies on words: the only way scientists know if people correctly read facial expressions is by seeing whether the subject can attach the "right" emotion word to them.

Because we understand our "true feelings" via these words, however inadequate they may be, I do not distinguish expressed feelings from "real emotions" in any essential way. To be sure, I hope that both my readers and I will imaginatively look for "that thing that's going on besides the words," as Al Pacino has said of the actor's ideal.[17] But we should also realize that, although we naturalize our own emotions – thinking that we know how *we* "really" feel – in fact we must interpret even our own feelings according to our own emotional community's norms and vocabularies. Many historians of emotions accept, however, a distinction between "real" and "expressed" emotions, preferring to speak of the "performance" of emotions. They thereby (sometimes, perhaps, unintentionally) distance themselves from the claim that these are the same as "felt" emotions.[18] But "performed emotions" are also felt: this was already the

---

could read into relatively static and "unemotional" donor images. Jacqueline Jung, *Eloquent Bodies: Movement, Expression, and the Human Figure in Gothic Sculpture of the Holy Roman Empire*, forthcoming, takes up the ambiguity of medieval emotional representations. I am very grateful to Professor Jung for letting me see chapters of her book prior to publication. See also the caption for Plate 6.2 below.

[15] See David Matsumoto, Dacher Keltner, Michelle N. Shiota, Maureen O'Sullivan, and Mark Frank, "Facial Expressions of Emotion," in *Handbook of Emotions*, 211–34.

[16] See Ruth Leys, "How Did Fear Become a Scientific Object and What Kind of Object Is It?" *Representations* 110 (2010): 66–104; Maria Gendron et al., "Perceptions of Emotion from Facial Expressions are not Culturally Universal: Evidence from a Remote Culture," *Emotion* 14 (2014): 251–62.

[17] Quoted in John Lahr, "Caught in the Act: What Drives Al Pacino?" *New Yorker*, September 15, 2014, 66.

[18] See Chapter 6, n. 29. Studies of the emotions involved in feuding sometimes fall into this category; see Chapter 4, n. 190.

conclusion of Arlie Hochschild's 1983 study of the emotional training of airline flight attendants: the successful trainees internalized the emotional norms that they were told to perform. They learned to really mean the smiles they gave to rowdy passengers; they learned to suppress feelings of fatigue and irritation.[19]

Of course, it is true that sometimes people feign their feelings, and this is something that the historian (like the psychiatrist) needs to be alert to. The feigning itself tells us what the emotional norms must be. But what interests me even more than whether this or that particular emotion – expressed by this or that particular person – is a pretense is to know how sensitive particular emotional communities are to issues of "sincerity," since worries about true intent are themselves historically contingent.[20]

Because I see words as crucial to emotional life (and my view here is seconded by some neuropsychologists),[21] I spend a lot of time in this book discovering emotional vocabularies, which I usually present in tabular form. These tables, which present the emotion words alongside their (rough) English equivalents, have many purposes. They allow for cross-community comparisons; they suggest the relative importance of various emotions in particular communities; and they are meant to present starting points for other researchers.[22] Perhaps most important, they show that notions of what is "emotional" have changed over time.

This last point is rarely recognized, certainly not by psychologists today. Consider the opening words of an article by Gerald Clore and

[19] Arlie Russell Hochschild, *The Managed Heart: Commercialization of Human Feeling* (Berkeley, 1983). The new field of "emotion regulation" confirms such findings. See, for example, Shauna L. Clen, Douglas S. Mennin, and David M. Fresco, "Emotion Regulation Strategies," in *The Wiley Handbook of Cognitive Behavioral Therapy*, ed. Stefan G. Hofmann et al., 3 vols. (Oxford, 2014), 1:85–105.

[20] Monique Scheer, "Topographies of Emotion," in Frevert et al., *Emotional Lexicons*, 32–61 at 60 considers the bourgeoisie to have made sincerity normative "as a mark of distinction opposed to the [inauthentic] aristocracy." But we shall see that emotional communities long before the rise of the bourgeoisie also valued sincerity.

[21] See, for example, Maria Gendron et al., "Emotion Words Shape Emotion Percepts," *Emotion* 12 (2012): 314–25.

[22] This sort of thing has been done with modern emotions. Anna Wierzbicka, *Emotions across Languages and Cultures: Diversity and Universals* (Cambridge, 1999), 49 speaks of the "some fifty emotion concepts such as fear, pride, relief, and admiration, which constitute the core of the English emotion lexicon." James R. Averill, "A Semantic Atlas of Emotional Concepts," *JSAS Catalog of Selected Documents in Psychology* 5/330 (1975) (Ms. No. 1103), 35–53, provides a list of 558 English words "with emotional connotations." Rated highest on the Amherst unemotional–emotional scale is "furious," with "unconcerned" at the lowest end (see 55–64). For frequencies of emotion word use in English, see Philip Shaver et al., "Emotion Knowledge: Further Exploration of a Prototype Approach," *Journal of Personality and Social Psychology* 52/6 (1987): 1061–86. For French emotion word frequencies, see Annie Piolat and Rachid Bannour, "Émotions et affects. Contribution de la psychologie cognitive," in *Le sujet des émotions au moyen âge*, ed. Piroska Nagy and Damien Boquet (Paris, 2008), 53–84.

Andrew Ortony: "Emotions are psychological states, but not all psychological states are emotional; for example, neither a state of exhaustion nor a state of confusion is an emotion."[23] How do they know that exhaustion and confusion are not emotions? Because those terms (and the concepts behind them) are not considered emotions by "most people." They are thinking of "most people" *today* who *speak English*. But in Chapter 1 we see that Cicero considered *aerumna* (weariness) and *pigritia* (indolence, sloth) to be emotions; and in Chapter 5 we learn that Thomas Aquinas considered *segnities* (slowness, sluggishness, inactivity) to be an emotion. As for "confusion," a frequent term for an "emotion" in both ancient and medieval theories was *perturbatio*, meaning, quite precisely, "confusion." By contrast with Clore and Ortony, I would not rule out *anything* as possibly having affective valence – in short, as possibly being "an emotion." It all depends on the culture and the emotional community. The historian must be open to the unexpected.

This is one reason why I do not pay much attention to the careful differentiation many modern psychologists make between "emotion" and "affect." In point of fact, there is no consensus on the difference between the two words today, nor was there in the past when, indeed, they were from time to time considered synonyms.[24] Nor do I shy away from using words like feeling, emotion, and even passion interchangeably. As we

---

[23] Gerald L. Clore and Andrew Ortony, "The Semantics of the Affective Lexicon," in *Cognitive Science Perspectives on Emotion and Motivation*, ed. Vernon Hamilton, Gordon H. Bower, and Nico H. Frijda (Amsterdam, 1988), 367–96 at 367. Clore and Ortony suggest (374) that if a word can be used with the same meaning in a phrase with "being" as with "feeling" (e.g. being angry; feeling angry) then it is an emotion word. The whole scheme thus belongs within the logic of the contemporary English language.

[24] Clore and Ortony, "Semantics," 373, say that affect is connected to "anything that is valenced or is positive or negative in value," giving the example of preference for one sort of ale over another as "affective." For them, emotions are a small subset of "affective conditions." But Nancy L. Stein, Marc W. Hernandez, and Tom Trabasso, "Advances in Modeling Emotion and Thought: The Importance of Developmental, Online, and Multilevel Analyses," in *Handbook of Emotions*, 574–86 at 578, report that "in our theory ... emotional responses are distinct from automatic, affective, and physical responses." Ruth Leys, "The Turn to Affect: A Critique," *Critical Inquiry* 37/3 (2011): 434–72 at 434 n. 2, argues that the distinction between affect and emotion "cannot be sustained." But see also the response to Leys by William E. Connolly, "The Complexity of Intention," *Critical Inquiry* 37 (2011): 791–98, and Ruth Leys, "Affect and Intention: A Reply to William E. Connolly," *Critical Inquiry* 37 (2011): 799–805. I thank Wojtek Jeziersky for references to the Leys/Connolly debate. Anne Schmidt, "Showing Emotions, Reading Emotions," in Frevert et al., *Emotional Lexicons*, 62–90 at 67, says that "until the late eighteenth century no strict distinction was made between [affects and passions]," while, in the same collection of articles, Scheer, "Topographies of Emotion," 54, notes that after 1970 German encyclopedias "almost always used synonymously" the words affect and emotion, while in Chapter 4 below we shall see that Aelred of Rievaulx used the word *affectus* sometimes as a sort of "drive" and at other times as the equivalent of love.

shall see, different writers used these words variously in different periods, but all of these words formed what we might call the "penumbra" of what we more-or-less mean by the word emotion.[25]

Words alone, however, will not tell us very much about emotional life. I am therefore also interested in which words emotional communities emphasize – and how they do so. Finally <u>I am interested in emotional sequences.</u> Psychologists frequently speak of "emotion scripts," by which <u>they mean</u> the circumstances that give rise to one emotion and the actions and expressions that accompany it.[26] I mean something quite different by an emotional "sequence." I mean that emotions do not normally come in singletons. Rather, emotional episodes often consist in a variety of emotions and emotional gestures, one after another. I feel angry, then feel guilty for feeling angry, then begin to cry, and at last laugh at myself and feel foolish. (This is a purely imaginary and hypothetical sequence, of course.)

Sequences are important because they tell us how emotions are felt differently according to the company they keep. If I feel angry and then guilty, that is a very different *feeling* of anger than if I feel angry and then euphoric. The sequence reveals how an emotion is valued. Explicit statements do so, as well. When Aelred of Rievaulx says that curiosity is "desire of the eyes" and a very bad emotion indeed, then *his* feeling when he felt curious (or when he did not feel curious) must have been very different from that of Thomas Hobbes, for Hobbes praised curiosity.[27]

All of the points I have made so far depend on words in texts – consciously shaped written sources. Am I therefore simply dealing with rhetoric rather than with feeling? The answer is no. <u>One cannot separate</u>

---

[25] See the articles in Frevert et al., *Emotional Lexicons*, which discuss the uses in modern encyclopedias in English, French, and German of "many individual words related to *emotions* ... [such as] *affect, appetite, emotion, sensation, feeling, temper, passion, fervour, sensibility,* and *drive.*" (Italics in the original.) On the eventual triumph of the word of emotion over all others, see Dixon, *From Passions to Emotions*; Otniel E. Dror, *Blush, Adrenaline, Excitement: Modernity and the Study of Emotions, 1860–1940* (Chicago, forthcoming).

[26] See, for example, Paula M. Niedenthal, "Emotion Concepts," in *Handbook of Emotions*, 593, Table 36.2, An Anger Script. There are five steps to this particular script: 1) a person is offended; 2) he or she (here I will use she) scowls at the offender; 3) she feels internal tension; 4) she desires retribution; 5) she strikes out and harms the offender. However, Stephen D. White, "The Politics of Anger," in *Anger's Past: The Social Uses of an Emotion in the Middle Ages*, ed. Barbara H. Rosenwein (Ithaca, NY, 1998), 127–52, uses the word "script" to refer to the ritual expressions of a variety of emotions in particular situations, in this case feuding. Sarah McNamer, *Affective Meditation and the Invention of Medieval Compassion* (Philadelphia, 2010), 12, takes the word "script" literally to describe the sequence of directives given in meditative texts.

[27] See below, Chapters 4 and 9, a point already cogently argued in Lorraine Daston and Katharine Park, *Wonders and the Order of Nature, 1150–1750* (New York, 2001), 304.

feeling from rhetoric, which is crucial for emotional expression. Put another way, emotional expression is always rhetorical to some degree. We don't speak emotion words alone; we embed them in constructed sentences. We don't say just the word "anger," for example. We say, "I am angry at him." That is the beginning of a speech, and we may well go on to say, "I am angry at him because he insulted me, and, because you are my friend, I hope you will join me in feeling angry at him." This is rhetoric: a statement designed to persuade. Small wonder that Aristotle embedded a long discussion of emotions in his book on rhetoric.

Nor should we dismiss the emotions that we find in texts as belonging to the boilerplate of particular genres and therefore meaningless from the point of view of "real feeling." Formal modern letters begin with "dear" as in "Dear Sir," but no one imagines that the Sir is "really" dear. Yet, desiccated as the emotion of that greeting may be, it nevertheless has a very different impact from the "Hi" that is the favorite opening of emails. "Hi" is cooler, breezier. Boilerplate has significance; it is used by different groups differently (I myself address people with "dear" in emails); and it can change over time. As a researcher of emotions, I actually welcome commonplaces, for they tell me precisely how people *think* they and others feel – or, at least, should feel.

All of these things – words, emphases, sequences, rhetoric, boilerplate – constitute the "emotional inheritances" that are available to contemporaries living at the same time and to new generations that come thereafter. Emotional communities adapt the traditions to their own needs. Sometimes, they produce new words and new sequences built on the older ones. That is what is meant by "generations of feeling": the constant availability and potentiality of older and coexisting emotional traditions. New traditions may be introduced: immigrants have always offered potent new norms wherever they settle, and today mass media such as movies and TV do similar work.[28]

Recent scientific work in the field of genetics suggests a metaphor for the variety, latency, potential, and interaction of emotional communities within any given society. While individual genes are unlikely to change quickly over time, nevertheless they *express* themselves differently depending on their environment.[29] These epigenetic changes, scholars

---

[28] See, for example, Rachel Spronk, "Media and the Therapeutic Ethos of Romantic Love in Middle-Class Nairobi," in *Love in Africa*, ed. Jennifer Cole and Lynn M. Thomas (Chicago, 2009), 181–203.

[29] Scientists speak of GEIs: "gene-environment interactions." See Daniel E. Runcie et al., "Social Environment Influences the Relationship between Genotype and Gene Expression in Wild Baboons," *Philosophical Transactions of the Royal Society B: Biological Sciences* 368/1618 (2013), online at dx.doi.org/10.1098/rstb.2012.0345;

note, are rapid and rampant.[30] Further, even one single individual carries not one genome but several: this is known as gene mosaicism.[31] It means that while some genomes may express themselves at certain times, others remain latent but potent. At the same time, because they are part of the same body, they must interact.

Why this book?

The history of emotions has become so popular lately that some scholars have started to speak of an "emotional turn."[32] Websites and blogs devoted to the subject are proliferating.[33] Nevertheless, I see some problems. Many of the new studies are only about the political uses of emotions, as though the state, broadly speaking, is still the only important topic for historians.[34] William Reddy has even claimed that "politics is just a process of determining who must repress as illegitimate, who must foreground as valuable, the feelings that come up for them in given contexts and relationships." Those who make this determination constitute what Reddy terms "emotional

William H. Durham, *Coevolution: Genes, Culture, and Human Diversity* (Stanford, 1991). I'm grateful to Mark Seymour for suggesting a cell-based metaphor.

[30] See Eva Jablonka and Marion J. Lamb, *Evolution in Four Dimensions: Genetic, Epigenetic, Behavioral, and Symbolic Variation in the History of Life* (Cambridge, MA, 2005); Daniel L. Smail, "Neurohistory in Action: Hoarding in Human History," *Isis* 105 (2014): 110–22.

[31] See, for example, Alexej Abyzov et al., "Somatic Copy-Number Mosaicism in Human Skin Revealed by Induced Pluripotent Stem Cells," *Nature* 492/7429 (2012): 438–42.

[32] Nicole Eustace et al., "*AHR* Conversation: The Historical Study of Emotions," *American Historical Review* 117 (2012): 1487–1531 at 1487.

[33] See, for example, *Les émotions au Moyen Âge (EMMA)* (editors: Damien Boquet and Piroska Nagy), emma.hypotheses.org/; Australian Research Council Centre of Excellence for the History of Emotions, www.historyofemotions.org.au/; Queen Mary Centre for the History of the Emotions publicizes lectures and conferences at www.qmul.ac.uk/emotions and hosts a History of Emotions Blog, emotionsblog.history.qmul.ac.uk ; H-Emotions, sponsored by H-Net Humanities and Social Sciences Online, networks.h-net.org/h-emotions; new in 2014 is *History of Emotions – Insights into Research* (editors: Margrit Pernau, Anja Laukötter) from the Max Planck Institute for Human Development, www.mpib-berlin.mpg.de/en/research/history-of-emotions.

[34] See, for example, François Foronda, *El espanto y el miedo. Golpismo, emociones políticas y constitucionalismo en la Edad Media* (Madrid, 2013); Laurent Smagghe, *Les Émotions du Prince. Émotion et discours politique dans l'espace bourguignon* (Paris, 2012); Régine Le Jan, "*Quem decet trinam observare regulam, terrorem scilicet et ordinationem atque amorem.* Entre crainte et amour du roi: les émotions politiques à l'époque carolingienne," in *Geschichtsverstellungen. Bilder, Texte und Begriffe aus dem Mittelalter. Festschrift für H.W. Goetz zu 65. Geburtstag*, ed. Steffen Patzold, Anja Rathmann-Lutz, and Volker Scior (Cologne, 2012), 392–411; Klaus Oschema, *Freundschaft und Nähe im spätmittelalterlichen Burgund. Studien zum Spannungsfeld von Emotion und Institution* (Cologne, 2006); Penelope Morris, Francesco Ricatti, and Mark Seymour, *Politica ed emozioni nella storia d'Italia dal 1848 ad oggi* (Rome, 2012).

regimes."[35] Granted, politics matters; granted, many emotions are "political." Nevertheless, as many historians of art and religion have shown, emotions are not *only* political.[36]

The second problem that I wish to highlight is how these works tend to fall into the traditional historical periods: medievalists work within the Middle Ages; modernists labor in the eras thereafter.[37] Over everyone looms the shadow of Norbert Elias and his more recent avatar – modernity. Writing during the 1930s in exile from Hitler's Germany, Elias concluded that the medieval period fostered emotionality, while the modern era learned, via the "civilizing process," to tame and restrain its emotions.[38]

In the wake of this enormously influential paradigm,[39] medievalists have been busy proving that the Middle Ages was *not* a period of untrammeled impulse. For the most part this has meant exploring the very political emotions of rulers.[40] Modernists, for their part, have been

[35] Reddy, *Navigation*, 129. Quotation from William M. Reddy, "Against Constructionism: The Historical Ethnography of Emotion," *Current Anthropology* 38 (1997): 327–51 at 335. A recent article, Nicole Eustace, "Emotion and Political Change," in *Doing Emotions History*, ed. Susan J. Matt and Peter N. Stearns (Chicago, 2014), 163–83, cites this quotation (169) as a starting point for her own inquiry.

[36] See, for example, the articles in *Love in Africa*, ed. Cole and Thomas, and Frevert et al., *Emotional Lexicons*; Scheel, *Das altniederländische Stifterbild*; McNamer, *Affective Meditation*. Even William M. Reddy, *The Making of Romantic Love: Longing and Sexuality in Europe, South Asia & Japan, 900–1200* CE (Chicago, 2012), is only somewhat about politics – that of the Church.

[37] There is room here to highlight only a very few recent examples of these studies. For the medieval period, see *Le sujet des émotions au Moyen Âge*, ed. Piroska Nagy and Damien Boquet (Paris, 2008), and *La chair des émotions. Pratiques et représentations corporelles de l'affectivité au Moyen Âge* = *Médiévales* 61 (2011), as well as *Vengeance in the Middle Ages: Emotion, Religion and Feud*, ed. Susanna A. Throop and Paul R. Hyams (Farnham, UK, 2010). For the modern period, see Ute Frevert, *Men of Honour: A Social and Cultural History of the Duel*, trans. Anthony Williams (Cambridge, 1995); Morris, Ricatti, and Seymour, *Politica ed emozioni*.

[38] Norbert Elias, *Über den Prozess der Zivilisation*, 2 vols. (Basel, 1939), in its latest English version *The Civilizing Process: Sociogenetic and Psychogenetic Investigations*, trans. Edmund Jephcott, rev. ed. Eric Dunning, Johan Goudsblom, and Stephen Mennell (Oxford, 2000).

[39] To show its overwhelming importance even today, let it suffice to cite Steven Pinker, *The Better Angels of our Nature: The Decline of Violence in History and its Causes* (New York, 2011). Chapter 3 is entitled "The Civilizing Process." On 59–60, discussing his contrarian desire to use a knife to guide food to his fork, Pinker reminisces: "Then one day, while doing research for this book, the scales fell from my eyes, the enigma evaporated, and I forever put aside my resentment of the no-knife rule. I owe this epiphany to the most important thinker you have never heard of, Norbert Elias." Elias is Pinker's theoretical guide for his survey of "the history of homicide." For Elias, homicide was the result of the same impulses that lay behind the expression of emotions. Similarly for Pinker, the "rage circuit" in the human mind is behind the human propensity to violence; see 485–88.

[40] Consider the work of Gerd Althoff, "Empörung, Tränen, Zerknirschung. 'Emotionen' in der öffentlichen Kommunikation des Mittelalters," *Frühmittelalterliche Studien* 30 (1996): 60–79, "*Ira Regis*: Prolegomena to a History of Royal Anger," in *Anger's Past*, 59–74, and "Demonstration und Inszenierung: Spielregeln der Kommunikation in

uninterested in finding continuities with the medieval past.[41] A few anthologies bridge the two periods, but individual articles within them do not.[42] There is no narrative, apart from Elias', that takes us across the medieval/early modern divide.

Hence this book. Elias spoke of France as the paradigmatic society: its warriors were for him representative of "medieval man." Its courtiers were exemplars of early modern "civilizing." This book, too, is limited in geographical scope, covering only France and England, and even then taking up only a few of their many possible emotional communities. No society speaks with one voice; I have attended to some groups that I consider "representative." Similarly, I discuss only certain periods. For example, I leap from Alcuin, a ninth-century thinker discussed in Chapter 3, to the twelfth and thirteenth centuries. Why? I have chosen to do what archaeologists call "judgmental sampling": I focus on moments that I consider important. However, there are other important moments that I leave out. I intend this book to present above all a *way* to look at emotional phenomena historically. I hope that others will fill the many gaps that it leaves.

The technique of this book is microhistorical: to look at particulars and yet to claim that they tell us something about larger groups in similar situations around the same time. For example, I spend much time on Rievaulx under Abbot Aelred not only because he represented the emotional community of one Cistercian monastery but because I hypothesize that Cistercian monasteries in general fostered similar (though surely not exactly the same) emotional styles and sensibilities.

But my intent is more ambitious than simply to provide examples of emotional communities. I want to show how later communities drew on the emotional repertories of past communities even as they changed the meaning of each repertory in its new context. I want to show, above all,

mittelalterlicher Öffentlichkeit," *Frühmittelalterliche Studien* 27 (1993): 27–50. For more recent work on the rationality of medieval emotions, see Smagghe, *Les Émotions du prince*.

[41] In effect, the Middle Ages functions as the "pre" for early modernists. See Daniel L. Smail and Andrew Shryock, "History and the 'Pre,'" *American Historical Review* 118 (2013): 709–37, esp. 713: "[The 'pre'] is a narrative space auto-populated by features that define temporal Otherness for the self-consciously modern observer." To be sure, there are many exceptions to the early-modernist neglect of the medieval. I cite two examples: David Aers and Nigel Smith, "English Reformations," *Journal of Medieval and Early Modern Studies* 40 (2010): 425–38, and Susan C. Karant-Nunn, *The Reformation of Feeling: Shaping the Religious Emotions in Early Modern Germany* (Oxford, 2010). However, Ute Frevert, *Emotions in History – Lost and Found* (Budapest, 2011), uses the notion of "modernity" to do much of the work of Elias' "civilizing." See Barbara H. Rosenwein, "Modernity: A Problematic Category in the History of Emotions," *History and Theory* 53 (2014): 69–78.

[42] See, for example, Jonas Liliequist, *A History of Emotions, 1200–1800* (London, 2012); *Emotions and Health, 1200–1700*, ed. Elena Carrera (Leiden, 2013).

that this process continued across the divide that historians still assume between the medieval period and the modern. The history of emotions suggests a more fluid paradigm – an open floor plan, if you will – rather than a series of rooms decisively entered and exited.

This book's shape, however, is less a floor plan than a work of masonry: stones held together by thin layers of mortar. Building chronologically, it alternates short chapters on theories of emotions with longer chapters that explore two or more coexisting emotional communities. The shorter chapters ground the vocabularies of the longer chapters in particular theories. These short chapters show that theories belong in historical contexts (no theory is timeless) and demonstrate in turn how emotional communities are to some degree both explained and created by prevailing theories.[43]

Chapter 1 begins with the theories and emotion words bequeathed to the medieval period by Cicero (first century BCE) and Saint Augustine (early fifth century CE). Chapter 2 takes up in summary form the emotional communities in Francia that I discussed in greater detail in my earlier book, *Emotional Communities in the Early Middle Ages*. These communities – one sentimental and tolerant of all sorts of emotions, another extremely restrained in emotional expression, and a third obsessed with anger and rancor – drew freely on the inheritance of antiquity. But soon, as Chapter 3 shows, the emotions were absorbed into discussions of the virtues and vices, as we see by analyzing a therapeutic manual by Alcuin, one of Charlemagne's courtiers.

Chapter 4 turns to the twelfth and thirteenth centuries. By studying two very different emotional communities – those of the English Cistercian monastery of Aelred of Rievaulx on the one hand and of the court of the counts of Toulouse (today southern France) on the other – we see, despite their differences, two overriding preoccupations in both: the love and the potential treacheries of friends. This chapter also allows us to see the affective vocabulary available in the vernacular (the Old Occitan of the troubadours who worked for the counts of Toulouse) and to compare it with the Latin of its day. There is extraordinary nuance in Old Occitan, and yet the emotions in many instances parallel those in the Latin texts.

From friendship, which is (at least in the groups studied in Chapter 4) based on the emotion of love, it is only a short step to Thomas Aquinas' theory of the "passions of the soul" (taken up in Chapter 5). For Thomas, love was the "root" of all the other emotions. His work signals a nascent

---

[43] The need for histories of "ideas" alongside and integrated with other sorts of histories is argued briefly but cogently in Darrin M. McMahon and Samuel Moyn, "Ideas Still Have Consequences," *The Chronicle Review* (February 21, 2014), B10–B12.

separation of theories of emotions from those of the virtues and vices, though many of the old traditions remain. Building on Aristotelian logic, Thomas argued that one emotion led to another: he saw *sequences* of emotions. That fact justifies and at the same time helps explain the pattern of emotions that we shall have seen in Chapter 4, where treachery followed love and friendship – to the dismay of all.

But Thomas' notion of love was more optimistic than that of the groups studied in Chapter 4. In general he saw the outcome of love's movement as union with the beloved, even ecstatic union. In Chapter 6 we see his ideas embraced, refracted, and rejected in three different emotional communities, which also variously drew on some of the earlier patterns noted in Chapters 2 and 4. At the court of the Duchy of Burgundy (which in the fourteenth and fifteenth century broke away from France politically but not in language or culture), love was downgraded, but dramatized emotions, particularly those of sorrow and joy, were highly valued. Drama was important in England, as well, but this time to the bourgeois matron Margery Kempe and her supporters. Her moments of despair alternated with those of ecstatic love focused on Christ in imagined dialogues. Entirely different were the Pastons, living in England very near Margery and at about the same time, but aspiring to the circles of the gentry. They cultivated emotional restraint, barely mentioning their feelings – focusing on their practical affairs – except for their often vain hope for emotional tranquility. These widely diverging emotional communities were nevertheless compassed in Jean Gerson's theory of the emotions, discussed in Chapter 7. Tying passions to the silent music of the heart, Gerson composed a little drama between the "worldly heart" and the "all-alone heart" to explain his theory. It was a dramatic dialogue in the service of silence!

Just as Chapter 2 focuses on France, so Chapter 8 concentrates on England. There, in the seventeenth century, the overriding emotion, heir (in part) to the community represented by Margery Kempe, was despair. But the same period also saw groups (the Levellers, for example) who put their emphasis on happiness, taking bits and pieces of the emotional patterns of both Margery and the Pastons. Still another group, the believers who joined a Puritan "gathered church" in London, more clearly drew on the norms of Margery's community. At about the same time, however, politician and diarist Samuel Pepys and his friend John Evelyn valued tranquility in their many occupations of daily life, much like the Pastons. We are lucky that Evelyn's friend Thomas Hobbes included a theory of the passions in his *Leviathan*. In Chapter 9 we see how that theory's emphasis on infinite motion and "curiosity" both help explain the emotional emphases of the seventeenth century and herald the scientific pursuits of the eighteenth.

The conclusion of the book likens emotional communities to "genome mosaicism." They persist over time but they also mutate. Within the body politic they nurture the possibilities of adaptations to new environments, partly because they are affected by those environments, and partly because their own internal changes fit new circumstances – or do not, leading to their marginalization and even, perhaps, their disappearance. There is, then, no teleology in the story of the emotions in France and England from 600 to 1700, and, certainly, no civilizing process. But there is, making up for that, a lively narrative of continuity and change.

1   Ancient theories

We begin with Cicero (d. 43 BCE). To be sure, long before his time many theories of the emotions had been elaborated, particularly within the Stoic and Epicurean philosophies of the Hellenistic era.[1] Cicero drew on these traditions when he wrote on emotions for the Latinate audience of the Roman West. Medieval people inherited his writings. But they read them through Christian lenses. Christianity, which became the official religion of the Roman Empire in the 380s, radically transformed ancient ideas about the emotions. To get a clear idea of some of the most important of those changes, we will focus in the second part of this chapter on Saint Augustine's reconsideration of the Ciceronian canon. Augustine (d. 430), perhaps the most influential of the Western Church Fathers, read Cicero on the emotions and reoriented the discussion. Armed with the theories and the vocabularies of Augustine and Cicero, we will be ready to look at some early medieval emotional communities in Chapter 2. In addition, the writings of Cicero and Augustine discussed here exerted an enormous influence on later emotional communities, especially those of the twelfth century and beyond, as we shall see in Chapter 4 and those thereafter.

Cicero's somber, "Stoic" emotions

While Cicero expressed many emotions in his writings, we are here interested in his theoretical works on the topic, particularly the *Tusculan Disputations* and *Laelius on Friendship*. Both were written near the end of Cicero's life, the first in 45 and the second in 44 BCE. This was a period of crisis for Cicero. Caesar was ready to end the Republic, and Cicero no longer had a role in the state, as he longed to have. Further, his beloved

---

[1] Good introductions to these theories include Martha C. Nussbaum, *The Therapy of Desire: Theory and Practice in Hellenistic Ethics* (Princeton, 1994); Juha Sihvola and Troels Engberg-Pedersen, *The Emotions in Hellenistic Philosophy* (Dordrecht, 1998); Simo Knuuttila, *Emotions in Ancient and Medieval Philosophy* (Oxford, 2004), 47–80; Richard Sorabji, *Emotion and Peace of Mind: From Stoic Agitation to Christian Temptation* (Oxford, 2000).

daughter had recently died.[2] Retiring to his estate at Tusculum, just southeast of Rome, he intended the writing of his *Disputations* to be a kind of therapy. In the course of his wide-ranging discussion, he offered what amounted to a summary of Stoic theory (which had been elaborated in the course of the third and second centuries) and a list in Latin of the *perturbationes animi* that were equivalent to the Stoic *pathé*, or "emotions." The Stoics intended to achieve *apatheia*, freedom from the effects of the *pathé*. Cicero wanted to demonstrate his "strength of mind" in the face of emotional turmoil. Was the discussion, then, Cicero's own? Yes and no. He did not accept every Stoic idea; he shaped their theories to conform to his own.

But his own ideas at the time were not the sum total of his thinking on the topic. Indeed, the *Tusculan Disputations*, with its jaundiced view of nearly every emotion, was but one side of his theory (and his disposition). As if writing to correct himself, Cicero shortly thereafter produced the *Laelius*, which claimed that a man without feeling was hardly a man at all.

Cicero's sorrows

In the *Tusculan Disputations*, Cicero wrote about the *perturbationes*, the Latin word that he chose for the emotions. The Greek word he was translating, *pathé*, was more precisely equivalent to the Latin word *passiones*, "passions," but "perturbations" was closer to Cicero's own dark feelings at the time he was writing. The *Tusculan Disputations*, written as a dialogue with "Brutus," began with Cicero vigorously lampooning the terrors of death and offering many reasons why "the dead were not in a bad way."[3] He turned in the second book to disparage pain, arguing that it was "clearly nothing (*nihil ... plane*)" when compared to disgrace (*turpitudo*).[4] In books 3 and 4, he belittled the emotions, organizing his discussion around the four genera of emotions – *voluptas* and *aegritudo* (pleasure and pain), *libido* (or *cupiditas*), and *metus* (desire and fear) – that had been elaborated by the Stoics. Let us now turn to these categories (noting in passing that in his fifth and final book, Cicero left off criticizing and became instead an advocate of virtue). Cicero's scheme is shown in Table 1.1.

Pleasure and pain were reactions to present stimuli; desire and fear to things anticipated. This was perfectly in accordance with Stoic views.

---

[2] For Cicero's circumstances at the time, see Margaret R. Graver, *Cicero on the Emotions: Tusculan Disputations 3 and 4* (Chicago, 2002), xi–xv.

[3] *M. Tulli Ciceronis Tusculanae Disputationes* 1.46.111b, ed. Michaelangelus Giusta (Turin, 1984) [henceforth: *TD*], 86: "nullo in malo mortuos esse."

[4] Cicero, *TD* 2.13.31, p. 116.

Table 1.1 *Cicero's genera of* perturbationes animi[a]

Present	Future
voluptas/*elatio animi*/*laetitia*, pleasure	*libido*/*cupiditas*, desire
aegritudo, pain/distress	*metus*, fear

[a] The slash (/) indicates synonyms or near-synonyms here, but in other tables may indicate antonyms; the context makes its meaning clear. Here and elsewhere, English translations must be considered only rough equivalents.

Table 1.2 *Cicero's* constantiae[a]

Present *constantiae*	(Corresponding *perturbationes*)
gaudium, joy	(*voluptas*), pleasure
(there is no *constantia* for present evil)	(*aegritudo*), pain/distress
Future *constantiae*	**(Corresponding *perturbationes*)**
voluntas, will	(*cupiditas*), desire
cautio, caution	(*metus*), fear

[a] Corresponding *perturbationes* are provided only for reference.

However, the emphases in Cicero's discussion were very much his own. First, Cicero hardly mentioned the Stoic "pre-passions," the bodily contractions, expansions, tears, pallor, blushes, and stings that told the wise man that an emotion was about to happen and that he must not assent to it.[5] Second, the Stoics considered certain emotions good: they were called the *eupatheiai* (*eu* meaning good) and there were many of them: varieties of *gaudium* (joy) like enjoyment, cheerfulness, and good spirits; kinds of *voluntas* (will) like good intent, benevolence, and affection.[6] Cicero mentioned these good emotions, which he termed *constantiae*, or consistencies, but unlike the Stoics, he did not bother to list their many kinds. Thus, reading Cicero's *Tusculan Disputations*, you would imagine that there were only three *constantiae* as shown in Table 1.2.

[5] On Stoic pre-passions, see Knuuttila, *Emotions*, 63–68. Cicero mentions them briefly in *TD* 3.34.83, p. 204. See Graver, *Cicero on the Emotions*, 124–26.

[6] Graver, *Cicero on the Emotions*, 138, lists some of the Stoic species of *eupatheiai*: for example, Diogenes Laertius and Pseudo-Andronicus named "enjoyment (*terpsis*), cheerfulness (*euphrosunê*), and good spirits (*euthumia*)" as species of joy; "good intent (*eunoia*), goodwill (*eumeneia*), welcoming (*aspasmos*) and affection (*agapêsis*)" were forms of will.

Table 1.3 *Cicero's* aegritudines

adflictatio, affliction
adflictari, to be miserable or afflicted
aemulatio, rivalry
aemulari, to rival
aerumna, weariness
aerumna adfici, to be weary
angor, anxiety
angi, to be vexed
desperare, to despair
dolor, sorrow, pain
dolere, to sorrow
invidentia, envying
invidere, to envy
invidia, envy, spite
lamentatio, lamenting, mourning
lamentari, to lament
luctus, grief
lugere, to grieve
maeror, sorrow
maerere, to sorrow
misericordia, pity
misereri, to pity
molestia, irritation, annoyance
(in) molestia esse, to be annoyed
obtrectatio, jealousy
obtrectare, to be jealous
sollicitudo, worry
sollicitari, to worry

Rather than consider the consistencies in detail, Cicero dwelled on the perturbations, and, of these, he emphasized distresses (*aegritudines*).[7] We may even say that Cicero treated *aegritudo*, pain/distress, as the type, or model, of emotions, and the worst of them all. Their many forms are listed in Table 1.3.

---

[7] The Stoics, too, emphasized distress (*lupé*) but they gave equal attention to desire (*epithumia*) and were keen to specify the many species under that rubric, including numerous kinds of rage, for example anger (*orgé*), heatedness (*thumos*), bile (*cholos*), hatred (*ménis*), rancor (*kotos*), and exasperation (*pikria*); see Margaret R. Graver, *Stoicism and Emotion* (Chicago, 2007), 56, Fig. 4. Nussbaum, *Therapy of Desire*, 287 n. 65 notes: "The reader of these lists [of Stoic passions] will be struck by the prevalence of terms designating angry and hostile feelings ... If one were to inquire into the motivations behind the Stoic condemnation of the passions on the basis of these lists alone, one would have to conclude that worries about malice and anger are central. The rest of the evidence confirms this."

Table 1.4 *Cicero's* perturbationes *(apart from the* aegritudines*)*

libido/cupiditas, desire
desiderium, desire, longing, yearning
discordia, discord
excandescentia, heatedness
indigentia, need
inimicitia, enmity
ira, anger
irasci, to be angry
odium, hatred
metus, fear, dread
conturbatio, agitation
exanimatio, petrifaction
formido, dread
pavor, panic
pigritia, indolence, sloth
pudor, shame, shyness
terror, terror
timor, fright
voluptas/elatio animi/laetitia (nimia)/amor, pleasure, gladness, love
delectatio, delight
jactatio, ostentation, vainglory
malevolentia, malice, spite, Schadenfreude

Cicero used many nasty adjectives to describe pain/distress: it was *taetra* (loathsome), *misera* (sad), and *detestabilis* (hateful).[8] He assimilated it to grief (*luctus, maeror, dolor*), *luctus* being the greatest (*maxima*) distress of all.[9] He took pleasure in elaborating on the folly of grieving.[10] For Cicero, the *aegritudines* covered a very large semantic field.

He dealt with the rest of the emotions far more perfunctorily, as Table 1.4 demonstrates.

In the *Tusculan Disputations* love (*amor*) was equated with *voluptas*, which Cicero called shameful (*turpis*). He said that love was "of such great triviality (*tantae levitatis*) that I find nothing to compare with it."[11] Not only did he ridicule homosexual love, but his treatment of *Medea*

---

[8] Cicero, *TD* 3.11.25, p. 164.

[9] Forms of *doleo, luctus*, and *maeror* are used to illustrate *aegritudo* in Cicero, *TD* 3.25.60, pp. 188–89; see also *ibid.*, 3.28.68, p. 194.

[10] *Ibid.*, 3.27.64–31.75, pp. 191–99. Graver, *Cicero on the Emotions*, 142, suggests some reasons for Cicero's focus: "The emphasis on distress, which is even more marked here than in Greek versions of the list, perhaps reflects the importance of grief and suffering in the literary tradition as well as Cicero's own interest in the subject."

[11] Cicero, *TD* 4.32.68, p. 254.

shows that he belittled heterosexual love as well.[12] He said nothing whatever of affection.[13]

Cicero's loves

Cicero belittled love when he wanted to explain the Stoic point of view. But the Stoics represented only one of the many traditions of Greek philosophy familiar to Cicero. One of those traditions was nourished by Aristotle's view of friendship as articulated in his *Nicomachean Ethics*. There, while recognizing (and talking a good bit about) friendships based on practical utility or pleasure, Aristotle considered friendships "between the good" as the most perfect. "It is those who wish the good of their friends for their friends' sake who are friends in the fullest sense, since they love each other for themselves."[14] Indeed, "a friend is another self."[15] Thus, still in forced retirement at Tusculum, Cicero wrote a much sunnier piece, *Laelius on Friendship*. (As befitted a good lawyer and politician – which Cicero was – he was glad to argue the case for and against emotions on both sides.) In his new work, written in the form of a dialogue set in the past and led by Laelius, the good friend of the just-deceased Scipio (d.129 BCE), Cicero argued on behalf of love (*amor*) and friendship (*amicitia*). Indeed, he had Laelius urge his interlocutors to "put friendship before all things human, for nothing is so fitting to nature."[16]

One important purpose of the dialogue was to distinguish friendship from political alliance, even though the same word might be used for both.[17] Political relationships were based on weakness and need. By contrast, friendships (Cicero argued) sprang entirely from love, and this made them benevolent. "For *amor* (love), from which the word *amicitia* (friendship) derives, is most necessary for establishing a bond of

---

[12] See *ibid.*, 4.32.69–33.71, pp. 255–56.

[13] See Graver, *Cicero on the Emotions*, 174–76.

[14] Aristotle, *Nicomachean Ethics* 8.3.6 (1156b10), trans. Harris Rackham (Cambridge, MA, 1932), 461.

[15] *Ibid.*, 9.4.5 (1166a30), p. 535.

[16] Cicero, *Laelius de Amicitia* 5.17, trans. William A. Falconer (Cambridge, MA, 1964) [henceforth *DA*], 108–211 at 126. On the philosophical schools on which Cicero drew for this piece, see Benjamin Fiore, "The Theory and Practice of Friendship in Cicero," in *Greco-Roman Perspectives on Friendship*, ed. John T. Fitzgerald (Atlanta, 1997), 59–76, esp. 59–66.

[17] See the discussion in David Konstan, *Friendship in the Classical World* (Cambridge, 1997), 123–29 and 136–37; Constant J. Mews, "Cicero on Friendship," in *Friendship: A History*, ed. Barbara Caine (London, 2009), 65–72, esp. 69–71; Sandra Citroni Marchetti, "'I Could Not Love Caesar More': Roman Friendship and the Beginning of the Principate," *The Classical Journal* 99 (2004): 281–99 at 286–88. Fiore, "Theory and Practice," 66–76, discusses political friendships and stresses the differences between Cicero's ideal and the reality.

benevolence *(benevolentiam coniungendam).*"[18] Benevolence is a pale word in English. By contrast, for Cicero it had enormous force: "If you were to rid nature of the bond of benevolence, neither home nor city could exist."[19] Benevolence was the antidote to hatreds *(odiis)* and discords *(discidiis).*[20]

Thus it is no surprise that Cicero's definition of friendship itself rested on benevolence, agreement, and love: "Friendship is nothing other than agreement *(consensio)* in all things divine and human along with benevolence *(benevolentia)* and love *(caritas).*"[21] Cicero's use of the word *caritas* rather than *amor* here was not particularly significant. He used the two words as synonyms alongside verb forms of *dilectio* (also love). Thus, following his definition of friendship, he added that it arose from "an inclination ... of the *animi* (soul/mind) along with a certain feeling of loving *(sensu amandi),*"[22] and, using the word *caritas*, he likened the love between children and parents to the "similar feeling of love *(similis sensus ... amoris)*" that takes shape when we meet someone in whom we see the light of virtue. "For there is nothing more lovable *(amabilius)* than virtue, nothing that leads more to loving *(diligendum).*"[23]

But now Cicero had to take on the Stoics, who, by striving to avoid anxiety (here Cicero used the word *angor*, one of the *aegritudines* in Table 1.3), ended up feeling nothing at all. That made their ideal "wise man" less than human: "For when emotion is taken away *(motu animi sublato)*, what difference is there – I don't say between an animal and a man – but between a man and a tree or a stone?"[24] Moreover, if we flee, like the Stoic, from cares and anxieties, "we must also flee from virtue *(virtus fugienda est)*," which always must "spurn and hate anything contrary to it, as goodness *(bonitas)* [opposes] malice *(malitia)*; temperance *(temperantia)* [rejects] lustful desire *(libido)*; and bravery *(fortitudo)* [hates] faintheartedness *(ignavia)* ... Therefore it is proper for the well constituted mind/soul *(animi)* both to rejoice *(laetari)* at good things and to sorrow *(dolere)* at their opposite."[25]

---

[18] Cicero, *DA* 8.26, p. 138. The etymology is correct: *amo* (I love)-icus→ *amicus* (friend)→ *amicitia* (friendship).

[19] *Ibid.*, 7.23, pp. 132–33. On the meanings of *benevolentia* in the *DA*, see Fiore, "Theory and Practice," 62.

[20] Konstan, *Friendship*, 130–35, points out that the hatreds and discords of which Cicero was thinking were those of his day. Citroni Marchetti, "I Could Not Love," 288, argues that the nature of friendship changed with the arrival of Caesar, when equality among "the élite of senators was substituted by a relationship of [Caesar's] benevolence that functioned for everybody from the top downwards."

[21] Cicero, *DA* 6.20, p. 130.

[22] *Ibid.*, 8.27, p. 138: "applicatione ... animi cum quodam sensu amandi."   [23] *Ibid.*

[24] *Ibid.*, 13.48, p. 158.   [25] *Ibid.*, 13.47, p. 158.

Table 1.5 *Cicero's "good" emotions*

amicitia, friendship
amor, love
amare, to love
redamare, to love in return[a]
benevolentia, benevolence, good will
caritas, love
concordia, concord
diligere, to love
fides, loyalty[b]
solacio, solace, comfort[c]

[a] Cicero, *DA* 13.49, p. 160. Cicero coined the term "*redamare*."
[b] *Ibid.*, 18.65, p. 174, where *fides* is termed the "*firmamentum* ...
stabilitatis constantiaeque (the prop of stability and consistency)."
[c] As a remedy for grief: see *ibid.*, 2.10, p. 118.

In this passage, then, Cicero named some "good emotions." Indeed, he spoke of the man of virtue as a person of *constantia* (consistency) – the very word that he used in the *Tusculan Disputations* for the Stoic good emotions (*eupatheiai*).[26] As he put it, good men are those who "so conduct themselves, so live, that of them is proved good faith (*fides*), integrity (*integritas*), justice (*aequitas*), generosity (*liberalitas*), nor is there in them any cupidity (*cupiditas*), libido (*libido*), audacity (*audacia*), and they are of great consistency (*magna constantia*)." We need, then, to add the good emotions discussed in *Laelius* to those that Cicero listed in his *Tusculan Disputations*. These are presented in Table 1.5.

In avoiding bad emotions and cultivating the good, Cicero's virtuous man engaged in what much later would be understood as the battle of the virtues against the vices. But where did that battle take place? What was the *animus* that was the seat of these emotions, which, as Cicero put it, "rejoiced at good things and sorrowed at their opposite"?[27] Cicero explored this question in the *Tusculan Disputations* in the course of discussing the nature of death.[28] Some, he reported, thought that the *animus* was the heart itself (*cor ipsum*).[29] But Empedocles said that the *animus* was the blood suffusing the heart (*cordi suffusum sanguinem*), while other philosophers thought that it pertained to a part of the brain (*pars ... cerebri*). Plato, too, put it firmly in the body, holding that the *animus* was divided into three parts, with one part (reason [*ratio*]) in the head (*caput*) and the other two parts (the irascible [*ira*] and the concupiscible

[26] *Ibid.*, 5.19, p. 128.   [27] Above, n. 25.   [28] Cicero, *TD* 1.8.16-1.11.25, pp. 12–20.
[29] *Ibid.*, 1.9.18, p. 14.

[*cupiditas*]) in the breast (*pectus*) and under the diaphragm (*praecordium*) respectively.[30] Meanwhile Aristotle, as reported by Cicero, claimed that "to love, to hate, to desire, to fear, to be anxious, and to rejoice" were among the activities of the mind (*mens*), which itself derived from a special "fifth nature (*quintam ... naturam*)" beyond the four elements of earth, fire, air, and water.[31] As for the Romans: they tended to identify the *animus* with the *anima* – the vital spirit.[32] Cicero's discussion tells us that the classical world had many different notions about the nature and the location of the *animus* and thus of the emotions. To some extent, this discussion persists today.[33]

In the *Tusculan Disputations*, Cicero called emotions into question; in the *Laelius* he celebrated them. In the end, he presented a huge thesaurus of emotion words and attitudes about them that nourished both the theories and the feelings of subsequent generations.

Augustine's willful emotions

Just after Cicero wrote, a revolution in values began to undermine the assumptions of the ancient world. Four hundred or so years later, the Roman Empire was Christian and the emotions of the ancient world had to be reevaluated in the light of the new religion. Augustine (354–430), bishop of Hippo (395–430), did that quite consciously. He knew Cicero's *Laelius* and the allure of its notion of friendship, but by the time he wrote his *Confessions* (397/401), he had rejected it.[34] He knew Cicero's *Tusculan Disputations*, but in various writings he disputed and modified it. Let us look at how he managed both of these things.

Augustine's reevaluation of friendship was straightforward. In his *Confessions*, he admitted that he had once sought "to love and to be loved"; he had felt that he and a boyhood friend had been "one soul in two bodies."[35] But now he wanted to redefine "true friendship." It was not a relationship forged between two men but rather the work of God, who, infusing their hearts with love, "glued" them together.[36]

---

[30] *Ibid.*, 1.10.20, p. 16.   [31] *Ibid.*, 1.10.22, p. 17.   [32] *Ibid.*, 1.9.19, pp. 14–15.

[33] See Scheer, "Topographies of Emotion," 32–61.

[34] For the dates of the works of Augustine discussed here, see Peter Brown, *Augustine of Hippo: A Biography* (Berkeley, 1969), Chronological Tables.

[35] Augustine, *Confessions* 3.1.1, in Saint Augustine, *Confessions*, ed. and trans. Pierre de Labriolle, 2 vols. (Paris, 1969, 1977) [henceforth *Conf.*], 1:45: "Amare et amari"; *ibid.*, 4.6.11, 1:74: "unam fuisse animam in duobus corporibus."

[36] Augustine, *Conf.* 4.4.7, 1:71: "tu [God] agglutinas inter haerentes tibi caritate diffusa in cordibus nostris (you glue together those adhering to you by the love diffused in our hearts)." On Augustine's debt to Cicero, see James McEvoy, "Friendship and Mutual Deception in Book IV of the *Confessions* of Augustine," in *Eklogai: Studies in Honour of*

Furthermore, two people could not be friends unless they shared the "right faith" – the right form of Christian doctrine. Here Augustine entered into a more general discussion about Christian friendship that was taking place during his lifetime and beyond.[37] (See Plate 1.1.)

Friendship was not the only affective issue that Augustine discussed theoretically. Although he did not write a treatise devoted to the emotions, he talked about them in works spanning much of his lifetime.[38] Already in the first book of *On Free Will* (388) he presented his view of human nature in the form of a dialogue. While the major crisis of Augustine's era would not happen until later (in 410 with the Sack of Rome), Augustine himself was in nearly continual personal crisis for the first thirty or so years of his life. Before writing *On Free Will* the year after his baptism (387), he had taken up and then repudiated Manichaeism; had similarly embraced and then rejected a common-law wife (originally in order to marry an heiress); had held prestigious posts in Rome and Milan; had been impressed by Ambrose, bishop of Milan; and only at age 32 had converted to Christianity.[39] His main design in *On Free Will*, as in so many of his writings, was to privilege permanence over transience. Free will for Augustine meant seeking the good – the permanent, eternal good: God. With the help of God, people could – and should – fix their wills on the good; their wills in turn would carry their emotions along.[40] Without this turn to the eternal, emotions would attach themselves to everything people were unwilling to lose and yet, ironically, would most certainly lose. These attachments perverted the right order of things. Again in the *City of God*, written many years later (413–20), perpetuity and ephemerality were Augustine's great themes. The City of God was eternal;

Thomas Finan and Gerard Watson, ed. Kiernan McGroarty (Maynooth, 2001), 3–19; John F. Monagle, "Friendship in St. Augustine's Biography: Classical Notion of Friendship," *Augustinian Studies* 2 (1971): 81–92; and Tarcisius Jan van Bavel, "The Influence of Cicero's Ideal of Friendship on Augustine," in *Augustiniana Traiectina*, ed. Jan den Boeft and Johannes van Oort (Paris, 1987), 59–72.

[37] See Stefan Rebenich, "Augustine on Friendship and Orthodoxy," in *A Companion to Augustine*, ed. Mark Vessey (Chichester, 2012), 365–74; Carolinne White, *Christian Friendship in the Fourth Century* (Cambridge, 1992). For Augustine's notion of friendship as the basis of his theory of family, society, and the state, see Donald X. Burt, *Friendship and Society: An Introduction to Augustine's Practical Philosophy* (Grand Rapids, 1999).

[38] See Emmanuel Bermon, "La théorie des passions chez saint Augustin," in *Les Passions antiques et médiévales. Théories et critiques des passions*, 1, ed. Bernard Besnier, Pierre-François Moreau, and Laurence Renault (Paris, 2003), 173–97, for an overview of Augustine's theory.

[39] Brown, *Augustine*, remains the classic biography.

[40] Augustine does not say much about the need for God's grace in *On Free Will*, but in his *Retractions*, he makes the point very clear. See Goulven Madec, "Unde malum? Le livre I du *De libero arbitrio*," and Ragnar Holte, "St. Augustine on Free Will (*De libero arbitrio*, III)," in *"De Libero Arbitrio" di Agostino d'Ippona*, commento di Goulven Madec et al. (Palermo, 1990), 16–17, 83–84.

Plate 1.1 An early icon of friendship in Christ

Plate 1.1

In the classical world, many sorts of relationships were termed friendships (*amicitiae*), including the bond uniting Roman patrons and their clients. Cicero's *Laelius* had been an attempt to lift the notion beyond practical advantage. During the course of the next few centuries, as Christianity gained purchase within the Roman Empire, Christ became (in some minds) the friend of the saints, much like a patron. Thus, in a hymn written for the martyr-saint Felix of Nola, the well-to-do Christian aristocrat Paulinus of Nola (d. 431) wrote, "Now I would like to give thanks to you, Felix, venerable father, eternal patron, my protector, Christ's dearest friend."[i] Augustine's Christ, however, was more than a patron: he "made" earthly friendships by gluing "together those adhering to you."[ii]

In the sixth- or seventh-century encaustic (colored wax) icon from Saint Catherine, Mount Sinai, pictured here, the two military saints Sergius and Bacchus carry the crosses of martyrs. Their three-jeweled collars (torcs) suggest the costume of the personal guards of Justinian, fitting garb for saints who were particularly venerated by that emperor.

Identical not only in clothing, accoutrements, and status, the two saints look exactly alike. This was a pictorial way to show their oneness in friendship. As their Greek hagiographer wrote, "The two chanted psalms together and prayed as if with one mouth." What united them was their love for Christ: "Being as one in their love for Christ, they were undivided from each other . . . united not by the way of nature, but in the manner of faith."[iii] The icon shows Christ's halo between the halos of the saints, as if forming the link of a golden chain that bound all three together. © The Bohdam and Varvara Khanenko National Museum of Arts, Kiev, Ukraine.

[i] Quoted in Rebenich, "Augustine on Friendship," 366.
[ii] Augustine, *Confessions* 4.4.7, 1:71.
[iii] Quoted in Stavroula Constantinou, "The Gift of Friendship: Beneficial and Poisonous Friendships in the Byzantine Greek Passion of Sergius and Bacchus," in *Friendship in the Middle Ages and Early Modern Age: Explorations*, ed. Marilyn Sandidge and Albrecht Classen (Berlin, 2011), 201–30 at 215–16.

the City of Man provided the evanescent things – food, friends, family, city – that were good only because they were of use to the pilgrims seeking the eternal city.

Those pilgrims had first to master the challenges of their fallen human nature. Original sin – for Augustine the sin of pride, of perverting the right order by which all are subordinate to God – corrupted and disordered human nature.[41] Man's task (with the help of God) was to reconstitute that right order. But how? The answer was in human nature itself and its natural superiority to other living things. True, people were like plants in that they took in nourishment, grew, and flourished. True, they were like animals in that they had senses and acted "to seek the pleasures of the body (*adpetere voluptates corporis*) and to avoid harm (*vitare molestias*)."[42] But they were unlike plants and animals in that they had higher faculties – the ability to jest and laugh (*jocari et ridere*) (a low sort of ability) and (a bit higher up) the "love of praise and glory (*amor laudis et gloria*) and the desire to dominate (*affectatio dominandi*)."[43] We shall soon see the importance of this latter desire. But now we need to understand that, for Augustine, none of these affective faculties made humans "superior to the beasts." On the contrary. They were what, in *On Free Will*, Augustine termed lusts (*libidines*), desires (*cupiditates*), and motions of the soul (*motus animae* or *motus animi*); they were, in effect, emotions, and for the most part they led to wallowing in sin. Elsewhere, Augustine used other terms as well: perturbations (*perturbationes*) (echoing Cicero), affections (*affectiones*), affects (*affectus*), and passions (*passiones*).[44] When these raged, a person's very life was shattered by "various and contrary tempests (*variis contrariisque tempestatibus*)," buffeted by fear (*timore*), desire (*desiderio*), anxiety (*anxietate*), empty and false happiness (*inani falsaque laetitia*), and the like.[45]

---

[41] Augustine, *De civitate dei* 14.3, ed. Bernard Dombart and Alphonse Kalb, Corpus Christianorum. Series Latina [henceforth CCSL] 47–48 (Turnhout, 1955) [henceforth: *Civ. dei*], 417, where pride (*superbia*) is the sin of the devil and where man's sin too is that "ille secundum se ipsum vivere voluit (he wanted to live by his own rule)."

[42] Augustine, *De libero arbitrio* 1.8, in Franco De Capitani, *Il "De Libero Arbitrio" di S. Agostino. Studio introduttivo, testo, traduzione e commento* (Milan, 1987) [henceforth *Lib. arb.*], 260.

[43] *Ibid*. For more on the desire to dominate, see Chapter 4, n. 118.

[44] For many of these, see Augustine, *Civ. dei* 9.4, p. 251. I adhere to the view of Knuuttila, *Emotions*, 156, that for Augustine these terms were interchangeable. However, Anastasia Scrutton, "Emotions in Augustine of Hippo and Thomas Aquinas: A Way Forward for the Im/passibility Debate?" *International Journal of Systematic Theology* 7 (2005): 169–77 at 171, thinks that Augustine generally used *passiones* in a "pejorative sense," while Sarah Catherine Byers, *Perception, Sensibility, and Moral Motivation in Augustine: A Stoic-Platonic Synthesis* (Cambridge, 2012), 61–62 at n. 22, says that Augustine uses *affectus* "when referring to emotions that he considers to be sins."

[45] Augustine, *Lib. arb.* 1.11, p. 268.

This was the wrong order, or, rather, it was total disorder. But there was a remedy: reason (*ratio*). This was a human faculty above all those pleasures, loves, and strivings. Augustine borrowed from the Platonic image of reason as the tamer of the soul's passions:

When reason (*ratio*) is master of these motions of the *anima* (*animae motibus*) a person is said to be well ordered (*ordinatus*) ... When this reason (*ratio ista*), therefore – or mind (*mens*) or spirit (*spiritus*) – rules the irrational motions of the *animus* (*animi motus*), then that [faculty of reason] – which rules by the law [of God] – truly reigns in a person.[46]

Augustine was impatient with terms. He did not care to define reason in contrast to mind and spirit, and earlier in the same chapter he explained why: "whatever it is (*hoc quidquid est*) by which man is placed above the beasts, whether it is called mind (*mens*) or spirit (*spiritus*) or more rightly both (*utrumque rectius*) since we find both in sacred scriptures," – whatever it is called, it justifies man's lordship over other things.[47] Similarly Augustine was unconcerned about the seat of the "motions," putting them in the *anima* in one sentence and in the *animus* in the next. Likewise, in the *City of God* he discounted any attempts to differentiate between various words for love because *caritas*, *amor*, and *dilectio* were all used as equivalents in Scripture.[48]

At bottom, the problem with the emotions was their desire for things that would always disappoint, since they were always ephemeral. Because people know that the things they desire are never secure, they "try to remove the impediments, and therefore they lead a wicked and sinful life (*facinorosam sceleratamque vitam*), which is better called 'death.'"[49]

All the bitter fruits of desire were for Augustine summed up in 1 John 2: 16–17: "For all that is in the world is the concupiscence of the flesh (*concupiscentia carnis*) and the concupiscence of the eyes (*concupiscentia oculorum*) and the pride of life (*superbia vitae*)." Both in his *Confessions* and his *Tractatus* on John's letter (begun perhaps 407/408, completed 416/417) Augustine spelled out the implications of this passage.[50] In the *Confessions*, he began with the desires of the flesh: lascivious emotions

---

[46] *Ibid.*, 1.8, pp. 260–62. The Platonic image is from the *Phaedrus*, 246a–254e.

[47] *Ibid.*, 260.

[48] Augustine, *Civ. dei* 14.7, pp. 421–22. See the introduction by Paul Agaësse to Saint Augustine, *Commentaire de la Première Épître de S. Jean*, ed. and trans. P. Agaësse, Sources Chrétiennes [henceforth SC] 75 (Paris, 1961) [henceforth *Tractatus*], 31–36, for some distinctions that Augustine nevertheless made from time to time among words for love.

[49] Augustine, *Lib. arb.* 1.4, p. 248.

[50] Augustine, *Conf.* 10.30–41, pp. 271–90; *Tractatus* 2.10–14, pp. 170–80. The classic discussion of the three desires and their legacy is Donald R. Howard, *The Three Temptations: Medieval Man in Search of the World* (Princeton, 1966).

(*lascivos motus*); the dangerous pleasure (*periculosa jucunditas*) of eating and drinking; the charm (*inlecebra*) of smells; the delights (*voluptates*) of hearing – in short, the concrete pleasures of the senses.[51] He enumerated the beauties of nature and man-made things. But even more dangerous than such desires of the flesh was a "certain empty, inquisitive desire (*curiosa cupiditas*) dignified by the name of cognition and knowledge."[52] Augustine attributed this curiosity to the concupiscence of the eyes because knowledge arrives mainly through the eyes, either literally, as when we read something, or metaphorically, as when we say, "I see!" Pleasure and curiosity have different objects: pleasure (*voluptas*) seeks the beautiful, the harmonious, the sweet, and so on; curiosity (*curiositas*), however, "may, for the sake of experiment, [seek] the contraries of these things – not in order to be discomfited, but out of the desire to experience and to know (*experiendi noscendique libidine*)."[53] Curiosity leads to gaping at corpses, searching out the secrets of nature, and even demanding God's signs and portents – not for the purposes of salvation but simply for the pleasure of the experience.

Curiosity could lead, if a person were not careful, to the "pride of life," which might include attributing to oneself the miracles that should be accredited to God.[54] As bishop of Hippo, Augustine was particularly subject to the allure of pride. "Has this third sort of temptation ceased from me, or can it [ever] cease in my whole life: to wish to be feared (*timeri*) and loved (*amari*) by people for no other reason than to gain joy (*gaudium*) from it, a joy that is not joy?"[55] A man who succumbed to the pride of life thought that he was a master even though he was in fact a slave to sin and passion, just like the devil. His enslavement was the culmination of the disordered life resulting from the Fall. In the right order, God was lord of all; with the loss of right order, people were infected by the "lust for domination (*libido dominandi*)," a miserable condition: "And certainly it is happier to be a slave to a person than [to be a slave] to lust, since the very lust for domination – not to mention all the other [lusts] – ravages the hearts of human beings with the cruelest despotism."[56]

Yet Augustine did not wholly condemn these desires. They could be turned around and attached to the right things – or, rather, they could be rightly attached to things used in ways that redounded to God's praise and glory. Then the desires became virtues. The key to this "turn around"

---

[51] Augustine, *Conf.* 10.34, p. 278.   [52] *Ibid.*, 10.35, p. 280.   [53] *Ibid.*, 281.
[54] Augustine, *Tractatus* 2.13, pp. 176–78, makes clear the connection between "desiderium oculorum (desire of the eyes)" and "ambitio saeculi [quae] superbia est (the ambition of the world, which is pride)."
[55] Augustine, *Conf.* 10.36, p. 284.   [56] Augustine, *Civ. dei* 19.15, p. 682.

was the human will. "The character of a man's will (*voluntas*) is at issue,"
he said. "For if it is turned the wrong way, it will turn these emotions (*hos motus*) awry; but if it is straight (*recta*), they will be not only blameless, but even praiseworthy."[57] Indeed, the emotions were themselves acts of will (*voluntas*): "the will is certainly in all of them, or rather, all are nothing other than wills."[58] Unlike Cicero and the Stoics, Augustine did not have one list of "good" and another of "bad" emotions. Rather, emotions were neutral: the issue was the will's ethical bent, not emotions per se. To make hard distinctions between *gaudium* and *laetitia* – as Cicero had done, assigning the first to the *eupatheiai* and the second to a wild sort of pleasure – to do this seemed pedantic to Augustine.[59] He was interested in how people really used these words and, again as with love, how they were used in Scripture.

For Augustine *voluntas* encompassed far more than it did for Cicero, who, as we have seen, used the word to translate the Greek *boulésis*, a sort of rational desire, and therefore one of the "good" emotions (see Table 1.2 above).[60] For Augustine, the will was the source of freedom of choice, the locus of moral responsibility, the site of will-power, and a component of all actions.[61] *Voluntas* could not be "good" by definition. Were it always good, why would the angels have had to qualify it as such when they wished for "peace on earth to men of good will."[62] So *voluntas* could be bad as well as good. At the same time, Augustine also argued that *by themselves* human beings could not choose the good. They had to have God's grace. As James Wetzel has put it, "When [Augustine] identifies emotions with expressions of will ... he is presupposing that redemptive consent, the kind that commends us to our better selves, is divinely mediated and no longer simply up to us."[63] Further, once Augustine adopted the notion of God's "gratuitous election," which he did in 396 when first presiding as bishop of Hippo, the role of the human will was further reduced. Thus, while expanding the role of will as moral arbiter, Augustine at the same time diminished it in favor of God's grace.[64]

---

[57] *Ibid.*, 14.6, p. 421.   [58] *Ibid.*   [59] *Ibid.*, 14.8, pp. 423–24.

[60] See Graver, *Cicero on the Emotions*, xxxviii.

[61] See Sorabji, *Emotions*, 319–40, esp. 335–37; Albrecht Dihle, *The Theory of Will in Classical Antiquity* (Berkeley 1982), 123–44. See, for example, Augustine, *Lib. arb.*, 1.11, p. 266: "Nulla res alia mentem cupiditatis comitem faciat quam propria voluntas et liberum arbitrium (Nothing may make the mind companion to desire other than its own will and free will)."

[62] Augustine, *Civ. dei* 14.8, p. 424.

[63] James Wetzel, "Augustine," in *The Oxford Handbook of Religion and Emotion* (Oxford, 2008), 349–63 at 351.

[64] James Wetzel, "Augustine on the Will," in *A Companion to Augustine*, 339–52.

Because he connected emotions to this new notion of human will, Augustine challenged the Stoic distinction between the passions and the pre-passions (those pricks, tears, blushes, contractions of the body and so on that signaled an emotion was on the way). For Augustine, the difference was purely semantic: the pre-passions were themselves initial emotions. Turning pale with fear was evidence of fear, not something "before" fear and "better than" fear. In fact, for Augustine fear was not necessarily (as the Stoics would have it) a bad thing. The real issue was "not *whether* [the pious soul/mind (*pius animus*)] is afraid (*timeat*), but *why* it is afraid. ... [It is good] to be afraid for someone in peril so that he may not perish."[65] Augustine considered will and love (*amor*) to be closely aligned and even to overlap. If your will was aimed at the good, you were a lover of the good and a hater of evil. Or, to put it in the reverse, if your will loved evil, you were a hater of the good.

The list of emotion words that results from Augustine's discussion (see Table 1.6) suggests that Cicero's emotions were assimilated into a more general treatment that centered above all on love and desire (words in majuscule). Even grief and pain, which were among the *aegritudines* for Cicero, were for Augustine the offspring of love, as when Saint Paul "felt great sorrow (*magnam tristitiam*) and ceaseless grief (*continuum dolorem*) in his heart" for the Israelites, who did not submit to God.[66]

Augustine rehabilitated the emotions. The Stoics – and even more fiercely Cicero in his *Tusculan Disputations* – had treated almost all emotions as bad, as vices. But for Augustine, emotions had both good and bad potential. If they were ruled by straightforward, godly intentions, they were good. Indeed, they were virtues. If they stemmed from wrong, ungodly intentions, they were bad; they were vices. Augustine concluded his discussion of the emotions in the *City of God* succinctly: "If these emotions (*motus*), these affects (*affectus*) deriving from love of the good (*amor boni*) and from holy *caritas* are to be called vices, then we might as well allow true vices to be called virtues. But since these feelings (*affectiones*) follow right reason when they are felt where appropriate, who would dare then to say that they were diseases or morally depraved feelings (*vitiosas passiones*)?"[67] He was standing the ancient legacy on its head.

---

[65] Augustine discusses this point in *Civ. dei* 9.5, p. 254. See also Knuuttila, *Emotions*, 155, 171. Nevertheless, Augustine retained the distinctions so dear to the Stoics between "suggestion," "pleasure," and "consent" when he discussed the difference between "fornication of the body" and "fornication of the heart." See Silvana Vecchio, "Peccatum cordis," in *Il cuore/The Heart = Micrologus* 11 (2003): 325–42 at 325–26.

[66] Augustine, *Civ. dei* 14.9, p. 427. See Rom 9:2.   [67] *Ibid.*

Table 1.6 *Augustine's emotion words*[a]

---

aegritudo, pain
   aegrescere, to suffer
AFFECTATIO, desire
AFFECTIO, affection/emotion
affectus, emotion
ambitio, ambition
AMOR, love
   AMARE, to love
anxietas, anxiety
avaritia, avarice
CARITAS, to love
cautio, caution
cavere, to beware
CONCUPISCENTIA, desire
contristare, to sadden
CUPIDITAS, desire
   CUPERE, to desire
DESIDERIUM, desire
   DESIDERARE, to desire
desidio, sloth
DILECTIO, love
   DILIGERE, to love
dolor, sorrow, pain
   dolere, to feel pain
gaudium, joy
   gaudere, to feel joy
invidia, envy
ira, anger
jocari, to joke
laetitia, joy
   laetari, to be joyful
LIBIDO, lust
luctus, grief
LUXURIA, lust
metus, fear
   metuere, to fear
motus [*animae/animi*], emotion
odium, hate
   odisse, to hate
passio, emotion
perturbatio, emotion
pervicacia, stubbornness
ridere, to laugh
superbia, pride
timor, fear
tremor, trembling
tristitia, pain/sorrow
vindicare, to avenge

---

[a] Love and desire words are in *CAPITAL ITALICS*.

If we put together the Ciceronian lists with Augustine's we have a virtual emotion "word hoard" from the ancient world. It is by no means complete, for neither Cicero nor Augustine claimed that their discussions were exhaustive. Indeed, they went out of their way to indicate that they were providing only examples. And, to be sure, there were other theories and somewhat different vocabularies and emphases in the Roman world. Nevertheless, those from Cicero and Augustine are enough to allow us to begin to explore in the next chapter some early medieval emotional communities, which drew on these words for their emotional expression.

2   Attachment and detachment

The emotion words and theories of Cicero and Augustine lasted long after the last Western Roman emperor was deposed in 476. That was true for the elites in the provinces as well as in Rome itself.[1] Yet such persistence hides a fact of equal importance: that different emotional communities did not deploy this heritage in the same way. There were in Gaul in the late sixth through seventh centuries at least three distinct emotional communities. In Austrasia the elites celebrated sentimental feelings of every sort, drawing on almost all of the vocabulary listed in Chapter 1. In Neustria just a bit later, however, the elites defined themselves (largely in reaction to the Austrasians) by their emotional detachment – except when heaven was their focus. They drew gingerly on words of love. Finally throughout Francia (as we may now call it) late seventh-century authors writing (again) for the elites emphasized the demonstrative emotions such as envy and anger. (For all the place names in this chapter, see Map 2.1.)

Family feeling in Austrasia

Clovis (d. 511), the Merovingian king who united Gaul under his rule, left his kingdom to four of his sons. Fractured by civil wars, the kingdom was eventually reunited under Clothar I after his brothers predeceased him. When he died (in 561), it was divided in turn among his surviving sons, Charibert (561–67), Guntram (561–93), Sigibert (561–75), and Chilperic (561–84).

---

[1] See discussions of the educational backgrounds of the various authors studied below. Some material in this chapter repeats that in Barbara H. Rosenwein, *Emotional Communities in the Early Middle Ages* (Ithaca, NY, 2006), chaps. 4 and 5, used by permission of the publisher, Cornell University Press. The interested reader will find a much fuller bibliography in those chapters.

Map 2.1 Early medieval Francia

The elites of Sigibert's kingdom, centered in the region later called Austrasia, cultivated an emotional style that may be glimpsed in the writings of Venantius Fortunatus (c. 535-c. 605) and Gregory of Tours (c. 538-c. 594).[2] Fortunatus studied in Ravenna, read the classical and patristic authors, and schooled himself in Virgilian poetry.[3] Arriving at Sigibert's court in 565, he earned his living as a

[2] Strictly speaking, Sigibert's kingdom, centered at Reims/Metz and including associated cities in the south such as Clermont, was not yet Austrasia.

[3] For Fortunatus' absorption of these authors, see Antonio V. Nazzaro, "Intertestualità biblico-patristica e classica in testi poetici di Venanzio Fortunato," in *Venanzio Fortunato tra Italia e Francia. Atti del Convegno Internazionale di Studi (Valdobbiadene-Treviso 1990)* (Treviso, 1993), 99–135, and Marc Reydellet, "Tradition et nouveauté dans les *Carmina* de Fortunat," in *ibid.*, 81–98 at 86–90, where Fortunatus' poetic forms and their inspiration are discussed. See also Franca Ela Consolino, "L'eredità dei classici nella poesia del

writer under the patronage of kings, bishops, and other members of the elites there. Around 567 or 568 he settled at Poitiers, where he became a priest and the friend of the nuns at the monastery of the Holy Cross. In c. 600 he became bishop of Poitiers.[4] His contemporary Gregory of Tours, born in Clermont, was probably educated in the household of his great-uncle Nicetius, bishop of Lyon. Even so, he well knew the techniques of classical rhetoric as well as the writings of the Church Fathers and, above all, Scripture.[5] He became bishop of Tours in 573.

Fortunatus and Gregory were good friends. Marc Reydellet has spoken of their "total communion of thought about matters divine and human."[6] Here I want to talk about their common emotional sensibilities.

Above all, they valued family feeling, drawing on the sorts of words we find in Cicero's list of *aegritudines* for mockery and for praise, as well as those we find in Cicero's vocabulary of friendship and Augustine's of love.

VI secolo," in *Prospettive sul tardoantico. Atti del convegno di Pavia (27–28 novembre 1997)*, edited by Giancarlo Mazzoli and Fabio Gasti (Como, 1999), 69–90, esp. 86–90; Luce Pietri, "Venance Fortunat, lecteur des Pères latins," in *Chartae caritatis. Études de patristique et d'antiquité tardive en hommage à Yves-Marie Duval*, ed. Benoît Gain and Pierre Jay (Paris, 2004), 127–41. Fortunatus, *Poems* 5.1.7, in Venance Fortunat, *Poèmes*, ed. and trans. Marc Reydellet, 3 vols. (Paris, 2002–4), 2:11, is a letter to Martin of Gallicia, outlining Fortunatus' educational background. He claims knowledge of Stoic and Peripatetic (Aristotelian) thought, but probably in digested form since he says that "Plato, Aristotle, Chrysippus and Pittacus are known to me only by reputation, not by reading," and, although he says he read Hilary, Gregory (of Nyssa? of Nazianzen?), Ambrose, and Augustine as if "nearly asleep (*dormitanti*)," this may have been more a gesture of humility than a fact. Pietri, "Venance Fortunat," 132, suggests that he read "large extracts" of Augustine, Hilary, Ambrose, and Jerome, possibly from florilegia such as the *Excerpta ex operibus s. Augustini* of Eugippius. For the education of both Fortunatus and Gregory, I thank Helmut Reimitz for bibliographical help.

[4] See the biographical introduction by Marc Reydellet in Venance Fortunat, *Poèmes*, 1: vii–xxviii; Judith W. George, *Venantius Fortunatus: A Latin Poet in Merovingian Gaul* (Oxford, 1992) [henceforth George, *A Latin Poet*], 4–34; Brian Brennan, "The Career of Venantius Fortunatus," *Traditio* 41 (1985): 49–78.

[5] On Gregory's education and training, see Max Bonnet, *Le latin de Grégoire de Tours* (Paris, 1890; rpt. 1968), 48–76. On his mastery of late antique rhetoric, his possible acquaintance with the works of Augustine, and his certain familiarity with Eusebius of Caesarea via the translation by Rufinus, see Guy Halsall, "The Preface to Book V of Gregory of Tours' Histories: Its Form, Context and Significance," *English Historical Review* 122 (2007): 297–317. For further reflections on Gregory's learning, see Conrad Leyser, "'Divine Power Flowed from this Book': Ascetic Language and Episcopal Authority in Gregory of Tours' *Life of the Fathers*," in *The World of Gregory of Tours*, ed. Kathleen Mitchell and Ian Wood (Leiden, 2002), 281–94.

[6] See Marc Reydellet, "Tours et Poitiers. Les relations entre Grégoire et Fortunat," in *Grégoire de Tour et l'espace gaulois*, ed. Nancy Gauthier and Henri Galinié (Tours, 1997), 159–67, quote on 159.

"The tears (*lacrimas*) of the parents dried, overcome by great happiness (*laetitiae mole*)," wrote Fortunatus as he recounted Saint Hilary's miraculous cure of a little boy named Probianus, who moments before had been at death's door.[7] This was a society in which the mother – and her feelings – mattered as much as the father and his.[8] Thus, Gregory wrote about a mother who retrieved her healed baby from the tomb of Saint Illidius "with trembling and joy (*cum tremore et gaudio*)."[9] When Gregory famously bewailed the Merovingian "civil wars" as bringing "pain (*dolorem*) to my mind (*animo*)" in the pages of his *Histories*, his lament arose less from an ideology of political unity or a principled stance against violence than from the bitter thought that brother was fighting against brother.[10] The dysfunctional family was his focus. Treating the first set of civil wars, he described Clothild's visit to the tomb of Saint Martin: "She knelt in prayer and stayed awake throughout the night, praying that civil war not arise between her sons (*inter filios suos*)."[11] When the sons of Clothar I went to war, Gregory stressed their fraternal ties: "King Sigibert stirred up the peoples who lived across the Rhine and, starting a civil war, determined to go against his brother (*fratrem suum*) Chilperic. When he heard this, Chilperic sent messengers to his brother (*fratrem suum*) Guntram. The two joined together [and] made a pact that neither would allow his brother (*fratrem suum*) to be destroyed."[12] The repetition of the word "brother" continued: the horror of the story was that the pact did not hold once Sigibert threatened to march against his brother (*fratre suo*) Guntram.

Similarly Gregory recounted the last part of the famous "war" (*bellum*) between Sichar and Chramnesind as a friendship and brotherhood gone awry.[13] Sichar had killed Chramnesind's kin, but eventually, with Gregory's intervention and with Chramnesind

---

[7] Venantius Fortunatus, *Liber de virtutibus s. Hilarii* c. 3, ed. Bruno Krusch, MGH AA 4.2 (Berlin, 1885), 7–11 at 8.

[8] Cristina La Rocca, "Venanzio Fortunato e la società del VI secolo," in *Alto medioevo mediterraneo*, ed. Stefano Gasparri (Florence, 2005), 145–67 at 155–61, points to the important change from the patrilineal Roman family to a new Frankish model that traced lineage through both father and mother.

[9] Gregory of Tours [henceforth Greg. Tur.], *Liber vitae patrum* [henceforth *VP*] c. 4, ed. Bruno Krusch, MGH SRM 1.2 (Hannover, 1885; rpt. 1969), 211–94 at 221.

[10] Greg. Tur., *Historiarum libri X* (henceforth *Histories*) 4.50, ed. Bruno Krusch and Wilhelm Levison, MGH SRM 1.1 (Hannover, 1951; rpt. 1993), 187.

[11] *Ibid.*, 3.28, p. 124.   [12] *Ibid.*, 4.49, p. 185.

[13] The feud is treated *ibid.*, 7.47, pp. 366–68 and 9.19, pp. 432–34. For recent discussions, see Warren C. Brown, *Violence in Medieval Europe* (Harlow, UK, 2011), pp. 38–41, and Ian Wood, "'The Bloodfeud of the Franks': A Historiographical Legend," *Early Medieval Europe* 14 (2006): 489–504.

compensated by Sichar (using money from Gregory's church coffers), each swore that he would "not say a word against the other."[14] Within three years, Sichar "had concluded a great friendship (*magnam amicitiam*) with [Chramnesind], and they loved one another with such mutual love (*caritate mutua*) that they often took their meals together and slept in one bed at the same time."[15] During one such feast, as Gregory imagined it, Sichar, reeling from wine, abused their affection: "You ought to give me great thanks, oh sweetest brother (*o dulcissime frater*), for killing your family members. Since you accepted compensation for them, gold and silver abounds in your house."[16] Gregory, always the ironist, played up their amity only to lay bare its fragility. When Chramnesind heard Sichar's words, he became "bitter in his mind" (*amaro animo*), just like (Gregory surely made the association) the Old Testament Anna, who was mocked for her sterility by her husband's second wife; or like David, enraged like a bear who had lost her cubs.[17] These were analogues of familial loss, and Chramnesind's anguish was, in Gregory's mind, nourished by similar fears: "'unless I avenge the death of my family members,' he said in his heart (*dixitque in corde suo*), 'I ought to lose the name man and be called a weak woman.'"[18] He then extinguished the lights and killed Sichar.

If loyalty to family members trumped a three-year-old friendship, that was only because the love among blood relatives was so intense. We have already seen how Fortunatus imagined parental tears shed over little Probianus. Gregory's mother, too, was (according to her son) utterly devoted to him. When he was ill, she considered it a "day of mourning (*maestum diem*)." He, in turn, cared about her pain: "Don't be sad (*nihil ... contristeris*)," he told her, "but take me back to the tomb of blessed bishop Illidius. For I believe ... that his power will bring happiness (*laetitiam*) to you and health to me."[19] When Fortunatus wrote to Gregory to ask him to help some members of his flock, he presented it as a family drama. He met on the road a father and mother who, he wrote, "mourn (*lugent*) their daughter with weeping (*fletibus*), filling the air with their cries and covering their cheeks with tears (*lacrimando*)." Through sobs and sighs they explained to Fortunatus that their daughter had been sold into slavery. "Investigate, follow up," Fortunatus admonished Gregory, "and if it be otherwise than it should be, sweet one and

---

[14] Greg. Tur., *Histories* 7.47, p. 368.   [15] *Ibid.*, 9.19, p. 432.   [16] *Ibid.*, p. 433.
[17] 1 Sam 1:10 and 2 Sam 17:8.
[18] Greg. Tur., *Histories* 9.19, p. 433. "Dixitque in corde suo" echoes Gen 27:41, where Esau vowed in his heart to kill his brother Jacob.
[19] Greg. Tur., *VP* 2.2, p. 220.

father, deliver her and join her to your flock. Return her to her father as well."[20]

Gregory's fatherly role, invoked by Fortunatus when he told him about the mourning parents, was a potent metaphor. He thought of himself in the same terms. When he wrote about the dysentery epidemic that ravaged "almost all of Gaul" in 580, he dwelled on "his" children and his feelings for them: "We lost children, so sweet and dear to us, whom we caressed on our laps or carried in our arms or whom we nourished with devoted zeal, providing them with food with our own hands. But, as we wipe away our tears, we say with blessed Job, 'The Lord gives; the Lord takes away.'"[21] Gregory's feeling for children not his own should not surprise us in a society in which godparenthood and adoption could establish ties as binding as "biological" kinship.[22]

---

[20] Fortunatus, *Poems* 5.14, 2:39, ll. 7–8 and 21–22. Nevertheless, for all his sentimentality about parents, Fortunatus, *Vita Germani episcopi Parisiaci* c. 1, ed. Bruno Krusch, MGH SRM 7 (Hannover, 1920; rpt. 1997), 372–418 at 372, reported that the mother of Saint Germanus tried to abort the saint in the womb. She had only a short time earlier given birth to another child, so "pudore mota muliebra (moved by womanly modesty)," presumably because her new pregnancy violated religious strictures against intercourse before weaning a previous child, she took an abortifacient and, when that did not work, attempted to crush the child in her belly. Thus "certabatur mater cum parvulo (the mother was struggling with the little one)." She succeeded in hurting only herself, while the saint "matrem redderet innocentem (restored his mother to her guiltless state)." But why would Fortunatus include this episode in the *Vita*? I suggest that he wished to signal Germanus' potency not only as a miracle worker (the main thrust of the *Vita*), but also as one who, even within the womb, had the power to "restore (*reddere*)" people to their original state. Compare *ibid.*, c. 5, p. 377, where the saint's prayers restore a bishop to health ("languidum saluti fuisse redditum"); *ibid.*, c. 14, p. 382, where the saint restores contracted fingers to their former state ("digitis redditur organum"); *ibid.*, c. 17, p. 383, where a certain Bobolinus, out of his mind, was restored to health by the saint's prayers ("sanus redditur"), and similarly in cc. 18, 27, 28, 33, 34, 37, 40, and 51. The attempted abortion episode is noted in Isabelle Réal, *Vies de saints, vie de famille. Représentation et système de la parenté dans le Royaume mérovingien (481–751) d'après les sources hagiographiques* (Turnhout, 2001), 400.

[21] Greg. Tur., *Histories* 5.34, p. 239. On attitudes toward children during this period, see Réal, *Vies*, 384–474; Cécile Treffort, "La vie et le corps de l'enfant au VIe siècle. Perception, signification et utilisation du thème de l'enfance dans l'oeuvre de Grégoire de Tours," in *L'enfant, son corps, son histoire*, ed. Luc Buchet (Sophia Antipolis, 1997), 115–27, who is not so much interested in "affection" as in the view, typified by Gregory, that the illnesses and deaths of children were part of the divine plan. Nevertheless, she also notes (p. 126) that cemeteries from the period buried newborns in privileged zones. Armelle Alduc-Le Bagousse, "Comportements à l'égard des nouveau-nés et des petits enfants dans les sociétés de la fin de l'Antiquité et du haut Moyen Âge," in *ibid.*, 81–95, surveys the evidence for the marginalization of infants, but also chronicles growing concern about them from the fifth through ninth centuries and emphasizes evidence of parental affection.

[22] See Bernhard Jussen, *Spiritual Kinship as Social Practice: Godparenthood and Adoption in the Early Middle Ages*, trans. Pamela Selwyn (Newark, 2000).

The affection between spouses was imagined as similarly tender. Gregory recounted a story of "two lovers (*duos amantes*)." Their chaste marriage, the genesis of which Gregory described in detail,[23] may not seem particularly loving to modern eyes. But for Gregory their "sleeping together in the same bed (*in uno stratu quiescentes*)," yet refraining from intercourse (*non coitu*), was a special secret between the two ("with them this most chaste life was in secret"), and it was only "by mutual consent" that eventually the husband, oddly named Injuriosus, or "noxious," "received the tonsure for Holy Orders, and the virgin [that is, his wife] put on the habit of a nun."[24] When she died, Injuriosus admitted their secret aloud, thanking God that he was returning his wife to her Maker still pure (*inpollutam*). But she, lying in the tomb, gently teased him: "Be quiet, be quiet, man of God; you don't need to confess our secret, since no one asked you." Upon his own death, Injuriosus was buried apart from his wife. "But in the morning, the tombs were discovered to be together, and they remain that way to this day. That's why the inhabitants now call them the 'two lovers.'"[25] Side-by-side to the end: that was Gregory's sentimental ideal for husbands and wives.

Fortunatus was similarly taken with marital love. In his epithalamium celebrating the marriage of King Sigibert and Brunhild, Fortunatus imagined how the couple felt about one another before their wedding. Sigibert, in love (*amans*), is seized by fire (*igne*) for his bride. She desires (*cupit*) him as well, though modesty (*verecundia*) holds her back. Cupid hovers above, shooting his "love-bearing" (*amoriferas*) arrows. At night, thinking of his Brunhild, Sigibert frolics in the embraces (*per amplexum*) of her image.[26]

Love of God was similarly spousal, tender, and passionate as Fortunatus portrayed it. He wrote a poem praising virginity to celebrate the appointment of Agnes by Radegund as abbess of Holy Cross.[27] Here the bride's spouse was Christ, and Fortunatus gave him voice: "She [Agnes] lay as though in vigil (in case I might come from somewhere) pressing her cold limbs on the now tepid marble. / She, turned to ice, preserved my fire (*ignem*) in her bones. / While her inward parts are rigid, her breast is inflamed with love (*amore calet*). / ... Although the moisture of her cheeks was exhausted (*exhausto humore*) by her continuous tears, / the earth swam with the waters of her [now] parched eyes. / And because,

---

[23] In Greg. Tur., *Histories* 1.47, pp. 30–31.

[24] This part of the story is recounted in Greg. Tur., *Liber in gloria confessorum* c. 31, ed. Bruno Krusch, MGH SRM 1.2:294–370 at 317.

[25] *Ibid.*   [26] Fortunatus, *Poems* 6.1, 2:45–46, ll. 37–57.

[27] For the little that is known about Agnes, see most recently *Venantius Fortunatus: Poems to Friends*, trans. Joseph Pucci (Indianapolis, 2010), 78.

while alive, she was unable to see me with her carnal eyes, she lovingly (*amata*) sent up prayers."[28]

In turn, Christ loved Agnes tenderly: "When she lay on the ground, resting but not overcome by sleep, / I often lay down with her to take care of her. / I shared her grief (*condolui*); I wiped away her river of tears (*lacrimarum flumina*), / giving her kisses (*oscula*) sweetened by shining honeycombs."[29] "Now let her reign and rejoice in a delightful love," Christ declares.[30] The celestial assembly voices its assent, and Agnes' name is written into the Book of Eternity. Adorned with jewels, crowned with a diadem, and clothed in garb befitting a virgin married to God, she will at last sit as queen in the bridal chamber (*thalamo regina sedebit*).[31]

Fortunatus left his own family behind in Italy, but he turned his friends and patrons into a sort of substitute family, writing poetic letters to them filled with words of affection.[32] He was particularly partial to the word *dulcedo*, sweetness, to express the feelings of love and friendship. We have already seen the word used by Gregory to describe the affection between Sichar and Chramnesind.[33] Fortunatus drew on the same vocabulary. To Lupus he wrote, "O name of Lupus, sweet (*dulce*) to me and always worth repeating, / ... the man whom the indestructible arc of my breast guards, once [he is] included on the tables of sweetness (*dulcedinis*) within."[34] He was captivated by Gogo's sweetness (*dulcedine*).[35] He assured Bishop Eufronius that "there is no bodily heart where the wonderful sweetness (*dulcedo*) of your soul is not received."[36]

Fortunatus turned especially to Gregory for familial warmth, dedicating his first letter collection to the bishop of Tours.[37] "O, highest of priests, ... beacon to my love; ... holding [you] in my heart by the pledge of friendship, ... I therefore pray you, father, ... that you deign by your sacred mouth to recall that I am yours."[38] Let us note that this very poem was also sent to Bishop Baudoald, a member of Fortunatus' circle of

---

[28] Fortunatus, *Poems* 8.3, 2:138–39, ll. 211–20.   [29] *Ibid.*, 2:140, ll. 253–56.

[30] *Ibid.*, p. 140, l. 257.   [31] *Ibid.*, p. 141, l. 277.

[32] In a poem to Agnes (*ibid.*, 11.6, 3:116–17, ll. 9–12) Fortunatus calls her both mother (*mater*) and sister (*soror*), "as if" (*ac si*) they had both nursed at the breasts of "mother Radegund."

[33] See above, n. 16.

[34] *Ibid.*, 7.8, 2:98, ll. 33–36. On Lupus, a friend and Austrasian courtier, as substitute family, see *ibid.*, 7.9, 2:101, ll. 11–12: "quod pater ac genetrix, frater, soror, ordo nepotum,/quod poterat regio, solves amore pio (What father, mother, brother, sister, a line of nephews could do, you fulfill with your tender love)."

[35] *Ibid.*, 7.1, 2:85, l. 11.   [36] *Ibid.*, 3.1, 1:81–82.

[37] Reydellet, introduction to *ibid.*, 1:lxx, dates this first collection of poems (consisting of books 1–7) to 576/577.

[38] *Ibid.*, 5.12, 2:38.

"sweet" friends.[39] Were his words simply boilerplate?[40] It is possible,
though Judith George has argued persuasively that Fortunatus' poems
were quite different for people with whom he had "no real tie of friendship
and those where there is such an affinity."[41] We will soon explore the
emotional community at the Neustrian court just after the time of
Gregory and Fortunatus. It eschewed most expressions of affection. So
even boilerplate can tell us about norms and comfort zones. In this case,
the *topoi* belonged to the tradition that C. Stephen Jaeger has illuminated,
where love language was understood to ennoble both lover and beloved.[42]

The issue for us is not whether Injuriosus "really" loved his wife or
whether Sigibert and Brunhild were "really" touched by Cupid, or
whether Agnes pined for Christ, or even whether Fortunatus "really"
liked his friends. We will never know, and even at the time, no one
could have been sure. Our task, therefore, is not to ascertain "real"
feelings – which are, as I argued in the introduction, themselves socially
shaped and understood – but rather to appreciate the expectations and
norms of Fortunatus and Gregory and to ask if they reflected those of a
larger group – an emotional community. The admittedly sparse evidence
suggests that they did. We can even name a few other members.

Brunhild was one. She met Fortunatus almost at the moment of her
arrival in Gaul for her marriage to Sigibert. The poet stayed on with
the royal couple for over a year.[43] Brunhild also knew Gregory, and
she was instrumental in promoting him to the episcopal see of
Tours.[44] She, Fortunatus, and Gregory met together at least once –
at Metz in 588 along with Brunhild's son, King Childebert II. While
Gregory went from there to Chalon as Childebert's emissary to King
Guntram, Fortunatus stayed behind, writing poems to the king and
dowager queen.[45] The fact that he addressed them both as "lords" and

---

[39] *Ibid.*, 9.8, 3:30.

[40] Pucci, *Poems to Friends*, 33, argues that the repetition of the poem in a later collection as
being addressed to Baudoald "reflects less on the sincerity of Fortunatus' poetic motivations (it seems impossible that he would recycle poems) than on the circumstances
surrounding the gathering and publication of the collection." This is certainly one good
interpretation. However, it does not obviate the fact that Fortunatus had some stock
phrases that he used to express high-flown affection for his friends; these typically used
the word *dulcedo* and its variants (literally, sweetness, but used to express approval,
flattery, and affection). See Rosenwein, *Emotional Communities*, 110–13, and John
M. Wallace-Hadrill, *The Frankish Church* (Oxford, 1983), 83.

[41] George, *A Latin Poet*, 143.

[42] C. Stephen Jaeger, *Ennobling Love: In Search of a Lost Sensibility* (Philadelphia, 1999).

[43] George, *A Latin Poet*, 28.

[44] According to Fortunatus, Gregory's appointment was by the *judicio* (judgment or approbation) of Brunhild and Sigibert: see Fortunatus, *Poems* 5.3, 2:17, ll. 13–16.

[45] Greg. Tur., *Histories* 9.20, p. 434. For Fortunatus' presence at Metz at this time, see his
Poems 10.7–9, 3:78–86; Wilhelm Meyer, *Der Gelegenheitsdichter Venantius Fortunatus*

"kings" suggests their equality.[46] Similarly, when we look at the bits of writing that we have from Brunhild, we find emotional norms consonant with those of the men whom we have been following. In a series of extant letters sent after the death of her daughter Ingund, she negotiated for the return of her young grandson Athanagild, who was living in Constantinople.[47] In one of these, directed to her "sweetest grandson (*dulcissimo nepoti*)," she spoke of the "great happiness that the longed-for occasion (*votiva magne felicitatis occasio*)" of writing to him brought her. Her letter – "direct and very love-worthy (*directis epistulis amabilibus*)" – constituted a way for her to be present to his eyes, and in him, she said, she could recall her "sweet daughter (*dulcis filia*)." Indeed, because her grandson remained alive, she had not entirely lost her daughter.

Baudonivia, a nun at Holy Cross, had the same emotional palette. She wrote a *Life* of Radegund (d. 587) that she said was intended to complement a slightly earlier one by Fortunatus.[48] Like Fortunatus' Agnes, so too Baudonivia's Radegund found her true bridegroom in heaven: "She gave herself to her celestial spouse (*sponso*) with such complete love (*toto amore*) that, as she embraced God with a pure heart, she felt Christ living within her."[49] A model mother, Baudonivia's Radegund loved her children passionately – in this case the nuns of her convent: "I have chosen you, my daughters (*filias*); you, my eyes; you, my life; you, my rest and entire happiness (*felicitas*); you, my new plantation (*plantatio*)."[50]

Another of Fortunatus' acquaintances was Dynamius, a Provençal nobleman, a regional governor (*rector provinciae*), and a writer of merit in his own right.[51] "I await you, my love," Fortunatus wrote to him,

(Berlin, 1901), 22; Richard Koebner, *Venantius Fortunatus. Seine Persönlichkeit und seine Stellung in der geistigen Kultur des Merowingerreiches* (Leipzig, 1915; rpt. 1973), 108–9.

[46] Fortunatus, *Poems* 10.7–9, 3:78–86. In *Poems* 10.7, p. 78, he addresses them both as lords (*dominis*) and in 10.8, p. 81, they are both kings (*praeconia ... regum*).

[47] *Epistolae Austrasicae* 27, ed. Wilhelm Gundlach, MGH Epistolae 3: Epistolae Merowingici et Karolini aevii 1 (Berlin, 1892; rpt. 1994), 139–40.

[48] Baudonivia, *De vita sanctae Radegundis liber II*, prol., ed. Bruno Krusch, MGH SRM 2 (Hannover, 1888; rpt. 1984), 377–95 at 377.

[49] *Ibid.*, 2.5, p. 382. In Fortunatus' version of the *Life* of Radegund, written before Baudonivia's, the former queen was "plus participata Christo, quam sociata coniugio (more a partner to Christ than companion for her husband)"; see Fortunatus, *De vita sanctae Radegundis liber I* c. 3, ed. Bruno Krusch, MGH SRM 2:364–77 at 366.

[50] *Ibid.*, 2.8, p. 383. The image of the *plantatio* echoes Matt. 15:13: "Omnis plantatio quam non plantavit Pater meus caelestis eradicabitur (every plant that my heavenly father did not plant will be destroyed)."

[51] On Dynamius, see Greg. Tur., *Histories* 6.11, pp. 280–82; Ian Wood, *The Merovingian Kingdoms, 450–751* (London, 1994), 101; George, *A Latin Poet*, 141–46, and Pucci, *Poems to Friends*, 47–48.

probably early in his career in Gaul.[52] In a later letter, he spoke as a lover pining for his long-absent beloved: "O Time, you have envied headlong love."[53] We have no idea if Dynamius responded in kind to Fortunatus, but we do have two extant missives from him. They suggest that, like Fortunatus, he wrote in one way to friends and in another to acquaintances. One was to an unnamed friend declaring that, though physically apart, they were nevertheless united by their "undivided affections" (*indivisis affectionibus*).[54] The other letter, addressed to Bishop Vilicus of Metz, was less demonstrative.[55]

Dynamius' *Life of Saint Maximus*, bishop of Riez, also reveals some of the norms of the Austrasian emotional community. Thus in Dynamius' telling, Maximus joined the monastery of Lérins where, "since he loved (*diligeret*) all with perfect love (*charitate*), he was himself likewise loved (*amabatur*) by all."[56] In writing about the miracles performed by Maximus, Dynamius stressed familial love and tenderness toward children; like Fortunatus and Gregory, he recorded sorrow at their illnesses or deaths, joy upon their recovery. Thus, when a widow's only daughter died as a child, "the mournful (*miserabilis*) mother" placed the girl in a bier "and hurried anxiously (*trepida*) to the blessed bishop [Maximus], signaling to him the cause of her sorrow (*doloris*) by tears (*lacrymis*) rather than words, and praying that he pour out prayers over the dead body." Maximus did so, and the girl returned to life. The mother was overcome by immense joy (*immenso afficitur gaudio*).[57]

It should be possible to look beyond Austrasia for others who shared the norms of Gregory and Fortunatus, for there is no reason to believe that other Merovingian royal courts at this time, however at loggerheads with

---

[52] Fortunatus, *Poems* 6.9, 2:80: "Expecto te, noster amor." George, *A Latin Poet*, 142–43, analyzes the poem, observing that the words "tua pars" in line 7 was a "particular phrase for a close personal tie ... used by the early Christian writers in consolations."

[53] Fortunatus, *Poems* 6.10, 2:81: "Tempora praecipiti vos invidistis amori." See George, *A Latin Poet*, 143–45, for further analysis of this poem.

[54] *Epistolae Austrasicae* 12, p. 127: "nos ... qui numquam indivisis affectionibus sequestramur (we ... who by our undivided affections are never separated)." Régine Le Jan, "Le lien social entre Antiquité et haut Moyen Âge: l'amitié dans les collections de lettres gauloises," in *Akkulturation. Probleme einer germanisch-romanischen Kultursynthese in Spätantike und frühem Mittelalter*, ed. Dieter Hägermann, Wolfgang Haubrichs, and Jörg Jarnut (Berlin, 2004), 528–46 at 532–35, speculates that the letter may have been destined for Fortunatus and notes that it alone (of all letters in collections of the fifth to seventh centuries) uses the word *amicus* in the address. Gogo, a correspondent of Fortunatus and also part of the Austrasian court, might equally be counted among the members of the emotional community we are exploring. See remarks *ibid.*, 534–35. For Fortunatus' poems to Gogo, see Fortunatus, *Poems* 7.1–4, 2:85–90, and for Gogo's letters, see *Epistolae Austrasicae*, Nos. 13, 16, 22, pp. 128, 130, 134.

[55] *Ibid.*, No. 17, pp. 130–31.

[56] Dynamius, *Vita sancti Maximi* c. 3, PL 80, cols. 31–40 at 34.   [57] *Ibid.*, c. 9, col. 37.

Austrasia politically, were very different from the point of view of emotional norms and expectations. This stands to reason: Guntram, Charibert, and Sigibert I were brothers; their mother was Ingund. Chilperic was their half brother by Aregund, Ingund's sister. They grew up together at the court of Clothar I and did not receive their own kingdoms until their father's death in 561.

Our knowledge of their emotional norms is, however, almost entirely indirect, coming once again from Fortunatus and Gregory.[58] The former expected his poetry to be appreciated in Paris, at the court of Charibert. His panegyric about Charibert was filled with familial metaphors. He claimed that the king was the guardian (*tutor*) and the father (*pater*) of the people of Paris;[59] he called Charibert "the brother (*frater*) and the very father (*ipse pater*) of the daughters" of his predecessor at Paris, King Childebert and Queen Ultrogotha.[60] Clothar I had ousted Ultrogotha and her daughters upon the death of Childebert, taking over the kingdom. When Charibert became king, he brought the women back to court.[61] This was astute politics. At the same time it suggests the sway of family sentiment. In the same vein, Fortunatus spoke of Clovis' joy at the birth of Childebert, "at last seeing his joy (*sua gaudia*) in a new offspring."[62]

Fortunatus was also welcome at the court of Chilperic and Fredegund. He went there at a moment of crisis for Gregory, who had been hauled before the royal couple at Berny-Rivière, charged with treason and slandering the queen. Fortunatus made a plea on behalf of Gregory by reminding the king of his father Clothar's special paternal love for him: "on you, dear head, your father rested all his cares; among so many brothers, you were thus his one love (*inter tot fratres sic amor unus eras*)."[63] While "living in the love (*in amore*) of the people here and of the father there," Chilperic was suddenly beset by dangers.[64] Fortunatus comforted him: "After long bearing so many hardships (*aspera*), now happy things follow (*laeta secuntur*), and through sorrows you reap newborn joys (*per maerores gaudia nata metis*)."[65] Turning to praise Fredegund as the king's excellent consort, he recalled her as one who wisely turned to Radegund for benefits (*mercedem*). May her progeny produce a grandchild, he continued. Gregory's life was on the line at Berny-Rivière; would Fortunatus not have changed his

---

[58] To be sure, one poem of King Chilperic has survived, a hymn praising Saint Médard of Soissons. Dag Norberg, *La poésie latine rythmique du haut moyen âge* (Stockholm, 1954), 31–40, cogently argues for its dependence on a now lost hagiography of Médard as well as lines from the *Carmen paschale* by Sedulius. It is full of praise but contains few emotions.

[59] Fortunatus, *Poems* 6.2, 2:53, ll. 10–12.   [60] *Ibid.*, p. 54, l. 24.

[61] See the notes to this poem *ibid.*, p. 54; George, *A Latin Poet*, 43–48; and *Venantius Fortunatus: Personal and Political Poems*, trans. Judith George (Liverpool, 1995), 34–35.

[62] Fortunatus, *Poems* 6.2, 2:54, l. 47.   [63] *Ibid.*, 9.1, 3:9, ll. 33–34.

[64] *Ibid.*, p. 10, l. 40.   [65] *Ibid.*, ll. 57–58.

rhetoric to fit a different set of emotional expectations if such had been called for there? He apparently had no need to do so.

Gregory's trial at Berny-Rivière took place just before two of Chilperic and Fredegund's sons died. When Fortunatus heard of the deaths, he wrote two more poems to console the bereaved parents. Of course, Fortunatus was a flatterer. Very likely, he was not "sincere." But this is beside the point. He played to his audience, and so we may imagine that his audience wanted to be consoled.

Even Gregory, who had nothing good to say about many of the Merovingians, could not describe their emotions without emphasizing family feeling, although in their case he laughed at their shallowness. Thus, rather than condemning outright Clothar I's multiple marriages, Gregory presented a scene between husband and wife that carried out – and then went hilariously beyond – the normative love story.

When [Clothar] had taken Ingund as his wife and loved her with a unique love (*unico amore diligeret*), he receive a request from her when she said, "... I ask that you deign to find for my sister [Aregund], your servant, a useful and wealthy husband so that I may not be abased (*humilier*) but rather, raised up, be able to serve you more faithfully." Hearing this, and since he was extremely lustful (*nimium luxoriosus*), he burned with love (*amore*) for Aregund. He went to the villa where she resided and married her.[66]

When it came to the next generation, Gregory recounted how Queen Fredegund deeply mourned her sons and went wild with anger (*furore commota*) when her daughter was humiliated.[67] (To be sure, Gregory later spoke of bitter enmities [*inimicitiae*] between Fredegund and her daughter.[68])

Thus it may be argued that up to the time of Gregory's death in 596, the Merovingian Gallic elites were largely part of a common emotional community. Their celebration of family feeling reflected their expansive *familiae*, their intertwined blood ties, their appreciation of both their maternal and paternal heritage, and their numerous offspring.[69] Their values reflected and buttressed the fact that Merovingian power was dispersed among brothers and their influential queens. Gregory mocked them and grieved when family affection turned into its opposite, with brothers fighting one another. He praised them when they expressed love between husbands and wives, parents and children. This ratified the political order, based, as it was, on family relations. The emotional palette of

---

[66] Greg. Tur., *Histories* 4.3, p. 136.

[67] For her fury when her daughter was mistreated, *ibid.*, 7.15, pp. 336–37.

[68] *Ibid.*, 9.34, p. 455. The main cause of her fury was her daughter's "adulteries (*adulteria*)."

[69] See Ian Wood, "Family and Friendship in the West," in *The Cambridge Ancient History*, vol. 14: *Late Antiquity: Empire and Successors, AD 425–600*, ed. Averil Cameron, Bryan Ward-Perkins, and Michael Whitby (Cambridge, 2001), 416–36, esp. 418–21.

members of this community also affirmed the ties binding together bishops and aristocrats.[70] When they expressed love for one another, they linked together more firmly the bonds of their group. The affection that they portrayed themselves feeling toward children and their commiseration with grieving parents fed into their role as regional leaders – whether as pastors caring for their flock, or, as in the case of Dynamius, as governors of a region.

Waiting for heaven in Neustria

"Let the pristine love [caritas] between ourselves and your – or rather our – [friend] Eligius remain unaltered ... Let us aid one another by mutual prayers so that we may merit to live together in the celestial palace of the High King in the same way as we were associates (socii) in the hall of the earthly prince."[71] Thus did Desiderius, former official at the court of Clothar II and now bishop of Cahors, write in the early 640s to Dado, a former fellow courtier (hence the reference to the "hall of the earthly prince") and now bishop of Rouen.[72] It was characteristic of Desiderius and his emotional community – a community linked to the Neustrian court a generation or two after the days of Gregory and Fortunatus – to express and appreciate most emotions only if they could be referred to the afterlife. Desiderius and his colleagues formed an emotional community quite different from the one at the courts of Gaul in Gregory's day. Let us consider the new norms and advance some reasons for the change.

In 613, the center of Merovingian power and patronage shifted from Austrasia to Neustria. There was one king now – Clothar II (d. 629) followed by his son Dagobert (d. 639) – though there were also aristocratic factions vying for their day in the sun.[73] The accession of

---

[70] For other elements of this group's episcopal identity, see Simon Coates, "Venantius Fortunatus and the Image of Episcopal Authority in Late Antique and Early Merovingian Gaul," *English Historical Review* 115 (2000): 1109–37, and Kirsten DeVries, "Episcopal Identity in Merovingian Gaul, 397–700" (PhD diss., Loyola University Chicago, 2009).

[71] Desiderius of Cahors, *Epistulae* 1.11, in *Epistulae S. Desiderii Cadurcensis*, ed. Dag Norberg (Stockholm, 1961) [hereafter Desiderius, *Ep.*], 30.

[72] For the careers of Desiderius and Dado (Audoenus), see Horst Ebling, *Prosopographie der Amtsträger des Merowingerreiches von Chlothar II. (613) bis Karl Martell (741)* (Munich, 1974), nos. 141 and 142, pp. 124–27.

[73] On the importance of factions in the political life of the Merovingian kingdoms, see Wood, *Merovingian Kingdoms*, 152, 155–57, and Paul Fouracre and Richard A. Gerberding, *Late Merovingian France: History and Hagiography, 640–720* (Manchester, 1996), 11–26, 56–58. Technically, one can speak of several kings at a time, since Clothar "created a sub-kingdom for his eldest son, Dagobert, who was set over a reduced Austrasia," while Dagobert did the same for Sigibert III (Wood, *Merovingian Kingdoms*, 145).

Dagobert's sons Sigibert III and Clovis II did not change the political situation immediately; this was not yet the period of the famous "do-nothing" Merovingian kings.[74] Under Clothar II, the royal court at Neustria became the close living quarters (*contubernium*) of young aristo-crats on the rise.[75] Régine Le Jan has stressed their diversity; unlike many of the Austrasian adherents, the youthful Neustrian court community often lacked blood ties, geographical commonalities, intertwined tradi-tions of friendship, or common class identification.[76] The central figure of the court, Clothar himself, had his own reasons to downgrade blood ties: his father was arguably not Chilperic but rather his mother's lover.[77] This may help to explain why the emotional norms of this group devalued family ties and scorned the sentiments of mothers. (See Genealogy 2.1.)

The new emotional norms were also inspired by the memory of Saint Columbanus, a fiery Irish monk who came to Gaul c. 591 to found monasteries, reform aristocrats and kings, and practice the sort of pil-grimage – permanent exile – that was highly valued by Irish ascetics.[78] At first he was welcomed at the Austrasian court and founded the monastery of Annegray and Luxeuil in Burgundy with the support of Childebert II. But Columbanus experienced a setback when Childebert's death in 596 transformed the political scene. Theuderic II took over Burgundy, while Theudebert became ruler of Austrasia. Brunhild was driven out of Austrasia in 602 and took refuge with Theuderic.[79] At this point, Columbanus repudiated Brunhild and the Burgundian court altogether. He moved on to Neustria, where he was welcomed with joy (*ovans*) by Clothar II.[80] Shortly thereafter, on his way to Italy to found the monastery of Bobbio, Columbanus traversed Gaul, bestowing his favor – in the form of blessings – upon select children of the aristocracy. Among them were

---

[74] Wood, *Merovingian Kingdoms*, 155–58. "Do-nothing" was in fact Carolingian propaganda.

[75] Desiderius, *Ep.* 1.10, p. 28. See also *ibid.*, 1.5, p. 18.

[76] Le Jan, "Le Lien," 538. However, courtiers Ado, Dado, and Rado were brothers, as were Desiderius, Rusticus, and Syagrius.

[77] See Ian Wood, "Deconstructing the Merovingian Family," in *The Construction of Communities in the Early Middle Ages: Texts, Resources and Artifacts*, ed. Richard Corradini, Max Diesenberger, and Helmut Reimitz (Leiden, 2002), 149–72 at 163–64.

[78] For the chronology of Columbanus' life, see Christian Rohr, "Hagiographie als historische Quelle: Ereignisgeschichte und Wunderberichte in der Vita Columbani des Ionas von Bobbio," *Mitteilungen des Instituts für Österreichische Geschichtsforschung* 103 (1995): 229–64.

[79] Wood, *Merovingian Kingdoms*, 130–31.

[80] On Clothar's joy, see Jonas, *Vitae Columbani abbatis discipulorumque eius libri duo* (here-after *Vita Columbani*), 1.24, ed. Bruno Krusch, MGH SRM 4 (Hannover, 1902), 64–152 at 98. For the reconstruction of Columbanus' politics, see Ian Wood, "Jonas, the Merovingians, and Pope Honorius: *Diplomata* and the *Vita Columbani*," in *After Rome's Fall: Narrators and Sources of Early Medieval History: Essays Presented to Walter Goffart*, ed. Alexander Callander Murray (Toronto, 1998), 99–120.

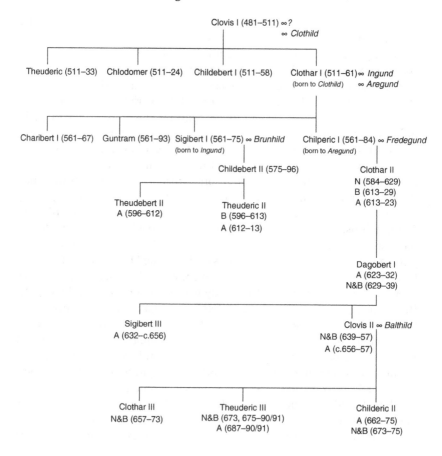

Genealogy 2.1 The Merovingians (simplified)

the brothers Ado and Dado, who, along with another brother, Rado, soon
became members of the Neustrian court as well as founders of
"Columbanian" monasteries.[81]

---

[81] Jonas, *Vita Columbani* 1.26, pp. 99–100. On these and other Columbanian monasteries,
which were characterized above all by the immunities and exemptions that they received,
see Barbara H. Rosenwein, *Negotiating Space: Power, Restraint, and Privileges of Immunity
in Early Medieval Europe* (Ithaca, NY, 1999), 42–96.

To this community of aristocrats, which retained its courtly ties even when it fanned out over Gaul as its members became bishops, we must add Eligius. He was goldsmith and minter for Clothar, diplomat for Dagobert, royal adviser to Queen Balthild (regent for her young son Clothar III), and finally bishop of Noyon. He was a member of the courtly trio united by "pristine love" as invoked by Desiderius' letter to Dado.[82] Jonas of Bobbio, the author of the *Life of Columbanus*, should also be counted a Neustrian courtier. A monk at Bobbio since at least 617, Jonas later (in the late 630s) joined Amandus, the bishop who was appointed and supported by Clothar II and Dagobert to be a missionary in the Scheldt region.[83] Jonas wrote the *Life of Columbanus* between about 639 and 642. There he took pains to denigrate Brunhild and her progeny and to elevate the dynasty of Clothar. The work is best seen as a partisan piece that reflects Jonas' connections with the Neustrian court and its adherents.[84] A second work by Jonas, the *Life of John of Réomé*, was explicitly written (in 659) for Queen Balthild.[85]

All of these texts downgraded sentimental family feeling. Perhaps it made sense for courtiers or monks like Jonas, who spent their boyhoods away from their parents, to belittle such emotions. But, as we shall see, they did not at the same time express intense feelings about their attachments to their friends. This is not to deny such attachments: why else would the former courtiers keep in frequent touch with one another? Why otherwise would Desiderius recall (in his letter to Dado) the *caritas* that united these men?[86] But in his hands *caritas* was a heavenly emotion; Desiderius was thinking of the afterlife when he used it.

---

[82] For Eligius, see Rosenwein, *Emotional Communities*, 133 n. 18.

[83] For the chronology of Jonas' life, see Rohr, "Hagiographie," 230–35.

[84] Rosenwein, *Emotional Communities*, 135; Wood, "Jonas, the Merovingians," points out that the *Vita* engages the concerns of the post-Columbanian generation; Alexander O'Hara, "The *Vita Columbani* in Merovingian Gaul," *Early Medieval Europe* 17 (2009): 126–53 at 144, stresses the aristocratic and royal readership of the *Vita* and "the close interrelationship between the Merovingian court [of Chlothar II and Dagobert I] and the Columbanians." In particular, he pinpoints the moment of its composition as an interregnum, when Clovis II was still an infant and Aega, hostile to the Columbanians, was mayor of the palace and regent, noting that (152) "The *Vita* may have been written partly to influence the contemporary rulers of Merovingian Gaul."

[85] See Jonas, *Vita Johannis abbatis Reomaensis*, ed. Bruno Krusch, MGH SRM 3 (Hannover, 1896; rpt. 1995), 502–17. Rohr, "Hagiographie," 234, expresses some doubt that the author was Jonas of Bobbio on "artistic (*künstlerisch*)" grounds, but Albrecht Diem, "The Rule of an 'Iro-Egyptian' Monk in Gaul: Jonas' *Vita Iohannis* and the Construction of a Monastic Identity," *Revue Mabillon*, n.s., 19 (2008): 5–50, firmly establishes Jonas of Bobbio's authorship by showing the *Vita Johannis*' correspondence to the *Vita Columbani* both in style (26–27) and larger purpose.

[86] The constant contact via writings is made clear in Desiderius' letter collection, which contains 17 letters written by him to others and 19 letters written by others to him, most

Jonas explicitly devalued family feeling every time that he spoke of mothers. In his view, mothers of saints loved their children too much, and their virtuous, chaste sons and daughters very properly rejected them. When Columbanus decides to leave home to pursue the monastic life,

his mother, struck with sorrow (*dolore*), begs him not to leave her. But he replies, "Haven't you heard: 'He who loves his father and mother more than me is not worthy of me'?" [Matt. 10:37] He begs his mother who is standing in his way and clinging to the threshold of the door, to let him go. She, wailing and prostrate on the floor, denies she will permit it. He leaps over both the threshold and his mother and tells his mother to be happy (*se laetam habeat*): she will never see him again in this life, but he will go wherever the path of salvation shows the way.[87]

Here the saint is not only unmoved by his mother's love but also positively contemptuous of her.

Similarly, when John of Réomé returned to a monastery near his home after a stint at Lérins, his mother,

putting to the test the desired entry of her reverend son, hastens to him so that, rejoicing (*ovans*), she might at last see his countenance, so long absent from her ... Taking to the road, she comes to the place where he was ... and begs the affection (*affectum*) of the servants that they might do as she deserved: to see with her own eyes her long-desired son. Hearing this, he declined and excused himself from giving in to the love (*affectum*) of his mother, recalling that "He who does not leave his father and mother is not worthy of me" [again Matt. 10:37].[88] Nevertheless, lest he injure by rash condemnation the faith of the mother ... he walked past her, appearing for a moment to her eyes so that he might satisfy her desire (*desiderium*) yet not weaken the vigor of his religion on account of her flatteries (*blandimenta*).

Thus the family feeling that was so valued by Gregory and Fortunatus was here repudiated. Weak mothers might importune, but their sons, eyes fixed on the afterlife, indulged them (if at all) not out of love of them but rather out of love of God.[89]

As Jonas told the tale, chaste women had the same jaundiced view of their mother's love. Deurechildis and her mother entered a monastery

---

involving fellow courtiers. Nor does this collection contain all of his correspondence; more letters were available to the author of the *Life of Desiderius*, writing circa 800; see *Vita Desiderii Cadurcae urbis episcopi*, cc. 9–11, ed. Bruno Krusch, MGH SRM 4:569–70. On the genre of letters and their role in friendships at this time, see Rosenwein, *Emotional Communities*, 135–36.

[87] Jonas, *Vita Columbani* 1.3, p. 69.   [88] Jonas, *Vita Johannis* c. 6, p. 509.

[89] The example of Jonas' own visit home (in Jonas, *Vita Columbani* 2.5, p. 118) had the same moral. After much begging, Jonas convinced his abbot to let him return home for a visit. However, no sooner had he arrived than he became feverish, a result of his abbot's prayers for him to return to his monastery. He left immediately, even his mother agreeing that "it is better for me ... to know you are healthy there than to weep (*deflere*) for you dead here."

together, but the daughter was more virtuous than her mother and was promised eternal life. As Deurechildis lay on her deathbed, her anxious (*anxia*) mother "amidst sobs and sighs (*singultus ac gemitus*) begs her daughter that, if she had strength, she should pray to be restored to the land of the living, or, if she were fulfilling the goal of her life [that is, dying], she would quickly take [her mother] from this world after her. For [she said], it was impossible for her to live after her daughter's departure." Deurechildis belittled her mother's feelings: "In asking such things over and over," she said, "you are goaded on by carnal desires (*carnalibus desideriis*)."[90] (Nevertheless, she did promise to bring her mother to heaven with her.)

While Gregory of Tours and Fortunatus approved of parental love, Jonas had nothing but disdain for Queen Brunhild's love of her great-grandchildren, whom she wanted Columbanus to bless. In Jonas' hands, Columbanus not only refused to give the blessing but repeated the dis-missive gesture that he had made with his own mother and "leaped across the threshold" in his haste to get away from her.[91]

Had Jonas wished to depict mother love more tenderly, he had plenty of models, and not just from Gregory of Tours. Needy, importuning mothers desirous of catching a glimpse of their beloved monk-sons were *topoi* in numerous early saints' *Lives*. But their sons did not usually jump over them. In the *Life of Simeon Stylites*, Simeon's mother comes to see him but is not allowed entry. But Simeon, hearing her voice, called out, "Wait a little while, mother, and we will see one another together [in heaven]." She began to weep (*flere*), and loosening her hair, rebuked him: "Son, why have you done this? For the womb in which I bore you, you have overwhelmed me with mourning; for the milk with which I suckled you, you have given me tears; for the kisses with which I kissed you, you have given me bitter heart pangs (*amaras cordis angustias*)." At this, every-one wept; even Simeon "put his face in his hands and cried bitterly (*ploravit amare*)."[92]

The cool stances of Jonas' heroes matched the flat emotional expres-sion of the other (male) members of the Neustrian courtly group. Thus, at the beginning of his letter to Dado – the one that referred to the friends' "pristine love" – Desiderius expressed in passive and disembodied fash-ion the emotion that he felt when contacting his old friend: "immense joy

---

[90] *Ibid.*, 2.15, pp. 134–35.

[91] *Ibid.*, 1.19, p. 87. Compare the gestures of leaping over the threshold ("dum limitem transiliret") here and in the episode with Columbanus' mother (above, n. 87: "ille limitem matremque transilit").

[92] Antonius, *Vita sancti Simeonis stylitae* c. 9, PL 73, cols. 325–34 at 329. For other examples of the mother-monk topos, see Rosenwein, *Emotional Communities*, 151–52.

(*gratulatio*) has now presented itself to my mind (*menti*)."[93] Compare this to an earlier bishop from a different emotional community, Avitus of Vienne (d. c. 518). He, like Desiderius, wrote "carefully and bombastically."[94] Even so, Avitus used *gratulatio* not passively but with the possessive, as in "my joy": "I, too, have been refreshed by the food with which you satisfied your mind while you were fasting in body. Whence this small fullness of my joy (*meae gratulationis*) bursts forth for you [in this letter]."[95]

Desiderius' letter continues: "I ask this more especially: that you grant and ever deign to be the one whose person you once showed me with a unique love (*unico amore*) in that flower of primeval youth, namely my Dado."[96] Then follows the passage already quoted: "Let the pristine love (*caritas*) between ourselves and your – or rather our – [friend] Eligius remain unaltered ... Let us aid one another by mutual prayers so that we may merit to live together in the celestial palace of the High King in the same way as we were associates in the hall of the earthly prince." In this letter, then, youthful *amor* was quickly converted into the *caritas* of heaven. Love's proper place was in the afterlife.

The letter's dryness is still more striking when Desiderius comes to speak of the loss of his two brothers, Rusticus and Syagrius. Both had been at Clothar's court: Rusticus held various clerical appointments under the king, including, at the end of his life, the bishopric of Cahors; Syagrius was among the ministers and familiars of the king at court, eventually becoming governor of Marseilles. When Syagrius died, Desiderius took his place at Marseilles, and when Rusticus was murdered, Desiderius became bishop of Cahors.[97] The Carolingian *Life* of Desiderius says that after his brother's murder, he was "so struck by unbearable sorrow (*dolore*) that in the death of his brother he seemed almost to undergo the death himself."[98] But such rhetoric reflects a later – a Carolingian – sensibility. In his own letter, Desiderius merely notes that, "although I have now lost two brothers from our fellowship, we have in

---

[93] Desiderius, *Ep.* 1.11, p. 30. On the various ways in which emotions were expressed via the body in the Middle Ages, see Barbara H. Rosenwein, "Les communautés émotionnelles et le corps," *Médiévales* 61 (2011): 55–76.

[94] Avitus of Vienne, *Letters and Selected Prose*, trans. Danuta Shanzer and Ian Wood (Liverpool, 2002), 85.

[95] Avitus of Vienne, *Epistularum ad diversos libri tres* 2.53, ed. Rudolf Peiper, MGH AA 6.2 (Berlin, 1883), 82. Shanzer and Wood, *Letters*, 317, translate *gratulationis* as "thanks," removing any hint of emotion. However, Desiderius, *Ep.* 1.8, p. 24 clearly uses *gratulor* as a synonym for joy, contrasting it with "I have sorrowed (dolui)."

[96] Desiderius, *Ep.* 1.11, p. 30.

[97] See *Vita Desiderii* 1.7–8, pp. 567–68, written c. 800 (see Krusch's prefatory remarks on 556) but essentially accurate on the *curricula vitae* of the brothers.

[98] *Vita Desiderii* 1.8, p. 568.

their place venerable Paulus and Sulpicius, no less praiseworthy in merits."[99] Interchangeable brothers! To be sure, this does not necessarily mean that Desiderius *felt* no grief – or indeed shame, guilt, or fear. What it does show is that he and his colleagues devalued the *expression* of those feelings.

Yet the letter to Dado was among the most emotional of all thirty-seven letters in Desiderius' collection. Another, addressed to Bishop Sallustius of Agen, was admittedly more studded with words of feeling. But the end result was very similar, referring to early friendships at court that remained "to this day in the name of God" and flowered into mutual *caritas*.[100]

Nor was Desiderius' emotional vocabulary very extensive. Of the many emotion words in the Latin vocabulary (see Chapter 1), Desiderius used very few.[101] The most often used was *caritas*, equivalent to *amor* for Augustine but evidently more ethereal for Desiderius. To be sure, some other words, like *consolatio*, were used by Desiderius in tandem with other emotion words; let us consider these associated words to be part of his emotional vocabulary, giving us a haul of twenty-four.

By far the most emotional of the letters in the collection was one – the only one – addressed to a woman, Abbess Aspasia. In this letter, Desiderius said that he had been moved (*motus*) by Aspasia's tears. He hoped she would find both divine consolation (*consolatio*) and fear (*timor*), quoting a version of Ecclesiasticus 2.1: "Coming to the service of God, stand in fear." He assured her that there was joy (*gaudium*) in her tears (*lacrimis*) and asked that her "soul have compassion (*compaciatur*) on my sorrow (*dolori meo*) so that I may rejoice (*possim laetificari*) over your well-being once the wound has been healed."[102] Was Desiderius suiting his rhetoric to a woman's idiom, adjusting his language to *her* emotional community? The letters of Herchenefreda, Desiderius' mother, suggest that women were less reticent than men about their feelings. Three of her letters to her son, presumably authentic, were included in the *Life of Desiderius*. They show an emotional effusiveness utterly absent in Desiderius' corpus. "To my sweetest (*dulcissimo*) and most beloved (*amantissimo*) son Desiderius," began the first letter. "To my sweetest (*dulcissimo*) and most desirable (*desiderantissimo*) son," was the salutation of the second, playing on Desiderius' name. In the third letter, relating the murder of Rusticus, Herchenefreda called herself a wretched (*misera*) and unhappy (*infelix*) mother, and she addressed her son as *dulcissimus* four times.[103]

---

[99] Desiderius, *Ep.* 1.11, p. 30.   [100] *Ibid.*, 1.1, p. 9.

[101] They are: *amabiliter/amare/amor, affectus/affectio, caritas, contristare, dilectio, diligere, dolere, dolor, gaudere, gaudium, laetari, motus, timor, desiderare.*

[102] Desiderius, *Ep.* 15, p. 37.   [103] *Vita Desiderii* 1.9–11, pp. 569–70.

Herchenefrede used emotion words far more frequently than did her son, but often less for emotional than for moral effect. To her "sweetest son" she wrote, "Have God constantly on your mind; do not consent to or act upon the bad works that God hates (*odit*); be faithful (*sis fidelis*) to the king; love (*diligas*) your fellow courtiers (*contubernales*); always love (*ames*) and fear (*timeas*) God." She wanted to rejoice (*letificari*) in her son's "life and good behavior (*de vita et bona conversatione vestra*)."[104] Only once, as we have already seen, did she reveal her feelings about a worldly event: when she reported on the murder of her son Rusticus and remembered her loss of Syagrius and their father as well, she called herself "a wretched mother (*misera*)." What would she do if she lost Desiderius as well? She relied on him for his virtue; he must never waver: "But you, my most pious pledge (*pignus*), my sweetest (*dulcissime*), guard yourself so constantly that, while you have lost the solace (*solatia*) of your brothers, you do not lose yourself ... Always beware the broad and spacious road [see Matt. 7:13] that leads to perdition." Avowing that she would "die of too much sorrow (*prae nimio dolore*)," she begged him to pray so that God, "for whose love I sigh day and night (*in cuius amore die noctuque suspiro*)," would receive her.[105] There are some echoes here of Jonas' emotional mothers. If we compare this letter to Desiderius' dry remark about losing his brothers, and if we adduce as well Aspasia's tears, we may reasonably conclude that the emotional norms for women were different from those for men. They were more "old fashioned," adhering still (to some degree) to the norms of the Austrasian court in the time of Gregory and Fortunatus.

Let us sum up: thus far we have looked at two emotional communities similar in that they were both composed largely of courtier bishops, but different in the ways in which they accepted and used words of feeling. The Austrasians were glad to express their emotions and expected others to do the same. The Neustrians were wary of emotions, accepting them only when they referred to clearly godly matters. Many of them drew from the "good emotions" that Cicero had discussed in his treatise on friendship (see Table 1.5). We would call them "positive emotions."

Wielded variously (passionately in Austrasia; delicately in Neustria), these positive words were pivotal in the ways in which these groups presented themselves and imagined others. Gregory, however, in particular, recognized how easily they might become their opposite, turning into hatred and discord, in effect the negative words on Cicero's list of "desires" (Table 1.4). In late seventh-century Francia, to which I now turn, writers used a less luxuriant emotional vocabulary than before; they

---

[104] *Ibid.*, 1.9, p. 569.   [105] *Ibid.*, 1.11, p. 570.

made the contrasts between positive and negative feelings starker; and they emphasized the dramatic and moral possibilities of all these emotions.

Late seventh-century factions and their discontents

Late seventh-century aristocratic groups enjoyed newly independent political clout. Before that time, as we have seen with Desiderius and his circle, aristocrats were largely dependent on kings. Even if they were not directly part of court culture, they adhered to one or another Merovingian. For example, once Theudebert and Brunhild fell, the aristocracy rallied around Clothar II. Even when aristocratic factions jockeyed for power, their reference point remained the king. As Ian Wood has noted, "Far from directing attention away from the court, or even from offering a challenge to Merovingian power, these rivalries were intimately connected with central politics."[106] This changed after 656 in Austrasia and after 664 in Neustria: now the aristocrats came to manipulate – indeed, to depose and raise – kings. No one of these factions permanently got the better of any other, least of all the Pippinids (the ones who would become the Carolingians), and from time to time Merovingian kings and queens managed to exploit rivalries to their own advantage.[107] Nevertheless, in the last three or so decades of the seventh century a clear political shift took place, one that both reflected and reinforced changes in emotional styles.

In the late seventh century, each faction wanted access to the king – and to close it off to others. Ebroin, mayor of the palace when the dowager Queen Balthild "retired," was the key player here. It seems very likely that he was one of those who eased her out. When her son Clothar III died in 673, Ebroin tried to be kingmaker, elevating Clothar's brother Theuderic III to the throne without allowing the other nobles their prerogatives or their access to the court.[108] Reaction was swift: a faction of the nobles invited Childeric II, Clothar's other brother and king of Austrasia, to take the Neustrian throne.

[106] Wood, *Merovingian Kingdoms*, 147–49 and 221–22.

[107] A point stressed *ibid.*, 221–34.

[108] The importance of access to the king is stressed in recent historiography because it counters the view that late seventh-century kings were weak. On the contrary, they were sufficiently strong for nobles to want to be associated with their power. For this and the general historical background presented here, see Wood, *Merovingian Kingdoms*, 227; Fouracre and Gerberding, *Late Merovingian France*, 21; Paul Fouracre, "The Career of Ebroin, Mayor of the Palace, c. 657–680" (PhD diss., University of London, 1981), 169. We shall see that the emotion connected with denial of access was not "desire" but "fear."

One member of this faction was Leudegar, Balthild's appointee as bishop of Autun. He intervened to save the lives of Ebroin and Theuderic, tonsuring rather than murdering them, and sent each into monastic exile: Ebroin at Luxeuil and Theuderic at Saint-Denis. Shortly thereafter, having alienated Childeric, Leudegar himself was sent to Luxeuil to be a fellow prisoner with Ebroin. Other nobles, too, fell out with Childeric, who was assassinated by some of them in 675. The two Luxeuil exiles then emerged, Leudegar to support the return of Theuderic, Ebroin to "discover" another Merovingian, one "Clovis." But as soon as he gained the upper hand, Ebroin abandoned Clovis, supported Theuderic, and began a campaign to kill his enemies, Leudegar among them. Leudegar's death backfired. While he was immediately recognized as a martyr, Ebroin became (in the extant sources) the wicked instrument of the devil. Like Brunhild, his memory was obliterated: we know nothing about his origins, and he left no posterity when he was assassinated (by yet another faction of nobles) in 680.

The 660s and 670s were hard on the written word. Almost no texts come from this period of turmoil. But in the 680s and 690s, when relative peace reigned, there was time to reflect, to remember, to shape, and to forget.[109] In these writings there was no trace of the distaste for strong emotions that had been characteristic of the first half of the seventh century. On the contrary, in the two decades before 700, emotions were seen as dramatic components of human action.

Many of the extant sources from the period are hagiographies, often martyrdom accounts. They concern the very figures and events – Leudegar, Ebroin, plots, and assassinations – that we have just discussed. The hagiographers, though usually anonymous, were clearly tied to the factions that roiled Francia. They wrote or commissioned stories of their leaders in the guise of martyrdom accounts. This is what happened, for example, in the case of Leudegar, whose cult seems to have been fostered by his episcopal successor (previously his opponent) at Autun.[110]

Paul Fouracre has pointed out that the development of these new martyrdom accounts marks a turning point in Christian literature. Previous such tales had depended on pagan persecutors or heretical opponents. The hagiographers of the later seventh century found a way "to deal within a traditional Christian framework with conflict between members of the faith, even between members of the same church, and

[109] See Patrick J. Geary, *Phantoms of Remembrance: Memory and Oblivion at the End of the First Millennium* (Princeton, 1994).
[110] See Paul Fouracre, "Merovingian History and Merovingian Hagiography," *Past and Present* 127 (1990): 3–38.

between rulers and ruled."[111] Their saints were Christian martyrs in a Christian context. Giving an enhanced role to the devil, who manipulated the weak, late seventh-century martyrdom accounts made the earth the battleground between heaven and hell, while the real political figures of the time became puppets of those supernatural forces.

But how do their authors constitute, let alone speak for, an emotional community? Gregory and Fortunatus were friends, and they knew and wrote to others who shared their sentiments. Desiderius had a coterie of fellow courtier-bishops. But the writers of the late seventh century were largely anonymous and they belonged to different factions, to boot. Disparate in political affiliation, they seem a tenuous community at best. On the other hand, people do not have to agree on all things to have the same norms of emotional comportment and feeling. The late seventh-century writers certainly read one another's works (as various literary borrowings indicate), and their audiences must have overlapped. Further, the elites that were behind these writings were supraregional. Already during the reign of Dagobert, the leading men of Burgundy had been absorbed into the political life of Neustria. The elites of Austrasia were moving in the same direction in the 670s when one faction there joined Ebroin in his bid to regain power in Neustria. In the 680s, the Austrasians ceased *de facto* to have a king, while one faction of its magnates, under the leadership of Pippin II, began to cannibalize Neustria. At first the process relied on wars, but soon it continued with the Pippinids and their followers marrying into Neustrian families, becoming Neustrian landowners, and slowly taking over patronage of the Neustrian church. Eventually they took over Francia as the "Carolingians."

There is another possible objection to using the writings of a group of seventh-century hagiographers as the voice of an emotional community: since they all (except one) wrote hagiographies, we might imagine that the emotions found in their writings reveal the *topoi* of the genre rather than the sensibilities of a community. In some ways this argument is easier to rebut than the issue of anonymity. We have seen hagiographies before: The joyous mother whose baby was cured by Saint Illidius was an episode in one of Gregory's hagiographical accounts, while Jonas' description of Columbanus' retort to his beseeching mother was *his* version of emotional virtue.[112] Hagiographies are flexible instruments of emotional expression.[113] Those of the late seventh century were quite different

---

[111] *Ibid.*, 29.   [112] See above at nn. 9 and 87.

[113] On the differences between Fortunatus' hagiographical writings and earlier examples of the genre, see Salvatore Pricoco, "Gli scritti agiografici in prosa di Venanzio Fortunato," in *Venanzio Fortunato tra Italia e Francia*, 175–93.

from those of the earlier periods. At the same time, as a group, they closely tracked one another emotionally.

Let us remember that, as I suggested in my introduction, historians may define emotional communities in a variety of ways. Larger and more amorphous ones, as in this case, will have more variants within them – subcommunities, as it were. We shall see some examples of this in the materials that follow.

Emotions of demons and their creatures

Largely written as propaganda for partisan causes, the hagiography of the period 675–700 was obsessed with the battle of good against evil.[114] We are here dealing with the sort of vocabulary Cicero drew on for his *aegritudines*. In the *Life of Germanus*, God knew beforehand (*praescivit*) that his "athlete" Germanus would be given the crown of martyrdom. And so it happened: the duke of the Alemanni, "incited with hatred (*excitatus est ... in zelum*)" against the people living around Germanus' monastery of Grandval, led an army against them. Germanus, fleeing the monastery, was knocked to the ground by "wicked men clearly possessed by the devil (*homines iniqui plene diabulo impleti*)."[115] Soon thereafter, men "full of the demon (*pleni daemonio*)" followed Germanus after he fruitlessly confronted the duke. Continuing to be "spurred by the demon (*repleti doemonio*)," they stripped him of his clothing, while the most audacious man among them, again "inspired by the demon (*repletus daemonio*)," stabbed him to death.

Similarly, in the *Martyrdom of Leudegar* Queen Balthild appointed the hero as bishop of Autun, and "at his coming, all the enemies of the church and city were terrified (*territi sunt*)."[116] Soon the devil (in his guise as the serpent in the Garden of Eden) began his dirty work:

But because malice (*malitia*) is always opposed to good will (*bona voluntate*), and the Ancient Serpent, who is envious (*invidus*), always finds those through whom he may sow temptation, some high-ranking men, ignorant of spiritual things but rather holding secular power, seeing Leudegar to be the inflexible pinnacle of justice, began to twist with envious spite (*invido livore*) and determined, if possible, to get in the way of his progress. Now, at that time the mayor of the palace (as we call him) was Ebroin. He ruled the palace under King Clothar [III], for the

---

[114] For an overview of the sources and their dates, see Rosenwein, *Emotional Communities*, 167–71.

[115] Bobolenus, *Vita Germani abbatis Grandivallensis* cc. 10–12, ed. Bruno Krusch, MGH SRM 5 (Hannover, 1910; rpt. 1997), 33–40 at 37–39.

[116] *Passio Leudegarii episcopi et martyris Augustodunensis I* c. 2, ed. Bruno Krusch, MGH SRM 5:282–322 at 284.

queen ... was now living in the monastery which she had prepared for herself
beforehand. The aforementioned envious men went to Ebroin and aroused his
mind (*animum*) to fury (*furore*) against the man of God.[117]

Divining the interests of a faction of aristocrats, the devil thus orche-
strated a succession of emotional transformations. First he incited men of
high rank to envy the privileges and power of Leudegar, Queen Balthild's
appointee. After helping to engineer her retirement, they made their way
to Ebroin, rousing him to fury.[118] Then Ebroin – who, the writer tells us,
was prone to greed (*cupiditas*), pride (*superbia*), and fear (*metus*) – used the
occasion of Clothar's death to control access to the new king, Theuderic
III.[119] The nobles, thwarted, then organized to enthrone a different king,
Theuderic's brother Childeric II. For a time they were successful:
Theuderic was deposed, Ebroin was exiled, and Leudegar became
Childeric's advisor. But Childeric did not "comply with his advice" and
soon, as the author of the *Martyrdom of Leudegar* reports, Leudegar
"recognized that the envy of the devil (*invidiam diaboli*) grew warm
again."[120] The devil clearly was a major player in this account.

He appeared again and again. In the *Life of Saint Gertrude* he was the
"enemy of the human race," envious (*invidus*) of all good works.[121] In the
Life of Wandregisel he could not abide the saint:

Because the devil longed to harm (*invidiosus est ad nocendum*) [the saint] and
because malice (*malicia*) fights against the very form of goodness, the devil
raged with the greatest envy against him (*invidia maxima in eum exarserat*), cease-
lessly harassing [Wandregisel] either personally or via his supporters (*per suos
fautoris*).[122]

The saint's torments came day and night. "Seeing that he was taking the
higher path, the devil, revealing great cruelty, raged against him (*in eo
exardiscebat*), causing him many disturbances both openly and in his
sleep."[123]

In the *Vision of Barontus*, written around the same time as these hagiographical texts, two demons attacked the monk Barontus on his apparent
deathbed (he eventually revived to tell the tale). Archangel Raphael tried
to stop them, but they resisted, saying "If the splendor of God may not

[117] *Ibid.*, cc. 3–4, p. 286.
[118] The *Vita Sanctae [Domnae] Balthildis A* c. 10, ed. Bruno Krusch, MGH SRM 2:482–508
at 495 makes clear that Balthild's move to her monastery was "permitted" by aristocrats
for their own purposes.
[119] For *cupiditas*, *Passio Leudegarii* c. 6, p. 288; *superbia*, c. 5, p. 287; *metus*, c. 4, p. 287.
[120] *Passio Leudegarii* c. 8, p. 290.
[121] *Vita Sanctae Geretrudis A* c. 2, ed. Bruno Krusch, MGH SRM 2:453–64 at 455.
[122] *Vita Wandregiseli abbatis Fontanellensis* c. 6, ed. Bruno Krusch, MGH SRM 5:13–24 at 16.
[123] *Ibid.*, c. 8, p. 17.

take him from us, you certainly cannot."[124] Barontus' soul was wrenched from his body: it had his head and body but was the size of a chick. Raphael held it on the right, trying to get the soul to heaven. At the same time, one of the demons "was grabbing me spitefully on the left side, and the other demon was giving me hard kicks on my back and, full of anger (*iracundia*), he said, 'I had you in my power once and hurt you badly, and now you will be tormented eternally in Hell.'"[125] Clearly the devil and his minions had feelings and inspired similar feelings in others.

The emotions of godly inspiration

But when the same texts talked about the emotions of the godly, they also drew on the Latin vocabulary ratified by Augustine. Those emotions were expressed as vividly and as strongly as the devil's. Often they were sentiments of joy or sorrow. Thus, when Germanus received permission from his bishop to be a hermit, he set out happily and cheerfully (*laetus et hilaris*). When he arrived at the monastery of Luxeuil, all the brethren there greeted him with happy faces (*hilari vultu*). But when he realized that the duke of the Alemanni was ravaging the valley, "he wept for a very long time (*flevit diutissime*)." Then, at the moment of his martyrdom, he heard a voice from heaven saying, "Come, faithful steward: the heavens are open to you. My angels rejoice (*congaudent*) for you and lead you into the heavenly Jerusalem." But on earth there was no rejoicing: when Germanus' brethren found his body they raised it up "with great lamentation (*eiulatu magno*)."[126]

Love, too, was invoked as a feeling of the godly. In the *Martyrdom of Leudegar*, the magnates who released the saint from his exile at Luxeuil were so "united in their love of him (*in eius conspirassent amore*)" that they were ready to die in his stead. They told "other powerful men (*potestatibus aliis*)" in the vicinity "that they had recognized divine grace in God's servant Leudegar," and all were "joined [together] in the devout love of Christianity (*religioso christianitatis amore*)" to offer their help to the beleaguered bishop. When, in their company, Leudegar re-enters his city of Autun, "the church is delighted (*laetatur*) by the renewed presence of its pastor, the streets are decorated with greenery, the deacons prepare their candles, the clergy celebrates with antiphons, and the whole city rejoices (*gaudet*) at the advent of its bishop after the storm of persecution."[127]

---

[124] *Visio Baronti Monachi Longoretensis* c. 3, ed. Wilhelm Levison, MGH SRM 5:377–94 at 380.
[125] *Ibid.*, c. 4, pp. 380–81.
[126] Bobolenus, *Vita Germani* cc. 4, 6, 12, 13, pp. 35, 38–39.
[127] *Passio Leudegarii* c. 17, p. 299.

In the *Life of Wandregisel*, the hero is full of both fear (*metus*) (of hell) and love (*amor*) (of Christ).[128] Characteristically cheerful, on his deathbed, he looked upward toward heaven "with a happy face (*hilare vulto*)." At the same time, to be sure, his disciples were "very depressed (*contristati sunt valde*), saying, 'What will we do, [seeing] that you leave us so suddenly, father?' ... And they prostrated themselves with sighs and tears in prayer (*cum gemito et lacrimis in oracione*), begging God not to permit him to part from his body before he offered them the grace of consolation (*confortacionis gracia*)."[129] Their sighs and tears signified both sadness and extreme piety. Dramatic and embodied, weeping was often meant as the equivalent of ascetic exercises, as another passage in the same *Life* makes clear, where Wandregisel "would afflict himself with fasts and vigils, [like Jerome] daily [pouring forth] sighs and tears."[130]

Barontus' monastic brethren were very sad when they saw him near death: "When they saw that no part of his body stirred, they began to weep very bitterly out of sorrow (*lacrimare prae dolore vehementer nimis*)." As his life was apparently draining out of him, they chanted the psalms until dawn. And then Christ's "wonderful power (*mira ... virtus*)" was made manifest, "which should not be passed over in silence throughout the whole Catholic Church, so that those who hear it may tremble (*expavescunt*) at their sins and convert with their whole hearts (*ex toto corde*) to the service of Christ, lest they lament (*plangant*) in the end in perpetual punishment."[131] "Trembling at sins": the author of the vision here made clear the proper place of fear in the lives of the godly. At this point, Barontus awoke and told his story.

The moral ambiguity of emotions

At first glance, then, it may seem that certain emotions (envy or anger) were always "bad" while other emotions (joy, sorrow, love, fear) were "good." But this was not quite the case. The emotions of bad people were indeed bad; they were vices. The contrary was true of emotions of good, which were virtues. However, while people were often depicted in these materials as if locked into one moral stance, either good or evil (though occasionally converting from one side to the other), the emotions

---

[128] *Vita Wandregiseli* c. 8, p. 17.   [129] *Ibid.*, c. 18, pp. 22–23.

[130] *Ibid.*, c. 8, p. 16: "se ieiuniis et vigiliis adfligebat, cotidiae gemitus, cotidiae lacrimas." Compare Jerome, *Libellus de virginitate servanda (Epistula 22)* c.7, ed. Isidor Hilberg, Corpus Scriptorum Ecclesiasticorum Latinorum [henceforth CSEL] 54 (Vienna, 1910), 143–211 at 153, a treatise in the form of a letter to Eustochium and likely the source for this passage of the *Vita Wandregiseli*.

[131] *Visio Baronti* c. 2, pp. 378–79.

themselves were morally ambiguous.[132] This was good Augustinianism: Augustine had made clear that the will, not the emotion, was the moral determinant.[133]

Thus, in the *Life of Wandregisel* the very devil could feel sorrow. The saint himself said so, telling his brethren to be virtuous, "so that the Lord may rejoice (*gaudeat*)" and "the devil may fall low and lament (*decidat et lugeat*), for he has the greatest sorrow (*maximam merorem habet*) when he sees anyone eagerly observing the commandments of God."[134] Similarly, bad people were perfectly capable of rejoicing, as happened when Leudegar came into his enemies' hands outside of Autun: "Rejoicing (*gavisi*), his enemies seized him as prey, they like wolves and he like an innocent sheep."[135]

The ungodly could also be fearful – of the wrong things. Thus Ebroin lived in fear of the leading men of Burgundy: "out of fear (*de metu*) [of them], all were suspected [by him]."[136] Similarly, bad people could love: those who delighted in love of the world (*amor saeculi*) were bad.[137] The *Vision of Barontus*, quoting 1 John 2: 15–17, made this clear: "Brothers, don't love (*diligere*) the world nor the things in the world. If anyone loves (*diligit*) the world, the love (*caritas*) of the Father is not in him."[138]

By the same token, good people could feel the emotions usually characteristic of the ungodly. The anger of God was by now a trope, having been the topic of a treatise by Lactantius in the fourth century.[139] But anger (*ira* in Latin) is not quite the same as fury (*furor*). Could the good rage? Not often, perhaps. But in the *Life of Saint Gertrude*, the heroine was described as feeling virtuous fury. Confronted by a suitor after she had pledged herself to Christ, Gertrude, "as if filled with fury (*quasi furore repleta*), rejected him with an oath."[140]

The use of *quasi* here is probably evidence of an authorial "tic" rather than an attempt to qualify Gertrude's fury.[141] However, emotions can indeed be "as if": people can feign them. Emotional communities are not always concerned about this possibility. Indeed, until the late seventh century, it does not seem to have been a major issue. But in the *Martyrdom of Leudegar*, when Ebroin found himself together with Leudegar at Luxeuil, he "pretended to be friends (*simulatam gerens concordiam*)" with the saint.[142] Moreover, he kept up the ruse. When the two emerged

---

[132] On the possibilities of emotional conversion, see Barbara H. Rosenwein, "The Emotions of Exclusion and Inclusion: The Case of Gregory the Great (590–604)," forthcoming.

[133] See Chapter 1.   [134] *Vita Wandregiseli* c. 15, p. 21.

[135] *Passio Leudegarii* c. 24, p. 306.   [136] *Ibid.*, c. 4, p. 287.

[137] *Visio Baronti* c. 20, p. 393.   [138] *Ibid.*, c. 21, p. 394.

[139] Lactantius, *On the Anger of God* in *Lactance, La colère de dieu*, ed. Christiane Ingremeau, SC 289 (Paris, 1982).

[140] *Vita Sanctae Geretrudis* c. 1, p. 454.

[141] See Rosenwein, *Emotional Communities*, 185–86.   [142] *Passio Leudegarii* c. 13, p. 296.

from Luxeuil and went together to Autun, Ebroin, "heedless of the friendship promised just a while ago," wanted to capture Leudegar. Prevented from doing this by Bishop Genesius, a stalwart partisan of Queen Balthild, Ebroin "again pretended a false friendship (*fictam rursus simulans amicitiam*)" with Leudegar, and the two entered the city together.[143] Later he feigned sorrow (*similans se dolere*) as a cover to persecute those whom he hated (*odisset*).[144]

The implications of one text are limited. It would go too far to suggest that feigned emotions had become a major preoccupation of the entire emotional community of the late seventh-century elites. But it may be that the particularly loud, public, and dramatic emotions commonly depicted by the larger emotional community inspired in at least one "subcommunity" thoughts about sincerity.

***

Three different, successive, but related emotional communities, each drawing on the same Latin vocabulary (albeit progressively watered down) of Cicero and Augustine, expressed feelings in different ways. Gregory of Tours and others of like sensibility, living in a world riven by civil wars among brothers, highly valued sentiment, put great premium on family feeling, and recognized and celebrated affection. At the same time, as we saw with Gregory, they well knew how easily such emotions could turn sour (as with Sichar and Chramnesind) or become risible in the wrong people (as with Clothar's "love" for his wife Ingund's sister).

In Neustria in the next generation, aristocratic competition was largely nonviolent, channeled via a political system that had mastered the tools of consensus and knew how to focus striving on access to the king. At the same time, Neustrian elites allied themselves with the new-style and exotic Saint Columbanus. Among these "monks manqués," family feeling was belittled; human affections were cultivated at arm's length, and men looked to heaven for real joy. To be sure, standards for women were rather different, as Desiderius' mother demonstrated in her emotionally charged letters to her son. Yet even there, emotions were largely expressed as moral stances: to love virtue, to hate vice.

The Neustrian consensus lasted until the 660s, fragmenting, later in the century, into competitive factions seeking to monopolize power. For the writers representing these factions, emotions were above all "political," telegraphing allegiances and claiming the high moral ground. Like

---

[143] *Ibid.*, c. 17, pp. 298–99. For Genesius, see Fouracre and Gerberding, *Late Merovingian France*, 168 and 198.
[144] *Passio Leudegarii* c. 29, p. 310.

the Neustrian emotional community, so this one was glad to include emotions of every sort, but the hardening of categories of good and evil and, no doubt, the decline of classical Latin education, meant that the emotions would be starker and the emotion words fewer.

We shall see in Chapter 3 how, around the year 800, Alcuin, an Anglo-Saxon-turned-Carolingian adviser, drew on these various developments when he wrote a treatise on the virtues and vices that was at the same time a theory of the emotions.

3   Alcuin's therapy

Not long after Leudegar was martyred (c. 678), the Austrasians, led not by a king but rather by a powerful courtier and aristocrat, Pippin II, began to take over Neustria bit by bit. Through wars, astute marriages, patronage of key monasteries, papal support, and key missionaries working on their behalf, the dynasty that would soon be known as the Carolingian gradually assumed power over all of Francia, the ancestor of today's France. Taking their name from Charles Martel (d. 741) (Charles is *Carolus* in Latin), the Carolingians legitimated their rule with the coronation and anointment of Pippin III (r. 751–68) as king of the Franks. His son Charlemagne (king 768–814; emperor 800–814) forged an empire that included much of today's Western Europe. Wealthy enough to support artists, architects, intellectuals, and poets, and powerful enough to ensure the allegiance of most of the Frankish aristocracy, the support of the papacy, and the adherence of other key groups, Charlemagne presided over a superficially united polity. Key to his success were the powerful laymen whom he enlisted as counts – local governors and judges. Overseeing the counts were chosen laymen and ecclesiastics, the *missi* [sing.: *missus*] *dominici* (literally, "the men sent out by the lord king").

It was Charlemagne's delight to surround himself with learned courtiers and brilliant advisers. He turned his court into a sort of "school," though one constantly in flux. But he could not find well-educated teachers in Francia alone. He had to turn to England – where Latin education had accompanied Christianization – and to Italy, where classical traditions had never entirely died out. These regions provided many of the scholars who came to praise, work for, teach, and advise Charlemagne.

Alcuin (c. 740–804) was one of these scholars, and perhaps the most famous.[1] Hailing from a "modest landowning family" in the Kingdom of

---

[1] The literature on Alcuin is enormous. I have profited greatly from Donald Bullough, *Alcuin: Achievement and Reputation. Being Part of the Ford Lectures Delivered in Oxford in Hilary Term 1980* (Leiden, 2004), with its five indispensible indexes. See also Douglas Dales, *Alcuin: His Life and Legacy* (Cambridge, 2012), and *Alcuin: Theology and Thought* (Cambridge, 2013).

Northumbria in England, Alcuin spent his boyhood with the community serving York cathedral.[2] It was an archbishopric, and when Alcuin joined it, its archbishop was Egbert (d. 765), brother of Northumbrian King Eadbert (r. 737–58). At York Alcuin learned Latin letters, prayer, and Christian doctrine, and, because of York's close relations with the king, he also learned about politics and powerful men. Throughout his life he contemplated the uses and abuses of rulership.

Alcuin was ordained deacon at York and never advanced in ecclesiastical rank. Rather, his promotions came in teaching and scholarship. In the 750s, the clerical community at York got its first schoolmaster, Ælberht.[3] Alcuin became his disciple and accompanied him to Italy and Francia. Then, shortly after Ælberht's consecration as archbishop of York in 767, Alcuin himself became the master of the cathedral school.[4] He remained in that position for nearly twenty years and seems during that time to have become a public figure with close connections to the royal court at York. How and when he came to the attention of Charlemagne is much disputed, but certainly by 786 he was in attendance at the Frankish king's court.[5]

If this is the right date, Alcuin's tenure there was quite short, lasting only to early 790.[6] After a sojourn in England from 790 to 793 he was back at Charlemagne's court between 794 and 796. During his time with Charlemagne he wrote numerous letters to and for the king, as well as poems and theological tracts. He was drafted to write capitularies – programmatic summaries of decisions reached at meetings of the king and high lay and ecclesiastical dignitaries. In 796 Charlemagne sent him, much to his dismay, to serve as abbot at the monastery of Saint Martin of Tours – there to care for a complex establishment and to oversee the production of an authoritative edition of the Latin Bible, the Vulgate.[7]

At Tours Alcuin continued his busy writing schedule. Among the works he produced there was a brief manual known as *On the Virtues and Vices.* Written (so it said) at the request of the powerful layman Wido, count and *missus,* it offered, I will argue here, a synthesis of two traditions: classical theories about the emotions and Christian ideas about the virtues and vices. Its intent was therapeutic: to help Wido deal with his troubles and gain joy.[8]

---

[2] Bullough, *Alcuin: Achievement,* 164.   [3] *Ibid.,* 238   [4] *Ibid.,* 305.   [5] *Ibid.,* 340.
[6] On the dates of Alcuin's terms with the court see *ibid.,* xxiv and 432–70. However, Dales, *Alcuin: His Life,* 31, dates Alcuin's first visit to the court of Charlemagne to 779 and then a long stay at court from 781, though admitting that Alcuin may not have arrived until 786.
[7] On his reluctance to leave court, *ibid.,* 470. On his time as abbot at Tours, see Dales, *Alcuin: His Life,* 129–38.
[8] See Barbara H. Rosenwein, "Taking Pleasure in Virtues and Vices: Alcuin's Manual for Count Wido," in *The Medieval Book of Pleasure,* ed. Naama Cohen and Piroska Nagy (Turnhout, forthcoming).

Could Wido really profit from a learned treatise written in Latin? It is more than probable that he could, for Latin literacy was widespread within the lay elites.[9] Did he really want a tract from a cleric, or was that claim simply an excuse for Alcuin to impose church norms on the unruly laity? No doubt the latter was one motive. But another motive came from the laity, who used the clergy in turn. They were as interested as clerics in their prospects of salvation, and they turned to clerics as specialists in Scripture and the Church Fathers. As Michel Sot has argued, clergy and laity belonged by and large to the same elite culture.[10]

Pre-Alcuinian schemes of virtues and vices

From the start, the virtues and vices tradition depended in part on theories of emotions. The Stoics had sought to avoid most – but not all – emotions in the interest of gaining calm tranquility.[11] Their method for doing so was to catch an emotion before it turned into one: to be aware of the pricking and tingling, blushing, and blanching that they considered to be "pre-passions (*propathê*)," and to refuse to "consent" to the oncoming "real" emotion. Stoic "bad" emotions – there were many, summarized in Cicero's *Tusculan Disputations* (see Chapter 1) – were one foundation of the Christian vices tradition. The emotions that were "good" – various Stoic *eupatheiai* – suggested virtues.[12] Evagrius (d. 399), an early ascetic and monk, drew on Stoic theory. He taught that demons infected people with "eight thoughts": gluttony, lust, avarice, distress, anger, acedia (sloth), vainglory (or vanity), and pride.[13] These were equivalent to the Stoic pre-passions in that they

---

[9] See Rosamond McKitterick, *The Carolingians and the Written Word* (Cambridge, 1989); *Documentary Culture and the Laity in the Early Middle Ages*, ed. Warren C. Brown et al. (Cambridge, 2013).

[10] Michel Sot, "Concordances et discordances entre culture des élites laïques et culture des élites cléricales à l'époque carolingienne: Jonas d'Orléans et Dhuoda," in *La culture du haut moyen âge. Une question d'élites?*, ed. François Bougard, Régine Le Jan, and Rosamond McKitterick (Turnhout, 2009), 341–61, esp. 351. And note the initial words of Jonas of Orléans (d. 843) who, like Alcuin, wrote a book of "instructions" for a layman (Count Matfrid d'Orléans) in Jonas d'Orléans, *Instruction des laïcs*, praef., ed. and trans. Odile Dubreucq, 2 vols. (SC 549–50) (Paris, 2012), 1:124, where he writes for lay people who do not want to – or cannot – "make their way through the vast expanse of divine Scriptures (aut cordi aut posse non est latos divinarum Scripturarum campos percurrere)."

[11] For bibliography and a quick review of the theory, see Rosenwein, *Emotional Communities*, 37–42. See Cicero's "take" on the Stoics in Chapter 1 above.

[12] Aristotle had already called *praotés* an emotion (*pathos*) in his *Rhetoric* but a virtue (*hexis*) in his books on ethics. See David Konstan, *The Emotions of the Ancient Greeks: Studies in Aristotle and Classical Literature* (Toronto, 2006), 79.

[13] See Columba Stewart, "Evagrius Ponticus and the 'Eight Generic *Logismoi*,'" in *In the Garden of Evil: The Vices and Culture in the Middle Ages*, ed. Richard Newhauser (Toronto, 2005), 3–34.

could be resisted – not consented to – by other "thoughts," equally dangerous in their own right but rendered null and void in battle. The ascetic
should, for example, enlist vainglory to counter lust.

Later Christian thinkers dispensed with the idea of pre-passions. For
Evagrius' pupil Cassian (d. 435), bad thoughts were already vices. They
were sins rather than forerunners to sins. He called them both vices (*vitia*) and
passions (*passiones*), a straightforward translation of the Greek *pathé*, which
closely tracks our own word "emotions." This hardening of the categories
was already clear in the *Psychomachia* of Prudentius (d. 405), whose long
poem on the virtues and vices described them in mortal one-to-one combat,
with each virtue always ultimately winning against its opposing vice.[14]

But Augustine, writing around the same time as Prudentius and
Cassian, changed the rules of the game (as we saw in Chapter 1).
Connecting the emotions to the will, he argued that when the will was
right (when it was directed toward God), the emotions were virtuous;
when the will was skewed, turned away from God, the emotions were
vices. There were, then, no invariable virtues or vices.

Pope Gregory the Great (d. 604) grafted this more positive view of
emotions/virtues and vices onto the ascetic's wariness of wayward
thoughts.[15] In general, Gregory condemned emotions as cogitations
(*cogitationes*) that tended to overwhelm the mind if not kept in check. In
a famous passage on these cogitations, he named the seven capital vices –
vanity (*inanis gloria*), envy (*invidia*), anger (*ira*), sadness (*tristitia*), avarice
(*avaritia*), gluttony (*ventris ingluvies*), and lust (*luxuria*). He visualized
them as forming a sort of tree, with pride (*superbia*) at its root. Gregory
aimed to extirpate all of them, root and branch. However, like Augustine,
Gregory also thought that, if rightly used, emotions (for example, *ira*,
tristitia) could be praiseworthy. And because he was a pastor, he thought it
essential that he and other clergymen use their emotions, "bending" them
to fit the feelings of their flock in order to guide their charges to salvation.
Gregory was here advocating that the pastor be a kind of moral therapist,
and, as we shall see, Alcuin expanded on this idea.

Thus transformed into sin and virtue, emotions *as* emotions were almost
never discussed theoretically until the scholastics took them up again.[16]
But Edward Peters has very helpfully noticed that the seemingly silent gap

---

[14] Donatella Marocco Stuardi, *Alcuino di York nella tradizione degli "Specula principis"*
(Milan, 1999), 49–50, sees the psychomachia as one of Alcuin's themes.

[15] On Gregory, see Rosenwein, *Emotional Communities*, 79–99, and Carole Straw,
"Gregory, Cassian, and the Cardinal Vices," in *In the Garden of Evil*, 35–58, esp. 48–58.

[16] Consider, for example, the survey of ancient and medieval theories of emotion in
Knuuttila, *Emotions*, which ends chap. 2 with Gregory the Great and begins chap. 3
with the twelfth century.

between the psychological theories of the Church Fathers and those of the scholastics is due to our rigid definition of "psychology." He suggests that the practical but no less psychological works of moral theologians dominated the period in between. He proposes calling their writings "palaeopsychology," citing Alcuin's work as one example.[17] We shall see that *On the Virtues and Vices* was, in effect, a guide to the emotions and a manual for dealing with them.

The text's influence and sources

Alcuin wrote *On the Virtues and Vices* between 801 and 804.[18] In a dedicatory letter, he says that he was responding to the request of Wido, count of the Breton march (that is, military frontier) in 799 and *missus* in 802.[19] The work was enormously popular, with more than 140 extant manuscripts, mostly in France, England, Spain, and Italy, but some in countries as far-flung as Sweden and Poland.[20] It was also translated, adapted, or glossed in a significant number of medieval vernacular languages, including Old Norse, Old English, and Middle English.[21]

This popularity must be understood together with the work's highly derivative nature. The manual (as Alcuin called it) is largely a pastiche of writings not by Alcuin but by (above all) Cassian, Isidore of Seville (d. 636), and Caesarius of Arles (d. 542).[22] Alcuin may also have made much use of the works of an author whom modern scholars call

---

[17] Edward Peters, "*Vir inconstans*: Moral Theology as Palaeopsychology," in *In the Garden of Evil*, 59–73.

[18] Alcuin, *De virtutibus et vitiis liber ad Widonem comitem*, PL 101, cols. 613–38 [henceforth *DVV*]. This edition dates from 1777 but it is the only one we have at present; see Franz Sedlmeier, *Die laienparänetischen Schriften der Karolingerzeit. Untersuchungen zu ausgewählten Texten des Paulinus von Aquileia, Alkuins, Jonas' von Orleans, Dhuodas und Hinkmars von Reims* (Neuried, 2000), 117–18; Paul E. Szarmach, "A Preliminary Handlist of Manuscripts containing Alcuin's *Liber de virtutibus et vitiis*," *Manuscripta* 25 (1981): 131–40 at 131, announces "an eventual [new] edition." For the date, see Alain Dubreucq, "Autour du *De virtutibus et vitiis* d'Alcuin," in *Alcuin, de York à Tours. Écriture, pouvoir et réseaux dans l'Europe du haut Moyen Âge*, ed. Philippe Depreux and Bruno Judic = *Annales de Bretagne et des Pays de l'Ouest* 111–13 (2004): 249–88, here 269–70, and Sedlmeier, *Die laienparänetischen*, 120–21.

[19] On Wido, see Julia M. H. Smith, *Province and Empire: Brittany and the Carolingians* (Cambridge, 1992), 52–53, 67–68. The dedicatory letter along with the final *peroratio* were edited as Alcuin, *Epistola* 305, ed. Ernst Dümmler, MGH Epistolae 4: Epistolae karolini aevi 2 (Berlin, 1895; rpt. 1994) [henceforth Alcuin, *Ep.* 305], 464–65.

[20] Szarmach, "A Preliminary Handlist," 135–40, supplemented by "The Latin Tradition of Alcuin's *Liber de Virtutibus et Vitiis*, cap. xxvii–xxxv, with Special Reference to Vercelli Homily xx," *Mediaevalia* 12 (1989): 13–41, esp. 14–16.

[21] Szarmach, "A Preliminary Handlist," 133–34.

[22] Liutpold Wallach, *Alcuin and Charlemagne: Studies in Carolingian History and Literature* (Ithaca, NY, 1959), also identifies among Alcuin's sources Peter Chrysologus, *Sermo* 53,

pseudo-Augustine, though Donald Bullough has argued that these were in fact Alcuin's own writings.[23] In any event, there is no question that much of the manual is made up of commonplaces. For some scholars, this diminishes its importance.[24] The opposite view might make *On the Virtues and Vices* utterly "representative" of its age. A middle way, the one taken here, is also possible. Alcuin did not borrow every word, phrase, and idea that he wrote, and even had he done so, he nevertheless made important choices and organizational decisions that allow us to see a creative mind at work.[25]

The work falls into several fairly coherent sections, though modern scholars count them somewhat differently.[26] It begins with the dedicatory letter to Wido. It then turns to a short chapter on wisdom. Thereafter come three chapters on the theological virtues (faith, charity, and hope) followed by a chapter on the importance of reading. Chapters 6–26 cover various virtues alongside what Donald Bullough has called "spiritual

and Gregory the Great, *Moralia in Job*; Dubreucq, "Autour," 274, adds Julian Pomerius, *De vita contemplativa*.

[23] The pseudo-Augustinian sources identified as cannibalized by Wallach, *Alcuin and Charlemagne*, 236–37 are his *Sermones* 98, 108, 254, 291, 297, 302, and 304. For all of these see *Clavis patristica pseudepigraphorum medii aevi*, 1: *Opera homiletica, pars A (Praefatio) (Ambrosius-Augustinus)*, ed. John J. Machielsen (Turnhout, 1990). Donald A. Bullough, "Alcuin and Lay Virtue," in *Predicazione e società nel medioevo: riflessione etica, valori e modelli di comportamento = Preaching and Society in the Middle Ages. Ethics, Values and Social Behaviour. Atti/Proceedings of the XII Medieval Sermon Studies Symposium. Padova, 14–18 luglio 2000*, ed. Laura Gaffuri and Riccardo Quinto (Padova, 2002), 85–87, points out that some of the Latin flourishes in pseudo-Augustine, *Sermo* 302 (for which see *Clavis patristica*, no. 1087) were characteristic of Alcuin and, further, that there is no independent MS tradition for that sermon until it was transmitted by Hrabanus Maurus, a student of Alcuin. Bullough concluded that "it is surely far more probable that Hrabanus's homily-text is one of a series in which he has combined extracts from one or more chapters of the *De virtutibus et vitiis* with prefatory and concluding passages of his own." The *Clavis Patristica* suggests that the same MS tradition was the case with pseudo-Augustine *Sermones* 98 (no. 883), 108 (no. 893), 291 (no. 1076), and 304 (no. 1089) – that is, there is no independent source for them until Hrabanus' homilary. That leaves pseudo-Augustine, *Sermo* 254 unaccounted for, but Bullough, *Alcuin: Achievement*, 354–55, argues that this, too, is Alcuin's, albeit heavily dependent on "two or three different works of Isidore," namely the *Sententiae*, the *Synonyma*, and the pseudo-Isidorian *Testimoniae divinae scripturae et patrum*.

[24] See, for example, Carla Casagrande and Silvana Vecchio, *I sette vizi capitali. Storia dei peccati nel Medioevo* (Turin, 2000), which mentions it only in passing.

[25] Certainly the range of Alcuin's reading was far wider than the sources he drew on for DVV; see Bullough, *Alcuin: Achievement*, 505, which indexes "Alcuin, his sources." Another way to consider Alcuin's borrowings is to assess not which sources but how closely (or loosely) Alcuin quoted them, as recommended by Sedlmeier, *Die laienparänetischen*, 130.

[26] Dubreucq, "Autour," 270 counts four parts; Bullough, "Alcuin and Lay Virtue," 87–89, implicitly counts five; Sedlmeier, *Die laienparänetischen*, 125–29, fixes on eight. Marocco Stuardi, *Alcuino di York*, 57 thinks that what we have today may possibly have originally been several separate tracts.

exercises."[27] These include compunction of heart, confession, and penance. Chapter 27–34 turns to the eight principal vices, and Chapter 35 summarizes what Alcuin said about the four cardinal virtues (prudence, justice, fortitude, and temperance) in an earlier treatise, his so-called *On Rhetoric*.[28] A final letter to Wido ends the work.[29]

In his dedicatory letter, Alcuin says that he wrote "so that you might always have at hand sentences of paternal admonition (*paternae ammonitionis sententias*)."[30] The "admonition" was a well-recognized genre in the Carolingian period.[31] It harked back to Gregory who, in his guide for pastors, *Pastoral Care*, told them how to admonish their flocks. A typical chapter in Gregory's manual, for example, prescribed "how to admonish in one way those who are happy and in another way those who are sad."[32] Gregory told the pastor to remind the happy about the tortures awaiting them but to tell the sad about the joys of heaven. With a lay audience, Alcuin's task was a bit different: it was to give Wido a basic guide to dealing with all his emotional states and moral dispositions. *Sentences of Paternal Admonition* might be a better title for this manual; the title *On the Virtues and Vices* comes from Alcuin's anonymous biographer, albeit with the terms reversed.[33]

Wido, Alcuin noted, had himself asked for the manual: he had requested exhortation (*exhortamentum*) – some emphatic advice – about his "bellicose occupation."[34] Alcuin saw this as cry for help, and he meant by his treatise to offer Wido solace (*solatium*): he gave his advice, he said, "so that your mind (*animus*), fatigued by external troubles, may have a joyful return to itself."[35] Troubles (*molestia*) and joy (*gaudium*): the first was among Cicero's emotional "distresses" (his *aegritudines*), while the second was among his "good emotions" (his *constantiae*). Had Alcuin

---

[27] Bullough, "Alcuin and Lay Virtue," 85 n. 53.

[28] Alcuin, *Disputatio de rhetorica et de virtutibus sapientissimi Regis Caroli et Albini magistri*, in *The Rhetoric of Alcuin and Charlemagne: A Translation, with an Introduction, the Latin Text, and Notes*, ed. and trans. Wilbur Samuel Howell (Princeton, 1941) [henceforth *DR*], 88–89.

[29] Alcuin, *Ep.* 305, pp. 464–65. In PL 101:638 this letter is (mistakenly) labeled c. 36.

[30] *Ibid.*, p. 464.

[31] For the admonitory tradition, see Mayke de Jong, *The Penitential State: Authority and Atonement in the Age of Louis the Pious, 814–840* (Cambridge, 2009), 112–47.

[32] Gregory the Great, *Pastoral Care* 3.3, in *Grégoire le Grand, Règle pastorale*, vol. 2, ed. Floribert Rommel, trans. Charles Morel, SC 382 (Paris, 1992), 272.

[33] *Vita Alcuini* c. 21, ed. Wilhelm Arndt, MGH SS 15.1 (Hannover, 1887), 182–97 at 195, called it "Homilies on the Principal Vices and Virtues (homilias de principalibus vitiis et virtutibus)."

[34] Alcuin, *Ep.* 305, p. 464.

[35] *Ibid.*: "ut animus exterioribus fatigatus molestiis, ad se ipsum reversus habeat, in quo gaudeat."

read Cicero? We shall see that he had, though not, it appears, the *Tusculan Disputations*.[36]

An emotional text?

Few scholars have previously asked what this text might have to do with emotions.[37] Unlike Alcuin's letters and poems, some of which employ what C. Stephen Jaeger has termed a "powerful erotic-religious language of romantic love," Alcuin's manual on virtues and vices is hardly "emotional."[38] Apart from calling Wido "most beloved son (*dilectissimo filio*)" on occasion, it contains not a word of affection. Compare this to a letter that Alcuin wrote to Archbishop Arn of Salzburg a few years before he wrote for Wido: "O would that I could be transported to you, like Habacuc: with what eager embraces I would enfold you, o sweetest son ... I would kiss all the limbs of your body with the sweetest greetings."[39]

Nevertheless, there are good reasons to consider the manual to be *about* emotions even if it is not very expressive itself. Indeed, Alcuin's opening letter explicitly claims that his manual will bring about an emotional transformation, from a troubled "*animus*" to a joyous one. What did Alcuin mean by the *animus*? We have already seen (in Chapter 1) that for Cicero the *animus* was the seat of the emotions. Alcuin knew this; in his dialogue *On Rhetoric*, in which he cast himself as teacher and Charlemagne as student, he borrowed extensively from Cicero's *On [Rhetorical] Invention*.[40] At its very start, Alcuin evoked the Ciceronian state of nature, where men "did nothing through reason of their *animus* (*ratione animi*) but depended rather on their physical strength (*viribus corporis*)."[41] Here the *animus* was the home of reason. But it was also the seat of what in Cicero's view were unreasonable feelings (*affectiones*). Alcuin copied Cicero here, writing about acts done on impulse (*impulsio*) – that is, "without thinking because of some feeling of the *animus* (*quandam affectionem animi*), such as love (*amor*), rage (*iracundia*), distress

---

[36] See Bullough, *Alcuin: Achievement*, 286.

[37] Wallach, *Alcuin and Charlemagne*, was interested in its sources; Bullough, "Alcuin and Lay Virtue," Dubreucq, "Autour," and Sedlmeier, *Die laienparänetischen*, wanted to discern Alcuin's contribution to the genre of lay mirrors. Marocco Stuardi, *Alcuino di York*, 13–21, locates it within the mirror of princes' tradition and (22–41) surveys its antecedents in writings from the first to seventh centuries. Dales, *Alcuin: Theology*, 218, like Peters, identifies its subject as moral theology.

[38] Jaeger, *Ennobling Love*, 48.   [39] Alcuin, *Ep.* 193, p. 319.

[40] Dales, *Alcuin: Theology*, 216, calls Charlemagne Alcuin's "pre-eminent layman and self-professed disciple." But an anointed king like Charlemagne was more than a "layman."

[41] Alcuin, DR, prol., p. 68, l. 35–36, echoing Cicero, *De inventione* 1.1.2, in *De inventione*. *De optimo genere oratorum. Topica*, trans. Harry M. Hubbell (Cambridge, MA, 1960), 4.

(*aegritudo*), intoxication (*vinolentia*), and the like.[42] Cicero wanted to explain how a prosecutor could convince his audience that a crime had been committed out of impulse. Alcuin's *On Rhetoric* repeated him:

[The prosecutor] will have to amplify on that urge (*impetum*) and, as it were, the agitation and emotion of the [criminal's] *animus* (*commotionem et affectionem animi*) with his words and phrases, and he will have to show how great is the force of love (*vis amoris*), how much perturbation of the *animus* (*perturbatio animi*) comes from rage (*iracundia*) or from any of those causes from which he says the impulse came. [He should do this] so that it will not seem strange that an *animus* agitated by such an emotion (*perturbatione*) should commit the crime.[43]

As we saw in Chapter 1, a "perturbation of the *animus* (*perturbatio animi*)" was Cicero's word for an emotion. Clearly in his *On Rhetoric*, Alcuin was glad to follow Cicero.

But in his treatise for Wido, which was less heavily dependent on Cicero, the *animus* was but one part of the human mental, spiritual, and moral apparatus. It was related (as, indeed, it had been in the ancient world) to the soul (*anima*), heart (*cor*), and mind (*mens*). Along with the body (*corpus, caro, carnis*), these mental faculties were responsible for human action, whether moral or immoral. Thus in *On the Virtues and Vices*, Alcuin was not systematic about which human faculty was associated with the emotions. While Cicero had associated anger (*ira*) with the *animus*, Alcuin said that it disturbed the *mens*.[44] And while Cicero had also placed love (in his case using the word *amor*) in the *animus*, Alcuin noted that the Lord himself had said (Matt. 22:37) "love (*diliges*) our Lord God with all your heart (*ex toto corde*) and all your soul (*ex tota anima*) and all your mind (*ex tota mente*)," helpfully explaining that this meant "with all your intellect (*intellectus*), will (*voluntas*), and memory (*memoria*)." Here Alcuin was quoting a text known as *De imagine dei*, which was in turn inspired by Augustine.[45]

---

[42] Alcuin, *DR* c. 16, p. 92, ll. 414–17; his source is Cicero, *De inventione* 2.5.17, p. 180.

[43] Alcuin, *DR* c. 17, pp. 92–94, ll. 430–35.

[44] Alcuin, *DVV* c. 24, col. 631: "Illa ira mala est, quae mentem turbat (anger is that evil thing that disturbs the mens)." The observation is in a chapter on *iracundia*, strongly suggesting that *ira* and *iracundia* were equivalent terms for Alcuin.

[45] John Marenbon, *From the Circle of Alcuin to the School of Auxerre: Logic, Theology and Philosophy in the Early Middle Ages* (Cambridge, 1981), 33–43, who gives the text of *De imagine dei* on 158–61 and attributes it to Alcuin or his "circle." However, Donald Bullough, "Alcuin and the Kingdom of Heaven: Liturgy, Theology, and the Carolingian Age," in *Carolingian Renewal: Sources and Heritage*, by Donald Bullough (Manchester, 1991), 161–240 at 181, concludes that it was more likely a "late fifth/ sixth-century work (perhaps of Gallic origin) which, with others similarly neglected for centuries, resurfaced at the Carolingian court in the 780s." Anita Guerreau-Jalabert, "'Aimer de fin cuer.' Le cœur dans la thématique courtoise," in *Il cuore*, 343–71, esp. 360, notes the importance of this passage in giving Christian thinkers a locus for love and associated words.

The essential equivalence of the *animus, anima, cor,* and *mens* in Alcuin's manual allowed him to associate many virtues and vices/emotions with more than one faculty. Thus anger (*ira*), if not ruled by reason (*ratio*), will turn into fury (*furor*) "such that a person will be powerless in his *animus* and will do something inappropriate." But anger can also seize (*insidit*) a person's heart (*cor*), affecting his good judgment. Again similarly, it can spawn a swollen *mens* (*tumor mentis*), leading to disputes, homicides, desire for revenge, and so on.[46] Here as elsewhere, Alcuin was drawing on a rich repertory of sources. When he spoke of a "seized heart," he was thinking of Cassian.[47] When he talked about anger's role in swelling the mind and producing brawls and bloodshed, he was drawing on Gregory the Great.[48]

Constructing a list of emotions

Not every chapter in *On the Virtues and Vices* named an emotion. The first chapter of the manual, on wisdom (*sapientia*), was about a goal, not an emotion. That is, unlike the moral virtues and vices, wisdom was not (in Alcuin's view) perfectible, changeable, or subject to human control. It did not exist in the human faculties of mind or body.[49] Wisdom, said Alcuin, is summed up in two commands: "turn from evil and do good" (Ps. 33:15). The rest of Alcuin's manual was, in effect, about how to carry out these injunctions. (See Plate 3.1.)

The emotions (or, in Alcuin's parlance, the virtues and vices) were under human control (with the grace of God, to be sure). They partook in human faculties such as the heart and soul. They could be changed and perfected. Consider Alcuin's discussion of love (using the term *caritas*). He notes that love "gets first place among the precepts of God, and without its perfection nothing can please God ... Hence, when the Lord himself was asked what was the greatest command, he

---

[46] Alcuin, *DVV* c. 31, col. 634.

[47] John Cassian, *De institutis coenobiorum et de octo principalium vitiorum remediis libri XII* 8.1, ed. Michael Petschenig, CSEL 17 (Vienna, 1888), 151: "hac [ira] enim in nostris cordibus insidente (for that anger seizes us in our hearts)." For the sins "of the heart" in the Carolingian period, see Vecchio, "Peccatum cordis," 328 n. 6.

[48] Gregory the Great, *Moralia in Job* 31.45, ed. Marcus Adriaen, CCSL 143B (Turnhout, 1985), 1610: "De ira, rixae[,] tumor mentis, contumeliae, clamor, indignatio, blasphemiae proferuntur (from anger are brought forth brawls, a swelled head, insults, din, indignation, and blasphemies)."

[49] Alcuin, *DVV* c. 1, cols. 614–15. However, Alcuin's apparent source, Boniface of Mainz, *Sermo* 7, PL 89, col. 857, *does* associate *sapientia* with an emotion in a passage not quoted by Alcuin, for he connects it to fear of God.

Plate 3.1 A Carolingian image of wisdom

Around the same time as Alcuin (now abbot of Saint Martin of Tours) was writing *On the Virtues and Vices*, he was preparing an authoritative edition of the Vulgate. We have several finely illustrated examples of the fruits of his labor from Tours somewhat after Alcuin's death. This page, which comes from one of those later bibles, the so-called Moutier-Grandval Bible (perhaps dated c. 830– c. 840), shows one of its few historiated initials (that is, an initial decorated with a figure or scene). Here, beginning the Book of Wisdom, is her personification. (Wisdom, *sapientia* in Latin, is a feminine noun and therefore always portrayed as a woman.) Standing upright in graceful pose, her flowing robe edged (like the initial D within which she stands) with gold, the haloed Wisdom carries a bejeweled book in her right hand and a flowering scepter in her left. She represents God's Holy Wisdom. But why did the artist single her out for special attention?

answered, 'Love (*diliges*) your Lord God with your whole heart and soul and mind.'"[50]

Let us draw up a list of Alcuin's emotion words by discovering those terms that he connected to the *animus, anima, mens,* and *cor. Corpus* (body) must be added here as well, partly because Alcuin made it the seat of gluttony (*gula*), which was also (according to him) in the *mens,* and partly because terms that were integral to classical theories of emotions, such as desire (*desiderium, concupiscentia*), were (for Alcuin) located in the body. In the next section I will use an associative method (explained below) to expand the list. In the end, it does not make sense to divide these emotions by the faculty they "belonged" to, since Alcuin quite blithely associated many of them (as we saw in the case of *ira*) with more than one.[51]

Let us begin with the *animus,* which, as we have seen, would rejoice when returned to a sort of quiet equilibrium within itself. Alcuin thought that the *animus* could also experience other delights, such as "spiritual happiness (*laetitia*) through hope (*spes*) in future things, the consolation (*consolatio*) of Scripture, and the fraternal talk in spiritual jocularity

---

Caption for Plate 3.1 (*cont.*)

One answer may come from Alcuin's emphasis on Wisdom as "the first of all things."[i] True wisdom, Alcuin said in his manual for Wido, was to turn from evil and to do good. For this, the virtues and vices – that is, the emotions – had to be tamed and trained. That was the purpose of the rest of the manual. Alcuin surely had the Vulgate's Book of Wisdom in mind. Indeed, it began with one of his emotion words, to love (*diligere*) in the form of a command: "Love justice (*diligite justitiam*), you that are the judges of the earth." The figure of Wisdom floats in the middle of the D of *diligite,* a stern reminder to a layman like Wido, who was in fact an earthly judge in his roles as count and *missus.* © The British Library Board, MS Add., 10546 f. 262v.

[i] The topic is from Isidore, but the words are directly from pseudo-Augustine, *Sermo* 302. See n. 23 for Alcuin's authorship of pseudo-Augustine.

---

[50] Alcuin, *DVV* c. 3, col. 615. The entire passage is taken from Boniface, *Sermo* 7, col. 857, and in turn Boniface may have been building on Isidore of Seville, *Sententiae* 2.3.3, ed. Pierre Cazier, CCSL 111 (Turnhout, 1998), 97, or possibly on Isidore's source.

[51] Other emotions associated with more than one human faculty include *amaritudo* (*cor/ animus*), *compunctio* (*anima/cor*), *gula* (*corpus/mens*), *humilitas* (*mens/cor*), *invidia* (*animus/ mens*), *patientia* (*anima/animus*), *spes* (*anima/animus*), and *tristitia* (*anima/animus*). But since *cor, anima,* and *mens* are so often associated, this can be only a partial list.

(*jucunditas*)"[52] Then, too, the classical virtues – fortitude (*fortitudo*), justice (*justitia*), patience (*patientia*), and temperance (*temperantia*) – were, among other things, positive feelings pertaining to the *animus*. For, as Alcuin declared, virtue "is the [good] disposition (*habitus*) of the *animus*," an idea that derived in part from Cicero's *On Invention*.[53] Alcuin explicitly made justice a part of the *animus*: "Justice is nobility of *animus* (*animi nobilitas*)."[54] Patience, sometimes connected to the *anima* rather than the *animus*,[55] was closely linked to forgiveness, which came from the heart: "True patience is to bear up bravely in the face of injuries and not seek vengeance in the future but forgive from the heart (*ex corde ignoscere*). We can be martyrs without sword or flames if in our *animus* we truly preserve patience (*patientia*) with our neighbors."[56] Compassion, too, was the preserve of the *animus*: "We merit the mercy (*misericordiam* ... *meremur*) of God and forgiveness of our sins by [our] compassion (*miseratione*) and alms to the poor, since he who does not turn his *animus* away from the poor quickly turns the Lord's ear to himself."[57]

At the same time, Alcuin associated the *animus* with feelings that were the equivalent of vices and not at all happy. Envy (*invidia*) was one: "Nothing can be more evil than envy," wrote Alcuin of this chief emotion of the devil, and "every envious man is tormented in his *animus*."[58] Meanwhile anger (*ira, iracundia*), which was a virtue when ruled by reason and directed against one's own sins, was a vice when it overcame reason (another attribute of the *animus*).[59] Thus, according to Alcuin, anger (*ira*) is that "which, if not ruled by reason, turns into fury (*furorem vertitur*), so that a person becomes powerless in his or her *animus* and does what is wrong."[60] In a later chapter, when speaking of sadness (*tristitia*),

---

[52] Alcuin, *DVV* c. 33, col. 635.

[53] *Ibid.*, c. 35, col. 637. See Cicero, *De inventione* 2.53.159, p. 326: "Virtus est animi habitus naturae modo atque rationi consentaneus (Virtue is the habit of the animus in harmony with the order of nature and reason)." Alcuin elaborated and Christianized the definition: "Virtus est animi habitus, naturae decus, vitae ratio, morum pietas, cultus divinitatis, honor hominis, aeternae beatitudinis meritum (Virtue is the habit of the animus, the dignity of nature, the rule of life, the goodness of morals, the worship of the divinity, the honor of man, the merit of eternal beatitude)."

[54] Alcuin, *DVV* c. 35, col. 637.

[55] *Ibid.*, c. 9, col. 619, quoting Luke 21:19: "In patientia vestra possidebitis animas vestras (in patience you will possess your souls)."

[56] *Ibid.*   [57] *Ibid.*, c. 17, col. 625.

[58] *Ibid.*, c. 22, col. 630. As we have seen in Chapter 2, envy was one of the emotions of the devil for the elites of the late seventh century, and this was the case for Alcuin a century later when he quoted Wisd. 2:24 on the devil's envy: "Invidia diaboli mors introivit in orbem terrarum (The envy of the devil brought death into the world)."

[59] *Ibid.*, c. 24, col. 631.

[60] *Ibid.*, c. 31, col. 634. On righteous anger, see Alcuin's discussion of *iracundia*, *ibid.*, c. 24, col. 631.

Alcuin treated many emotions that we would classify as forms of anger but that for him were the fruits of sorrow. They, too, were connected to the *animus*: "The other [sadness, the bad sort] is the sadness (*tristitia*) of this world ... which perturbs the *animus* and often sends it into despair (*desperationem mittit*) ... From [sadness] are born malice (*malitia*), rancor (*rancor*), cowardice (*animi pusillanimitas*), bitterness (*amaritudo*), and despair (*desperatio*)."[61]

Alcuin worried a lot about despair. When talking about mercy, he described the good judge, who balanced mercy with discipline. Too much mercy would lead sinners to think that they were free to sin. But too much discipline would "turn the offender's *animus* to despair (*in desperationem*)."[62] In the section of his manual in which he considered the nature of penance and confession, Alcuin wrote:

True penance is not counted by years but by bitterness of *animus* (*amaritudine animi*). Thus Saint Peter quickly received the Lord's indulgence, for he wept most bitterly (*amarissime flevit*) over his sin of triple denial. However short it may be, penance, if carried out (*agitur*) in the intimate bitterness of the heart (*intima cordis amaritudine*), is not despised by God, the just judge, who looks into the heart's secrets (*cordis secreta*). For God does not so much require length of time as he weighs the feeling of sincerity (*affectum sinceritatis*) of the penitent. For he who believes in Christ with his whole mind (*tota mente*), even if he were to die in multiple sins, lives eternally by his faith.[63]

Here we see that the *animus* was where bitterness (*amaritudo*) resided as it spilled out in plangent weeping. In his chapter on sadness, Alcuin explicitly tied that emotion to the *animus*: "sadness (*tristitia*) is salvific when the *animus* is saddened (*contristatur*) by the very sins of the sinner, and it is made so sad (*contristatur*) that [the sinner] seeks to make confession and do penance."[64]

But Alcuin also associated *tristitia* with the heart (*cor*), and the heart inevitably evoked its companions, the soul (*anima*) and the mind (*mens*). As we have seen, these words were linked together by Scripture in passages that exhorted men and women to love God.[65] Compunction (*compunctio*) was typically paired with the heart in the phrase *compunctio cordis*.[66] An offspring of humility, compunction, as Alcuin said, stood at the beginning of a chain of worthy spiritual events leading to confession,

---

[61] *Ibid.*, c. 33, col. 635.   [62] *Ibid.*, c. 7, col. 618.

[63] *Ibid.*, c. 13, col. 622. The passage is equivalent to pseudo-Augustine, *Sermo* 254, PL 39, cols. 2215–16 at 2216, but Bullough, *Alcuin: Achievement*, 354, has identified the ultimate sources as "two or three different works of Isidore [of Seville]."

[64] Alcuin, *DVV* c. 33, col. 635.

[65] Matt. 22:37; Luke 10:27; Deut. 6:5 and others make the link.

[66] A quick search in the PL database yields 95 "hits" in volumes 1–100, that is, roughly the period before Alcuin.

penitence, and pardon. Like bitterness of *animus*, compunction was humility of *mens* (*humilitas mentis*), and, like bitterness (*amaritudo*), it was accompanied by tears (*lacrymae*).[67] Alcuin took care to explain the qualities of the emotions (*qualitates affectionum*) with which "the thought of the just (*cogitatio justi*) is pricked [the root meaning of compunction] to salubrious loathing (*salubri taedio compungitur*)." These emotional "qualities" – a better translation might be "causes" – included the "memory of acts neglected and mindfulness of future punishments."[68] Here both heart (*cor*) and mind (*mens*) were involved in compunction, and soon Alcuin made clear that the soul (*anima*) participated as well: "The *anima* of a person, which is pricked in prayer, is extremely effective for his salvation. When compunction is poured forth through prayer, it is certain that the presence of the Holy Spirit is there in our hearts."[69]

Finally, the flesh (*carnis, corpus*) was the site of desire (*desiderium, concupiscentia*), gluttony (*gula*), and worldly happiness (*laetitia*). "Let a person oppose the flames of eternal torment to the desire of the flesh (*desiderio carnis*)," wrote Alcuin.[70] And the first of the corporal sins (which were equally the eight vices of the *mens*) was gluttony (*gula*).[71]

The result of this survey is presented in Table 3.1.

Expanding the list

It is possible, however, to expand this list by looking at how each word was deployed by Alcuin to evoke others of its kind or its contraries.[72] Thus, for example, bitterness (*amaritudo*) is already on Table 3.1. But Alcuin also spoke of a bitterness of fear (*timoris amaritudo*); it was the opposite of the

---

[67] Alcuin, *DVV* c. 11, col. 621.

[68] *Ibid.* Many of these ideas and even their expression here were borrowed from Isidore of Seville, *Sententiae* 2.12.4, p. 118, or from Defensor of Ligugé, *Liber Scintillarum* c. 6, in *Defensor de Ligugé, Livre d'étincelles*, vol. 1, ed. Henri-Marie Rochais, SC 77 (Paris, 1961), 124. Marocco Stuardi, *Alcuino di York*, 67–70, 78–81, compares these and a few other sources with Alcuin's treatise, concluding that they hardly influenced his treatment of virtue but were decisively influential on his treatment of vice.

[69] Alcuin, *DVV* c. 11, col. 621. Some, but not all, of this was from Defensor of Ligugé, *Liber Scintillarum* c. 6, p. 120, where it was attributed to Gregory the Great.

[70] Alcuin, *DVV* c. 18, col. 626. In the same chapter, Alcuin quoted Ecclus 18:30, which associated *concupiscentia* with the soul (*anima*).

[71] *Ibid.*, c. 28, col. 633: "Primum est corporale peccatum gula (The first [of the principal vices after pride] is the 'corporal sin' gluttony)." Earlier, *ibid.*, c. 27, cols. 632–33, Alcuin had said that from the eight principal vices "every [aspect] of the corrupt mind or the unchaste body spawns the vices of diverse iniquities (omnia corruptae mentis vel incasti corporis diversarum vitia pullulant iniquitatum)."

[72] Here using the "associative method" that I first proposed in Rosenwein, *Emotional Communities*, 43–45, and discussed further in my "Thinking Historically about Medieval Emotions," *History Compass* 8/8 (2010): 828–42 at 833.

Table 3.1 *Alcuin's emotion words*

acedia, tedium, boredom
affectio, emotion, affection
amaritudo, bitterness
avaritia, avarice
cenodoxia/vana gloria, vainglory
caritas, love
compunctio, compunction
concupiscentia, ardent desire, concupiscence
consolatio, consolation
desiderium, desire
desperatio, despair
   desperare, to despair
diligere, to love
fides, good faith
fornicatio, fornication
fortitudo, courage, fortitude
furor, fury
gaudium, joy
gravitas, gravity, dignity
gula, gluttony
humilitas, humility
   humiliare, to humble
ignoscere, to pardon
invidia, envy
ira/iracundia, anger
   irascor, to be angry
jucunditas, jocularity
justitia, justice
laetitia, joy, happiness
malitia, malice
misericordia, mercy
patientia, patience
pusillanimitas, cowardice, pusillanimity
rancor, rancor
spes, hope
superbia, pride
taedium, weariness
temperantia, temperance
tristitia, sorrow
   contristari, to sadden
tumor mentis, mental excitement

emotion markers:
flere, to weep
lacrymae, tears

fear of God born of the sweetness of charity (*ex charitatis dulcedine*).[73] This authorizes us to call fear in its guise as *timor* one of Alcuin's emotions. In turn, *timor* and its corresponding verb *timere* (to fear) were for Alcuin equivalent to *metus* (another word for fear) and its verb (*metuere*),[74] and paralleled love (*amor*), desire (*cupiditas*), and hate (*odium*) in perverting justice.[75] *Caritas* (charity, a form of love) destroyed discord (*discordia*), which was a branch of vanity (*cenodoxia, vana gloria*). And so on. The result is the expanded list of emotions in Table 3.2.[76]

Implications

Because Alcuin meant his manual to help Wido, it was not a simple exposition of virtues and vices (or, as we would say, emotions). It was meant to be therapeutic and offer solace. It assumed that human beings were responsible for their feelings and actions and, by understanding the sources of these things, could change them. In his discussion of sorrow, Alcuin explained how Wido – and by implication, everyone – could anticipate the course of a feeling and prod it in the right direction:

There are two sorts of sadness, one salvific, the other destructive. Sadness is salvific when the mind of the sinner is made sad (*contristatur*) by its own sins; and [the sinner] is so saddened (*contristatur*) that he seeks to do confession and penance and desires to turn himself to God. The other is the sadness of this world, which brings about the death of the soul (*animae*), which does not manage to produce anything good, which perturbs (*perturbat*) the mind and often drives it to despair (*desperationem*), so that it takes away the hope (*spem*) of future good things. From [this sort of sadness] are born malice, rancor, cowardice, bitterness, and despair. Often there is even no delight (*delectatio*) in the present life. [This sadness] is conquered by spiritual happiness (*laetitia spiritualis*) and hope (*spes*) of

---

[73] Alcuin, *DVV* c. 15, col. 624.

[74] As *ibid.*: "qui timore sancto Deum metuunt (those who fear God with a holy fear)."

[75] *Ibid.*, c. 21, col. 629.

[76] Further citations for Table 3.2: *arrogantia ibid.* c. 34, col. 635, is a branch of *cenodoxia/ vana gloria*; *blasphemia ibid.*, c. 24, col. 631, is associated with *amaritudo* and *ira* in Eph. 4:31, quoted by Alcuin; *clamor ibid.*, c. 24, col. 631, is associated with *amaritudo* and *ira* in Eph. 4:31, quoted by Alcuin; *cupido (inanis gloriae)* is associated with *cenodoxia/vana gloria ibid.*, c. 34, col. 635; *eleemosynis in pauperes* (alms to the poor) is the opposite of avarice (*avaritia*) *ibid.*, c. 3, col. 634; *erubescere ibid.*, c. 10, col. 620, is associated with lack of humility; *hypocrisis* is a branch of *cenodoxia/vana gloria ibid.*, c. 34, col. 635; *indignatio ibid.*, c. 24, col. 631, is associated with *amaritudo* and *ira* in Eph. 4:31, quoted by Alcuin; *jactantia ibid.*, c. 34, col. 635, is a branch of *cenodoxia/vana gloria*; *pietas in miseros* (pity toward the miserable) is the opposite of *avaritia ibid.*, c. 30, col. 634; laughter (*risus*) *ibid.*, c. 27, col. 633, is *in laetitia*; *vindicta* (vengeance) *ibid.*, c. 9, col. 619, is the opposite of *ex corde ignoscere* (forgiving from the heart).

Table 3.2 *Alcuin's emotion words enhanced*

acedia, sloth
affectio, emotion, affection
amaritudo, bitterness
amor, love
arrogantia, arrogance
avaritia, avarice
blasphemia, blasphemy
cenodoxia/vana gloria, vainglory
caritas, love
clamor, noise, complaint
compunctio, compunction
concupiscentia, ardent desire, concupiscence
consolatio, consolation
cupiditas/cupido, desire, cupidity
desiderium, desire
desperatio, despair
  desperare, to despair
dilectio, love
  diligere, to love
discordia, discord
eleemosyna, alms
fides, good faith
fornicatio, fornication
fortitudo, courage, fortitude
furor, fury
gaudium, joy
gravitas, gravity, dignity
gula, gluttony
humilitas, humility
  humiliare, to humble
hypocrisis, hypocrisy
ignoscere, to pardon
indignatio, indignation
invidia, envy
ira/iracundia, anger
  irascor, to get angry
jactantia, ostentation, boasting
jucunditas, jocularity
justitia, justice
laetitia, joy, happiness
malitia, malice
metus, fear
  metuere, to fear
misericordia, mercy
odium, hate
patientia, patience
pietas, piety
pusillanimitas, cowardice, pusillanimity

Table 3.2 (*cont.*)

rancor, rancor
sinceritas, sincerity
spes, hope
superbia, pride
taedium, weariness
temperantia, temperance
timor, fear
timere, to fear
tristitia, sadness
contristari, to sadden
tumor mentis, mental excitement
vindicta, vengeance
emotion markers:
erubescere, to blush
flere, to weep
lacrymae, tears

future things, the consolation (*consolatio*) of Scripture, and fraternal talk in spiritual jocularity (*jucunditas*).[77]

This offered a program for self help. Did Wido feel sad? He must first diagnose which sort of sadness he felt. Did it come from awareness of his sins? Then his sadness was salvific, and the next step was to confess and do penance. From there he could convert himself (*converti se*) to God. Or was it worldly sadness, stirring up the mind with the sorts of confused anxieties that had led Cicero to call *all* emotions *perturbationes*? This sort of sadness led to despair. Alcuin offered specific antidotes to avoid despair and get back on the right track.

Further, Alcuin wanted Wido to consider whether his emotions were "real" or "fake." Thus, when he came to penance, Alcuin wrote about the importance of "sincerity": "[Penance], if carried out in the intimate bitterness of the heart is not despised by the just judge God, who looks into the heart's secrets. For God does not so much require length of time as he weighs the feeling of sincerity (*affectum sinceritatis*) of the penitent."[78]

We have not seen the "feeling of sincerity" before this, and it apparently was not a very common notion before Alcuin's day, though the late seventh-century emotional community we explored in Chapter 2 did think about "simulated" emotions.[79] To be sure, the word *sinceritas* per

---

[77] *Ibid.,* c. 33, col. 635.   [78] *Ibid.,* c. 13, col. 622.

[79] As revealed by a search of the databases of the PL, Library of Latin Texts A, and the e-MGH. A *Confessio fidei* concerned with simulated piety was once thought to be by Alcuin

se had long been in circulation, with its basic meaning connected to the notion of purity – a bell's tone or the clarity of a liquid. A *sincerus* writer was straightforward. When Ambrose (d. 397) wrote on the psalms, he paired *simplex mens* (a straightforward mind) with *pura sinceritas* (pure sincerity).[80] Augustine did the same in his treatise *On the Magnitude of the Soul* when he spoke of "so much purity, so much sincerity."[81] When he used it alongside the word heart, however, sincerity began to take on the affective hue that it had in Alcuin's manual for Wido.[82] Thus there is no point in arguing for a time let alone a moment in which "sincerity" was "discovered," but it seems to have become a preoccupation with the progressive melding of the virtues and vices tradition and theories of emotions.

Alcuin took Gregory the Great's ideas about pastoral care seriously. But the pope had considered managing the emotions too dangerous to entrust to the laity. He wanted the rectors of the church to have a monopoly on therapy. Alcuin did not. He was not a church rector; he was just a deacon. More important, he was above all a teacher. He was willing to trust that his pupils would learn their lessons and be able to apply it themselves. He wrote a manual for Wido to use for life, whether or not Alcuin was around to admonish him.

Many of Alcuin's emotions clustered around words of sorrow, vanity, and anger. Indeed, for Alcuin these feelings were not really separate. Surely this melded sentiment was pertinent to the salvation of a man like Wido, who acted as both a judge and a military authority. The elites of the late seventh century had thought about similar uses and abuses of

---

but is almost certainly by John of Fécamp (c. 990–1078); see pseudo-Alcuin, *Confessio fidei*, pars IV, c. 14, PL 101, col. 1096: "Fac me Deus meus ... sine simulatione sanctum, et sine manifestis vitiis, simulatisque virtutibus suo semper servitio deditum (Keep me, my God, ... holy without feigning, without evident vices and feigned virtues, dedicated always to His service)." On the attribution to Alcuin, see *Clavis scriptorum latinorum medii aevi. Auctores Galliae, 735–987*, vol. 2: *Alcuinus*, ed. Marie-Hélène Jullien and Françoise Perelman (Turnhout, 1999), 514. On John's authorship or at least his revision of this work into its present form, see Lauren Elisabeth Mancia, "Affective Devotion and Emotional Reform at the Eleventh-Century Monastery of John of Fécamp" (PhD diss., Yale University, 2013), 33 and chap. 2. I am grateful to Lauren Mancia for discussing John with me and sending me a copy of her dissertation.

[80] Ambrose, *Expositio psalmi CXVIII* c. 21, ed. Michael Petschenig, CSEL 62 (Vienna, 1913), 163.

[81] Augustine, *De quantitate animae* c. 33, § 76, ed. Wolfgang Hörmann, CSEL 89 (Vienna, 1986), 131–231 at 225.

[82] Augustine, *Epistula* 149, ed. Alois Goldbacher, CSEL 44 (Vienna, 1904), 348–80 at 348: "sinceritati cordis tui." R. Jay Magill, Jr., *Sincerity* (New York, 2012), 23, traces the first use of the English word "sincere" to 1533. But he regards that use of the term to represent the first time in any language that it applied to people. "*Sincerus*, the Latin term, had been used to describe physical things ... that were unaltered, pure, and whole if they were to be of any value" (29).

power, and it should not surprise us that their vocabulary was not so different from Alcuin's. But they rather rarely spoke of love, while Alcuin spoke of it often, using the nouns *amor* and *caritas* and the verb *diligere*. Moreover, he called *caritas* "the first of God's precepts."[83] In Chapter 4 we shall see love taking center stage in two emotional communities. But we shall also see how that emotion brought in its train many other feelings and preoccupations, as well.

---

[83] Alcuin, *DVV* c. 3, col. 615: "In praeceptis vero Dei charitas obtinet principatum (indeed, among the precepts of God caritas gets first place)."

4   Love and treachery

The empire of Charlemagne – an attempt to unify continental Europe – came to an end a few decades after Alcuin wrote. It collapsed from its own internal weaknesses and the invasions of outsiders, especially Vikings. Gone was Francia, while "France" was still far in the future. The area that we call France today (and shall do so here for convenience) disintegrated into small units, each ruled by more or less independent men and occasionally women. Their power was based not only on military might and castles that served them as fortified centers of exploitation and rule, but also on personal bonds and the prestigious attributes of leadership. As already implied by Alcuin's handbook for the count-warrior Wido, the new regional rulers cultivated the image (and to some degree the reality) of piety and virtue. They distributed gifts to demonstrate their generosity; they founded and supported monasteries where monks might carry out vicariously for them lives dedicated to God; and they surrounded themselves with vassals and others with whom they pledged mutual fidelity. As towns rose and the economy burgeoned, these regional rulers grew rich; with their money they employed officials, legal advisers, physicians, and entertainers, creating thriving courts. The new economy in turn supported the rise of centers of learning – cathedral schools and eventually universities. Here scholars drew on the writings of both ancient and more recent authorities to create daring new syntheses and theories – about emotions, among other things, as we shall see.

The invasions that shattered the Carolingian empire ironically helped create a united England. In the course of the fifth and sixth centuries, Roman Britain had become Anglo-Saxon England, a global name for a shifting group of kingdoms. But with the Viking invasions came vigorous military action. Alfred the Great (d. 899) and his successors defeated the invaders and established a single kingdom with a real tax base and considerable military strength. At times ruled by kings who also reigned in Denmark and Norway, England was invaded in 1066 by one of the Continental rulers, Duke William of Normandy. He cut the links between England and Scandinavia, establishing in their place new ties with France.

Kings and local rulers were joined by two other important players on the twelfth- and early thirteenth-century stage: popes and monasteries. The late eleventh century was the age of the "Gregorian Reform," a movement named after Pope Gregory VII (1073–85) to "free the church from the world." In practice this meant imposing strict rules of celibacy on the clergy, ending (to some degree) lay control over clerical appointments, and enhancing the role of the papacy in *both* the church and the world.

The monasteries were part of this movement insofar as they, too, sought worldly detachment even as they depended on the world for support and tried to guide it by advising and pressuring secular rulers. The eleventh century was the heyday of the monastery of Cluny. Monks at Cluniac monasteries, like all monks, followed a rule, took vows of stability, and dedicated themselves to intercessory liturgy, chanting psalms and other texts at the "offices" – seven during the day and one at night. Cluny's liturgy was particularly elaborate, and it was carried out in splendid Romanesque churches of astonishing and lavish beauty.[1] But in the twelfth century newly ascetic monastic movements reacted against both Cluniac opulence and commercial profits.[2] The Cistercian Order was particularly successful. It began as one house, Cîteaux, founded in 1098 by Robert of Molesme. Soon it founded new abbeys; by 1115 there were four of them. These were known as Cîteaux's "daughter houses," and they in turn "began to found their own offspring."[3] Expansion of the order increased rapidly between 1130 and 1150 during the abbacy of Bernard, abbot of Clairvaux (d. 1153). By the middle of the twelfth century, there were more than 350 monasteries across Europe that followed – or claimed to follow – the customs of Cîteaux. (Women's houses that followed Cistercian customs were not always formally associated with the order.[4]) Vowing to return to the traditions of Saint Benedict and the Benedictine Rule, the Cistercians in fact created a form of monasticism all their own. They emphasized asceticism and simplicity: a simple liturgy; a simple, unadorned architecture; simple food; simple, undyed clothing. At the same time, they cultivated a rich interior life of private prayer and contemplation, emphasizing love or, as they termed it, "charity." Indeed, as they grew and organized, the Cistercians issued a

[1] The bibliography on Cluny is enormous. Happily, much of it is summed up in, and surpassed by, *Cluny. Les moines et la société au premier âge féodal*, ed. Dominique Iogna-Prat et al. (Rennes, 2013).
[2] See Lester K. Little, *Religious Poverty and the Profit Economy in Medieval Europe* (Ithaca, NY, 1978).
[3] Martha G. Newman, "Foundation and Twelfth Century," in *The Cambridge Companion to the Cistercian Order*, ed. Mette Birkedal Bruun (New York, 2013), 25–37 at 27.
[4] See Constance H. Berman, "Were There Twelfth-Century Cistercian Nuns?" *Church History* 68 (1999): 824–64.

Charter of Charity that was in effect a constitution of the Order, the title emphasizing the links of love rather than law that bound the monks together. This was to be a "voluntary" love; the Cistercians did not accept children into their monasteries, recruiting only grown men with some experience of the world.

These men were of two sorts. The shaved monks, who ordinarily came from the knightly or literate classes, carried out the spiritual labor of prayer and contemplation. The bearded "lay brothers," who were normally recruited from the rural and illiterate poor, did the manual labor for the monastery – tilling the fields or shepherding, for example.[5]

Cistercian monasteries formed a hierarchical Order: mother houses exercised jurisdiction over daughter houses; father abbots made yearly Visitations to the daughter houses; and abbots of daughter houses came to the mother house for the so-called Chapter meetings.[6] There was, therefore, considerable contact among all Cistercian houses.

This was a very different world from that of the Merovingians or of Alcuin. Yet, just as Alcuin melded ancient thought about the passions with newer traditions about the virtues and vices, so (as we shall see) twelfth- and thirteenth-century emotional communities drew on older emotional vocabularies and sensibilities even as they created their own emotional norms and values. The past was useful: Alcuin's popular "palaeopsychology" authorized ways for laypeople to be righteous *and* emotional. At the same time, it gave ascetics the justification for a passionately affective life within the monastery. Not that everyone read Alcuin; but ideas like his were not unusual (hence the popularity of his treatise) and by now had been absorbed into a common heritage.[7]

In this chapter we shall focus on two emotional communities separated by about 1000 miles and equally distant in goals. Nevertheless, we shall see many commonalities. Under its third abbot, Aelred, the Cistercian monastery of Rievaulx in England was dedicated to worship, prayer, and withdrawal from the world. Nevertheless, it throve under Aelred in the context of a long civil war (1135–54) that pitted against one another the forces of two female heirs to the English throne. Just a bit later, the court of the Raimondin counts of Toulouse in the Midi – today southern France – was dedicated to fostering, supporting, and exercising the power of the count in the world. It, too, was involved in a decisive war. I chose Rievaulx as an example of a monastic community because it

---

[5] See James France, "The Cistercian Community," in *The Cambridge Companion to the Cistercian Order*, 80–86.

[6] See Brian Patrick McGuire, "Constitutions and the General Chapter," in *ibid.*, 87–99.

[7] For example, Szarmach, "A Preliminary Handlist," 135–40, notes many Latin copies of Alcuin's *DVV* now in English libraries and usually of English origin; also extant are Old English texts that borrowed from Alcuin's treatise, including one dating from as late as the second half of the twelfth century.

boasted an exceptionally rich literary output and yet was a relatively "typical" Cistercian house.[8] I chose the Raimondin court as an example of a twelfth- and thirteenth-century aristocratic warrior community because its sources included early vernacular writings as well as Latin charters; I wanted to see how a vernacular vocabulary might affect emotional expression.

We begin with Rievaulx's emotional community because it comes first chronologically. However, as we shall see, neither community can be properly understood without the other. (For all the place names in this chapter, see Map 4.1.)

Aelred and Rievaulx

Born the son of a priest in Hexham, Yorkshire, Aelred (1110–67) was likely educated at the cathedral school at Durham. Unable to succeed his father as priest in the wake of new rules following the Gregorian Reform, Aelred entered the service of King David I of Scotland (r. 1124–53) some time after 1124.[9] Soon he was serving as the king's steward and, in the words of his biographer, Walter Daniel, "nothing was done, inside or out, apart from him."[10] In 1134 he entered the monastery of Rievaulx, which had been founded in Yorkshire only two years earlier by Walter Espec, a "childless Norman knight and patron of several religious houses."[11] Less

---

[8] As Marsha L. Dutton makes clear in "The Sacramentality of Community in Aelred," in *A Companion to Aelred of Rievaulx*, ed. Marsha L. Dutton (Turnhout, forthcoming), chap. 10, it is not just wishful thinking to call Aelred's Rievaulx a real community. Insofar as he inspired its spirituality and organization, it was designed as "a model community, a small-scale representation of the community begun in creation by God and developing with God at its heart." I am very grateful to Professor Dutton for sending me her chapters in this *Companion* prior to publication, as well as for making it possible for me to read some of the other papers in the collection.

[9] For Aelred's biography, see most conveniently Marsha L. Dutton, introduction to *The Life of Aelred of Rievaulx by Walter Daniel* (Kalamazoo, 1994), 7–88, and "Aelred of Rievaulx: Abbot, Teacher, and Advisor to Kings," in *A Companion to Aelred*, chap.1. The bibliography on Aelred is enormous. The classic study is Aelred Squire, *Aelred of Rievaulx: A Study* (London, 1969); the most recent book is Pierre-André Burton, *Ælred de Rievaulx (1110–1167). De l'homme éclaté à l'être unifié. Essai de biographie existentielle et spirituelle* (Paris, 2010).

[10] Walter Daniel, *The Life of Ailred of Rievaulx*, ed. and trans. Frederick M. Powicke (Oxford, 1978) [henceforth *VA*], 4.

[11] See Marsha L. Dutton, "The Conversion and Vocation of Aelred of Rievaulx: A Historical Hypothesis," in *England in the Twelfth Century: Proceedings of the 1988 Harlaxton Symposium*, ed. Daniel Williams (Woodbridge, Suffolk, 1990), 31–49, quote at 42. Dutton argues that Aelred's entry into Rievaulx was well planned in advance by both King David and himself. The more traditional view, that Aelred's conversion was spontaneous, following Walter, *VA* c. 5, p. 10, that Aelred learned about Rievaulx only by chance, is maintained by Burton, *Ælred*, 127–46. On the foundation of Rievaulx, see Emilia Jamroziak, *Rievaulx Abbey and Its Social Context, 1132–1300: Memory, Locality, and Networks* (Turnhout, 2005), 28–40.

Map 4.1 England and France in the twelfth and thirteenth centuries

than a decade later (probably in 1141), Rievaulx's abbot appointed Aelred master of the "novices," the would-be monks who had not yet taken their vows.[12] Aelred held this office for only two years before he was elected abbot of Revesby, one of Rievaulx's daughter houses. In 1147 Aelred returned to Rievaulx to become its abbot, an office that he held until his death in 1167.

We may consider Aelred's Rievaulx an emotional community and, more generally, an example of a Cistercian monastic emotional community, even though we know about its emotions mainly from the writings of Aelred himself. That is because, as Elizabeth Freeman has noted, even though Aelred wrote for a variety of patrons and purposes, he always had the monks of Rievaulx in mind.[13] What he wrote – whether in reporting his own emotions, directing those of his monks, or imagining those expressed by others – both reflected and helped to shape the emotions of his monks.

At the same time, Aelred looked beyond the monastery.[14] He was, after all, a product (at least in part) of King David's court. Early in the English civil war – thus shortly after Aelred entered Rievaulx – David invaded northern England on behalf of one of the claimants to the throne. These incursions badly afflicted the region around Hexham, Aelred's home.[15] Given his personal investments in these places, events, and people, it is perhaps not surprising that, unlike most monastic writers of the period, Aelred wrote histories at the same time as he penned spiritual works. Between 1153 and 1163, he produced four works of history aimed at guiding Henry II of Anjou, who became king of England in 1154.[16] Aelred's secular writings melded his thoughts about the monastery – its virtues and its perils – with his image of a harmonious society beyond its walls.

---

[12] On the considerable responsibilities of the master of the novices, see Emilia Jamroziak, *The Cistercian Order in Medieval Europe, 1090–1500* (London, 2013), 59–60.

[13] Elizabeth Freeman, *Narratives of a New Order: Cistercian Historical Writing in England, 1150–1220* (Turnhout, 2002), 57.

[14] As Damien Boquet kindly reminded me, we have lost the numerous letters that Walter, *VA* c. 32, p. 40, reports Aelred wrote to the pope, the king of France, the king of England, the archbishops of Canterbury, and so on "in quibus viventem sibi reliquit imaginem (in which he left a living image of himself)." I am very grateful to Damien Boquet for reading and commenting on this chapter.

[15] See Jean A. Truax, "A Time for Peace: Ælred of Rievaulx and the End of the Anglo-Norman Civil War," *Cistercian Studies Quarterly* 46/2 (2011): 171–87.

[16] See Marsha L. Dutton, "That Peace Should Guide and Society Unite: Ælred of Rievaulx's Political Philosophy," *Cistercian Studies Quarterly* 47/3 (2012): 279–95, emphasizing the role of the people as well as the monarch in Aelred's "political philosophy."

Supplementing Aelred's works are the writings of another member of this community. Walter Daniel lived as a monk at Rievaulx under Aelred for seventeen years.[17] He was close to Aelred, represented one of three interlocutors in Aelred's important dialogue *On Spiritual Friendship*, and became Aelred's biographer after the abbot's death. Together, these men serve to represent the emotional community at Rievaulx. As we shall see, their major emotional concerns centered on love and friendship.

Love and the affectus

Aelred wrote about love constantly, but he devoted two works in particular to the topic: *On the Mirror of Charity* and *On Spiritual Friendship*, inspired by Cicero. The *Mirror*, as I will call it henceforth, and the first book of *On Spiritual Friendship* were early works.[18] The last two books of *On Spiritual Friendship* were written later.[19] In its modern edition, the *Mirror* is prefaced by a letter from Bernard of Clairvaux requesting Aelred to take up the topic. Evidently it was well known that Aelred had "long meditated . . . on the excellence of charity (*caritas*)."[20] The subject was of considerable concern to the Cistercians, not only because of their emphasis on love (as in their *Charter of Charity*) but also because, by the 1140s, they were stung by critics who charged that they lacked charity in their pursuit of a selfishly austere way of life.[21]

---

[17] Walter, *VA* c. 31, p. 40.

[18] Aelred, *De speculo caritatis* [henceforth *Spec. car.*] in *Aelredi Rievallensis. Opera Omnia* [henceforth *OO*] 1: *Opera ascetica*, ed. Anselme Hoste and Charles H. Talbot, Corpus Christianorum. Continuatio Mediaevalis [henceforth *CCCM*] 1 (Turnhout, 1971), 3–161. Traditionally dated 1142–43, it may possibly be later than 1143. See Charles Dumont's introduction to Aelred of Rievaulx, *The Mirror of Charity*, trans. Elizabeth Connor, intro. and notes Charles Dumont (Kalamazoo, 1990), 55–59, suggesting that the work may well have been written over the course of several years. See also Aelred of Rievaulx, *Spiritual Friendship*, trans. Lawrence C. Braceland, ed. and intro. Marsha L. Dutton (Collegeville, 2010), 21.

[19] Aelred, *De spiritali amicitia* [henceforth *SA*], in *OO*, 1:287–350. Traditionally its first book is dated 1143–44?, the second and third books after 1159. Dutton in Aelred, *Spiritual Friendship*, 22, notes that Book II refers to anti-pope Victor IV (1159–64), suggesting that the treatise "can be dated between April 1164 and Aelred's death in 1167." On the various titles by which *SA* is known, see *ibid.*, 25.

[20] Aelred, *Spec. car.*, "Epistola Bernardi," §6, p. 4. Julian P. Haseldine, "Monastic Friendship in Theory and in Action in the Twelfth Century," in *Friendship in the Middle Ages and Early Modern Age*, 349–94 at 352, considers Bernard's request "a conventional contrivance to offer a dedicatory letter, and so a public seal of approval, for a work which Bernard knew was well advanced."

[21] See Aelred, *Spec. car.*, "Epistola Bernardi," §6, p. 4, where Bernard argues that the "affliction of the outer man (*hominis exterioris afflictio*)" does not, "as some think (*ut*)

Bernard asked Aelred to take up three topics. First, he should talk about the sweetness (*dulcedo*) of *caritas* (love, charity) and, by contrast, the heavy feeling (*oppressio*) wrought by its opposite, *cupiditas* (greed, lust, desire, cupidity). Second, he should address the Cistercians' critics to show that the "mortification of the exterior man (*hominis exterioris afflictio*)" – in other words, the rigors of the Cistercian life-style – did not decrease charity but in fact augmented its sweetness. And third, he should show what was involved in the practice of charity.[22] Aelred scrupulously followed these directives, dividing his treatise into three books and taking up each of Bernard's topics in turn.[23]

To understand Aelred's argument, let us recall the theories of emotion of Cicero and Augustine. In Chapter 1 we saw that Cicero had had a jaundiced view of most emotions. He did, however, admit a few that were good, and among these was love (*amor*).[24] Augustine, however, thought that *any* emotion had the potential to be good. It all depended on the will: if the will aimed in the right direction (toward God), the emotions would be right. But the will could not aim rightly without God's grace. And so the good aim of the will, and the emotions that reflected that will, were "divinely mediated."[25] Aelred's thought was permeated by this idea.

For Aelred, *amor* was one of the original attributes of man. (Here Aelred was speaking of "man" in the generic sense, as a "human being"; the word implied no gender.) God created man in his image, and love or will (*amor sive voluntas*) was one of the ways – the others were memory and understanding – in which man participated in that image. Because of his love, man savored divine sweetness (*dulcedo*) and was happy (*beatus*).[26]

The Fall, brought about by Adam and Eve's original sin, ended that idyllic state. Just as memory was now infected by forgetfulness and

---

quidam putant)," diminish but rather increases charity. Charles Dumont, "Pourquoi le 'Miroir de la charité' a-t-il été publié? L'identité cistercienne hier comme aujourd'hui," *Collectanea Cisterciensia* 55 (1993): 14–27, referring not so much to the writing as to the publication of the *Mirror*, surveys the critics of Cistercian austerity. See also Burton, *Ælred*, 188–89.

22 Aelred, *Spec. car.*, "Epistola Bernardi," §6, p. 4.
23 As Aelred notes *ibid.*, praef., §4, p. 6.   24 See above, Table 1.5.
25 Wetzel, "Augustine," 351.
26 Aelred, *Spec. car.* 1.3, p. 16. On Aelred's cosmology and anthropology, see John R. Sommerfeldt, *Aelred of Rievaulx: Pursuing Perfect Happiness* (New York, 2005), esp. 28–40, and *Aelred of Rievaulx: On Love and Order in the World and the Church* (New York, 2006), esp. 1–17.

Figure 4.1 Aelred's two forms of *amor*

understanding by error, so love was now prone to cupidity – the wrong sort of love.[27] The only way back to heaven was through *caritas*, the good form of love. Indeed, for Aelred, as for Bernard,[28] love (*amor*) had two opposing forms: *caritas* on the one hand, *cupiditas* (or *concupiscentia*) on the other (see Figure 4.1).[29]

Charity and cupidity are pale words compared to the force of the Latin, but let us fall back on them for this discussion.[30] Charity was the good form of love, cupidity the bad. Unlike Augustine, who considered *dilectio*, *amor*, and *caritas* to mean more or less the same thing, Aelred thought that only *amor* and *dilectio* were interchangeable. *Caritas* was something else. Much like a body attacked by its own immune system, love "as if by opposing appetites, is obviously divided against itself."[31] What could that mean? Aelred explained: love has to be considered in two ways. It is, first, "a power (*vis*) or attribute (*natura*) of the rational soul (*animae rationalis*), whereby [the soul] naturally possesses the faculty of loving (*facultas amandi*) something or not loving something."[32] The faculty of loving is always good, for the soul is created by God and is always good. However, in the second place, love is also the act (*actus*) through which the rational soul exercises its power, and that act may go awry, loving what ought not to be loved or not loving what ought to be loved. Thus the act of love, not the faculty of loving is the real ethical hinge of Aelred's theory. The way a person uses his or her inborn capacity to love determines whether love is going to be good or evil. Charity is the right use, cupidity the abuse.[33] Indeed, Aelred made his theory of love an explanation for the virtues and vices: "The root (*radix*) of all evil is cupidity, and the root of all good is charity."[34] So "charity is

---

[27] Aelred, *Spec. car.* 1.3, pp. 16–17.

[28] Bernard already spoke of *cupiditas* as the opposite of *caritas* in his letter to Aelred.

[29] For *concupiscentia* as the equivalent of *cupiditas*, see Aelred, *Spec. car.* 1.10, p. 23.

[30] Aelred of Rievaulx, *The Mirror of Charity*, 93, 100, etc. translates *cupiditas* as "self-centeredness." I prefer "cupidity," nearly obsolete as the word may be, because love of self is in fact one of the objects of charity. See below at n. 59.

[31] Aelred, *Spec. car.* 1.9, p. 23.   [32] *Ibid.*, 3.7, p. 114.   [33] *Ibid.*, 115.

[34] *Ibid.*, 3.8, p. 116.

love ... but not all love is charity."[35] Or, to put it another way, not all love is charity because some love is cupidity!

Both charity and cupidity followed a three-step sequence beginning with love's choice (*electio*), continuing with its movement (*motus*), and ending with its enjoyment (*fructus*).[36] People choose what they think will make them happy. It is always a "rational" choice, not because it is always reasonable or right but because, in choosing, love "discerns with careful consideration (*vivaci circumspectione discernat*) what it selects from what it rejects."[37] Then love moves toward the beloved, driven by desire and doing what must be done to obtain it. Finally, when the beloved is obtained, love enjoys the fruits of its labor. If love chooses, moves toward, and enjoys the right object, then it is charity; if it goes through the whole sequence for the wrong object, then the whole act of love is wrong and is cupidity.

The act of love needs something to ignite it, to spur it into choosing, moving, and enjoying. Occasionally the spur may be reason itself.[38] Much more often, it is something that Aelred called *affectus*. When he used the word, he did not mean it as Augustine had done. For Augustine, the word *affectus*, like *affectiones*, *passiones* and *perturbationes* was an "umbrella" term, more or less equivalent to our word "emotions." Aelred meant nothing so all-embracing. He defined *affectus* along the lines of Cicero's notion of friendship (*amicitia*), which arose, in Cicero's account, "from an inclination of the *animus* along with a certain feeling of loving (*sensu amandi*)."[39] Aelred used Cicero's words but also added to them in important ways: for Aelred *affectus* (or "affect," as I will term it here) was "a kind of spontaneous (*spontanea*) and sweet (*dulcis*) inclination of the *animus* toward someone."[40]

Let us unpack this definition. By speaking of affect as "spontaneous," Aelred made it unlike reason, which always had its explanations. Affect's spontaneity made it unpredictable as well as active and dynamic; its direction – its inclination – would be good only by the grace of God. By adding that its inclination was sweet (*dulcis*), Aelred made affect's very activation a source of pleasure: recall that man's happiness in heaven involved savoring God's sweetness. Sweetness was itself a sort of emotion, as indeed it had been when Fortunatus invoked it at the end of the sixth

---

[35] *Ibid.*, 3.7, p. 114.   [36] *Ibid.*, 3.8, p. 115.   [37] *Ibid.*

[38] Similarly, love could also result from nature (*ex natura*) or from duty (*ex officio*). See Aelred, *Spec. car.* 3.20, p. 128.

[39] See above, Chapter 1, n. 22.

[40] Aelred, *Spec. car.* 3.11, p. 119. On Aelred's *affectus*, see Damien Boquet, *L'ordre de l'affect au Moyen Âge. Autour de l'anthropologie affective d'Aelred de Rievaulx* (Caen, 2005), and James McEvoy, "Les *affectus* et la mesure de la raison dans le livre III du *Miroir*," *Collectanea Cisterciensia* 55 (1993): 110–25.

century (see Chapter 2). Finally, let us consider *animus*. Is it mind, heart, spirit? In fact, as Damien Boquet has noted, Aelred was inconsistent, speaking of *various* seats of affect: the *mens*, the *anima*, the *animus*, *pectus*, *cor*, and even *spiritus*.[41]

By spontaneity Aelred meant that affect "poured out" like tears and, indeed, was often accompanied by weeping. In his *Eulogy for King David of Scotland*, written c. 1153, shortly after the king's death, Aelred recalled that during his last visit, he and the king had embraced and kissed each other tearfully. Now (with David dead), "I pour out (*libo*) and let loose (*resolvo*) my tears for you; I pour fourth (*refundo*) my affect and all my spirit (*totum spiritum*)."[42] Thinking about the death of his dear fellow monk Simon, Aelred paused in the middle of the first book of his *Mirror* to record his grief and to consider his weeping. At first the tears had not come. But then "the shock (*stupor*) gave way to affect (*affectui*), gave way to sorrow (*dolori*), gave way to compassion (*compassioni*)."[43] He wept just as (Aelred noted) Christ had wept at Lazarus' death: for Christ "took on the affect (*affectum*) of our [human] weakness" (though only because he wanted to; he could have refrained). If some people – hard people (*aliqui fortes*) – judged Aelred's love for Simon as "too carnal (*nimis carnalem*)," Aelred didn't care. "Let them interpret [my tears] as they please," wrote Aelred. They could not see how he suffered within; only God could see that.[44] Tears were a bodily sign of affect.

That helps explain why Aelred – and Walter Daniel as well – highly valued tears.[45] In a lament that Walter wrote after Aelred's death, he repeatedly addressed his tears as if they were a second self: "O tears: are you pouring out or not?" They answered, "We are pouring out, Walter."[46] Walter knew that some people called tears "shameful (*verecundas*)." But he himself considered them a necessary step on the way to

---

[41] Damien Boquet, "Affectivity in the Spiritual Writings of Aelred of Rievaulx," in *A Companion to Aelred*, chap. 7. I thank Damien Boquet for sending me his chapter before publication.

[42] Aelred, *Eulogium Davidis regis Scotorum* [henceforth *Lament*] in *Pinkerton's Lives of the Scottish Saints*, ed. William M. Metcalfe, 2 vols. (rev. ed., Paisley, 1889), 2:269–85. It was written 1153–54, most likely 1153, right after the king's death in May. About a year later, Aelred used it to preface his *Genealogia Regis Anglie Henrici iunioris* [henceforth *Gen.*], PL 195, cols. 711–37. Although Aelred meant the *Lament* to be the preface to the *Gen.*, the version there is only in abbreviated form; thus references to it here will be to Pinkerton's edition.

[43] Aelred, *Spec. car.* 1.34, p. 63.

[44] *Ibid.*: "Interpretentur eas, ut volent," echoing Augustine, *Conf.* 9.12.33, 2:235, when he mourns the death of his mother with tears and remarks "Legat qui volet et interpretetur, ut volet (Let them who wish read and interpret this as they like)."

[45] It was already a highly valued aspect of the ascetic life; see above, Chapter 2, n. 130, where Saint Wandregisel afflicts himself with fasts and pours forth tears.

[46] Walter, *Lamentatio*, l. 84, in Charles H. Talbot, "La Lamentation de Walter Daniel sur la mort du bienheureux Aelred," *Collectanea Cisterciensia* 5 (1938): 9–20 at 17.

reason, moderation, and living well (*bene vivere*). Thus in his *Life of Aelred*, Walter proudly reported that Aelred "hardly ever prayed without tears; because of tears, he said ... embassies (*legaciones*) exist between God and man; because of tears, all the affect of the heart is shown ... When he spoke to his Lord, our Aelred bathed his whole face with a fountain of tears."[47]

So affects "poured out" like tears. And sometimes Aelred equated affects with love itself.[48] Evidently he did not consider it terribly important to decide whether love was pushed by affect or was an affect itself. The important point was that love's inclination (and thus its choice) was the starting point of all human feeling and ethical behavior. That is why love could also be induced through reason, as when we love our enemy. "Love of enemy" resulted *not* from a "spontaneous inclination" but from our dutiful obedience to follow God's commandments.[49]

And the end point of love? To be sure, it could be unhappy. Charity sometimes meant loving "those who are a burden and a pain to us."[50] However, in the best scenario, the *animus* chose well, pursued the beloved successfully, and ended by "resting (*quiescit*) in the use [of its beloved] with joy and delight (*cum gaudio ac delectatione*)."[51] However, "if the *animus* chooses foolishly, if it is moved indecently, if it misuses [the beloved] filthily,"[52] then this must be called cupidity, and it yields no rest or joy and delight but rather "labor and groans, sorrow and affliction of spirit."[53]

Aelred knew very well Augustine's discussion of cupidity in the *Confessions*.[54] There were three sorts, as 1 John 2:16 made clear: craving of the flesh (*concupiscentia carnalis*); longing of the eyes (*concupiscentia oculorum*), "which the holy Fathers called curiosity (*curiositatem*)"; and pride of life (*superbia vitae*).[55] These were passions (*passiones*), and all

---

[47] Walter, *VA* c. 11, p. 20.

[48] Aelred, *SA* 1.19, p. 292. But although here Aelred equated affects with love, in Aelred Spec. car. 3.16, p. 123, he said that the *affectus* were the "roots (*radices*)" of love, but not love.

[49] Aelred, *SA* 3.1, p. 317.   [50] *Ibid.*, 2.19, p. 306.   [51] Aelred, *Spec. car.* 3.8, p. 116.

[52] *Ibid.*   [53] *Ibid.*, 1.28, p. 46.   [54] See Chapter 1 at n. 50.

[55] In a collection of "sentences," written perhaps as a sort of exercise, Walter Daniel, too, mentioned the three sorts of cupidity and their culmination in unjust dominion: Walter Daniel, *Centum sententiae* c. 39, in Charles H. Talbot, "The *Centum Sententiae* of Walter Daniel," *Sacris Erudiri* 11 (1960): 266–374 at 292: "Tres sunt generales anime corruptiones, concupiscentia carnis, concupiscentia oculorum et superbiae vite (There are three kinds of corruptions of the soul: craving of the flesh, longing of the eyes, and pride of life.)" A bit earlier (c. 33, p. 289) Walter talked about the offspring of *concupiscentia*, namely *libido* (lust) and *carnalitas* (carnality), relating the former to unjust dominion: "Libido indebitum affectat dominium (libido aims at irresponsible rule)." It is worth noting that in c. 39 Walter says that the various types of *concupiscentia* were true *especially* (*specialiter*) of women. Clearly, then, these sorts of discussions were not meant to be limited to men. Talbot (p. 227) dates the *Centum* c. 1157 but gives no reasons.

were bad. But the pride of life, which led to the lust to dominate (*libido dominandi*), was the worst passion (*pessima passio*) of all.[56] We will return to it when we explore the emotions of power.

Just as there were three sorts of cupidity, so there were three objects of charity. These formed a clear order: first came love of self, then of neighbor, finally of God. Each necessitated the other: "these three loves (*amores*) are engendered by one another (*ab invicem concipiuntur*), nourished (*nutriuntur*) by one another, and aroused (*accenduntur*) by one another." With the completion of the sequence, the three loves were "brought to perfection together (*simul omnes perficiuntur*)."[57]

The pursuit of each of these loves went through all of the stages: choice, movement, and rest. It was the times of rest (*quies/requies*) that most delighted Aelred. He called them Sabbaths after the weekly day of rest prescribed in the Bible.[58]

Here is how the first Sabbath, achieved through love of self, "feels (*sentiatur*)":

When a person withdraws from exterior tumult (*exteriori tumultu*) into the secret retreat (*secretarium*) of his *mens* and ... surveys his inward treasures (*gazas*) and finds nothing restless (*inquietum*), nothing disordered (*inordinatum*), nothing that bites or barks at him, but rather everything joyous (*jucunda*), harmonious (*concordantia*), peaceful (*pacifica*), and tranquil (*tranquilla*), the entire throng of his thoughts, words, and deeds, like a very well-ordered and very peaceful family will smile (*arriserit*) in his *animus* like a father's household (*patrifamilias domus*).[59]

The well-ordered and happy family is the metaphorical core of the self. Thoughts, words, and deeds all "smile" – a gesture, although here secret and interior, that recalls the *hilaris vultus* of the saints of the late seventh century. In Aelred the tranquility of the saint has been interiorized. Aelred continues: the feeling is of "marvelous security (*mira securitas*)," ending in "marvelous joy (*mira jucunditas*)."

If love of self is familial happiness, love of neighbor, the second Sabbath, involves a whole panoply of feelings about others:

Yet if, from that very secret retreat in which a person celebrates this first Sabbath, he directs himself to that lodging (*diversorium*) of his breast, that place where he is accustomed to rejoice with those who rejoice (*ibi solet gaudere cum gaudentibus*), to weep with those who weep (*flere cum flentibus*), to be weak with those who are weak

---

[56] Aelred, *Spec. car.* 2.26, p. 102.   [57] *Ibid.*, 3.2, p. 107.

[58] *Ibid.*, 106: "requies animi, pax cordi, tranquillitas mentis." See Joseph Molleur, "The Notion of the Three Sabbaths in Aelred's *Mirror of Charity*," *Cistercian Studies Quarterly* 33/2 (1998): 211–20, and Domenico Pezzini, "Il riposo come categoria della vita spirituale. I tre sabati nello *Specchio della carità* di Aelredo di Rievaulx," *Vita consacrata* 36 (2000): 357–74.

[59] *Ibid.*, 3.3, pp. 107–8.

(*infirmari cum infirmis*), to burn (*uri*) with those who are tempted to evil (*cum scandalizatis*); and if he will sense there that his *anima* is united with the *animae* of all his brothers by the glue of charity and that it is not agitated *(agitari)* by any pricks of envy (*invidiae*), inflamed by any fire of indignation (*indignationum*), weakened by darts of suspicion (*suspicionum*), consumed by the bites of voracious sadness (*tristitiae*), so that he may snatch (*rapiat*) them up to the very tranquil lap of his *mens*, where he may embrace and nourish (*amplectatur et foveat*) all of them with a certain sweet affect (*dulci affectu*) and make [them] one heart and one soul with himself (*secum unum cor et unam animam faciat*), then, at the delightful taste of this sweetness (*dulcedinis*), the whole tumult of the cupidities (*cupiditates*) soon falls silent (*silet*) and the din of vices becomes quiet (*conquiescit*), and there, inside, absolute freedom (*vacatio*) from everything harmful is realized, along with grateful and joyous rest (*grata et iucunda pausatio*) in the sweetness of brotherly love (*in fraternae dilectionis dulcedine*).[60]

Here Aelred begins with compassion: rejoicing with others when they rejoice, weeping when they weep, and so on. He itemizes some of the emotions that can disrupt harmonious interpersonal relations: envy, indignation, suspicion, and sadness. He turns to acts of love: snatching others to one's bosom, embracing and nourishing them. Finally, he praises the sweetness, joy, and peace that come from this brotherly love, the love of neighbor.

In the third Sabbath, the one that results from the love of God, the *mens* exults (*gestit*) in the happy embraces (*felices amplexus*) of the divinity and is absorbed into unaccustomed sweetness (*inusitata dulcedine*). All things corporal, sensible, and mutable fade away. The *mens* sees that the Lord himself is God, and it returns to the Creator.[61]

Charity in action

Thus charity was a feeling, but it was also an action, a process. It required "entering" into the feelings of others, as described in Aelred's second Sabbath: rejoicing when they rejoiced, weeping when they wept. The idea came from Paul in Rom 12:15: "*Gaudere cum gaudentibus, flere cum flentibus* (Rejoice with the rejoicing, weep with the weeping)." Aelred called this compassion (*compassio*), just as the late sixth-century Pope Gregory the Great (590–604) had done. Gregory had obliged the holy man (he was thinking of bishops like himself) to descend from heavenly contemplation to attend to the feelings of his fellow creatures. This he called "compassion" – co-feeling is one way to translate the Latin *compassio*.[62] Aelred, as we have seen, considered compassion an essential

---

[60] *Ibid.*, 3.4, p. 108.   [61] *Ibid.*, 3.6, p. 113.
[62] For example, in Gregory, *Moralia in Job* 3.12, p. 127. See Rosenwein, *Emotional Communities*, chap. 3.

component of the second Sabbath. To convey this co-feeling he used verbs like *collacrymare* (weeping together with) and *collaetare* (rejoicing with).[63]

However important compassion had been for Gregory the Great, he had not associated it with thinking about Christ's life. Aelred did. He worked out a particularly compassionate way to meditate on the life of Christ.[64] In his *Formation of Anchoresses*, written 1160–62, he gave step-by-step instructions for how the recluse should mentally "participate" in key moments in Christ's life. The process should begin with the birth of Christ and continue through the Passion and Resurrection. The first step, said Aelred, is to enter Mary's room and read along with her "the books in which is prophesized the virgin birth and the coming of Christ." The second step is to "wait for the advent of the angel so that you may see him arriving. Hear his greeting. And so, full of amazement (*stupore*) and ecstasy (*extasi*), greet your most sweet (*dulcissimam*) Lady as the angel greets her."[65] As Rachel Fulton Brown has put it, the recluse is to become "not only an onlooker but also an actress, herself part of the historical spectacle to which, in her imagination, she is a witness."[66]

Sarah McNamer suggests that it was Aelred's sister who was the anchoress addressed in this treatise and who inspired his thinking about compassion and meditation.[67] But, as we have seen, Aelred had already written in his *Mirror* about the importance of compassion for the Christ-centered life. We can see how it was supposed to work "in action" in Walter Daniel's biography. Early in his story, while at the court of King David, Aelred was confronted by a military man (*militaris*) who went crazy (*insaniens*) because "[Aelred] was loved above all others by the king and was pleasing to all in the palace."[68] Envious (*invidens*) and gnashing his teeth (*frendens dentibus*), the man persecuted Aelred out of his great hatred (*gravi odio*) and tried to rouse the others at court to indignation (*indig-natio*) against Aelred. His attempts were fruitless. At last his fury (*furor*) and anger (*ira*) spilled out in the foulest possible words (*spurcissimis verbis*)

---

[63] Aelred, *Spec. car.* 3.39, p. 159.

[64] Wolfgang Riehle, *The Secret Within: Hermits, Recluses, and Spiritual Outsiders in Medieval England*, trans. Charity Scott-Stokes (Ithaca, NY, 2014), 28, calls Aelred's teaching in this regard "new and groundbreaking."

[65] Aelred, *De institutione inclusarum* c. 3 [hereafter *Inclus.*], in *OO*, 1:637–82 at 663. Walter, *VA* c. 32, p. 41, says that Aelred wrote "unum librum sorori sue incluse (a book for his recluse sister)," and Aelred, *Inclus.*, prol., 637, calls the recluse "*soror* (sister)," but Dutton, "Sacramentality of Community," speaks of the book's "anchoress-audience," implicitly making the point that no sure evidence ties the book's recipient to Aelred's family.

[66] Rachel Fulton Brown, *From Judgment to Passion: Devotion to Christ and the Virgin Mary, 800–1200* (New York, 2002), 420.

[67] McNamer, *Affective Meditation*, 84–85.   [68] Walter, *VA* c. 3, p. 5.

before the entire court, to the horror (*horror*) of all. But Aelred himself, blushing (*rubore faciei*), replied to those foul words: "You say well, you speak well, O best of knights, and everything you declare is true, for, as I believe, you hate lying and you love me (*me diligis*). For who is worthy enough to fight for King David? Who, I ask, is fit to serve him?" In this way, by agreeing with the man's insulting words, Aelred led his accuser to reconsider and finally to repent and ask Aelred's pardon (*indulgenciam*). Then the man promised Aelred in secret that he would be in future his faithful and firm friend (*fidelem ... et firmum amicum*).[69]

We will soon see the importance of a "faithful and firm friend" at Rievaulx. But let us here note that Aelred's mirroring of the man's foul words was understood to have made Aelred a better man. As he told his new friend: "By your hatred (*odio tuo*) I grew in love (*amorem*) of my Lord." The hatred of the one thus became the love of the other. Aelred's patience (*paciencia*) had been tested (*probata*) and, as Aelred put it (as quoted by Walter), "I have perhaps advanced a bit in God's eyes."[70] Walter waxed eloquent about his hero: "Behold a new Joseph in Egypt, another Daniel in Babylon, a modern Lot in Sodom. What can I say? Here is certainly something that the peacemakers (*pacifici*) will gladly hear."[71] Let us recall that in Aelred's first Sabbath, the self feels "everything joyous (*jucunda*), harmonious (*concordantia*), [and] peaceful (*pacifica*)." Aelred had not only attained the joyous and peaceful goal of the first Sabbath but, by his example, had given joy to others of like mind.

In his *Letter to Maurice*, written to buttress the miracles of his *Life of Aelred*, Walter wrote about a similar incident. While the abbot was in great pain and lying in agony on a mat near the hearth, a lay brother charged into the room "looking like a bull (*aspectu taurino*)," wrote Walter, and "criminally enraged (*iratus ... criminaliter*)."[72] As the crazed brother gnashed his teeth (as once the military man at David's court had done), he tried to throw the sickly abbot into the fire. Walter, who was present, "felt the ardor of indignation against the tyrant (*concepi ardorem indignacionis contra tirannum*)" and grabbed the man by the beard. Other monks soon entered the fray. But Aelred, "the man of peace (*pacificus Alredus*)" and "mindful of charity (*caritatis memor*)," begged the monks to stop: "No, no! I say. No my sons: do not take from your father the tunic of patience (*paciencie*)." The raging brother, he said, had purified (*purgavit*), not harmed (*peremit*), him. "To be sure, [Aelred continued], I am not well in body; but [that brother], who is sick (*infirmus*), has healed me in my soul (*sanavit me in anima*)." Then, recounted Walter, Aelred "kissed [the

---

[69] *Ibid.*, 7–8.   [70] *Ibid.*, 8.   [71] *Ibid.*, 8–9.
[72] For the episode, see Walter Daniel, *Epistola ad Mauricium* c. 4, in *VA*, 78–81.

brother], blessed him, and embraced him . . . and gently tried to soften the fury of the man enraged against him without cause. O the charity of the man, greater than many miracles!" He ordered no punishment for the lay brother, for, as Aelred put it, he could always take revenge but would never do so "because the charity of your [abbot] . . . ought to be perfected." In the emotional economy of this community, patience, which involved welcoming the feelings of those hostile to you, enhanced charity.

Again toward the end of his life (Walter reported) Aelred returned to Scotland to visit Dundrennan, one of Rievaulx's daughter houses. There, Aelred found a petty king (Fergus) enraged (*iratus*) against his sons (Gilbert and Uchtred), while the sons were furious (*savientes*) against their father – as well as against one another.[73] No one – neither King Malcolm (David's successor), nor the local bishop – had been able to calm their mutual hatred (*odia*), rancor (*rancores*), and tyranny. Then Aelred "the peacemaker (*pacificus*)," convening them all, bound the angry sons by words of peace "in a single bond of love (*unum dileccionis vinculum*)," while he convinced the father to become a monk. In the end, the sons venerated their father and "until now live in tranquil peace (*tranquilla pace*)."[74]

Note how much work went into charity. It required diplomacy, intervention in the feelings of others, and enormous physical and emotional efforts. But consider the end results:

The day before yesterday [Aelred reported in his *On Spiritual Friendship*] as I was walking around the cloister, with the brothers sitting in a most loving circle (*amatissima corona*), I marveled at the leaves, blossoms, and fruits of each single tree as if I were in the fragrant bowers of paradise. Finding no one among them whom I did not love and no one by whom I was not loved, I was filled with a joy (*gaudio*) that surpassed all the delights of the world.[75]

The joys and pains of friendship

Not all of those monks were Aelred's "friends."[76] Friends were special. The topic of friendship had been dear to ancient authors; Cicero was one example, as we have seen.[77] We have also seen that the Christianization of

---

[73] For the episode, see Walter, *VA* c. 38, pp. 45–46.

[74] Walter could not know that Gilbert later murdered his brother! See Powicke's remark in Walter, *VA*, 46 n. 1.

[75] Aelred, *SA* 3.82, p. 334.

[76] But Dutton, "Sacramentality of Community," points out that for Aelred, "monastic community . . . begins in the intimate friendships of a few but then grows to include many."

[77] See above, Chapter 1.

the Roman Empire meant adapting the classical forms to suit Christians.[78] Fortunatus had reveled in the potential of friendship, modeled on family relations, to knit together the Merovingian aristocratic elites.[79] Now, in the twelfth century, Aelred picked up the theme again for new purposes. In *On Spiritual Friendship*, Cicero's form (the dialogue) and Cicero's definition of the term ("friendship is nothing other than agreement [*consensio*] in all things divine and human along with benevolence [*benevolentia*] and love [*caritas*]") were Aelred's starting points.[80] However, where Cicero used Laelius as his spokesman, Aelred used the persona "Aelredus"; and where Cicero created two interlocutors, Aelred used three: Ivo, Gratian, and Walter.[81] Like Cicero, Aelred derived friendship from the word *amor*, love.

Amor, we recall, was for Aelred both a faculty and an act; as an act, it could result in cupidity as well as in charity. Certainly there were false friendships that grew out of cupidity. Aelred talked about two sorts of non-spiritual friendships, one carnal (*carnalis*), which is under the influence of affect alone and blows this way and that; and the other worldly (*mundialis*), which is intoxicated by cupidity for temporal and material things and is always full of fraud and deception (*plena fraudis atque fallaciae*).[82]

Real friendship came from charity. That meant that once a friend is chosen, "he is to be so tolerated, so treated, and so supported that, as long as he [no doubt Aelred was thinking of other men rather than women]

---

[78] See White, *Christian Friendship*, esp. 164–84. But C. Stephen Jaeger, "Friendship of Mutual Perfecting in Augustine's *Confessions* and the Failure of Classical *amicitia*," in *Friendship in the Middle Ages and Early Modern Age*, 185–200 at 193, argues that "*amicitia* joined comfortably with Greek and Roman philosophy, but not with Christianity, and certainly not with the monastic life."

[79] See above, Chapter 2.

[80] Cicero, *DA* 8.26, p. 138. For the context, see Chapter 1. For Aelred's notion of friendship, see Adele Fiske, "Aelred's of Rievaulx [*sic*] Idea of Friendship and Love," *Cîteaux* 13 (1962): 5–17, 97–132, and more recently Boquet, *L'ordre de l'affect*, 275–323, and Aelred, *Spiritual Friendship*, with useful introduction and bibliography. Forthcoming is Domenico Pezzini, "Aelred's Doctrine of Charity and Friendship," in *A Companion to Aelred*, chap. 9, which stresses the connections between the *Mirror* and *On Spiritual Friendship*. I thank Don Pezzini for allowing me to read his chapter prior to publication.

[81] Aelred, *SA*, is organized into three books. In the first, Aelred visits a daughter house and engages in discussion with Ivo. In the second, which is set at a later time at Rievaulx itself and takes place in the wake of Ivo's death, Walter is the initial interlocutor with Gratian arriving toward the end of the dialogue. Walter and Gratian then continue the discussion in book 3. (Walter, *VA* c. 31, p. 41, makes the claim that Walter Daniel himself was the "Walter" of the dialogue.)

[82] Aelred, *SA* 1.42, p. 296.

does not depart irrevocably from the original foundation, he should be so much yours, and you his – both in bodily and in spiritual matters (*tam in corporalibus quam in spiritalibus*) – that there should be no separation of souls (*animorum*), affection (*affectionum*), wills (*voluntatum*), or opinions."[83]

"No separation of souls": for Aelred this was possible only in *spiritual* friendship, a love triangle in which Christ participated. Everything good about friendship "begins with Christ, is advanced through Christ, and is perfected in Christ."[84] Acts 4:32 said that those who believed in Christ were "of one heart and one soul." Aelred made the idea apply to friendship: "A friend adhering to a friend (*amicus ... adhaerens amico*) in the spirit of Christ becomes one heart and one soul with [his friend]. And so, by mounting the steps of love (*amoris gradus*) to the friendship of Christ, he is made one spirit with him in one kiss."[85] Saints had long been known as "friends" of Christ; that is why saints Sergius and Bacchus could be portrayed in the sixth or seven centuries with their halos joined by Christ's own halo (see Plate 1. 1). Aelred's contribution was to make *human* friendships the way to friendship with Christ. And to add a kiss, so important to the bonds of fidelity in Aelred's world.[86]

Being "one spirit" with Christ was the ultimate joy of these human friendships. But there were intermediate joys as well. Above all, since there was "no separation of souls" among friends, they could confide in one another. We love many people, but only to friends do we "bare our soul and pour out our guts."[87] In the *Mirror*, Aelred noted that friends are united through an "intimate affect (*affectu intimo*)"; a friend is someone "in whom your spirit may rest, to whom your *animus* may pour itself out."[88] In *On Spiritual Friendship* he added: "We call 'friends' only those to whom we are unafraid of committing our heart (*cor*) and whatever is in

---

[83] Aelred, *SA* 3.7, pp. 318–19. Because Aelred admitted "bodily" union, some commentators have speculated he was homosexual. But whether he was one or not, or was a latent homosexual or not, love of men was certainly one of his most important emotional themes, and that is what we must explore here. For the debate on Aelred's homosexuality and relevant bibliography, see Boquet, *L'ordre de l'affect*, 307–23.

[84] Aelred, *SA* 2.20, p. 306.

[85] *Ibid.*, 2.21, p. 306. See Katherine M. Yohe, "Adhering to a Friend in the Spirit of Christ," *Cistercian Studies Quarterly* 33/1 (1998): 29–44.

[86] Italo Sciuto, "Le passioni e la tradizione monastica," *Doctor Seraphicus* 45 (1998): 5–39, esp. 33–35, sees Aelred's chief contribution to the monastic understanding of the passions to be his insistence on the human origins of spiritual friendship. On the kiss of fidelity, see below at n. 184. Consider, too, the key role of kisses in the poems of the troubadours, discussed below.

[87] Aelred, *SA* 3.84, p. 335: "nostrum propalare animum, et effundere viscera."

[88] Aelred, *Spec. car.* 3.39, p. 159.

it; and in turn they are bound to us by the same law of loyalty (*fidei*) and security (*securitate*)."[89]

And yet such security, being of this world, was also a source of sorrow. Aelred wrote about a dear friend of his, Simon, who had died. Addressing himself, Aelred counseled: "Weep, then, poor me, for your dearest father, weep for your most loving son, weep for your sweetest friend."[90] To Simon he said, "Allow me to offer you my tears, to release my affect (*affectum meum*) to you and, if possible, to pour back into you (*refundam tibi*) my whole *animus*."[91] Just as Augustine had justified his own tears when he lost a dear friend, so Aelred explained: "I grieve (*doleo*) for my most beloved (*dilectissimum meum*), because the one-in-heart with me (*unicordem meum*) has been wrenched from me; but I rejoice (*gaudeo*) because he has been elevated to eternal tabernacles."[92]

Nor was death the only source of grief in friendship. As Walter (in his guise as interlocutor in *On Spiritual Friendship*) put it: "I almost join the camp of those who say that friendship should be avoided as something full of anxiety (*sollicitudinis*) and cares, not free of fear (*timoris*), and even liable to many pains (*doloribus*)."[93] A mutual "commitment of hearts" might mean that friends shared their vices! That, too, felt very sweet (*tanta ac talis experiatur dulcedo*), though not as sweet as friendship without impure desire (*libido*), avarice (*avaritia*), or lust (*luxuria*).[94] No one was perfect after the Fall. Suppose, wrote Aelred, we have two persons: one is gentle, affable, charming, and so on, but less perfect in certain virtues; the other is advanced in the highest virtue, but is not at all charming. Now, by a sort of spontaneous affect, the *animus* is moved to love the first; but reason and the rule of ordered charity urge the *animus* to love the second. "And so, when a person feels his *animus* embracing the first with a certain sweetness (*illum quadam amplecti dulcedine*), but hardening toward the one lacking all agreeableness (*omni vacuum suavitate*), he is anxious (*anxiatur*), he grieves (*dolet*), and he fears (*timet*) going beyond the rule of charity, for he thinks that he loves the first more than necessary and the second less than necessary."[95]

Thus, people "waver" because they are not sure that they have chosen the right love or that they love it (or him or her) rightly. Aelred used words like "agitation" and even "anxiety" to describe the human

---

[89] Aelred, *SA* 1.32, p. 294.   [90] Aelred, *Spec. car.* 1.34, p. 59.   [91] *Ibid.*, 57.

[92] *Ibid.*, p. 60. See Augustine, *Conf.* 4.5.10, 1:73.

[93] Aelred, *SA* 2.45, pp. 310–11. The "camp" referred to those whom Epicurus rebuked in a letter to Lucilius. Presumably Aelred knew about this letter from Seneca, *Ad Lucilium Epistulae Morales* 1.9, ed. L. D. Reynolds, 2 vols. (Oxford, 1965), online at www.intratext.com/IXT/LAT0230/_P9.HTM.

[94] Aelred, *SA* 1.36, p. 295.   [95] Aelred, *Spec. car.* 3.18, p. 125.

condition. Recall that to achieve the second Sabbath, people must not be "agitated (*agitari*) by any pricks of envy (*invidiae*), inflamed by any fire of indignation (*indignationum*), weakened by darts of suspicion (*suspicionum*), or consumed by the bites of voracious sadness (*tristitiae*)."[96] In his treatise *On Spiritual Friendship*, Aelred made clear that these emotions impeded true friendship such as the one between David and Jonathan in 1 Sam 23:17: "This is true, perfect, stable, and eternal friendship, not corrupted by envy (*invida*), not weakened by suspicion (*suspicio*), not destroyed by ambition (*ambitio*)." Thus, when choosing a friend you should avoid people who are irascible (*iracundi*), unstable (*instabiles*), suspicious (*suspiciosi*), and verbose (*verbosi*).[97] The irascible were rebellious, the unstable were unfaithful, the verbose were never serious, and the suspicious saw treachery everywhere.[98]

And yet, as the interlocutor Walter pointed out in *On Spiritual Friendship*, Aelredus himself cultivated a friendship with a man who was exceedingly irascible (*iracundissimo*). Why didn't he follow his own advice? Aelredus excused himself: his friend knew how to keep his passion (*passionem*) under control.[99] Then another interlocutor, Gratian this time, boldly accused Aelredus of playing favorites regarding a different irascible monk, preferring "above all of us [a monk who] was overcome by anger (*ira*)."[100] Playing favorites: we must now look at Aelred's notion of the emotions involved in power relations.

Emotions of power

The monastery, like the court of King David, knew all about preferment and power. Being an abbot meant ruling; and ruling, whether of a kingdom or a monastery, called forth certain emotions both in the ruler and the ruled.[101] For Aelred and Walter, worldly political life was in effect monastic life writ large. After David died, Aelred wrote a *Lament* for him in which he noted that the king "always hoped to be loved rather than feared."[102] The phrase directly echoed the Benedictine Rule's precept: "let the abbot be zealous to be loved more than feared."[103] When Aelred

---

[96] Above at n. 60. On Aelred's notion of envy and its implications, see Jonah Wharff, "Ælred of Rievaulx on Envy and Gratitude," *Cistercian Studies Quarterly* 43/1 (2008): 1–15.

[97] Aelred, SA 3.96, p. 338; ibid., 3.14, p. 319.   [98] *Ibid.*, 3.29, p. 323.

[99] *Ibid.*, 3.16–17, p. 320.   [100] *Ibid.*, 3.18, p. 320.

[101] There is a huge literature on the emotions of the ruler. See above, Introduction, n. 40, for some examples.

[102] Aelred, *Lament*, 271: "magis amari quam timeri."

[103] *The Rule of Saint Benedict*, ed. and trans. Bruce L. Venarde (Cambridge, MA, 2011) [henceforth RB], 64:15, p. 208: "studeat plus amari quam timeri."

enumerated King David's virtues, he borrowed two of them (humility and chastity) from those of monks, and he took one, justice, from those that Benedict had applied to the abbot.[104] It is thus not surprising to find Aelred praising David as founder of several monasteries or to read that "among [the brothers] he was like one of them."[105] Indeed, Aelred recalled visiting David during Lent and found "in the king a monk, a cloister in the court, in the palace the discipline of a monastery."[106]

Like the monastery, political life was supposed to be regulated by charity and made still sweeter by friendships.[107] In his *Genealogy*, Aelred remembered King David as his "sweetest lord and friend."[108] In the same work, he praised King Alfred for being "amiable (*amabilem*) to the good, terrifying (*terribilem*) to the impious, in awe (*pavidum*) of the ministers of the church, [and] joyful (*jucundum*) to his friends and associates (*amicis et sociis*)."[109] It was important to Aelred to stress that when Alfred had a vision prophesying his victory over the Danes, he gathered his friends around him along with the rest of his army. They all exchanged embraces and kisses and shed tears together while the king gave thanks to God.[110]

But if the joys of ruling a kingdom and a monastery were the same, so were the problems. When Aelred was elected abbot of Rievaulx, Walter commented: "certain men think that he ascended to the government of this house out of his own ambition (*ambicione*), which every good man knows is false." But, continued Walter, "virtue never lacks envy (*invidia*). And how many wickedly jealous men (*male zelantes*) did the peaceful [Aelred] endure?"[111] The powerful had to put up with the worst sides of human nature.

At the same time, the powerful had to contend with temptations of their own. Consider the dilemma of an abbot, who might well be tempted to promote the monks he loved the most. In *On Spiritual Friendship* Aelred warned against this: merit should be the sole criterion for promotion. "Let us offer a friend all of our love (*amoris*), grace (*gratiae*), sweetness (*dulcedinis*), and charity (*caritatis*). But as for those futile honors and burdens: let us impose them on [the monks] whom reason (*ratio*) [rather than

[104] Aelred, *Lament*, 270. Justice first appears in RB 2:19, p. 22, on the discretion of the abbot to promote one monk over another "justitia dictante (at the dictate of justice)." The same chapter also has four other invocations of *justitia*. See Terrence Kardong, "Justitia in the Rule of Benedict," *Studia Monastica* 24 (1982): 43–73.
[105] Aelred, *Lament*, 272.   [106] *Ibid.*, 278.
[107] For this and other Cistercian notions of rulership, see Martha G. Newman, *The Boundaries of Charity: Cistercian Culture and Ecclesiastical Reform, 1098–1180* (Stanford, 1996), esp. chap. 7.
[108] Aelred, *Gen.*, PL 195, col. 716: "dulcissime domine et amice."   [109] *Ibid.*, col. 717.
[110] *Ibid.*, col. 721.   [111] Walter, *VA* c. 26, p. 33.

affect] singles out."[112] Nevertheless, Aelred admitted that he had once given the office of subprior to a friend. In that case (he explained), it was on account of the man's "gray hairs, as it were (*quosdam canos*)" in virtue and grace. Indeed, his friend had feared that the appointment would mean that he would not love or be loved as much as before: high office jeopardized friendships. In the event, it did nothing of the sort. To the contrary, their friendship had grown more and more perfect, allowing Aelred to experience the bliss (*beatitudo*) – the peace (*pax*) and quiet (*quies*) – of the Sabbath.[113] Thus the usual solution – *not* appointing a friend – had to be weighed alongside other options. There were no simple answers.

There was, however, one simple principle: love and friendship should be subordinated to what was in the interest of the whole community: "Well-ordered friendship (*amicitia ordinata*) is this: that reason (*ratio*) should so rule affect (*affectus*) that we pay attention not so much to what the sweetness of friends entreats [us to do] as to what the common good (*multorum . . . utilitas*) requires."[114]

Thus leaders were buffeted by many temptations, some coming from those who loved them and whom they loved in turn, others from people who envied them and invited revenge. The antidote, on the whole, was compassion and reason. But sometimes the very emotions that threatened charity were also good and righteous. Long after Aelred had become abbot of Rievaulx, he suffered virulent abuse from the abbot of a daughter house who evidently came to Rievaulx for a Chapter meeting.[115] In the words of Walter, the abbot "burst in on the father [Aelred], attacking him violently with the darts of curses." In this instance, Aelred did not feel compassion. Instead, the man's insults "moved his spirit to indignation (*indignacionem*) against him and made [Aelred] rightly angry against him (*et merito in se provacavit iratum*)." Indeed, "he bore the man's malice (*maliciam*) with difficulty (*graviter*)," and called upon God to "quickly (*cito*)" put an end to it. A few days after the abbot had returned home without Aelred's blessing, he died. Walter painted his hero in glowing colors during this episode.[116]

How can we explain Walter's unapologetic, indeed laudatory, attitude toward Aelred's anger and indignation? It is clear that those emotions, like love, had (in the view of Aelred and Walter) both good and bad

---

[112] Aelred, *SA* 3.118, p. 345.   [113] *Ibid.*, 3.124–25, p. 346–47.   [114] *Ibid.*, 3.118, p. 345.

[115] Powicke in Walter, *VA*, lxx, speculates that this was Philip, abbot of Revesby (d. 1166). The episode is described *ibid.*, c. 37, pp. 44–45.

[116] In his *Epistola ad Mauricium*, in Walter, *VA*, pp. 66–81, a letter that Walter Daniel wrote to someone named Maurice to corroborate all the miracles in his *Life of Aelred*, Walter (68) declined to name the witnesses to this episode, suggesting some ambivalence about its virtues. For the possible identities of Maurice, see Powicke's introduction to Walter, *VA*, xxx–xxxi.

possibilities. We have already seen this point made by Augustine and turned to practical account by Alcuin.[117]

Other temptations of rulers were clearly vices. Aelred singled out the "lust to dominate" (*libido dominandi*) as the worst. A major concern of Augustine, the lust to dominate took on new importance in Aelred's writings.[118] He identified it as the fruit of cupidity and an offshoot of pride: "when an opportunity for promotion to some kind of honor is offered, a person is so inflamed with the lust to dominate that, in his hope of reaching the top, he does not dread committing any crime."[119] In his *Genealogy of the Kings of England*, Aelred offered many examples of kings past. Some of them, like Cnut (r. 1016–35) and Edmund II Ironside (r. April–November 1016), could not resist the desire to dominate.[120] King Æthelwulf (r. 839–56), however, "considered the needs of others rather than satisfying his own will to dominate (*voluntati dominando*)."[121] Aelred meant the parade of kings in his *Genealogy* to function as a prelude to the young Henry of Anjou, on whom rested the spirit (*spiritus*) of the most Christian of all kings, David I of Scotland.[122] Writing in 1153–54, the moment that marked the end of the civil war that had broken out after the death of King Henry I (d. 1135), Aelred knew that the second Henry had been designated the next king even though Stephen was still on the throne. He exulted (*maxime gaudeo*) that the prince had been knighted in 1149 by David: "through his hands may Christ's grace have poured into you [, Henry,] the virtue of his chastity, humility, and piety."[123] At the end of the *Genealogy*, Aelred begged God that Henry be free of cupidity, free of pride, and ignorant of cruelty. He was hoping, in short, that Henry would not be overcome by the lust to dominate.[124]

---

[117] See Chapters 1 and 3 above.
[118] See, for example, Augustine, *Civ. dei*, praef. l. 21, p. 1; 1.30, l. 29, p. 31; 3.14, l. 55, p. 77; and so on; Herbert A. Deane, *The Political and Social Ideas of St. Augustine* (New York, 1963), 49–53. Beyond Augustine, concern about the "lust to dominate" was expressed by, among others, Cyprian of Carthage, Jerome, Gregory the Great, and various Carolingian commentators before it was taken up again in the twelfth century (according to the results of an online PL database search). On Aelred's quite original ideas about the vices, see Elias Dietz, "Aelred on the Capital Vices: A Unique Voice among the Cistercians," *Cistercian Studies Quarterly* 43/3 (2008): 271–93, esp. 279–93.
[119] Aelred, *Spec. car.* 2.2, p. 68. In a sermon on the feast of Saint Benedict, Aelred, *Sermo* 54 §8, in Aelred, *Sermones XLVII-LXXXIV*, ed. Gaetano Raciti, CCCM 2B (Turnhout, 2001), 69, told the monks "that the first discord from the devil began with pride, which prefers to dominate than to be subdued. For truly 'all who exalt themselves shall be humbled.' (Luke 14:11) ... Yet even so pride did not give up its lust to dominate, but [chose] a seat for itself in the cold hearts of human beings," stirring up all the vices.
[120] Aelred, *Gen.*, PL 195, col. 731.   [121] *Ibid.*, col. 718.   [122] *Ibid.*, col. 713.
[123] *Ibid.* On the idea that Henry inherited David's virtues, see Marie Anne Mayeski, "Secundum naturam: The Inheritance of Virtue in Aelred's *Genealogy of the English Kings*," *Cistercian Studies Quarterly* 37/3 (2002): 221–28.
[124] Aelred, *Gen.*, PL 195, col. 738.

This lust was a problem for monks as well as for kings. Commenting on Adonias in 1 Kings 1:5–6, who hoped to succeed David as king even though his younger brother, Solomon, had already been designated, Aelred explained: "Adonias signifies one who in religious life is puffed up in heart (*in religione corde tumidum*), greedy for honors, devoted to carnal desires ... Without question, they imitate Adonias who try to put themselves in front of others, who plan to depose those ahead of them (*praelatos deponere*), who are tortured by the promotion of their betters (*de promotione meliorum torquentur*)." Turning directly to his monks, Aelred warned: "Take note that those who are vexed by the lust to dominate are violently shaken (*pulsantur*) by carnal desires."[125] Everyone was liable to the impulse: "In these days there is hardly a bishop or abbot or prior or even [just a] monk or nun (*claustralis*) 'who is lacking in love to dominate (*amore dominandi*) and does not hanker for human glory.'"[126]

If the lust to dominate infected both the cloister and the world, so too did the vices that ruined friendship. To enumerate them, Aelred drew on Ecclesiasticus/Sirach. No friend will abandon you except on account of "slander (*convicio*), reproach (*inproperio*), and pride (*superbia*), and betraying a secret (*mysterii revelatione*), and deceitful injury (*plaga dolosa*)."[127] For Aelred, the last two of these were by far the worst. If a friend was, above all, the person to whom you opened your heart, how terrible if he betrayed your secrets! There was "nothing worse (*turpius*), nothing more execrable (*execrabilius*)." When a secret was violated, the sweetness of friendship drained away, leaving only bitterness (*amaritudo*), indignation (*indignatio*), hatred (*odium*), and pain (*dolor*).[128] "Let us consider it a sacrilege to reveal the secrets of friends; [by that act] trust (*fides*) is lost."[129] And when trust is lost, despair (*desperatio*) is the result. Aelred was here thinking of Achitophel, a character in 2 Kings, who hanged himself after betraying the biblical King David and "earned the fate reserved to a traitor (*proditori*)." But he could have had Judas Iscariot in mind as well.

Betrayal haunted the world of Aelred's kings. In the *Genealogy*, Edmund I died prematurely "because of a wicked betrayal (*nefanda proditione*)."[130] Similarly Edmund II was assassinated by "a traitor (*proditor*)" who devised "an utterly wicked and disgraceful kind of treachery (*nefandissimum ac turpissimum insidiarum*)," hiding himself under a latrine and striking the king from below.[131] A ruler like King David, whose court Aelred knew

---

[125] Aelred, *Sermo* 74.31–33, in *Sermones XLVII-LXXXIV*, 254–55.

[126] Aelred, *Sermo* 113.10, in *Sermones LXXXV-CLXXXII*, ed. Gaetano Raciti, CCCM 2C (Turnhout, 2012), 155, quoting Augustine, *Enarrationes in psalmos* 1.1, in Augustine, *Enarrationes in Psalmos 1–50*, ed. Clemens Weidmann, CSEL 93/1A (Vienna, 2003), 67.

[127] Aelred, *SA* 3.23, p. 321, drawing on Ecclus. 22:27.   [128] *Ibid.*, 3.24, p. 321.

[129] *Ibid.*, 3.27, p. 322.   [130] Aelred, *Gen.*, PL 195, col. 725.   [131] *Ibid.*, col. 733.

well, had to sort out true from unfaithful followers by knowing whose accusations of treachery were true and whose were false. In Aelred's *Battle of the Standard*, written perhaps 1153–54, Robert de Bruce, tied to King David "not only by friendship but also by fidelity (*non solum amicitia, sed et fidei*)," warned the king of the treachery (*proditio*) of the Scots.[132] But David's nephew William Fitzduncan (in effect the leader of the "Scots" accused by Robert) warned the king in turn about Robert's own treachery (*ipsum Rodbertum . . . arguit proditionis*).[133] David made the mistake of listening to his nephew and lost the battle.

Thus, as we see from the writings of Aelred and Walter, the community of Rievaulx was both driven and riven by love, whose two branches – charity and cupidity – competed with each other. Love was good as a faculty; but as an act, it could go awry. Nor was it easy for a person to know if he or she was practicing charity for certain, since every virtue could also be a vice, every vice a virtue. How could you know if you loved the right person and in the right way? Your inclinations might bend one way while reason told you to love another.

And yet you could not – should not – avoid love. At Aelred's Rievaulx, it was expected that you would feel. If you did not, you were nothing but a stone. Cicero had already said something like this (see Chapter 1, n. 24), and Aelred repeated it. But he also went further. "Those who say they should live such that they are of consolation (*consolationi*) to no one, nor indeed a burden (*oneri*) or pain (*dolori*) to anyone; who feel no delight (*nihil delectationis*) at the good of another, who inflict no bitterness (*nihil amaritudinis*) on others out of their own perversity (*sua perversitate*), who love no one (*amare nullum*) and don't care to be loved by anyone (*amari a nullo*) – I would call such people not so much human beings as beasts."[134] At Rievaulx, feelings, even "perverse" feelings that might pain others, were better than none at all. To be sure, it was best to feel alongside others – to have compassion. It was best to love the good and the virtuous. And yet it was well understood that in this world you could make mistakes.

At the court of Toulouse

At Toulouse c. 1200, love was similarly valued and at the same time surrounded with analogous fears and anxieties. We have already seen the importance of family ties and affection at the court of Metz, as exemplified

---

[132] Aelred, *De bello standardii* [henceforth *BS*], PL 195, cols. 701–12 at 709. For its date, see Marsha L. Dutton's arguments in *Aelred of Rievaulx: The Historical Works*, trans. Jane Patricia Freeland, ed. Marsha L. Dutton (Kalamazoo, 2005), 24–31. Burton, *Ælred de Rievaulx*, 418–25, suggests that it must have been while King David was still alive, thus before May 24, 1153.

[133] Aelred, *BS*, col. 710.   [134] Aelred, *SA* 2.52, p. 312.

largely in the writings of Gregory of Tours and Fortunatus. Their words of love – *amor, dilectio, dulcedo* – remained potent in the twelfth century. But family feeing was less emphasized in this later period than were the affective ties that bound men to other men, as we have already seen at Rievaulx and will see again at the court of Toulouse. The counts there – Raimond V (1148–94), Raimond VI (1194–1222), and Raimond VII (1222–49) – were lords within a political system badly termed "feudalism." No historians, I suppose, will adopt the terms "amicism" or "amorism" in its stead, but that is what it was. We shall see that tremendous faith was put in "friendship" and "love," as well as in the emotions of anger and indignation, to correct – and bitterly complain about – love gone awry.

To explore these feelings at the court of Toulouse, we have the *acta* of the counts, drawn up largely in Latin, as well as many works in Old Occitan written by the troubadours supported by the counts.[135] The case of one countess – Eleonor of Aragon, the last (the fifth) wife of Raimond VI – makes it possible to see whether a woman at this court supported different values and emotions. We shall see that she did not.[136]

The context: the count and his court

Until 1213, the counts of Toulouse (who also styled themselves dukes of Narbonne and marquises of Provence) ruled a wide swath of the French Midi.[137] (See Map 4.1.) Raimond V warred with the king of England, the count of Barcelona, and local lords. Raimond VI, however, negotiated

---

[135] The *Acta* are catalogued (and the hitherto unpublished ones are edited) in *Catalogues raimondins (1112–1229). Actes des comtes de Toulouse, ducs de Narbonne et marquis de Provence* [henceforth *Cat. Rai.*], ed. Laurent Macé (Toulouse, 2008). At Toulouse, I was privileged to be allowed access to all the *Acta*, which have been collected and keyed to the *Catalogues* by Professor Macé. The most important study of the court of the counts of Toulouse is Laurent Macé, *Les comtes de Toulouse et leur entourage. Rivalités, alliances et jeux de pouvoir, XIIe–XIIIe siècles* (Toulouse, 2003). I wish to express my deepest gratitude here to Professor Macé and to the staff of the Bibliothèque d'études méridionales, Toulouse, for their generosity and help during my stay there. I also owe much to conversations with Claudie Amado, Pilar Jiménez-Sanchez, and Dominique Iogna-Prat on issues raised here. Finally, I wish to record my enormous debt to William D. Paden, who not only taught me Old Occitan but also helped me immeasurably with the translations here. These translations are quite literal, as they attempt to get at the emotional vocabulary in the poems rather than their rhythmic or literary qualities. All translations (and, it goes without saying, all errors) are ultimately my own. A study that similarly considers the poets alongside the aristocrats is Jan Rüdiger, *Aristokraten und Poeten. Die Grammatik einer Mentalität in tolosanischen Hochmittelalter* (Berlin, 2001), which, however, does not focus on emotions and ranges far beyond the court.

[136] Eleonor of Aragon was still young at her marriage in 1204 and alive until at least the end of 1226. See Aimeric de Belenoi, *Le Poesie*, ed. Andrea Poli (Florence, 1997) [henceforth Aimeric de Belenoi], 8.

[137] For the historical background summarized here, see Macé, *Les comtes*, 33–50 and 431. See also Jean-Luc Déjean, *Quand chevauchaient les Comtes de Toulouse, 1050–1250* (Paris, 1979).

treaties with these erstwhile enemies and focused on the Toulousain. His successes were checked when the church accused him of protecting "Cathar heretics."[138] The heresies of these men and women, sometimes also called Albigensians by their accusers, were largely figments of the imagination of post-Gregorian churchmen.[139] But such prelates were not wrong to see dissenters in the Midi – men and women who felt that the Gregorian Reform had not gone far enough in freeing the Church from the world – and some of the local rulers (the Raimondin counts among the least of them, however) offered these people protection.[140]

Raimond, excommunicated in 1207 by Pope Innocent III (1198–1216), at first took the cross, battling on the side of the crusading French army against the Cathars (more correctly against the lords who supposedly protected them) in the Midi. But after he was excommunicated a second time in 1211, Raimond turned against the French, now led by Simon de Montfort. With the Battle of Muret (1213), he lost most of his lands, some of which were confiscated by Innocent.[141] After a protracted war, during which Raimondet succeeded his father as Raimond VII, the count's cause failed in 1229. Thereafter, the count's power was severely curtailed in favor of the king of France and his men.[142]

When in power, the counts gained support from members of their family and from the many lords whose interests they guaranteed.[143] "Interest" was not the term they or their adherents used, however; as we shall see, they spoke rather of bonds of love with one another. Under Raimond V, the lesser aristocrats formed the backbone of the count's entourage.[144] But with the Albigensian Crusade (the crusade against the Cathars), the great princes formed a bloc in support of Raimond VI and his son, as did the lesser urban nobility and middle-class townsmen.[145] All of these groups came to see the Toulousain count as the champion of what the *Chanson de la Croisade albigeoise* would call *paratge* – cognate of the word "peerage," and signfying a community of equals defined by its nobility and virtue.[146]

---

[138] Mace, *Les comtes*, 340–46, traces the growing hostility between the counts and Rome in the course of the twelfth century as the counts imposed what they saw as their "rights" on the bishops and monasteries of the Midi.

[139] As argued by Robert I. Moore, *The War on Heresy* (Cambridge, MA, 2012).

[140] Pilar Jiménez-Sanchez, *Les catharismes: modèles dissidents du christianisme médiéval, XIIe–XIIIe siècles* (Rennes, 2008).

[141] Mace, *Les comtes*, 33–34. This Simon de Montfort (d. 1218) was the father of the Simon de Montfort (d. 1265) who led a revolt against King Henry II of England.

[142] *Ibid.*, 99.

[143] Family members included the Sabran family (Mace, *Les comtes*, 103–4) and Bernard IV, count of Comminges (see *Cat. Rai.*, 423, p. 320 [1218, 30 May]).

[144] Mace, *Les comtes*, 107.   [145] *Ibid.*, 99, 110, 118–19.

[146] *Chanson de la Croisade albigeoise*, ed. and trans. Eugène Martin-Chabot, 3 vols. (Paris, 1957–61) [henceforth *Chanson*], 2:16, laisse 137, ll. 1–2: "Totz lo mons ne valg mens, de ver o sapiatz,/Car Paratges ne fo destruitz e decassatz (The whole world is worth

A glaring exception to this widely shared adherence to the Raimondin counts was found among the higher clergy. While an uncle of Raimond V, Aldebert (1141–82), had been archbishop of Nîmes, and while Fulcrand, bishop of Toulouse (1179–1201), had been a partisan of the count, the thirteenth-century clergy was purged by the papacy. In the decades after 1200, the major ecclesiastical office-holders of the Midi were hostile to the Toulousain house.[147] The same was true of the regular clergy, even though the counts were generous donors to the Cistercians. Only the Hospitalers, which the counts had favored above the others, remained supportive.[148] Laurent Macé suggests that the counts of Toulouse, thoroughly secular in outlook, did not *want* to surround themselves with clergymen.[149] This was a fatal flaw, as it later turned out.

Among those who accompanied the counts and depended on their largesse were bureaucrats: chancellors, notaries, and other men concerned with drawing up and sealing documents; seneschals and bailiffs, who acted as judges and dues collectors on the counts' estates.[150] Despite their wariness of clerics in general, the counts had chaplains, and we know the names of a few of them.[151] Women populated the court – the counts' mistresses and countesses, for example.[152] But the former were almost entirely anonymous, while the latter were honored mainly by their sons.[153] Finally there were troubadours (but no *trobairitz*, women troubadours).[154]

---

less, know that truly, / For Paratges was destroyed and unseated)." These, the opening lines of the poem's anonymous continuator, who wrote on the side of the counts of Toulouse, was the first of his many references to the term. See C. P. Bagley, "*Paratge* in the Anonymous *Chanson de la Croisade albigeoise*," French Studies 21 (1967): 195–204; Rüdiger *Aristokraten*, 440–46; Eliza Miruna Ghil, *L'Age de Parage. Essai sur le poétique et le politique en Occitanie au XIIIe siècle* (New York, 1989), which, however, concentrates on the period after the Albigensian Crusade.

[147] Macé, *Les comtes*, 100–2.

[148] *Ibid.*, 101–2. On their generosity and privileges to the Hospitalers in Occitania, see Dominic Selwood, *Knights of the Cloister: Templars and Hospitallers in Central-Southern Occitania c. 1100–c.1300* (Woodbridge, 1999), 101–3 and 43–44, on the support of the Hospitalers of the Toulousain counts during the Albigensian Crusade.

[149] Macé, *Les comtes*, 102.   [150] *Ibid.*, 123–38.   [151] *Ibid.*, 171–73.

[152] For the counts' mistresses, *ibid.*, 174–78. For the countesses, *ibid.*, 168; Hélène Débax, "Les comtesses de Toulouse. Notices biographiques," *Annales du Midi* 100 (1988): 215–34, and "Stratégies matrimoniales des comtes de Toulouse (850–1270)," *ibid.*, 131–51.

[153] Macé, *Les comtes*, 211–16.

[154] With the possible exception of Alamanda de Castelnau, as proposed in Angelica Rieger, "Alamanda de Castelnau – Une *trobairitz* dans l'entourage des comtes de Toulouse?" in *Les troubadours et l'État toulousain avant la Croisade (1209). Actes du Colloque de Toulouse (9 et 10 décembre 1988)*, ed. Arno Krispin (Bordeaux, 1994), 183–92. But even if so, we have no corpus of poems by her.

The troubadours in the counts' entourage

Numerous troubadours wrote one or two poems for the counts of Toulouse, but it would go too far to consider them part of the emotional community of the court. Rather, we must look at those who spent some time in Toulouse and presumably knew the emotional norms that obtained there.[155] I make the assumption that the troubadours could not have pleased their patrons if they had sung songs that made no emotional sense at their court.

A few decades ago, in both published and unpublished works, Ariane Loeb listed the main courtier-troubadours and the poems that they wrote for the counts of Toulouse.[156] The most important and prolific were Peire Vidal,[157] Gaucelm Faidit,[158] Bernart de Ventadorn,[159] and

---

[155] I thus list here only poets who wrote more than two poems for the court.

[156] Ariane Loeb, "Les relations entre les troubadours et les comtes de Toulouse (1112–1229)" (M.A. thesis, Université de Toulouse-Le Mirail, 1982), with poems listed on p. 74 [henceforth Loeb, "Les relations thesis"]; Loeb, "Les relations entre les troubadours et les comtes de Toulouse (1112–1229)," *Annales du midi* 95 (1983): 225–59; Loeb, "Aimer et servir: le vocabulaire féodo-vassalique dans la poésie des troubadours" (PhD diss., Université de Toulouse-Le Mirail, 1992). More recent surveys of the poets at court are Sergio Vatteroni, "Le corti della Francia meridionale," in *Lo Spazio letterario del Medioevo 2. Il Medioevo volgare*, vol. 1: *La produzione del testo*, pt. 2 (Rome, 2001), 353–98, and Rüdiger, *Aristokraten*, 150–56.

[157] Peire Vidal, *Poesie*, ed. Silvio Avalle d'Arco, 2 vols. (Milan, 1960) [henceforth Peire Vidal], No. 1, *Be m'agrada la covinens sazos*; No. 2, *Bels Amics cars, ven s'en ves vos estius* (before October 3, 1187); No. 3, *Ajostar e lassar* (before October 3, 1187); No. 4, *Tant me platz jois e solatz* (Spring, 1188–1192); No. 8, *Tant ai lonjamen sercat* (after 1188); No. 30, *Son ben apoderatz* (after October 3, 1187); No. 37, *Plus qu·l paubres, quan jai el ric ostal* (before August 18, 1186 [date of death of Geoffrey of Brittany]). On the other hand, note that Antonio Sánchez Jiménez, "Catalan and Occitan Troubadours at the Court of Alfonso VIII," *La corónica: A Journal of Medieval Hispanic Languages, Literatures, and Cultures* 32 (2004): 101–20 at 111, puts Vidal at the court of Alfonso VIII of Castille "around 1187 or 1188 ... and possibly again between 1198 and 1204." Moreover, he says that "the poet had a close relationship with Alfonso VIII, whom he praises in *Plus qu·l paubres*." Even so, I consider it here as part of Raimond's court culture. Veronica M. Fraser, *The Songs of Peire Vidal: Translation and Commentary* (New York, 2006), offers slightly different dates for many of these poems. She gives the texts in Avalle's edition followed by English translation. For a French translation of his own edition, see *Les poésies de Peire Vidal*, ed. and trans. Joseph Anglade (Paris, 1913). To sum up: the best guess is that Peire wrote poems addressed to Raimond V from before 1187 to c.1192, but this guess assumes that the poet's exile to the Holy Land and his return thereafter – chronicled only in the poems – were facts rather than poetic fancies.

[158] *Les poèmes de Gaucelm Faidit. Troubadour du XIIe siècle*, ed. and trans. Jean Mouzat (Paris, 1965) [henceforth Gaucelm Faidit], No. 19, *D'un amor, on s'es asis*; No. 20, *D'un dotç bell plaser*; No. 22, *Si tot noncas res es grazitz*; No. 23, *Oimais taing que fassa parer*; No. 27, *Jauzens en gran benananssa*; all written for Raimond V.

[159] *The Songs of Bernart de Ventadorn*, ed. and trans. Stephen G. Nichols, Jr. et al. (Chapel Hill, 1965) [henceforth Bernart], No. 12, *Be m'an perdut lai enves Ventadorn*; No. 16, *Conortz, era sai eu be*; No. 29, *Lo rossinhols s'esbaudeya*; all written between c. 1150 and c. 1180 for Raimond V.

Raimon de Miraval.[160] I consider as well the anonymous author of the
Chanson de la Croisade albigeoise to have been among the courtiers of
Raimond VII, since he identified fully with the counts and their cause
and was on hand for many of their confrontations and battles.[161] Among
those who wrote for Countess Eleonor,[162] the most prolific were
Aimeric de Belenoi[163] and Cadenet.[164]

---

[160] *Les poésies du troubadour Raimon de Miraval,* ed. and trans. L. T. Topsfield (Paris,
1971) [henceforth Raimon de Miraval], No. 8, *Chansoneta farai, Vencut;* No. 9,
Dels quatre mestiers valens; No. 10, *S'a dreg fos chantars grazitz;* No. 11, *Be
m'agrada·l bels tems d'estiu;* No. 13, *Tot quan fatz de be ni dic;* No. 15, *Enquer non
a guaire;* No. 16, *Cel qui de chantar s'entremet;* No. 17, *Si tot s'es ma domn'esquiva;*
No. 19, *Tuich cill que vant demandan;* No. 21, *Pueis onguan no·m valc estius;* No. 23,
Tals vai mon chan enqueren; No. 27, *Er ab la forsa dels freys;* No. 28, *Selh, cui joys
tanh ni chantar sap;* No. 32, *Cel que no vol auzir chanssos;* No. 33, *Ben aia·l
messagiers;* No. 34, *Un sonnet m'es belh qu'espanda;* No. 35, *Aissi cum es genser
pascors;* No. 37, *Bel m'es q'ieu chant e coindei;* all written for Raimond VI.

[161] *Chanson,* vols. 2 and 3 (vol. 1 was by William of Tudela, who supported the
crusaders). Saverio Guida, "L'autore della seconda parte della *Canso de la crotzada,*" *Cultura neolatina* 63 (2003): 255–82, identifies Gui de Cavaillon as the
author of the anonymous portion of the *Chanson.* Certainly Gui was allied with
the count of Toulouse against the crusaders. And he wrote a *partimen,* a joint song,
Senh'en coms, saber volria, in Saverio Guida, "L'attività poetica di Gui de Cavaillon
durante la crociata albigese," *Cultura neolatina* 33 (1973): 235–71, with the count
of Toulouse, whom Guida (238–39) identifies as Raimond VII. See also
Saverio Guida, "Per la biografia di Gui de Cavaillon e di Bertran Folco
d'Avignon," *Cultura neolatina* 32 (1972): 189–210. However, more recently
Marjolaine Raguin, "Propagande politique et religieuse dans la *Chanson de la
Croisade albigeoise,* texte de l'Anonyme" (PhD diss., Université Montpellier III,
2011), 40 (forthcoming), argues convincingly for a poet who redacted his work c.
1228–29 in the service of Roger Bernard II, the count of Foix. I am very grateful to
Dr. Raguin for allowing me to read her dissertation prior to publication.

[162] They are listed in *Les Poésies du troubadour Cadenet. Edition critique avec introduction,
traduction, notes et glossaire,* ed. and trans. Josef Zemp (Bern, 1978) [henceforth
Cadenet], 290. But most wrote only one or two poems for (and possibly not at) the
court. For example, according to Alfredo Cavaliere, *Le Poesie di Peire Raimon de
Tolosa. Introduzione, testi, traduzioni, note,* ed. and trans. Alfredo Cavaliere
(Florence, 1935), iii, Peire Raimon wrote two cansos for Toulouse, one (No. 1,
Ar ai ben d'amor apres) for the count (Raimon V or VI) and the other (No. 6,
Anqera·m vai recalivan) for a countess, probably Eleonor. I consider Eleonor an
integral part of the court not only because she was Raimond VI's wife but because
Savaric de Mauleon wrote a poem, of which we now have only a fragment,
Dompna, be sai that promises her the troops he will bring the count to counter
the Albigensian Crusade. See Henry John Chaytor, *Savaric de Mauléon, Baron and
Troubadour* (Cambridge, 1939), 21. See also *Chanson,* 1:152–54, laisse 61, and
1:206, laisse 87.

[163] Aimeric de Belenoi, No. 5, *Aissi co·l pres que s'en cuia fugir* (1204–26); No. 7, *Nulls hom
non pot complir adreizamen* (1185–1217); No. 8, *Per Crist, s'ieu creses Amor* (1204–26). I
also include No. 4, *S'a midons plazia* (1203–11), which was written for Indie, half sister
of Raimond VI. The dates are given by Poli.

[164] Cadenet, No. 15, *Meravilh me de tot fin amador* (written for Raimond VI); No. 16, *No sai
qual cosselh mi prenda;* No. 17, *Oimais m'auretz avinen;* No. 22, *S'ieu pogues ma voluntat;*
the latter three were written for Eleonor, at least according to Zemp, who identifies the

Emotion words

The troubadours allow us to confront a new – vernacular – vocabulary. But how can we determine which words had emotional force for them? The worst answer would be to look for analogues to modern English emotion words! I suggest that we can discover the troubadours' emotion words by recalling that theories of the emotions – those of Alcuin and of Aelred, for example – connected emotions to the mind (*mens* and *animus* in Latin), the body (*corpus*), especially the heart (*cor*), and the soul or spirit (*anima*).[165] Although the troubadours wrote in Old Occitan, they certainly knew about hearts and minds. They also used the soul – the *espirit* (spirit) – in connection with clearly affective language.[166] Some troubadours at the Toulousain court talked about the mind (*sens*), though generally when that faculty was in accord with or opposed to the heart (*cor*).[167] Thus Peire Vidal sang that his heart and mind gladly went to the place where *solatz* – solace, conversation, companionship – gave him joy,[168] while Bernart de Ventadorn complained that love eliminated good sense (*sen*).[169]

---

pros regina with the wife of Raimond VI, explaining that "the majority of those who served her called her *regina* (as daughter of king Alfonso II of Aragon)." However, Zoltán Falvy, "La cour d'Alphonse le Sage et la musique européenne," *Studia Musicologica Academiae Scientiarum Hungaricae* 25/1–4 (1983): 159–70 at 160, asserts that Cadenet was at the court of Aragon. If so, it is just possible that the "queen" of Cadenet's poems refers to the Eleonor who was queen-consort of James I of Aragon 1221–30, after which time the marriage was annulled. However, the first redaction of the 16th century vida by Jehan de Nostredame (Cadenet, 71) refers to Cadenet "retiring" to the court of the king of Castile; this would have been Alfonso VIII (1158–1214), whose daughter, Eleonor, married James I. We thus cannot be entirely sure that Cadenet was writing for Eleonor of Toulouse.

[165] Guerreau-Jalabert, "Aimer de fin cuer," 358–65, discusses the rich symbolism of the heart in vernacular courtly literature and traces its source largely to Christian texts.

[166] See below, n. 176. Already Cicero (see Chapter 1, n. 29) and Alcuin (see Chapter 3) knew theories that made the heart the site of emotions. This role persists in the modern world: see Scheer, "Topographies of Emotion," 49–50.

[167] The heart, like the mind, was also sometimes the site of intention, for example in Raimon de Miraval, No. 8, *Chansoneta farai*, l. 39: "Et ai vos o ben en cor a carvendre (And I have well in mind to sell you at a high price)."

[168] Peire Vidal, No. 1, *Be m'agrada*, ll. 6–8. For the meaning of *solatz*, see Claudie Amado, "Effets de la Croisade albigeoise sur les valeurs nobiliaires méridionales," in *La Croisade albigeoise. Actes du Colloque du Centre d'Etudes Cathares Carcassonne, 4–6 octobre 2002*, ed. Michel Roquebert (Carcassonne, 2004), 211–17.

[169] Bernart, No. 16, *Conortz, era sai eu be*, ll. 31–32: "car, qui en amor quer sen,/cel non a sen ni mezura (for he who seeks sense in love, /that person has neither mind nor moderation)." See also Aimeric de Belenoi, No. 5, *Assi co·l pres*, ll. 12–13: "mas anc mos sens no·s poc tan afortir/qe·m get del cor celei qui m'a conques (but never can my mind so fortify itself/that I [can] eject from my heart she who has conquered me)." The will (Latin: *voluntas*/Old Occitan: *voluntat*) was also part of the human mental apparatus. For Cadenet, No. 22, *S'ieu pogues ma voluntat*, ll. 1–4: "S'ieu pogues ma voluntat/ Forsar de segre mo sen, /Greu m'agra Amors tornat / A faire son mandamen (If I could force my

But the heart seems to have been the chief organ by far of the emotions for the troubadours.[170] I have therefore taken for my preliminary survey the words that the troubadours associated with the *cor*, heart. Moreover, in Old Occitan *cor* was so close to the word for body (*cors*) that sometimes the words were used interchangeably; sometimes, too, *cors* meant person or self.[171] Thus these words are extremely sensitive conveyers of emotions. Sometimes the eyes (*olh*), as well, were affected by the heart or vice versa.[172] I have included all these instances. Table 4.1 gives the results of this inquiry.[173]

These constituted, as it were, the "core emotions" for the Toulousain poets. But they were associated with other words that had like force as synonyms or antonyms. These are listed, along with the words on Table 4.1, in Table 4.2. Thus, for example, Peire Vidal wrote of being grief-stricken (*marritz*) and heavy (*grieus*).[174] Since *greu* is already on Table 4.1 and *marrit* is used to reinforce it – functioning, then, as a

will/ to follow my reason, /Love would have a hard time / getting me to follow its commands)."

[170] This accords with the observations of Glynnis M. Cropp, *Le vocabulaire courtois des troubadours de l'époque classique* (Geneva, 1975), 254–64, who bases her study on a different set of poets, the only overlapping ones being Bernart de Ventadorn and Gaucelm Faidit. See also Christopher Lucken, "*Chantars no pot gaire valer, si d'ins dal cor no mou lo chans.* Subjectivité et *poésie formelle* dans le *grand chant* des troubadours et des trouvères," in *Il cuore*, 373–413 at 392–401, who affirms the heart's central place as the wellspring, site, and container of love in troubadour poetry.

[171] See the forms and definitions for these words in William D. Paden, *An Introduction to Old Occitan* (New York, 1998), s.v., and Frede Jensen, "Provençal 'cor' and 'cors': A Flexional Dilemma," *Romance Philology* 28 (1974): 27–31.

[172] As in *Chanson*, 2:42, laisse 143, ll. 23–24: "De pietat e d'ira n'a·l cor tant doloiros/Qu'en sospira e·n plora de sos olhs ambedos. (His heart is so full of pity and sorrow and sadness that he sighs and weeps about it from both his eyes.)"

[173] In order to come up with a "common vocabulary" of emotion words used at the court, Table 4.1 lists only words that are associated with the *cor* by two or more authors. (I have included in this table an additional four poems of Peire Vidal not listed in n. 157. Four of them were identified by Loeb, "Les relations thesis," 74, as written for the Toulousain court: No. 5, *De chantar m'era laissatz*; No. 39, *Nulhs hom non pot d'amor gandir*; No. 41, *S'ieu fos en cort on hom tengues dreitura*; and No. 42, *Quant hom honratz torna en gran paubreira.* I also include No. 7, *Ges quar estius*, because it mentions Na Vierna.) I take *coratge* (*cor* + *-atge* [makes the noun abstract]) as equivalent to *cor*. Note that many, though not all, of these words are also listed in Cropp, *Le vocabulaire* as part of the troubadour's "courtly vocabulary," namely: *alegransa/alegra*; *amar/amor*; *amistat/amic*; *bon*; *coral*; *dezir*; *dolor*; *dous*; *gaug/jauzir*, and so on; *ira/irat*; *paor/espaven*; *pezansa/pezar*; *ric* (93–97). Georges Lavis, *L'expression de l'affectivité dans la poésie lyrique française du moyen âge (XIIe–XIIIe s.).* Etude sémantique et stylistique du réseau lexical joie-dolor (Paris, 1972), takes up a similar task with, however, a much larger corpus of texts (including those of the trouvères). Rather than find criteria within the poems for determining whether a word is "affective," Lavis takes a definition from his own day, and the words that he finds are grouped under modern French emotion terms.

[174] Peire Vidal, No. 5, *De chantar*, l. 52: "En sui sai marritz e grieus (About it I am here, grief-stricken and heavy)."

Table 4.1 *Old Occitan words associated with* cor[a]

---

alegransa (n.), joy
  alegrar (vb.), to rejoice[b]
amar (vb.), to love
  amor (n.), love
amistat (n.), friendship, love
  amic (n.), friend, lover
bon (adj.), (in *de bon cor*) sincere
coral (adj.), sincere
dezesperar (vb.), to despair
destrenher (vb.), to torment
dezir (n.), desire
  dezirar (vb.), to desire
  dezirier (n.), desire
  dezirion (adj.), desirous
doler (vb.), to grieve
  dolor (n.), grief
dousor (n.), sweetness
  adolzar (vb.), to sweeten
dur (adj.), hard
  endurzir (vb.), to make hard
esclairar (vb. refl.), to glow
felon (adj.), cruel
  esfelnir (vb. refl.), to make furious
  felnia (n.), treachery, sorrow, gall, anger
fin (adj.), sincere
gaug (n.), joy
  jauzir (vb.), to rejoice
  jauzen (past part./adj.), rejoicing
  joi (n.), joy
  joia (n.), joy
greu (adj.), heavy
ira (n.), anger, grief
  irat (adj.), angry, sad
leial (adj.), loyal
paor (n.), fear
  espaventar (vb. refl.), to be afraid
pezansa (n.), grief
  pezar (vb.), to grieve
plorar (vb.), to weep
  ploros (adj.), tearful
ric (adj.), noble[c]
sospirar (vb.), sigh

---

[a] Most of the translations into English come from Paden, *An Introduction* with
  additional help from Emil Levy, *Petit dictionnaire provençal-français*
  (Heidelberg, 1909). Here and in other tables listing vernacular words, parts of
  speech are labeled.
[b] With the verb form, all tenses (for example, the present and past participles,
  which often are used adjectivally) should be understood.
[c] For this sense of the multivalent *ric*, see Cropp, *Le vocabulaire*, 95–96.

Table 4.2 *Old Occitan emotional vocabulary at the Toulouse court*

adorar (vb.), adore
afan (n.), grief
alegramen (n.), joy
  alegransa (n.), joy
  alegrar (vb.), to rejoice
  alegria (n.), joy
amar (vb.), to love
  amor (n.), love
amic (n.), friendship, lover
  amistat (n.), friendship, love
angoisa (n.), anguish
anta (n.), shame
ardor (n.), ardor
baudor (n.), joy
  baut (adj.), joyous
benanansa (n.), happiness
bon (adj.), (in *de bon cor*) sincerely
caitiu (adj.), miserable
  caitivier (n.), misery
chantar (vb.), to sing
clamar (vb. refl.), to complain, lament
clar (adj.), gay
cochatz (adj.), tormented[a]
consir (n.), worry
  consirar (vb.), to be pensive (about)
coral (adj.), sincere
  coralmen (adv.), sincerely
corrosos (adj.), angry
dan (n.), grief
destemprar (vb.), (in *destemprar los cors*) to trouble
destorbier (n.), trouble
destrenher (vb.), to torment
dezesperar (vb.), to despair
dezir (n.), desire
  dezirar (vb.), to desire
  dezirier (n.), desire
  dezirion (adj.), desirous
dezonor (n.), dishonor
dol (n.), grief
  doler (vb.), to grieve
  dolor (n.), grief
  doloros (adj.), full of grief
dousor (n.), sweetness
  adolzar (vb.), to sweeten
dur (adj.), hard
  endurzir (vb.), to make hard

Table 4.2 *(cont.)*

---

esbaudir (vb., sometimes refl.), to rejoice
esclairar (vb. refl.), to glow
esfre (n.), fear
   esfredar (vb., sometimes refl.), to be troubled, to fear
esmai (n.), lamentation
esperansa (n.), hope
fe (n.), faith, good faith
   fezel (adj.), faithful
felon (adj.), cruel
   esfelnir (vb. refl.), to make furious
   felnesamen (adv.), bitterly
   felnia (n.), treachery, sorrow, gall, anger
fin (adj.), sincere, true
fremir (vb.), to shudder
gaug (n.), joy
   jauzir (vb.), to rejoice
   jauzen (past part./adj.), rejoicing
   joi (n.), joy
   joia (n.), joy
gemer (vb.), to moan
greu (adj.), heavy
honrar (vb.), to honor
ira (n.), anger, grief
   iraiser (vb. refl.), to become angry
   irat (adj.), angry, sad
lagrema (n.), tear
langor (n.), melancholy, languor[b]
leial (adj.), loyal
mal (1) (n.), pain
mal (2) (adj.), (in *ab mal cor*) angry
marrimen (n.), sadness
   marrit (adj.), grief-stricken
martelar (vb.), (in *martelar las dens*) gnash (the teeth)
merce (n.), pity
morn (adj.), sad
ner (adj.), black (with emotion)
oltracuidamen (n.), presumption
orgolh (n.), pride
orgolhos (adj.), prideful
paor (n.), fear
   espaventar (vb. refl.), to be afraid
   espaventier (n.), fear
paratge (n.), parity, peership
pena (n.), pain, suffering
penedir (vb.), to atone
pensiu (adj.), pensive

Table 4.2 (*cont.*)

perilh (n.), sorrow
pes (n.), burden
pezansa (n.), grief
   pezar (vb.), to grieve
pietat (n.), pity
planher (vb.), to lament
plazer (n. formed from vb. inf.), pleasure
plor (n.), weeping
   plorar (vb.), to weep
   ploros (adj.), tearful
rancura (n.), complaint
   rancurar (vb. refl.), to complain
regart (n.), fear
reprovier (n.), bitter words
ric (adj.), noble
rire (vb.), to laugh
salut (n.), greeting (of love)
sobrafan (n.), extreme sorrow
sofrir (vb.), to suffer
solatz (n.), solace
sospir (n.), sigh
   sospirar (vb.), sigh
talen (n.), desire
temensa (n.), fear
   temer (vb.), to fear
   temoros (adj.), fearful
tenchar (vb.), to color (the complexion [red, black], from emotion)
tenson (n.), dispute
tormen (n.), torment
trebalh (n.), worry, torment
tremer (vb.), to tremble
tristeza/tristor (n.), sorrow
   trist (adj.), sad
vergonha (n.), shame
voler (vb.), to want

[a] Or, more properly, the pp. of the verb *cochar*, to torment.

[b] On this word and its many ramifications in poetry as well as in scholastic and monastic thought, see Valentina Atturo, "*Languor carnis*. Echi di memoria salomonica nella fisiologia emozionale dei trovatori," in *Dai pochi ai molti. Studi in onore di Roberto Antonelli*, ed. Paolo Canettieri and Arianna Punzi (Rome, 2014), 49–78.

synonym – it is included in Table 4.2. In another poem, Vidal sings of not being joyous (*jauzens*) because of a sadness (*marrimens*) that has come over him; here *marrimens* is an antonym of *jauzens* and is also included on Table 4.2.[175] Table 4.2 thus represents the emotional vocabulary of the Toulouse poets better than Table 4.1 does (though it could not have been arrived at without the latter). But it, too, is unquestionably incomplete.[176] Compared to the lists of Latin emotion words we have seen, the vernacular list appears exceptionally rich and subtle. That the Toulousain court could draw on both languages gave it multiple advantages for feeling and expressing those feelings.

For there were others at court who mainly wrote in Latin, as we see from most of the counts' *acta*. How can we be sure which words in the charters had emotional force? There is only one mention of the "heart" in all of the charters – and that one is in Old Occitan.[177] But in that fact we have a key: we may gather a short list of the words in the vernacular documents that correspond to those on Table 4.2. And because the clauses of the *acta* are quite formulaic, we find corresponding clauses in Latin. In a further step, I have identified other Latin words that seem to correspond fairly closely to the language of the poets. Finally I have culled the synonyms and antonyms of those words. Table 4.3 presents the result of this inquiry.

"Official" feelings: the emotions of the charters

This last list is made up of words drawn from the charters of the counts. An earlier generation of historians would have dismissed such documents as utterly unemotional even if they contained an "emotion word." This is no longer the assumption.[178] Nor is the formulaic nature of the *acta* a serious objection, since emotions are generally expressed via much

---

[175] *Ibid.*, No. 7, *Ges quar estius*, ll. 3–6: "Non sui jauzens,/ Qu'us marrimens/Me ven de lai (I am not joyous/ because a sadness comes/ to me from there)."

[176] Unlike the words on Table 4.1, the additions on Table 4.2 are not necessarily found in more than one of the Toulousain authors. But in order to be included, they are associated with that common vocabulary. I have not included associations with the word *amor*, as that would be an endless list; love is connected with nearly every feeling, attribute, and action. This explains why *grat* (thanks) is not on the list even though it is connected to *amor* in *Chanson*, 2:220, laisse 174, l. 30. Directly connected with the *espirit* in these poems are *clamar*, *doler*, *jauzir*, *pezar*, and *plorans* (derived from *plorar*). The only word among these not already on Table 4.1 is *clamar*, which I include on Table 4.2, not only because of its association with *espirit* but because it is linked to *doler* in *Chanson*, 2:68, laisse 149, l. 6.

[177] *Cat. Rai.*, 536, p. 386 (1226).

[178] Undermined above all by the work of Fredric L. Cheyette, as (for the Midi) in his *Ermengard of Narbonne and the World of the Troubadours* (Ithaca, NY, 2001).

Table 4.3 *Emotion words in the* acta[a]

affectuose (adv.), affectionately
　affectuosus (adj.), full of affectionate feeling
<u>*amar*</u> (vb.), to love
　<u>*amor*</u> (n.), love
amicabiliter (adv.), in friendly manner
　amicus (n.), friend
　amic (n.), friend
　amicabilis (adj.), friendly
　amicitia (n.), friendship
　<u>*amistat*</u> (n.), friendship, love
calliditas (n.), trick
carus (adj.), dear
　carissimus (adj.), dearest
compania (n.), companionship
<u>*clamor*</u> (n.), complaint
<u>*decipio*</u> (n.), deception
　decipere (vb.), to deceive
devotio (n.), devotion[b]
dilectio (n.), love
　dilectus (adj.), beloved
dolus (n.), treachery
fe (n.), good faith
fealtad (n.), loyalty, fidelity
fidelitas (n.), loyalty, fidelity
<u>*fidelis*</u> (adj. and n.), worthy of belief; loyal person, vassal
　fideliter (adv.), loyally, faithfully
　fides (n.), good faith (in *in bona fide*), faith (in *in Dei fide*)
　<u>*fin*</u> (adj.), sincere, faithful
fraus (n.), fraud
　defraudatus (adj.), defrauded
gaudere (vb.), to rejoice
hilarissime (adv.), most cheerfully
honor (n.), honor
　honorare (vb.), honor
indignatio (n.), indignation
ingenium (n.), trick
inimicus (n.), enemy
injuria (n.), injury, insult
<u>*ira*</u> (n.), anger
<u>*leial*</u> (adj.), loyal
machinatio (n.), plot
　machinari (vb.), to plot
<u>*misericordia*</u> (n.), pity
offendere (vb.), to offend, hurt (feelings)
osculari (vb.), to kiss, exchange kisses
<u>*pietas*</u> (n.), piety
<u>*salus*</u> (n.), greeting (to *amici*)
<u>*sincerus*</u> (adj.), sincere

Table 4.3 (*cont.*)

societas (n.), fellowship
specialis (adj.), special
timere (vb.), to fear
voluntas (n.), (in *bona voluntas* and *spontanea voluntas*), good will

[a] Old Occitan and Latin words are here interleaved. Underlined words correspond directly or closely with those on Table 4.2. All other words are associated with those underlined as synonyms or antonyms. I have regularized spellings; for example, *karissimus* in the charters is here rendered *carissimus*.

[b] This is termed an *affectus* in *Cat. Rai.*, 243, p. 204 (1193): "vestre devocionis affectum attendentes."

repeated phrases ("I love you"; "I'm furious at him") that nevertheless have (or at least are meant to have) real affective meaning. Furthermore, although few of the charters express any emotions, those that do are quite clearly associated with specific recipients. Feelings, even in charters, are not directed randomly.

Precisely because emotions have objects, we need to know the contexts – the scenarios and fantasies that evoked them – to understand their meaning, their usage, and the ways in which they worked together. Since the *acta* are less complex than the poems and also refer to real-life events, we begin with them. Three sorts of charters were particularly replete with emotion words: those that gave fortifications (*castra*) to men in return for oaths of fidelity and other obligations; those that granted privileges to especially favored monasteries and towns; and those that were directed to some of the counts' bailiffs (*bajuli*).

Laurent Macé has already observed the affective charge in many of these charters.[179] In them, the count professes his love for his *fideles* – his faithful followers, all male; his bailiffs (again all male); and his favored institutions, whether towns or religious houses. He uses terms of love (*amor* and *dilectio*) when speaking of his *fideles*. If he writes to his bailiffs, he calls them his friends (*amici*), and greets them with love (*dilectio*). And so on.

Let us look at a few examples. In a charter from 1218, Raimond VI spoke to "his beloved and faithful men (*dilectis ac fidelibus suis*)," in the town of Agen, offering them "greeting and sincere love (*salutem et*

---

[179] Macé, *Les comtes*, 251–84, a chapter entitled "Amour, colère et pardon." See also Macé, "Amour et fidélité: le comte de Toulouse et ses hommes (XIIe–XIIIe siècles)," in *Les sociétés méridionales à l'âge féodal (Espagne, Italie et sud de la France X[e]–XIIIe s.). Hommage à Pierre Bonnassie*, ed. Hélène Débax (Toulouse, 1999), 299–304.

sinceram dilectionem)" and authorizing them to clear a blockage in the Garonne river.[180] A charter concerning the same count and men, but this time drawn up in Old Occitan, was addressed to his "beloved and faithful men *(als sieus amatz e fidels)*" of Agen, offering them "greeting and friendship *(salus et amisteit)*" and informing them of the appointment over them of his beloved and faithful *(amat et fidel)* seneschal Guilhem Arnaud.[181] To his bailiffs, and particularly to Doat Alaman (1194–1234), Raimond VI wrote in exceptionally affectionate language. "To all his friends and bailiffs and especially Doat Alaman whom this letter reaches: greeting and love *(salutem et dilectionem)*. We bring to the attention of your love *(dilectioni vestre)*" that the count is taking the Cistercian monastery of Bonnecombe under his protection.[182] Doat Alaman was, as Laurent Macé has pointed out, an "assiduous" member of the count's entourage, a man raised from the petty nobility to become one of Raimond's most trusted aides.[183] Let us conclude our survey of the terms of affection in Raimond VI's charters by noting that in one of them a kiss accompanied his profession of fidelity.[184] Many others paired fidelity with love *(dilectio)*.[185]

Nor were the terms different in the charters of Raimond's son. For example, in 1222, not yet count, Raimondet issued letters to all his "friends and armed men *(amicis et valitoribus)*" to inform them that he had put under his own power – as well as that of his friends and armed men – the hospital at Aubrac. He ordered his men to guard and defend the hospital "from every injury and loss if they want to have our love *(si amorem nostrum habere desiderant)*."[186]

Side by side with professions of love, however, were somber worries. Just as Aelred had talked about the vicious emotions of cupidity – envy, suspicion, and ambition – that destroyed sweet friendship, so the counts anticipated – and tried to stave off – deceit and fraud. The charters repeated constantly that all promises were made, all gifts were given and taken, and every loyalty was offered "in good faith and without deceit *(bona fide et sine dolo)*."[187] When Raimond VI issued a charter of

---

[180] *Cat. Rai.*, 424, pp. 320–21 (1218). A few charters of Raimond V may be cited as examples of love language. Indeed, Cheyette, *Ermengard of Narbonne*, 214, cites one of them, *Cat. Rai.*, 99, p. 120 (c. 1163), for the scribes' skill in turning "the plain speaking of the counting house into the finely spun language of deference and fidelity, loyalty and love."

[181] *Ibid.*, 430, p. 323 (1218).   [182] *Ibid.*, 300, p. 240 (c. 1200).

[183] Macé, *Les comtes*, 108, 166. Rieger, "Alamanda de Castelnau'" argues that Alamanda belonged to his family and was at the Toulouse court. The identification is based on the name association of Alamanda with Alaman.

[184] *Cat. Rai.*, 315, p. 250 (1202).

[185] For example, *ibid.*, 316, pp. 250–51 (between 1202–3); *ibid.*, 424, pp. 320–21 (1218).

[186] *Ibid.*, 485, p. 356 (1222).

[187] For example, from Raimond V: *ibid.*, 156, p. 153 (1176); 158, pp. 154–55 (1176); 201, pp. 178–79 (1185); 208, p. 183 (1185/1186); 224, pp. 192–93 (1189); 252, p. 210

protection and exemption from tolls for the abbot and monks at the Cistercian abbey of Candeil, he added a warning to "any of our other friends (*coetero ullus amicorum nostrorum*)" not to dare to take anything from the monks, and "we cast out (*ejicimus*) from our love (*dilectione*) and fidelity (*fidelitate*) him who would hold this command in contempt."[188] When the same count received a promise of fidelity from Raimond Aerradus and Raimond de Mauguio for the fortification of La Rouquette, they agreed to return it at the command of the count and promised that "we will not devise any trick or plot (*aliquam fraudem vel machinacionem*)" to avoid such a requisition. And if anything should be taken by anyone from the count or his men "we will not have love or society or fidelity with him except for the purpose of recovering the fortification (*non habebimus cum illo amorem vel societatem vel fidelitatem, nisi propter causam recuperandi castellum*)."[189]

When confronted with evidence of such fraud, the counts threatened to wreak their anger and indignation on the wrongdoer. The charter of Raimondet in favor of Aubrac warned that if any of those men he had called his friends "should attack the brethren and other men living in the Hospital of Aubrac or their properties in any place or cause them harm or injury: in that very hour let him feel overcome by our anger (*ira*) and indignation (*indignatione*) and separated from our love (*amore*)."[190]

(1194): "bona fide, sine fraude et dolo"; from Raimond VI: 325, p. 259 (1203); 344, p. 270 (1204/1205); 351, pp. 274–77 (1206); 362, pp. 282–83 (1208); and so on. Interestingly, the formula was rather little used in the charters of Raimond VII, but see words attributed to him in the humiliating Treaty of Meaux and Paris, *ibid.*, 554, pp. 394–95 (1229): "bona fide, sine fraude et malo ingenio." On fears of treason at the court of Toulouse, see Laurent Macé, "La trahison soluble dans le pardon? Les comtes de Toulouse et la félonie (XIIe–XIIIe siècles)," in *La trahison au Moyen Âge*, ed. Mäité Billoré and Myriam Soria (Rennes, 2010), 369–84. Reddy, *The Making of Romantic Love*, 45–67, considers trickery a regular and admired characteristic of "aristocratic speech" at this time. But both Aelred (see above at n. 127) and the counts of Toulouse evidently detested it.

[188] *Cat. Rai.*, 316, pp. 250–51 (betw. 1202–3).   [189] *Ibid.*, 350, p. 273 (1206).

[190] *Ibid.*, 485, p. 356 (1222). Studies of the emotions of feuding and vengeance may be helpful here. Briefly, some historians, for example Althoff, "Ira Regis," argue that the "anger" and "enmity" involved in feuds were highly calculated and ritualized. They "performed" power in an age that valued gestures rather than written constitutions. The meanings of these performances were understood and accepted by others at the time; they served political and legal – not particularly "emotional" – functions. Other historians, however, for example Richard Kaeuper, "Vengeance and Mercy in Chivalric *Mentalités*," in *Peace and Protection in the Middle Ages*, ed. T. B. Lambert and David Rollason (Toronto, 2009), 168–80, argue that feuding was essentially irrational, the expression of a basic human urge for revenge. Putting these two views together is Stephen D. White, for example in "The Politics of Anger," who, while emphasizing the strategic aspects of displays of anger and other such emotions in feuds, nevertheless does not deny their emotionality.

The disappointments of love

Thus, the charters professed love but also anticipated disappointments deriving from faithlessness and deceit. The troubadour poets at the court of Toulouse had a larger palette of words with which to say many of the same things about their own loves.[191] However, there was one major difference between the woes of the counts and those of the poets: the poets were ostensibly speaking of love for a woman, while the counts' charters were concerned about love between men. I suggest that this was a displacement of the very serious anxieties of the male world onto women, who hardly "counted" at the court.

Most of the songs written for the counts of Toulouse were about the poet's pure love, grounded in the sincerest of motives. This was contrasted with the treachery of the poet's lady, who thwarted his just hopes and expectations at every turn. And nevertheless, the poet – the lover – persisted in loving, serving, and lamenting. If he invoked his *ira*, it meant, in Old Occitan, a *mixture* of sorrow and anger, not anger alone.

Thus Bernart de Ventadorn, writing for Raimond V at some point between c. 1150 and c. 1180 begins *Be m'an perdut lai enves Ventadorn* with a lament about his lady: how much he loves her, how beastly and harsh (*salvatj' e grama*) she is toward him. By the end of the poem he is accusing her of deceiving him: "As for me, I say to you that evil has come to me,/ for the badly-disposed beauty has betrayed me."[192] In *Conortz, era sai*, his lady once favored the poet with greetings, "friendship" (*amistatz* – here the friendship of lovers), and messages. Now she shows him a "savage heart, hard and wrathful" (*fers cors, durs et iratz*). She blames him for something that he did in good faith (*per bona fe*) for Count Raimond. Nevertheless, the poet swears to continue to serve her and by the end of the poem he has high hopes: "for from my Conort [that is, Consolation, Bernart's *senhal* or nickname for his lady] I expect/ still good fortune."[193] In *Lo rossinhols s'esbaudeya*, the poet laments that because he is too faithful and *not* treacherous he is unlucky in love: "He has more of Love who courts with pride (*orgolh*) and deceit (*enjan*)/ than he who

---

[191] Some of these ideas were already suggested by Loeb, "Les relations" and "Aimer et servir." See also Mario Mancini, *Metafora feudale. Per una storia dei trovatori* (Bologna, 1993). I cannot begin to cite all the research that has been done on the troubadours here discussed. I cite only selected recent literature.

[192] Bernart, No. 12, *Be m'an perdut lai enves Ventadorn*, ll. 34–35: "per me·us o dic que mals m'en es vengutz,/car träit m'a la bela de mal aire." On Bernart, see Simon Gaunt, "A Martyr to Love: Sacrificial Desire in the Poetry of Bernart de Ventadorn," *Journal of Medieval and Early Modern Studies* 31/3 (2001): 477–506, and Mancini, *Metafora*, 63–86, who (67) speaks of his "retorica dell'antitesi (rhetoric of antitheses)."

[193] *Ibid.*, No. 16, *Conortz, era sai*, ll. 53–54: "car de Mo Conort aten/ enquera bon' aventura."

implores all day/ and goes about too humbly./ For Love hardly wants the one /who is as honest (*francs*) and faithful (*fis*) as I am./ That [fact] has ruined all my affairs/ since I was never false (*faus*) nor treacherous (*trichaire*)."[194] The poems of Bernart reflect the charters' preoccupations with love, good faith, and the likelihood – indeed, in his case, the near certainty – of betrayal.

Peire Vidal, writing after Bernart, created a "cycle" of songs about his unrequited love for a lady named *Na Vierna*. In *Ajostar e lassar* the poet's lady "is tormenting me (*auci me*)." He continues: "When I saw her, she struck /my gluttonous heart/ so that ever after I take pains for her good/ and she does nothing but bad to me."[195] This sets up the theme for the rest of the poem, which contrasts the lover who "served with a faithful heart (*servi ab cor fi*)," to his beloved, who wishes him banished and has given him nothing but a ribbon for his pains. Well, admits the poet, he got a bit more from her than that: "Yes, I had: for one morning/ I entered her house/ and I kissed in secret/ her mouth and her chin."[196] At this point, his recompense has become erotic, and to make the point even clearer, the poet adds: "I have had that and nothing more/ And I am totally dead, if she holds more back."[197]

In the next stanzas the poet sighs and weeps while his beloved shows him "the heart of a dragon (*cor a de drago*)." Because of her he was exiled, forced to become a pilgrim to the Holy Land. The moral: "Every man should pursue his wellbeing,/ before a cruel lord mistreats him."[198] In this poem, the lord is the lady. She "says bad things to me, and smiles to the others who are around," playing the cruel lord who feigns mildness.[199] Yet the poet persists, locked in the prison (*preizo*) of Love, hoping against hope for her fidelity: "And then, because I love her so and believe in her,/ I should never find bad faith (*mala fe*) in her."[200]

Another song in the cycle, *Tant me platz*, has the poet back from the Holy Land and still talking about the kiss: "I would have been better paid

---

[194] *Ibid.*, No. 29, *Lo rossinhols s'esbaudeya*, ll. 9–14: "Mais a d'Amor qui domneya/ ab orgolh et ab enjan/ que cel que tot jorn merceya/ ni·s vai trop umilian./ C'a penas vol Amors celui/ qu'es francs e fis si com eu sui./ So m'a tout tot mon afaire/ c'anc no fui faus ni trichaire."

[195] Peire Vidal, No. 3, *Ajostar e lassar*, ll. 10–13: "Quant la vi si·m feri/ Mon coratge gloto,/ Qu'ades poinh el sieu pro,/ E no·m fai si mal no."

[196] *Ibid.*, ll. 25–28: "Si agui, qu'un mati/Intrei dins sa maizo/E·lh baiziei a lairo/ La boca e·l mento."

[197] *Ibid.*, ll. 29–30: "So n'ai agut e no mais re/ E sui totz mortz, si·l plus rete."

[198] *Ibid.*, ll. 44–45: "Totz hom deu percassar son be,/Ans que mals seinhers lo malme." On the significance of "feudal metaphors" like the lady's "lordship," see Mancini, *Metafora*, 163–86.

[199] *Ibid.*, ll. 36–37: "Qu'a me di mal e ri/ Als autres deviro."

[200] *Ibid.*, ll. 74–75: "E doncs pus tan l'am e la cre,/Ja no·i dei trobar mala fe."

than any man born,/if she had given me the stolen kiss/ Or even conceded it."[201] In *Tant ai lonjamen sercat*, he complains that "She has mistreated and deceived me;/ by her beautiful companionship/ she has so quickly stolen my heart/ that I could hardly believe it. I love her more than myself, which is why she reproaches me/ and seeks my harm knowingly/ for with her I find neither 'friendship' [*amistat* again] nor pity."[202] In the charters, the count threatened to wreak his anger against those not his "friends." Here Vidal's lady is the lord, and she is punishing her man: "Good lady, if you please, I surrender to you,/ and if it doesn't please you, I do it all the same;/ for I know well that in no way/ have I power over you : much grievous torment suffers/ a wretch who falls under the anger of a lord (*ira de senhor*)/ and finds neither support nor help."[203]

In another poem, *Son ben apoderatz*, however, he blames the count himself for abusing him and exiling him from court.[204] This is the count's *ira et indignatio* in action, and Peire "reproaches" Raimond for exercising it.[205] He chastises the count, peppering his lines with as many words of anger, deceit, shame, and torment as of joy and love, and ending with bitter upbraiding: "Lady Vierna, he is a proven/ and badly educated villein/ who has distanced us/ from our 'friendship' (*amistatz*)./ And that is why my Castiat,/ if he is burned by Rome,/ it's just as well, but it's a pity,/ since he is not wholly corrupted there."[206] He blames the count for preventing him from gaining the just recompenses of friendship. Calling the count by the *senhal* "Castiat" may be another way of unbraiding him: the word can mean "chastised one."

Let us sum up the main emotional themes of Bernart and Peire at the court of Toulouse under Raimond V. Deceit followed upon faithfulness; disappointment followed upon love. The poets served their lords (who were sometimes their ladies), but they were not rewarded, or not rewarded enough.

---

[201] *Ibid.*, No. 4, *Tant me platz*, ll. 25–28: "Mielhs pagatz fora qu'om natz,/ Si·l bais emblatz mi fos datz/ O neis autreyatz."

[202] *Ibid.*, No. 8, *Tant ai lonjamen sercat*, ll. 19–25: "Trait m'a e galiat;/ Ab bella paria/ M'a si tot mon cor emblat,/ Que ja no·l creiria./ Lei ami plus que mi, per que·m repren/ Et enquier me mon dan ad escien;/ Qu'ab lieis non truep amistat ni pitansa."

[203] *Ibid.*, ll. 65–70: "Bona domna, si·us platz, a vos mi ren,/ E si no·us plaz, si m'o fatz issamen; / Que be conosc que per nugun'esmansa/ No·us ai forsa: mout trai greu malanansa/ Chaitius que chai en ira de senhor/ E non troba sosteing ni valedor."

[204] For the abuse, see *ibid.*, No. 30, *Son ben apoderatz*, ll. 17–18: "Q'enqer par als costatz/ Con ieu fui laig menatz (which still appears by my ribs/ when I was treated in ugly manner)."

[205] *Ibid.*, l. 25: "Auzir deu repropchier (he should hear reproach)."

[206] *Ibid.*, ll. 71–78: "Na Vierna, proatz/Vilas mal enseignatz/Es qi nos a loignatz/ De nostras amistatz./ Per qe, mos Chastiatz/ S'es per Romas crematz,/Si·lh fai, mas es pechatz,/ Pos totz no·i es taratz."

Gaucelm Faidit, another poet writing for Raimond V, was only slightly less disappointed. He says he was far more successful than Peire Vidal in romancing his lady: "Sweetly and graciously she conquered me,/when she was willing that I see/ her beautiful body prone, white and joyous,/from which may good come to me!/ And don't imagine that I would have left/ if she had allowed it to me/when I saw that which I most wanted to see!"[207] And indeed, he says, she soon allowed more than that: "Therefore, I am so well submitted to her/ since that which I sought of her/ she gave me, that it cannot please me/that another lady retain me."[208] Even so, following the pattern that we have seen in both the charters and the poems of Bernart and Peire Vidal, Gaucelm fears that deceits will mar his happiness: "Because of her, in whom I have good hope/may that joy come/ about which may neither blabbermouths,/ adversaries,/ false ones,/ nor jealous ones,/ have a thought!/ Nor let the blabbing/ nor the rude crying of 'false love!'/ overcome us or our love!"[209]

Gaucelm's *D'un dotç bell plaser* alternates love and deceit continually. He begins by crediting his poetic abilities to his lady and the "sweet and beautiful pleasure" (*dotç bell plaser*) that she brings him. Yet he fears his poems are too unrestrained: "for in restraint/ my mouth/ is not held back."[210] He is torn, fearing to say too much and wanting to speak: "Will I die if I silence my praise/ or if my words do not have savor for her?"[211] He professes his loyal fealty (*lial fe*) to her, but "I fear/ that she will hold me a liar."[212] He tries to banish such thoughts from his mind: "Go away! (*vai t'en!*)." Here the poet fears his own deceit, but in the end good faith triumphs.

Gaucelm's *Oimais taing que fassa parer* has a similar theme. The poet is so full of joy that "I scarcely know/ who I was or who I am, I am so happy!"[213] But, as in *D'un dotç*, he must restrain himself: "Now I make

---

[207] Gaucelm Faidit, No. 19, *D'un amor, on s'es asis*, ll. 49–55: "Soau e gient me concis,/can volc c'ieu vis/ son bell cors blanc gioios giaser,/ don bes me vegna!/ e no cresatç ce ieu partis,/s'il m'o sofris,/ can vi so qu'ieu plus volc veser!"

[208] *Ibid.*, ll. 65–67: "Pero tan be·l soi aclis,/ can so que·ll quis/ me det, qe [g]es no·m pot plaser/ c'autra·m retegna."

[209] *Ibid.*, ll. 71–80: "per lieis, en cui ai bon esper/ ce giois m'en vegna;/ don janglos,/ contrarios,/ fals, ni gelos,/ no·i ag' entendensa!/ ce·l ganglars,/ ni·l cridars/ braus: 'fals amars!'/ nos ni nostr' amor vensa!" On the joy of the troubadour, which is often anticipatory rather than expressing pleasure in present well-being, see William D. Paden, "The Beloved Lady in Medieval Galician-Portuguese and Occitan Lyric Poetry," *La corónica: A Journal of Medieval Hispanic Languages, Literatures, and Cultures* 32/2 (2004): 69–84, esp. 78.

[210] *Ibid.*, No. 20, *D'un dotç bell plaser*, ll. 43–45: "car en fre/ no·s te/ ma boca; ... "

[211] *Ibid.*, ll. 67–68: "ni morai, si·n tais lausor,/ o si·l dir no l'an sabor!"

[212] *Ibid.*, ll. 84–85: " ... ai paor/ que·m tegna per mentidor."

[213] *Ibid.*, No. 23, *Oimais taing que fassa parer*, ll. 15–16: "c'a penas sai/ qui fui ni qui sui, tant be·m vai!"

the effort, for now I have power,/ since such great and rich joy falls to me,/ to hide and keep my joy."[214] In part he fears outside betrayers: "I know to hide my heart,/ so that the gossips (*lausengier*) full of deceit/ will never know what I best remember."[215] But he also fears that he himself might offend his lady, as lovers do. More triumphantly than in *D'un dotç*, the poet decides in the end that the pleasures are worth the risk: "No man should fear loving/ for, more than he offends in a thousand days/ Love makes up for in just one evening."[216] Here, all the follies and desperation that love brings in its train – and that the poem has recounted in detail before this – are dispelled by a night of lovemaking. Unlike Bernart de Ventadorn and Peire Vidal, Gaucelm advertises his bedroom successes to Count Raimond V.

When we turn to the court of his son and successor, Raimond VI, for whom Raimon de Miraval wrote, sexual allusions are yet more abundant. If this correlates with the fact that Raimond had five wives and at least three children out of wedlock, it is only to suggest that both count and troubadour had the dispoisiton of the duke of Mantua in Verdi's *Rigoletto*: "La donna è mobile."

Thus, Raimon's allusions to women were often bitter, pointing to deceits, not love. As he puts it in one poem, "Because of the wrongs that the ladies do/ the service of Love turns into decadence./ For they demonstrate so much deceit/ that the most faithful lover gets angry (*s'irais*)."[217] In *Chansoneta farai, Vencut* the poet's lady has prostituted herself to the highest bidder: "He can enter first who gives more."[218] She had previously given herself to the poet; now he feels sullied: "And although I have had joy of it,/ now I want to be pure and rid of it."[219]

---

[214] *Ibid.*, ll. 41–43: "Ara m'effortz, c'ar ai poder,/ pois tant rics jauzimens m'eschai,/ de mon joi celar ni tener."

[215] *Ibid.*, ll. 48–50: " ... sai mon cor escondire,/ qe ja lausengier d'engan ple/ no sabran don plus mi sove." The *lausengiers* appear again, still trying to spoil the poet's happiness, in *ibid.*, No. 27, *Jauzens en gran benananssa*, l. 36.

[216] *Ibid.*, No. 23, ll. 61–63: "Nuills hom d'amar no·is deu temer,/ que, plus q'en mil jorns non forfai, /esmend' Amors en un sol ser."

[217] Raimon de Miraval, No. 19, *Tuich cill que vant demandan*, ll. 17–20: "Pels tortz que las dompnas fan/ Torna dompneis en abais,/ Que tant li mostron d'engan/ Per que·l plus fis drutz s'irais." In Miraval, No. 21, *Pueis onguan no·m valc estius*, his lady is deceitful but no one will believe him because in l. 23: "C'als sieus bels digz lo mieus dregz par niens (for [in comparison] to her beautiful words my right seems nothing)." For Raimon de Miraval, see Paul Andraud, *La vie et l'oeuvre du troubadour Raimon de Miraval. Étude sur la littérature et la société méridionales à la veille de la guerre des albigeois* (Marseille, 1973; rpt. of Paris 1902 ed.).

[218] *Ibid.*, No. 8, *Chansoneta farai, Vencut*, l. 8: "Pus premiers pot intrar selh que mais dona."

[219] *Ibid.*, ll. 9–10: "E, si tot m'en ai joy avut,/ er en vuel esser mons e blos."

In *Dels quatre mestiers valens*, one out of ten ladies are ignorant (*desconoisens*).[220] Happily, however, in that poem the poet claims to "know one lady whose heart is noble/ and whose merit is true."[221] He renders to her "my heart and both my eyes,/ and Miraval and my songs."[222] This lady may have been the one he called *Mais d'amic* (More than a Friend/Lover) in several poems. In *S'a dreg fos chantars grazitz*, she has him serve her for three years. He demurs: "for in a love affair without any treachery/ a term of three years is grievous."[223] No doubt it was foolish to enter into an agreement like that, but he was powerless to resist: "Lady, you are my guide in all,/ for I have neither folly nor sense/ but at your command."[224]

In other poems, Raimon reveals that his lady has given him no recompense whatever for his service. In *Be m'agrada* he complains that "it does not please you to deign to thank me for anything,/ but it pleases you that I die of desire."[225] He wants to make love: "For I desire that your desiring body/ grant me the precious pleasure."[226] He assures her that "I desire you so well without any deceit."[227] But others – the wicked gossips at court – speak evil and "turn the lovers/ and turn the precious ladies/ and turn many joyous men into miserable people."[228] Nevertheless, Raimon is the perfect servant: rewarded or not, "in serving a powerful lord/ the good server is happy."[229]

But this does not prevent him from complaining. In *Enquer non a guaire* he cannot understand why his lady gives him nothing. He has served her for "five months and two years" and she still has not kissed him.[230] He takes recourse in the usual assurances: "that I am not a trickster to her,/ nor a false lover nor a prankster."[231] In another poem she neglects to send

---

[220] *Ibid.*, No. 9, *Dels quatre mestiers valens*, l. 10.

[221] *Ibid.*, ll. 48–50: "La say don sos cors es gens/ E sa valors/ Fin' ... "

[222] *Ibid.*, ll. 57–58: "Mon cor li ren e·ls huils amdos,/ E Miraval e mas chansos."

[223] *Ibid.*, No. 10, *S'a dreg fos chantars grazitz*, ll. 53–54: "Qu'en domney ses totz enguans/ Es greus termes de tres ans."

[224] *Ibid.*, ll. 46–48: "Domna, vos m'etz del tot guitz,/ Qu'ieu non ai foldat ni sen/ Mas al vostre mandamen."

[225] *Ibid.*, No. 11, *Be m'agrada·l bels tems d'estiu*, ll. 7–8: " ... vos non platz que re·m deingnes grazir,/Mas agrada·us car me muor de desir."

[226] *Ibid.*, ll. 11–12: "Qar desir que·l rics benestans/ Vostre cors desiran m'aiziu."

[227] *Ibid.*, l. 14: " ... tan be·us desir ses totz engans."

[228] *Ibid.*, ll. 26–28: "Lausengier que viro·ls amans,/ E viron las domnas presanz/ E manz jais viron en chaitiu." However, in his No. 23, *Tals vai mon chan enqueren*, the poet is quite unusually well rewarded, as in ll. 29–31: "Qu'ab lieys ai tot quan volia/ D'amor e de drudairia (For from her I have as much as I wanted/ of love and of the matters of love)."

[229] *Ibid.*, No. 11, *Be m'agrada·l bels tems d'estiu*, ll. 41–42: "Per servir en ric seingnoriu/ Es bons servire benanans."

[230] *Ibid.*, No. 15, *Enquer non a guaire*, l. 49: "Passat son cinc mes et dui an."

[231] *Ibid.*, ll. 40–41: "Qu'ieu no·lh sui trichaire/ Fals drutz ni bauzaire."

him a "greeting or anything with which I might rejoice/ nor does she want me to return to her."[232] In still another, following a pattern that we have come to expect, "although [my lady] is cool/ and shows me pride and disdain,/ I will never tire of being her servant."[233] As befits a *fidelis*, he is the best of servants, for in him "there is no deceit at all."[234] In these poems love is a source of great pain, contrary to the way things should be. To his lady he writes: "Mais d'Amic, the best and the worst/ one should share in common./ But you have the joy and the merit and the profit,/ and I have no more than sorrow mingled with anger (*ira*) and a melancholy heart (*cor fello*)."[235] Sexual and love relations at court, so bound up with ideas about service without recompense, are ordinarily unhappy affairs.[236]

Was the same true of the poets patronized by Countess Eleonor, the one woman at court who commanded an entourage of sorts? Cadenet, who wrote three poems for her, also wrote one for her husband, Raimond VI. It begins with love's presumed advantages: "The good reputation that [a lover] has from it [Love], since he is noble and worthwhile,/ compensates him for his pains and his torments./ And also he ought then to rejoice/ about the other good that he hopes to enjoy from it./ And in that way, he can destroy his complaint."[237] Is the poet serious? Does good reputation really compensate for pain and torment? Does the hope of enjoying sex really make up for all the lover's frustrations? Soon the poet reveals his caustic take on the whole matter: he *praises* the gossips at court. Their lies tell the ultimate truth – that loving is indeed, as Cadenet's editor Josef Zemp puts it, nothing but "vain ambition."[238]

Cadenet's poems for the countess are similar to his one poem for the count. Indeed, in *S'ieu pogues ma voluntat* the poet takes up an analogous

---

[232] *Ibid.*, No. 16, *Cel qui de chantar s'entremet*, ll. 8–10: "ma dompna no·m tramet/ Salutz ni ren don m'esclaire/ Ni vol q'ieu ves liei repaire."

[233] *Ibid.*, No. 17, *Si tot s'es ma domn'esquiva*, ll. 1–3: "Si tot s'es ma domn'esquiva/ Ni·m mostr'orguoill ni soan,/ Ges del sieu servir no·m las."

[234] *Ibid.*, l. 26, "Q'en mi non a pont d'enjan."

[235] *Ibid.*, No. 19, *Tuich cill que vant demandan*, ll. 49–52: "Mais d'amic, los bes e·ls mals/ Degr'om partir comunals,/ Mas vos n'avetz lo gaug e·l pretz e·l pro,/ Et ieu no n'ai mais ir'e cor fello."

[236] *Ibid.*, No. 32, *Cel que no auzir chanssos* explicitly rejects material signs of favor for sex in ll. 9–13: "De la bella, don sui cochos,/ Desir lo tener e·l baisar, /E·l jazer e·l plus con-quistar,/ Et apres, mangas e cordos,/ E del plus qe·il clames merces (Of the beautiful lady for whom I am in haste,/ I desire to hold her and kiss her,/ and lie with her and obtain the most of her,/ and [only] afterward sleeves and collars,/ and of more favors that I may ask of her)."

[237] Cadenet, No. 15, *Meravilh me de tot fin amador*, ll. 16–20: "El pretz qu'en a, quar es pros e quar val,/ Emenda·lh ben las penas e·ls turmens/ Et atressi deu pueis esser jauzens/ De l'autre ben qu'en espera jauzir./ Et enaissi pot la clamor delir."

[238] *Ibid.*, 92.

theme. He weighs the ennobling effects of love against its unreasonable demands. Love is a lord who never helps and never thanks those who serve him. One ought not to love such a lord, and yet one does so, out of loyalty: "And the lord who always wants to take/ from his men and spurs them to ruin/ ought not to be loved (*amatz*) nor held dear (*car tengutz*)/ but only as much as loyalty (*leialtatz*) suggests."[239]

In *Oimais m'auretz avinen* the poet hides his joy: "I know so well how to constrain my heart/ that never would anyone know from my song/ that I have great joy."[240] Even while "singing and laughing (*chantan e rizen*)," a wise man can be "silent and sealed (*quetz e selatz*)."[241] The theme of saying one thing while feeling another appears as well in *No sai qual cosselh mi prenda*. Here the poet's lady's mouth says "no" but her glances say "yes." Is she deceiving him? Or simply acting like a woman? "Don't believe that I understand/ by the 'no' that she says to me/ that she is now a deceiving woman (*enjanairitz*)!/ Nor is it hardly right that I reproach her for it./ For ladies are thus accustomed/ – to such who inquire of them – to hide their desire."[242] The poet never resolves his doubt, ending on a bitter note: "It doesn't matter to her if I am grief-stricken."[243]

Love, deception, and pain: those were the intertwined themes circulating at the court of the Raimondins. Aimeric de Belenoi, who wrote three songs for Eleonor, announces those very themes in the first stanza of his poem to Raimond VI's half-sister Indie: "If it pleased my lady,/ whom I love without deception (*bauzia*)/ I would make a gay descort [a kind of poem]/ that I would send her,/ and if I reproached her/ [saying] how night and day/ her love was killing me/ and I find no defense/ because no one [but you] can protect me now,/ no one other exists/ but you, sweet love (*amia*):/ I don't know anyone more noble."[244] He is on his way to her; no pilgrim is more desirous of heaven than he desires to serve her "beautiful,

---

[239] *Ibid.*, No. 22, *S'ieu pogues ma voluntat*, ll. 21–24: "E·l senher qu'ades vol traire/ Dels sieus e·ls ponh' en desfaire,/ Non deu esser amatz ni car tengutz,/ Mas sol aitan cum leialtatz adutz."

[240] *Ibid.*, No. 17, *Oimais m'auretz avinen*, ll. 8–11: " ... be sabria/ Mon cor destrenher d'aitan/ Que ja nulhs hom a mon chan/ Gran joi no·m conoisseria." I am grateful to Professor Paden for devoting an entire seminar session to this poem.

[241] *Ibid.*, ll. 12–13. But note that the poet seems to contradict himself in stanza 5 when he bursts out with a volley of reasons why he loves his lady prefaced (l. 44) by the admission "I speak madness (dic folhia)."

[242] *Ibid.*, No. 16, *No sai qual cosselh mi prenda*, ll. 11–16: "Ges no cugetz qu'ieu entenda/ Per lo no que·m ditz/ Qu'ilh ja sia enjanairitz!/ Ni·s tanh ges qu'ieu la·n reprenda./ Quar donas son costumadas d'aitan,/ Qui las enquier, d'escondir lur talan."

[243] *Ibid.*, l. 53: "No·lh cal s·ieu n·estauc marritz."

[244] Aimeric de Belenoi, No. 4, *S'a midons plazia*, ll. 1–12: "S'a midons plazia/ cuy am ses bauzia/ guay descort faria/ que l'enviaria,/ e si·lh retrazia/ cossi nueg e dia/ s'amors m'aucizia/ e no·y truep guandia, /quar ia no·m guerria/ nulh'autra que sia/ mas vos, douss'amia:/ gensor no·n say mia."

smooth body (l. 38, *son belh cors lis*)." But she is far nobler than he, and he knows that "love according to wealth hardly goes/ but rather to the truest one."[245]

In *Per Crist, s'ieu crezes Amor*, written for countess Eleonor, Aimeric sounds similar themes. Here again, his heart is struck by an "amorous expression/ that came to me from a joyous, attractive person."[246] She did him a great honor: she pulled her hand out of her glove when he was about to depart. That "broke the lock of his heart (l. 17, *frais del cor la serradura*)," but he restrained himself from expressing his love. Upon his return to her, however, restraint fled, and now he cares about nothing except to admire her. May he please her, "for I love her without deceit (l. 34, *qu'ieu l'am ses engan*)." To be sure, he is not as noble as she; but he is a loyal lover (l. 42, *leial aman*), and his poems bring her "honor so great/ that if she measures it against her nobility,/ her nobility will be found lacking."[247] An idle boast? No doubt; but surely it enhanced his value with his patroness, if not with his "lady."

In other poems for Eleonor, however, Aimeric's focus on loyalty and deception drops out, leaving only love and pain. In *Aissi co·l pres que s'en cuia fugir*, love is a "prison (l. 4, *preson*)." The poet flees, leaving his lady's very country "so that I might not see her noble self/body."[248] But flight is not the same as escape: "Never can my good sense (*sens*) so fortify itself/ that I eject from my heart her who has conquered me."[249] When he thinks of her, he hardly hears what people around him are saying. "But I feign the appearance of it to them by looking/ and smiling and saying 'yes' and 'no.'"[250] He is in pain (*dan*), but her virtue (*valors*) makes his suffering pleasing (*abelir*). As a true lover (*fis amics*), he is ready to return to her simply in order to be where she is praised. Similarly in *Nulls hom non pot complir adreizamen*, his lady's worth is so extraordinary that even though he loves her utterly, "I love her little according to my understanding/ for I have only so much honor or good as I love her/ and if I loved her as much as was fitting for her/ I would have been king of Love and of Youth/ and of noble deeds."[251] His inadequacy gives him great grief (*gran pezansa*).

---

[245] *Ibid.*, ll. 64–66: "mas ges amor/ segon ricor/ no vay mas al plus fi."

[246] *Ibid.*, No. 8, *Per Crist, s'ieu crezes Amor*, ll. 6–7: " . . . d'un amoros semblan/ que·m venc d'un gai cors benestan."

[247] *Ibid.*, ll. 43–45: "e port a leis honor tan gran/ s'ab sa ricor la mesura/ ricors li fara fraitura."

[248] *Ibid.*, No. 5, *Aissi co·l pres que s'en cuia fugir*, l. 10: " . . . que no vis son cors gen."

[249] *Ibid.*, ll. 12–13: "mas anc mos sens no·s poc tan afortir/ qe·m get del cor celei qui m'a conques."

[250] *Ibid.*, ll. 27–28: "mas faz lor en ab esgardar parven/ et ab rire et ab 'oc' e 'non' dir."

[251] *Ibid.*, No. 7, *Nulls hom non pot complir adreizamen*, ll. 9–13: "Petit l'am ieu segon so qu'eu enten,/ c'onor ni be mas tan com l'am non ai;/ e s'ieu l'ames tan com a lieis s'eschai/ eu·n fora reis d'Amor e de Ioven/ e de rics fatz . . . "

Raimond VII, caught in the most furious phase of the Albigensian Crusade, did not have the luxury of surrounding himself with troubadours. Nevertheless, one anonymous poet closely followed his movements and chronicled them in his continuation of William of Tudela's epic Old Occitan poem, the so-called *Chanson de la Croisade albigeoise*. Here deceit loomed large, as did loyalty, friendships, enmities, and pains both physical and mental. Small wonder, since the *Chanson* was made ready for publication in 1228–29, when Raimond was supported only by the city of Toulouse and the count of Foix, Roger Bernard II, who was very likely the patron of the anonymous poet.[252]

The *Chanson* is very long, and it is impossible to discuss the full range of its emotional expression here. Rather, I propose following the lead of Marjolaine Raguin, who analyzes in detail an early episode in the poem: the confrontation of the two sides of the war at the Lateran palace in 1215. On one side were: the count of Toulouse, Raimond VI; his young son, Raimondet; the count of Foix, Raimond-Roger (1188–1223 – he was the father of Roger Bernard II); and other lords of the Midi.[253] On the other were: Pope Innocent III; numerous prelates, including the bishop of Toulouse; and Guy de Montfort (representing his brother Simon). During that meeting, Raguin argues, the clash of two notions of right – lordly claims of the right to inherit, ecclesiastical claims of the right to pursue heretics – announced the political and religious themes of the rest of the poem. Let us, in turn, explore some of the emotions the poet invoked.

Unlike the troubadour poems that we have seen, the Lateran episode, like all others in the *Chanson*, included numerous protagonists, many expressing emotions. The poet clearly wanted to present the feelings of all sides. Consider his treatment of the pope when Raimond, Raimondet, and the count of Foix throw themselves on their knees before him:

The pope looks at the child [Raimondet] and his face/ and recognizes the lineage and knows the offenses/ of the Church and of the clergy, who are hostile./ From pity (*pietat*) and grief mingled with anger (*ira*), he has a heart so sorrowful (*doloiros*)/ that he sighs (*sospira*) and weeps (*plora*) with both his eyes./ But no right or good faith (*fes*) or reason avails for the counts there.[254]

---

[252] Raguin, "Propagande politique," 40.

[253] For the dates of Raimond Roger, see Macé, *Les comtes*, 34.

[254] *Chanson*, 2:42, laisse 143, ll. 20–25: "L'Apostolis regarda l'efant e sas faisos,/ E conosc lo linatge e saub las falhizos/ De Glieza e de clercia, que son contrarios:/ De pietat e d'ira n'a·l cor tant doloiros/ Qu'en sospira e·n plora de sos olhs ambedos./ Mas lai no val als comtes dreitz ni fes ni razos." On the sighs of this passage, see Raguin, "Propagande politique," 113.

The pressure of the other prelates overwhelms the pope, "and out of fear (*paor*) of the clergy, of whom he is fearful (*temoros*)/ he afterward kept for himself the [count's] land and became its possessor."[255]

The count of Foix could not have known that would be the verdict. He spoke up to invoke the values of fidelity and good faith, which, as we have seen in both the charters and the troubadour poems, were supposed to overcome adversities: "I came to your court for a fair decision,/ I and the powerful count, my lord, and his son as well,/ who is handsome (*bel*) and good and wise and a little boy,/ and never acted or spoke deceitfully (*engan*) or falsely (*falhiment*)."[256] Here Raimondet had the characteristics of both the faithful troubadour and the beautiful beloved.

But the pope was a new sort of character, a sympathetic villain! This was an innovation over the charters, with their swift turns from friendship to enmity, and the troubadour poems, with their beautiful but treacherous ladies. The poet of the *Chanson* tells us that the pope wept over the injustices done to the Raimondin counts. Why then does he prolong the damage? The poet's answer: because he is weak and therefore duplicitous. When Raimond de Roquefeuil cries out to him, "Right Lord Pope, have mercy and pity," the pope replies, "Friend (*amix*), . . . it will be well attended to now."[257] But he does not attend to it well at all.

Did the poet think "friendship" a sham? By no means: for prior to the episode at the Lateran, in the very first scene of the poem's continuation, Pedro of Aragon rallied his "friends (*amics*)" to fight the crusaders. He made a speech: "The clergy and the French [that is, the crusaders from the Kingdom of France] want to disinherit/ the count my brother-in-law and drive him from his land;/ . . . and I pray my friends (*amics*), those who want to honor me,/ that they take care to equip themselves and arm their bodies./ . . . And they answer, 'Lord, it's good to do just that./ We never want to oppose you in anything you wish.'"[258] In effect, the poet contrasted two emotional communities: one deceitful, mouthing honorable sentiments but acting on shameful ones; the other straightforward, "sincere," beautiful, worthy of love.

---

[255] *Ibid.*, ll. 33–34: "E per paor de clercia de qu'el es temoros,/ Li retenc pueih sa terra e·n devenc poderos."

[256] *Ibid.*, 2:44, laisse 144, ll. 16–19: "Soi vengutz en ta cort per jutjar leialment,/ Eu e·l rics coms mos senher, e sos filhs ichament,/ Qu'es bel e bos e savis e de petit jovent,/ Ez anc no fe ni dig engan ni falhiment."

[257] *Ibid.*, 2:58, laisse 146, l. 48: "'Amix,' ditz l'Apostolis, 'ja er be emendat.'"

[258] *Ibid.*, 2:1, laisse 132, ll. 1–10: "Li clergue e·ls Frances volon dezeretar/ Lo comte mon cunhat e de terra gitar;/ . . . E pregue mos amics, sels que·m volen ondrar,/ Que·s pesson de garnir e de lor cors armar;/ . . . E eli responderon: "Senher, be·s tanh a far;/ Ja de re que vulhatz no·us volem contrastar."

The earlier troubadours had displaced all the doubts and worries about love in the counts' charters from men to women. Their poems painted women as the deceivers. Because women hardly mattered at the court of Toulouse (an opinion apparently held by Countess Eleonor as well!), this displacement made the poems both comforting and entertaining. They deflected anxieties about treachery from the political realm to the erotic.[259] But the poet of the *Chanson*, writing later and in the wake of a horrible war, was willing to explore male treason. As he did so, he "entered into" the feelings of those – like the pope – who were deceitful. The poet painted the pope as weak rather than evil, a man unhappily under the thumb of truly wicked clerics.

***

Superficially, the Cistercian monastery of Rievaulx and the Toulousain court expressed the same emotions, though certainly not in the same way. The monastic community wrote Latin treatises, sermons, letters, and *Lives*; the court produced Latin charters and vernacular poems. If any proof is needed to show that genre does not control or determine which emotions are expressed, it should be these two different source sets.

Yet these two communities were not saying the same thing.[260] Indeed, the Cistercian emotional community is best understood as carefully repurposing and circumscribing the love and friendship of the court. I speak not of the Toulousain court specifically, since that flourished after Aelred's Rievaulx, but rather of courts – very common at the time – organized around the notion that friendship and love was the way to bind men to one another and ensure loyalty.[261] Cistercian monks, who joined the monastery as adults, often knew a great deal about such courts.

---

[259] See Reddy, *The Making of Romantic Love*, for a very different recent view of the role of the erotic in the emotional economy of the poets.

[260] Yet see Jaeger, *Ennobling Love*, esp. 109–16, for the argument that a notion of "sublime love" united both court and monastery.

[261] I list only a few titles out of the enormous bibliography on the topic. For a more complete list, see Bertrand Haan and Christian Kühner, "D'intérêt comme d'émotion. L'amitié, lien social et politique par excellence in France et en Allemagne du XIIᵉ au XIXᵉ siècle," (2013) at www.perspectivia.net/content/publikationen/discussions/8-2013/haan-kuehner_interet. Most recent is Sean Gilsdorf, *The Favor of Friends: Intercession and Aristocratic Politics in Carolingian and Ottonian Europe* (Leiden, 2014). See also Anne Vincent-Buffault, *Une histoire de l'amitié* (Montrouge, 2010); Andreas Schinkel, *Freundschaft. Von der gemeinsamen Selbstverwirklichung zum Beziehungsmanagement. Die Verwandlungen einer sozialen Ordnung* (Fribourg-en-Brisgau, 2003); Gerd Althoff, *Verwandte, Freunde und Getreue. Zum politischen Stellenwert der Gruppenbildungen im frühen Mittelalter* (Darmstadt, 1990); Verena Epp, *Amicitia. Zur Geschichte personaler, sozialer, politischer und geistlicher Beziehungen im frühen Mittelalter* (Stuttgart, 1999); Claudia Garnier, *Amicus amicis-inimicus inimicis. Politische Freundschaft und fürstliche Netzwerke im 13. Jahrhundert* (Stuttgart, 2000).

Walter's father had been a "lord."[262] Aelred's first experience beyond
school was, as we have seen, at the court of King David of Scotland. He
called David his friend; he lamented his passing; he saw the monastery as
a miniature kingdom.

Nevertheless, the monastery was a kingdom in which all the faults of the
world were not only recognized but also accounted for. Love was rede-
fined as being radically divided into two opposite tendencies. The bad
part – cupidity – was condemned. The good part – charity – was largely
the preserve of monks, who, by including Christ in their notion of friendship, claimed the joy that the troubadours lacked and in addition avoided
the treason that the counts anticipated.

The religious life of the Cistercians involved a critique of lay practices
as well as wholesale adoption of some of them. Carefully dividing out the
insecurity of cupidity from the security of charity, they claimed a better
form of life. In that way, even as the Cistercian Order implicitly chided the
lay elites, it also made claims on their generosity. This helps explain why
even the counts of Toulouse supported Cistercian houses like Candeil
and Bonnecombe: such houses seemed to carry out successfully the very
practices on which the count depended.

To be sure, the monks at Rievaulx were well aware of the imperfections
of their own charity; they too were heir to the deceits, lusts, and envy that
evoked the anger and indignation of the Toulousain counts. Aelred had
even (as Walter recounted) responded to a furious abbot exactly as the
counts threatened recalcitrant *fideles*. It was in cases like this, when the
sins of the world knocked at the door of the monastery, that even monks
had to perform lordly emotions in order to make their point.[263]
Nevertheless, while the counts threatened and the troubadours complained, the Cistercians had a great asset: a theory that explained *why*
love (in this world) was bound to produce anxieties and uncertainties
even as it sought the peace that was perfect only in heaven.

But the critique and the imitation did not go only one way. Aelred's
image of the court of David as a kind of monastery was partly his fantasy;
but it was also, it would seem, a model that David himself adopted. It is
no accident that Aelred, steward to that king, joined Rievaulx; its founder, Walter Espec, was "one of David's most important Norman
supporters."[264] Aelred's writings were meant not just to manage emotions in the monastery but also in the lay world. And although the
influence must have been indirect, we can see the court of Toulouse

---

[262] See Powicke's introduction in Walter, *VA*, xvii–xxvi.
[263] On "performing" emotions, see above, n. 190.
[264] Dutton, "Conversion and Vocation," 42. See also *ibid.*, 44–46, arguing that David was
very much involved in Aelred's entry into Rievaulx.

responding to the emotional norms espoused by the Cistercians (and no doubt others) at the time. Not tears – courts would come to value tears only later (as we shall see in Chapter 6) – but compassion. It is true that the twelfth-century poets at the Raimondin court did not seem to care much about compassion. But the anonymous poet of the *Chanson* went even further than Walter and Aelred. Not only did he show that he himself was empathetic – even to anti-heroes (such as the pope) – but he also attempted in his description to make his readers feel empathy.[265] When Walter wrote about Aelred's empathy with the military man who swore at him, he marveled at this trait, possible only in a saint. But the *Chanson* poet expected *all* his readers to resonate with the fears and weaknesses of his anti-heroes.

Beyond the various similarities and differences, the paramount concern of both communities was love: its many potentials and its failings. It stands to reason that in the thirteenth century Thomas Aquinas would elaborate a theory of emotions that made love the linchpin of all emotions. We shall explore his theory of the "passions of the soul" in the next chapter.

---

[265] For further examples, see Barbara H. Rosenwein, "Love, Anger, and Empathy at the Court of the Counts of Toulouse c. 1200," forthcoming.

5   Thomas' passions

Thomas Aquinas (1224/5–74), who wrote the most influential medieval theory of the emotions, takes us from the court and monastery to the schools.[1] Thomas knew about courts, for he was born to a family of the lower nobility; his father was lord of the castle of Roccasecca, located about halfway between Rome and Naples and, at the time, part of the Kingdom of Sicily. Thomas also knew about ties of love and fidelity; indeed, two of his brothers fought for Emperor Frederick II (ruler of the Kingdom of Sicily), and one of them was executed for participating in a conspiracy against Frederick. Monasteries were also familiar to Thomas: around the age of five, he became an oblate (a child "offering") at the monastery of Monte Cassino.

Still as an oblate, Thomas left Monte Cassino around 1239 to study the liberal arts in Naples. Between the time of Aelred's studies in a cathedral school and the capitulation of Raimond VII of Toulouse to the crusaders, universities had come to dominate higher education – at Paris, Montpellier, Oxford, Salerno, Bologna, and elsewhere. In general, the teachers (masters, scholastics) of the liberal arts stressed logic (also called dialectic); beyond the arts, at a few universities, some masters taught the "higher" studies of theology, law, and medicine. The university of Naples, founded by Frederick II to rival the already famous University of Bologna, was fairly unusual in offering lectures on Aristotle's natural philosophy and metaphysics. But even before finishing his education in the liberal arts, Thomas left the Benedictines and joined the Dominican Order in Naples in 1244. He was around twenty years old.

The Dominicans were "mendicants" (the Franciscans were another such group). "Mendicant" means "beggar," and the chief features uniting the mendicant religious orders were their vocation of poverty and their

---

[1] For biographical information I rely largely on Denys Turner, *Thomas Aquinas: A Portrait* (New Haven, 2013); Bernard McGinn, *Thomas Aquinas's "Summa theologiae": A Biography* (Princeton, 2014); and James A. Weisheipl, *Friar Thomas d'Aquino: His Life, Thought, and Works, with Corrigenda and Addenda* (Washington, DC, 1983). I thank Peter John Hartman and Blake D. Dutton for reading and commenting on an earlier draft of this chapter.

begging of alms. Such orders were at home in the cities. The Dominicans, who received papal confirmation from Honorius III in 1216 – about a year after Raimond VI and his son petitioned Innocent III to restore their lands – were officially known as members of the Order of Friars Preachers. They were soon drawn to the universities, in part to recruit students and masters to their order and in part to study and prepare themselves to preach. They also set up schools within their convents so that their university-trained lectors could teach the rank and file the practical skills of preaching and confessing.[2]

Although the Dominicans lived in accordance with a rule (like monks), they did not take vows of stability and could move from house to house as their pastoral mission required. Around the time of Thomas' death they had more than 450 houses for men and nearly 60 for women.[3] By the end of Thomas' life the Dominicans were extremely powerful, producing cardinals, papal secretaries, and, starting with Innocent V in 1276, popes.

Almost immediately after joining the Dominicans, Thomas was sent northward to continue his studies. (He was, however, waylaid by his family – vainly hoping he might pursue a more traditional monastic career – and kept at his home for about a year.[4]) After a stint at the Dominican convent at Saint-Jacques in Paris 1245–48, Thomas went to Cologne to study with Albert the Great, a famous master of theology and also a Dominican. Between 1252 and 1256 Thomas was back in Paris, preparing to lecture to fledgling Dominicans at Saint-Jacques and studying at the university there. By 1256 he had completed the curriculum for theology and – once the opposition of the non-mendicant masters was overcome by papal fiat – became a master of theology at the University of Paris in 1257.[5] His itinerary from 1259 on had him shuttling among various Dominican convents in Italy as a teacher, and he also taught again in Paris for a brief stint (1268/9–72). In 1273, once more in Naples, he had a sort of breakdown and stopped writing. He died a year later.

A "breakdown": until that moment, Thomas had churned out *summae* and other works at breathless speed. Dense summaries of scholarly and

---

[2] On these points, see M. Michèle Mulchahey, *"First the Bow is Bent in Study ... ": Dominican Education before 1350* (Toronto, 1998), esp. 26–33, 130–203. The Franciscans connected their mission with the universities a bit later. See Neslihan Şenocak, *The Poor and the Perfect: The Rise of Learning in the Franciscan Order, 1209–1310* (Ithaca, NY, 2012).

[3] William A. Hinnebusch, *The History of the Dominican Order*, vol. 1: *Origins and Growth to 1500* (New York, 1965), 262.

[4] William of Tocco, *Ystoria sancti Thome* c. 8, in *Ystoria sancti Thome de Aquino de Guillaume de Toco (1323)*, ed. Claire le Brun-Gouanvic (Toronto, 1996), 105–6.

[5] McGinn, *Aquinas's Summa*, 25–26, briefly explains the reasons for the non-mendicant opposition.

creative thought, the *summa* (the singular of *summae*) was the character-istic product of medieval university scholars. Thomas' theory of emotions was largely embedded in the so-called *prima secundae*, the "first section of the second part," of his *Summa theologiae*, which he wrote in 1271, during his second term at Paris.[6] However, the topic of emotions interested him throughout his life.[7]

The passions of the soul

To be sure, Thomas did not speak of a "theory of the emotions." Rather, he wrote about "passions of the soul (*passiones animae*)" or, occasionally, the "affections (*affectiones*)."[8] We have seen that previous writers were uncertain (and in fact not very concerned) about where to put the emo-tions: the *mens*, the *animus*, the *anima*, even the heart were all possible. By contrast, Thomas firmly placed the passions in the *anima*, as Aristotle had

---

[6] For the date, I follow the catalogue of the works of Thomas by G. Emery in Jean-Pierre Torrell, *Saint Thomas Aquinas*, vol. 1: *The Person and His Work*, trans. Robert Royal (rev. ed., Washington, DC, 2005), 333. The *Summa theologiae* [hereafter ST] is cited conventionally by part, question, and so on. In its typical form the ST takes up a question, divides it into articles, and presents each article with a number of "objections," each of which quotes a text that claims the position Thomas disagrees with. This is followed by an "on the contrary" that quotes a text on Thomas' side and introduces his own argument, which is presented in a section beginning "I answer that." The article is then concluded by Thomas' replies to each of the objections.

[7] They are (in chronological order) *Scriptum super Sententiis* (1252–56) [henceforth *Super Sent.*], *De Veritate* (1256–59), *De Malo* (1266–70), and *Sententia libri Ethicorum* (1270). Dates are from Emery's catalogue in Torrell, *Aquinas: The Person*, 330–61. For more on Thomas' lifelong interest in the passions, see Mark D. Jordan, "Aquinas's Construction of a Moral Account of the Passions," *Freiburger Zeitschrift für Philosophie und Theologie* 33 (1986): 71–97, here 75–76. Italo Sciuto, "Le passioni dell'anima nel pensiero di Tommaso d'Aquino," in *Anima e corpo nella cultura medievale*, ed. Carla Casagrande and Silvana Vecchio (Florence, 1999), 73–93 at 78 *et passim*, puts emphasis on the differences in Thomas' formulations between his *De Veritate* and the ST. For all of Thomas' works I use the *Corpus Thomisticum* at www.corpusthomisticum.org/, a website maintained by the Departamento de Filosofia, Universidad de Navarra, under the supervision of Enrique Alarcón. On rare occasions I have needed to correct these texts by using subsequent editions.

[8] Of recent writers on Thomas' theory of the passions, Robert Miner, *Thomas Aquinas on the Passions: A Study of* Summa Theologiae, *1a2ae 22–48* (Cambridge, 2009), 1, considers Thomas' "passions" to be an ancestor of our term "emotions." Nicholas E. Lombardo, *The Logic of Desire: Aquinas on Emotion* (Washington, DC, 2011), 18, undertakes "to see what Aquinas has to say about the particular psychological phenomena that we typically identify as emotions." Thus modern emotion words constitute his starting point. As these two studies show, entire books have been written on Thomas' so-called treatise on the passions. I can present only a simplified summary here. For a rapid survey of thought on the passions prior to Thomas', see the introduction by Silvana Vecchio of Tommaso d'Aquino, *Le passioni dell'anima*, trans. and intro. Silvana Vecchio (Florence, 2002), 5–18, as well as Carla Casagrande and Silvana Vecchio, "Les théories des passions dans la culture médiévale," in *Le sujet des émotions*, 107–22.

done before him. Following Aristotle's *De Anima*, Thomas understood man's soul to consist of five faculties. Aristotle explained:

[human beings have a faculty] for nourishment, for appetite, for sensation, for movement in space, and for thought. Plants have the nutritive faculty only, but other living things have this and the faculty for sensation. But if for sensation, then also for appetite, for appetite consists of desire, anger, and wish, and all animals have one of the senses, that of touch. But that which has sensation knows pleasure and pain ... and that which knows these has also desire. For desire is an appetite for what is pleasant.[9]

In this scheme, of all living things only human beings had all five of the faculties, including the intellective, the one for thought. (See Figure 5.1.)

The word passion comes from the Latin *pati*, meaning "to suffer" (as Christ suffered during his "Passion"); it also means simply "to receive." In the sense of receiving, human beings have many sorts of passions. When the sun shines on our skin, for example, the skin "receives" warmth. The soul, too, can be receptive in that way. When it "receives" new knowledge, its very reception of that knowledge is a "passion."[10] But the skin's new warmth and the mind's new knowledge are very "dispassionate" sorts of passion.

A more passionate kind of passion engages both body and soul. This is the sort of passion that involves bodily transformations (*transmutationes corporales*).[11] As another glance at Figure 5.1 shows, the soul and the body are a "composite (*compositum*)," or "a unity."[12] The body needs the soul

---

[9] Aristotle, *On the Soul* 2.3 (414a–414b), in Aristotle, *On the Soul. Parva Naturalia. On Breath*, trans. W. S. Hett (Cambridge, MA, 1935), 1–203 at 81. Thomas was not the first to emphasize the various faculties of the soul, which had already been utilized by John of Damascus, *De Fide Orthodoxa: Versions of Burgundio and Cerbanus*, ed. Eligius M. Buytaert (Louvain, 1955), 118–19. For the classic study of the faculties in writings before Thomas Aquinas, see D. Odon Lottin, *Psychologie et morale aux XIIe et XIIIe siècles*, vol. 1: *Problèmes de psychologie* (Louvain, 1942), 394–404. See also Daniel A. Callus, "The Powers of the Soul: An Early Unpublished Text," *Recherches de Théologie ancienne et médiévale* 19 (1952): 131–70.

[10] ST I-II, q. 22 a. 1 co.: "Dicitur quod sentire et intelligere est quoddam pati (it is said [by Aristotle, *On the Soul* 1.5 (410a), 57] that to think and to understand is a kind of passion)."

[11] ST I-II, q. 22 a. 1 co.

[12] *Ibid.*, Sciuto, "Le passioni," 74, calls them a "unity (unità)" and notes (76) that the soul "governs and moves (amministra e muove)" the body. Turner, *Thomas Aquinas*, 58–62, has clarifying remarks on Thomas' notion of the unity of body and soul. See also Umberto Galeazzi, "Le passioni secondo Tommaso d'Aquino: De veritate, q. 26," *Aquinas. Rivista internazionale di filosofia* 47/3 (2004): 547–70 at 556–58. Technically, the soul is the "substantial form" of the body: see Thomas Aquinas, *Summa contra Gentiles*, 2, 68, n. 2: "Relinquitur quod anima humana sit intellectualis substantia corpori unita ut forma (It remains that the human soul is an intellectual substance united to the body as its form)." See Shawn D. Floyd, "Aquinas on Emotion: A Response to some Recent Interpretations," *History of Philosophy Quarterly* 15/2 (1998): 161–74 at 163, and B. Carlos Bazán, "The Human Soul: Form and Substance? Thomas Aquinas' Critique of Eclectic Aristotelianism," *Archives d'histoire doctrinale et littéraire du moyen âge* 64 (1997): 95–126, esp. 116–17.

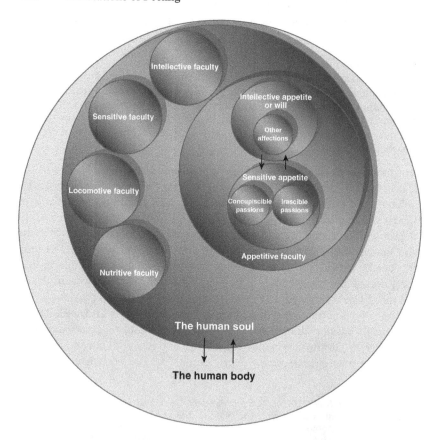

Figure 5.1 Aquinas' body-soul composite

to give it life, and the passions that Thomas wants to talk about – love, sorrow, pleasure, and the like – pertain to the body as well as the soul.[13] Indeed, "passions of the soul" is only a manner of speaking, since they are also passions of the body.

The bodily transformations that Thomas is thinking about include blushing and blanching, as well as contractions, expansions, and other movements of the heart.[14] In Thomas' theory, the Stoic "pre-passions" – those "first movements" that warned the wise man that an emotion was on the way – are treated as the bodily concomitants of the passions

---

[13] Peter King, "Emotions," in *The Oxford Handbook of Aquinas*, ed. Brian Davies and Eleonore Stump (Oxford, 2012), 209–26 at 211, says that the soul "vivifies the body."

[14] Sciuto, "Le passioni," 90 and n. 59, helpfully refers to Thomas' *De motu cordis* and further bibliography.

themselves. Some of these bodily transformations are for the worse. Thomas says that those are most properly called "passions." So the transformations that accompany sorrow make it more of a passion than joy. But in all cases, the passions that are more than just "reception" come with bodily transformations. This is thoroughly Aristotelian.[15]

Insofar as the passions are in the soul, where exactly are they? The notion of faculties gave the soul a kind of geography. Thomas put the passions in the appetitive faculty. We have already seen that Aristotle had written that "appetite consists of desire, anger, and wish." Thomas agreed: "the word *pati* is used when a thing is drawn to (*trahitur ad*) an agent."[16] For Thomas, the soul is "drawn to" things in a variety of ways. The intellective faculty is "drawn to" something not "as it is in itself (*in seipsis*)" but as it forms a complex mental image of the thing (*secundum intentionem rei*).[17] It has no "passions". The appetitive faculty has two parts: the intellective and the sensitive. The intellective appetite is drawn to things in themselves, and so it has passions. But because they do not involve bodily transformations, they are best not called passions but rather "other affections."[18] The part of the appetitive faculty that is home to the passions as such is the sensitive appetite. There the soul is drawn to the agent *as it is in itself*. This does not mean that it has no mental image at all of the agent, but rather that its image is limited to recognizing its pleasantness or usefulness.[19] Something presents itself (via the senses of touch, sight, taste, and so on) to the sensitive appetite as a good or an evil and induces us to want it (or to want to avoid it).

Thomas divided the passions of the sensitive appetite into two sorts, the concupiscible and the irascible.[20] Originating with Plato, this division was well accepted by Thomas' day.[21] The word "concupiscible" referred to desire; we have already seen it used that way in Aelred. "Irascible" derived from the word *ira*, or anger.[22] In Thomas' scheme, the two sorts of

---

[15] Aristotle, *On the Soul* 1.1 (403a15), p. 15: "Probably all the affections of the soul are associated with the body – anger, gentleness, fear, pity, courage, and joy, as well as loving and hating; for when they appear the body is also affected."

[16] ST I-II, q. 22 a. 1 co.   [17] *Ibid.*, a. 2 co.

[18] Peter King, "Aquinas on the Passions," in *Aquinas's Moral Theory: Essays in Honor of Norman Kretzmann*, ed. Scott MacDonald and Eleonore Stump (Ithaca, NY, 1999), 101–32 at 105 n. 7, calls these *affectiones* "pseudo-passions." On these affections, see Lombardo, *The Logic of Desire*, chap.3, and Miner, *Aquinas on the Passions*, 35–38.

[19] On the meanings of *in seipsis* and *secundum intentionem*, see Mark P. Drost, "Intentionality in Aquinas's Theory of Emotions," *International Philosophical Quarterly* 31/4 (1991): 449–60, and Miner, *Aquinas on the Passions*, 21–25, 69–82.

[20] ST I-II, q. 23.

[21] It already inspired the Cistercian abbot Isaac of Stella (d. c. 1169), for example, in his *Sermo* 17 c. 13, in *Isaac de L'Étoile, Sermons*, ed. Anselme Hoste, SC 130 (Paris, 1967), 318. Knuuttila, *Emotions*, 178, says that Parisian scholastics were using the terminology of concupiscible and irascible by the 1230s.

[22] As Thomas notes in ST I-II, q. 46 a. 1 arg. 1.

Table 5.1 *Aquinas' concupiscible and irascible passions*

concupiscible	irascible
amor vs. *odium*, love vs. hate	*spes* vs. *desperatio*, hope vs. despair
desiderium vs. *fuga*, desire vs. avoidance	*timor* vs. *audacia*, fear vs. courage
delectatio/gaudium vs. *dolor/tristitia*, delight/ joy vs. pain/sorrow	*ira*, anger

passions had different objects. "The object of the concupiscible is a good or an evil as received directly by the senses, that is, something that is pleasurable or painful. But because the soul sometimes must experience difficulty or struggle to obtain some such good or to avoid some such evil ... this same good or evil, insofar as it has an arduous or difficult nature, is the object of the irascible."[23] The concupiscible passions pursued their objects, and when the pursuit got tough, the irascible passions came to their aid. Thomas named eleven kinds of passions: six were concupiscible, five were irascible.[24] Table 5.1 presents them in schematic form.

Apart from anger (*ira*), each passion has a contrary. Why? In offering his answer, Thomas introduces a new and fundamental theme: "passion is a kind of motion (*motus*)."[25] Here he refers to Aristotle's *Physics*, which he read (in Latin translation) and commented on in 1268–69 – thus almost immediately before writing his treatise on the passions.[26] But he had other thinkers to draw on, as well. Thomas knew, for example, the work of John of Damascus (d. 749), whose *On the Orthodox Faith* had been translated into Latin in the twelfth century.[27] Quoting John, Thomas wrote that "'passion is a motion of the sensitive appetitive faculty when imagining good or evil.' In other words, 'passion is a motion of

[23] ST I-II, q. 23 a. 1 co.

[24] Here he modified Aristotle's scheme of fourteen *pathé*, which were (in rough English equivalents) anger vs. mildness; love vs. hate; fear vs. confidence; shame vs. shamelessness; benevolence vs. lack of benevolence; pity vs. indignation; and envy vs. desire to emulate. See Konstan, *The Emotions of the Ancient Greeks*.

[25] ST I-II, q. 23 a. 2 co.

[26] For the date, see Emery's catalogue in Torrell, *Aquinas: The Person*, 342. See Thomas Aquinas, *Commentaria in octo libros Physicorum*. For a discussion of the translation Thomas used, see the introduction by Vernon J. Bourke to Thomas Aquinas, *Commentary on Aristotle's Physics*, trans. Richard J. Blackwell et al. (London, 1963), xvi–xviii. For "passion is a kind of motion" see *ibid.*, 146 (Aquinas, *Commentaria* 3.5.310).

[27] John of Damascus, *Fide Orthodoxa*, 132. The editor (xiv) dates Burgundio's translation, which Thomas used, to 1153–54. John of Damascus was in turn following Nemesius of Emesa, a late fourth-century bishop.

the non-rational [faculty] of the soul caused by the thought of good or evil.'"[28] This quotation makes two important points. First, Thomas, following John, said that the sensitive appetite did not react to an object per se but rather to a cognition of it, namely of its usefulness or pleasantness. Second, Thomas considered passions to be motions. For that latter point, he hardly needed Aristotle or John, however. The idea that emotions – and their kin, passions and affections – were "motions" was traditional and widespread. When Augustine talked about *hos motus* turned awry by the will and leading to vice, he was referring to the emotions.[29] Gregory of Tours had used the word as we do, in a phrase like "moved to mercy (*misericordia motus*)."[30] Aelred's sequence for love involved choice (*electio*), motion (*motus*), and enjoyment (*fructus*).[31]

Aristotle, however, gave Thomas some precise arguments about kinds of motions. Working with Aristotle's discussion of the contrariety of motion, Thomas outlined two ways in which the passions may be contrary.[32] In the first, their objects are contrary. This is the contrariety of the concupiscible passions: utterly goal-oriented, they have opposite objects (good or evil). In the second way, the motion rather than the object is contrary. The irascible passions, more flexible than the concupiscible because their purpose is to fight obstacles, can move in both ways. For example, fear may be the opposite of courage when it has a different motion vis-à-vis the same object, as when fear flees while courage advances toward an enemy. But fear and courage may also have different objects, as when fear runs from well-armed knights while courage attacks a vulnerable castle.

Anger (*ira*) has no contrary. Its purpose is not to overcome obstacles that prevent the concupiscible passions from gaining their object, for the object has already been lost. Rather, anger is "caused by a difficult evil already present."[33] It is the outcome of the other irascible passions, which "end (*terminatur*)" in it when their pursuit has been unsuccessful. "The motion of anger does not arise except because of some sorrow endured (*tristitiam illatam*) and unless there is desire and hope for revenge

---

[28] ST I-II, q. 22 a. 3 s.c. The Corpus Thomisticum, which is usually accurate, has *susceptionem*, which here must be corrected to *suspicionem* according to the more recent Leonine edition (Rome, 1981), as reprinted in Tommaso d'Aquino, *Le passioni dell'anima*, 27.

[29] See Chapter 1, n. 57.   [30] Greg. Tur., *Histories* 6.22, p. 290.

[31] See Chapter 4, n. 36.

[32] Aristotle discussed contrariety of motions in *Physics* 5.3 (229a30) (see the translation by R. P. Hardie and R. K. Gaye at www.logicmuseum.com/authors/aristotle/physics/physics.htm#15c3), and Thomas commented in *Commentaria* 5.8.715–26; Aquinas, *Commentary on Aristotle's Physics*, 325–30.

[33] ST I-II, q. 23 a. 3 co.

(*desiderium et spes ulciscendi*)."[34] That means that anger is a product of the "flowing together (*ex concursu*) of many passions."[35] It has no contrary because "it contains contrariety in itself": the passions of hope (*spes*), whose object is the good and agreeable, and of sorrow (*tristitia*), whose object is the bad and disagreeable.[36]

The sequence of the passions

The nature of motion also allows Thomas to distinguish among the passions even though they have common objects. It is true that the cause of all the passions is also their object. The good that activates the motion of the concupiscible passions is also the object of those same passions: the good "has, as it were, the force of attraction."[37] And, by the same token, the evil that activates those same concupiscible passions is also their repulsive object. Even so, the motion of each particular concupiscible passion is not the same even with their common causes and objects. In the first place, the good "causes, in the appetitive power, a certain inclination or aptitude or affinity for the good (*quandam inclinationem seu aptitudinem connaturalitatem*), and this pertains to the passion of love (*quod pertinet passionem amoris*)."[38] In the case of evil, the inclination to move in the opposite direction pertains to the passion of hate. What's next? "If the good object is not yet achieved, it causes the appetitive power to move to attain the beloved good."[39] That is the role of desire or concupiscence (*pertinet ad passionem desiderii vel concupiscentiae*). In the case of evil anticipated but not yet present, the inclination to good causes the motion of fleeing (*fuga vel abominatio*). Third and last, when the good is obtained, the good (as both cause and object) causes the appetitive power to "rest," in the beloved, and that rest or quiet (*quietatio*) belongs to pleasure or joy (*pertinet ad delectationem vel gaudium*). Last in the order of an evil cause/object is when the evil is present. Then the result is pain or sorrow (*dolor vel tristitia*). Figure 5.2 represents the sequences in schematic form.

---

[34] ST I-II, q. 46 a. 1 co.   [35] *Ibid.*   [36] *Ibid.*, a. 1 ad 2.   [37] ST I-II, q. 23 a. 4 co.

[38] *Ibid.* Compare Aelred's definition of affect as a "spontaneous and sweet inclination of the *animus* toward someone." Above, Chapter 4, n. 40.

[39] *Ibid.* Gianmarco Stancato, *Le concept de désir dans l'œuvre de Thomas d'Aquin. Analyse lexicographique et conceptuelle du* desiderium (Paris, 2011), includes tables of all the grammatical contexts in which the word *desiderium* appears in Thomas' works. The most frequent subject (as reflected in the possessive genitive) is *hominum* (his Table 1.4); the most frequent object (as reflected in the "génitif déclaratif") is *finis* (Table 1.5). He notes (67–68) that *concupiscentia* refers essentially to bodily pleasures while *desiderium* refers to all types of pleasures.

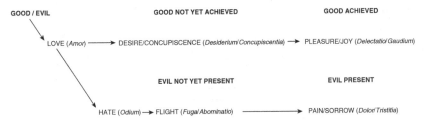

Figure 5.2 Aquinas' sequence of the concupiscible passions

Note that Figure 5.2 shows an arrow leading from love to hate, indicating that hate follows on love. Love comes before hate since, in the first place, good "naturally (*naturaliter*) comes before evil."[40] We will soon discuss the role of love in greater detail. But a similar argument allows Thomas to add the irascible passions to his sequence: "the concupiscible passions regard absolute good; but the irascible passions regard a restricted good, namely the arduous."[41] That makes the concupiscible passions "come before (*sint priores*)" the irascible. The concupiscible passions both move (think of desire moving toward the beloved) and rest (as when joy finds quiet in the beloved). The irascible move but never rest.

Now, according to the Aristotelian theory of motion, "rest is the end of movement."[42] (We shall see in Hobbes in Chapter 9 the consequences of a different theory of inertia.) The irascible passions must end in the concupiscible because only the concupiscible can rest. This is easiest to see in the case of pursuit of the good, when joy is the result. For joy "feels" restful and peaceful. But it is also true in the case of the avoidance of evil, for the sorrow that comes when evil is present engenders anger. And anger, once it has carried out its mission, brings joy.[43]

Thus, first come the concupiscible passions of love or hate. They are followed by desire or avoidance. As soon as those appear, the irascible passions are ready to enter the fray. For the good not yet obtained, hope and despair (*spes et desperatio*) come to help; for the evil not yet present, fear and courage (*timor et audacia*) arrive. Once the pursuit of the beloved is successful, no further irascible passion is needed. But anger (*ira*) is aroused by the evil that is present, and it sets off its own sequence, driven by its own good object (vengeance) and ending in pleasure once its object is achieved.[44] Figure 5.3 sets out the whole sequence, with the exception of anger's progeny.

---

[40] ST I-II, q. 25 a. 2 co. Thomas goes on to explain that "eo quod malum est privatio boni ([this is] because evil is the privation of good)."
[41] *Ibid.*, a. 1 s.c.   [42] *Ibid.*, a. 1 co.   [43] *Ibid.*   [44] *Ibid.*

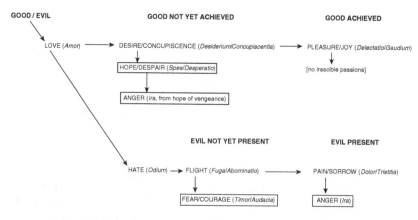

Figure 5.3 Aquinas' sequence of the concupiscible and irascible passions[a]

[a] Irascible passions are inside rectangular frames.

We see in Figure 5.3 that the irascible passions come between the concupiscible passions that involve motion toward good (or away from evil) and those that involve rest in good or evil. Thus the irascible passions are both initiated by and terminate in the concupiscible.[45] Indeed, "the concupiscible passions are the cause of the irascible passions."[46]

The whole sequence worked rather like the three-and-four voice motets that were being sung on the streets of Paris as Thomas was writing. The first theme, in the treble, is sounded by love, soon joined by desire. In chimes the tenor voice of hope or despair, lamenting or anticipating the possibility of obtaining the beloved. The bass line, always slow and somber, often taken from a liturgical text, is represented by anger, slow to burn and yet ready to achieve its own very different "good" objective. And then comes the end: rest and pleasure. To be sure, in a motet pleasure is felt throughout the performance, not only when it is over. But even here there is a similarity with the sequence of the passions. For in his long discussion of love (which we will get to in a moment), Thomas defines love as, among other things, a *complacentia boni*, which in English sounds like a "complacency in the good" but means something much closer to a "pleasure in the good."[47] Falling in love in Thomas' scheme is

---

[45] *Ibid.*   [46] ST I-II, q. 46 a. 3 ad 3.

[47] ST I-II, q. 26 a. 1 co.: "Et similiter coaptatio appetitus sensitivi, vel voluntatis, ad aliquod bonum, idest ipsa complacentia boni, dicitur amor sensitivus, vel intellectivus seu ratio-nalis (And similarly, the aptitude of the sensitive appetite or of the will [the intellective appetite] to something good – i.e. its complacency in the good – is called 'sensitive love' or 'intellective' or 'rational' love)." See below at n. 58 for the context of this quote.

pleasurable from the start, though *that* pleasure (*placentia*, a "pleasing") is not the same as the pleasure (*delectatio* or *gaudium*) gained when the beloved is obtained. The pleasure is that of *delectatio morosa*, the pleasure of dwelling on and longing for the beloved, even when it or she or he is far off or unobtainable. It is the pleasure of so many of the troubadours at the comital court of Toulouse.[48]

Considering that a person always hates the opposite of what he or she loves, the two sequences must often happen together. And since people usually fix on more than one love at the same time – an ice cream cone, God, a friend – there must be about as many motions taking place within the human soul as there were voices on the Paris streets.

Beyond eleven passions

Thus far, it seems that Thomas recognized only eleven passions of the soul. But this is not correct. Each of the eleven was an umbrella term for a multitude of words. Table 5.2 lists the ones that Thomas mentioned. But, like Cicero, he did not consider his examples to be exhaustive.[49]

Moreover, even the eleven passions must be understood to have had various internal registers. Consider sorrow. It was not just "sorrow" and that's that! It was accompanied by tears and groans and sometimes by words, and these things softened the sorrow, assuaged it, and even offered a bit of pleasure:

tears and groans naturally lessen sorrow (*mitigant tristitiam*). This is for two reasons. First, certainly, because every interior hurt is more painful [when] contained ... But when it is let out .... it is then dispersed (*disgregatur*), and in that way the inner pain is diminished. And because of this, when people who sorrow show their sorrow outwardly in tears or groans or even words, the sorrow is lessened. Second, [tears and groans lessen sorrow] because an action that befits a man according to his actual disposition is always pleasant to him. Well, tears and groans are certain actions (*quaedam operationes*) that befit the sad or grieving person, and so they become pleasant (*efficiuntur ... delectabiles*) to him or her.[50]

---

[48] Thomas talks about *delectatio morosa* in ST I-II, q. 74. Poets and scholastics had different but related ideas about this form of longing; see Charles Baladier, *Ërôs au Moyen Âge. Amour, désir et "delectatio morosa"* (Paris, 1999).

[49] Thomas also had in ST I-II, q. 25 a. 4 co. a restricted list of four principal passions (*passiones principales*), namely joy (*gaudium*), sorrow (*tristitia*), fear (*timor*), and hope (*spes*). The first two "are called principal because they are the fulfillment (sunt completivae) and the end (finales) of all the passions." The second two do not fully complete the others, but they do complete "the motion of the appetitive faculty toward something (motus appetitivi ad aliquid)." In other words they "complete" the motion of desire or of aversion.

[50] ST I-II, q. 38 a. 2 co. On this passage, see Turner, *Thomas Aquinas*, 145–46.

Table 5.2 *Aquinas'* passiones animae

abominatio, avoidance
acedia, a kind of sorrow; torpor
achthos, a kind of sadness; distress
admiratio, a kind of fear; wonder
   miror, wonder at
agonia, a kind of fear; anxiety
amor, love
angustia, anxiety
anxietas, a kind of sadness; anxiety
audacia, courage
benevolentia, a kind of love equivalent to friendship's love
caritas, a kind of love
complacentia, love[a]
concupiscentia, desire
cupiditas, desire
delectatio, pleasure
desiderium, desire
desperatio, despair
dilectio, a kind of love, mainly intellectual
dolor, sorrow, pain
erubescentia, a kind of fear; embarrassment
excandescentia, burning
exultatio, joy
fel, a kind of anger
fuga, avoidance
furor, a kind of anger
gaudium, joy
invidia, a kind of sadness; envy
ira, anger
jucunditas, jocularity
laetitia, joy, happiness
luctus, mourning
   lugere, to mourn
mania, a kind of anger
mansuetudo, meekness; the opposite of anger
metus, fear
misericordia, a kind of sadness; pity
nemesis, indignation; a kind of envy
odium, hatred
penitentia, penitence
pigritia, a kind of fear; indolence
securitas, a kind of courage
segnities, a kind of fear; laziness
spes, hope
stupor, a kind of fear; wonder
thymosis, a kind of anger
timor, fear
tristitia, sorrow
verecundia, a kind of fear; shame

Table 5.2 (*cont.*)

emotion markers/effects:
afflictio, an effect of hope; affliction
aggravatio, an effect of sorrow; depression
dilatatio, an effect of pleasure; expansion
extasis, an effect of love; ecstacy
fervor, a fever from anger; a fever stemming from love
fruitio, an effect of love; pleasure
inhaesio, an effect of love; indwelling
languor, a kind of sadness from love; languor
liquefactio, an effect of love; melting
zelus, an effect of love; a kind of envy

[a] ST I-II, q. 25 a. 2 co.: "amor, qui nihil aliud est quam
complacentia boni (love, which is nothing other than
complacency/pleasure in the good)."

Love

Not all of the passions are equal in Thomas' theory. Love has a special
place, its origins in God himself. The love of God, "tending (*tendens*)
toward his son as if toward an object, is the reason why God gave all the
effects of love (*omnem effectum amoris*) to his creature (*creaturis*) [including
mankind]. And it is why the Holy Spirit, which is the love (*amor*) by which
the Father loves his son, is also the love (*amor*) by which he loves his
creature, allowing him to participate in his perfection."[51] Human love
could not exist if God's had not existed first.[52]

Love (*amor*) orchestrates every other emotion. Even hate (*odium*) is
caused by love, for nothing can be hated "unless it is contrary to an
appropriate thing that is loved."[53] Thomas spells it out: love is the "tap-
root (*prima radix*) of all the other passions."[54] And again: "There is no
other passion of the soul that does not presuppose love of some kind."[55]

Unlike Aelred, Thomas did not think that the passions were degraded
by the Fall of mankind from the Garden of Eden. Following Aristotle, he
saw all of them as natural; they were as God had created them.[56] The Fall
perverted the natural order, which had subjected the human mind to God
and human passions to reason.[57] But the passions, even before the Fall,
had been part of human nature and a necessary part of human virtue.

[51] *Super Sent.*, lib. 1 d. 14 q. 1 a. 1 co.
[52] On this point, see Jean-Pierre Torrell, *Saint Thomas d'Aquin, maître spirituel. Initiation 2*
(Fribourg-Paris, 1996), 234.
[53] ST I-II, q. 29 a. 2 co.   [54] ST I-II, q. 46 a. 1.   [55] ST I-II, q. 27 a. 4 co.
[56] See Sciuto, "Le passioni," 79.   [57] See ST I-II, q. 82 a. 2 co.

Thomas' discussion of love began by recognizing three kinds: natural, sensitive, and intellective (or willful). The first is "love" only by analogy: a rock falls to the ground because it "naturally" seeks the earth. The other two are real loves, one sensitive and the other intellective. The "joining together (*coaptatio*) of the sensitive appetite or of the will [i.e. the intellective appetite] with some good, that is, its very complacency in the good is called [on the one hand,] 'sensitive love' or [on the other] 'intellective' or 'rational love.'"[58] These two loves have different names: the first is *amor*, the second *dilectio*.

In Chapter 1 we saw that Augustine disparaged any careful discrimination between words like *dilectio*, *caritas*, and *amor*.[59] If the will was directed toward God all the words for love were synonyms for the same virtue; if it was directed away from God, they were vices. Thomas knew Augustine's discussion very well and even quoted it.[60] But he could not entirely accept it because his scheme had two appetitive faculties. The intellective (the will) had "passions" and apprehensions without bodily concomitants. By contrast, the sensitive appetite depended on the body both to apprehend and to express its passions. Thus, Thomas distinguished among *amor*, *dilectio*, and *caritas*: "For among them, *amor* is the most general; every *dilectio* or *caritas* is *amor*, but not vice versa." *Dilectio* implied choice (Thomas derived it from the word *electio*), and that made it the will's sort of love. And *caritas* implied "a certain perfection (*perfectionem quandam*)" of love.[61]

But Thomas did not leave the question there, with its suggestion that the *amor* of the sensitive appetite – the love that was the root of all the other passions and had been the form of love on which he had spent so much time – was inferior to the *dilectio* of the intellective appetite. To the contrary, he added a point that corresponded not to any of the three objections he adduced for his agrument but treating instead the topic of his *sed contra*.[62] In that new point, he noted that Dionysius in *On the Divine Names* had said that some people thought that *amor* was more divine than *dilectio* even in the intellective appetite because *amor* (unlike *dilectio*) implied a certain passivity, especially insofar as it was also in the sensitive appetite. Why did this passivity make *amor* "more divine"? Thomas explained: "A person can make his way better to God through *amor*, in a way passively drawn by God himself, than he can lead himself to God by means of his own reason, which pertains to the nature (*rationem*) of *dilectio*. And on account of this, *amor* is more divine than *dilectio*.' "A person can make his way better to God though *amor*, in a way passively drawn by God himself, than he can lead himself to God by means of his own reason, which pertains to the nature (*rationem*) of *dilectio*. And on account of this, *amor* is more divine than *dilectio*."

---

[58] ST I-II, q. 26 a. 1 co.   [59] See Chapter 1, n. 48.   [60] ST I-II, q. 26 a. 3 arg. 3.
[61] *Ibid.*, a. 3 co.   [62] Miner, *Aquinas on the Passions*, 121, emphasizes this point.

This is a key passage. It helps explain why Thomas considered the passions of the sensitive appetite foundational for his discussion of human beings in his larger story. The general narrative of the *Summa theologiae* has been described as an *exitus-reditus* (exit and return), with man a sort of Prodigal Son, begotten by God and coming back to him.[63] How and why man returns to God necessitates a discussion of human nature. In Thomas' scheme, the passivity of the passions is not a fault. Rather the passive becomes habit (Thomas' next topic) and thereby turns into virtue or vice.[64]

After discussing *amor*'s divine potential, Thomas turns to two kinds of love: desire's love (*amor concupiscentiae*) and friendship's love (*amor amicitiae*). The idea came from earlier scholastics. Geoffrey of Poitiers, for example, writing c. 1214, named two forms of "voluntary love (*dilectio voluntaria*)": concupiscent love and friendship.[65] Taking his cue from Aristotle's discussion of friendship, where "those who wish the good of their friends for their friends' sake ... are friends in the fullest sense,"[66] Thomas distinguishes between "simple" love of something for its very self (this is friendship's love) and love of something for something else (desire's love). The two are related as prior (friendship's love) and posterior (desire's love): a person first of all loves himself for himself and then will love other things for contributing to that love because they are useful or pleasurable.[67] Thomas' conclusion is that "insofar as [a friendship] is

---

[63] This analysis of the structure is the traditional one, first offered by Marie-Dominique Chenu, *Toward Understanding Saint Thomas*, trans. A.-M. Landry and D. Hughes (Chicago, 1963), 310–18. Torrell, *Aquinas: The Person*, 150–59, problematizes it and suggests that the *Summa* is better seen as a study of God. Brian Davies, *Thomas Aquinas's* Summa Theologiae: *A Guide and Commentary* (Oxford, 2014), 15, suggests that Thomas did not have a fixed agenda for the work.

[64] See Mark D. Jordan, "Ideals of *Scientia moralis* and the Invention of the *Summa theologiae*," in *Aquinas's Moral Theory*, 88–90. Leonard E. Boyle, "The Setting of the *Summa theologiae* of Saint Thomas," in *The Gilson Lectures on Thomas Aquinas*, intro. James P. Reilly (Toronto, 2008), 19–45, esp. 36–39, argues that Thomas' *Summa theologiae* was an implicit critique of the way the Dominicans had previously presented ethics, namely via *summae* on the individual virtues and vices.

[65] Geoffrey of Poitiers, *Summa*: "Dilectio voluntaria dividitur in duas: prima dicitur concupiscentia ... Secunda est amicitia (Voluntary love is divided in two: the first is called concupiscence; the second is friendship)." BnF cod. lat. 15747 fol. 23, quoted in Artur Landgraf, "Studien zur Erkenntnis des Übernatürlichen in der Frühscholastik," *Scholastik* 4 (1929): 376 n. 2. On the date of this *Summa*, see Paul Anciaux, "La date de composition de la Somme de Godefroid de Poitiers," *Recherches de Théologie ancienne et médiévale* 16 (1949): 165–66.

[66] Aristotle, *Nicomachean Ethics* 8.3.6 (1156b10), 461. See the discussion in Chapter 1 at n. 14 above.

[67] ST I-II, q. 26 a. 4. Note that what I here term "friendship's love" as the translation for *amor amicitiae* is usually translated into English as "love of friendship," while "desire's love" for *amor concupiscentiae* (as here) is usually translated as "love of concupiscence." The problem is the genitive with the word "love." In the phrase "love of someone" the someone is the object. In the phrase "the coat of someone," the coat is properly someone's. By *amor amicitiae*, Thomas does not mean that someone "loves friendship" but rather that there is a form of love that is proper to friendship, namely friendship's (form

pulled toward (*trahitur ad*) desire's love, it falls short (*deficit*) of the character of true friendship."[68]

It "falls short." Yet this love that falls short is a necessary preliminary to friendship's love. We have already seen in Aelred that love of self constituted the first Sabbath, prior to love of neighbor. Thomas saw the love of self as generating the first steps toward friendship's love. People often needed more than the irascible passions to overcome obstacles. They needed others to help, and they loved those who helped them.[69] "The love by which someone loves himself is the form and root of friendship (*forma et radix amicitiae*)."[70] And again, "every sort of friendship includes concupiscence or desire and adds something above and beyond that."[71]

Both sorts of love – desire's love and friendship's love – have, in different ways, three extraordinary "effects": union, mutual indwelling, and ecstasy (*extasis*). In elaborating on "union," Thomas noted that "lovers seek a union that is appropriate and fitting, namely that they spend time together (*simul conversentur*), talk together (*simul colloquantur*), and in other ways of this sort be joined together (*conjungantur*)."[72] In the instance of desire's love, the union is about the particulars: it involves the pleasures of good conversation, for example. In the instance of friendship's love, the union is, as it were, with the very being of the beloved, whether or not he (or she) is a good conversationalist. Recall Aelred's dialogue *On Spiritual Friendship*. In it, he pictured himself sitting with friends and discoursing on friendship. A friend, he said, "should be so much yours, and you his – both in bodily and in spiritual matters – that there should be no separation of souls, affection, will, or opinion." This describes Thomas' notion of friendship's love. But remember that, unlike Aelred's *caritas*, at the root of friendship's love in Thomas' theory is self-interested love – desire's love.

As if the closeness of union were not enough, Thomas also saw lovers dwelling in one another. Indeed, this enlisted not only the appetitive faculty but also the intellective: "As to the intellective faculty (*secundum apprehensionem*), the lover (*amans*) is said to be in the beloved (*amato*)

---

of) love. Hence my translation. On *amor amicitiae*, however translated, see Daniel Schwartz, *Aquinas on Friendship* (Oxford, 2007). For further background and bibliography on the notion, see Abelardo Rivera, "El Amor de Amistad" (Extract of PhD diss., University of Navarra, 2003), online at encuentra.com/revista/wp-content/uploads/2008/07/amistad_el_amor_de_amistad.pdf.

[68] ST I-II, q. 26 a. 4 ad 3.

[69] ST I-II, q. 40 a. 7. See David M. Gallagher, "Thomas Aquinas on Self-Love as the Basis for Love of Others," *Acta philosophica* 8/1 (1999): 23–44.

[70] ST II-II, q. 25 a. 4 co.

[71] *Super Sent.*, lib. 3 d. 27 q. 2 a. 1 ad 1: "quaelibet amicitia concupiscentiam seu desiderium includit, et aliquid super eam addit."

[72] ST I-II, q. 28 a. 1 ad 2.

insofar as the lover is not content with superficial knowledge of the beloved but strives to investigate everything that intimately pertains to the beloved, and thus he enters into his very interior (*ad interiora eius ingreditur*)."[73]

Indwelling works in the opposite way in the appetitive faculty. There the beloved (*amatum*) is said to be in the lover (*amante*) "as it is in [the lover's] affections through a certain 'complacency,' such that when [the beloved] is present, [the lover] takes pleasure in it [in the case of desire's love] or in its good [in the case of friendship's love]."[74] And when the beloved is not present? Then it is in the lover through longing (*desiderium*). When the longing is that of desire's love, the lover simply "tends toward the beloved itself (*tendat in ipsum amatum*)." When it is caused by friendship's love, the lover tends toward the good that he wishes for the beloved.

Beyond union and indwelling is *extasis*, transport beyond oneself. The word itself is in the Vulgate in Acts 3:10: "And they [the people who see a man healed by Peter] were filled with wonder and rapture (*stupore et extasi*)," as are the words *stupore mentis* (trance) (Acts 22:17), *mentis excessu* (ecstasy of mind) (Ps. 67:28) and *raptus* (snatched) (II Cor. 12:2–4), when Saint Paul is snatched up to the third heaven.[75] But the Bible did not connect these experiences with love, and, indeed, Augustine tended to connect them with fear.[76] Love's role in generating ecstasy was the invention of the Neoplatonists, especially the fifth-century mystic pseudo-Dionysius, whose words "divine love produces transport (*extasim*)" became a favorite passage of thirteenth-century theologians at Paris.[77] Thomas' writings on the topic were, however, more "explicit and complete" than others.[78] In his treatise on the passions, Thomas argued that "every sort of love causes ecstasy."[79]

Again, as in the case of mutual indwelling, Thomas distinguished between the ecstasy of the intellective faculty and that of the appetitive. When intellective love dwells on the beloved, "intense meditation on one thing draws him away (*abstrahit*) from other things."[80] By contrast, the

---

[73] *Ibid.*, a. 2 co. Thomas found the idea of mutual indwelling in 1 John 4:16: "He who abides in charity abides in God and God in him." But Thomas generalized this indwelling to every sort of love (*quilibet amor*). See *ibid.*, a. 2 s.c.

[74] *Ibid.*, a. 2 co.

[75] See Barbara Faes de Mottoni, "*Excessus mentis, alienatio mentis*, estasi, *raptus* nel Medioevo," in *Per una storia del concetto di mente*, ed. Eugenio Canone (Florence, 2005), 167–84, and in particular 170–71 for further biblical passages. Thomas himself distinguished between *raptus* and *extasis* in ST II-II, q. 175 a. 2 ad 1: "extasis importat simpliciter excessum a seipso ... sed raptus supra hoc addit violentiam quandam (*extasis* means simply a going beyond oneself, but *raptus* adds to this a kind of violence)."

[76] Faes de Mottoni, "*Excessus mentis*," 173. [77] *Ibid.*, 176. [78] *Ibid.*, 181.

[79] ST I-II, q. 28 a. 3 s.c.: "quilibet amor causet extasim." [80] *Ibid.*, a. 3 co.

second kind of ecstasy, that of the appetitive faculty, is the effect of love directly (*directe*): simply (*simpliciter*) in the case of friendship's love and not simply in the case of desire's love. In this "non-simple" instance the lover, dissatisfied with the good that he has, "goes out from himself" to find something beyond him. Yet, because his love is ultimately self-interested, "the affection is, in the end, confined (*concluditur*) within him."[81]

Here, too, Thomas echoed the ideas of Aelred regarding love's special effects, and he helped legitimate the burgeoning mystical movements of which we shall see an exemplar in the next chapter.[82]

The morality of the passions

Considered simply as themselves (*secundum se*), as motions of the sensitive appetite, the passions are neither good nor evil. They are involuntary, irrational, and natural. But we cannot, in the real world, consider them "simply as themselves." The sensitive appetite has what we might call a semipermeable membrane. It is subject to sensations and to cognitions about them. Even an animal "knows" that the food it eats is a good thing. This is all the more true in the case of human passions. And thus the passions are moral insofar as they are "subject to the command (*imperio*) of reason and the will."[83] Or, to put it another way, "insofar as the passions of the soul are regulated (*ordinatae*) by reason, they pertain to virtue."[84] They even "contribute to the perfection of human good (*ad perfectionem humani boni*) if they are moderated by reason."[85] Would human beings nevertheless be more perfect if they had no passions? By no means. We have already seen that God created human beings *with* passions; we have already noted how *amor* is more divine than *dilectio*; and we have also explored how friendship's love cannot exist without desire's love. In sum, Thomas says that the passions are *necessary* to the perfection of human virtue. "For it pertains to the perfection of moral good that a person be moved to the good not only by his will *but also* by the sensitive appetite."[86]

This confluence of the will and the sensitive appetite happens only when the passions follow the judgment of reason. Thomas outlines two such virtuous scenarios. In the first, the superior part of the soul (*superior pars animae*) – the intellective appetite – wants something so badly (or, as Thomas puts it, "is moved so intensely [*intense movetur*]") that, through a

---

[81] *Ibid.*

[82] Torrell, *Thomas d'Aquin*, v, argues that Thomas was not only a "maître spirituel" but also "un mystique."

[83] ST I-II, q. 24 a. 1 co.   [84] *Ibid.*, a. 2 ad 3.   [85] *Ibid.*   [86] *Ibid.*, a. 3 co., italics mine.

kind of overflowing (*per modum redundantiae*), the passions of the soul are carried along, "and thus the passion that consequently exists in the sensitive appetite is a sign of the force of the will (*signum intensionis voluntatis*). And this indicates a greater moral goodness (*et sic indicat bonitatem moralem maiorem*)."[87] In a second scenario, a person chooses to be affected by a passion in order to make reason's work more effective (*promptius*). "And so the passion of the soul (*passio animae*) adds (*addit*) to the goodness of the act."[88]

There are other possibilities. Passions might be mitigated or modified by reason's power.[89] Peter King gives an example of how this might work: "Grief over the death of a friend can be mitigated by thinking of the general truth that we all die."[90] On the other hand, for higher cognition to have any intensity – for it to *care* about the fact that we all die – it needs the passions: "For the will cannot be moved intensely toward anything but that some passion in the sensitive appetite be excited."[91]

This idyllic working relationship between reason and the passions is, however, very hard to achieve. In the first place, since the Fall, reason itself is not a guarantor of good judgment. Original justice (*justitia*) was the ordering principle of the Garden of Eden. The loss of that justice was the original sin, severing the "subjection of the human mind to God."[92] Since then, the will has always moved toward "a good," but that good might be only an apparent one.[93]

In the second place, the harmony of will and passion always depends on the will's guiding role, which it does not always manage to take. Sometimes the passions divert the will, either by "distracting (*secundum quandam abstractionem*)" it from the judgments of reason or by overwhelming reason itself with mad illusions.[94] Sometimes the will is blinded by its own limitations: it may know something is wrong in the abstract but

---

[87] *Ibid.*, a. 3 ad 1.   [88] *Ibid.* See Miner, *Aquinas on the Passions*, 91–93.

[89] See ST I-II q. 24 a. 3 co. See the remarks in Torrell, *Thomas d'Aquin*, 346–48; Elisabeth Uffenheimer-Lippens, "Rationalized Passion and Passionate Rationality: Thomas Aquinas on the Relation between Reason and the Passions," *The Review of Metaphysics* 56 (2003): 542–57; Sciuto, "Le passioni," 81–82; and Galeazzi, "Le passioni," 558–65, takes up the point in connection with Thomas' *De veritate*.

[90] King, "Emotions," 216–17, enumerates many other ways in which "the sensitive appetite is subordinate to the will."

[91] ST I-II, q. 77 a. 6 co. See further Lombardo, *The Logic of Desire*, 89–93.

[92] ST I-II, q. 82 a. 2 co.: the cause of original sin is the "privatio originalis justitiae per quam sublata est subjectio humanae mentis ad Deum (loss of original justice, through which [loss] the human mind's subjection to God was destroyed)."

[93] ST I-II, q. 77 a. 2 co.: "voluntas sit boni vel apparentis boni (the will is [moved to] a good or an *apparent* good)." (Emphasis mine.)

[94] *Ibid.*, a. 1 co. "Impeditur enim judicium et apprehensio rationis propter vehementem et inordinatam apprehensionem imaginationis (for judgment and apprehension is impeded because of a vehement and inordinate apprehension of the imagination)."

nevertheless not apply that knowledge correctly in the particular. Love and anger are particularly prone to be so intense and to cause such great bodily transmutations that a person "loses the use of his reason entirely."[95]

Were the passions always seething and reason newly called upon to guide them at every moment, human life would be virtuous only very sporadically. Happily, the passions can *routinely* come under the control of reason. This happens through habit (*habitus*). A habit is a "disposition (*dispositio*) according to which that which is disposed [namely the person] is disposed well or badly (*bene aut male*)."[96] The trick to being well disposed is to have good habits. These good habits constitute the moral virtues.

What is a virtue and how exactly does it relate to the passions? Thomas defines virtue as "a certain perfection of a faculty (*quamdam perfectio potentiae*)."[97] Different sorts of virtues are proper to different faculties. The perfection of the intellective faculty, for example, involves "a habit of intellectual virtue (*habitum virtutis intellectualis*)."[98] But having a perfected intellective appetite is nothing unless a person acts on that virtue. Moral virtues – virtues that incline a person to act in a good way[99] – are necessary. Those are the virtues that perfect the appetitive faculty, "whose function it is to move all the [other] faculties to their acts."[100]

As we have seen, the appetitive faculty does not always follow the intellective, the seat of reason. The role of the moral virtues pertaining to the sensitive appetite is to help ensure that reason rules the passions. If this subordination happens just here and there, it is not virtue, though it is virtuous. Virtue, by definition, is *habitual*.[101] "The virtue that is in the irascible and concupiscible [powers] is nothing other than a certain habitual conformity (*quaedam habitualis conformitas*) of those powers to reason."[102] Virtue does not eliminate the passions (here Thomas, like Aelred, Augustine, and Cicero argued against the Stoics). Rather "virtue overcomes inordinate (*inordinatas*) passions even as (*autem*) it produces well moderated (*moderatas*) passions."[103]

Different passions are moderated by different moral virtues. The concupiscible passions, all directed to obtaining the same good or avoiding the same evil, require only one virtue: temperance

---

[95] *Ibid.*, a. 2 co.   [96] ST I-II, q. 49 a. 1 co.
[97] ST I-II, q. 55 a. 1 co. Miner, *Aquinas on the Passions*, 287–95, is helpful on the relationship between virtue and the passions.
[98] ST I-II, q. 58 a. 2 co. Prudence is an example of an intellectual virtue.
[99] *Ibid.*, a. 1 co.   [100] *Ibid.*
[101] ST I-II, q. 51 a. 3 co.: "habitus virtutis non potest causari per unum actum, sed per multos (the habit of virtue cannot be caused by one act but by many)."
[102] ST I-II, q. 56 a. 4 co.   [103] ST I-II, q. 59 a. 5 ad 1.

(*temperantia*).[104] The irascible passions are more complicated, for they are "directed to different things (*ad diversa ordinantur*)."[105] While fear and courage are directed at danger, hope and despair are about a difficult good, and anger tries to overcome something that has caused harm. Thus fortitude (*fortitudo*) is the virtue that moderates fear and courage; magnanimity (or great-souledness, *magnanimitas*) is needed for hope and despair; and meekness (*mansuetudo*) regulates anger.

Other moral virtues correspond to the objects of the passions rather than to the passions themselves. These also regulate the passions, but not in a one-to-one manner. Thus the object "money" is not particularly pleasurable to touch. If it were, it would be the role of temperance to moderate desire for it. But "in the case of money considered as a good absolutely, as an object of concupiscence or pleasure or love, there is [the virtue of] liberality (*liberalitas*)." Or, if we consider money as a "good difficult to get and thus as an object of hope, there is magnificence (*magnificentia*)."[106] And so on. In all, Thomas named eleven moral virtues, one of which (justice, *justitia*) pertained to the will. Thomas recognized the four classical virtues – prudence, justice, fortitude, and temperance – as the "cardinal virtues" among the moral virtues.[107] As for the theological virtues – faith, hope, and charity – these "were something added for man supernaturally (*supernaturaliter*) to direct (*ordinandum*) him to his supernatural end."[108]

In these ways, Thomas incorporated the virtues into his discussion of the passions. Alcuin had treated the virtues as essentially equivalent to emotions. Thomas, although not equating them, nevertheless linked the two indissolubly. See Table 5.3.

Alcuin had also considered the vices to be emotions. And Thomas? Thomas said that vices are the contrary of virtues. Virtues are essentially good habits; vices are bad habits. They both have the potential to generate acts, one good, the other bad. The word merit (*meritum*) is sometimes used to designate a virtuous act; the word for a bad act is sin (*peccatum*).[109] As a bad habit, vice is intimately connected to the passions by disposing them to

---

[104] On how temperance works to order the concupiscible passions, see Giuseppe Butera, "On Reason's Control of the Passions in Aquinas's Theory of Temperance," *Mediaeval Studies* 68 (2006): 133–60.

[105] ST I-II, q. 60 a. 4 co.   [106] *Ibid.*, a. 5 co.

[107] ST I-II, q. 61 a. 2. Of these four, only prudence is not about the passions but rather is the virtue that should rule the intellective faculty. Justice should rule the will, temperance the concupiscible passions, and fortitude the irascible.

[108] ST I-II, q. 62 a. 3 co.

[109] ST I-II, q. 71 a. 1 co. and ad 2 provide the definitions of making sin the contrary of a virtuous act and vice the contrary of virtue. In q. 71 a. 5 arg. 1, Thomas uses the word *meritum* (merit) to signify the act of virtue. In a. 5 co., he notes that sometimes a sin of omission does not involve an actual act.

Table 5.3 *The moral virtues that regulate Aquinas' passions and affections*

Virtue	Passion(s) regulated
affabilitas, affability[a]	concupiscible
eutrapelia, pleasures of games	concupiscible
fortitudo, fortitude	irascible, *timor* and *audacia* (fear and courage)
justitia, justice[b]	will (affections)
liberalitas, liberality[c]	concupiscible
magnanimitas, magnanimity[d]	irascible, *spes* and *desperatio* (hope and despair)
magnificentia, magnificence	irascible
mansuetudo, meekness	irascible, *ira* (anger)
philotimia, love of honor	concupiscible
sinceritas, sincerity	concupiscible
temperantia, temperance[e]	concupiscible

[a] *Affabilitas*, *eutrapelia*, and *sinceritas* regulate the concupiscible passions for the *good of others* rather than self.

[b] *Justitia* regulates external activities (*operationes*). All the other virtues regulate the passions of the sensitive appetite. Thus, if you hit someone out of anger, you lack *justitia* in your external behavior, but you lack *mansuetudo* internally. See ST I-II, q. 60 a. 2 co.

[c] *Liberalitas*, *magnanimitas*, *magnificentia*, and *philotimia* regulate concupiscible and irascible passions aroused by a good for the *benefit of self* (for example, money and honor).

[d] *Magnanimitas* regulates hope and despair aroused when a good is arduous. For example, when honor is apprehended as an arduous good and therefore the object of hope, *magnanimitas* is the proper regulating moral virtue.

[e] *Temperantia* regulates all the concupiscible passions in that it guarantees that they follow the rational mean. It also regulates those passions that are aroused by a good apprehended by the sense of touch and that pertain to the preservation of human life (for example, food).

disorder rather than order. "The vice of any one thing (*uniuscuiusque rei*) seems to be that it is not disposed in accordance with what befits its nature."[110] What befits the nature of the sensitive appetite? To be in accord with reason. Vice is the contrary of that. Why do people do things contrary to nature? Thomas explains that human nature has two parts: rational and sensitive. "It is through the operation of his senses (*operationem sensus*) that man arrives at (*pervenit*) acts of reason." The process has two steps, but "more people get to the beginning of something than arrive at its completion."[111]

---

[110] *Ibid.*, a. 1 co. and repeated in a. 2 co.   [111] *Ibid.*, a. 2 ad 3.

We have seen that some virtues are differentiated by the passions they correspond to, while others are differentiated by their objects. Thomas says that the various sins "are better distinguished according to the objects of their acts than according to their opposites. However, even if they were distinguished according to their opposite virtues, it would come to the same thing (*in idem rediret*)."[112] Because he looks at the objects of the vices, Thomas' discussion of vices and sins seems less anchored than the virtues in his treatise on the passions. But this is illusory. The vices and sins are as fully rooted in the sensitive appetite as the virtues. The difference is that the vices are chained by bad habits and, deaf to reason's command, they are entirely disordered.

Let us conclude our discussion of Thomas' theory with his image of the human condition. Appetites, both intellective and sensitive, are at its core, for appetites determine both loves and acts. In the ideal, rightly ordered world, human reason would follow God's law, the human will would want that law, the sensitive appetite would love and desire all the good commanded by that law, and the body would move in accordance with those loves. But we do not live in an ideal world: "for original sin passes away as guilt (*reatu*) and [yet] remains as act (*actu*)."[113] No one ever wittingly seeks evil. But since "some evil (*aliquod malum*) is an apparent good (*apparens bonus*), the will sometimes desires some evil (*aliquod malum*)."[114] The result, for the ordinary person, is a life necessitating continual and unflagging vigilance:

the corruption of the *fomes* [the effect of original sin] does not prevent a person with rational will from being able to repress (*reprimere*) the individual inordinate motions of sensuality if he is aware [of them], as for example by diverting a thought to other things. But when a person diverts a thought to something else, some inordinate motion can arise even around that. Thus, when someone, wanting to avoid the motion of desire (*concupiscentiae*), transfers his thought from the delights of the flesh to the contemplation of knowledge, sometimes some unpremeditated motion of vainglory rises up (*insurgit*). Because of the corruption [of original sin], a person cannot avoid all these motions. But this alone is sufficient [remedy] for voluntary sin: that he avoid each single one.[115]

We are almost back to Evagrius with his "eight thoughts," each of which had to be used to drive out the other.[116]

***

Thomas drew on the inheritance of both ancient and medieval thinkers for his lengthy account of the passions. His list of terms was not very

---

[112] ST I-II, q. 72 a. 1 ad 2.   [113] ST I-II, q. 74 a. 3 ad 2.   [114] *Ibid.*, a. 1 ad 1.
[115] *Ibid.*, a. 3 ad 2.   [116] See Chapter 3 at n. 13.

different from the ancient word-hoards that Cicero and Augustine had provided. His physics and logic came from Aristotle. His outlook on the morality of emotions came from Augustine and reflected the same conviction that Alcuin had had when advising the layman Wido: you can read, hear, think, and act on knowledge about the passions to help you become virtuous.

Love was the root of Thomas' scheme, as it had been when Aelred counseled his fellow monks about friendship in Christ, when the counts of Toulouse professed to love their men, and when the troubadours praised and blamed their ladies. Thomas made explicit and logical what the troubadours sang: love's inclination starts a whole chain of human desire, and all the other passions come to its aid in one way or the other.[117] Anger, too, was key in Thomas' scheme, since it was the potential outcome of two scenarios and because the joy of its success in revenge was always a live possibility. This mirrored the importance of anger and indignation in Thomas' world.

Although Alcuin had also seen a sequence – in the transformation of the wrong sort of sadness into the right sort, for example – Thomas' emotional sequence was worked out in far greater detail. Each of Thomas' passions played a particular role; each role had a particular virtue.

In the next chapter we shall see that the primacy of love remained true in the fifteenth century for Margery Kempe, who acted out her love for God and Christ (and theirs for her) in dramatic dialogue. For this, she drew on the forms of meditation that Aelred had written about to his sister. But love gave way to other emotions – especially to a new emphasis on pity – in a different fifteenth-century emotional community, the equally dramatically inclined court of Burgundy. Finally, in the same period, the Paston family hardly mentioned love and, indeed, tamped down all of its emotional expressions.

---

[117] See Baladier, *Érôs au Moyen Âge*, and more recently, Valentina Atturo, "*Languor carnis*", 49–78, esp. 53–60.

6   Theatricality and sobriety

It was no accident that Saint Thomas' theory associated emotions with the body. Even before his day, mystics like Saint Francis, Christina Mirabilis, and Marie d'Oignies had made such an association a regular – though not, as with Thomas, a theoretical – part of their affective lives. In the fifteenth century some emotional communities highly valued bodily gestures – openly and publicly expressed – of ardor, joy, sorrow, and other emotions. In Johan Huizinga's famous and influential view, this made it an age of passionate extremes. He spoke of the "vacillating moods of unrefined exuberance, sudden cruelty, and tender emotions" in the medieval city; of a "surplus of tears" among the masses; of the "flaming passion and childish imagination" reigning in daily life; and of "the most primitive emotions of mutual loyalty" prevailing in relations between servants and masters.[1]

Huizinga gathered his examples from the chronicles of the time. As we shall see, he missed much of their emotional import.[2] But even had he gotten everything right, he would still mislead, for the chroniclers represent only one emotional community. For example, in the very same cities where Huizinga saw "vacillating moods of unrefined exuberance" were groups – the New Devout (or brethren of the common life) – whose highest values centered on "inwardness" and "interiority" rather than public display.[3]

---

[1] Johan Huizinga, *The Autumn of the Middle Ages*, trans. Rodney J. Payton and Ulrich Mammitzsch (Chicago, 1996), 2, 8, and 10, a translation of *Herfsttij der middeleeuwen* (Haarlem, 1919).

[2] For a critique and appreciation of Huizinga's method, see Jan-Dirk Müller, "Johan Huizinga (1872–1945) und der Herbst des Mittelalters," in *Kulturwissenschaftler des 20. Jahrhunderts. Ihr Werk im Blick auf das Europa der frühen Neuzeit*, ed. Klaus Garber with Sabine Kleymann (Munich, 2002), 263–82.

[3] Recognizing the diversity of the Burgundian Netherlands is Scheel, *Das altniederländische Stifterbild*, 18–25, with interesting things to say about the sensibilities of the New Devout on 199–200, 230–42 *et passim*. For the New Devout in particular, see *Devotio Moderna: Basic Writings*, trans. John Van Engen (New York, 1988), 27. Jan Dumolyn and Elodie Lecuppre-Desjardin, "Propagande et sensibilité. La fibre émotionnelle au cœur

169

Across the Channel, English communities showed a similar variety. Margery Kempe, deeply influenced by the model of mystics, nevertheless brought the bodily expression of emotion to such an extreme that she alienated many – though by no means all – with whom she associated. Hers was presumably a small, but real, emotional community. The Paston family, which lived around the same time as Kempe and, in fact, not very far away from her, provides an example of a very different sort of emotional community. And there were many others I do not treat here.[4] (For all the place names in this chapter, see Map 6.1.)

"Troubled, sad, and upset at heart": the Burgundian chroniclers

Late medieval Burgundy was the dazzling creation of its dukes, the most important for our discussion here being Philip the Bold (1363–1404), John the Fearless (1404–19), and Philip the Good (1419–67).[5] When Philip the Bold inherited Flanders in 1384, he became the ruler of an hourglass-shaped territory that stretched in fits and starts from south (with its center at Dijon) to north (with its capital at Lille). (See Map 6.1.) He and later dukes added bits and pieces to the mix to form the Burgundian "constellation."[6] They held it together by tireless travel from one end to another. Historians speak of Burgundy as a "theater state" to call attention to the rulers' use of ceremony, lavish display, and the trappings of chivalric romance to bolster their power (at least in part) and give a measure of unity to their mismatched

---

des luttes politiques et sociales dans les villes des anciens Pays-Bas bourguignons. L'exemple de la révolte brugeoise de 1436–1438," in *Emotions in the Heart of the City (14th-16th century). Les émotions au Coeur de la ville (XIVe–XVIe siècle)*, ed. Elodie Lecuppre-Desjardin and Anne-Laure Van Bruaene (Turnhout, 2005), 41–62, reveals the existence of at least two quite separate emotional communities at Bruges in the fifteenth century.

[4] For example, did the London chroniclers of the fifteenth century form an emotional community? The fact that all these chronicles were written in English by lay Londoners with considerable education, the leisure to write, and lively interest in matters broadly definable as "civic," suggests as much. See Mary-Rose McLaren, *The London Chronicles of the Fifteenth Century: A Revolution in English Writing* (Cambridge, 2002). The Lollards are another group that now has its own study: Fiona Somerset, *Feeling Like Saints* (Ithaca, NY, 2014). I thank the author for sending me her manuscript in advance of publication.

[5] Newer historiography continues the tale, at least of Netherlandish Burgundy, into the sixteenth century. See Wim Blockmans and Walter Prevenier, *The Promised Lands: The Low Countries under Burgundian Rule, 1369–1530*, trans. Elizabeth Fackelman, rev. and ed. Edward Peters (Philadelphia, 1999).

[6] "Constellation" is suggested by Jean Richard, "Le contexte. L'Etat bourguignon," in *Les Chroniques de Hainaut, ou, Les ambitions d'un Prince Bourguignon*, dir. Pierre Cockshaw, ed. Christiane Van den Bergen-Pantens (Turnhout, 2000), 9–11 at 1. I give the names of the dukes in their usual English form, but I give other names in the form that the chroniclers present them (albeit regularizing the spelling).

Map 6.1 France, England, and Burgundy in the fifteenth century

regions.[7] The Order of the Golden Fleece (the Toison d'Or), created by Philip the Good in 1430, helped to integrate urban and courtly society.[8] The court itself did the same, drawing members of the lower nobility and even the bourgeosie into the magnetic field of the ruler.

The chroniclers were among them. The court and its adherents, particularly in the Low Countries, formed their social matrix.[9] They covered a tumultuous period: the Hundred Years' War and its aftermath, assassinations, shifting political alliances, city revolts. They "romanced the past" – to borrow the phrase of Gabrielle Spiegel – by grafting history onto the vocabulary and to some extent the fantasies of vernacular romances, while adopting the sober form of prose.[10] Spiegel's romancers helped bolster the prestige of the thirteenth-century Franco-Flemish aristocracy as it faced threats from above (the monarchy) and from below (the bourgeoisie). Their late-medieval Burgundian counterparts were equally concerned to "authenticate [their] claim to historical legitimacy," asserting the moral authority of the ducal house while nevertheless validating the French state.[11] Indeed, we may see them as continuing a regional tradition, since the chroniclers with whom Spiegel worked also spoke for groups in northwest Europe. However, the Burgundian chroniclers not only translated from earlier Latin sources, but also represented something new, writing as eyewitnesses, or nearly so, of contemporary events.[12] Why did they write in prose? It was already a well-accepted idiom for history, as

---

[7] For example, David Nicholas, "In the Pit of the Burgundian Theater State: Urban Traditions and Princely Ambitions in Ghent, 1360–1420," in *City and Spectacle in Medieval Europe*, ed. Barbara A. Hanawalt and Kathryn L. Reyerson (Minneapolis, 1994), 271–95, who, however, queries the relevance of the idea of the "theater state" for Flemish cities like Ghent. *Court and Civic Society in the Burgundian Low Countries c. 1420–1530*, ed. Andrew Brown and Graeme Small (Manchester, 2007), 21–35, concludes that the epithet is a "term of convenience" that hides the polyvalent meaning of rituals.

[8] *Ibid.*, 132–34, denying that the Order helped integrate ducal domains but giving credence to the observation of Richard Vaughan, *Philip the Good: The Apogee of Burgundy* (New York, 1970), 160–62, that the Order's function was "to unite the nobility of the different Burgundian territories and bind them in close personal dependence on the duke." On the structure of the court, see Werner Paravicini, "The Court of the Dukes of Burgundy: A Model for Europe?" in *Princes, Patronage, and the Nobility: The Court at the Beginning of the Modern Age, c. 1450–1650*, ed. Ronald G. Asch and Adulf M. Birke (Oxford, 1991), 69–102.

[9] For the ways that the urbanized southern Netherlands and northern France influenced the activities of the court, see *Court and Civic Society*, 4–5. On the growing interest of northern French (and Burgundian) princes in historical works and the role of the chroniclers vis-à-vis that interest, see Graeme Small, "Chroniqueurs et culture historique au bas Moyen Âge," in *Valenciennes aux XIVe et XVe siècles. Art et Histoire*, ed. Ludovic Nys and Alain Salamagne (Valenciennes, 1996), 271–96.

[10] Gabrielle M. Spiegel, *Romancing the Past: The Rise of Vernacular Prose Historiography in Thirteenth-Century France* (Berkeley, 1993).

[11] Quoted in Spiegel, *Romancing*, 3.

[12] For example, Jean [Jehan] Wauquelin, *Chronique des ducs de Brabant*, ed. Edmond de Dynter, 3 vols. (Brussels, 1854–60).

the *Grandes Chroniques de France* – the "official" royal chronicles, begun in 1274 – attest.[13] Prose was said to foster adherence to the facts.[14] Why in the vernacular? Because it was the language that educated laymen could read, and it had even become the language of government and business. When he wrote the *Chronique du religieux de Saint-Denys*, its author, Michel Pintoin (1349–1421), had to "translate" both common speech and official documents into Latin.[15] The Burgundian chronicles could claim to combine the best aspects of two domains: romance and fact.[16]

Enguerrand de Monstrelet (c.1390/95–1453) wrote his *Chronicle* between 1444 and 1453, covering the period 1400 to 1444.[17] We are not well informed about his life.[18] The best guess is that he came from a petty (and relatively impoverished) noble family in Picardy.[19] Fairly well educated (judging by references to Cicero and other classical Latin authors in his *Chronicle*), he held a variety of offices: working for Duke Philip of Burgundy, he was captain of the castle at Frévent; working for Jehan de Luxembourg (a close associate of Philip), he was tax collector (*gavenier*) at Cambrai; employed by the cathedral canons at Cambrai, he was again *gavenier* as well as prévôt of the city. He married and had several

---

[13] *Les Grandes chroniques de France*, ed. Jules Viard, 10 vols. (Paris, 1920–53); see Gabrielle M. Spiegel, *The Chronicle Tradition of Saint-Denis: A Survey* (Brookline, MA, 1978), 72–89.

[14] See Spiegel, *Romancing*, 55–56, on the "truth of prose" and the "deforming medium of verse."

[15] *Chronique du religieux de Saint-Denys*, ed. and trans. M. L. Bellaguet, 6 vols. (Paris, 1839–52). For the identity of Michel Pintoin as author, see Nicole Grévy-Pons and Ezio Ornato, "Qui est l'auteur de la chronique latine de Charles VI, dite du Religieux de Saint-Denis?" *Bibliothèque de l'École des Chartes* 134 (1976): 85–102. For Michel Pintoin as "translator," see Bernard Guenée, *Un roi et son historien. Vingt études sur le règne de Charles VI et la Chronique du Religieux de Saint-Denis* (Paris, 1999), 9.

[16] Catherine Emerson, "Je Doncques: The Voice of the Author in Fifteenth-Century Historical Prologues," in *Auctoritas: Authorship and Authority*, ed. Catherine Emerson, Edward A. O'Brien, and Laurent Semichon (Glasgow, 2001), 21–38 at 21, points out that the genres of chronicle and poetry were clearly distinguished at the ducal court. Gabrielle M. Spiegel, "Theory into Practice: Reading Medieval Chronicles," in *The Medieval Chronicle: Proceedings of the 1ˢᵗ International Conference on the Medieval Chronicle, Driebergen/Utrecht, 13–16 July 1996*, ed. Erik Kooper (Amsterdam, 1999), 1–12, discusses the problems of using chronicles as historical texts.

[17] *La Chronique d'Enguerran de Monstrelet*, ed. L. Douët-D'Arcq, 6 vols. (Paris, 1857–62) [henceforth Monstrelet]. A continuation of this work by another author begins 6:109.

[18] I cobble together here the findings of Cyrille Thelliez, "Enguerrand de Monstrelet. Prévost de Cambrai, chroniqueur," *Mémoires de la Société d'émulation de Cambrai* 92 (1968): 9–23; Denis Boucquey, "Enguerran de Monstrelet, historien trop longtemps oublié," *Publications du Centre européen d'études bourguignonnes (XIVᵉ–XVIᵉ s.)* 31 (1991): 113–25, who proposes a birth date of c.1390–95; and *Dictionnaire des lettres françaises: Le Moyen Age*, ed. Geneviève Hasenohr and Michel Zink (rev. ed., Paris, 1994) [henceforth DLFMA], 409–10.

[19] A variety of evidence, much of it contradictory, is presented in Denis Boucquey, "Une conception de l'histoire à la fin du Moyen Âge: la *Chronique* d'Enguerran de Monstrelet" (Mémoire de licence, Louvain-la-Neuve, 1989), 30–32.

children. Throughout his life he was attached to Jehan de Luxembourg. It
is thus fair to say that he was a spokesman for the Burgundian (and
perhaps northern French) courtly emotional community of his day.[20]
Monstrelet began his history with the year 1400 because, as he tells us,
that is when Jean Froissart, the great Picard chronicler of the first half of
the Hundred Years' War, ended his own *Chroniques*.[21] He thus self-
consciously worked within a regional vernacular chronicle tradition.

After Monstrelet's death, a small group of court chroniclers came to the
fore.[22] George Chastelain (c. 1415–75) did not, apparently, know
Monstrelet personally, but he relied on Monstrelet's *Chronicle* for the first
two books of his own history. Pantler (butler) to Philip the Good, Chastelain
wrote his *Chronique* under the duke's patronage, starting in 1455, as the first
"official historian" of the Burgundian house. His *Chronicle* began with the
assassination of John the Fearless in 1419 and ended, unfinished, in 1474.[23]
For more members of the court's emotional community, we may draw upon
not only his works but also the writings of two of Chastelain's close associates
at the ducal court: Jean Lefèvre de Saint-Rémy (c. 1396–shortly after 1468)
and Olivier de La Marche (1425–1502).[24] Lefèvre, who served the duke as
an administrator and diplomat, was named the first *roi d'armes* – the chief
herald – of Philip's Order of the Golden Fleece; thereafter he was known by
the epithet Toison d'or. His *Chronique* covered the period 1408–36.[25] La

---

[20] Jehan was named count of Ligny and a knight of the Order of the Golden Fleece; see
Jean Lefèvre, *Chronique*, ed. François Morand, 2 vols. (Paris, 1876, 1881) [henceforth
Lefrèvre], 1:28; 2:172. To be sure, one may imagine that the Burgundian court consisted
of various overlapping (and evolving) emotional communities.

[21] Monstrelet, 1:5.

[22] I do not here take up the work of Mathieu d'Escouchy (1420–82), who was more courtier
to the king of France than to the duke of Burgundy, though he did cover some of the same
materials and paid homage to Monstrelet at the beginning of his work: see
Mathieu d'Escouchy, *Chronique*, ed. G. du Fresne de Beaucourt, 3 vols. (Paris, 1863–
64), 1:2: "ce noble homme et vaillant historien, Engueran de Monstrelet (this noble man
and worthy historian, Enguerrand de Monstrelet)."

[23] Georges Chastelain, *Chronique*, vols. 1–6 of *Oeuvres de Georges Chastellain*, ed. Kervyn de
Lettenhove, 8 vols. (Brussels, 1863–66). The essential modern study of this writer is
Graeme Small, *George Chastelain and the Shaping of Valois Burgundy: Political and
Historical Culture at Court in the Fifteenth Century* (Woodbridge, 1997), who documents
his subject's urban origins as Joris Chastelain. For the office of pantler and other courtly
offices, *ibid.*, 54–55; for Chastelain's appointment as ducal historian, *ibid.*, 65.

[24] For Chastelain's relationship with Lefèvre and La Marche, see *ibid.*, 73–75. I speak of
these men as forming an emotional community, but this should not imply that I adopt the
old view that they belonged the same "school" – whether of *rhétoriqueur* or anything else.
For a review of the origins of the idea of the *rhétoriqueurs*, see Catherine Emerson, *Olivier
de La Marche and the Rhetoric of 15th-Century Historiography* (Woodbridge, 2004), 75–77.

[25] Lefèvre, 1:2, himself called it his "petites récordacions et memoires (little minutes and
reminders)." Emerson, "Je Doncques," 22–23, points out that the term Mémoires was
used to distinguish writings of "less polished style" from chronicles. For a general overview of Jean Lefèvre, see DLFMA, 804–5. For his official positions, see Jacques Paviot,

Marche was also an officer of the court (he progressed from page to pantler to maître d'hôtel); at the opening of his *Mémoires*, he referred to Chastelain as "my father in teaching, my master in learning, and my particular friend."-[26] His *Mémoires* were written in the thirty-year period that began in c. 1470 and continued to shortly before his death, though in the main it is a very late work, a product of the years when part of Burgundy came under Hapsburg rule.[27] It treats the period 1435–88.

The sorrow and the pity

How can we identify what was "emotional" for the chroniclers? I here take Monstrelet as my "model" text and use the technique first introduced in Chapter 4. Table 6.1 gives the words that Monstrelet associated with the heart.[28]

The emotional emphasis of this list is entirely new. The key emotions for Monstrelet were sadness (*tristesse*) and its many near synonyms (*deul, dolent, douleur, ennuy, pleurer, triste*). Closely related to sadness were words of discontent or anguish (*admiracion, besogneux, desplaisir, ennuieux, souspirer, troublé*). These, along with terms for rancor of various sorts (*courroucie, hayne, indignacion, ire, vengence*) and the competitive emotions of shame (*vergogne*) and envy (*envieux*), round out most of Monstrelet's "heartfelt feelings." To be sure, there were positive emotions: joy (words like *joieux,*

"Étude préliminaire," in *Les Chevaliers de l'Ordre de la Toison d'or au XVe siècle. Notices bio-bibliographiques*, ed. Raphaël de Smedt (2d ed., Frankfurt, 2000), xv–xxxii at xvii.

[26] Olivier de La Marche, *Mémoires*, ed. Henri Beaune and Jean d'Arbaumont, 4 vols. (Paris, 1883–88) [henceforth La Marche],1:184: "George Chastelain, mon pere en doctrine, mon maistre en science et mon singulier amy." For a précis of his biography and writings, see DLFMA, 1085–86. See also Henri Stein, *Étude biographique, littéraire et bibliographique sur Olivier de La Marche* (Brussels, 1888). La Marche came from a family of ducal officials: see Henri Stein, *Nouveaux documents sur Olivier de La Marche et sa famille* (Brussels, 1922), 4.

[27] See Emerson, *Olivier de La Marche*, chap.1.

[28] That is, the terms that were *au cuer, de cuer, en cuer*, and so on, when "heart" signified an internal organ of feeling. I include in Table 6.1 a few words (*vergogne* is one) with which a person was *rempli* (filled). I have considered only the materials written by Monstrelet, not the speeches of others that he quoted, often extensively. Some of these used a rather different emotive vocabulary. For the heart as the seat of emotions, see the examples under *coeur* (heart) in the *Dictionnaire du Moyen Français (1330–1500)* at atilf.atilf.fr, as well as articles in *Il cuore*. In Monstrelet, the heart could also have moral meaning, as for example courage in Monstrelet, 2:43, when Jehan de Montagu, grand master of the royal household, was taken into custody but then took heart: "le cuer lui fut revenu"; purity of heart *ibid.*, 2:352: "cuer pur et net"; national feeling *ibid.*, 4:27: "natif de Haynau, anglois en cuer de toute ancienneté"; something strongly felt, *ibid.*, 5:397: "qui avoit la chose moult fort au cuer [who took the matter very much to heart]." The heart might also be associated with obstinancy or willingness: *ibid.*, 2:194: "qu'il vouloit et de tout son cuer désiroit [which he wanted and desired with all his heart]"; *ibid.*, 4:55: "Si se mirent de tout leur cuer et puissance [if they applied themselves with might and main]."

Table 6.1 *Emotions associated with the heart in Monstrelet,* Chronique*ª*

admiracion (n.), wonder [at something bad]
appaisié (adj.), calmed
besogneux (n.), need
courroucié (adj.), angered
desplaisir/desplaisance (n.), displeasure
douleur (n.), sorrow
deul (n.), mourning
dolent (adj.), sad
ennuy (n.), deep sorrow
ennuieux/anoyeux (adj.), troubled
envieux (adj.), envious
hayne (n.), hatred
indignacion (n.), hatred
joie (n.), joy
joieux (adj.), joyous
léesce (n.), happiness
pleurer (vb.), to weep
souspirer (vb.), to be anguished
tristesse (n.), sadness
triste (adj.), sad
troublé (adj.), troubled
vengence (n.), revenge
vergogne (n.), shame
yre/ire (n.), anger

ª Spellings are as in Monstrelet. English translations are very approximate.

léesce, rejoys/joie) and, indeed, the soothing of a troubled mind (*appaisié*). But without doubt the weightiest part of the list consists of words of sorrow.

Moreover, these dolorous feelings often came in clusters. Thus Duke John the Fearless was "as troubled, sad, and upset at heart as he could possibly be" when the Flemish citizens in his army refused to serve after the normal stint to fight his archenemy, the duke of Orléans.[29] When

---

[29] Monstrelet, 2:183: "tant troublé, triste et ennuieux en cuer que plus ne povoit." On the emotions of the Burgundian dukes discussed as a performance of power or political strategy, see Smagghe, *Les émotions du prince*; Smagghe "*Sur paine d'encourir nostre indignation.* Rhétorique du courroux princier dans les Pays-Bas bourguignons à la fin du Moyen Âge," in *Politiques des émotions au Moyen Âge,* ed. Damien Boquet and Piroska Nagy *Micrologus* 34(2010), 75–92. Emphasizing the latter but nevertheless recognizing an affective side as well is Manuel Guay, "Les émotions du couple princier au XVᵉ siècle: entre usages politiques et *affectio conjugalis*," *ibid.,* 93–111. In this chapter I do not separate the emotions of the prince from the other emotional norms and modes of expression valued or devalued by the chroniclers of the court.

King Charles VI of France attacked the city of Bourges, which had taken the side of the English, "the lords who were besieged within were sad and sorrowful at heart."[30] Such feelings transcended gender: the wife and niece of Waléran, count of Saint-Pol, who rushed to his side when he was on his deathbed, "were very sad and sorrowful at heart."[31] Sadness also bridged classes, as when all the besieged within the city of Meaux-en-Brie were "sad at heart at this event."[32]

How did Monstrelet know how the citizens of Meaux felt? He didn't. Rather, he was imaginatively reconstructing their emotional lives from his own experiences and assumptions about human nature. To be sure, the people of Meaux might have felt sad. But had *they* been reporting on their feelings, they might have used other terms, such as fear, anger, or resignation. When Monstrelet described emotions, he did so from his own vantage point and that of the emotional community of which he was a part. It is wrong to use Monstrelet to reveal the emotional life of the people he wrote about, at least those outside of his courtly milieux.[33] Rather, Monstrelet tells us about *his* emotional life – or, at least, the norms about it that he wished to reveal.

Already Froissart (1337–after 1404), Monstrelet's predecessor as chronicler of the Hundred Years' War, had anticipated this emotional palette.[34] Michel Zink has traced the career of this earlier writer, who limned so many different cultures.[35] Born into a family of merchants at Valenciennes, which was part of the Hanseatic League of commercial

---

[30] Monstrelet, 2:282: "Les seigneurs qui dedens estoient asségez estoient de cuer tristes et dolens."

[31] *Ibid.*, 3:68: "furent moult tristes et ennuieuses en cuer."

[32] *Ibid.*, 4:82: "tristes de cuer pour ceste adventure."

[33] It is true that a new strand of historiography, represented by, for example, Graeme Small, "When *Indiciaires* meet *Rederijkers*: A Contribution to the History of the Burgundian 'Theatre State,'" in *Stad van koopmanschap en vrede: literatuur in Brugge tussen Middeleeuwen en Rederijkerstijd*, ed. Johan Oosterman (Leuven, 2005), 133–61, questions "the assumption of cleavage between city and court" (133). This certainly would be worth pursuing from the point of view of emotional vocabulary. There may well have been city chroniclers who echoed courtly emotional values – and, as Small suggests, a "bottom-up" effect in which the townspeople influenced the court.

[34] Jacqueline Picoche, *Le vocabulaire psychologique dans les chroniques de Froissart*, 2 vols. (Paris, 1976–84), 1:123 finds no general word for the "passions" or "emotions" in Froissart. This and the special place of adjectives and adverbs in his work show (in her view) the "animated (*vivant*) character and the weak degree of abstraction" of his vocabulary. But Froissart knew Latin and thus presumably knew some of the Latin treatises on the *passiones animae*. See Michel Zink, *Froissart et le temps* (Paris, 1998), 5– 7. Christiane Raynaud, "Le courroux et la haine dans les Chroniques de Jean Froissart," *Bulletin du C.R.I.S.I.M.A.* 2 (2001): 113–234, remarks on "une grande sobriété du vocabulaire" of Froissart (119) by contrast with the terms available (117–19). For some of those terms, see Tables 6.1 and 6.2.

[35] Zink, *Froissart*, esp. 5–29.

cities and tied politically to England, Froissart at first worked as court poet in the entourages of various nobles, then obtained the church appointments that would give him the chance to work on his magnum opus: four books chronicling the Hundred Years' War. Though often said to celebrate chivalry, Froissart saw how maladapted knightly ideals were to the new realities of the battlefield.[36] His chronicle progressively became both more autobiographical and more disillusioned. Jacqueline Picoche has studied its subjective vocabulary, including emotion words.-[37] Words of fear and melancholy dominate.

Monstrelet inherited these words. To the sorrowful events that pre-occupied him, Monstrelet had one constant response, pity, and one constant adjective, piteous.[38] Indeed, although he recognized and cele-brated the "*proesses* (acts of prowess)" and "*valliances* (valiant deeds)" of the heroes of his day,[39] Monstrelet considered his most important task to consist in explaining why "the divisions, discords, and wars arose between the very noble, very excellent and very renowned lords of France. From these originated, on account of so many evils and misfortunes, great destruction and devastation in the kingdom, which piteous thing ought to be recorded."[40] A moment later, Monstrelet was speaking of the "*piteuse aventure* (piteous event)" that took place on the road to Le Mans, when King Charles VI went insane; the affliction was to last all his life.[41] This "loss of memory," as Monstrelet delicately described it, "was the main reason for the devastation of [Charles'] entire kingdom."[42]

Devastation was paramount in Monstrelet's consciousness. When the henchmen of Duke John the Fearless of Burgundy murdered Louis, the duke of Orléans, Monstrelet did not take the Burgundian side in any

---

[36] *Ibid.*, 52.

[37] Picoche, *Le vocabulaire*, 1:13, reports that she attempted to talk about frequencies from the digitized materials available to her but considered the sample too small. Today the whole has been digitized at "The Online Froissart: A Digital Edition of the Chronicles of Jean Froissart," ed. Peter Ainsworth and Godfried Croenen, www.hrionline.ac.uk/onli-nefroissart/.

[38] Pity (*eleos*) was one of the *pathê* of Aristotle, and *misericordia* was among Thomas' *passiones animae*. For the classical and early Christian meanings of pity, see David Konstan, *Pity Transformed* (London, 2001).

[39] Monstrelet, 1:4.

[40] *Ibid.*, 1:6: "les divisions, discordes et guerres s'esmurent entre la très noble, très excel-lente et très renommée seigneurie de France, dont à cause de ce tant de maulx et inconvéniens sont venus ou grant dommage et désolacion dudit royaume, que piteuse chose sera du recorder."

[41] *Ibid.*, 1:8.

[42] *Ibid.*, 1:8–9: "Et pour ceste doloreuse maladie perdi, toute sa vie durant, grant partie de sa bonne mémoire; qui fut la principale racine de la désolacion de tout son royaume. (And because of this terrible illness, lasting throughout his life, a large measure of his good memory was lost, and that was the main reason for the devastation of his entire kingdom.)"

obvious way.[43] Rather he called the assassination "the most dolorous and piteous event that had ever happened for a long time in the most Christian kingdom of France."[44] He spoke of the grief of Louis' men: "When they heard the news of the death and murder of their lord, so piteous, all wept and, painfully sorrowing at heart – the nobles as much as the non-nobles – they ran to him and found him dead there on the paving stones."[45] Later the two sides – the Burgundians and the Armagnacs (the followers of Orléans) – clashed in Paris, and the king of France took the Burgundian side, issuing "a spate of royal *ordonnances*" in favor of John.[46] Monstrelet reported that "in many and diverse places a great number of those who were of the party of Orléans were taken and arrested, and some were executed and the others made prisoner and ransomed as enemies of the kingdom. It was thus a piteous thing to hear recounted the grave persecutions which every day were carried out between these parties."[47] After a grievous battle, the English retreated, the French sought their friends among the dead, and the bodies "were entirely denuded of their clothes, and many were even despoiled of their underwear ... by the peasants, men and women, from the nearby villages." The young Philip, son of Duke John, "knowing the hard and piteous misfortune of the French, had great sorrow in his heart about it."[48] These examples could be multiplied many times over.[49] The "hard and piteous misfortune" of battle was even illustrated visually (see Plate 6.1).

---

[43] Already noted by George T. Diller, "The Assassination of Louis d'Orléans: The Overlooked Artistry of Enguerran de Monstrelet," *Fifteenth-Century Studies* 10 (1984): 57–68.

[44] Monstrelet, 1:154: "la plus doloreuse et piteuse adventure que en long temps par avant fut advenue ou très chrestien royaume de France."

[45] *Ibid.*, 1:159: "quant ils oyrent nouvelles de la mort et occision de leur seigneur, tant piteuse, tous pleurèrent, et griefment au cuer courroucez, tant les nobles comme non nobles, accoururent à lui, et là, le trouvèrent mort sur les quarreaulx."

[46] Richard Vaughan, *John the Fearless: The Growth of Burgundian Power* (New York, 1966), 92.

[47] Monstrelet, 2:196: "en plusieurs et divers lieux furent prins et arrestez très grant nombre de ceulx qui tenoient la partie d'Orléans, dont aucuns furent exécutez, et les autres mis prisonniers et raençonnez comme ennemis du royaume. Si estoit alors piteuse chose d'oyr raconter les griefves persécucions qui chascun jour se faisoient entre icelles parties."

[48] *Ibid.*, 3:121–22: "ilz furent tous desnuez de leurs vestemens et mesmement la plus grant partie furent despoullez de leurs linges ... par les paysans, hommes et femmes, des villages à l'environ ... Phelippe de Charrolois sachant la dure et piteuse adventure des François, de ce aiant au cuer grant tristesse."

[49] See, for example, *ibid.*, 2:346, 3:94, 3:112, 4:17, 4:128, among many others. Rather than pity, Froissart stressed "comfort" (Picoche notes more than 150 occurrences): it ordinarily meant an altruistic action on behalf of the weak. Inspiring the court of Burgundy was the poet and musician Guillaume de Machaut (1300–77), who regularly used words of pity, as is made clear in the word entries in atilf.atilf.fr. For one of Machaut's writings at the ducal court, see Joyce Coleman, "The Text Recontextualized in Performance: Deschamps' Prelection of Machaut's *Voir Dit* to the Count of Flanders," *Viator* 31 (2000): 233–48.

Plate 6.1 Wauquelin's "piteous words"

In short, pity at the sorrowful events of his time dominated Monstrelet's writings. It is true that joy, too, figured among Monstrelet's "heartfelt" emotions.[50] But this was not because he "vacillated" in his feelings, as Huizinga would have it, nor did he ordinarily

---

Plate 6.1

This page shows one of the many narrative illustrations in the *Chronicles of Hainaut*, a work commissioned by Philip the Good as part of his attempt to link his lineage, as well as his duchy, to an ancient past stretching back to Troy. Some of the books he ordered involved taking Old French poetic romances and turning them into prose works of "history." Others, like this one (produced in 1446–52), were translations into the vernacular of regional annals and chronicles originally written in Latin.

The text was written by Jehan Wauquelin, who not only translated the original work by Jacques de Guise but also chose the episodes to be illustrated, as well as the artists to do the job. The miniature shown here was placed above a chapter titled "the second battle of Africa," referring to the Second Punic War between Rome (led by Scipio Africanus) and Carthage (led by Hannibal). The foreground shows a battle; the Roman army is on the right, holding up a gold banner sporting the two-headed eagle of the Holy Roman Empire. However, the text itself focuses on some marvels reported in Augustine's *City of God* of "talking oxen, infants not yet born calling out certain words from the wombs of their mothers, serpents flying, women turned into men, and hens turned into roosters and other things of this sort."[i] Wauquelin added drama to these prodigies. He wrote that the oxen wailed and the babies in the wombs of their mothers were heard making "terrible cries (*cris mervilleux*)" and calling out "piteous words (*paroles piteuses*)." The artist (or artists working collaboratively) illustrated those dramas, as well: on a hill above the battle are three women (turning into men?), some oxen, and hens and roosters, all looking heavenward and no doubt uttering terrible cries and piteous words. Above the whole scene hover flying serpents. Wauquelin's addition of "paroles piteuses" is perfectly in keeping with the concerns of the emotional community at the Burgundian court.

In the next few lines, Wauquelin added material about an earthquake that toppled the Colossus of Rhodes following Scipio's battle. The original illustrative program apparently had not included a depiction of that event, but Philip later ordered the miniature that spills over the margin here. © Bibliothèque royale de Belgique, Chroniques de Hainaut, MS 9242 fol. 156r.

[i] Augustine, *Civ. dei*, 3.31, p. 97.

---

[50] For example, for the period 1420–29 Monstrelet speaks of joy at least 34 times.

depict others doing so. Joy was almost always connected to two events: when leaders, vassals, or loved ones met or arrived at a predetermined place; and when good fortune smiled.

Consider, for example, the joyous advent – or "reception."[51] It was an ancient topos with longstanding emotional significance, giving luster and éclat to the ruler. Monstrelet used it when he noted that Parisians greeted the ceremonial entry of King Charles VI into Paris in 1412 with boundless joy, crying "Noël," lighting bonfires, and shouting throughout the night, "Long live the king!"[52] But other meetings were occasions for joy as well. When the duke of Burgundy called up his men-at-arms, he "received them joyously."[53] Good fortune and lucky breaks were also joyous. "For love of the peace" between warring factions, Parisians celebrated "two days and nights of great joy and great happiness."[54] After the count of Waudément and the duke of Bar made peace, "the subjects of both sides had very great joy in their hearts."[55] Citizens also rejoiced when a hated king retreated. Thus, after the Neapolitans were temporarily successful in their rebellion against King Jaques de Bourbon, they "held a great celebration and showed great joy there and lighted fires and torches throughout the city, and the next day the ladies and demoiselles of the city danced at the castle [where the king and queen were cowering] and there manifested great joy."[56] Combatants rejoiced when their luck turned for the better: the English reinforcements sent to the embattled counts of Alençon and Richemont were received "with joyous hearts."[57]

These occasions for joy were so predictable that they could be manipulated, and joy could be a pretense. When the count of Penthièvre invited the duke of Brittany to sup at his house, he promised that "madame his

---

[51] On entries, see *Court and Civic Society*, 165–209, with bibliography in the notes. The entry recalled Christ's advent into Jerusalem: see Wilhelm Josef Schlierf, *Adventus Domini: Geschichte und Theologie des Advents in Liturgie und Brauchtum der westlichen Kirche* (Mönchengladbach, 1988). On imperial entries, see Michael McCormick, *Eternal Victory: Triumphal Rulership in Late Antiquity, Byzantium, and the Early Medieval West* (Cambridge, 1986); on various aspects of ruler entries, see articles in *Adventus. Studien zum herrscherlichen Einzug in die Stadt*, ed. Peter Johanek and Angelika Lampen (Cologne, 2009).

[52] Monstrelet, 2:302.   [53] *Ibid.*, 4:74: "qui les receut joieusement."

[54] *Ibid.*, 2:399: "si furent deux jours et deux nuis fait grant joye et grant léesse par toute la ville pour amour de la paix." Nicolas Offenstadt, *Faire la paix au moyen âge. Discours et gestes de paix pendant la guerre de Cent Ans* (Paris, 2007), 196, emphasizes the functional role of joy in accompanying announcements of peace.

[55] Monstrelet, 5:49: "les subjetz de chascune partie eurent au cuer très grant joie."

[56] *Ibid.*, 3:170: "ceulx de ladicte cité de Naples firent grant feste et menèrent grant joye, et alumèrent parmy la ville feux et torches, et lendemain furent les dames et les damoiselles de la cité danser audit chastel, et y menèrent grant joye."

[57] *Ibid.*, 2:291: "de cuer joieux."

mother, who was there, would be very joyous about it and would receive him very honorably, as well as she was able."[58] In fact the invitation was a ploy to take the duke prisoner.

Love was strikingly absent from Monstrelet's heartfelt emotions (see Table 6.1). Nothing more clearly suggests a major shift in emotional sensibilities from the twelfth- and thirteenth-century cases we have analyzed. Love had been (as we have seen) the key passion for Thomas Aquinas, and it dominated the vocabulary of the communities at Rievaulx and Toulouse. For Monstrelet, however, love was largely a synonym of the word "peace," and it was routinely associated with treaties, whether formal or patched up.[59] We have already remarked on the Parisians' celebration "for love of the peace."[60] The marriage between Jehan of Brabant and Jacqueline of Bavaria – who was countess of Hainault, Holland, and Zeeland – was arranged "in the hope" that their various territories "would have greater friendship and cordial love together."[61] (In the event, however, Philip the Good got her counties as well as Brabant.) When two quarrelling princes came to terms, they showed "great signs of happiness and love."[62]

If not signifying a formal alliance, love was nevertheless a public gesture, a show of support. After his father was assassinated, the young Duke Philip the Good came before the royal family, who "showed him a very great sign of love."[63] Two masters of arts went to Tournai as royal ambassadors to "admonish and instruct the people in the love of King Charles."[64] The people knew what that meant: they gave the masters gifts and paid their expenses. A Carmelite, Friar Thomas, who went about northern France preaching against finery and clerical vice, "acquired great love and renown among all the people in all the regions where he went."[65]

---

[58] *Ibid.*, 4:28: "madame sa mère, laquelle y estoit, en seroit moult joieuse et le recevroit à son povoir moult honnorablement."

[59] Offenstadt, *Faire la paix*, 185, notes the connection between love and peace in many representations of the period. Oschema, *Freundschaft und Nähe*, 280–90, points out that the terms "love" and "friendship" were regularly used in association with alliances.

[60] Monstrelet, 2:399, as above, n. 54. See, however, *ibid.*, 3:58, where, notwithstanding a peace, there was little security or love.

[61] *Ibid.*, 3:280: "sur espérance que les pays dudit duc et d'elle . . . eussent plus grande amitié et cordiale amour ensemble."

[62] *Ibid.*, 3:323: "grant signe de léesse et amour."

[63] *Ibid.*, 3:378: "lui monstrèrent très grant signe d'amour."

[64] *Ibid.*, 4:178, chap. title: "comment deux maistres en ars furent envoyez en la cité de Tournay pour admonester et entretenir le people en l'amour du roy Charles."

[65] *Ibid.*, 4:304: "il acquist grand amour et renommée de tout le peuple par tous les pays où il aloit." On the significance of this passage, see Rosenwein, "Thinking Historically."

Given its political significance, shows of love were easily manipulated for public consumption. When Philip the Good, John, duke of Bedford, and John V, duke of Brittany, met at Amiens in 1423 to sign the Triple Alliance of 1423, they "did great reverence to one another and made a show of being in love."[66] The Breton contender Olivier de Penthièvre pretended to be reconciled to Duke Jehan de Montfort, "showing each day the semblance of great love towards duke Jehan for public consumption."[67] We have seen that for Thomas Aquinas *amor* was the highly praised enabler of mystical union.[68] But other voices, especially by the end of that century, emphasized love's more malign potential. In Monstrelet, a jaundiced view of love between family members, spouses, and the affianced was frequent. Like Gregory of Tours, he recorded family feeling gone sour.[69]

Thus, when Jaques de Harcourt came to see his cousin, the count of Harcourt, he "did love and reverence to him in appearance," but in fact he meant to enter the count's castle and seize him.[70] Monstrelet milked the pathos of the scene: the count greeted his cousin and his entourage with a "very joyous face, saying 'Cousin, be welcome.'" But, after some dilatory conversation, Jaques grabbed him by the sleeve, saying, "'My lord, I make you prisoner of the King [Henry V].' And then the count, very taken aback, said to him, 'Dear cousin, what are you saying?'"[71] At another time, Philip the Good and his brother-in-law Charles of Bourbon met and exchanged "a few words of salutation, not at all embracing one another with a show of great love and joy, as people so closely related by blood as they were ... customarily do."[72]

Love's farcical potential played out in the story of King Lancelot of Naples, who "fell in love with the daughter of one of his physicians." The doctor at first refused to consent to the union, but eventually he "gave his consent and feigned that he was happy, which was not at all the case." The physician continued the pretense with his daughter, telling her how to

[66] *Ibid.*, 4:147: "firent l'un à l'autre grande révérence, et semblant de tout amour."
[67] *Ibid.*, 4:28: "moustrast audit duc Jehan chascun jour semblant de grant amour à la veue du monde."
[68] See Chapter 5 above on Thomas Aquinas' theory.
[69] The ducal library seems to have had a translation of Gregory of Tours; see Small, *George Chastelain*, 131.
[70] Monstrelet, 3:258: "lui faire amour et révérence, comme il monstroit semblant."
[71] *Ibid.*, 3:258: "lui fist très joieuse chère, disant: 'Cousin, vous soiez le bien venu.' ... [Jaques] print ledit conte de Harecourt par la manche en disant: 'Monseigneur, je vous fais prisonnier du Roy.' Et adonc ledit conte, moult esbahi, lui dist: 'Beau cousin, que distes-vous?'"
[72] *Ibid.*, 4:360: "en disant aulcunes parolles de salutacions, non mie en embrassant l'un l'autre par manière de grand amour et joieuseté, ainsi que ont accoustumé faire si prouchains de sang qu'ilz estoient l'un à l'autre."

keep the king's love forever ("pour avoir l'amour du roy à tousjours"). Then he prepared an ointment for her to apply on the king's stomach when he entered the marriage bed. The king "was soon burning with fire, and the girl was as well. And, in the end, they finished their days soon afterwards in this way, very miserably and in great pain."[73] The story ends with the doctor's flight.

When Jaques became king at Naples, occasioning a rebellion (as we have seen), "the queen his wife, who was old and hostile by nature, was not very happy with him because she had been informed that he was amorous of some young women in the region more than he was of her."[74] No wonder love was not among the terms Monstrelet associated with "the heart."

What had happened to love's emotional content? Monstrelet quoted many people who used the word in the old ways, but he himself used it sparingly and even then mainly in its institutional meaning – as a term for an alliance – or as something to be mistrusted because so often feigned or foolish. Thus for the period 1400–8, for example, he quoted others who used the term fifty-one times, but he himself used it only five times. Nevertheless, because it was sometimes associated with Monstrelet's "heartfelt" emotion words, we may tentatively include it in an expanded list (see Table 6.2).

Table 6.2 is worth careful consideration. Not only does it reinforce the impression of Table 6.1, namely that words of sorrow and pity predominate. But it is also rather short. In Chapter 4, the emotion word-hoard of the troubadours at Toulouse might have suggested the hypothesis that the vernacular world had a larger vocabulary of emotion words than the Latinate. Table 4.2 contains 87 Old Occitan words, not counting the variants listed in the form of subentries. That is almost twice the number of words as those given by Cicero (fifty) or Thomas Aquinas (forty-three). But now we have Monstrelet overturning the hypothesis, for his list equals that of Thomas: forty-three. Did the emotional vocabulary determine the nature of the emotional community? Or vice versa? The answer is surely: both! But let us also remember that theorists never claimed their lists to be exhaustive, and I do not

---

[73] *Ibid.*, 3:45–46: "il fut amoureux de la fille d'un sien phisicien … bailla son consentement et feigni qu'il en estoit content, ce qui n'estoit point … Quant le roy vint à elle pour son désir … il fut tantost exprins de feu et la fille pareillement. Et en la conclusion, par le moien de ce, finèrent leurs jours assez tost après, très misérablement et à grant douleur."

[74] *Ibid.*, 3:170: "la royne sa femme, qui estoit vielle et de diverse condicion, n'estoit pas bien contente de lui, pour ce qu'elle avoit esté advertie qu'il estoit amoureux de aucunes jeunes dames du pays plus qu'il n'estoit d'elle."

Table 6.2 *Enhanced list of emotions associated with the heart in Monstrelet,* Chronique

admiracion (n.), wonder (at something bad)
amour (n.), love
appaisié (adj.), calmed
besogneux (n.), need
confusion (n.), mental turmoil
  confus (adj.), troubled
consolacion (n.), consolation
content (mal) (adj.), displeased
courroux (n.), anger
  courroucié (adj.), angry; pained
crainte (n.), fear
désolé (adj.), sad
desplaisir/desplaisance (n.), displeasure
  desplaisant (adj.), displeased
dommage (n.), hurt
doubte (n.), fear
douleur (n.), sorrow
  deul (n.), mourning
  dolent (adj.), sad
ennuy (n.), deep sorrow
  ennuieux/anoyeux (adj.), troubled
envie (n.), envy
  envieux (adj.), envious
esmerveillez (adj.), amazed (often in a negative way)
esmeu (adj.), moved (often by ire)
fraieur (n.), fear
fureur (n.), fury
gémissement (n.), groaning
gré (mal) (adj.), badly
griefment (adv.), painfully
hayne (n.), hatred
honte (n.), shame
indignacion (n.), hatred
joie (n.), joy
  joieux (adj.), joyous
  joyeusement (adv.), joyously
léesce (n.), happiness
lamenter (vb.), lament
larmes (n.), tears (sorrowful)
Noël (interj.), sound of joy
piteux (adj.), worthy of pity
pleurer (vb.), to weep
souspirer (vb.), to sigh; be anguished

Table 6.2 (*cont.*)

tribulacion (n.), fear
tristesse (n.), sadness
triste (adj.), sad
troublé (adj.), troubled
vengence (n.), revenge
vergogne (n.), shame
yre/ire (n.), anger

claim that the lists I have gathered from the troubadours and Monstrelet are exhaustive, either. Measured against one another, however, they do suggest tendencies. The court at Toulouse was more demonstrative, more welcoming of emotions of every sort, than the court of Burgundy two centuries later.

The next generation of chroniclers at the Burgundian court (Chastelain, Lefèvre, La Marche) seems to have employed a similar vocabulary of emotions.[75] However, Lefèvre was far drier – far more parsimonious in expressing emotions – than Chastelain. When he described John the Fearless on the road to Montereau – where he was ambushed by the Dauphin's men and put to death for his role in the assassination of the duke of Orléans – Lefèvre's John was the model of prudence, asking for counsel and following the best advice the whole way.[76] By contrast, Chastelain turned John into a tormented and tragic figure, all but seeking his own death: "His repentance was great towards God." He therefore went against the advice of his men to the bridge of Montereau, where he was "villainously and inhumanely put to death" before the eyes of the dauphin. "O you Lords, then, who hear about this most piteous and most valiant death, ought not ... to take sides in judging between these two princes."[77]

Chastelain's chronicle provided the tastiest grist for Huizinga's mill. However, it represented but one extreme in the expressive norms of

[75] I have made a systematic survey of the emotional vocabulary in the first vol. of each of their chronicles.

[76] Lefèvre, 1:370–79. This may well be because he drew directly on the language of annals: see Claude Buridant, "La phrase des chroniqueurs en moyen français: l'exemple de Monstrelet – Le Fèvre," in *Le moyen français: philologie et linguistique. Approches du texte et du discours*, ed. Bernard Combettes and Simone Monsonégo (Paris, 1997), 319–38 at 320.

[77] Chastelain, *Chronique*, 1:31–32: "sa repentance estoit grande envers Dieu ... [il] vilainement et inhumainement fut mis à mort devant royal conspect de regardeur. O vous! seigneurs doncques, qui oyez ceste très-piteuse et très-vilaine mort, ne devez ... tenir faveur en jugement entre ces deux princes."

Plate 6.2 Jean de la Huerta's mourner

the Burgundian court. Thus, according to the dispassionate Lefèvre, when Philip the Good learned of the murder of his father at Montereau, "he had such great sorrow and displeasure that ... for some days his officers could not comfort him nor make him drink or eat."[78] Such "quiet" mourning was not just his idea: see Plate 6.2 for

---

Plate 6.2

This 16 in. high alabaster mourning figure was once part of the tomb of Duke John the Fearless and his wife Margaret of Bavaria. Commissioned considerably after John's murder in 1419 by his son Philip the Good, it was made by the Spanish sculptor Jean de la Huerta during 1443–45 and put into place at the Carthusian monastery of Champmol in 1470.[i]

The sculpture should be imagined in context. The effigies of John and Margaret lie atop a large tomb made of black marble and black-painted stone with some polychrome (in blue and red) and gilded alabaster.[ii] With open eyes (as though resurrected), they raise their hands in prayer while their feet rest on lions. Angels kneel at their heads. Beneath, along all sides of the tomb, are flamboyant Gothic arcades within which are numerous alabaster mourners, two in each space separated by columns.

The mourners are meant to signify the funeral procession for John and its attendant emotion. Some represent laypersons, others clerics. Some wear their hoods to hide their faces, others to cover their hair, and still others – like the one here – have hoods draping over their backs. The Cleveland mourner (known as "mourner 67") raises his eyes to heaven. His mouth is slightly open, exposing his teeth. Sometimes bared teeth indicate vice, but here they appear to signify emotion under control.[iii] © The Cleveland Museum of Art

[i] The tomb was dismantled during the French Revolution, and this particular figure found its way to the Cleveland Museum of Art. Today at Champmol it has been replaced by a cast.

[ii] The tomb is 96 7/8 x 148 x 142 ½ inches (246 x 376 x 362 cm). See Sophie Jugie, *The Mourners: Tomb Sculptures from the Court of Burgundy* (New Haven, 2010), 44–50.

[iii] For the ambiguity of meaning in the facial expressions found in medieval art, see Elina Gertsman, "The Facial Gesture: (Mis)Reading Emotion in Gothic Art," *Journal of Medieval Religious Cultures* 36/1 (2010): 28–46, and Jacqueline E. Jung, "Gothic Sculpture and the Decorum of Emotions in the Medieval Church," paper presented at the New England Medieval Conferences, RISD, November 9, 2013, and kindly sent to me by the author, as well as a MS of her forthcoming her book *Eloquent Bodies*.

---

[78] Lefèvre, 1:380: "il eult si grand tristresse et desplaisir que ... par aucuns jours ne povoient ... ses gouverneurs le conforter, ne faire boire ne mengier."

the figure of one of a large group of mourners commissioned by Philip the Good for the tomb of his father.[79]

But Chastelain's account of the same episode was more melodramatic:

The young, unhappy prince, conquered and overcome by sorrows – letting out a loud and horrible cry lamentable in every way – flung himself on a bed, and there stretched out, suddenly became disfigured in his face, deprived of speech and entirely inert in spirit. His eyes began to turn inward, his lips became black, his teeth clenched, his arms and legs moved him toward death. Only in his stomach, near his heart, did he retain some life. [That organ] was so distended and puffed up that it was necessary very quickly to cut the lacings of his clothing and to pry open his teeth with constant force or he would certainly have died from his sorrow. Those who were there felt such great pity that their hearts burst into tears, shouts, and pounding of hands, as if they saw the entire fabric of the world come to an end before their eyes.[80]

This is the stuff of opera. Though opera was not yet a genre, the analogy may not be far from the mark.[81] The florid description of a prince falling on his bed half dead was the rhetoric of a chronicler used to writing poetry and drama for the ducal court. Lefèvre admired the style, calling Chastelain the "*noble orateur.*"[82] Just as ancient rhetoricians understood that the orator must employ emotions to sway a jury, so the ducal court appreciated the propaganda value of elaborated passions. "With his

---

[79] The image of pity, equivalent to the Man of Sorrows, was popular at this time, as well: see Joachim Jacoby, "The Image of Pity in the Later Middle Ages: Images, Prayers and Prayer Instructions," *Studi medievali*, ser. 3ª, 46 (2005): 569–605.

[80] Chastelain, *Chronique*, 1:49: "Le jeusne desconforté prince vaincu et paroultré de douleurs, gectant un haut effrayeux cry avec toutes manières lamentables, se rua sur un lit; et là gisant, subitement devint défiguré de visage, privé de parole et tout amorty d'esprit. Les yeux luy commencèrent à tourner, les lèvres à noircir, les dents à estreindre, les bras et les jambes à tirer à la mort; seulement en l'estomac vers le cœur se retrahy la vye, lequel tellement s'engrossy et enfla que très-hastivement luy falloit couper la lachure de ses habillemens et deffermer les dents à force continuelle, ou il eust esté estaint infailliblement en son deuil. Sy fu la pitié si grande par léans que les cœurs fondoient en larmes, en clameurs et en battures des mains, comme s'ils vissent toute la fabricque du monde finir devant eux."

[81] See Isabelle Cazeaux, *French Music in the Fifteenth and Sixteenth Centuries* (New York, 1975), chap. 2; Howard Mayer Brown, *Music in the French Secular Theater, 1400–1550* (Cambridge, MA, 1963); Jeanne Marix, *Histoire de la musique et des musiciens de la cour de Bourgogne sous le règne de Philippe le Bon (1420–1467)* (Strasbourg, 1939), 37–43. For Chastelain's association with at least one musician in the ducal chapel, see Small, *George Chastelain*, 73 and n. 112.

[82] Lefèvre, 1:2. On Chastelain as one of the "Grands Rhétoriqueurs" of the late Middle Ages and its implications for the theatrical nature of his writing, see Estelle Doudet, "Mettre en jeu, mettre en écrit. Les Grands Rhétoriqueurs bourguignons face aux textes de théâtre," in *L'écrit et le manuscrit à la fin du Moyen Âge*, ed. Tania Van Hemelryck and Céline Van Hoorebeeck (Turnhout, 2006), 99–110.

dramatization of history, Chastelain pushes to the outer limits the theatricality of his other texts," observe Gillette Tyl-Labory and Sylvie Lefevre.[83] Chastelain's *Mystère sur la paix de Péronne*, for example, brought passionate emotions – expressed at the beginning and end by characters named *Bouche* (mouth) and *Cœur* (heart) – to bear on the signing of the Treaty of Péronne (1468).[84] In his *Les Epitaphes d'Hector* (1454), Chastelain enlivened the marriage negotiations for the future Charles the Bold with a drama – largely in verse – about reconciliation. This was staged with the help of Chastelain's close compatriots at court, including Olivier de La Marche.[85] It posed the question: Whom should Alexander honor more: Achilles or Hector? At first Alexander, musing on the epitaphs of both men, glorified Achilles as victor over Hector. Then Hector himself appeared to make a long complaint. Once a fierce leader, he was literally stabbed in the back:

> Power, speed, aggressiveness, proud manner
> All were changed into something plaintive.
> My lance, once murderer of a thousand men
> In just one day became weak as a reed,
> And the terrifying body ranged in battle,
> Became an image of weeping:[86] a painting of sorrow.
> The proud saddle became a bier,
> The fiery horse, a funeral bed.
> Alas: the right hand, once quick as lightning,
> Fell to the ground and putrefaction.[87]

Performed with music and dance, as was the practice,[88] pageants like Chastelain's *Epitaphes* privileged florid emotional expression to provide

---

[83] DLFMA, 511. Small, "When *Indiciaires* Meet *Dederijkers*," 140–42, suggests that experience with city guilds provided Chastelain with models for dramatic performances.

[84] Chastelain, *Mystère sur la paix de Péronne*, in *Oeuvres* 7:423–52.

[85] Small, *George Chastelain*, 65 and 74; Estelle Doudet, "Un dramaturge et son public au XVe siècle: George Chastelain," *European Medieval Drama* 9 (2005): 61–86. However, Small, "When *Indiciaires* Meet *Dederijkers*," 146 and n. 65, points out that only Chastelain's *Mystère par manière de lamentacion de la mort du duc Philippe* was "undeniably intended for performance," since the manuscript contains stage directions.

[86] See Plate 6.2.

[87] Chastelain, *Complainte d'Hector* [recte *Les Epitaphes d'Hector*], in *Oeuvres*, 6:167–202 at 176: "Force, vitesse, aigreur, fière manière, / Tout est tourné en plaintive nature./ Lance jadis de mille hommes meurtrière /Par un seul jour est devenue fougière,/ Et corps horrible en bataille rangière,/ Plourant ymage et dolente peinture./ Selle orguilleuse est devenue bière,/ Cheval bruiant, amattie litière;/ Dextre jadis comme fouldre légière/ Las! sy est cheue en terre et pourriture." Doudet, "Un dramaturge," 64–67, argues that Achilles represented the assassins of John the Fearless, while Hector was John the Fearless and then, because Hector forgives Achilles in the play, also Philip the Good. At the same time, Doudet emphasizes Chastelain's desire to make his symbols ambiguous, capable of several interpretations.

[88] La Marche, 3:143–48 describes an entertainment at a different wedding feast; it depicted the Labors of Hercules: each labor was introduced by the sound of trumpets, and the

proof of profundity of feeling and sensitivity. It was in part because of his
pleasure in the *Epitaphes*, performed in September 1454, that Philip the
Good appointed Chastelain (on June 25, 1455) as the first official ducal
chronicler.[89]

In the *Mémoires* of Olivier de la Marche, close friend of Chastelain at
court, we have a long description of courtly entertainment embedded
directly in a chronicle-like text.[90] At the "Feast of the Oath of the
Pheasant" held at Lille in 1454, La Marche marveled at the three tables
of different sizes laden with tableaux vivants: a nude child on a rock
pissing rose water; Melusine in her castle; a serpent battling a tiger
("marvelously true to life"). Twenty-eight musicians in a giant pie played
"diverse instruments."[91] Some tableaux became animated. La Marche
dwelled on the one that was "pitiable, which seems to me the most special
of all."[92] It began with a giant, representing a Saracen, leading an elephant
topped by a howdah in which was a woman (or, rather, possibly
La Marche)[93] dressed as a religious and meant to symbolize "Holy
Church." She wore "white satin, and over that a cloak of black fabric, and
on her head was a white bonnet, like that . . . of a recluse. And as soon as she
entered the [banquet] hall and saw the noble company that was there . . . she
said to the giant who accompanied her, 'Giant: I want to stop here/ for I see
noble company/ to whom I must speak.'"[94] When at last he stopped, she
continued, now as a musical lament: "Alas, alas! How miserable,/ sad,
unhappy, troubled, /sorry I am, alas,/ more than anyone!/ Everyone looks
at me and sees me/ But no one wants to recognize me/ . . . Weep for my
suffering, for I am Holy Church,/your mother/ driven to ruin and bitter
pain."[95] Her lamentation over, Toison d'Or (Jean Lefèvre) entered, holding
a grandly bejeweled pheasant. Addressing the duke, he spoke of the

performance was followed by music and dance. The next day (*ibid.*, 148–54) the entertainment boasted various "animals" playing instruments and singing songs and motets.
[89] Small, *George Chastelain*, 65; Doudet, "Un dramaturge," 67.
[90] La Marche, 2:348–78. It was described in even greater detail (and with some variations)
in d'Escouchy, *Chronique* 2:116–237. For modern bibliography on the feast, see *Court
and Civic Society*, 36–39.
[91] La Marche, 2:351: "jouans de divers instrumens."
[92] *Ibid.*, 2:362: "pitoyable qui me semble le plus especial des aultres."
[93] *Ibid.*, 2:340: "Et voulut le duc que je fisse le personnage de Saincte Eglise." But later
(2:368), he speaks of *seeing* the pageant.
[94] *Ibid.*, 2:362: "satin blanc, et par dessus avoit ung manteau de drap noir, et la teste avoit
affulée d'ung blanc couvrechief, à la guise . . . de recluse, et si tost qu'elle entra en la sale,
et elle veit la noble compaignie qui uy estoit . . . elle dit au geant qui la menoit: (*La dame*):
Geant, je veulz cy arrester,/Car je voy noble compaignie/ A laquelle me fault parler."
[95] *Ibid.*, 2:363: "(*Complainte de la dame*): Helas! helas! moy douloureuse,/ Triste, desplaisant, annuyeuse,/ Desolée, las, peu heureuse,/ La plus qui soit!/ Chascun me regarde et
me voit;/ Mais ame ne me recongnoit,/ . . . Plourez mes maulx; car je suis Saincte Eglise,/
La vostre mere,/ Mise à ruyne et à douleur amere."

"ancient custom" of presenting such a bird to lords.[96] The duke, "who knew his purpose in organizing this banquet, looked at the Church and then, as if taking pity on her," took out a letter containing his vow to go on a crusade against the Turks, who had taken Constantinople the year before.[97]

Despite its jaundiced view of love, the Burgundian court drew on the patterns of sentimentality we long ago saw in the emotional community of Gregory of Tours and Fortunatus (see Chapter 2). No doubt in part because it flourished in a time of war, it valued sorrowful feelings. But this emphasis was not inevitable, as we shall see with the Pastons (below), who cultivated a very different emotional response to the Wars of the Roses and their own engagement in local battles.

Further, the Burgundian courtiers reinforced their expressions of sorrow by invoking pity at every turn. *Misericordia* was an *aegritudo* for Cicero – a pain and distress. For Aelred of Rievaulx, it was a technique – one of many – to employ when contemplating Christ. At the court of Toulouse the Albigensian Crusade seems to have brought with it a sense of empathy, but the anonymous poet who demonstrated this sensibility used the word *pietat*, pity, only sparingly. For Thomas Aquinas *misericordia* was simply a form of sorrow, *tristitia*. Contrast these uses of the term to those at the court of Burgundy, where pity had a pivotal character, justifying and encompassing all the other emotions.

All of the court's emotions were expressed in the new theatrical idiom that Carol Symes has called "a common stage," blurring the boundaries between public life and entertainment.[98] We shall see some of the same theatricality – but also its determined rejection – across the English Channel at the same time.

Finding it "full merry to be reproved": Margery Kempe

Around the time that Monstrelet was beginning his chronicle, the religious mystic Margery Kempe (c. 1373–c. 1439) enacted her own dramas. She is, at first glance, an odd subject for a book on emotional communities. Indeed, she was in many ways a social misfit, subjected to "public scorn, threats upon her safety ... and even episcopal inquiries into the nature of her faith."[99]

---

[96] The "tradition" was recent and more literary than historical; see Gail Orgelfinger, "The Vows of the Pheasant and Late Chivalric Ritual," in *The Study of Chivalry: Resources and Approaches*, ed. Howell Chickering and Thomas H. Seiler (Kalamazoo, 1988), 611–43.

[97] La Marche, 2:367: "le duc, qui savoit à quelle intencion il avoit fait ce bancquet, regarda l'Eglise, et ainsy, comme ayant pitié d'elle, tira de son seing ung brief."

[98] Carol Symes, *A Common Stage: Theater and Public Life in Medieval Arras* (Ithaca, NY, 2007).

[99] *The Book of Margery Kempe*, trans. Lynn Staley (New York, 2001) [hereafter Staley], vii.

Nevertheless, her *Book*, which is nearly our only source about her, details not only the social opprobrium that she inspired, but also the admiration of supporters.

Margery Kempe was a member of an important burgess family in Bishop's Lynn (later King's Lynn) in Norfolk, England. Until the early 1400s, her father, John Brunham, was a pillar of the community, frequently serving as mayor and in other civic posts. But between 1411 and 1413, having taken an unpopular political stance and lost a great deal of money, he came to be vilified by many citizens.[100] Meanwhile, at the age of twenty, Margery married John Kempe, also a Lynn townsman.[101] She bore fourteen children, started two unsuccessful business enterprises (brewing beer; milling flour), and never abandoned her marriage. Eventually, however, she and her husband took mutual vows of chastity and lived in separate quarters. Later, when John became too ill to live alone, Margery returned to care for him.

Only one of her children figured to any degree in her story; Margery was far more focused on the Holy Family.[102] Much of her time was spent making pilgrimages and visiting religious people of note; she revealed her "contemplations" to them and sought their approval. For a number of years, starting around 1413 (thus, right around the time of her father's fall), she came under suspicion as a Lollard. However, she weathered that storm and ended her life as a member of the prestigious Guild of the Trinity at Lynn.[103]

By the mid-1420s, Margery had begun to dictate – in the vernacular English of her region – an account of her spiritual life that became for modern commentators the *Book of Margery Kempe*.[104] Although extremely

---

[100] See Kate Parker, "Lynn and the Making of a Mystic," in *A Companion to* The Book of Margery Kempe, ed. John H. Arnold and Katherine J. Lewis (Cambridge, 2004), 55–73, and Anthony Goodman, *Margery Kempe and Her World* (London, 2002), 15–55.

[101] *The Book of Margery Kempe*, ed. Sanford Brown Meech and Hope Emily Allen (Oxford, 1940) [henceforth BMK], Appendix 3, 362–68. For John Kempe's "social self," see David Gary Shaw, "Social Selves in Medieval England: The Worshipful Ferrour and Kempe," in *Writing Medieval History*, ed. Nancy F. Partner (London, 2005), 3–21.

[102] Deborah S. Ellis, "Margery Kempe and King's Lynn," in *Margery Kempe: A Book of Essays*, ed. Sandra J. McEntire (New York, 1992), 139–63 at 147, rightly points out that "Kempe expresses her relationship with Christ in domestic terms." See below at n. 165.

[103] For a chronology of events in Margery's life, see Charity Scott Stokes, "Margery Kempe: Her Life and the Early History of Her Book," *Mystics Quarterly* 15 (1999): 3–67. On the chronology of her trials as a Lollard, see John H. Arnold, "Margery's Trials: Heresy, Lollardy and Dissent," in *A Companion to* The Book of Margery Kempe, 82–88.

[104] Stokes, "Margery Kempe," 40–41. The text is called a "schort tretys" (BMK, prol., p. 1) and a "booke" (*ibid.*, 4). (I use throughout the translations of Staley.) The literature on Margery Kempe and her *Book* is enormous. The publication of the *Book* and general trends in its reception are surveyed (to 2004) in Marea Mitchell, *The Book of Margery Kempe: Scholarship, Community, and Criticism* (New York, 2005). The literature on just the question of who was responsible for the text – a real woman named Margery Kempe, a woman "created" by Margery Kempe, the scribes of the *Book* – is vast. I myself treat the *Book* as essentially the work of Margery Kempe, matron of Bishop's Lynn, but I would be equally happy to accept the argument of Felicity Riddy, "Text and Self in *The Book of Margery Kempe*," in *Voices in Dialogue: Reading Women in the Middle Ages*, ed.

intimate, it was told largely in the third person, using the term "this creature" to refer to its subject.[105] The emotional life depicted in it had precedents in the distant past, in the writings of Aelred, whose emotional community we surveyed in Chapter 4, and in hagiographical and mystical models closer to Margery's day.[106] By then Aelred's assumptions about lay people had been overturned. While Aelred had seen the kingdom as a miniature monastery, the only lay person he saw inhabiting a monastic role was the ruler. As for women: he wrote for an anchoress, not a laywoman. Margery, by contrast, never withdrew from the world. When she wept and roared, she did so in public.[107]

How do we know which words in the *Book* had emotional force? Again, assuming that the heart (*hert* in Middle English) was a touchstone of emotion, I have gathered a list of the terms that were "in" the *hert* or "filled" it or "were of" it, and the like. I have then noted the words associated with such terms, yielding a hoard of Kempian emotion words (see Table 6.3).[108]

Although the *Book* does not put it quite this way, in effect it suggests two emotional communities around Margery.[109] One was hostile to her

---

Linda Olson and Kathryn Kerby-Fulton (Notre Dame, 2005), 435–53, who thinks that the text was a collaborative effort, for this emphasizes that the emotional norms expressed therein were not sui generis but rather shared by others.

[105] BMK, prol., p. 1: "þis creatur."   [106] See below at n. 144.

[107] Fiona Somerset, "Excitative Speech: Theories of Emotive Response from Richard Fitzralph to Margery Kempe," in *The Vernacular Spirit: Essays on Medieval Religious Literature*, ed. Renate Blumenfeld-Kosinski, Duncan Robertson, and Nancy Bradley Warren (New York, 2002), 59–79 at 70, writes of "Margery's wish to present herself as a social activist." Jeffrey Jerome Cohen, *Medieval Identity Machines* (Minneapolis, 2003), 172, argues that Margery's vocalizations "ensure the impossibility of claustration."

[108] Margery knew the writings of Richard Rolle, who stressed the heart as the seat of his passionate love for God. See Richard Rolle, *The Fire of Love*, trans. Clifton Wolters (New York, 1972), 45, discussed in Raymond A. Powell, "Margery Kempe: An Exemplar of Late Medieval English Piety," *Catholic Historical Review* 89/1 (2003): 1–23, esp. 6–9. Note, too, that the Lollard Bible translated Ps. 20:3 "desiderium animae" as "desire of his herte," suggesting that the Latin word *anima*, seat of the emotions for Thomas Aquinas and others, was, in the English vernacular, thought equivalent to the heart. I do not suggest that Margery was Lollard. Rather, I suggest that the Lollard Bible, meant to attract a wide readership, is a useful tool for finding vernacular equivalents to Latin emotion words and associated concepts. For all references to the Lollard Bible I have used *The Holy Bible . . . made from the Latin Vulgate by John Wycliffe and his Followers*, ed. Josiah Forshall and Frederic Madden, 4 vols. (Oxford, 1850; rpt. 1982) [hereafter LB].

[109] See Ellis, "Margery Kempe," 151, who speaks of "a new transient group" at Lynn centered on Kempe; and Janet Wilson, "Communities of Dissent: The Secular and Ecclesiastical Communities of Margery Kempe's *Book*," in *Medieval Women in their Communities*, ed. Diane Watt (Toronto, 1997), 155–85. See also Nicholas Watson, "The Making of *The Book of Margery Kempe*," in *Voices in Dialogue*, 395–434 at 396 and nn. 4–5; *The Book of Margery Kempe*, ed. Barry Windeatt (Harlow, 2000), 4. For bibliography on town and country groups that chose to be – or not to be – orthodox, semi-dissenters, or Lollards, see the notes in Rob Lutton, "Connections between Lollards, Townsfolk and Gentry in Tenterden in the Late Fifteenth and Early Sixteenth Centuries," in *Lollardy and the Gentry in the Later Middle Ages*, ed. Margaret Aston and Colin Richmond (Stroud, 1997), 199–228.

Table 6.3 *Margery's heart-felt terms and those associated with them*[a]

a-feerd, afraid
affeccyon, affection
blysse, bliss
care, care
charite, charity
comfort, comfort
compassyon, compassion
contricyon, contrition
compunccyon, compunction
cryin, to cry
delectacyon, delectation; delight
despysed, despised
desyr, desire
devocyon, devotion
dispeyr, despair
diswer, doubt
drede, dread
dredyn, to dread
felyng, feeling
gladnes, gladness
hatyn, hate
heuynes, heaviness
joy, joy
kyssyn, to kiss
lofe, love
lowness, lowness
mekenes, meekness
mercy, mercy
mery, merry
mornyn, to mourn
pety, pity
petows, piteous
peyne, pain
plesyn, to please
rewful, rueful
roryngys, roarings
sadnes, sadness
schame, shame
sobbyng, sobbing
sorwe, sorrow
sorweful, sorrowful
swetnesse, sweetness
syhyngy, sighing
teerys, tears
tribulacyon, tribulation

Table 6.3 *(cont.)*

unkyndnesse, unkindness
wepyn, to weep
wepyng, weeping
worshipyn, to worship
wreth, wrath

[a] In bold are the words associated directly with the *hert* (heart).
Note that an entirely different approach to Middle English
emotion words is taken by Ayumi Miura, *Middle English Verbs
of Emotion and Impersonal Constructions: Verb Meaning and
Syntax in Diachrony* (Oxford, 2015), where (19) the verbs of
emotion chosen for study are "based on the classification in
the Historical Thesaurus of the Oxford English Dictionary."

constant weeping and crying; the other supported – and sometimes
joined – her emotional displays. The first group is the most visible to the
reader because the text emphasized it. The hostility of the world was, in
fact, an essential element in Margery's emotional life. It was painful, but
the pain was sweet. As she put it, "Then this creature thought it was full
merry to be reproved for God's love. It was to her great solace and comfort
when she was chided and scolded."[110] "Full merry": this was how (she
tells us) it felt in heaven.[111]

Margery's enemies are easy to find. They despised her extravagant sobs
and roars and even wanted to kill her, accusing her of being a Lollard.
They disliked her rebukes and pretensions of holiness, and for that
reason, too, they wanted to put an end to her. Finally, they thought that
she could restrain herself and accused her of feigning lack of emotional
control. As an example of the first point, consider Canterbury, where

[110] Staley, 23; BMK c. 14, p. 29: "Than thys creatur þowt it was ful mery to be reprevyd for
Goddys lofe; it was to hir gret solas & cowmfort whan sche was chedyn & fletyn." On
Margery's merriment in the face of spite, see Karma Lochrie, *Margery Kempe and
Translations of the Flesh* (Philadelphia, 1991), chap. 4. This merriment was not just
Margery's image. The fifteenth-century text *The Lanterne of Liȝt*, ed. Lilan
M. Swinburn (London, 1917; rpt. 1971), 76, has a section on "joy in tribulation (ioye
in tribulacioun)" and a translation by the anonymous author of "gaudete et exulatate"
(Matt. 5:11–12) as "ioye & be myry (rejoice and be merry)." *The Lanterne* was a Lollard
text, but its vocabulary surely was not limited to that group.

[111] BMK c. 3, p. 11: "Alas, þat euyr I dede synne, it is ful mery in Hevyn (Alas, that ever I
did sin; it is full merry in heaven)." See Chaucer, "The Nun's Priest's Tale," in *The
Riverside Chaucer*, ed. Larry D. Benson, 3d ed. (Boston, 1987), 263–61 at 259, ll.*4447–
49: "Wommennes conseil broghte us first to wo/ And made Adam fro Paradys to go,/
Ther as he was ful myrie and wel at ese. (Women's counsel brought us first to woe/ and
made Adam from Paradise to go,/ there where he was full merry and well at ease.)"

(Margery reported) "she was greatly despised and reproved because she wept so hard, both by the monks and the priests and by secular men, nearly all day, both morning and afternoon, also in so much that her husband went away from her as if he had not known her."[112] When later she thanked her persecutors for their "shame, scorn, and despite as I was worthy," they retorted, "You shall be burnt, false Lollard."[113]

Her rebukes to others for their impiety were more rare but no less provocative. When she got to London and visited Lambeth palace, "there were many of the Archbishop's clerks and other reckless men, both squires and yeomen who swore many great oaths and spoke many reckless words, and this creature boldly rebuked them and said they should be damned unless they left off their swearing and other sins that they used. And with that came forth a woman of the same town in a pilche [a fur-trimmed garment] and reviled this creature [and] banned her."[114] Again, in the course of her pilgrimage to Jerusalem, her companions told the papal legate at Constance that "she should no longer be in their company unless he would command her to eat meat as they did and leave her weeping and that she should not speak so much of holiness."[115] When the legate refused, they became "wroth and in great anger" and left her behind, taking her maid with them.[116]

Finally, there were many who doubted that her tears and cries were involuntary:

And, as soon as she perceived that she should cry, she would keep it in as much as she might, so that the people should not have heard it, for it annoyed them. For some said it was a wicked spirit vexed her; some said it was a sickness; some said she had drunk too much wine ... Some great clerks said our lady [the Virgin Mary] cried never so, nor no saint in heaven, but they knew full little what she felt,

---

[112] Staley, 21; BMK c. 13, p. 27: "Sche was gretly despysed & repreuyd for cawse sche wept so fast bothyn of þe monkys & prestys & of seculer men ner al a day boþe a-for-noon & aftyr-noon, also jn so mech þat hyr husbond went a-way fro hir as he had not a knowyn hir & left hir a-loon a-mong hem."

[113] Staley, 22; BMK c. 13, p. 28: "schame, skorne, & despyte as I was worthy ... Than sche went owt of þe monastery, þei folwyng & crying vp-on hir, 'Þow xalt be brent, fals lollare." Andrew Cole, *Literature and Heresy in the Age of Chaucer* (Cambridge, 2008), 160, observes that "vociferous crying, which seizes Kempe so often, was by the late fourteenth century thought to be a patent feature of 'Lollard' heresy."

[114] Staley, 27–28; BMK c. 16, p. 36: "ther wer many of þe Erchebysshoppys clerkys & oþer rekles men boþe swyers & ȝemen which sworyn many gret oþis & spokyn many rekles wordys, & þis creatur boldly vndyrname him & seyd þei schuld ben dampnyd but þei left her sweryng & oþer synnes þat þei vsyd. & wyth þat cam forth a woman of þe same town in a pylche & al for-schod þis creatur [&] bannyd hir."

[115] Staley, 47; BMK c. 27, pp. 63–64: "[seyd] vttyrly sche xulde no lengar be in her company les þan he wolde comawndyn hir to etyn flesch as þei dedyn & levyn hir wepyng & þat sche xulde not speke so mech of holynes."

[116] Staley, 47; BMK c. 27, p. 64: "wroth & in gret angyr."

nor would they not believe that she might have abstained from crying if she wished.[117]

To be sure, none of this is enough to define a non-Kempian emotional community, especially as it is all reported by someone glad to vilify it. But it does suggest that there were emotional and behavioral norms quite different from Margery's.

It is hard to find people sharing Margery's emotional norms in the *Book*, so focused is the text on those who scorned her. Yet, as she says in one passage of her book, she was writing to give "an example for those who come after."[118] And, indeed, almost in spite of herself, Margery appears to have had many friends and supporters. There was, first of all, her husband, who "though he sometimes for vain dread let her alone for a time," as we have seen above, "yet he resorted evermore again to her, and had compassion for her, and spoke for her as much as he dared for dread of the people."[119] But Margery did not think very highly of him.[120] More important to her were men of the church. "This creature showed her manner of living to many a worthy clerk, to worshipful doctors of divinity, both religious men and others of secular habit, and they said that God wrought great grace with her and commanded that she should not be afraid ... They counseled her to be persevering."[121] When Margery went to York, "our Lord of his mercy ever he made some men to love her and support her."[122] She found "good friends" in some members of the Yorkshire clergy: John Aclom, John Kendale, "and another priest who sung by the bishop's grave."[123]

---

[117] Staley, 51; BMK c. 28, p. 69: "&, as sone as sche parceyvyd þat sche xulde crye, sche wolde kepyn it in as mech as sche myth þat þe pepyl xulde not an herd it for noyng of hem. For summe seyd it was a wikkyd spiryt vexid hir; sum seyd it was a sekenes; sum seyd sche had dronkyn to mech wyn ... Sum gret clerkys seyden owyr Lady cryed neuyr so ne no seynt in Heuyn, but þei knewyn ful lytyl what sche felt, ne þei wolde not beleuyn but þat sche myth an absteynd hir fro crying yf sche had wold."

[118] Staley, 12; BMK c. 4, p. 14: "I purpos to wrytyn for exampyl of hem þat com aftyr."

[119] Staley, 25; BMK c. 15, p. 32: "Þow þat he sumtyme for veyn dred lete hir a-lone for a tyme, ȝet he resortyd euyr-mor a-geyn to hir, & had compassyon of hir, & spak for hir as he durst for dred of þe pepyl."

[120] BMK c. 2, p. 9: "hym semyd neuyr for to a weddyd hir (Staley, 8: he seemed never the man to have married her)." Raphaela Sophia Rohrhofer, *Familial Discourses in* The Book of Margery Kempe: "*Blyssed be the wombe that the bar and the tetys that yaf the sowkyn,*" (Frankfurt am Main, 2014), 112–13, suggests that John Kempe conformed to the image of Saint Joseph.

[121] Staley, 33; BMK c. 18, p. 43: "Thys creatur schewyd hyr maner of leuyng to many a worthy clerke, to worsheful doctorys of divinyte, boþe religiows men & oþer of seculer abyte, & þei seyden þat God wrowt gret grace wyth hir & bodyn sche xuld not ben aferde. ... Þei cownseld hir to be perseuerawnt."

[122] Staley, 89; BMK c. 51, p. 121: "And owr Lord of hys mercy euyr he mad sum men to louyn hir & supportyn hir."

[123] *Ibid.*: "þes wer hir good frendys of þe spiritual-te (Staley, 89: these were her good friend of the spirituality)."

Moreover, some people not only befriended her but also appear to have shared her emotional norms. In Rome she found a priest who could not understand English, but "desiring to please God," he prayed to understand her, enlisting the prayers of others as well.[124] In the end he understood her English (but only hers), and she revealed to him all her secrets. "Then this priest received her full meekly and reverently, like his mother and his sister."[125] He promised to support her against all her enemies. He was reviled for standing by her, but nevertheless continued to "support her in her sobbing and in her crying."[126] When she was ready to leave Rome for England, the two said their good-byes in tears. Then "she, falling on her knees, received the favor of his blessing, and so parted asunder those whom charity joined both in one."[127] This was, surely, an affective community, at least of two. It was echoed when, again at Rome, Margery "met casually with a good man . . . With him she had many good tales and many good exhortations till God visited him with tears of devotion and of compunction, to his high comfort and consolation. And then he gave her money."[128] A man at Newcastle "was so drawn by the good words that God put in her to say of contrition and compunction, of sweetness and of devotion, that he was all moved, as if he had been a new man, with tears of contrition and compunction, both days and nights . . . so that sometimes when he went into the fields he wept so sorely for his sins and his trespasses that he fell down and might not bear it."[129]

Much less frequently Margery found affective sisterhood. Some women took compassion on her, to be sure, like the well-heeled Italian woman who invited her to dinner every Sunday and gave her food and money.[130] There were also other "good women" who "having compassion for her sorrow and greatly marveling at her weeping and at her crying,

---

[124] Staley, 60; BMK c. 33, p. 82: "Desyryng to plese God."

[125] Staley, 61; BMK c. 33, p. 83: "þan þis preste receyued hir ful mekely & reuerently as for hys modyr & for hys syster."

[126] Staley, 61; BMK c. 33, p. 83: "he wolde supportyn hir in hir sobbyng & in hir crying."

[127] Staley, 73; BMK c. 42, p. 100: "Sche, falling on hyr knes, receyued þe benefys of hys blyssyng, & so departyd a-sundyr whom charite ioyned bothyn in oon."

[128] Staley, 68; BMK c. 38, p. 93: "[Sche] met casualy wyth a good man. . . . to whom sche had many good talys & many good exhortacyonys tyl God visited hym wyth terys of deuocyon & of compunccyon to hys hey comfort & consolacyon. & þan he ȝaf hir mony."

[129] Staley, 79; BMK c. 45, p. 108: "& he was so drawyn be þe good wordys þat God put in hir to sey of contricyon & compunccyon, of swetnes & of deuocyon þat he was al meuyd as he had ben a newe man wyth terys of contricyon & compunccyon, boþe days & nyghtys . . . þat sum-tyme whan he went in þe feldys he wept so sor for hys synnes & hys trespas þat he fel down & myth not beryn it." The Book, ed. Windeatt, 223, identifies the place as most likely Newcastle under Lyme, Staffordshire.

[130] BMK c. 38, p. 93.

much the more they loved her."[131] In around 1413, Margery met with the anchoress Julian of Norwich, who lectured her on charity, chastity, and "tears of contrition, devotion, or compassion." Julian said that the Holy Ghost "makes us ask and pray with mournings and weepings." And she praised the "despite, shame, and reproof" that Margery weathered in the world, since they betokened merits in heaven.[132] Nevertheless, although the two spent time together sharing in their love of Jesus, Julian did not actually join Margery in tears and cries, the key elements of her public emotional life.[133] Indeed, only the women at Beverley did so, according to the *Book*. Locked up there in 1417 to await trial as a Lollard, Margery told "many good tales to those who would hear her, in so much that women wept sorely and said with great heaviness of their hearts, 'Alas, woman, why shall you be burnt?'"[134] It is doubtful that these were the only women who partook in Margery's emotional norms. But her *Book* preferred to stress the men who joined her.

At Bishop's Lynn, her hometown, Margery had many friends. Reassuring her that her revelations were Godly rather than demonic, one of her confessors "took it on charge of his soul that her feelings were good and sure and that there was no deceit in them."[135] When leaving for the Holy Land, she said good-bye to another of her confessors, praying "him for his blessing, and so forth from other friends."[136] Deborah Ellis has sketched the social tensions and cohesions at Bishop's Lynn in Margery's time, naming many of her "like-minded neighbors and allies" there.[137] Did

---

[131] Staley, 72; BMK c. 41, pp. 98–99: "Þe good women, hauyng compassyon of hir sorwe & gretly meruelyng of hir wepyng & of hir crying, meche þe mor þei louyd hir."

[132] Staley, 32–33; BMK c. 18, p. 42: "terys of contrisyon, deuosyon, er compassion"; *ibid.*, 43: "he makyth vs to askyn & preyn wyth mornynggys & wepyngys"; *ibid.*: "despyte, schame, & repref."

[133] Did Julian of Norwich belong to Margery's emotional community? A preliminary survey suggests that, while both drew on affective mystical traditions, they were quite different in the emotions that they emphasized and in the scripts that their emotional trajectories followed.

[134] Staley, 96; BMK c. 53, pp. 130–31: "many good talys to hem þat wolde heryn hir, in so meche þat women wept sor & seyde wyth gret heuynes of her hertys, 'Alas, woman, why xalt þu be brent?'" A woman at Bishop's Lynn who went mad after childbirth, roaring and crying, became meek and quiet when in Margery's company: see BMK c. 75, pp. 177–79.

[135] Staley, 33; BMK c. 18, p. 44: "toke it on charge of hys sowle þat hir felyngys wer good & sekyr & þat þer was no disseyt in hem."

[136] Staley, 45; BMK c. 26, p. 60: "& preyd hym of hys blyssyng, & so forth of oþer frendys."

[137] Ellis, "Margery Kempe," 147. Margery was admitted to Lynn's prestigious Trinity guild at the end of her life; see BMK, 358 (recording her entry in the Account Roll of the Trinity Guild). That *she* considered it prestigious is shown by her proud assertion of her father's membership there: BMK c. 2, p. 9: "for hir fadyr was sum-tyme meyr of þe town N. and sythyn he was alderman of þe hey Gylde of þe Trinyte in N. (Staley, 8: For her father was sometime mayor of the town N., and since then he was an alderman of the high Guild of the Trinity in N.)"

they constitute an "emotional community"? I think so. But Margery courted Christ's love, and that was gained through enmities: "Daughter," Christ said to her, "the more shame, despite, and reproof that you suffer for my love, the better I love you."[138] This is no doubt why she treated her soul mates only in passing.[139]

Moreover, if we look beyond Bishop's Lynn, we will see many people involved in the sort of "affective spirituality" that Margery practiced. Her discussions with Christ, their pledges of mutual love, her marriage to God Himself: these were not odd in the larger context of late medieval religious life. Already Aelred had talked about friendship with Christ and the ascent to his kiss and advised meditative participation in Christ's life; by Margery's day, his text was available in Middle English.[140] The Beguine Marie d'Oignies (d. 1213) claimed that she held the Christ child "close to her so that He nestled between her breasts like a baby."[141] The Dominican mystic Henry Suso (d. 1366) "had a heart filled with love" for the eternal Wisdom of Christ.[142] After carving the name of Jesus into the flesh over his heart, he not only spoke with God but also attempted, by "conforming himself to Christ," to feel "sympathy for everything his Lord and God, Christ, had suffered before him."[143] Even though Margery could not read or write, her *Book* suggests that she knew about various exemplars of the religious life from hearing texts by or about them. Her emotional community was inspired by the charismatic dead – the saints – who lived on through pious writings.[144]

---

[138] Staley, 60; BMK c. 32, p. 81: "dowtyr, þe mor schame, despite, & reprefe þat þu sufferyst for my lofe, þe bettyr I lofe þe."

[139] Ellis, "Margery Kempe," 150, observes that "she demands acceptance, yet at the same time she validates her self-image ... through her rejection by others. Though she dreads being alone, Kempe provokes everyone to desert her."

[140] See Chapter 4. Riehle, *Secret Within*, 258, stresses this point. Two Middle English versions of Aelred, *Inclus.* (one from a manuscript [MS Vernon] dated c. 1400, the other [Bodley 423] c. 1430–80) are published in *Aelred of Rievaulx's De institutione inclusarum: Two English Versions*, ed. John Ayto and Alexandra Barratt (London, 1984), xvi and xxix for the dates. Clarissa W. Atkinson, *Mystic and Pilgrim: The Book and the World of Margery Kempe* (Ithaca, N.Y., 1983), 134, argues that "when Margery Kempe placed herself in meditation ... she was obeying the instructions of Ailred as well as later writers."

[141] Jacques de Vitry, *The Life of Marie d'Oignies*, trans. Margot King, in *Medieval Women's Visionary Literature*, ed. Elizabeth Alvilda Petroff (New York, 1986), 179–83 at 182. On late medieval devotion to Mary and the Christ Child, see Henk van Os, *The Art of Devotion in the Late Middle Ages in Europe, 1300–1500*, trans. Michael Hoyle (Princeton, 1994).

[142] Henry Suso, *The Life of the Servant*, in *Henry Suso: The Exemplar, with Two German Sermons*, ed. and trans. Frank Tobin (New York, 1989), 61–204 at 67.

[143] *Ibid.*, 84.

[144] BMK c. 20, p. 47, concerns Saint Bridget's "book"; *ibid.*, c. 62, p. 153, mentions Mary d'Oignies; *ibid.*, 154, brings up Elizabeth of Hungary and Richard Rolle. For these and other writings that Margery probably absorbed, see *The Book*, ed. Windeatt, 9–18, and

Thus far, we have mentioned Margery's most histrionic and public expressions of emotion – sobbing, crying, and (later) roaring – and the reactions to them of her "friends" and "enemies." But she evinced more "private" emotions as well, though the line between public and private is hard to draw. The *Book* focused on Margery's love for God alone – by now a topos within Western culture[145] – and "the reproofs and scorns" that others heaped on her, which (as we have seen) brought her great joy.[146] All of these were embedded in contexts – sequences unfolding over time – that involved many other emotions, as well.

The first such sequence, reported very early in the *Book*, described Margery's emotional life after the birth of her first child. She recalled that, "what for the labor she had in childing and for the sickness going before, she despaired of her life, thinking she might not live."[147] Calling a priest, she tried to confess a "thing in conscience which she had never shown before that time," but her confessor "was a little too hasty and began sharply to reprove her before she had fully said her intent." Thus she kept silent, and "for the dread she had of damnation on the one side and his sharp reproving on that other side, this creature went out of her mind ... for half a year, eight weeks and some odd days."[148]

more recently Barry Windeatt, "1412–1534: Texts," in *The Cambridge Companion to Medieval English Mysticism*, ed. Samuel Fanous and Vincent Gillespie (Cambridge, 2011), 195–224. On the cult of Bridget in Norwich and its importance for both Margery Kempe and the Pastons, see Carole Hill, *Women and Religion in Late Medieval Norwich* (Woodbridge, 2010), 107–17. There is a huge bibliography on mystical models for Margery, including Atkinson, *Mystic and Pilgrim*, chaps. 5–6; Lochrie, *Margery Kempe*, chap. 2. Santha Bhattacharji, "Tears and Screaming: Weeping in the Spirituality of Margery Kempe," in *Holy Tears: Weeping in the Religious Imagination*, ed. Kimberley Christine Patton and John Stratton Hawley (Princeton, 2005), 229–41, stresses traditions of weeping, both male and female. To the models of contemporary mystics, Catherine Sanok, *Her Life Historical: Exemplarity and Female Saints' Lives in Late Medieval England* (Philadelphia, 2007), chap. 5, adds models from the early church, such as Mary Magdalene.

[145] BMK c. 3, p. 12: "Þe lofe of myn hert & myn affeccyon is drawyn fro alle erdly creaturys & sett only in God. (Staley, 10: The love of my heart and my affection is drawn from all earthly creatures and set only in God.)"

[146] Above, n. 110. For "reproofs and scorns," see BMK c. 3, p. 13: "[sche] was as mery whan sche was repreuyd, skornyd, or japyd for ower Lordys lofe (Staley, 11: she was as merry when she was reproved, scorned, or mocked for our Lord's love)."

[147] Staley, 6; BMK c. 1, p. 6: "what for labowr sche had in chyldyng & for sekenesse goyng beforn, sche dyspered of hyr lyfe, wenyng sche mygth not leuyn."

[148] Staley, 7; BMK c. 1, p. 6: "a thyng in conscyens whech sche had neuyr schewyd be-forn þat tyme"; *ibid.*, 7: "hir confessowr was a lytyl to hastye & gan scharply to vndyrnemyn hir er þan sche had fully seyd hir entent ... [&] for dreed sche had of dampnacyon on þe to syde & hys scharp repreuyng on þat oþer syde, þis creatur went owt of hir mende ... half ȝer viij wekys & odde days."

Tempted by devils during this time to deny God and all whom she loved, she followed their bad advice: she "slandered her husband, her friends and her own self; she spoke many a reproving word and many a harsh word."[149] She also turned against her own body, biting her hand and violently tearing at the "skin ... against her heart grievously with her nails."[150] It was at this juncture that Jesus first appeared to her – as a beautiful man at her bedside, asking, "Daughter, why have you forsaken me, and I forsook never you?"[151] After this vision, she returned to her senses.

The emotional sequence announced here – despair, sense of sinfulness, dread, fear of abandonment, and eventual certainty of Christ's love – recurred time and again in the *Book*, though often, as here, complicated by intervening emotions. Here despair first led Margery to attempt (unsuccessfully) to salve her conscience; then came fear of the priest's reproof, which led in turn to her slandering her loved ones and harming herself. The sequence culminated in the calming words of Christ: "I forsook never you."

A slightly different emotional sequence unfolded about two years later. Although finding sex with her husband "horrible," Margery was nevertheless tormented by lecherous thoughts.[152] A man "whom she loved well" told her that he "would lie by her and have his lust of his body." Sure "that God had forsaken her" because she could think of nothing but his proposition, she agreed to it. But then *he* refused *her*, and she "went away all shamed and confused," seeing how "she had consented in her will to do sin. Then she fell half in despair."[153]

---

[149] Staley, 7; BMK c. 1, p. 7: "Sche slawndred hir husbond, hir frendys, and her owyn self; sche spak many a repreuows worde and many a schrewyd worde."

[150] Staley, 7; BMK c. 1, p. 8: "skyn ... a-ȝen hir hert wyth hir nayles spetowsly."

[151] Staley, 8; BMK c. 1, p. 8: "Dowtyr, why hast þow forsakyn me, and I forsoke neuyr þe?" Christ's question here echoes his cry to his Father during the Crucifixion in Matt. 27:46, which in turn echoes Ps. 22:1. It was used in dramas that Margery was very likely familiar with, as in *The Towneley Plays*, ed. George England and Alfred W. Pollard (London, 1897; rpt. 1973), 276, line 580, online at quod.lib.umich.edu/c/cme/Towneley/1:23?rgn=div1;view=fulltext. On Margery's use of contemporary plays, see Claire Sponsler, "Drama and Piety: Margery Kempe," in *A Companion to* The Book of Margery Kempe, 129–44.

[152] BMK c. 4, p. 14: "sche had no lust to comown wyth hir husbond, but it was very peynful & horrybyl vn-to hir. (Staley, 12: she had no lust to common with her husband, but it was very painful and horrible to her.)"

[153] Staley, 12–13; BMK c. 4, p. 14: "a man whech sche louyd wel seyd on-to hir ... þat for any-thyng he wold ly be hir & haue hys lust of hys body"; *ibid.*, p. 15: "Þe Deuyl put in hir mende þat God had forsakyn hir"; *ibid.*: "Sche went a-way al schamyd & confusyd in hir-self"; *ibid.*, 16: "& now sche saw how sche had consentyd in hir wyl for to don synne. Þan fel sche half in dyspeyr."

Table 6.4 *Margery's typical emotional sequence*

Despair →
sense of sinfulness (accompanied by shame; the scorn of others) →
dread of damnation/fear of God's abandonment →
compunction via tears/weeping →
joy/merriment associated with assurance of God's love

Numerous confessions did not help, for she was still beset by "temptations of lechery and despair," with no respite except for two hours each day, when the Lord "gave her ... compunction for her sins with many bitter tears."[154] The temptations continued, as did her certainty that God had abandoned her. Finally, near Christmas, as she "wept wonder sore," Christ "ravished her spirit" and said, "I am come to you, Jesus Christ ... I bid and command you, boldly call me Jesus your love, for I am your love and shall be your love without end ... I shall help you and keep you so that there shall never devil in hell part you from me, nor angel in heaven, nor man on earth."[155] Here the sequence went from lechery to despair and shame to fear of abandonment, to contritition and weeping, and finally, once again, to the certainty of Christ's love. In the *Book* a similar sequence is described for a sinful monk, who went from dispair and lechery to virtue – once Margery intervened with God on his behalf.[156] Table 6.4 sums up the general sequence. Although different in details from Thomas Aquinas' sequence of the passions (see Fig. 5.3), Margery's emotional trajectory from despair to joy was in effect already present in his theory.

In the first third or so of the *Book*, Margery was compelled (by Christ, as she understood it) to speak "with God's servants, both anchorites and recluses and many other of our Lord's lovers, with many worthy clerks

---

[154] Staley, 13; BMK c. 4, p. 16: "[Sche] was labowrd wyth horrybyl temptacyons of lettherye & of dyspeyr ... [but the Lord] ʒaf hir ... compunccyon for hir synnys wyth many byttyr teerys."

[155] Staley, 13–14; BMK c. 5, pp. 16–17: "wept wondir sore ... [Jesus] rauysched hir spyryt & seyd on-to hir: 'Dowtyr, why wepyst þow so sor? I am comyn to þe, Ihesu Cryst ... iI bydde þe & comawnd þe, boldly clepe me Ihesus, þi loue, for I am þi loue & schal be þi loue wyth-owtyn ende ... I schal helpyn þe & kepyn þe þat þer schal neuyr deuyl in Helle parte þe fro me, ne awngel in Heuyn, ne man in erthe.'" For the meaning of the word "ravish" in this period and in texts probably known by Margery Kempe, see Mary Dzon, "Margery Kempe's Ravishment into the Childhood of Christ," *Mediaevalia* 27 (2006): 27–57, esp. 27–32. Thomas Aquinas had long before identified ecstasy as an effect of love; see Chapter 5 at n. 79.

[156] BMK c. 12, pp. 26–27.

[and so on] ... to learn if any deceit were in her feelings."[157] These encounters were often emotional. At Bishop's Lynn a local anchorite, her principal confessor, responded to her revelations with "great reverence and weeping."[158] At Lincoln the bishop, Philip Repingdon, was, if not in tears, at least "right glad of her coming."[159] In London, "many worthy men desired to hear her dalliance and her communication, for her communication was so much of the love of God that the hearers were oftentimes stirred through it to weep right soberly."[160] Nevertheless, because she did not always understand her revelations, Margery herself continued to "dread" that they were deceptions of "her ghostly enemies," and "her confessor feared that she should have fallen into despair therewith."[161] Here the sequence of emotions went from fear to despair. But, as always, she was reassured, in this case because "it would be showed unto her soul how the feelings [that is, revelations] should be understood."[162]

Some of these sequences were highly dramatic. While the court of Burgundy acted out its favored emotions in public entertainments, Margery's were generally played out in her mind – in "contemplation," as she put it. But they borrowed from contemporary York and other Mystery plays.[163] Music figured in her visions, as well.[164] Many of her encounters with Christ were presented in the form of dialogues. Sometimes she took a role in apocryphal stories of the

---

[157] Staley, 20; BMK c. 11, p. 25: "wyth Goddys seruawntys, boþen ankrys & reclusys & many oþer of owyr Lordys louerys, wyth many worthy clerkys ... to wetyn yf any dysseyt were in hir felyngys."

[158] Staley, 14; BMK c. 5, p. 18: "gret reuerens & wepyng."

[159] Staley, 26; BMK c. 14, p. 33: "rygth glad of hir comyng."

[160] Staley, 28; BMK c. 16, p. 37: "many worthy men desyred to heryn hir dalyawns & hir comunycacyon, for hir communycacion was so mech en þe lofe of God þat þe herars wer oftyn-tyme steryd þerthorw to wepyn ryt sadly."

[161] Staley, 40–41; BMK c. 23, pp. 54–55: "dred þat sche had of illusyons & deceytys of hir gostly enmys. ... hir confessowr feryd þat sche xuld a fallyn in dyspeyr þerwyth."

[162] Staley, 41; BMK c. 23, p. 55: "it xuld ben schewyd vn-to hir sowle how þe felyngys xuld ben vndyrstondyn."

[163] See Sponsler, "Drama and Piety," 129–43. The sequences may also have been inspired by the narrative art that Margery would have seen. See Plates 6.3 and 6.4. Clifford Davidson, *Corpus Christi Plays at York: A Context for Religious Drama* (New York 2013), devotes a chapter (33–62) to "visual piety," that is, the ways in which the plays stimulated and reinforced images and sequences already embedded in the viewers' memory.

[164] For music, see, for example, BMK c. 35, p. 88: "Þes sowndys & melodijs had sche herd ny-hand euery day ... & specialy whan sche was in deuowt prayer, also many tymes whil sche was at Rome & in Inglond boþe. (Staley, 64: These sounds and melodies had she heard nearly every day ... and especially when she was in devout prayer, also many times while she was at Rome and in England both.)"

Holy Family, as when she saw herself caring for the young Virgin Mary. She fed, dressed, and spoke to the child like a new Archangel Gabriel. "'Lady, [said Margery,] you shall be the mother of God.' The blessed child answered and said, 'I would I were worthy ... ' The creature said, 'I pray you, Lady, if that grace fall on you, forsake not my service.'" The vision continued, following the biblical story. Margery continued to play the role of servant in a kind of time-lapse contemplation: the Virgin grew up and, now carrying the Christ child, assured Margery that "your service pleases me well." Saint Elizabeth appeared, and Margery begged her to intercede with the Virgin so that she might remain her servant, and Elizabeth answered, "You do right well your duty." When Christ was born, Margery was there, swaddling him "with bitter tears of compassion ... [and] saying to him, 'Lord I shall fare fair with you; I shall not bind you sorely [tightly].'"[165] The domestic setting here comported with the majority of Margery's visions, in which she was a daughter of Christ and Mary or bride of the Godhead.[166] The emotional sequence here went from fear of abandonment (by the Virgin) to assurance that she was wanted, to tears of compassion. (See Plates 6.3 and 6.4.)

Margery's roaring was embedded in a similar script, this time moving from tears to love, then to pity and compassion and ending with a profound sense of loss. The context was the story of Christ's Passion. At the Holy Sepulcher in Jerusalem, it was "as if Christ had hung before her bodily eye in his manhood. And, when ... it was granted this creature to behold so verily his precious tender body,

---

[165] The drama unfolds in Staley, 15; BMK c. 6. pp. 18–19: "'Lady, ȝe schal be þe Modyr of God.' The blyssed chyld answeryd & seyd, 'I wold I wer worthy ... ' Þe creatur seyd, 'I pray ȝow, Lady, ȝyf þat grace falle ȝow, forsake not my seruyse.' ... [Mary assures Margery] 'ȝi seruyse lykyth me wel.' ... [Elizabeth tells Margery,] 'þu dost ryght wel þi deuer.' ... [Margery swaddles the baby Christ child] "wyth byttyr teerys of compassyon ... seyng to hym, 'Lord, I schal fare fayr wyth ȝow; I schal not byndyn ȝow soor.'" See The Book, ed. Windeatt, 75–80, for notes on other texts that parallel Margery's account. A similar, but far longer, drama is recorded in BMK cc. 79–81, pp. 187–97, where Margery again plays the role of Mary's handmaid, this time in the episodes of Christ's torments and Passion, Mary's mourning, and Christ's resurrection. On the familial imagery in this episode, see Dzon, "Kempe's Ravishment," 33–43, and Rohrhofer, Familial Discourses, 145–47.

[166] The Father of the Trinity weds her with words that derive from traditional wedding vows in The Sarum Missal: "I N. take the N. to my weddyd wyfe, to have & to holde, for better for wurs, for rycher for porer." See Missale ad usum Sarum, ed. Francis H. Dickinson (Burntisland, 1861–83), 831. For God's vows, see BMK c. 35, p. 87: "I take þe, Margery, for my weddyd wife, for fayrar, for fowelar, for richar, for powerar. (Staley, 64: I take you, Margery, for my wedded wife, for fairer, for fouler, for richer, for poorer.)"

Plates 6.3 and 6.4 Christ's Passion at Norwich

completely rent and torn with scourges ... the grisly and grievous
wound in his precious side shedding out blood and water for her
love and her salvation, then she fell down and cried with loud voice,
wonderfully turning and twisting her body on every side, spreading
her arms abroad as if she should have died, and could not keep
herself from crying or from these bodily movings, for the fire of

---

Plates 6.3 and 6.4

Probably dating from c. 1400–c. 1425, these wooden panels (mea-
suring about 13×12 in.) painted with tempera and gilded with gold,
are fragments of a larger, continuous narrative of Christ's Passion.
The original relationship between these particular fragments is
uncertain. The upper fragment (**6.3**) shows Christ bearing the
Cross. A soldier above him shouts, showing his teeth, as does
another man on the right. The soldier behind Christ strikes him
on the head. In the bottom left corner are the Virgin Mary and
Saint John, who will stand at the foot of the Cross during the
crucifixion.

Pictured underneath here (**6.4**) is Christ standing before Pilate
(though the crown suggests Herod). It illustrates John 19:5-6:
"Jesus therefore came forth, bearing the crown of thorns and the
purple garment. And [Pilate] said to them: Behold the Man. When
the chief priests, therefore, and the servants, had seen him, they
cried out, saying Crucify him, crucify him." The banners below
Christ's accusers read "Crucifige, crucifige," reminding the viewer
of what they are shouting. While Christ is surrounded by people
gesturing with their hands and arms (as well as shouting), and while
his own face, neck, and hands stream blood, Christ himself remains
calm. Below, on the left, you can make out another representation
of Christ that was originally part of another scene: the top of his
halo, crown of thorns, and some dripping blood are all that are
visible.

For full color reproductions of these images, see "Christ Before Pilate,"
http://webapps.fitzmuseum.cam.ac.uk/explorer/index.php?oid=786; and
"Christ Bearing the Cross," http://webapps.fitzmuseum.cam.ac.uk/
explorer/index.php?oid=785.

Since the provenance of these fragments appears to be Norwich, it is
quite possible that Margery Kempe saw them and, as was appropriate in
meditation (see the discussion of meditation in Chapter 4), entered into
the scenes herself with her mind's eye.[i] © The Fitzwilliam Museum,
Cambridge.

---

[i] For other artifacts and buildings pertinent to Margery, see illustrations in
Goodman, *Margery Kempe and Her World*, plates between page 140 and
page 141.

love that burnt so fervently in her soul with pure pity and compassion."[167] Margery compared her reaction to people who grieve for a loved one. Let us take up Margery's challenge and compare this passage with Chastellain's description of Philip the Good reacting to the death of his father.[168] Overcome by sorrow, he fell down, uttering a horrible cry. He stretched; he writhed; he swelled. Those witnessing his torment felt "such great pity that their hearts burst into tears, shouts, and pounding of hands." Margery Kempe mentioned very similar acts and feelings. She did not belong to the emotional community of the courtiers of Burgundy, for her pity and her dramas centered on Christ rather than on worldly events. But her emotional norms overlapped theirs in many ways. Yet not far from Margery's Bishop's Lynn, the Paston family was, emotionally speaking, a world apart.

"Neither too heavy nor too merry": The Pastons

Margery's contemporary Clement Paston lived about fifty miles east of Bishop's Lynn.[169] Born a peasant – perhaps even a serf, as

---

[167] Staley, 51; BMK c. 28, p. 70: "as yf Crist had hangyn befor hir bodily eye in hys manhode. &, whan ... it was grawntyd þis creatur to beholdyn so verily hys precyows tendyr body, alto-rent & toryn wyth scorgys ... þe gresly & grevous wownde in hys precyows syde schedyng owt blood & watyr for hir lofe & hir saluacyon, þan sche fel down & cryed with lowde voys, wondyrfully turnyng & wrestyng hir body on euery syde, spredyng hir armys a-brode as 3yf sche xulde a deyd, & not cowde kepyn hir fro crying,–and þese bodily mevyngys for þe fyer of lofe þat brent so feruently in hir sowle wyth pur pyte & compassyon." The Dominican Félix Fabri's report on one of his pilgrimages to the Holy Land make clear that Margery's behavior at the Holy Sepulcher was in fact quite normative, at least for a slightly later period. See Félix Fabri, *Les errances de Frère Félix, pélerin en Terre sainte, en Arabie et en Égypte (1480–1483)*, vol. 2: *Troisième et quatrième traités*, ed. and trans. Jean Meyers and Nicole Chareyron (Montpellier, 2002), 113: "Vidi ibi quosdam peregrinos quasi destitutis viribus resolutos in terra jacere ... Aliqui stabant fixis in terram nudis genibus et brachiis in modum crucis extentis cum fletu orabant ... Super omnes autem mulieres peregrinae sociae nostrae et sorores quasi parturientes clamabant, ullulabant et flebant. (I saw some pilgrims there lying enervated on the ground, as if deprived of their strength ... Others knelt on the ground on bare knees, and, with arms extended in the form of a cross, they prayed tearfully ... Above all the women pilgrims – our companions and our sisters – cried out, shrieked, and wept as if they were giving birth.)" Note that in LB, the verb *clamare* was translated as "cry" (3 Kings 1:40).

[168] See above, n. 80.

[169] The scholarship on Kempe and the Pastons is almost entirely separate. An exception is Wendy Harding, "Medieval Women's Unwritten Discourse on Motherhood: A Reading of Two Fifteenth-Century Texts," *Women's Studies* 21 (1992): 197–209.

was his wife – he benefited from the dislocations of the Black Death and the social mobility that it offered to a lucky few. Clement's son, William I (1378–1444), sent to law school by his uncle, rose to be a justice of the Common Bench; was well paid; purchased many properties, mainly in Norfolk; traveled a great deal; married well; and had five children. He took the family name from Clement's original fields at Paston. His son John I (d. 1466) also studied law, made his way into the gentry, and gained the confidence of the very wealthy Sir John Fastolf (the original of the Falstaff of Shakespeare's plays.)[170] (See Genealogy 6.1.)

Fastolf wanted to found a chantry – an endowment where priests would celebrate masses for his soul – at Caister, where he had already built a castle. He died before accomplishing this, leaving an unsigned will dated two days before his death in which he entrusted John Paston to set up the foundation. In return, the will granted John all of Fastolf's manors in Norfolk and Suffolk. Fastolf had other trustees and agents, and they contested the will. The dukes and other landowners of Norfolk and Suffolk made claims on Paston manors, as well; the armed men of Lord Moleyns ousted them from their purchased estate at Gresham, for example. In part, this outright violence was made possible by the wars between the Yorkists and the Lancastrians, later dubbed the Wars of the Roses (1453–87). But the Wars were only one problem: the Pastons faced many other troubles, among them a raging plague epidemic, property disputes (the ones over Caister and Gresham being only among the most bitter), and even brief stints in jail.

---

[170] Clement Paston had likely been a serf; see the testimony of "A Remembraunce of the wurshypfull Kyn and Auncetrye of Paston …," written between 1444 and 1466 and printed in *Paston Letters and Papers of the Fifteenth Century*, pts. 1 and 2, ed. Norman Davis, pt. 3, ed. Richard Beadle and Colin Richmond (Oxford, 2004–5) [henceforth Paston, cited by vol., page, document number, and date (the latter two if relevant)], 1:xli–xlii. (Pt. 1 is available online at the Corpus of Middle English Prose and Verse website: quod.lib.umich.edu/c/cme/browse.html). See further discussion of the origins of the Pastons in Caroline Barron, "Who were the Pastons?" *Journal of the Society of Archivists* 4 (1972): 530–35, and Colin Richmond, *The Paston Family in the Fifteenth Century: The First Phase* (Cambridge, 1990), 13–22. In 1466 Edward IV declared the Pastons "gentlemen discended lineally of worshipfull blood sithen [since] the Conquest hither"; the document is in Paston, 2:549, no. 896A. On the interconnections of townsmen and the rural middling and gentry classes, see Rob Lutton, *Lollardy and Orthodox Religion in Pre-Reformation England: Reconstructing Piety* (Woodbridge, 2006), 218–21.

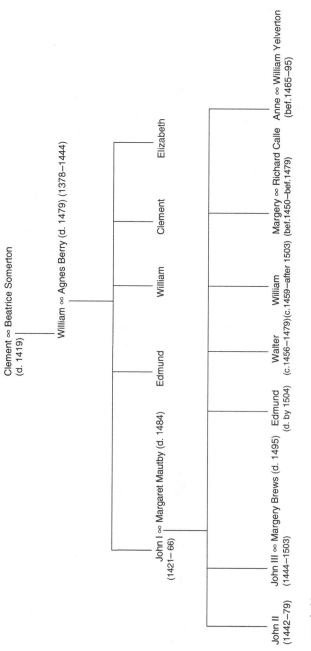

Genealogy 6.1 The Pastons[a]

Clement ∞ Beatrice Somerton
(d. 1419)

William ∞ Agnes Berry (d. 1479) (1378–1444)

John I ∞ Margaret Mautby (d. 1484)
(1421– 66)

Edmund   William   Clement   Elizabeth

John II
(1442–79)

John III ∞ Margery Brews (d. 1495)
(1444–1503)

Edmund
(d. by 1504)

Walter
(c.1456–1479)

William
(c.1459–after 1503)

Margery ∞ Richard Calle
(bef.1450–bef.1479)

Anne ∞ William Yelverton
(bef.1465–95)

∞ **married to**

[a] Based on Colin Richmond, *The Paston Family in the Fifteenth Century: Fastolf's Will* (Cambridge, 1996), xvi.

In the midst of these upheavals, the Pastons wrote more than 400 calm and judicious letters to one another.[171] Or, rather, in many instances, they dictated their missives to an amanuensis. To what extent can we know about the emotional community of the Pastons if our only sources for them – their letters – were often dictated? Let us note that Margery Kempe's *Book* was also dictated; that is why some scholars treat it as almost a work of fiction, certainly a text with a "rhetorical structure."[172] No matter who writes them, letters, too, have a rhetorical structure. The *ars dictaminis* gave the rules for medieval letters, though their influence had diminished by the Pastons' day.[173] Since a letter always has a recipient, it is (almost by definition) a presentation of self, not a revelation of self – unless the revelation has a social purpose. This must be true whether the initiator writes, dictates, or composes a rough draft that will later be smoothed out by someone else. Let us note, too, that inner feeling is both a construct and a value that may change with the emotional community. Our culture today values revelations of inner life. But we should not expect every group or every age to privilege that. We need to be contented with knowing the emotions that letters value and devalue and wish to reveal; these are the major issues, not "true feelings," whatever those might be.

Did the scribes get in the way of revealing the feelings of the Pastons? At least one letter suggests that they did not. In 1477, Margery Brews wrote to

[171] Richmond, *Paston Family: Fastolf's Will* (Cambridge, 1996), 1, notes the presence in Norfolk, at precisely the same time as the Pastons were there, of Joan the Meatless, a girl who ate only the Eucharist, and with "great joy" and was "as unlike Huizinga's fifteenth-century universe as Caroline Walker Bynum's twentieth-century world. Yet there Joan was. She makes me think that I might have mistaken the Norfolk of the Pastons, or indeed the Pastons themselves." Richmond treats the "character" of the Pastons in a thoughtful and sensitive chapter (chap. 1), but he reverts to business in the rest of the book, suggesting that business is mainly what we can know from the letters, even if it is not all that there was to the Pastons. To be sure, the letters are limited. But Richmond's first chapter paves the way to our considering here the infrequent but telling moments in which emotions do emerge. It is also important to appreciate that dryness itself is an emotional style. If business was key for the Pastons, so be it. There were doubtless a variety of emotional communities in fifteenth-century East Anglia. Some, like that of Joan (which likely intersected at many points with Margery's), centered on religious feeling; others, like the Pastons', were (as we shall see) focused on business, labor, and practical affairs. (Margery was initially focused in this way, as well – hence her brewing and milling.) For the emotional implications of another set of fifteenth-century family letters, see Gerhard Fouquet, "Fürsten unter sich – Privatheit und Öffentlichkeit, Emotionalität und Zeremoniell im Medium des Briefes," in *Principes: Dynastien und Höfe im späten Mittelalter*, ed. Cordula Nolte and Karl-Heinz Spiess (Stuttgart, 2002), 171–98.

[172] Wilson, "Communities of Dissent," 156.

[173] Jennifer Douglas, "Kepe wysly youre wrytyngs: Margaret Paston's Fifteenth-Century Letters," *Libraries and the Cultural Record* 44/1 (2009): 29–49, esp. 36–36. See also John Taylor, "Letters and Letter Collections in England, 1300–1420," *Nottingham Mediaeval Studies* 24 (1980): 57–70.

John Paston III, at that time her fiancé. Addressing "my right well-beloved Valentine," Margery expressed her longing for her beloved in romantic prose and verse. She said that she meant the missive to be private: "I beseech you that this bill be not seen by any earthly creature save only yourself."[174] Yet this letter was written out in its entirety by Margery's father's clerk, Thomas Kela. It is possible, then, that amanuenses were invisible to letter-dictators, the equivalent (in the eyes of the person dictating them) of tape recorders rather than human beings. In that case, what the Pastons revealed about themselves in their letters was as unmediated as if they were writing directly.[175] And yet this too will not mean that they revealed themselves in ways that a modern sensibility might expect or wish.

Did the Pastons and their acquaintances constitute an emotional community? They were a very small social group, to be sure.[176] But I make the assumption that they represented a wider phenomenon: that is, I assume that their emotional norms were shared by others of the up-and-coming gentry in their day.[177]

The Paston letters and other writings were systematically collected and preserved beginning in the time of John I, and possibly at his behest.[178] The tradition continued with his wife and their sons. To be sure, the collection needs a bit of pruning since it includes materials both written and received by the Pastons. Some of these were documents written by people outside the family – servants and legal clients, for example.[179] I don't normally count such documents as evidence of Paston emotional norms unless the person writing was deeply involved with the family. This

---

[174] Paston, 1:662–63, no. 415 (1477, February): "my ryght welebeloued Voluntyne … I besech ȝowe þat this bill be not seyn of non erthely creature safe only ȝour-selfe."

[175] Douglas, "Kepe wysly," 34–36, argues this point in some detail.

[176] Note that the "community" of interests of the Pastons was emphasized by John I, who called the household akin to a "felaship, or company … [that] euery persone of it be helpyng and fortheryng aftir his discrecion and powyre (fellowship or company … that every member is helping and furthering according to his discretion and power)." (Paston, 1:127–28, no. 72 [1465, 15 January]).

[177] Similarly, Joel T. Rosenthal, *Margaret Paston's Piety* (New York, 2010), uses a case study of Margaret Paston as a way to "reconstruct the religious life of the late medieval English laity" (1). *Ibid.*, 146–50, attempts to find some evidence of her emotional life, if only in relation to her piety, but Rosenthal concludes that, although she *must* have had feelings about at least certain major events in her life, "we know nothing" (148) for certain about them.

[178] Charles Lethbridge Kingsford, *English Historical Literature in the Fifteenth Century* (Oxford, 1913), 199, argues that John I's "business-like character … made him such a careful keeper of papers" that he must have begun the letter collection. Rosenthal, *Margaret Paston's Piety*, 152 n. 5, favors crediting Margaret, as does Douglas, "Kepe wysly," 42.

[179] Valerie Creelman, "'Ryght worchepfull mastres': Letters of Request and Servants' Scripting of Margaret Paston's Social Self," *Parergon* 26/1 (2009): 91–114, discusses the rhetorical strategies of the twenty-six letters in the Paston archive addressed to Margaret Paston by non-kin males, particularly servants.

was true, for example, of someone like Richard Calle, who was the chief Paston estate manager and who married one of John I's daughters.

The letters are immensely convenient in that they provide the historian of emotions with a significant dossier of texts. However, the fact is that these letters are most notable for their *lack* of emotion. Colin Richmond, a learned commentator on the Pastons, had to turn to an account roll of John I's personal expenses to find John's "gentler side."[180] Norman Davis, who prepared the most recent edition of the letters, spoke of the modern reader's need for "relief from [the letters'] prevailing attention to property."[181] Roger Dalrymple writes, "any glimpses of emotion are summarily displaced by the resurgence of the pragmatic."[182] If there are hardly any emotions in the letters, what is the point of studying them for their emotions?

The first response must be that *lack* of emotions is also part of emotions history. If an emotional community hardly expresses emotions – devalorizing them and finding them repugnant or perhaps simply irrelevant – that fact is as much a part of the history of emotions as are the norms of groups that loudly and proudly proclaim their feelings.[183] But in the second place, we cannot really know how devoid of emotions the Pastons were until we study them closely. And for that, we need to know what to look for. Once again, I have sought the words associated with the heart. In the Paston letters, there are eight such words: comfort, desire, devout, ease, heavy or heaviness, love, sorrow, and troubled.[184] But there is no reason to be limited to them. Kempe's vocabulary, from the same time period and indeed the same geographical region – East Anglia – must have been potentially in the Paston vocabulary. The question is whether or not they used them and, if so, to what effect.

It turns out that they used many of them – and some particular to their own discourse besides. I calculate about forty-nine words to have had emotional force for the Pastons (see Table 6.5).

The variety is impressive, nearly equal to Margery Kempe's. Indeed, as a simple list, it seems in many ways similar to hers. It even contains the ingredients of some of her emotional scripts: despair, dread, love, shame, weeping, and fear. But the sequence of these emotions in Paston writings

---

[180] Richmond, *Paston Family: Fastolf's Will*, 13.

[181] Norman Davis, *The Paston Letters: A Selection in Modern Spelling* (London, 1963), xix.

[182] Roger Dalrymple, "Reaction, Consolation and Redress in the Letters of the Paston Women," in *Early Modern Women's Letter Writing in England*, ed. James Daybell (New York, 2001), 16–28.

[183] Rosenthal, *Margaret Paston's Piety*, 5, notes that "much of what I have to say in introducing Margaret Paston takes the peculiar form of discussing what she was not."

[184] The word "troubled" was also associated with the mind as in Paston, 1:361–62, no. 214 (c. 1472): "so trobled in my mende."

Table 6.5 *Paston emotion words*[a]

aferd/affrayd, afraid
affeccion, affection
angry
belovyd, beloved
care
comfort
compassion
dere, dear
desyre, desire
devowte, devout
dought, doubt
drede, dread
dyspeyre, despair
envye
eas, ease
fere, fear
gereue, distress
glad
heuy, heavy
heuynesse, heaviness, grudge
jalous, jealous
joye
lekyth, like
love
mercy
mery, merry
pensyly, sorrowfully
petowse, piteous
peyn, pain
pité, pity
plesyd, pleased
shame
sorow, sorrow
sory, sorry
trowblyd, troubled
wroth, angry
wypyng, weeping

[a] Words that the Pastons connected with the heart are indicated
in boldface. Variant spellings have been included only sparingly. Translations, where supplied, are only approximate; in
most instances I have used modern English cognates, though
this has its dangers: we use these words differently, and in
different contexts.

was very little like Margery Kempe's. Consider a letter that spoke a good bit about fear. It is from Margaret to her husband John Paston I:

Right worshipful husband, I recommend me to you. Please know that I have spoken with the wife of Thomas Denys, and she recommends herself to your good mastership. And she prays you to be her good master, and prays you of your good mastership that you will give her your advice on how she should proceed regarding her person and her goods. For, as touching her own person, she dare not go home to her own place, for she faces the threat that, should she be taken, she would be slain or put in the fearful position of shortening the days of her life, and so her heart is heavy, God help her ...

Item: the last time I spoke with her, she made such a piteous moan and said that she knew not what she would do for money, and so I lent her 6 s, 8 d.

Item: I sent my kinsman Berney the letter that John Pampyng [an agent for the Pastons] wrote by your command to me, and he has sent a letter of intent about it to you and to [William] Rokewode; also, unless it please you to take better care of his matter than he can do himself, I think he shall otherwise fare the worse, for, in faith, he is daily in great fear of the false and hostile party against him.

Item: for the reverence of God, beware of wicked and evilly disposed companions if you ride or go. I am daily put in fear of abiding here, and counseled by my mother and by other good friends that I should not abide here, except if the world were quieter than it is. God for his mercy send us a good world, and send you health in body and soul and good speed in all your affairs.[185]

Some context is needed. Thomas Denys, the coroner of Norfolk, had many enemies and already had written several times to John, his "right worshipful and my especially good master," to come to the aid of both himself and his wife.[186] In November, a few days before Margaret's

---

[185] Paston, 1:267–68, no. 160 (1461, 9 July): "Right worchepful hosbond, I recommand me to yow. Please yow to wete þat I have spoke wyth Thomas Denys wyffe, and she recommand hyr to your good masterchep. And she prayeth yow to be here good master, and prayet you of your good masterchep þat ye wolle geve her your advice howe to be demenid for hyr person and hyr goodys; for as towchyng hyr owne person she dare not goo home to hyr owne place, for she is thret if þat she myght be take she shuld be slayne or be put in ferfull place in shorttyng of hyr lyve-dayes, and so she standyth in gret heuynes, God her helpe .... Item, þe last tyme þat I spake wyth hyre she mad suche a petows mone, and seyd þat she wost ner howe to do for mony, and so I lent vj s. viij d. Item, I sent my cosyn Barney þe bylle þat John Pampyng wrot be your commanddement to me, and he hath sent a letter of hys entent to yow and to Rokwod therof; and also but yf it please yow to take better hed to hys mater than he can do hym-selff I can thynk he shall ellis fare þe wors, for j feyth he standyth daly in gret fere for þe false contrary party ageyns hym. Item, at þe reuerence of God be ware howe ye ryd or go, for nowgty and euyll desposyd felachepys. I am put en fere dayly for myn a-bydyng here, and cownsellyd be my moder and be other good frendys þat I shuld not a-beyd here but yf þe world wher in more quiete than it is. God for hys merci send vs a good world, and send yow helthe in body and sowle and good speed in all your maters."

[186] Paston, 2:230–31, no. 626 (1461, probably April-May); Paston, 2:234–35, no. 629 (1461, May): "Right wurshipfull and myn especiall good maister." On Thomas Denys,

letter to John, Thomas was abducted and murdered by the parson of Snoring, who was probably working for the duke of Norfolk, a claimant to Caister castle.[187] John I had helped broker the marriage between Denys and his wife, Agnes, so Margaret felt some responsibility for Agnes' fate. Meanwhile John Berney, Margaret's uncle, was also under attack by Norfolk's party. It goes without saying that John and Margaret were in danger, as well. How could the letter not speak of fear? But the "script" began with someone else's fear – that of Agnes. It emphasized her deference to her "master" and her dependence on the Pastons, and it took into account *her* feelings, her "heavy heart." Margaret saw her plight as piteous. Immediately, however, pity was left behind as Margaret took up family matters: her uncle, her husband, her concern for both. Pity and fear: these were the emotions of an Aristotelian tragedy, but here they were embedded in an itemized list. They were matters to be acted upon.

The same may be said of love. The Pastons certainly talked about it, and "beloved" and "well-beloved" were common epithets in many of their letters to one another.[188] Yet when the idea of love was broached, it was generally as an issue to be addressed, as when Margaret wrote to her son John II in 1463:

Item: I would that you speak with Wykes [John, usher of the King Edward IV's chamber] and know his attitude toward Jane Walsham. She has said since he departed that unless she might have him, she would never be married; her heart is very set on him. She told me that he said to her that there was no woman in the world he loved so well. I would not like for him to trifle with her, for she really means it, and if he will not have her, let me know in haste and I shall make other arrangements for her. As for your harness and the gear that you left here, it is in Daubeney's keeping. [John Daubeney was a Paston servant.] It was not moved since your departure because he didn't have the keys . . . I sent your grey horse to Ruston to the blacksmith, who says it shall never be good to ride nor to plow nor to cart . . . Your grandmother would like to hear some tidings from you. It would be well done to send a letter to her telling her how you are doing as quickly as you can.[189]

see the index of Paston 3, s.v., and Richard Barber, *The Pastons: A Family in the Wars of the Roses* (London, 1981), 46.

[187] Denys names some of his enemies in Paston, 2:234, no. 629 (1461, May), including John Heydon, who had long been hostile to Paston interests in the region. Useful background is in Barber, *The Pastons*, 30–64, 86–87.

[188] For example, in letters of John II to his brother John III, such as Paston, 1:449, no. 269 (1472, 4 November): "Worshypffull and weell belovyd brother"; 1:455, no. 272 (1473, 3 February): "Weell belovyd brother"; 1:457, no. 274 (1473, 12 April): "Best belovyd brother."

[189] Paston, 1:288, no. 175 (1463, 15 November): "Item, I wold ye shuld speke wyth Wekis and knowe hys dysposysion to Jane Walsham. She hathe seyd syn he departyd hens but

Here a harness, a lame horse, and obligations to a grandmother jostled with a love affair. Even when, in May 1469, the affair involved a daughter of John and Margaret – Margery, who fell in love with and married Richard Calle, the Paston estates' manager – it was treated, at least by John III, as simply the start of a doleful letter to John II: "[Calle] will never have my consent to make my sister sell candles and mustard in Framlingham!"[190] Following this, he renewed his request for some gear unavailable in Norfolk and reported on more threats to the castle at Caister.

But, while they were forced to live apart, Richard Calle wrote a devoted love letter to Margery, filled with sorrow, love, and longing, and detailing his many difficulties in communicating with "my own lady and mistress and before God very true wife."[191] He spoke of "the great bond of matrimony that has been made between us, and also the great love that has been, and as I trust still is, between us, and for my part never greater."[192] And less than a decade later, when John III finally was about to marry, his fiancée, also named Margery, wrote perhaps the first valentine, which I have already mentioned:

Right reverend and worshipful and my right well-beloved Valentine, I commend myself unto you full heartily, desiring to hear of your welfare, which I beseech Almighty God to long preserve unto his pleasure and your heart's desire. And if it please you to hear of my welfare, I am not in good health of body nor of heart, nor shall be until I hear from you.[193]

Even the formidable Margaret once – as a young bride expecting her first child – wrote in affectionate tones to her absent husband: "You have left

she myght have hym she wold neuer be [deleted in MS] maryyd; hyr hert ys sore set on hym. She told me þat he seyd to hyr þat ther was no woman in þe world he lovyd so welle. I wold not he shuld jape hyr, for she menythe good feythe, and yf he wolle not have hyr late me wete in hast and I shall purvey for hyr in othyr wysse. As for your harneys and gere that ye left here, it ys in Daubeneys kepyng. It was neuer remeuyd syn your departyng be-cause that he had not þe keyes ... I sent your grey hors to Ruston to þe ferrore, and he seythe he shall neuer be nowght to rood nowthyr ryght good to plowe nore to carte ... Your grandam wold fayne her sum tydyngys from yow. It were welle do þat ye sent a letter to hyr howe ye do as astely as ye may."

[190] Paston, 1:541, no. 332 (1469, May): "he shold neuer haue my good wyll for to make my sustyr to selle kandyll and mustard in Framlyngham."
[191] Paston, 2:498, no. 861 (1469): "Myn owne lady and mastres, and be-for God very trewe wyff."
[192] *Ibid.*: "the gret bonde of matrymonye þat is made be-twix vs, and also the greete loue þat hath be, and as I truste yet is, be-twix vs, and as on my parte neuer gretter."
[193] Paston, 1:662, no. 415 (1477, February): "Ryght reuerent and wurschypfull and my ryght welebeloued Voluntyne, I recommande me vn-to yowe full hertely, desyring to here of yowr welefare, whech I besche Almyghty God long for to preserve vn-to hys plesure and ȝowr hertys desyre. And yf it please ȝowe to here of my welefare, I am not in good heele of body ner of herte, nor schall be tyll I here from yowe."

me such a remembrance that it makes me think upon you both day and night when I want to sleep."[194]

But soon, as Caroline Barron has put it, "the cares of her family and estate cramped her expressions of affection."[195] Or, to put it another way, Margaret quickly adapted to the set of emotional norms that the Pastons expected. The Margery who wrote the valentine did the same. After marrying, her letters to her husband took on the familiar tone of any of the brothers John or their mother Margaret. Similarly Richard Calle, so ardent as a lover, nevertheless continued to serve the family right through the crisis – writing about business to John II in May and July of 1469 – and afterwards, as with his letters about selling wood at Sporle to Margaret in 1472 and 1473.[196] Clearly these people were acquainted with a variety of emotional communities, and they knew well enough how to conform to the "Paston norms" when needed.

Those norms included not only dry expression but also certain highly valued words. We have seen that love and fear were often mentioned; without doubt, they signified very strong emotions, even when embedded in a list of other sorts of items. Let us not conflate dryness with lack of feeling. Philippa Maddern long ago called attention to the importance of affective bonds for the Pastons, not only within the family but also in the instance of "supporters and adherents."[197] Maddern also stressed the importance the Pastons placed on shame, the avoidance of which was crucial to the honor and status of the family. Thus John Paston III wrote to his mother Margaret, "in good faith I shall never, while God gives me life, dread death more than shame." In the context, what he was referring to was his uncle's claims on his father's will and his own efforts "to labor in hindering the execution of my unkind uncle's intent."[198]

On the whole, however, the emotion words most used by the Pastons tended to emphasize quiet and equilibrium. Thus John II wrote to his mother, Margaret, in 1469: "And to comfort you, do not despair about your lack of provisions and gunpowder, and be neither too heavy nor too merry

---

[194] To John I from Margaret, Paston, 1:217, no. 125 (probably 1441, 14 December): "Ye haue lefte me sweche a rememravnse þat makyth me to thynke vppe-on yow bothe day and nyth wanne I wold sclepe."

[195] Barron, "Who Were the Pastons?" 532.

[196] To John II, Paston, 2:395–98, nos. 759 (1469, 22 May), 761 (1469, 3 July); to Margaret Paston, 2:356–58, nos. 728 (probably 1472, 27 November), 729 (perhaps 1473, c. October). John Paston II knew about the affair already in May 1469; see above, n. 190.

[197] Philippa Maddern, "Honour among the Pastons: Gender and Integrity in Fifteenth-Century English Provincial Society," *Journal of Medieval History* 14 (1988): 357–71, here 368.

[198] Paston, 1:618–19, no. 384 (1479, December): "In good feyth I shall never, whyll God sendyth me lyff, dred mor dethe then shame ... I am drevyn to labore in lettyng of th'execucyon of myn vnkynd onclys entent."

about it. For if heaviness or sorrow would have been the remedy for such things, I never knew any matter in my life that I could have been so heavy or sorry about."[199] Thus did John II encourage Margaret and her defenders, John III and his men, to face a concerted attack on Caister by the duke of Norfolk and his soldiers.[200] After John III was forced to surrender, he wrote, possibly ironically, to John II, who had remained at court and apparently had not helped out during the crisis, "God preserve you, and I pray you be of good cheer until I speak with you, and I trust to God to ease your heart in some things."[201] Irony or not, "ease" was the word that came most readily to hand. Meanwhile the Pastons were often "glad," and they spoke of others as being so. Thus Margaret told her husband that "I would be very glad to hear some good news from you."[202] And later the same month she reported that "all your tenants at Hellesdon and Drayton except these three [Will Herne, Piers, and another] are very glad that we are there among them, and so are many others of our old neighbors and friends."[203]

Even the most emotional moments show the Pastons valuing equanimity over passion. When the bishop of Norfolk insisted on speaking with Margery and Richard Calle to see if they were indeed bound to one another, Margaret reported on the meeting to her oldest son.[204] The bishop, she said, began by reminding Margery of her friends and family and of "what rebuke and shame and loss it should be to her if she were not guided by them."[205] He had heard that vows had been exchanged and

---

[199] Paston, 1:406, no. 243 (1469, 15 September): "And to encomfort yow, dyspeyre yow not fore lak of vytayle ner of gonne-powder, ner be natt to heuy ner to mery there-fore. Fore and heuynesse ore sorow wolde haue ben the remedy there-of, I knew neuyre matere in my lyffe þat I kowde haue ben so heuy ore sory fore."

[200] Paston, 1:344, no. 204 (1469, 12 September): "your brothere and his felesshep stond in grete joparté at Cayster and likke vetayll; and Dawbeney and Berney be dedde and diuerse othere gretly hurt, and thei fayll gonnepowder and arrowes (your brother and his company stand in great jeopardy at Caister and lack provisions; and Daubeney and Berney are dead and many others badly injured, and they lack gunpowder and arrows.)"

[201] Paston, 1:546, no. 334 (1469, about 25 September): "God preserue yow, and I pray yow be of good cher tyll I spek wyth yow; and I trust to God to ese your hert in some thynggys." On the sequence of these letters and their circumstances, see Barber, *The Pastons*, 155–58.

[202] Paston, 1:290, no. 176 (1464, 6 May): "Sere, I wold be ryte glad to here swmme gode tydynggys fro ȝow."

[203] Paston, 1:303, no. 183 (1464, 27 May): "All youre tenauntys at Haylesdon and Drayton except thes iij be ryght glad that we erre there a-mongys hem, and so be many othere of oure old nebors and frendys."

[204] On the doctrine of consent and its role in this episode, see Jacqueline Murray, "Individualism and Consensual Marriage: Some Evidence from Medieval England," in *Women, Marriage, and Family in Medieval Christendom: Essays in Memory of Michael M. Sheehan*, ed. Constance M. Rousseau and Joel T. Rosenthal (Kalamazoo, 1998), 121–51.

[205] Paston, 1:341–44, no. 203 (1469, 10 or 11 September), here 342: "wat rebuke and schame and los yt xuld be to here yf sche were not gydyd be them."

wanted to know if they "made matrimony or not. And she [Margery] repeated what she had said and said boldly that if those words did not make it legally binding, she would make it legally binding before she left, for she said she thought in her conscience she was bound, whatsoever the words were. These foolish words grieve me and her grandmother [Agnes] as much as all the rest."[206] Taking his time, the bishop postponed the verdict, and Margaret barred the door to her daughter: "When I heard say what her conduct was, I charged my servants not to receive her in my house. I have given her warning; she might have realized this before if she had been well-disposed. And I sent on to one or two others that they should not receive her if she came."[207] Margery ended up at the house of one Roger Best and his wife. Her mother was pleased: "I am better off that she is there for the while than if she had been in another place, because of the wisdom and good disposition of himself and his wife, for she shall not be allowed to play the ne'r-do-well there."[208] And then the calm conclusion: "I pray and require you not to take it sorrowfully, for I well know it goes right to your heart, as it does to mine and to others. But remember, as do I, that in her we have lost nothing but a ne'r-do-well, and take it less to heart." Margaret nevertheless counseled against pursuing divorce, for it would "offend God and your conscience ... For know well that she shall fully repent her foolishness hereafter, and I pray God she might do so. So I pray you, for my heart's ease: be of good comfort in all things."[209]

Why would the Pastons express feelings in such attenuated ways? One answer may lie in the notion of the ne'r-do-well, the *brethele*, as Margaret put it. The term was more usually spelled *brothel* or *brodel*: a worthless

---

[206] *Ibid.*: "wheythere yt mad matramony ore not. And sche rehersyd wat sche had seyd, and seyd yf thoo worddys mad yt not suhere, sche seyd boldly þat sche wold make yt suerhere ore þat sche went thens; fore sche sayd sche thowthe in here conschens sche was bownd, wat so euere þe worddys wern. Thes leud worddys gereue me and here grandam as myche as alle þe remnawnte." On the developing role of individual conscience, see Maddern, "Honour among the Pastons."

[207] *Ibid.*, 343: "wan I hard sey wat here demenyng was I schargyd my seruantys þat sche xuld not be reseyued in myn hows. I had ȝeuen here warnyng, sche mythe a be ware afore yf sche had a be grasyows. And I sent to on ore ij more þat they xuld not reseyue here yf sche cam."

[208] *Ibid.*: "I am better payed þat sche is there fore þe whyle þan sche had ben in othere place, be-cause of þe sadnes and god dysposysion of hym-sylfe and hys wyfe, fore sche xal not be souerd there to pleye þe brethele."

[209] *Ibid.*: "I pray ȝow and requere ȝow þat ȝe take yt not pensyly, fore I wot wele yt gothe ryth nere ȝowr hart, and so doth yt to myn and to othere; but remembyre ȝow, and so do I, þat we haue lost of here but a brethele, and setyt þe les to hart ... [but divorce would] offend God and ȝowr conschens ... Fore wottyt wele, sche xal ful sore repent here leudnes here-aftyre, and I pray God sche mute soo. I pray ȝow, fore myn hard ys hese, be ȝe of a good cownfort in alle thynggys."

person, deriving from an Old English verb meaning "to go to ruin, to degenerate."[210] Margery Kempe compared herself to one when she sought the world's opprobrium. The morality play *The Castle of Perseverance* used the word as a synonym for Sloth. Calling Margery a brethel was Margaret's way of saying that her daughter had repudiated the values of the family.

These were, above all, the values of the busy, enterprising man or woman of business. Although the Pastons moved into the nobility (in 1466 they were so designated by Edward IV), they did not in fact share many values with noblemen. Their major focus was on productivity, not gentlemanly idleness.[211] That is the clear implication of their busy, practical, itemized letters to one another.[212] And it became explicit when they were displeased with the behavior of family members or exhorted them to do better. Thus in the first generation, Agnes wrote in a memorandum of errands to do in London: "To ask Grenefeld [tutor to her son Clement Paston] to send me faithfully word by writing how Clement Paston has done his duty in learning. And if he has not done well, or will not amend, pray him that he will truly beat him until he amend ... And tell Elizabeth Paston that she must accustom herself to work as readily as other gentle-women do and to help herself somewhat thereby. Item, to pay the Lady Pole [with whom Elizabeth was boarding] 26 s 8 d."[213]

John I accused his son John II, who spent most of his time at the royal court, of "playing games." He considered his courtly pastimes as frivolities. Of his oldest son's behavior, his father wrote: "I understand in him

---

[210] See the online Middle English Dictionary, *brethel* as form and headword and also the Oxford English Dictionary under *brethe*. In Paston 1:230, no. 131 (1449, 15 February), Margery called Moleyns' men "a cumpany of brothell" when they threatened the Pastons' hold on Gresham.

[211] See Edward IV to the Bailiffs of Yarmouth, Paston, 2:549, no. 896A (1466, 26 and 27 July): "we ... take and repute them as gentlemen discended lineally of worshipfull blood sithen the Conquest hither (of honorable blood since the Conquest.)"

[212] Helen Fulton, "Autobiography & the Discourse of Urban Subjectivity: *The Paston Letters*," in *Early Modern Autobiography: Theories, Genres, Practices*, ed. Ronald Bedford, Lloyd Davis, and Philippa Kelly (Ann Arbor, 2006), 191–216 at 201, argues that the *Paston Letters* exemplified a new, secular, urban discourse; their correspondence was modeled on "business formats."

[213] Paston 1:41–42, no. 28 (1458, 28 January): "To prey Grenefeld to send me feythfully word by wrytyn who Clement Paston hath do his devere in lernyng. And if he hathe nought do well, nor wyll nought amend, prey hym that he wyll trewly belassch hym tyl he wyll amend ... And sey Elyzabet Paston that che must vse hyr-selfe to werke redyly as other jentylwomen don, and sumwhat to helpe hyr-self ther-wyth. Item, to pay the Lady Pole – xxvj s. viij d." Even when Margaret fended off an outside attack by the duke of Suffolk's men on the manor of Hellesdon, John I praised her not for her courage or skill or resourcefulness but rather for her "labowr and besynes"; see Paston, 1:134, no. 74 (1465, 13 July). Ann S. Haskell, "The Paston Women on Marriage in Fifteenth-Century England," *Viator* 4 (1973): 459–71 at 463, notes that Englishwomen of the gentry during this period were expected, like their husbands, to be excellent managers of their "part of the family corporation."

no disposition for management nor of governance as a man of the world ought to have, but he lives only, and ever has, as a dissolute man, without any provision, nor does he exert himself to understand such matters as a man who makes a living must needs understand."[214] (A modern commentator, however, has noted that John II was up to "gamesmanship," not games.[215]) The "at home" Pastons did not understand the norms of the court, but John II knew those of his family very well. Attempting to smooth out ruffled feelings, he wrote to his sober-minded brother: "Right worshipful and truly well-beloved brother, I heartily commend me to you, thanking you for the labor and diligence that you have [shown] in keeping my place at Caister so securely, both with your heart and mind, and to your great effort and trouble."[216] Labor, diligence, earning a living: these were the goals to which the Pastons devoted themselves. The norms of their emotional community accorded with and reinforced these goals.

***

Huizinga was right: there were ostentatious expressions of emotions in the Late Middle Ages. That is, there were certain emotional communities that privileged dramatic outpourings. That was true of the Burgundian chroniclers as well as of Margery Kempe and her supporters. However, their values and goals were very different, and therefore,

---

[214] Paston, 1:132, no. 73 (1465, 27 June): "I vnderstand in hym no dispocicion of polecy ne of gouernans as man of the werld owt to do, but only leuith, and euer hath, as man disolut, with-owt any prouicion, ne that he besijth hym nothinge to vnderstand swhech materis as a man of lyuelode must nedis vnderstond."

[215] Richmond, *Paston Family: Fastolf's Will*, 167 and, in general, chap. 4. On the other hand, the same author suggests that the Paston family would have been happy with John had he been a more successful courtier; see Colin Richmond, "The Pastons Revisited: Marriage and the Family in Fifteenth-century England," *Bulletin of the Institute of Historical Research* 58 (1985): 25–36 at 27. John I called John II "a drane amonges bees whech labour for gaderyng hony in the feldes and the drane doth nought but takyth his part of it (a drone among bees that labor to gather honey in the fields, while the drone does nothing but take his portion)" in Paston, 1:128, no. 72 (1465, January). Two years later, John III expressed his disapproval of John II's chivalric, courtly ventures in Paston, 1:535, no. 327 (1467, April): "and wher as it plesyth yow for to wyshe me at Eltam at the tornay for the good syth þat was ther, by trowththe I had leuer se yow onys in Caster Halle then to se as many kyngys tornay as myght be betwyx Eltam and London (and whereas it pleases you to wish me [to have seen you] at Eltham at the tournament for the good sight that was there, on my honor I had rather see you once at Caister Hall than to see as many kings' tourneys as might be between Eltham and London." John II's invitation to "see him" is quoted in the headnotes for Paston, 1:396, no. 236.

[216] Paston, 1:396, no. 236 (1467, probably March, and thus slightly before no. 327 above): "Ryght worschypful and verrely welbelouyd brothere, I hertely comande me to yow, thankyng yow of yowre labore and dyligence that ye haue in kepyng of my place at Castre so sewerly, both wyth yowre hert and mynde, to yowr gret bisynesse and troble."

in context, they did not express the same emotional norms. The Burgundians were preoccupied with pathos; they saw the tragedy of war and dynastic folly. Margery was concerned with her own experiences, which led her to despair and then bliss. Her compassion was for Christ alone.

Kathleen Ashley has rightly put Margery in her bourgeois context: "For roughly 1300 to 1650 … a new group we now call the 'middle class' consolidated their socioeconomic power by developing a self-conscious identity."[217] Margery, Ashley argues, demonstrates how a member of that class negotiated a religious justification for lay life. Margery's non-religious life – as a brewer, as a miller – was devoted to business and busyness. Even when she imagined herself part of Christ's life, she gave herself the job of nursemaid.

The Burgundian chroniclers were part of and valued a more exalted kind of service. To be sure, they were busy: they wrote; they organized pageants; Chastelain served as a pantler; Lefèvre was a herald and diplomat; La Marche was a court official. But these men worked for a duke. Their service was more like that of John II Paston at the English royal court, seen as utterly frivolous by his family.

The Pastons valued diligent and practical work, and they cultivated an emotional style to match.[218] When they wrote to one another, passionate matters were treated alongside harnesses and lame horses. They itemized everything. Their feelings were measured; they carefully doled out their words, barely hinting at their unhappiness or pleasure. They were a family on the rise, from peasantry to nobility. Whence their emotional norms? Did they reflect those of a silent peasantry? It is possible. But I suggest that these norms had at least two other origins, as well. First, they were habitual among certain groups within the gentry, the class into which the male members of the family married.[219] We have already seen in

---

[217] Kathleen Ashley, "Historicizing Margery: *The Book of Margery Kempe* as Social Text," *Journal of Medieval and Early Modern Studies* 28 (1998): 371–88, quote on 382.

[218] John II was at Lynn in 1462: see Paston, 1:393–94, no. 233. See also Paston, 1: xlvi, for John's patron, John Wykes, who was, among other things, controller of customs at Lynn. There was also a vague Burgundian connection: John II and John III traveled to Bruges in service to Princess Margaret when she married Duke Charles the Bold in 1468; see, for example, Paston, 1:538–40, no. 330 (1468, 8 July). In this letter of John III to Margaret, he suggests the wonder of the Burgundian court, and his delight in it. Nevertheless, he seems happy enough to return to England: "I shall tell yow [more] when I come home, whyche I tryst to God shalnot be long to (I'll tell you more when I get home, which I trust to God will not be long)."

[219] See Paston, 1:liii and lv, noting that Agnes Paston was "daughter and heiress of Sir Edmund Berry" while Margaret was "daughter and heiress of John Mautby … through whom she was related to Sir John Fastolf."

France a Neustrian court that practiced understatement and emotional restraint. I do not suggest that that particular court was "remembered" or had any direct effect on the Pastons centuries later. But I do suggest that just as bits of the human genome "come from" ancient sources and are expressed from time to time, so ancient emotional patterns and norms remain part of the repertory on which later communities may draw. Second, and complementing this last point, the Paston norms may have been common to some bourgeois groups living right in their region and at the same time – for example, those people who were *not* supportive of Margery, who were dismayed by Margery's tears, cryings, and roarings.

In the next chapter, we shall explore the theory of emotions of the fifteenth-century scholastic and preacher Jean Gerson. Linking the passions to a silent "chant of the heart," Gerson helps us see how the same era could support emotional communities spanning the spectrum from utterly dramatic to nearly mute.

7 Gerson's music

Although the fifteenth century has been called "the century of Gerson," it is not because of his theory of emotions.[1] Indeed, Gerson (1363–1429) is hardly mentioned as an emotion theorist. In part that is because, with the exception of three short texts, his theory of emotions masqueraded under other guises, particularly as a form of music.[2] But Gerson was a scholastic with a humanist bent, and thus he knew and valued the passions; in his view, writing that did not rouse them was sterile. However, Gerson did not mean to appeal to *all* the passions. Unlike Thomas Aquinas, he was wary of most: many of them were bad, and others were at best morally neutral. Gerson was most interested in the emotions of the heart, which he saw as expressing the free will of reason. These emotions, the *Canticordum*, were "sung" silently.

Gerson was born in relatively modest circumstances in the hamlet of Gerson-lès-Barby, a bit northeast of Reims.[3] A scholarship student at the College of Navarre in Paris, Gerson learned the liberal arts in a milieu saturated by the works of both Italian and French humanists. Soon he began to study theology. From the first, he was the protégé of Pierre d'Ailly (1350–1420), a "rising star" (Brian McGuire's epithet) of both university politics and intellectual life. In 1395, Gerson followed d'Ailly to

---

[1] *Histoire de l'Église*, ed. Augustin Fliche and Victor Martin, vol. 14.2: *L'Église au temps du grand schisme et de la crise conciliaire (1378–1419)*, ed. Etienne Delaruelle, Edmond-René Labande, and Paul Ourliac (Paris, 1962), chap. 5: "Le siècle de Gerson." I thank Brian McGuire and Daniel Hobbins for reading and commenting on this chapter in draft.

[2] *A Companion to Jean Gerson*, ed. Brian Patrick McGuire (Leiden, 2006), has no chapter on the emotions and only sporadic reference to them. Daniel Hobbins, *Authorship and Publicity Before Print: Jean Gerson and the Transformation of Late Medieval Learning* (Philadelphia, 2009), treats them as a given for Gerson, unproblematic and ready to be roused by rhetoric. Knuuttila, *Emotions*, 284, devotes one paragraph to Gerson.

[3] For biographical information, see Brian Patrick McGuire, *Jean Gerson and the Last Medieval Reformation* (University Park, PA, 2005); McGuire, "In Search of Jean Gerson: Chronology of His Life and Works," in *A Companion to Jean Gerson*, 1–39; Hobbins, *Authorship*, 3–5; Palémon Glorieux, "La vie et les oeuvres de Gerson. Essai chronologique," *Archives d'Histoire doctrinale et littéraire du Moyen Âge* 25–26 (1950–51): 149–91.

become chancellor of Notre Dame cathedral and thus of the University of Paris. Meanwhile he gained fame as a preacher at courts and to princes. Duke Philip the Bold of Burgundy appointed him chaplain in 1393 and gave him a deanship at the collegial church of Saint Donatian at Bruges. However, the assassination of the duke of Orléans by the Burgundian duke's henchmen in 1407 effectively ended Gerson's association with the Burgundians. In any event, throughout this period his primary home was Paris until February, 1415.

At that point, Gerson went to the Council of Constance (1414–18) as a member of the French delegation. The council's main goal was to end the Great Schism (1378–1417), which by this time had split the church among three papal claimants. Already around the time of the Council of Pisa (1409), Gerson had written an important work that put him in the conciliarist camp, *De auctoritate concilii* (*On the Authority of the Council*) (1408–9), and he followed that with a spate of other writings.[4] At Constance Gerson had a starring role, at least for a while.[5] But he could not return to Paris when it was over: the Burgundians had allied themselves with the English, and Paris was under their rule.

Now an exile from Notre Dame, Gerson made his way to join one of his younger brothers, also Jean, who had become prior of the Celestine monastery at Lyon in 1421. There, in a cloister near the cathedral, Gerson remained until the end of his life. This was a stable and productive period for him, even though he liked to think of himself as a pilgrim "with no abiding home."[6]

During this time "in exile" Gerson wrote his most important work on the passions: the so-called *Tractatus de canticis* (*Treatises on Songs*) (c. 1423– c. 1429) as well as a vernacular piece on the same topic, the *Canticordum au pélerin*, a sort of "pilgrim's guide" to the song of the heart.[7] Earlier, around

---

[4] Listed in Francis Oakley, "Gerson as Conciliarist," in *A Companion to Jean Gerson*, 179– 204, here 194.

[5] McGuire, "In Search," 25, points out that Gerson's constant diatribes at the Council against tyrannicide, directed against the Burgundians, wore out his welcome there. On Gerson as "a cautious and conservative theologian," seeking unity in the church above all, see G. H. M. Posthumus Meyjes, *Jean Gerson – Apostle of Unity: His Church Politics and Ecclesiology* (Leiden, 1999), quote on 2, and Oakley, "Gerson as Conciliarist."

[6] McGuire, "In Search," 26. *Gershon*, as Gerson knew, means "pilgrim" in Hebrew; see Hobbins, *Authorship*, 76. On the "deeper meaning" of the term for Gerson, see *ibid.*, 74, and Jeffrey Fisher, "Gerson's Mystical Theology," in *A Companion to Jean Gerson*, 205–48 at 211.

[7] For the dates, texts, and suggested titles (since Gerson himself did not provide titles), *La doctrine du chant du Coeur de Jean Gerson. Edition critique, traduction et commentaire du "Tractatus de canticis" et du "Canticordum au pélerin,"* ed. and trans. Isabelle Fabre (Geneva, 2005). [Henceforth the *Tractatus de canticis* is cited as TC and the *Canticordum au pélerin* as CP followed by the page number in Fabre.] G. Matteo Roccati, "La production *de canticis* de Jean Gerson: les circonstances de composition et de diffusion. À propos d'un ouvrage récent," *Le*

the time of the Council of Pisa, Gerson had written *De passionibus animae* (*On the Passions of the Soul*) (1408–9), a scholastic work on the emotions divided into considerations (*considerationes*) – "convenient points," which as Hobbins explains, were "organizational devices ... easily committed to memory."[8] Also at some point during his extended stay in Paris (1400–15), Gerson composed a short "pamphlet" with the same title: *On the Passions of the Soul*.[9] Supplementing these was his even briefer *Enumeratio peccatorum ab Alberto posita*; it listed ten of Thomas Aquinas' eleven emotions, each followed by its many species and circumstances.[10]

Thus Gerson thought about the emotions when he was young as well as in his final years. Although, as we shall see, he took many of his ideas from Thomas Aquinas and from pseudo-Dionysius (who, to be sure, also inspired Thomas), Gerson articulated a theory both more practical and more capacious than the thirteenth-century master. We shall follow this theory from its first appearance in the "scholastic mode" (mainly the two treatises *On the Passions*) to its later, more ecstatic form as a theory of music.[11]

Practical lists and a theory

Gerson's short treatise on the passions (DP short) reads like notes to himself (or to others) about the nature, causes, and effects of the passions. Above all, Gerson was interested in emotion words. What were they? What were the precise circumstances in which they were invoked? The result was less a treatise than something like a thesaurus. Insofar as Gerson had an organizing principle, it was a loose combination of two schemes: the Stoic grid (we have already seen Cicero's version of it in

Moyen Age 112/2 (2006): 355–61 at 356–57, points out that the title *Tractatus* is somewhat misleading, given that it is composed of a miscellany of works on the chant brought together only after Gerson's death.

[8] Gerson, *De passionibus animae*, in Jean Gerson, *Oeuvres complètes*, ed. Palémon Glorieux, 10 vols. (Paris, 1960–73) [henceforth OC], 9:1–25, No. 423 [henceforth DP long]; quote from Hobbins, *Authorship*, 107–8. For the date, Glorieux, "La vie," 173.

[9] Gerson, *De passionibus animae*, in OC, 9:155–57, No. 437 [henceforth DP short]; date is from OC, 9:xi.

[10] Gerson, *Enumeratio peccatorum ab Alberto posita*, in OC, 9:160–66, No. 438 [henceforth EP]. In this work, Gerson made Thomas' courage (*audacia*) a species of despair (*desperatio*).

[11] In TC, 340, Gerson referred to his DP long, suggesting that he saw his later work as a natural development of his earlier thoughts. Music had long been associated with emotions. For a convenient summary of thought on the topic before Gerson, see Brenno Boccadoro, "La musique, les passions, l'âme et le corps," in *Autour de Guillaume d'Auvergne (†1249)*, ed. Franco Morenzoni and Jean-Yves Tilliette (Turnhout, 2005), 75–92.

Table 7.1 *The Stoic emotional grid*

	Assessed as a good	Assessed as an evil
Present	pleasure	pain
Future	desire	fear

Table 1.1, and Table 7.1 summarizes it slightly differently) and the distinction between the concupiscible and irascible emotions.

Let us consider pain, for example, which Gerson paired with sorrow (*tristitia vel dolor*). Like all the passions, it was a "motion," in this case one responding to a present evil but not an "arduous" one.[12] (In Gerson's short treatise on the passions, only anger [*ira*] and its opposite, meekness [*mansuetudo*], responded to present arduous evils.[13]) Pain or sorrow was called one thing (*achos*) when you recognized your own misfortune; it derived from the idea of being "without a voice." But you used a different word – not *achos* but *acedia* – when you spoke of laboring hard. You used the word *aggravatio* (close to our term "oppression") when paying dues and services. *Nemesis* was the pain that came from realizing that something good belonged to an unworthy person. There were similar conditions for envy (*invidia*) (the pain felt when realizing that a worthy person had something good), zeal (*zelus*) (feeling badly about another's fault), and compassion (*misericordia*) (sadness about another person's wrongful punishment).[14] Later in the same short work, Gerson expanded the list of sorrows slightly, adding anxiety (*anxietas*) and anguish (*angustia*).

Still longer, ironically, was the entry for sadness in Gerson's even more abbreviated *Enumeratio peccatorum*, where he named 33 species.[15] That's because the *Enumeratio* was truly just a bunch of lists. Putting together the emotion words from the short version of *De passionibus* and the *Enumeratio*, we get the lengthy list of words for pain/sorrow in Table 7.2.

In the same works, Gerson provided similar, though shorter, lists for pleasure (*delectatio*) and fear (*timor*), and still shorter ones for love (which

---

[12] Given Gerson's later treatises on the connections between the passions and music, it is relevant that some medieval writers, for example Robert Grosseteste, considered music to be the best example of motion. See Nancy van Deusen, *Theology and Music at the Early University: The Case of Robert Grosseteste and Anonymous IV* (Leiden, 1995), 2.

[13] DP short, 156. But note that Gerson added that there were all sorts of angers: light, sharp, quick, bitter (*levis, acuta, velox, amara*).

[14] See notes for Table 7.2.

[15] Perhaps it was an oversight that he did not include *invidia* there, though it is possible that *aemulatio* took its place.

Table 7.2 *Gerson's terms of pain and sorrow*

acedia,[a] torpor (in one's work)
achos,[b] voiceless distress (about oneself)
aemulatio, envious emulation
angustia, distress
anxietas, anxiety
aspernatio, contempt
attritio, being "rubbed the wrong way"
clamor, cry out
compassio, compassion
concussio viscerum, internal shaking
contritio, contrition
displicentia, displeasure
dolor, pain, sorrow
ejulatus, lamentation
fletus, weeping
gemitus, groan
indulgentia, mildness
invidia,[c] envy
languor,[d] longing
mansuetudo,[e] meekness
misericordia,[f] compassion
moeror, grief
nemesis,[g] indignation
plangor, shriek
poenitentia, penance
prostratio, prostration
rugitus, roaring
singultus, sobbing
sollicitudo, anxiety
stridor, shout
torsio manuum, wringing of the hands
tunsio frontis, striking the forehead
tunsio pectoris, striking the chest
zelus,[h] compassionate sorrow

[a] Qualified in DP short, 156, as "ex apprehensione proprii laboris, et est aggravatio per angariam (from the apprehension of one's own labor; and it is oppression by service obligations)"; similarly glossed in EP, 161, as "aggravatio, angaria ex apprehensione proprii laboris (oppression [from] service obligations [and] from apprehension of one's own labor)."

[b] Qualified in DP short, 156, as "ex apprehensione proprii infortunii (from the apprehension of one's own misfortune)."

[c] Qualified in DP short, 156, as "ex apprehensione boni digne habiti (from the apprehension of a good held worthily [by another])."

[d] Qualified in EP, 161, as "ex absentia rei amatae (because of the absence of the beloved)."

[e] Qualified in EP, 161, as "dum non potest assurgere in vindictam ([mildly biding one's time] while one is unable to rise in revenge)."

[f] Qualified in DP short, 156, and EP, 161, as "tristitia de malo poenae alterius (sorrow about another's wrongful punishment)."

[g] Explained in DP short, 156, as "ex apprehensione alieni boni quo indignus est possidens (from the apprehension of another's good that is possessed unworthily)." EP, 161, is similar, but garbled.

[h] Qualified in DP short, 156, as "tristitia de malo culpae alterius, tam illius quem amat et quem odit (sorrow about the evil of a fault committed by another, whether by someone loved or hated)." In EP, 161, is the same idea but garbled.

for Gerson, as for Thomas, directed the movement of desire) as well as for desire itself. But more important than the number of words or even the rubrics into which they were divided was Gerson's concern to link feelings to their real-world contexts. Breaking from the scholastic interest in logic, Gerson considered the circumstances that elicited each shade of emotion.[16] Thus meekness – which had been the opposite of anger for Aristotle because it was a feeling of "satisfaction" – was for Gerson a kind of sadness.[17] It was not the calm feeling of one who has been appeased (as it had been for Aristotle) but rather the slow burn you feel while waiting to carry out vengeance. Similarly specific, Gerson's pity (*misericordia*), like Aristotle's (in the guise of *eleos*), was a kind of pain. But there was an important difference: for Aristotle pity was felt about wrongful harm suffered by another only when "one might expect oneself ... to suffer" the same sort of thing.[18] For Gerson, however, it was a more universal feeling that applied to the unjust suffering of another regardless of whether you might expect the same thing to happen to you. Here Gerson was drawing out the implications of Aelred's "compassion" and, closer to home, adhering to the Burgundian court's emphasis on *pitieux* moments. Similarly, *zelus* was a moral emotion for Gerson; it was sorrow about someone else's fault or failure. The feeling against the fault was enough to override any personal feelings about the person committing it.

Gerson was equally keen to note the sounds, silences, physical symptoms, and gestures that betrayed emotions even without words. Thus, where Thomas had simply listed *achos/achtos* as one type of sorrow, Gerson explained that it was a sorrow that could not be expressed by the voice; it was silent.[19] (During his exile, as we shall soon see, Gerson worked out a complex and totally voiceless form of song.) In the same list, as if they were themselves forms of sadness, Gerson included words like roaring (*rugitus*) and sobbing (*gemitus*), the sounds of pain that (as we have seen) were familiar to Margery Kempe. Again as if equivalent to *tristitia*, Gerson added dramatic gestures – striking the chest, wringing the hands. He even included a bodily symptom that no one but the self could see or hear: a shivering or shaking inside the body (*concussio viscerum*).

In his longer *On the Passions of the Soul* (DP long) Gerson was less interested in emotion words than in the "force (*fervor*), effect, and origin"

---

[16] For Gerson's quarrels with the scholastics, see Hobbins, *Authorship*, 120–25.
[17] See Konstan, *Emotions of the Ancient Greeks*, 77–90.
[18] Konstan, *Pity Transformed*, 49; see also Konstan, *Emotions of the Ancient Greeks*, 201–18.
[19] ST I-II, q. 35 a. 8 arg. 1 explains that John of Damascus identified four types of *tristitia*: *acedia*, *achthos*, *misericordia*, and *invidia*.

of the passions.[20] Addressing a learned audience in Latin, he wrote "for souls called to the school of devotion."[21] To be sure, "ignorant and simple people" knew something about emotions through experience; "nevertheless, the addition of doctrine adds a lot."[22] Bypassing the thirteenth-century scholastics, Gerson drew on the twelfth-century mystic Hugh of Saint Victor to define devotion as an affective activity: "There is no devotion without feeling (*sine affectione*), for what else is devotion but the extension or elevation of the mind (*mens*) to God through pious and humble emotion (*affectum*)?"[23]

Crediting the thinker we know as pseudo-Dionysius with the idea, Gerson said that a passion is "a certain inclination or joining (*coaptatio*) and conformity or inclination and tendency to Himself."[24] Compare this with Thomas' notion of the effect of the good on love.[25] Gerson likened passion to fire, which draws forth new fire.

Like Thomas, whose treatise on the passions he recommended to his readers, Gerson named six concupiscible emotions, three "with respect to simple good, and three similarly with respect to bad."[26] The first three were love, desire, and delight; the second were hatred, avoidance, and pain/disquietude (*amor, concupiscentia, delectatio, odium, fuga, dolor vel inquietudo*). Thus "a man affected by love for something is inclined to it, and if he does not have it, he desires or longs for it, and if he gains it, he rests and delights in it." This was the sequence of the first three. But there was also the contrary sequence, for by the same token the man in love with one thing "truly hates the opposite [of what he loves] and abhors its likeness,

---

[20] DP long, 1. Note that in this work *affectus* = *passio*. In DP short, 156–57, Gerson briefly covered words for the causes, conditions, and effects of key emotions, for example the causes of love (*amor*) were goodness (*bonitas*), knowledge (*cognitio*), and similarity (*similitudo*).

[21] DP long, 1. See the remarks in Daniel Hobbins, "Gerson on Lay Devotion," in *A Companion to Jean Gerson*, 41–78 at 46–49.

[22] DP long, 1: "verumtamen additio doctrinae multum confert." On Gerson's attempt to combine philosophy with affective mystical theology, see Gerhard Krieger, "'Theologica perscrutatio labi debet ad inflammationem affectus.' Der Zusammenhang von mystischer Theologie und Philosophie bei Johannes Gerson," in *Scientia und ars im Hoch– und Spätmittelalter*, ed. Ingrid Craemer-Ruegenberg and Andreas Speer, 2 vols. (Berlin – New York, 1994), 2:605–19, esp. 618–19. But on Gerson's view that the laity should limit itself to devotion and not learn theology, see Geneviève Hasenohr, "Religious Reading amongst the Laity in France in the Fifteenth Century," in *Heresy and Literacy, 1000–1530*, ed. Peter Biller and Anne Hudson (Cambridge, 1994), 205–21, esp. 217.

[23] DP long, 1; for the origin of this idea in Hugh, see Hobbins, "Gerson on Lay Devotion," 46.

[24] DP long, 2: passion is "assimilatio quaedam vel coaptatio et convenientia, vel inclinatio et tendentia ad ipsum."

[25] Above, Chapter 5 at n. 38.   [26] DP long, 2.

and if he is joined to it, he is sad."[27] Here, then, were the next three passions, abhorrence (*horret*) being a form of avoidance.

Still following Thomas, Gerson named the irascible passions, which were directed at objects difficult to obtain. "If the [irascible power aims] confidently at future goods to be obtained, it is called hope (*spes*); if [it is aimed] diffidently, it is termed despair (*desperatio*)."[28] If it seeks to repel a future evil with confidence of success, it is called courage (*audacia*); if without, it is fear (*metus* or *timor*). Anger (*ira*) is the final irascible passion, which "rises to avenge an injury."

All of this is familiar from Thomas, who also named the same eleven passions. But then Gerson problematized the number. He could see that a different point of view might reduce them to the Stoic four (*delectatio*, *dolor*, *spes*, and *metus*), or even just to two (*delectatio* and *dolor*).[29] On the other hand, he could also expand their number to over one hundred.

Riffing on a passage about "irrational animals" in pseudo-Dionysius, Gerson did not hesitate to add their stereotypical characteristics to his list of emotions. "All the passions in brute animals are to be considered good and beautiful, as for example courage (*audacia*) and boldness (*animositas*) in the lion and the rooster; anger (*ira*) in the tiger and the boar, pleasure (*voluptas*) in the pig, he-goat, and sparrow," and so on.[30] But while these were good and beautiful in animals, they were not so in human beings, who had free will and therefore should be motivated by "spiritual passions (*passiones spirituales*)" rather than the "passions of the body (*passiones corporis*)."[31]

Yet the body was the site of the heart, which was a spiritual as well as physical organ for Gerson. As a part of the body it was affected by sensual emotions, the lower-level passions. Happiness (*laetitia*), for example, made the heart expand; sorrow (*tristitia*) caused it to contract. Anger (*ira*) overheated it; fear (*timor*) made it cold; and so on.[32] Table 7.3 lists all the emotions of animals and men that Gerson named in his longer treatise on the passions.

---

[27] *Ibid.* Compare Pseudo-Dionysius, *De divinis nominibus* 4.10, in *Dionysiaca. Recueil donnant l'ensemble des traditions latines des ouvrages attribués au Denys de l'Aréopage*, ed. Philippe Chevalier, 2 vols. (Paris, 1937–50), 1:199, trans. in Pseudo-Dionysius, *The Divine Names*, in *Pseudo-Dionysius: The Complete Works*, trans. Colm Luibheid with Paul Rorem (New York, 1987), 79: "all things must desire, must yearn for, must love, the Beautiful and the Good."

[28] DP long, 4: "Et siquidem hoc fiat respectu boni futuri cum fiducia adipiscendi, sic dicitur spes; si cum diffidentia, sic nominatur desperatio."

[29] *Ibid.*, 5.

[30] *Ibid.*, 6, elaborating on Pseudo-Dionysius, *De divinis nominibus* 4.25, in *Dionysiaca* 1:286, versio S: "Sed neque in animalibus irrationabilis est malum. Si enim auferas furorem et concupiscentiam et alia, quaecumque dicuntur et non sunt simpliciter eorum naturae mala, etenim animorum et superbum leo cum perdiderit, neque leo erit ... "; trans. in *The Divine Names*, in *Pseudo-Dionysius: The Complete Work*, 92: "Nor is evil to be found among the irrational animals. Take away anger, desire, and such like, which are said to be naturally evil but in fact are not so, then the lion, minus its courage and pride, will no longer be a lion ... "

[31] *Ibid.*, 7, for the *passiones corporis*; *ibid.*, 11, for *passiones spirituales*.   [32] *Ibid.*, 10.

Table 7.3 *Gerson's list of the passions of animals and men*[a]

adulatio, adulation
aegritudo, distress
amicitia, friendship
amor, love
   libido, a form of love
animositas, boldness
audacia, courage
avaritia, greed
benignitas, kindness
concupiscentia, desire
   cupiditas, desire
   cupido, desire
   desiderium, desire
      prosecutio, pursuit
delectatio, pleasure
   gaudium, joy
   laetitia, happiness
   voluptas, delight
desperatio, despair
detestatio, execration
dolor, pain, sorrow
   angustia, constriction
   inquietudo, disquietude
   tristitia,[b] sorrow
fervor, rage
fraudulentia, deceit
fuga, avoidance
   abominatio, loathing
   horror, dread
furor, fury
ira, anger
   zelus, zeal
justitia, justice
malitia, malice
metus, fear
   timor, fear
      pusillanimitas, cowardice
odium, hatred
   indignatio, indignation
   rancor, rancor
pertinacia, stubbornness
spes, hope
superbia, pride
timiditas, timidity
verecundia, shame

[a] In this table synonyms are listed by subordinating them (i.e. indenting them beneath) the keyword. For example, Gerson spoke of "amor vel libido" (DP long, 4). In Table 7.3 I list *amor* as the keyword and *libido* as subordinate to it.

[b] DP long also mentions the *tristitia in melancholica* (melancholic sorrow) of the cat (6) and of people after consuming too much wine (18).

These were the passions in general. But Gerson was particularly interested in how they manifested themselves when spiritualized. Here the heart was also the point of origin. For in that capacity, it "sang" the passions in a particular way: it "psallit (sings)," rather than "cantat (chants)" or "citharizat (plucks)." Let us see what he had in mind.

The song of the heart

At leisure (albeit also in exile) in Lyon, Gerson composed two substantial works on the song of the heart: one, a collection of treatises in Latin for the learned, the other a dialogue for the French-reading "pilgrim." He died before finishing these works, which may never have reached the audiences for which they were intended.[33]

Here Gerson distinguished between the "song of the mouth" and the "song of the heart." The mouth's song was audible; the heart's song was silent. Yet both depended on the same theory of music: the hexachord.[34] Rather than think in terms of letter notes of the octave (C, D, E, and so on), medieval music theorists worked with interlocking sequences of six notes: ut, re, mi, fa, sol, and la. Starting at ut, which today we call G, the intervallic pattern between these notes was whole step (ut to re, or G to A), then whole step (re to mi; A to B), then half step (mi to fa; B to C), then whole step (fa to sol; C to D), and finally whole step (sol to la; D to E). The next hexachord began at fa, and it too followed the intervallic pattern without problem. However, the third hexachord, which again began at fa (in this case equivalent to our F), had to have a soft B (our B♭) to conform to the pattern. (The fourth hexachord used the hard B

---

[33] The texts are now published as TC, CP; emphasizing their unfinished state is Roccati, "La production," 358. But Thomas Connolly, *Mourning into Joy: Music, Raphael, and Saint Cecilia* (New Haven, 1994), chap. 5, esp. 137–50, argues that Gerson's "song of the heart" was well known to at least one influential Bolognese spiritual director in the early sixteenth century. Geneviève Hasenohr, "Aperçu sur la diffusion et la réception de la littérature de spiritualité en langue française au dernier siècle du Moyen Age," in *Wissensorganisierende und wissensvermittelnde Literatur im Mittelalter*, ed. Norbert R. Wolf (Wiesbaden, 1987), 57–90 at 69, argues that churchmen like Gerson expected only a "thin fringe" of lay society to benefit from their vernacular writings. See also Hasenohr, "Religious Reading," 207–8, quoting from Gerson's list of readings intended to more fully understand his doctrine of the heart in the CP, 514; Hasenohr remarks that "this programme of books, not all of which were available in French, could only have been useful to those already well advanced in the spiritual life." Hasenohr (*ibid.*, 214) points out that there are only six surviving manuscripts of CP, suggesting minimal popularity. Perhaps, but Hobbins, *Authorship*, suggests that Gerson often, if not always, wrote for a wide public; further, as Brian McGuire has pointed out to me (email communication), Gerson preached his vernacular sermons "in parish churches all over Paris and thus reached a large audience."

[34] I here follow the explanation of the hexachord in Connolly, *Mourning into Joy*, 139–42, and Richard H. Hoppin, *Medieval Music* (New York, 1978), 63–64.

	1/2 step			1/2 step			1/2 step				

1st hexachord	ut G	re A	mi B	fa C	sol D	la E					
2nd hexachord				ut C	re D	mi E	fa F	sol G	la A		
3rd hexachord							ut F	re G	mi A	fa B♭	sol C	la D

Figure 7.1 The hexachord system

[B♮] once again.) Because the sequence of hexachords began with G, *gamma* in Greek, the whole system (spanning nearly three octaves) was called the gamma ut, or gamut. (See Figure 7.1 to visualize the scheme.)

This theory was first clearly articulated by Guido d'Arezzo (d. 1050). It governed Gerson's song of the mouth and was the musical starting point for Gerson's song of the heart. The emotional starting point, however, was constituted by the vowels: AEIOU. Each stood for a passion: A stood for love or joy (*amor* or *gaudium* in Latin, *bonne amour* or *joye* in Gerson's Middle French); E for hope (*spes* in Latin, *espoir* or *desir* in French); I for pity (*compassio* in Latin, *pitié* or *compassion* in French); O for fear (*timor* in Latin, *paour* in French); and U for sorrow and pain (*tristitia* and *dolor* in Latin, *tristesse* or *douleur* in French).[35] The six notes of the hexachord were equivalent to the five vowels because fa and la, both containing the vowel A, could be merged under one passion.

Guido's hexachord system was taught by using the image of the palm of the left hand: you associated the first ut (the sound of G) with the tip of the thumb, re was associated with the thumb's joint, and mi was at the joint of thumb and palm; fa was where the index finger joins the palm, and so on. Gerson himself occasionally used the hand to teach his emotional song of the heart (see Figure 7.2), particularly as a mnemonic device.[36]

---

[35] On the merging of theories of music and affect and Gerson's contribution to this, see Günter Bader, *Psalterspiel. Skizze einer Theologie des Psalters* (Tübingen, 2009), 46–58.

[36] TC, 431. On the Guidonian hand as a memory aid, see Karol Berger, "The Guidonian Hand," in *The Medieval Craft of Memory: An Anthology of Texts and Pictures*, ed. Mary Carruthers and Jan M. Ziolkowski (Philadelphia, 2004), 71–82.

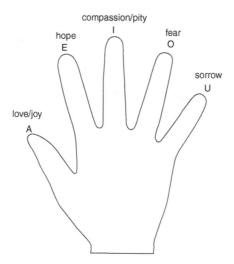

Figure 7.2 Gerson's hand of the passions

But mainly Gerson used a different image: the cross. At the top was A, the passion of joy and love; at the bottom was U, sorrow; the right branch was E, hope; the left branch was O, fear. And in the middle was the sum of all passions: I, symbolizing compassion, Christ, and Mary, mother of Jesus. (See Figure 7.3 and Plates 7.1 and 7.2.)

As we have come to expect from earlier theorists, however, Gerson's "simple" passions embraced many terms. Indeed, passions were like notes of a scale, which may be divided into half-tones and quarter-tones, and so on. The music of the heart (*musica cordis*) had "as many voices and sounds as we find the number of the inner motions of the inner passions or affections (*passionum interiorum vel affectionum*)."[37] That number had no limit, for the passions are "innumerable (*innumerabiles*)," even though philosophers, theologians, and doctors – including Gerson – "reduced them to a few."[38] This explains why Gerson was able to expand or contract his schemes of emotion terms as his purposes required. It also explains why he almost always provided synonyms whenever he brought up an emotion word, as if no one term would ever do. Finally, it helps us see why he could, without blinking an eye, add an extended discussion of a passion that had not appeared in his other works on the topic, consolation (*solatium*), in one section of the *Tractatus de canticis*. Consolation, a

[37] TC, 339: "musicam cordis, cuius tot sunt voces et soni quot inveniuntur motus interiores numerosi passionum interiorum vel affectionum."
[38] TC, 350.

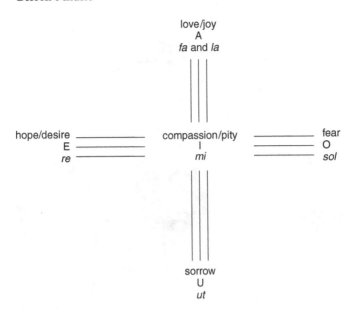

Figure 7.3 Gerson's cross of the passions

"soothing passion (*mulcebris passio*)," extended to all beings, from the angels to the animals.[39] It was a joy (*gaudium*), but a special sort of joy, since it came in the midst of sorrows. It sometimes arose from love, but since there were two sorts of love (love of God, love of self) there were also two kinds of solace. And so on.[40] Unlike many modern psychologists who reify and harden emotions into several basic forms, Gerson could not – did not want to – pin them down.

But if passions came in infinite forms and numbers, nevertheless there was one, compassion (*compassio/pitié*), that contained them all. At the center of the cross was Christ, compassion itself. Compassion was also Mary.[41] She was Gerson's model musician: she "drank up the multiform

---

[39] TC, 467. It is worth recalling that Gerson was later known as *doctor consolatorius*, the consoling doctor. See McGuire, "In Search," 13. *Consolatio* was among Alcuin's emotion words (see Table 3.1) and, more importantly for Gerson, *consolacion* was an emotion word at the Burgundian court (see Table 6.2).

[40] TC, 467–68.

[41] After quoting Adam of Saint-Victor, *Prose Supernae matris gaudia*, 5, vv. 17–18: "confusa sunt hic omnia,/ Spes, metus, meror, gaudium (Here are all mingled: hope, fear, sorrow, joy), Gerson TC, 424, remarks that "compassion" is the sum of those four passions, or "voices," which we may also call "commiseration" (*miseratio*) and "mercy" (*misericordia*), of which Mary is the "mother and queen," an allusion (as Fabre points out *ibid.*, n. 10) to the antiphon *Salve regina* ("Hail, Queen"), where Mary is called the "mother of mercy (*mater misericordiae*)."

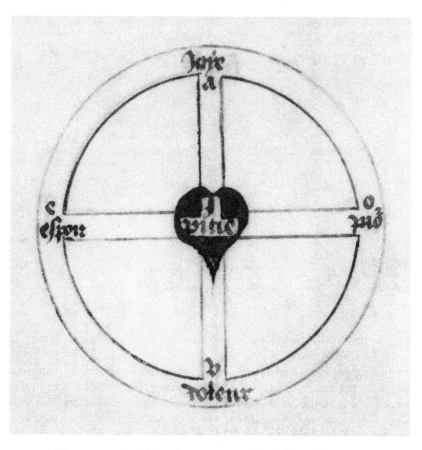

Plates 7.1 and 7.2 Gerson's *canticordum* as a cross

These two figures are here pictured side by side as they are in a fifteenth-century manuscript containing the *Canticordum au pélerin*, Gerson's vernacular dialogue on the *canticordum*. Conceptually, the two should be merged into one; the illustrator has divided Gerson's image for pedagogical purposes. The heart is at the center of the cross in both illustrations. On the left (**7.1**), it is labeled i, *pitié*=compassion; on the right (**7.2**), it is assigned the sound of mi. The top arm of the cross in **7.1** has the vowel a and its passion, *joye*=joy; on **7.2**, the top of the cross is associated with the sounds of fa and la. The left arm of the cross (as the viewer sees it) in **7.1** is associated with the vowel e and the passion *espoir*=hope; in **7.2** it is given the sound of re. The right arm of the cross in **7.1** is associated with the vowel o and the passion *paor*=fear, and in **7.2** with the sound of sol. The foot of the cross is labeled u and *doleur*=sorrow on **7.1** and ut on **7.2**. The whole scheme nicely traces the emotional journey of the crucifixion and resurrection, with joy at the top and sorrow at the bottom. Christ himself, then, becomes the incarnation of pity and the heart becomes a symbol of Christ. © Bibliothèque nationale de France. MS 2176, fols. 62v-63r.

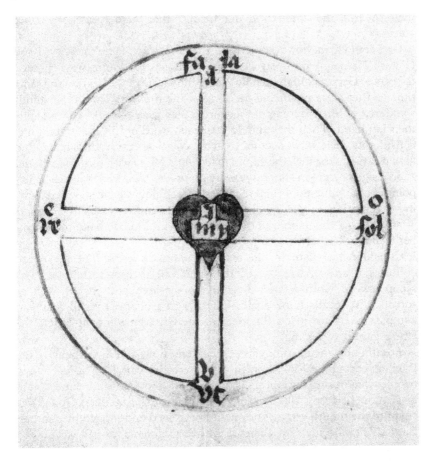

Plates 7.1 and 7.2 (*cont.*)

affections," and they became the voices of her heart's song.[42] Every mother was a bit like Mary: "Doesn't the mother every day hear her child saying 'Oh, I'm hurt! Oh, I'm scared' and form in her spirit the emotion of pain or fear or compassion?"[43] Everyone's heart was something like that: hearing cries of emotion, they were "roused" to feel something similar.[44] But God and the saints didn't need audible shouts;

---

[42] TC, 409: "affectiones hausisse multiformes."
[43] TC, 413: "Nonne sic omni die mater audiens filium dicentem 'O doleo! O timeo!' format in spirtu suo vel doloris vel timoris vel compassionis affectum?"
[44] *Ibid.*

they "heard" the "desires of our hearts" that were created by inner voices.[45]

One could learn how to practice the *Canticordum*. Here Gerson's hand (Figure 7.2) came into play. Addressing monks or canons who chanted the office, Gerson told them how to sing the music of the heart at the same time as they were practicing the song of the mouth. When their minds wandered off the meaning of the words, they were to look at or imagine their left hand. Then they should take each word of the chant at a time, consider its vowels, connect those to the vowel-affects of their hand, and in that way run through the gamut of feelings. Along with this, they should "add a sigh or a groan (*suspirium vel gemitum*)."[46] As Mary Carruthers has pointed out, "mnemonic and recollective techniques have all relied heavily on emotion as the quickest and surest way to catch the mind's attention."[47] Gerson utilized the well-known Guidonian hand to remember feelings themselves.

Consider, for example, the text *Puer natus est nobis*. The first word contains u and e, which lead the singer to sorrow and hope. The second word, with a and u, conjures up love and joy as well as sorrow. *Est* recalls hope again. The o and i of *nobis* recall fear and compassion. Thus just a fragment of the Christmas introit covers the entire gamut of feelings.

To sum up: when people express their emotions aloud, the heart of the listener reacts (like Mary's) with what we today call "empathy." When people want to sing the emotions of the heart, they can learn a method to do so more perfectly. But that song is inaudible, heard only by God: "The chant of the mouth can be known and perceived and judged by another. But only he who sings the chant of the heart understands it – except God and those to whom God wants it made known."[48] Is it, then, not a lonely song?

---

[45] TC, 415.

[46] TC, 435. Writers before Gerson had also connected passions to prayers. See Carla Casagrande, "Agostino, i medievali e il buon uso delle passioni," in *Agostino d'Ippona. Presenza e pensiero. La scoperta dell'interiorità*, ed. Alfredo Marini (Milan, 2004), 65–76. She notes (74), for example, that Hugh of Saint-Victor's *De modo orandi* "suggests how [in prayer] to join love, admiration, and joy first to humility, sorrow, and fear, and then to indignation, zeal, and hope." See also Emma Dillon, *The Sense of Sound: Musical Meaning in France, 1260–1330* (Oxford, 2012), esp. 178–85 on song and affect and 195–202 on sounds and distractions; and see Peter V. Loewen, *Music in Early Franciscan Thought* (Leiden, 2013), which takes up not only emotions connected to music but also Franciscan solutions to the problem of lukewarm prayer.

[47] Mary Carruthers, *The Craft of Thought: Meditation, Rhetoric, and the Making of Images, 400–1200* (Cambridge, 1998), 117.

[48] TC, 379.

In his vernacular dialogue on the music of the heart, Gerson faced that issue directly. Organized as a series of "collations," in the style of John Cassian (d. 435), who wrote up the sayings of the desert fathers, Gerson's *Canticordum au pélerin* has Cuer Mondain (Worldly Heart) converse with Cuer Seulet (Lonely or Single Heart). Cuer Mondain speaks first: "Tell me, please, Cuer Seulet, why you stay here in this deserted place? How can you live or last so shut off, away from everyone, without the companionship of others and without their consolation? Doesn't this make you melancholy and sad?" Cuer Seulet answers: "I'm not at all sad or melancholy; indeed I am joyful, cheerful, happy, and in love every day. The one who consoles me is with me."[49] True joy comes from the "sweet chant of the Canticordum."[50] Cuer Mondain learns about the uses of the cross and the hand and the significance of the five vowels that stand for each of the "passions, emotions, or affections."[51] Table 7.4 provides what Gerson called the "names of the voices" in his *Tractatus*[52] and in his *Canticordum au pélerin*.[53]

Of these emotions, Cuer Seulet wants particularly to teach its worldly friend about pity (*pitié*). Surely, says Cuer Seulet, Cuer Mondain sometimes has pity for the sorrows of others or for itself, "especially regarding your family members (*tes parens*) and members of your lineage (*affins de lignaige*)."[54] Well, because we are all "sons of God," we are all of His lineage. Cuer Mondain admits that it never feels pity; rather it feels "cupidity and iniquity." Then Cuer Seulet tells his worldly counterpart that, just as one can make a smooth transition from one hexachord to another on a particular note (a process called a mutation), so Cuer Mondain can make "the marvelous mutation (*la merveilleuse muance*)" from false to true music.[55]

The heart's mutation is an emotional transformation. The worldly heart goes from sorrow to happiness and from happiness to fear, but these are the wrong kinds of sorrow, happiness, and fear. They bring no sweet pity (*doulce pitié*) but rather lack of pity (*impieté*): rather than find consolation, they lead to desolation, deception, and discord.[56] The music of the heart, by contrast, moves easily from *good* sorrow to *good* joy, from good fear to good hope. And pity usually (*generalement*) joins, "now to one voice, then to another, then to all together, in many guises and modulations and always in harmony (*in accord*)."[57]

---

[49] CP, 481.   [50] CP, 483: "doulz chant."
[51] CP, 485: "passions, mouvemens ou affections."   [52] TC, 441–42.   [53] CP, 509–10.
[54] CP, 485.   [55] CP, 494.   [56] CP, 497.   [57] CP, 496.

Table 7.4 *Names of the voices of Gerson's* canticordum

Latin	Middle French[a]
A: *gaudium*, joy	***joye*, joy**
alacritas, eagerness	*alacrité*, eagerness
defectio, swoon	*beneir*, bless
delectatio, delight	*deffection par joye*, swooning from joy
ebrietas, intoxication	*ebrieté*, intoxication
hylaritas, hilarity[b]	*glorifier*, glorify
jocunditas, jocularity	*hillarité*, hilarity
letitia, happiness	*jocundité*, jocularity
liquefactio, liquefaction[c]	*leesse*, happiness
satietas, satiety[d]	*liquefaction*, liquefaction
voluptas, pleasure	*loer*, praise
	magnifier, magnify
	regracier, thank
	sacieté, satiety
	saulter, jump
	transformacion, conversion
	volupté, pleasure
E: *spes*, hope	***espoir/desir*, hope/desire**
anhelatio, breathlessness	*ardeur*, strong desire
ardor, strong desire	*concupiscence*, desire
audacia bona, good audacity, courage	*emulacion*, rivalry
concupiscentia bona, good desire	*expectacion*, hope
emulatio bona, good rivalry	*fain*, desirous; eager
esuries, hunger	*hardiesse*, audacity, courage
expectatio, impatience	*jalousie*, zealous desire
ira bona, good anger	*soif*, thirst
sitis, thirst	*souspire*, sigh, ardent desire
suspirium, sigh, ardent desire	*tendance*, striving
tendentia, striving	
zelus bonus, good zeal	
I: *compassio*, compassion	***pitié*, pity**
benignitas, kindness	*benivolence*, benevolence
elemosina, act of mercy[e]	*benignité*, kindness
liberalitas, generosity	*clemence*, clemency
mansuetudo, meekness	*compassion*, compassion
miseratio, commiseration	*humanité*, benevolence
misericordia, mercy	*liberalité*, generosity
mititas, sweetness	*mansuetude*, meekness
munificentia, munificence	*miseracion*, compassion
pietas, piety/pity	*misericorde*, mercy
	mittité ou debonnaireté, sweetness or benevolence
	munificence, munificence
O: *timor*, fear	***paour*, fear**
abhominatio peccati, loathing of sin	*abhominacion*, loathing
admiratio, astonishment	*admiracion*, astonishment
agonia, anxiety	*desperacion*, despair
desperatio bona, good despair	*ennuy*, pain, torment
erubescentia bona, good blushing for shame	*erubescence*, blushing for shame
fastidium bonum, good disgust	*espoentement*, fear
formido, fear	*formidacion*, fear
fuga, avoidance	*fuite*, avoidance
horror, dread	*horreur*, dread
	nauseacion, disgust

Table 7.4 (*cont.*)

Latin	Middle French[a]
nausea voluptatis male, disgust of bad pleasure	*paresse*, weariness
segnities bona, good disinclination to act	*resilicion dedans soy ou exilicion a chose qui peut aidier a sa neccessité*, recoiling
stupor bonus, good wonder	into oneself or leaping at something
tedium bonum vite huius, good weariness of this life	that can aid in an emergency
timor reverentialis, reverential fear[f]	*resverie*, confusion
trepidatio, agitation	*trepidacion*, agitation
verecundia bona, good shame	*vergoingne*, shame
U: *tristitia*, sorrow	***tristesse*, sorrow**
contritio, contrition	*contricion*, contrition
cruciatus, torment	*cruciacion*, torment
detestatio, detestation	*detestacion*, detestation
dolor, pain	*doleur*, pain
gemitus, groan	*envie*, envy
invidia bona, good envy	*gemissemens*, groans
lamentum, lamentation	*haine*, hatred
langor, prolonged dejection	*lamentacion*, lamentation
odium bonum, good hatred	*langueur*, prolonged dejection
planctus seu plangor, lament	*plainte*, lament
rugitus, roar	*rugissement comme les lyons*, roar like the lions
torsio, torture	*torcion*, torture
ululatus, howling	*ululacion*, howling

[a] Definitions taken from atilf.atilf.fr/ and from the glossary compiled by Fabre, 579–91. I have tried, where possible, to coordinate the Latin and French meanings.

[b] I translate this as hilarity rather than cheerfulness because TC, 441, explains that *hylaritas* manifests itself externally, on the face and especially with the eyes, "in horrore leto (in a paroxysm of joy)."

[c] TC, 441, explains that liquefaction, like air or water, cannot keep itself within bounds but rather "labitur in rem amatam (sinks into the beloved)."

[d] TC, 441, explains that this satiety does not preclude desire, but it is indeed free of any disgust.

[e] Gerson explains (TC, 442) that *elemosina* is the emotion of commiserating (*affectus miserendi*) about disadvantages (*incommodis*), whether spiritual or corporal.

[f] Gerson means this to be equivalent to the French *resilicion*, for he explains that *timor reverentialis* is a certain recoiling (*resilitio*) into one's own littleness when considering a superior majesty, or it is a fearful recoiling (*resilitio formidabilis*) to an appropriate aid (*ad proprium adiutorem*) in an emergency (*cum consideratione urgentis necessitatis*).

Gerson's dialogue of two hearts took place over the course of seven meetings punctuated by pauses of indeterminate duration. Presumably it could have been performed. It nicely fits into the theater culture to which Carol Symes has called attention and which was so prominent a feature of the emotional lives of the Burgundians that we explored in Chapter 6.[58]

***

Indeed, even though Gerson broke with the Burgundians long before he wrote most of his works on the passions, his emotional emphases and vocabulary both make sense of and mirror those of the Burgundian chroniclers. (Compare his vernacular list of emotions in Table 7.4 with the Table of Monstrelet's emotion words in Table 6.2.) Gerson's five voices were the affects we find stressed in Monstrelet and Chastelain. Virginie Minet-Mahy has argued that the cross formed by Gerson's song of the heart helped inspire the iconography of Chastelain's *Douze Dames de Rhétorique*. She also shows that a number of texts by Gerson were most assuredly in the ducal library.[59] If music and drama were among the ways that emotions were expressed and valued at that court, they were equally so for Gerson, however unusual these media might seem among the ordinary pursuits of a university chancellor and priest.

Above all, Gerson's stress on the pivotal emotion of pity, at the very center of his theory and of his ruminations on the *Canticordum*, helps explain why the Burgundian emotional community responded to sad events with pity; why Monstrelet was so anxious to record the piteous events of his day; and why he so evidently wanted his readers to know that the right response to those events was pity. These men no longer saw love as the root of emotions. They sought an emotion that would embrace all feelings at once. Aelred of Rievaulx had seen compassion as a by-product of love; Gerson dethroned love to make compassion's twin – pity – the chief mark of the "feeling human being." And the feeling human being was indeed what he was advocating, for if someone really practiced the canticord assiduously, he would cover all the emotions again and again in the course of just one chant. Gerson's chant of the heart had the potential to create an emotional virtuoso.

Gerson's drama was a morality play, but it was far from the theatricality of a Margery Kempe. Indeed, Gerson had some harsh things to say about people who spent their time in weeping and contrition. There were two kinds of pain (*dolor*), Gerson advised. One was the pain of reason under the control of free will: it was *dolor* about sin. The other, however, was a motion of the sensitive appetite, and it could become excessive. The

---

[58] Symes, *A Common Stage*.

[59] See Virginie Minet-Mahy, "L'iconographie du cœur et de la croix dans le *Mortifiement* de René d'Anjou et les *Douze Dames de Rhétorique* de George Chastelain. Un dialogue avec Jean Gerson," *Le Moyen Age* 113/3–4 (2007): 569–90.

"vigorous and virile heart (cor . . . strenuum et virile)" was not given to tears: "it can hardly or even never weep."[60] But there was also the "feminine" heart. It was soft (mollis) and prone to tears. People wrongly judged as the "most virtuous" those – mainly women – who were "most devout in compunction and in tears."[61] This was probably not meant as a rejection of the sometimes tearful spirituality of Aelred and other Cistercians.[62] Rather, it was Gerson's reaction to the sort of piety being practiced by certain kinds of mystics who tended to be women. Gerson did not know about Margery Kempe, but he certainly knew about – and criticized – the ecstatic spirituality of Bridget of Sweden.[63] Even so, the fact that Gerson included howling, laments, roars, and groans among his emotion words suggests that he understood very well that such sounds were expressions of feeling.[64]

At the same time, the absolute silence of Gerson's music of the heart must recall the restrained emotional palette of the Pastons. To be sure, their rational, down-to-earth, and businesslike lives seem worlds away from the ecstatic harmonies that Gerson was advocating. But, as we have seen, the Pastons did feel emotions, and they expressed them, albeit in sober and attenuated ways. Gerson's theory touched on such modes. His emphasis on internal emotions helps us make sense of the Pastons' avoidance of verbalization. His stress on the special place of "consolation" parallels the Pastons' constant recourse to words of "comfort."

Gerson's theory also looks forward to the future. It should seem odd that he spoke of "good despair" as an emotion of the Canticordum. For Margery Kempe despair was always the pit: it was the emotion so far down that she could either commit suicide or ascend. But, as we shall see in Chapter 8, despair became the emotion most highly valued by many overlapping emotional communities in seventeenth-century England.

---

[60] TC, 391: "Vel vix vel nunquam flere possit."

[61] TC, 395.

[62] See McGuire, Jean Gerson and the Last Medieval Reformation, 92–93.

[63] On Gerson's attitude toward women, see Wendy Love Anderson, "Gerson's Stance on Women," in A Companion to Jean Gerson, 293–315, who argues that Gerson's critique focused on those who advised women rather than on women themselves, and Yelena Mazour-Matusevich, "La Position de Jean Gerson (1363–1429) envers les femmes," Le Moyen Age 112/2 (2006): 337–53, and esp. 339–40 on Gerson's notion of discretion. Both argue that Gerson thought a lot about and appreciated women. Such positive views are challenged by Nancy McLoughlin, Jean Gerson and Gender: Rhetoric and Politics in Fifteenth-Century France (New York, 2015).

[64] It is also worth noting that some of Gerson's writings were aimed at a female audience, including his sisters. For example, see McGuire, "In Search," 11–12.

8   Despair and happiness

"All my joyes to this are folly,/Naught so sweet as melancholy . . . All my griefes to this are jolly,/ Naught so sad as Melancholy." Thus wrote Robert Burton (d. 1640) in his *Anatomy of Melancholy*.[1] In early modern England, melancholy was both celebrated and decried. To be sure, sad emotions had been well known before this time. Alcuin had much to say about sorrow.[2] The Burgundian chroniclers had been "troubled, sad, and upset at heart."[3] Gerson's *Cuer Mondain* wrongly thought that a hermit like *Cuer Seulet* must be "melancholy and sad."[4] These emotional communities had dwelled largely on sorrow's pain.

Yet even before the early modern period, sorrow had had a positive side as well. Alcuin had talked about two sorts of *tristitia*, one a vice, the other a virtue. The Burgundians highly valued the pity that sorrows awakened. Margery Kempe found despair, however painful, to be the necessary springboard to joy. In Quattrocentro Italy, Marsilio Ficino (d. 1499) wrote about the wonders of melancholy, which he identified as the source of creativity, discovery, and scholarship.[5] The Reformation brought new appreciation of despair. Luther made it the beginning of salvation as well

---

[1] Robert Burton, *The Anatomy of Melancholy*, ed. Thomas C. Faulkner, Nicholas K. Kiessling, Rhonda L. Blair, commentary J. B. Bamborough and Martin Dodsworth, 6 vols. (Oxford, 1989–2000), 1:lxix. I thank Robert Bireley, Robert Bucholz, Gary O'Neill, Joad Raymond, and Fabrizio Titone for help with the bibliography for this chapter.

[2] See Chapter 3.   [3] See Chapter 6.   [4] See Chapter 7.

[5] See, for example, Marsilio Ficino, *Three Books on Life*, ed. and trans. Carol V. Kaske and John R. Clark (Binghamton, N.Y., 1989), 117: "So far, let it suffice that we have shown why the priests of the Muses either are from the beginning or are made by study into melancholics, owing to causes first celestial, second natural, and third human. This [Pseudo-]Aristotle confirms in his book of *Problems*, saying that all those who are renowned in whatever faculty you please have been melancholics." For Ficino's view and its critics, see Noel L. Brann, *The Debate over the Origin of Genius during the Italian Renaissance: The Theories of Supernatural Frenzy and Natural Melancholy in Accord and in Conflict on the Threshold of the Scientific Revolution* (Leiden, 2002). Burton knew Ficino's work and quoted it (see Burton, *Anatomy*, 1:331) but, in the words of his modern commentator, Bamborough, "does not devote much space to it" (*ibid.*, 1:xxviii).

as, in Angus Gowland's phrase, "a pathology of the soul."[6] Calvin
thought that by falling "into deep despair," man's conscience would at
last seek God. He lauded the "dread of death" and despair because "both
these emotions engender humility and self-abasement."[7] The first sermon that was regularly delivered in English parish churches was on "the
misery of all mankind."[8]

In seventeenth-century England, sorrowful emotions gained prestige
even as they led some to suicide. If a whole society may be described as
an emotional community, then early modern England was one obsessed by
melancholy. With William Reddy, we might call this an emotional regime.[9]
But if so, the regime's power came not from political clout but rather the
prestige of intellectuals, physicians, and divines who valued (variously)
genius, inspiration, and religious authenticity. Looked at this way, the
regime was hardly monolithic. And to its own variations on the theme
must be added some contemporary groups that cared very little about
melancholy at all. (For all the place names in this chapter, see Map 6.1.)

The "great divide"? From medieval to early modern

In moving to the seventeenth century, we have crossed the "great divide"
between the medieval and early modern periods. It is a division that has long
organized departments of history. And it is deeply engrained in Western
ways of thinking about the past. Above all, Western historians privilege the
notion of "modernity." Heir to Quattrocentro writers' self-conscious
glances right past the benighted "middle age" in order to pattern themselves
on the glamorous ancient world, modernity is everything the Middle Ages
was not. For Norbert Elias in the 1930s, it brought "the civilizing process,"
placing restraints on the hitherto impulsive expression of emotions.[10] For
Ute Frevert in the twenty-first century, modernity was and is an active
historical force that has promoted some emotions (like compassion) and
taken unprecedented interest in the topic of emotions itself.[11]

Reinforcing the boundary between the medieval and the modern is the
dual thesis of social discipline and confessionalization that dominates studies
of the Reformation era. This thesis holds that in the early modern period,
church and state introduced new controls over behavior, institutions, and

---

[6] Angus Gowland, "The Problem of Early Modern Melancholy," *Past and Present* 191
(2006): 77–120, here at 104.

[7] Calvin, *Institutes of the Christian Religion* 2.8.3, ed. John T. McNeill and trans. Ford
Lewis Battles, 2 vols. (Philadelphia, 1960), 1:369–70.

[8] Church of England, *The Two Books of Homilies Appointed to be Read in Churches* (Oxford,
1859), 16.

[9] See Introduction at n. 35.   [10] See this book's Introduction.

[11] Frevert, *Emotions in History*, 16–17, and my review of this book, Rosenwein, "Modernity."

emotions, tamping down impulsivity, self-assertion, and emotional expression.[12] Insofar as this view is challenged, dissent comes mainly from historians who argue that social control is from the bottom up rather than the top down. In this view, in the words of Heinz Schilling, "the family, the neighborhood, brotherhoods, or other corporations" created the leaders – and hence the controlling policies – of church government.[13]

---

[12] Although confessionalization, strictly speaking, concerns the hardening of the boundaries among confessions, the topic soon merged with that of social control. See Susan R. Boettcher, "Confessionalization: Reformation, Religion, Absolutism, and Modernity," *History Compass* 2 (2004): 1–10; Thomas A. Brady, Jr., "Confessionalization: The Career of a Concept," in *Confessionalization in Europe, 1555–1700: Essays in Honor and Memory of Bodo Nischan*, ed. John M. Headley, Hans J. Hillerbrand, and Anthony J. Papalas (Aldershot, 2004), 1–20; and Heinz Schilling, "Confessionalization: Historical and Scholarly Perspectives of a Comparative and Interdisciplinary Paradigm," in *Confessionalization in Europe*, 21–36. On the paradigm of social control, see Gerhard Oestreich, "Strukturprobleme des europäischen Absolutismus," *Vierteljahresschrift für Sozial- und Wirtschaftsgeschichte* 55 (1968): 329–47, translated as "The Structure of the Absolute State," in Gerhard Oestreich, *Neostoicism and the Early Modern State*, ed. Brigitta Oestreich and H. G. Koenigsberger, trans. David McLintock (Cambridge, 1982), 258–73. For the history of the idea of social control, see Pieter Spierenburg, "Social Control and History: An Introduction," in *Social Control in Europe*, vol. 1: *1500–1800*, ed. Herman Roodenburg and Pieter Spierenburg (Columbus, 2004), 1–22. On Elias' influence on these ideas, see Heinrich Richard Schmidt, "Sozialdisziplinierung? Ein Plädoyer für das Ende des Etatismus in der Konfessionalisierungsforschung," *Historische Zeitschrift* 265 (1997): 639–82, esp. 639–40; Giorgia Alessi, "Discipline. I nuovi orizzonti del disciplinamento sociale," *Storica* 4 (1996): 7–37, who (esp. 16–25) traces the *idea* of social discipline – though not the term – from Max Weber to Norbert Elias and Michel Foucault; see also Winfried Schulze, "Gerhard Oestreichs Begriff 'Sozialdisziplinierung in der frühen Neuzeit,'" *Zeitschrift für historische Forschung* 14 (1987): 265–302; and Heinz Schilling, "Disziplinierung oder 'Selbstregulierung der Untertanen'? Ein Plädoyer für die Doppelperspektive von Makro- und Mikrohistorie bei der Erforschung frühmodernen Kirchenzucht," *Historische Zeitschrift* 264 (1997): 675–91. For the National Socialist origins of Oestreich's emphasis on "social discipline," which began as "Wehrgeschichte," in effect the process by which the state imposed military discipline, see Peter N. Miller, "Nazis and Neo-Stoics: Otto Brunner and Gerhard Oestreich before and after the Second World War," *Past and Present* 176 (2002): 144–86, here 173. Oestreich himself mentioned Elias in the context of the triumph of ancient notions of *prudentia* and *virtus* in his "'Police' and Prudentia civilis in the Seventeenth Century," in Oestreich, *Neostoicism*, 164: "[At the court], as Elias puts it, social constraint became self-constraint." However, unlike Elias, Oestreich thought that social constraints began in the cities and spread thence to the universities and the courts.

[13] Schilling, "Disziplinierung," 680. For England, see Robert von Friedeburg, "Sozialdisziplinierung in England? Soziale Beziehungen auf dem Lande zwischen Reformation und 'Great Rebellion, 1550–1642,'" *Zeitschrift für historische Forschung* 17/4 (1990): 385–418, who reviews the historiography and ends by stressing the difficulties met by the gentry and yeomanry in attempting to impose social control on the indigent, while Peter Iver Kaufman, "Reconstructing the Context for Confessionalization in Late Tudor England: Perceptions of Reception, Then and Now," in *Confessionalization in Europe*, 275–87, notes the many different sorts of groups involved in England's reform. For Italy, see William V. Hudon, "Religion and Society in Early Modern Italy – Old Questions, New Insights," *American Historical Review* 101 (1996): 783–804. Similarly, Alessi, "Discipline,"

To be sure, a few scholars question the validity of the thesis altogether, often grounding their demurral on the nature of religious emotions.[14] Susan Karant-Nunn argues that Luther and his followers did not support total emotional inhibition: "The goal was to reduce the intensity of some forms of expression, to suppress others entirely, and to shape appropriately still other approved types of feeling."[15] She thus emphasizes the "shaping," rather than the snuffing-out, of emotions.[16] Some scholars of English Protestantism make the same point. In the face of assertions of social control in England (implied as well by Eamon Duffy's classic study *The Stripping of the Altars*, which saw a brutal break between "traditional piety" and the "iconoclasm" of the reformers), Alec Ryrie has recently made clear that the English Reform was in many ways an intensely emotional religious movement.[17]

esp. 14–15, 25–27, reviews new (in 1996) work on the topic as represented above all by the articles in *Disciplina dell'anima, disciplina del corpo e disciplina della società tra medioevo ed età moderna*, ed. Paolo Prodi (Bologna, 1994), and shows how they opened up "nuove questioni e modelli interpretativi" (27). Even historians of modern totalitarianism are questioning the ability of such regimes to impose their standards and values on essentially passive populations; see Paul Corner, *Popular Opinion in Totalitarian Regimes: Fascism, Nazism, Communism* (Oxford, 2009).

[14] An exception is Nikolaus Buschmann, "Zwischen Leidenschaft und Disziplinierung: 'Treue' als gefühlspolitischer Kampfbegriff an der neueren deutschen Geschichte," *Arcadia* 44/1 (2009): 106–20, which argues for the persistence of "fidelity" (*Treue*) as a "political feeling" well into the modern period.

[15] Susan C. Karant-Nunn, "'Christians' Mourning and Lament Should not Be Like the Heathens': The Suppression of Religious Emotion in the Reformation," in *Confessionalization in Europe*, 107–29, here 107.

[16] Susan C. Karant-Nunn, *The Reformation of Feeling: Shaping the Religious Emotions in Early Modern Germany* (Oxford, 2010), esp. 101–32, for the Reformed churches. Karant-Nunn looks largely at sermons; other scholars have found emotional expression in early modern music, art, theatre, dance, and literature: see *Passion, Affekt und Leidenschaft in der frühen Neuzeit*, ed. Johann Anselm Steiger, 2 vols. (Wiesbaden, 2005).

[17] Eamon Duffy, *The Stripping of the Altars: Traditional Religion in England c. 1400–c. 1580* (New Haven, 1992), implicitly countered by Alec Ryrie, *Being Protestant in Reformation Britain* (Oxford, 2013), esp. Part I: The Protestant Emotions (17–98). Already Ted A. Campbell, *The Religion of the Heart: A Study of European Religious Life in the Seventeenth and Eighteenth Centuries* (Columbia, SC, 1991) devoted a chapter to "Affective Piety in Seventeenth-Century British Calvinism." Peter Marshall, *Religious Identities in Henry VIII's England* (Aldershot, 2006), discussed common attitudes toward fear held by both evangelical and Catholic writers in the Henrician period. Matthew Milner, *The Senses and the English Reformation* (Farnham, 2011), 3, has made the related point that "protestantism was itself dependent on sensual experience." But new theories of the senses heralded in 1603 by Kepler's work on vision leads Milner to end his study when the seventeenth century begins. Similarly, on the ambivalent attitudes toward sensuality of early English reformed piety, see Joe Moshenska, "'A Sensible Touching, Feeling and Groping': Metaphor and Sensory Experience in the English Reformation," in *Passions and Subjectivity in Early Modern Culture*, ed. Brian Cummings and Freya Sierhuis (Burlington, VT, 2013), 183–99. For continuities with Catholicism across the medieval/early modern period, see Elena Carrera, "The Spiritual Role of the Emotions in Mechthild of Magdeburg, Angela of Foligno, and Teresa of Avila," in *The Representation of Women's Emotions in Medieval and Early Modern Culture*, ed. Lisa Perfetti (Gainesville, 2005), 63–89.

Although there are other ways to bridge the medieval/early modern divide,[18] the study of emotions has unusually good potential to knit together the two sides and yet point up their differences.[19] This is because emotions do not depend on particular developments like industrialization or absolutism; nor do they need historical movements, like rebellions, or special conditions, like epidemics, to manifest themselves. To be sure, emotions respond to all of these things and change alongside them. But they also have persisted over the long haul.

Political and religious reforms

Certainly much had changed between fifteenth-century England, when we last saw it, and the seventeenth-century England treated in this chapter. The Wars of the Roses, the circumstances of which so affected the Pastons, were over. The Ottomans had taken over the former Byzantium and were now a permanent presence in European politics. The New World had been "discovered," and Spanish and other accounts of the "manners, ceremonies, lawes, governments, and warres of the Indians" had been swiftly translated, joining the travel literature created by English explorers.[20] The Copernican Revolution had destabilized cosmologies and hierarchies.[21]

---

[18] For example, Aers and Smith, "English Reformations"; Euan Cameron, *Enchanted Europe: Superstition, Reason and Religion, 1250–1750* (Oxford, 2010), esp. 141–45, dealing with attitudes toward superstition. See also the articles in *Découper le temps. Actualité de la périodisation en histoire = Atala. Cultures et sciences humaines* 17 (2014), especially the article by Philippe Hamon, "Du Moyen Âge aux Temps modernes: une 'charnière' canonique et ses remises en cause," 133–45. Richard Newhauser, "'These Seaven Devils': The Capital Vices on the Way to Modernity," in *Sin in Medieval and Early Modern Culture: The Tradition of the Seven Deadly Sins*, ed. Richard G. Newhauser and Susan J. Ridyard (York, 2012), 157–88, argues (174) for continuities in the history of ideas about sins even as it accepts the notion of modernity, which "disconnect[s] the vices from a purely sacramental significance," giving them new, if different, life.

[19] Peter N. Stearns, "Modern Patterns in Emotions History," in *Doing Emotions History*, 17–40, makes the same point at 18 but focuses not on continuities but shifts, arguing that focus on emotional communities "risks obscuring larger cultural systems" (23). I suggest here, to the contrary, that focus on emotional communities is a good way to see larger patterns "on both sides of the premodern-modern divide" (24).

[20] See, for example, José de Acosta, *The naturall and morall historie of the East and West Indies Intreating of the remarkable things of heaven, of the elements, mettalls, plants and beasts which are proper to that country: together with the manners, ceremonies, lawes, governments, and warres of the Indians*, trans. Edward Grimeston (London, 1604); Richard Hakluyt (d. 1616) in Richard Hakluyt, *The principal navigations, voyages, traffiques & discoveries of the English nation made by sea or overland to the remote and farthest distant quarters of the earth at any time within the compass of these 1600 years*, intro. John Masefield, 8 vols. (London, 1927).

[21] The classic is Thomas S. Kuhn, *The Copernican Revolution: Planetary Astronomy in the Development of Western Thought* (Cambridge, MA, 1957).

Under the Tudor and Stuart dynasties, the monarchy was relatively strong. Once Henry VIII (d. 1547) initiated England's break with Rome, the Reformation came to England. It meant doctrinal and ceremonial changes, though to greater or lesser degrees depending on who was on the throne. By the seventeenth century, England was largely Protestant. But there were many forms of Protestantism.

To simplify, we may say that these forms fell into two groups, one "hotter" than the other. The "hotter" sort nurtured a reformist agenda, anxious to eliminate all Catholic elements – hierarchies, ornaments, vestments, and rituals – and to foster a more active, fervent faith.[22] The "less hot" was contented with the severing of the church from the Roman papacy, but accepted hierarchy and ceremony. After Charles I came to the throne in 1625 and William Laud became archbishop in 1633, the two sorts of Protestantism increasingly went their separate ways, the "Anglican" affirming the exalted status of bishops and the importance of communion, the "Puritan" focusing on predestination and godliness.[23] The rift culminated in the 1640s, when a largely Puritan Parliament ended up challenging the Anglican Church, organizing an army, and fighting royalist forces. In the next phase, Parliament organized the New Model Army (1645), won the Civil War, and (now shrunken to a Rump) put the king to death. The Commonwealth, which lasted from 1649 to 1660, was dominated by men like Oliver Cromwell (d. 1658), who identified with the Puritans, tolerated (but barely) the Anglicans, and prohibited Catholics from worshipping in public.[24]

The melancholic turn

And yet people of every religious persuasion seem to have been obsessed with melancholy.[25] They expressed it in literary and autobiographical

[22] See Peter Marshall, *Reformation England, 1480–1642* (London, 2003).

[23] To be sure, the term "Puritan" is problematic, since it was not just one movement and it was (and to some extent continues to be) defined by those hostile to it. See John Coffey and Paul C. H. Lim, "Introduction," in *The Cambridge Companion to Puritanism*, ed. John Coffey and Paul C. H. Lim (Cambridge, 2008), 1–16, and Peter Lake, "The Historiography of Puritanism," in *ibid.*, 346–71.

[24] For a useful introduction to the main historiographical debates concerning the English Reformation, see Lake, "Historiography," 360–65. The study of Ryrie, *Being Protestant*, effectively *ends* in 1640 "because the jungle of Protestant exotica which spread across Britain after 1640 would need a different book" (4).

[25] For an overview, see Gowland, "The Problem," 77–120. J. B. Bamborough, *The Little World of Man* (London, 1952), 103–18, speaks of young people who affected melancholic airs. Similarly, see Michael MacDonald, *Mystical Bedlam: Madness, Anxiety, and Healing in Seventeenth-Century England* (Cambridge, 1981), 2: "Scientific writers popularized medical lore about melancholy ... Gentlemen and ladies proclaimed themselves melancholy." See also *ibid.*, 135. Valentine Cunningham, "The Novel and the Protestant Fix:

accounts; they analyzed it in medical treatises and philosophical tracts. Edmund Spenser (d. 1599) was of modest – even poor – birth and a Church of England man. William Shakespeare (d.1616) was from the middle class and, perhaps, a closet Catholic. John Bunyan (d. 1688) was a tinker and a dissident from the established church. Robert Burton spent most of his life as a member of Christ Church, Oxford, and came from a family "of some antiquity, if no great distinction."[26] All of these men thought and wrote a great deal about melancholy or its close relations, despair and sorrow. (And, as we shall see, some women did as well.)

Let us explore some representative literary works of the period with the idea in mind that they must have appealed to a wide and literate public. Here, then, I postulate an emotional community of writers and their audience. In Spenser's *The Faerie Queene*, published in 1590, the hero-knight Redcrosse is a man whose "cheere did seeme too solemne sad."[27] Spenser (d. 1599) meant the entire poem to be understood as "a continued Allegory, or darke conceit."[28] In the first book, Redcrosse (the Red Cross Knight) was summoned to fairyland by Una, who represented Truth.[29] Of

---

Between Melancholy and Ecstasy," in *Biblical Religion and the Novel, 1700–2000*, ed. Mark Knight and Thomas Woodman (Aldershot, 2006), 39–58 at 43, thinks melancholy (and its manic counterpart, ecstasy) was a European-wide, if largely Protestant, phenomenon. Note, however, that calling melancholy "fashionable" tends (wrongly) to minimize its emotional significance. On melancholy's negative effects, see Michael MacDonald and Terence R. Murphy, *Sleepless Souls: Suicide in Early Modern England* (Oxford, 1990), 103. For earlier literature on the topic, see Stanley W. Jackson, *Melancholia and Depression: From Hippocratic Times to Modern Times* (New Haven, 1986); Susan Snyder, "The Left Hand of God: Despair in Medieval and Renaissance Tradition," *Studies in the Renaissance* 12 (1965): 18–59; Raymond Klibansky, Erwin Panofsky, and Fritz Saxl, *Saturn and Melancholy: Studies in the History of Natural Philosophy, Religion, and Art* (London, 1964). Michael Heyd, *"Be Sober and Reasonable": The Critique of Enthusiasm in the Seventeenth and Early Eighteenth Centuries* (Leiden, 1995), points out the close connection in the minds of contemporaries between melancholy and "enthusiasm." The latter was a term of opprobrium and theological/philosophical criticism. It was connected to elite groups who positioned themselves against both the Catholics and the radical Protestants. In the context of a history of emotions based on emotional communities, it may be postulated that in England the anti-enthusiasts became normative with the Restoration. See below, at Pepys and Evelyn.

[26] J. B. Bamborough, "Burton, Robert (1577–1640)," *Oxford Dictionary of National Biography* [henceforth DNB] (Oxford, 2004); online ed., Oct. 2009, www.oxforddnb.com/view/article/4137, accessed June 19, 2014.

[27] Edmund Spenser, *The Faerie Queene*, ed. A. C. Hamilton, 2d. rev. ed. Hiroshi Yamashita and Toshiyuki Suzuki (London, 1977) [henceforth FQ], 1.1.2, p. 31 (cited by book, canto, stanza). In this discussion of Spenser I rely importantly on Paola Baseotto, *"Disdeining life, desiring leaue to die": Spenser and the Psychology of Despair* (Stuttgart, 2008). Christopher Tilmouth, *Passion's Triumph over Reason: A History of the Moral Imagination from Spenser to Rochester* (Oxford, 2007), 37–48, stresses the negative effects of the passions of lust, pity, and anger in the poem. Despair is briefly discussed at 48–50.

[28] Spenser, "Letter to Raleigh," in FQ, p. 724.   [29] FQ 1.2 argument, p. 44.

royal lineage, Una's parents had been expelled from their kingdom by "that infernall feend with foule vprore." To save them, Una "had this Knight [Redcrosse] from far compeld,"[30] taking him as "my liege Lord and my loue."[31] But Redcrosse soon came to believe (by the evil magic of the evil Archimago) that Una was a wanton woman. Abandoning her, now "Will was his guide, and griefe led him astray."[32] After a long series of misadventures, Redcrosse was imprisoned and left to rot by the giant Orgoglio, but he was saved by Una together with the young Arthur, here a squire to Merlin. Still weak spiritually and physically, Redcrosse and Una set off together only to encounter a knight, one Trevisan, with a noose around his neck. Fleeing Despayre (Despair), Trevisan had already witnessed the suicide – at the promptings of Despair – of Terwin, his companion, who had been "sad and comfortlesse" because of unrequited love.[33] Redcrosse rushes off to do battle with Despair, sure he will win, asking Trevisan only "Of grace do me vnto his cabin guyde."[34]

But Redcrosse needed grace of a different sort. His outrage at Despair's advocacy of voluntary death was immediately dampened by Despair's "suddeine wit": "What iustice euer other iudgement taught,/ But he should dye, who merites not to liue?" asked the demon.[35] Redcrosse was immediately stricken by his own sins: "The knight was much enmoued with [Despair's] speach,/That as a swords poynt through his hart did perse,/ ... And to his fresh remembraunce did reuerse [revert],/ The vgly vew of his deformed crimes."[36] He was about to stab himself when Una "snatcht the cursed knife,/ And threw it to the ground," quickly leading him away to the House of Holiness.[37]

The emotional sequence embedded in this literary text is not far from the ones familiar from Margery Kempe's *Book* (see Table 6.4). Despair leads Redcrosse to see and bewail his sins. Una takes the place of God, whom Redcrosse abandoned at the start and through whose interventions he is saved and (in the end) redeemed. With variations, despair was reiterated across Spenser's entire oeuvre.[38]

---

[30] FQ 1.1.5, p. 31.   [31] FQ 1.1.51, p. 42.   [32] FQ 1.2.12, p. 46.

[33] FQ 1.9.28, p. 118.

[34] FQ 1.9.32, p. 119. On this episode with Despair, see Harold Skulsky, "Spenser's Despair Episode and the Theology of Doubt," *Modern Philology* 78 (1981): 227–42; Baseotto, *"Disdeining Life,"* 48–69; Baseotto, "Godly Sorrow, Damnable Despair, and *Faerie Queene* I.ix," *Cahiers Élisabéthains* 69 (2006): 1–11.

[35] FQ 1.9.38 and 1.9.41, pp. 120–21.   [36] FQ 1.9.48, p. 122.

[37] FQ 1.9.52, p. 123. Even in the House of Holiness, Redcrosse remained burdened by suicidal thoughts. See Baseotto, *"Disdeining Life,"* 69–74.

[38] *Ibid.*, 97–166.

It appeared in other works of literature, as well. Not long after Redcross met Despair, for example, Hamlet was in doubt about himself, his mother, and even his father's apparition:[39]

> .... The spirit that I have seen
> May be a de'il, and the de'il hath power
> T'assume a pleasing shape. Yea, and perhaps
> Out of my weakness and my melancholy,
> As he is very potent with such spirits,
> Abuses me to damn me! I'll have grounds
> More relative than this. The play's the thing
> Wherein I'll catch the conscience of the king.[40]

Hamlet's melancholy was one of his sins, and he, too, contemplated suicide (the famous "To be, or not to be" speech),[41] only at last to pull out of his gloom and vacillation long enough to slay the king and die in turn.

John Bunyan (d.1688), writing *Pilgrim's Progress* (1677) more than three-quarters of a century later, was likewise inspired by the theme of despair. His book was meant as its remedy:

> Wouldst thou divert thy self from Melancholy?
> Wouldst thou be pleasant, yet be far from folly?
> ... O then come hither,
> And lay my book, thy head and heart together.[42]

Bunyan's hero, Christian, "wept and trembled" as he contemplated the future of mankind. "What shall I do to be saved?" Shunning him, his family and neighbors let him take off on his quest for Mount Zion. His first obstacle was the Slough of Despond, where "many fears and doubts and discouraging apprehensions [arise]."[43] Once out of the Slough, temptations vied for attention with strange scenes (each of allegorical meaning) and figures. Despair sat in an iron cage, unable to repent. The sight of the cross, however, lifted Christian's spirits. He "stood looking and weeping," and, clothed anew, he gave "three leaps for joy" and sang:

> Thus far did I come loaden with my sin,
> Nor could aught ease the grief that I was in,
> Till I came hither: What a place is this![44]

Overcoming still more obstacles and finding help in the ministrations of Charity, Piety, and Discretion, Christian meets up with his neighbor Faithful, who is making the same pilgrimage but finding different

---

[39] On the date see William Shakespeare, *Hamlet*, ed. Ann Thompson and Neil Taylor (London, 2006), 43–59; it is possible that a version existed as early as 1589 and the latest date is 1602 or 1603.

[40] Shakespeare, *Hamlet* 2.2.533–40, pp. 278–79.   [41] *Ibid.*, 3.1.55, p. 284.

[42] John Bunyan, *Pilgrim's Progress*, ed. Roger Sharrock (London, 1966), 145.

[43] *Ibid.*, 151.   [44] *Ibid.*, 169–70.

temptations. The two are tormented at the Vanity Fair, and Faithful is brought to trial (the jury made up of Mr. Blind-man, Mr. No-good, Mr. Malice, and so on). After a horrible execution, Faithful is "carried up through the clouds, with sound of trumpet," while Christian escapes with Hopeful.[45] Like Redcrosse, they meet with Giant Despair, who imprisons them and tells them to kill themselves. They need no Una to save them; Hopeful's arguments against suicide and Christian's hand key (called Promise) release them from prison. The allegory gave Bunyan opportunity to present arguments for and against suicide and other issues of morality and faith. It was half sermon, half testimonial.

These were literary representations of melancholy. Alongside them were scientific discussions. The physician Timothie Bright (d. 1615) published *A Treatise of Melancholie* in 1586.[46] He treated emotions (which he called "perturbations" or "affections") as if they corresponded to medieval medical "simples" and "compounds." There were two sorts of simples: four "primitives" – love, hate, like, and dislike (or mislike) – and four "derivatives" – joy (or rejoicing), hope (or expectation), heaviness of heart (or sadness), and fear.[47] Bright's scheme for the simples is summarized in Table 8.1.

"Compound" emotions were mixtures of the "simples." When the ingredients (like, dislike) were unequal, the result (when "like" predominated) was a sort of nasty joy (today we would say *Schadenfreude*) that spilled over into merriment and laughter; when "dislike" was heavier, the result was compassion and pity. When the proportions of primitives and derivatives were equal the mixtures produced envy, jealousy, trust, distrust, anger, revenge, shame, bashfulness, malice. When derivatives alone were mixed together, despair and assurance were the results.[48] While seeming to adhere to the traditional emphasis on love, Bright's real

Table 8.1 *Bright's "primitive" and "derivative" emotions*

"Primitives"	present "derivatives"	future "derivatives"
love/like	joy, rejoicing	hope, expectation
hate/dislike	heaviness of heart/sadness	fear

---

[45] *Ibid.*, 218.

[46] Timothie Bright, *A Treatise of Melancholie. Containing the causes thereof, and reasons of the strange effects it worketh in our minds and bodies ...* (London, 1586) [where the pagination and chapter numbers of the original publication are incorrect, they will be cited here followed by (*sic*) and the correct number]. Other books on the subject are surveyed in Jackson, *Melancholia*, 78–95.

[47] Bright, *Treatise of Melancholie* c. 15, p. 82.   [48] *Ibid.*, 82–84.

interest was in forms of joy and sadness.[49] These, as we shall see, more or less sum up the preoccupations of the various emotional communities we shall study here.

According to Bright, all of the perturbations were rational, the mind objectively assessing the stimuli of the outer world and communicating its judgments to the heart, the seat of the passions. The perturbations and the humors of the body – a heritage of Galenic medical theory that postulated four humors (blood, two kinds of bile, and phlegm) – were entirely different things.[50] How, then, "cometh it to passe, that melancholicke persons are more sad than other, & cholericke more angrie &c. if these humoures beare no sway herein?"[51] There was no question that this happened. Some people had every external comfort – security, wealth, friendship – yet were "ouerwhelmed with heauines, and dismaide with such feare, as they can neither receiue consolation, nor hope of assurance."[52] They were under the sway of the melancholic humor, "surcharged . . . for want of free vent, by reason of obstruction." In this case the body was not healthy; the humors distorted the perturbations, making them "disorderly" and "otherwise then nature hath disposed."[53] Continuing his discussion of the humors, Bright turned to their hot (burned or adust) forms. The adust melancholic humor produced "monstrous terrors of feare and heauinesse without cause"; the adust choleric humor caused fury and madness.[54] And so on.

"Of all the actions of melancholie, or rather of heauinesse and sadnesse, none is so manifolde and diuerse in partes, as that of weeping."[55] Bright devoted five chapters to the topic of tears. They were always caused by sorrow. Even "such weeping as seemeth to proceed of ioy is of a mixt cause as shall hereafter be declared . . . We see no man weep but in sorow."[56] He associated tears with children and women, since they were "of a moist, rare, and tender body, especially of brayne and heart."[57] And he considered them the gestures of a mediocre sort of sorrow, neither very strong nor very weak, thus demoting it from its special role in the lives of men and women like Aelred and Margery Kempe.[58]

---

[49] *Ibid.*, c. 23, p. 132, makes the point that "feare is the verie ground and roote of that sorowe, which melancholick men are throwne into."

[50] On Galenic models of melancholy in this period and the body-soul composite that they stressed, see Angus Gowland, "Melancholy, Passions and Identity in the Renaissance," in *Passions and Subjectivity*, 75–93.

[51] Bright, *Treatise of Melancholie* c. 15, p. 86.   [52] *Ibid.*, c. 16, p. 90.   [53] *Ibid.*, 89-90.

[54] *Ibid.*, c. 18, pp. 110–11.   [55] *Ibid.*, c. 24, pp. 135–36.

[56] *Ibid.*, 158 (*sic*) 138. On tears, Bright's and others of the period, see Bernard Capp, "'Jesus Wept' but Did the Englishman? Masculinity and Emotion in Early Modern England," *Past and Present* 224 (2014): 75–108, who, however (76) claims that "Bright presented melancholy as a medical affliction, with tears a natural physiological response." True; but note that sorrow and other passions caused that response.

[57] *Ibid.*, 143–44.   [58] *Ibid.*, 158 (*sic*) 138, 140–41.

Yet Bright's treatise was in other ways not so distant from them. Though a medical doctor, his treatise was directed to an anonymous friend who suffered from "the affliction of conscience for sinne." No misery was worse; it was "not to be described to the capacity of any, but of such as have felt the anguish, as your selfe at this present."[59] This sorrow was due to a correct assessment of real sinfulness; it was a despair of the perturbations, not the humors. Nevertheless, people of melancholy humor fell most often into this sort of sorrow because they were most prone to doubt "not only of this life, but also of the life to come."[60] In a long chapter, Bright analyzed the work of the devil on the human spirits and counseled patience.[61] It was the sort of despair that most concerned Bright. "If I be tedious," he wrote, it is because "I ... comprehend the estate of many one at this day in like sort affected and afflicted, who if they receiue any meanes of comforte by this my travaile, they may be more beholding unto my friend M. & pray for his release."[62] Thus did Bright identify religious despair as the malady of a large number of his contemporaries.

Robert Burton (d. 1640), who published the first edition of *The Anatomy of Melancholy* in 1621, had still grander ambitions. Taking on the persona of heir to the ancient writer Democritus, Burton offered a treatise to "cure [melancholy] in himselfe, [and] by his writings and observations, teach others how to prevent & avoid it."[63] In an address to the reader, Democritus Junior pointed to "the generalitie of the Disease, the necessitie of the Cure, and the ... common good that will arise to all men by the knowledge of it."[64] His definition of the term was capacious: "take Melancholy in what sense you will, properly or improperly, in disposition or habit, for pleasure or for paine, dotage, discontent, feare, sorrow, madnesse, for part, or all, truly, or metaphorically, 'tis all one."[65] Moreover, it was everywhere: you had only to look around to know that "all the world is mad, that it is melancholy, dotes [is deranged] ... & needs to be reformed."[66] England, notwithstanding all its glories, was full of beggars and idlers; it had no cities, no tradesmen, few navigable rivers, unreformed laws and manners.[67] Democritus Junior despaired of real change, but he could at least create an ideal polity in his mind: "I will yet to satisfie & please my selfe, make an *Utopia* of mine owne, a new *Atlantis*, a poeticall commonwealth of mine owne, in which I will freely domineere, build Citties, make Lawes, Statutes, as I list my selfe." In this commonwealth, no one was idle and no one melancholy.[68]

[59] *Ibid.*, c. 32, p. 186.   [60] *Ibid.*, c. 35, p. 199.   [61] *Ibid.*, c. 30 (*sic*) 36, pp. 207–42.
[62] *Ibid.*, 241.   [63] Burton, *Anatomy*, 1:6.   [64] *Ibid.*, 23.   [65] *Ibid.*, 25.   [66] *Ibid.*, 24.
[67] *Ibid.*, 75–84.   [68] *Ibid.*, 85.

In creating this utopia, Burton joined those who, inspired in part by sixteenth-century voyages of discovery, created ideal worlds reached either through effort or magic.[69] Initially Burton sought another Hercules to purge the world and "fight against Envy, lust, anger avarice, &c. and all those feral vices & monsters of the mind."[70] He thought, too, of a magic ring that would give one the power to

transport himselfe in an instant, to what place he desired, alter affections, cure all manner of diseases, that he might range over the world, & reforme all distressed states & persons . . . He might root out Barbarisme out of *America*, & fully discover *Terra Australis Incognita* . . . End all our idle controversies, cut off our tumultuous desires, inordinate lusts, roote out Atheisme, impiety, heresy, schisme, and super-stition, which now so crucifie the World.[71]

In the end he contented himself with his "poeticall" skills.

Using the words affections, perturbations, passions, and motions with-out distinction, Burton followed scholastic thought in dividing them into concupiscible and irascible.[72] His theory reads like a combination of Thomas Aquinas' – with its emphasis on the soul – and Timothie Bright's, with its emphasis on the body:

All affections and perturbations arise out of these two fountaines [that is, concu-piscible and irascible], which, although the *Stoickes* make light of, we hold naturall, and not to be resisted. The good affections are caused by some object of the same nature [that is, an object appraised by the senses as good]; and if [such objects are] present, they procure joy, which dilates the Heart and preserves the body: If absent, they cause Hope, Love, Desire, and Concupiscence. The *Bad* are *Simple* or *mixt: Simple* for some bad object present, as sorrow which contracts the Heart, macerates [that is, torments] the Soule, subverts the good estate of the Body, hindering all the operations of it, causing Melancholy, and many times death it selfe.[73]

Burton thus saw melancholy as a part of the human condition: "*Cain* was melancholy, as *Austin* [Saint Augustine] hath it, and who is not? Good discipline, Education, Philosophy, Divinity (I cannot deny) may mitigate and restraine these passions in some few men at some times, but most part they domineere and are so violent, that . . . they overwhelme reason, judge-ment, and pervert the temperature of the body."[74]

---

[69] The classic study is J. C. Davis, *Utopia and the Ideal Society: A Study of English Utopian Writing, 1516–1700* (Cambridge, 1981), esp. 86–104 for Burton. See also Nicole Pohl, "Utopianism after More: The Renaissance and Enlightenment," in *The Cambridge Companion to Utopian Literature*, ed. Gregory Claeys (Cambridge, 2010), 51–78, esp. 51–63.

[70] Burton, *Anatomy*, 1:84, borrowing from Apuleius.   [71] *Ibid.*, 85.   [72] *Ibid.*, 154.

[73] *Ibid.*

[74] *Ibid.*, 248. The reference to Augustine is perhaps to *City of God* 15.7, which quotes Gen. 4:6: "And the Lord said unto Cain, why art thou wroth, and why is thy countenance cast down?" See Burton, *Anatomy*, 4:290 (Commentary).

Much of Burton's *Anatomy* was thus taken up with the miseries of men and women whose passions, experiences, and bodily frailties turned them into melancholics.[75] The entire third part of his treatise was devoted to "love melancholy" – the seventeenth-century version of lovesickness[76] – to jealousy, and to "religious melancholy." It should not be surprising, then, that Burton's emotion words, listed in Table 8.2, centered on sorrow and pain.

All were natural and inescapable but could be mitigated. Prayer would help.[77] Friends, music, and merrymaking might soothe the trouble spirit. Even better was prudent exercise of body and mind: "some employment or other."[78]

Treatises on melancholy continued to be written after Burton's day. But the humors were beginning to be challenged by new – chemical and corpuscular – theories of disease. We see this "new science" in Thomas Willis, *Two Discourses Concerning the Soul of Brutes* (1672).[79] However, Timothy Rogers, *A Discourse Concerning Trouble of Mind and the Disease of Melancholly* (1691), writing some twenty years later, put all his emphasis on religious despair.[80]

Feeling despair, seeking comfort: the believers in a gathered church

Religious despair was indeed a widespread experience in seventeenth-century England. Although treatises on melancholy were most interested in cure, autobiographies – Bunyan's is a good example – described an emotional trajectory that led from despair to joy.[81]

---

[75] However, Bridget Gellert Lyons, *Voices of Melancholy: Studies in Literary Treatments of Melancholy in Renaissance England* (New York, 1971), chap. 5, treats Burton as a satirist.

[76] On lovesickness, a topic growing out of medical theories and influential in literature, see Mary Frances Wack, *Lovesickness in the Middle Ages: The* Viaticum *and Its Commentaries* (Philadelphia, 1990); Lesel Dawson, *Lovesickness and Gender in Early Modern English Literature* (Oxford, 2008); Jacalyn Duffin, *Lovers and Livers: Disease Concepts in History* (Toronto, 2005). I am grateful to Annalese Duprey-Henry for bibliographical help on this topic.

[77] Burton, *Anatomy*, 2:5–6.   [78] *Ibid.*, 68, here translating a Latin version of al-Razi.

[79] The changes in theory and their impact on Willis' work are discussed in Jackson, *Melancholia*, 110–15.

[80] Timothy Rogers, *A Discourse Concerning Trouble of Mind and the Disease of Melancholly* (London, 1691).

[81] On the proliferation of spiritual autobiographies in England, most written by members of the clergy rather than laity, see Owen C. Watkins, *The Puritan Experience: Studies in Spiritual Autobiography* (New York, 1972); Kaspar von Greyerz, *Vorsehungsglaube und Kosmologie. Studien zu englischen Selbstzeugnissen des 17. Jahrhunderts* (Göttingen, 1990); *Early Modern Autobiography*; and Kathleen Lynch, *Protestant Autobiography in the Seventeenth-Century Anglophone World* (Oxford, 2012).

Table 8.2 *Burton's emotions*[a]

affliction
ambition
anger
anguish
anxiety
appetite
avarice
care
concupiscence
contention
covetousness
cross (to bear)
despair
desire
discontent
emulation
epichairekakia (*Shadenfreude*)
envy
fear
grief
hatred
hope
indignation
jealousy
joy
love
malice
mercy
misery
perplexity
pride
self-love
shame
sorrow
vainglory
vexation
zeal

[a] Note that nowhere does Burton purport to give a complete
list of emotion words. All the terms here are from Burton,
Anatomy, vol. 1.

Here I want to focus in some detail on the stories contained in
Spirituall Experiences, the testimonials of sixty-one members of a
"gathered church" (we may loosely term it Puritan) probably led by

Henry Walker in London in the 1650s.[82] Before joining these unofficial congregations, prospective members were required to give an oral or written narrative of their conversions. Sometimes, as in the case of *Spirituall Experiences*, the testimonials were collected together. Introducing the second edition of *Spirituall Experiences*, the Welsh divine Vavasor Powell wrote that the accounts were in a sense God's own words:

> The special and unspeakable love, and care of our good Lord ... hath so manifestly appeared to his people (especially of late yeares) that out of his fulnesse he hath communicated so bountifully that many of them (like good Scribes) ... have been able to bring things new and old for the refreshing, comforting, and supplying of many poore souls, which otherwise had been in extreame want and distress.[83]

Such accounts, then, were published in order to bring comfort to their readers. The genre was popular for a short time on both sides of the Atlantic Ocean.

As Watkins long ago noted, Protestant testimonials tended to follow a common pattern, and those in *Spirituall Experiences* were no exception.[84] Rather than decry this in the vain search for "real" emotions, let us consider the general emotional sequence to be normative, allowing us to

---

[82] *Spirituall experiences, of sundry beleevers. Held forth by them at severall solemne meetings, and Conferences to that end. With the recommendation of the sound, spiritual, and savoury worth of them, to the sober and spirituall Reader, By Vavasor Powel, Minister of the Gospel* (2d ed., London, [1653]) [henceforth SE]. Accessed through Early English Books Online [Henceforth EEBO]. The book was thus "recommended" by Vavasor Powell, a Welsh divine, who wrote an introductory epistle for this, its second, augmented edition. On its connection to the church led by Henry Wallace, see Watkins, *Puritan Experience*, 41; Lynch, *Protestant Autobiography*, 130–40, where Walker's movements are traced from an unspecified parish to another in Wood Street, Cheapside, to a third, in 1650, in Knightsbridge. The evidence certainly points to Henry Walker. Thus the testimony of SE, 227: "Providence was pleased to cast my lot at *Westminster*, where once I heard Mr. *Henry Walker*." Or, again SE, 384–85: "I have had an earnest desire that the Lord would make my way to be joined unto Mr. *Walkers* Fellowship." (Italics in original.) For Westminster, see Norman G. Brett-James, *The Growth of Stuart London* (London, 1935), maps opposite 132 and 366. Tai Liu, *Puritan London: A Study of Religion and Society in the City Parishes* (Newark, 1986), 106, points out that gathered churches might draw their clientele and pastors from many different parishes. Nevertheless, Lynch, *Protestant Autobiography*, 140, cautions that "it is doubtful that the publication [of SE] represented any single fully gathered church." For a portrait of one gathered church, see Ellen S. More, "Congregationalism and the Social Order: John Goodwin's Gathered Church, 1640–60," *Journal of Ecclesiastical History* 38/2 (1987): 210–35.

[83] SE, [i]. On Puritanism and melancholy, see Julius H. Rubin, *Religious Melancholy and Protestant Experience in America* (New York, 1994).

[84] Watkins, *Puritan Experience*, 30–31, dates the end of such testimonial collections to around the date of SE's publication. He describes (38) the "normal pattern of a Puritan conversion" as going from "peace, disturbance, and then peace again." See also Geoffrey F. Nuttall, *Visible Saints: The Congregational Way, 1640–1660* (Oxford, 1957).

see how people understood their own emotions and what emotions they expected from others. However, in point of fact, the sequence was not so uniform as to obliterate all individual voices, even though each narrative was attributed to a set of initials rather than to names. Of the sixty-one accounts, twenty-four represented the experience of a female, eighteen of a male, leaving nineteen as indeterminable.[85]

I propose to explore the testimony of the witnesses in *Spirituall Experiences* through the glossed experience of one exemplar, A. O.[86] I give his or her experience (the gender of this believer is uncertain) in italics, with key emotions underlined. Interspersed, in Roman font, are excerpts from other experiences, both male and female, to fill out A. O.'s account. For convenience – to avoid constant use of the phrase "he or she" – I will consider A. O. a man.

I have undergone sad troubles of spirit for my sins . . .

As was typical of these testimonials, A. O. began with his sins. He did not say what they were. Nor did S. P., who "was called out to be a souldier, and having had much experience of God's deliverance from enemies in the high places of the field, it brought me to a consideration of my wayes and of the evill of sinne."[87] T. G. however, named his sins: "The first grosse one was, many kinds of unlawfull gameing, which held mee as a bondslave some thirty years." Vowing to God never to play again, the devil soon "drew me into a liking of Tobacco," and when he had rid himself of that vice, the devil persuaded him "that to drinke with my neighbours, was acceptable to God, (which may be used with restraint of excesse, but) I gave wil the ful reins, which brought me back againe from my former courses."[88] D. M. identified her sin as loving too much "my Husband in a fleshly love, making an idoll of him."[89]

---

[85] The best clue to gender is the Table of Contents, which often refers to the believer as "him" or "her" (whereas the testimonials use the first person, "I"). Lynch's statistics (*Protestant Autobiography*, 133) are a bit different: "When gender can be determined, women outnumber men by fifty percent." Two narratives belong to the same man, H. W. (SE, 103–10; 286–90). This was very likely Henry Walker himself. See Nigel Smith, *Perfection Proclaimed: Language and Literature in English Radical Religion, 1640–1660* (Oxford, 1989), 43, and Lynch, *Protestant Autobiography*, 136; at 130–31 Lynch outlines the book's organization. The testimonials range in length from 2 to 32 pages, counting fractions of a page as a page.

[86] In fact, there are two experiences attributed to an A. O., the first at SE, 87–93, and the second, used here, on 134–39. They are quite different, and the best guess is that they were by separate individuals. For some other ways to consider the emotions in SE, see Barbara H. Rosenwein, "Transmitting Despair by Manuscript and Print," in *Crying in the Middle Ages: Tears of History*, ed. Elina Gertsman (Routledge, 2012), 249–66.

[87] SE, 349.   [88] SE, 309–11.   [89] SE, 34.

More dramatic and voluble than most, M. K. called her "life upon the stage of this world" a "comicall Tragedy, or a tragical Comedy, or a labyrinth from one sin to another." In particular, after her mother died, she was "suddenly made my fathers house-keeper, so as it were a mother to ten children [her siblings], a mistresse over six servants, none to doe any thing without my command or consent ... It did not onely stop my sorrow, but caused an exceeding joyfull pride, or proud joy." When her father died, "I asked my heart, 'What was the cause of my father's death?' It made answer thus, 'Because thou hast sinned against God, thou hast not onely omitted much good, but thou hast committed much evill, thou hast spent thy time idlely and loosely, and for thy sake, all thy brothers and sisters are now made fatherlesse and motherlesse.'"[90]

... [sins] which I have had a great sight and sense of, and shed many tears for, and desire to be truly sorry for them, and hate them, and to have no more communion with them. About five years since, and for some two years space I lay under very great temptations, and was ready to despair, and for several nights could not take any rest in my bed; but was very weak with weeping and much grieved for my evil thoughts [.]

In this phase, A. O. reported many unhappy emotions. He hated his sins and wanted to feel sorry – evidently rather unsuccessfully – about them. He was ready to despair; he wept; he was grieved. Other accounts echo these feelings. After D. M. realized that she had loved her husband too much, she reported that "this wrought upon me great troubles, and despaire; that I cryed untill I was almost blinde: And I had a great feare and trembling upon me." A few months later, "I had a temptation by Satan to drown my selfe in a Pond neare *Leeds*."[91] N. B., who was born a Protestant but "fell to the Church of *Rome*," was persuaded by his wife to be "somewhat softned." In the event, he had a "troubled spirit ... which drove me into, almost, a despairing condition."[92] A. H., too, was "drawn away to Popery," and "was much distempered in my minde." The devil tempted her "to make away myselfe."[93]

M. K., the woman whose heart told her that she had caused her mother's and father's deaths, reported that "this consideration made such a deep impression upon my spirit, that I refused all comfort for the space of halfe a year, crying out continually, 'My sins, my sins, woe is me my sins!'" She "wearied all my friends with my excessive sorrow." Moving to London, she married, but she and her husband fell in with bad company: there was "one man espcially [*sic*], who gave his minde to drinking, and other vices." She tried to persuade her husband to see less of the man, but he would not listen. Then she yielded to the devil and determined to kill the man.[94]

Yet the Lord drew forth my heart to call upon him and hope *in him for mercy. But I had many sore conflicts, insomuch that I could not lie in the chamber alone; I made what use I could of opportunities to* desire comfort *from such godly Christians as I could meet withal to counsel me in the wayes of God, and I laboured to hearken to them, but found my* heart very dul and heavy *for that time until about three yeares since, I began to finde* comfort *from some sermons that I heard, and books that I read, and some thoughts that the Lord settled upon my heart by his spirit, hoping that there was mercy for me.*

In this phase, God intervened, giving A. O. hope and leading him to seek – and sometimes to find – comfort. Nevertheless, he could not sleep alone, and periods of relief alternated with heaviness of heart. Similarly, M. H., who alternated between delighting in the word and straying from it, "found much comfort" in "able ministers of the Gospel . . . and more particularly, hearing Mr. Bridges of Yarmouth opening that comfortable Scripture, Ps. 42:11."[95]

M. K. had a dream in which the man who was corrupting her husband entered a chamber where she was as well. She seized a weapon to kill him, but then heard "a voice in my eare, saying, 'Vengeance is mine'; to which voice I answered aloud, 'And thou wilt repay, O Lord.'" She found in her heart "a whole nest of most Diabolicall and wicked intentions, which my God was pleased by his preventing graces to smother in their birth." Then began a little drama in which she "ran away from my Captain, but for all this he had a favour towards me, and sent an Herauld after me to bring mee backe againe." She found comfort in sermons of Mr. Dod, "for this minister did not onely preach to the people, but shewed me as it were in a looking-glasse, mine owne condition, and told me that by the gates of hell many times God was pleased to bring his servants to heaven." The minister became M. K.'s special guide, for "after he was sensible of my condition, which I made knowne to him privately, he was very laborious to bring my soule out of the jawes of death, and to raise it to Jesus Christ."[96]

And I did believe that I had all the prayers of all the Saints in the world put up to the Throne of grace for me, and that my Saviour had satisfied for my sins, and

---

[94] SE, 165–68.   [95] SE, 220.   [96] SE, 168–69, 178–80.

through him God was reconciled to me, and in particular I found comfort from
these and some other promises.

John 6:35: Jesus said unto them, I am the bread of life, he that cometh to me,
shall never hunger, and he that believeth on me, shall never thirst.

[John 6:] 37: All that the Father giveth me, shall come to me, and him that
cometh to me, I will in no wise cast out.

John 14:1: Let not your hearts be troubled, ye believe in God, believe also in
me.

Jer. 31:23: But this shall be the Covenant that I will make with the house of
Israel; After those dayes saith the Lord, I will put my Law in their inward parts,
and write it in their hearts, and I will be their God, and they shall be my people.

A. O.'s account ended, as did most of the others, with comforting
quotations from Scripture and the sense of reconciliation with God.
M. K. reported that "by faith I see my Saviour Jesus Christ suffering for
mee, nailed upon the Crosse for mee, wounded, buffeted, stript, and spit
upon for me; dead, buryed, rose againe ... making intercession for mee;
which give me assurance of my Gods everlasting and unchangeable love,
in, and through my Saviour Jesus Christ towards mee." She found certainty in God's love, as had A.O., in texts from the Gospel of John.[97]
Similarly, M. H. quoted Scripture, in his case many citations from the
Old Testament as well as, yet again, John 6:37.[98]

And I do find in my heart a testimony of my believing; and that I do love God;
wrought in me by his blessed Spirit, by these particulars.

1. *I do so love God, not through slavish fear, but for his name and glory, that I*
   can leave all for him, and nothing is so dear and precious to me, as the love of
   God; and nothing so great a joy to me, as that Christ who dyed for me, hath
   not left me.
2. *I find such comfort from the Lord, that he by his Spirit revives my drooping*
   heart, and fills my empty soul, and when I am in my poor spirit even fainting
   away, I find comfort from his glorious power and presence.
3. *When I cannot come to Ordinances it is a grief to me; and when I am in*
   duty,[99] it is a grief to me, that I am so dull and finde no more inlargement; yet
   my affections are groaning after the Lord Jesus Christ in the duties, and I
   have a great longing to receive more of Christ. And I find more comfort when

---

[97] SE, 187–88.   [98] SE, 226.

[99] The Ordinances were God's laws and more specifically the sacraments, especially baptism and communion. Here A. O. is probably referring to communal worship, such as
singing the psalms, bible reading, and alms-giving. Being "in duty" refers mainly to
praying. See Thomas Shepard, "The Sincere Convert," in *The Works of Thomas
Shepard: First Pastor of the First Church, Cambridge, Mass.: With a Memoir of His Life and
Character*, 3 vols. (Boston, 1853), 1:105–6, in *Sabin Americana*. Gale, Cengage Learning,
Loyola University Chicago, accessed December 8, 2014.

my heart is inlarged in duty than in any other thing in the world, and I know that all my comfort is from Jesus Christ.

4. *What I desire to injoy, I seek to injoy it in God through peace of conscience, that it may be to the comfort of my faith, for God is pure, and it is a great grief to me that I can serve my God no better.*

5. *I do not fear death, for my faith is so settled in God, that I long to be with my Saviour, when he shall be pleased to call me to him; Christ hath dyed for me, to take away the fear of the second death.*

A. O.'s account ended with his love of God, his assurance of God's love, comfort, and joy. At the same time, he admitted to occasional "dullness." This sort of sporadic backsliding was the case in other accounts, as well. T. A. admitted that: "'Tis about a yeare, since God brought me to some settlement of comfort upon the Promises afore-mentioned, only some clouds of doubts sometimes interpose; but God is pleased to rebuke them, and to assure me, 'his grace shall bee sufficient for me [2 Cor. 12:9].'"[100] Similarly, J. B. explained that, "though I cannot serve God so well as I would, I do as well as I can; and am troubled in my spirit for my failings, and therefore I beleeve I shall never be condemned."[101] L. P. spoke of "The peace I finde with my God in my soule, which is sweet, though not without much heaviness of spirit for my failings. I doe not live without waines and changes in my Spirituall life, and faith towards the Lord, for sometimes I can trust God with all, and at other times I meet with some doubtings, yet (blessed be God) I find still more and more, my doubtings asswaged, and my communion with Christ every day more sweet, and more full."[102] Table 8.3 sums up the general sequence of emotions of the testimonials in *Spirituall Experiences*.

This sequence is quite similar to Margery's in Table 6.4. The key emotions are very similar, and even the order in which they unfold is nearly

Table 8.3 *General sequence of emotions in* Spirituall Experiences

sense of sinfulness →
despair →
dread of damnation/fear of God's abandonment →
tears →
comfort associated with assurance of God's love

---

[100] SE, 4–5.   [101] SE, 57.   [102] SE, 232–33.

the same. Despair is at or near the beginning, along with a sense of sinfulness. Fear of God's abandonment is at a critical midpoint, and the comfort that comes from the assurance of God's love is at the end. There are, however, important differences. Margery suffered from – though ultimately welcomed – the scorn of others who were annoyed by her constant crying. Even so, Margery herself found her weeping very consoling. For the Protestant believers, tears were, by contrast, often associated with grief rather than consolation. On the other hand, these believers did not face scorn for weeping but rather were offered comfort.[103] The final emotions of the two sequences were also a bit different, with Margery speaking of joy, even merriment, while the Protestants emphasized a quiet sort of comfort, admitting at the same time some backsliding and "heaviness." Their restrained joy was more reminiscent of the Pastons, for whom, we should recall, comfort and heaviness were among the eight words that they associated directly with the heart.[104]

There are other differences. While the Puritans in the gathered church did occasionally report that Jesus or God spoke to them, these incidents were normally brief, and they melded seamlessly into quotations from Scripture. Protestant theology exchanged the Bible for visions of God. At the same time, some of the accounts in *Spirituall Experiences* reported little dramas that recall Margery's much more extensive dramas with the Holy Family. One was the account of T. M., who had a dream that included a dragon and a child.[105] "I asked [the child] what was its name; it said, *Emanuel*; I asked it, who was its father; it said, *I am*," and so on, in an extended interview. We have already seen M. K.'s dramatic confrontations with God.[106]

Thus we see in the seventeenth century the repurposing of some of the emotional vocabularies and the sequences of the fifteenth. Precisely because they were repurposed, they no doubt *felt* differently. In the context of a religion that emphasized a radically transcendent God who had predetermined salvation and damnation, the believers in *Spirituall Experiences* were never entirely sure of their salvation. Their comfort alternated with doubts. In the face of a religious doctrine that offered no Purgatory, the believers could not feel like the triumphant Margery, who

---

[103] W. F. in SE, 304, speaks of the "persecution, shame, reproach, or scorne of the world," but this seems theoretical rather than personal. Two testimonies speak of the pain of being called a "Puritan": M. H. in SE, 217, and J. H. in SE, 376. See the remarks on spiritual tears in Capp, "Jesus Wept," 96–101.

[104] See Table 6.5.   [105] SE, 369–75.

[106] See above at n. 96. It is true that the English theaters were closed in 1642, but, as N. W. Bawcutt, "Puritanism and the Closing of the Theaters in 1642," *Medieval and Renaissance Drama in England* 22 (2009): 179–200 at 192, notes, "allusions to plays and theatrical language" continued thereafter, even within Puritan circles.

was assured by Christ that she would bypass Purgatory and go straight to Heaven. In these ways, the gathered believers were more anxious. On the other hand they received the emotional support of their community, while Margery had to bear the scorn (or imagine she bore the scorn) of others.

We may take the argument about repurposed emotions somewhat further if we accept, as is very likely, that Henry Walker headed up the church to which the "sundry believers" applied for admission. Walker was a failed ironmonger, a university dropout, and a successful journalist and preacher.[107] During the Civil War he was a Cromwellian partisan and may have been the author of a pamphlet on Cromwell's final days. If so, he was "one that was then Groom of [Cromwell's] bedchamber."[108]

Walker published news, opinions, and religious pamphlets. Although he did not write an autobiography (unless the two testimonials by H. W. in *Spirituall Experiences* are his), he did write about other people, and here we find emotional sequences rather close to those of his church members:

There is no misery can exceed the misery of an evill Conscience .... [Such a conscience is] seared up with hardnesse, and sensing it selfe against the breathings and workings of Gods Spirit ... or else it becomes so fearfull, that it casteth a man into utter desparation, so that it is as impossible for such a man or woman to looke up to God with comfort, as for a blinde man to behold the Sunne ... Hence it hath come to passe, that some have been so farre perplexed in this sad condition, that they have been so confident that they should bee damned in hell, that though the Lords Ministers have come after a most sweet and heavenly manner ... yet still they have cast off all, nothing could yeeld them any comfort.[109]

The woes that arose from this evil conscience included "feares, and troubles, and doubts." Walker followed this discussion with the "happiness a good Conscience is." Here the talk was all of comfort: comfort from the help of the Spirit; comfort from union with Christ; comfort from the certainty of eternal life.[110]

Nor was this discussion of conscience purely theoretical. In his newspaper, *Perfect Occurrences*, which he began to edit in 1644, Walker was compassionate toward men impressed into the royal army and harsh in his judgments about the consciences of their persecutors:

---

[107] Joad Raymond, "Walker, Henry (*fl.* 1638–1660)," DNB (Oxford, 2004); online ed. www.oxforddnb.com/view/article/40242, accessed December 6, 2014.

[108] *A Collection of Several Passages concerning his late Highnesse Oliver Cromwell, In the time of his Sickness* (London, 1659); another version of the same text, but with the title *An Account of the Last Houres of the late Renowned Oliver Lord Protector* (London, 1659), styles the author "one who was an Eye and Ear-witness of the most part of it." Lynch, *Protestant Autobiography*, 137–40, surveys Walker's writings.

[109] [Henry Walker], *The Heavenly Guide to True Peace of Conscience* (London, 1641), 2–3.

[110] *Ibid.*, 4–5.

... it would pittie any mans heart to see them [the impressed soldiers] languish in
their bloud, for the Cavalier [the royalists] they say do so cut, and beat them (*into
Allegiance as they call it.*[)] ... They are in terrible feare of the Lord Generals forces,
and are continually in a posture of running away ... It is a grievous thing to be
troubled in conscience as these Cavaliers are.[111]

In his eulogy on Ferdinando Fairfax's death in 1648, Walker's acrostic
poem invoked tears: "Adieu, brave Honour, *England* with brinish teares
may say, Night clad in sable blacke, mournes for the losse of day." And for
the eulogy proper he wrote: "His death sets sluces ope, to powre out
tears."[112] The account of Cromwell's death, likely by Walker, spoke of
Cromwell as "a most indulgent and tender Father" to his daughter, who
died a month before Cromwell himself.[113] When the leader's own

time was come ... neither prayers nor tears could prevail with God to lengthen out
his life ... although abundantly and uncessantly poured out on his behalf, both
publickly and privately (as was observed) in a more than ordinary way. Besides
many a secret sigh, yet like *Moses* Cry, more loud, and strongly laying hold on
God, though neither perceived nor heard by man, than many vocal
supplications.[114]

Thus, tears and sighs were normative and even considered potentially
efficacious: "All which [tears, sighs, and cries] (the hearts of Gods people
being thus mightily stirred up) did seem to beget confidence in some, and
hopes in all, yea some thoughts in himself that God would restore him."[115]
Although Timothie Bright earlier had associated tears with women, Walker
saw them as manly and useful. Gender did not always count.

Walker approved of certain emotions while decrying others. In one of
his pamphlets, he offered a "gad of steele" – a dagger, in other words –
that would "defend [the heart] from being battred by Sathans temptation," a formulation that seems to suggest a tool for suppressing
emotions.[116] But the purpose of this gad was "meanes to procure thee
more happinesse to thy Soule, then the richest Diadem in the world can
procure to thy Body."[117] Happy and sad emotions suffused this "enchir-
idion": both joy in seeing "others endued with goodnesse" and sadness in
seeing the ephemeral joy of those who revelled in "Drunkennesse,

[111] [Henry Walker], *Perfect Occurrences of Parliament And chief Collections of Letters from The
Lord Generall, Sir William Waller, the Lord Fairfaxes quarters, and others concerning Lyme,
Derby, York, Oxford, Gloster, and other parts of the Kingdome*, no. 23 (May 24, 1644).
[112] H[enry] Walker, *An Elogie or Eulogie on the Obits of the Right Honorable Ferdinando Lord
Fairefax* (London, 1648).
[113] *An Account of the Last Houres*, 1.   [114] *Ibid.*, 2.   [115] *Ibid.*, 2–3.
[116] Henry Walker, *A Gad of Steele, wrought and tempered for the Heart to defend it from being
battred by Sathans temptation, and to give it a sharpe and lasting edge in heavenly Consolation*
(London, 1641).
[117] *Ibid.*, i.

Swearing, Cosening [that is, deceit]," and other sins.[118] Certainty of God's salvation brought comfort; sin brought misery. Walker had his readers imagine the unrepentant man at the hour of death: "God the Father will not give him one smile, but is full of displeasure against him; God the Son, gives him sentence to depart from him, and will not spare him one drop of his Bloud; God the Holy Ghost, leaves him a despairing Conscience."[119]

In a sermon published in 1642, Walker spoke of bad humors and tempers, two words for emotions, among other things.[120] He railed against the man of bad humor, the "Papsticall Atheist," who thought predestination "*a very dangerous Doctrine, able to drive men to despaire.*"[121] Those of "a more indifferent temper" were not so impious as the papists, but "yet through idle *curiosity*, are dangerously transported, from embracing the means and way of salvation prescribed to make question how many, or what others shall be saved?"[122] Indeed, the sermon was largely aimed at the "humor" of curiosity, for it was found in "the most part of men."[123] Curiosity was an emotion that Walker (like Augustine and Aelred) condemned.[124]

In a sermon preached at Whitehall in 1649, Walker expounded on the various spirits that filled men. Some "had a spirit but theirs was a spirit of fears and of bondage"; others were "quick and nimble to act for God: when the Spirit of God is powerfull upon the heart of a believer, it doth make him act powerfully and couragiously."[125] Courage was good, fear bad. Love was good: "Let this stirre up your affection to an holy duty, be in love with the Word of God, with the Ordinances of God, with the People of God, with Prayer; for, by this meanes there is a great injoyment

---

[118] *Ibid.*, 1–2. "Happiness," based on the Middle-English *happ*, was coming increasingly to be used in place of "felicity," and (according to Phil Withington, "The Modern Invention of Happiness," paper read at conference on Renaissance Continuities and Discontinuities, July 22–23, 2014, Northwestern University), reached a high frequency of use (based on the materials in EEBO) during the period 1651–60. See below at n. 171 for the changing meanings of happiness during the seventeenth century. Middle English *Happi* could be used as a synonym for blissfull, as in the 1425 *Medulla Grammatice* (a Latin-Middle English glossary), but its usual Middle English meaning was "chance," "luck," or "fortune." It does not figure as an emotion on the lists for Margery Kempe or the Pastons.

[119] *Ibid.*, 6.

[120] See Burton, *Anatomy*, 1:372: "bad humours are radicall in every one of us, causing these perturbations, affections, and severall distempers."

[121] *The Sermon of Henry Walker, Ironmonger: Having beene twice Apprehended, for Writing seditious Pamphlets* (London, 1642), [2].

[122] *Ibid.*, [3].   [123] *Ibid.*

[124] See the discussion of curiosity in Chapters 1 (at n. 52) and 4 (at n. 55).

[125] Henry Walker, *A Sermon, Preached In the Kings Chappell at White-Hall* (n.p., 1649), 4, 6.

of God."[126] Such enjoyment brought "comfort" and roused men "to doe [any duty] chearfully."[127]

A year later, preaching at Somerset House the day after Thomas Fairfax had resigned as Commander in Chief of the army and Cromwell had taken his place, Walker took up the issue of Lot and Abram's separation (Gen. 13).[128] Fairfax and Cromwell had been like Lot and Abram, sharing their journey until they had prospered so well that they could no longer "dwell together" (Gen. 13:6). Walker's preoccupation was whether they still loved one another. They did: "Their separation one from the other ... was Personal, not in affection, their Love was as sincere as before."[129] Abram's desire to avoid strife was a "humble motion unto *Lot*, for continuance of love and affection between them."[130] Further, God comforted Abram, as he later comforted Silas and Timothy when Paul was separated from them (Acts 17:14). And in general, while "a naturall man that is unregenerated" – an unbeliever – finds no enjoyment and no comfort, a "believer ... receives inward consolations from his spirit, and there he doth chearfully repose himself."[131] The sorrows of an unbeliever are legion: "he murmures, repines, and wasteth himself in discontent." The believer, however, "hath communion with his God, and the sweete smiling fatherly countenance of God in Christ to him, fills his heart with an abundance of matter to stir him up to praise the Lord his God."[132]

Like Margery Kempe, Walker saw redemptive value in shedding tears and bearing the scorn of others:

When the people of God are weeping and humbling themselves for sinne, prophane persons deride and scorne them, and despise their fastings, and mournings; but herein they professe themselves to be not enemies only to the Lords people, but even to God himselfe: and believers have this comfort, that let ungodly men malign them never so much, they know that as for them their prayers are to God.[133]

In short, Henry Walker did not seek to tamp down *all* emotions; rather, he valued and emphasized some (and their objects) and devalued others. Table 8.4 offers a list of his approved and disapproved emotions.

---

[126] *Ibid.*, 11.

[127] *Ibid.*, 12, 15. Cheer is also invoked (17) as a proper emotion for the army marching into Ireland: "How much have we had *Gods* love appeared to us, and have much more, should we go cheerfully to destroy Idolaters and Rebels."

[128] Henry Walker, *A Sermon Preached in the Chappel at Somerset-House in the Strand* (London, 1650).

[129] *Ibid.*, 3.   [130] *Ibid.*   [131] *Ibid.*, 7–8.   [132] *Ibid.*, 9.   [133] *Ibid.*, 15.

Table 8.4 *Emotions valued and devalued by Walker*

Valued emotions	Devalued emotions
cheerfulness	curiosity
comfort	despair
courage	discontent
enjoyment of God	fear
happiness	misery/sorrow/ephemeral joy
hope	
love/affection	
pity	
sadness at others' sins	

Privileging justice and happiness

Not long before *Spirituall Experiences* was published, a different group – known, to their chagrin, as the Levellers – sought not comfort but justice.[134] They were certain that God's law was equivalent to natural law, equity, and justice.[135] The chief propagandists, writers, and spokesmen for the Levellers were John Lilburne, Thomas Prince, Richard Overton, and William Walwyn.[136] Women "signed Leveller petitions and participated in Leveller demonstrations," and at least one, Katherine Childley, was "of the second rank of leadership."[137] Most Levellers were Londoners, and on the whole the men had experience in London city government.[138] From the start, their supporters were "the tradesmen, craftsmen, and apprentices who populated sectarian congregations."[139] They met in nonconformist

---

[134] A recent study of Leveller thought is Rachel Foxley, *The Levellers: Radical Political Thought in the English Revolution* (Manchester, 2013). Although treating Leveller language and its notions of human nature, Foxley does not touch on Leveller emotions.

[135] See J. C. Davis, "The Levellers and Christianity," in *Politics, Religion and the English Civil War*, ed. Brian Manning (London, 1973), 225–50 and below at n. 157, for Lilburne's conflation of the various laws.

[136] Others included John Wildman, Edward Sexby, Colonel Thomas Rainsborough, Maximilian Petty, Captain William Bray; see *The Writings of William Walwyn*, ed. Jack R. McMichael and Barbara Taft [henceforth WW] (Athens, GA, 1989), 30–31, 46.

[137] Ian Gentles, "London Levellers in the English Revolution: The Chidleys and Their Circle," *Journal of Ecclesiastical History* 29 (1978): 281–309 at 282.

[138] Philip Baker, "*Londons Liberty in Chains Discovered*: The Levellers, the Civic Past, and Popular Protest in Civil War London," *Huntington Library Quarterly* 76/4 (2013): 559–87.

[139] WW, 23. Walwyn generally claimed that he was not part of a separatist church, but, according to David R. Como, "An Unattributed Pamphlet by William Walwyn: New Light on the Prehistory of the Leveller Movement," *Huntington Library Quarterly* 59/3 (2006): 353–82 at 357, "By 1645, Walwyn's sympathies and associations appear to have been entirely with the sects."

churches much like the one led by Henry Walker, and they joined forces as pamphleteers.[140] Some, like Lilburne, joined the army, though Leveller support from the army rank and file was relatively muted.[141] On the whole, "support for the Levellers was neither broad nor deep."[142] But the group was well organized and capable of taking a constructive leadership role.[143] The Levellers identified themselves with "the people" and recognized only the jurisdiction of elected representatives. After the execution of Charles I in January 1649, Lilburne, Walwyn, Prince, and Overton summed up their ideas:

finding after eight years' experience and expectation, all endeavours hitherto used or remedies hitherto applied to have increased rather than diminished our distractions, and that if not speedily prevented, our falling again into factions and divisions will not only deprive us of the benefit of all those wonderful victories God hath vouchsafed against such as sought our bondage, but expose us first to poverty and misery, and then to be destroyed by foreign enemies; and being earnestly desirous to make a right use of that opportunity God hath given us to make this nation free and happy; to reconcile our differences and beget a perfect amity and friendship once more amongst us, that we may stand clear in our consciences before Almighty God as unbiased by any corrupt interest or particular advantages, and manifest to all the world that our endeavours have not proceeded from malice to the persons of any, or enmity against opinions, but in reference to the peace and prosperity of the commonwealth and for prevention of like distractions and removal of all grievances: we the free people of England, to whom God hath given hearts, means and opportunity to effect the same, do with submission to His wisdom, in His name, and desiring the equity thereof may be to His praise and glory, agree to ascertain our government, to abolish all arbitrary power and to set bounds and limits both to our supreme and all subordinate authority, and remove all known grievances.[144]

Note the emotions. "Free and happy" are paired, as though the one implies the other. "Amity and friendship" recall the language of Cicero and Rievaulx, now repurposed for a whole people. The Levellers constituted an emotional community. They knew one another; they strongly agreed on matters that they cared about deeply; they valued some emotions and devalued others (as we shall see); and they agreed on modes of emotional expression (especially strong claims delivered via pamphlets). That they were also interested in imposing their norms on others

---

[140] Baker, "*Londons Liberty*," 566; Como, "An Unattributed Pamphlet," 358; WW, 21.

[141] On Lilburne, see Andrew Sharp, "Lilburne, John (1615?–1657)," DNB (Oxford, 2004); online ed., Oct. 2006, www.oxforddnb.com/view/article/16654, accessed December 6, 2014.

[142] WW, 23.   [143] WW, 35.

[144] [John Lilburne et al.], *An agreement of the free people of England* [1 May 1649], in *The English Levellers*, ed. Andrew Sharp (Cambridge, 1998), online at www.constitution.org/lev/eng_lev_12.txt, accessed May 1, 2015.

illustrates precisely one of the points of this book: emotions should not be separated from whatever else communities were engaged in.[145] We must look for the ways in which emotions worked in tandem with these groups' political ideologies, self-interest, values, and beliefs (among other things). Emotions are not *only* political, but they are certainly *also* political.

Leveller thought grew out of at least two traditions: the religious sensibilities of the Puritans and the civic consciousness of Londoners.[146] David Como has identified the beginning of the movement with pamphlets printed in the wake of an anti-sectarian Presbyterian initiative.[147] In September 1645, a group of Presbyterians petitioned Parliament to act against the "many strange sects ... incorporating themselves into separate assemblies, setting up illiterate persons to be their pastors"– in short, calling for a ban on the sort of church that Henry Walker led.[148] The Presbyterians, generally members of propertied urban classes, had at one time been allies of the Puritans, but during the Civil War of the 1640s they sought greater social and religious stability.[149] They and their Parliamentary allies clamped down on sectarian spokesmen, imprisoning them for illegal pamphleteering. John Lilburne was among the victims.[150]

Responding to the Presbyterian challenge came a flurry of pamphlets from men who would soon form the core of the Levellers: *Strong Motives*, almost certainly by William Walwyn; *Englands Birth-right Justified*, probably by John Lilburne; and *Englands Lamentable Slaverie*, almost certainly by Walwyn.[151] The works were printed by at least one press operated by Richard Overton, another Leveller leader. David Como concludes that "a discrete and coherent network, or perhaps more colorfully a 'propaganda

---

[145] On the Levellers as a political movement, see David Wootton, "Leveller democracy and the Puritan Revolution," in *The Cambridge History of Political Thought, 1450–1700*, ed. J. H. Burns with Mark Goldie (Cambridge, 1991), 412–42.

[146] For the Puritan background, see D. B. Robertson, *Religious Foundations of Leveller Democracy* (New York, 1951), chap. 2; for the civic protest traditions, Baker, "*Londons Liberty*," 561–65.

[147] Como, "An Unattributed Pamphlet," 365–67.

[148] *To the Right Honourable the Lords and Commons assembled in Parliament, the Humble Petition of [blank]* (1645) (accessed through EEBO).

[149] Keith Lindley, *Popular Politics and Religion in Civil War London* (Aldershot, 1997), 356–403; Michael Mahony, "Presbyterianism in the City of London, 1645–1647," *The Historical Journal* 22/1 (1979): 93–114.

[150] Como, "An Unattributed Pamphlet," 354.

[151] John Lilburne, *Englands birth-right justified against all arbitrary usurpation* (1645) (accessed via EEBO); Como, "An Unattributed Pamphlet," 367–70, noting (365 n. 20) that if Lilburne did not write all of *Englands Birth-right*, he almost certainly wrote the first seven pages; [William Walwyn], *Strong Motives or Loving and Modest advice, unto the Petitions for Presbiterian Government*, ibid., 377–82; William Walwyn, *Englands lamentable slaverie* (1645), bcw-project.org/texts/englands-lamentable-slaverie, accessed May 1, 2015.

collective,' had come together in London; at its core were Overton, Walwyn, and Lilburne."[152]

John Lilburne (1615?–57), the rallying figure of the collective, began his activist career as a committed religious Independent distributing illegal religious books. He was arrested in 1637 and, refusing to take the oath demanded of him by the Star Chamber, was condemned to be whipped through the streets and pilloried.[153] Back in prison, he wrote about the experience in *A Worke of the Beast*. The title page claimed that his account was "very usefull for these times both for the encouragement of the Godly to suffer, And for the terrour and shame of the Lords Adversaries," thus advertising the emotions it wished to evoke. Following a well-worn emotional path, Lilburne wrote that on the morning before his whipping, he prayed "to undergoe my Affliction with joyfullnes and courage." Finding consolation in words of Scripture, he "went to my suffering with as willing and joyfull a heart as if I had been going to solemnize the day of my maraige with one of the choysest Creatures this world could afford." When he was stripped and bound, he said (he reported) "Welcome to the Crosse of Christ."[154] Courage, cheerfulness, merriment, as well as a "holy disdaine" toward his tormenters: these were the emotions he reported feeling as he was whipped through the streets.[155] He focused on the prerogatives God's love gave him rather than the uncertainty of his faith, "I being one of his chosen ones."[156] We have seen most of these emotions, apart from Lilburne's absolute conviction of being among God's elect, already in the testimonials in *Spirituall Experiences*. But Lilburne connected liberty of faith with a new stress on the laws of the state. For him there should be no distinction between "the Law of God, the Law of the Land, the glory of God, the honour of the King of state."[157] Indeed, all of these were the equivalent of "natural law": when he refused to take the oath demanded by the Star Chamber, he "refuted [it] as a sinfull and unlawful Oath: it being the High-Commission Oath, with which the Prelates ever have and still do so butcherly torment, afflict and undoe, the deare Saints and Servants

---

[152] Como, "An Unattributed Pamphlet," 370; affirming that the Levellers constituted an organization, see Norah Carlin, "Leveller Organization in London," *The Historical Journal* 27/4 (1984): 955–60.

[153] On the Star Chamber, see Daniel L. Vande Zande, "Coercive Power and the Demise of the Star Chamber," *American Journal of Legal History* 50/3 (2008–2010): 326–49, esp. 331–34.

[154] John Lilburne, *A Worke of the Beast or A Relation of a most unchristian Censure, Executed upon Iohn Lilburne, (Now prisoner in the fleet) the 18. of Aprill 1638 with the heavenly speech uttered by him at the time of his suffering* (1638), 3–5 (accessed via EEBO).

[155] *Ibid.*, 6.

[156] *Ibid.*, 4. On the Leveller belief in universal salvation, see Davis, "The Levellers," 230–31.

[157] Lilburne, *A Worke of the Beast*, 20.

Table 8.5 *A Leveller list of vices*

ambition
arbitrary will
carelessness
corruption
covetousness
cowardliness
injustice
negligence
severity
simplicity
slavery
unfaithfulness
variableness

of God, It is also an Oath against the Law of the Land ... Againe it is absolutely against the Law of God ... With all this Oath is against the very law of nature."[158]

Walwyn's *Englands Lamentable Slaverie*, among the first identifiably "Leveller" tracts, began with a series of grievances – sounding very much like vices, old mingled with new: "Proceeding from the Arbitrarie will, severitie, and Injustices of Kings, Negligence, corruption, and unfaithfulnesse of Parliaments, Coveteousnesse, ambition and variablenesse of Priests, and simplicitie, carelesnesse, and cowardlinesse of People."[159] The grievances/vices in this tract are summarized in Table 8.5.

Covetousness (in the guise of greed and cupidity) had already been one of Cicero's "perturbations." Aelred of Rievaulx had classed ambition with envy and suspicion as charity's chief enemies, and he had depicted sinful human beings, buffeted by many contrary emotions, as variable. Unfaithfulness had been bewailed at the court of Toulouse. Gerson had made courage one of the passions; its opposite was cowardliness. In short, some of Walwyn's grievances had long been considered emotions. The others, while perhaps not quite emotions themselves, were, by their association with the others, meant to energize a new political program. The Levellers redirected old vices and emotions toward public outrages.

Writing as "a true Lover of his Countrey and a faithfull friend to that worthy Instrument of Englands Freedome, Lieuten. Collonnell Lilburn,"

---

[158] *Ibid.*, 12–13.
[159] All quotations are taken from the online version bcw-project.org/texts/englands-lamentable-slaverie .

Walwyn's good faith and friendship were directed not just to one or a few people, but to England itself. Similarly he praised Lilburne "for your constant zealous affection to the Common Wealth, and for your undaunted resolution in defence of the common freedome of the People." He spoke of his compassion for Lilburne, drawing on an emotion already highly prized by Aelred and Gerson: "who are they that would be thought Christians, and can exempt themselves for suffering with [men who suffer]? . . . If one suffer, all ought to suffer with that one, even by having a sympathie and fellow feeling of his miserie, and helping to beare his burden; so that he may be eased in the day of tentation." That Lilburne was in prison "was very sad newes to all that love you," and when they heard that he was in the worst prison of all, "they were confounded with griefe."

For Walwyn, Lilburne's imprisonment mirrored England's bondage. Just as Lilburne had once been a free man, so England had once been a free land. Walwyn invoked the "peoples rights and liberties." Before the Norman Conquest, those had been guaranteed to Englishmen. With that conquest they had to be once again "wrestled out of the pawes of those Kings, who by force had conquered the Nation, changed the lawes and by strong hand held them in bondage." The struggle had involved "much striving and fighting" and the shedding of "the blood of our Ancestors." Now Parliament threatened to revoke those hard-won liberties, and Lilburne, a true hero, had defied it, "alledging it to be against your liberty, as you were a free borne Englishman, to answer to questions against your selfe, urging MAGNA CHARTA to justifie your so doing." Walwyn praised Lilburne as the first to liken the Parliamentary Committee of Examinations to the royal Star Chamber. No one – no king, no Parliament – had the right to infringe certain human rights. "A Parliamentary authority is a power intrusted by the people (that chose them) for their good, safetie, and freedome; and therefore . . . a Parliament cannot justlie doe any thing, to make the people lesse safe or lesse free, then they found them."

Although the printer of Walwyn's pamphlet put the words Magna Carta in capital letters, Walwyn considered that document a paltry concession, made by one of the conquering kings and abridged by successive monarchs thereafter, often with "the unnaturall assistance of Parliaments to helpe them." Meanwhile, Parliament occupied itself with ridiculous matters. Here Walwyn used wry irony: "See how busie they have been about the regulating of petty inferiour trades and exercises, about the ordering of hunting, who should keep Deere and who should not, who should keep a Greayhound, and who a Pigeon-house, what punishment for Deere stealing, what for every Pigeon killed, contrary to law, who should weare cloth of such a price, who Velvet, Gold, and Silver, what wages poore Labourers should have and the like precious and rare businesse, being most of them put on of purpose to divert them from the very thoughts of freedome."

Whence this emphasis on political freedom, which we have not seen before? It came, to be sure, from the Reformation, which emphasized the "freedom of the Christian."[160] But it was also embedded in the language of citizenship, which talked of "liberties," "privileges," "franchises," and "immunities."[161] Already in 1642, Henry Colthrop, "sometime Recorder of London," collected and commented on *The liberties, usages, and customes of the city of London*. His discussion was organized alphabetically in order to serve as a handy reference tool for looking up the rights and exemptions of London's citizenry.[162] Four years later, Lilburne, writing on behalf of the thwarted attempt of some London citizens to vote for mayor, published in full the privilege for London issued by King John: he had it printed in Latin, provided an English translation, and added a long commentary.[163] Here he revealed yet another direct inspiration: the Roman Republic: "All free Cities, lest their government should become a tyranny, and their Governours, through ambition and misgovernment, take liberty to oppresse and inslave the people to their lusts and wils; have in their first Constitutions provided, that all their Officers and Magistrats should be elective *By Votes and Approbation* of the free people of each City; and no longer to continue then a yeare, (as the *Annuall Consuls in Rome*.)."[164]

In the same pamphlet, Lilburne asserted "that all lawfull powers reside in the people, for whose good, welfare, and happiness, all government and just policies were ordained."[165] The happiness that good government was

---

[160] For example, in England, Friedrich van Hulsius, *The character of a Christian as hee is distinguished from all hypocrites and hereticks. With the freedome of the faithfull: as they are proposed by our Saviour, in the words of the Gospell* (London, 1627); George Downame, *The Christians freedome wherein is fully expressed the doctrine of Christian libertie* (Oxford, 1635); John Milton, *The doctrine and discipline of divorce: restor'd to the good of both sexes, from the bondage of Canon Law, and other mistakes, to Christian freedom, guided by the Rule of Charity* (London, 1643). On the relationship between religious and Leveller ideas, see Foxley, *Levellers*, 119–49.

[161] See *ibid.*, 91–118; Baker, "*Londons Liberty*"; Ian V. Archer, "Popular Politics in the Sixteenth and Early Seventeenth Centuries," in *Londinopolis: Essays in the Cultural and Social History of Early Modern London*, ed. Paul Griffiths and Mark S. R. Jenner (Manchester, 2000), 26–46; Rosenwein, *Negotiating Space*, 184–212.

[162] Henry Colthrop, *The Liberties, usages, and customes of the city of Lond; confirmed by especiall Acts of Parliament ...* (London, 1642).

[163] John Lilburne, *Londons Liberty in Chains discovered* (London, 1646). He followed up with a collection of other important city charters. See Baker, "*Londons Liberty*," 572–78.

[164] Lilburne, *Londons Liberty*, 2. On p. 7 Lilburne asks rhetorically, "Did *Rome* ever so flourish, as when, no any thing was done but by the Senate and People there?"

[165] *Ibid.*, 2.

to provide was matched by the sorrow that bad government induced. Nor was this purely abstract: "though I am not a Citizen, yet no stranger, nor foreigner, but a freeman of *England*, who hathe freely hazarded all, for the recovery of the common Liberty, and my Countries freedome; and it is no small griefe unto me; yea, it lyes more heavy upon me, then all other my troubles undergone, to see our *Nationall and Fundamentall Lawes, Rights, and Priviledges, then trodden under foot.*"[166]

By 1649, after Charles I had been executed, Lilburne, Walwyn, Prince, and Overton, "(Now Prisoners in the Tower of *London*) And others, commonly (though unjustly) styled Levellers," declared happiness their ultimate goal: "Since no man is born for himself only, but obliged by the Laws of Nature (which reaches all)[,] of Christianity (which ingages us as Christians) and of Publick Societie and Government, to employ our endeavours for the advancement of a communitive Happinesse, of equall concernment to others as our selves: here have we . . . laboured with much weakness indeed, but with integrity of heart, to produce out of the Common Calamities, such a proportion of Freedom and good to the Nation, as might somewhat compensate its many grievances and lasting sufferings."[167] This "communitive happiness" was not the same as private contentment, which the writers could easily have: "'Tis a very great unhappinesse we well know, to be always struggling and striving in the world, and does wholly keep us from the enjoyment of those contentments our severall Conditions reach unto." The authors set the higher happiness that they sought against the passions that opposed them: "In doing thereof we have hitherto reaped only Reproach, and hatred for our good Will, and been faine to wrestle with the violent passions of Powers and Principalities."[168] They spoke of the "sincerity of our actions," and accused others of "being fed with Jealousies that there is more in our designs then appears, that there is something of danger in the bottom of our hearts, not yet discovered."[169] They could forgive all that, "but since the ends of such Rumors are purposely to make us uselesse and unserviceable to the Common-wealth, we are necessitated to open our breasts and shew the world our insides." Setting the record straight about their political program, the Levellers found a new way to achieve "Tranquillity of mind, and peace of Conscience."[170] Stoic *apatheia*, Aelredian peace, and the comfort that the believers of Walker's church

---

[166] *Ibid.*, 10.
[167] John Lilburne et al., *A Manifestation* ([April 16] 1649), 3. On the appearance of "happiness" as a value during the English Civil War, see Darrin M. McMahon, *Happiness: A History* (New York, 2006), 176–77.
[168] Lilburne et al., *A Manifestation*, 3.   [169] *Ibid.*, 4.   [170] *Ibid.*, 5.

sought and found were emotions here harnessed by men obsessed with politics.[171]

Curiosity and delight

A generation later, Leveller happiness seemed abstract and too "enthusiastic" to men like Samuel Pepys (1633–1703) and John Evelyn (1620–1706).[172] Pepys and Evelyn enjoyed life intensely, but it was a pleasure that grew, in the first place, from their curiosity and delight in sights, books, gardens, antiquities, arts, and the sciences. It also stemmed from their sense of doing all that duty required – of their work on behalf of their patrons, their monarch, and their professional undertakings. It grew equally out of the pleasures of friendship and association. And – particularly for Pepys – it came from being a "goodfellow" – a *bon vivant*.[173]

Evelyn and Pepys came from different social strata. Evelyn was of the gentry class. When confronted by some angry Frenchmen at Vanves (a suburb near Paris), he and his party were glad when their attackers came "at last to consider that we might be persons of quality (for at first they took us for burgers of Paris)."[174] Pepys *was* a burger: the son of a London tailor. Nevertheless, he had relatives in high places, and he made good use of the patronage of his well-connected cousin Edward Mountagu, later earl of Sandwich. Both Evelyn and Pepys came into their own with the Restoration of the monarchy under Charles II in 1660. Acquainted by the mid-1660s, they had become good friends by the end of Pepys' life in 1703.[175] Their initial work together involved their engagement in the Royal Navy Office in the 1660s, Pepys as Clerk of the Acts and Evelyn

---

[171] The use of the term "happiness" for the purposes of civil society was in part related to its new importance as the word for secular felicity (based, perhaps, on its Anglo-Saxon – hence popular – origins), and in part to the importation of classical ideas about individual and collective goals. On the new uses of the word happiness, see Paul Slack, "The Politics of Consumption and England's Happiness in the Later Seventeenth Century," *English Historical Review* 122/497 (2007): 609–31, esp. 629–31.

[172] See Michael Heyd, *Be Sober and Reasonable*; George Williamson, "The Restoration Revolt against Enthusiasm," *Studies in Philology* 30 (1933): 571–603. Michael MacDonald, "Religion, Social Change, and Psychological Healing in England, 1600–1800," in *The Church and Healing*, ed. W. J. Sheils (Oxford, 1982), 101–25, argues that a new elite railed against both religious enthusiasm and melancholy as forms of "madness" in order to suppress popular beliefs and the political subversion that (as the Civil War taught) came with radical religion.

[173] Samuel Pepys, *The Diary of Samuel Pepys*, ed. Robert Latham and William Matthews, 11 vols. (Berkeley, 1970), 1:xix. On Evelyn, see the articles in *John Evelyn and his Milieu*, ed. Frances Harris and Michael Hunter (London, 2003).

[174] John Evelyn, *The Diary of John Evelyn*, ed. E. S. de Beer, 6 vols. (Oxford, 1955), 3:5 (7 May 1650).

[175] *Particular Friends: The Correspondence of Samuel Pepys and John Evelyn*, ed. Guy de la Bédoyère (Woodbridge, 1997), 10–11.

as commissioner for the sick and wounded.[176] They attended the same church in London (the chapel at Exeter House), and both were early members of the Royal Society, founded in 1660.

They were – or aspired to be – "virtuosi": men of letters, connoisseurs of the arts and sciences. Evelyn's translation of the first book of Lucretius' *De rerum natura* included a "commentary in which he showed the relationship between Lucretius's views and the findings of modern scientists."[177] He wrote a large number of books.[178] His gardens, extensive library, and art collections were much admired. For his part, Pepys "by 1660 had already acquired ... the elements of the best general culture of the day: a classical and mathematical education, together with a curiosity about the fine arts and the sciences, if not yet an informed interest in them."[179] He played several musical instruments and "sang well."[180] But, by contrast to Evelyn, Pepys published only one book: *Memoires Relating to the State of the Royal Navy* (1690).[181]

Both men were acutely aware of their images. Pepys' diary, which was begun in 1660 and ended in 1669, was written in shorthand, but its "clean and shapely" appearance suggests that "he intended it to have some of the qualities of a printed book, something akin to the shorthand *Book of Psalms* that had recently been printed."[182] Evelyn's "diary," which covered nearly his entire life, was, like everything else he wrote, much worked over. Many parts were written long after the fact.[183] When the two friends wrote to one another, they (especially Evelyn) "sometimes made drafts [of their letters], and also additional copies in a letter-book."[184] They meant these writings for posterity. We shall not get "spontaneous" emotions from these two; lack of spontaneity was, indeed, one of the values of their emotional community.[185]

In point of fact, neither Pepys nor Evelyn regularly mentioned or expressed emotions. When they did, the emotions were often quite attenuated.[186] This must remind us of the Pastons. Pepys was the man of action. His diary gives the impression of constant motion:

---

[176] *Particular Friends*, 29.   [177] *The Diary of Evelyn*, 12 (de Beer's intro.).
[178] *The Writings of John Evelyn*, ed. Guy de la Bédoyère (Woodbridge, Suffolk, 1995), contains a selection of these writings.
[179] *Diary of Pepys*, 1:xix.   [180] *Ibid.*, 1:xxi.   [181] *Ibid.*, 1:xxxviii.   [182] *Ibid.*, 1:xlv.
[183] *Particular Friends*, 11–12.   [184] *Ibid.*, 12.
[185] Greyerz, *Vorsehungsglaube*, 16–18, points out that one should not expect "intimacy" in these diaries and that even Pepys wrote for an imagined public.
[186] Nevertheless, I take issue with Williamson, "Restoration Revolt," 599, when he writes that with the Restoration "emotion was definitely discredited." Certain forms of emotionality were undoubtedly discredited, but being "unemotional" is itself an emotional norm and value in the context of an emotional community.

19 [April 1664] Up and to St. James's [Palace] where long with Mr. [William] Coventry, [Thomas] Povey, &c. in their Tanger [Tangier Committee] accounts. But such the folly of that coxcomb Povey that we could do little in it. And so parted for that time, and I to walk with [John] Creed and [Philibert] Vernatz in the physique garden [the Physic Garden, a medicinal garden] in St. James Park, where I first saw Orange trees and other fine trees. So to Westminster-hall and thence by water to the Temple; and so walked to the Change [the Royal Exchange] and there find the Change full of news from Guiny [Guinea]: some say the Dutch have sunk our ships and taken our fort, and others say we have done the same to them ... So home to dinner and then to the office, and at night with Captain [John] Taylor, consulting how to get a little money by letting him the *Elias* [a warship] to fetch masts from New England. So home to supper and to bed.[187]

Entries such as this project a man of affairs, not sentiment. Or, rather, sentiment was often linked to business. Thus Pepys spoke of his "short melancholly leave of my father and mother, without having time to drink or say anything of business one to another."[188] The drink signified conviviality; the business gave him a sense of well-being. For March 13, 1662, his entire entry was as follows: "All day either at the office or at home, busy about business till late at night – I having lately fallowed my business much. And I find great pleasure in it, and a growing content."[189] He was fulfilling Burton's utopia, where everyone was busy and no one melancholy.[190]

Evelyn's diary was less concerned with movement than with observation and description. While Pepys contented himself with a quick mention of the orange trees in St. James's Park, Evelyn's diary entry not long afterward paid close attention to Sir John Shaw's new house:

the place is pleasant if not too wett, but the house not well contrived, especially the roofe, & roomes too low pitch'd & *Kitchins* where the Cellars should be: The *Orangerie* & *Aviarie* handsome, & a very large plantation about it.[191]

Evelyn himself drew up plans for buildings and published that same year a book on trees.[192] He knew whereof he spoke. Like Pepys, he was a man of affairs, attuned to the outer, not the inner world. His own busyness – and pride in it – is clear in his letters connected with his work as commissioner

---

[187] *Diary of Pepys*, 5:127. For the annotations, I have relied on those available at www.pepysdiary.com/archive/1664/04.

[188] *Ibid.*, 1:93 (March 20, 1660).   [189] *Ibid.*, 3:45 (March 13, 1662).

[190] See above at n. 68.   [191] *Diary of Evelyn*, 3:376 (July 14, 1664).

[192] For his book on trees, John Evelyn, *Sylva, or a Discourse of Forest Trees*, published in 1664 together with *Pomona*, a treatise on fruit trees, and *Kalendarium Hortense*, a garden almanac, see *Diary of Evelyn*, 1:16 (intro.). For his buildings, see his plans for a new infirmary at Chatham in *Particular Friends*, 60–65.

for the sick and wounded during the Second Anglo-Dutch War (1665–67). To Pepys he wrote in his official capacity:

I have ... put all things in perfect order, save my selfe, who have never been in bed since Saturday last ... Unless you be pleased to allow some covering to the poor creatures [wounded and sick sailors], who are (many of them) put stark naked and mortified on the shore, multitudes of them must perish. And therefore ... I have adventured to give way that some of the miserable should have shirts or stockings (according to their needs) to preserve them from perishing: and I do by these beg of you, to Order your Slope sellers [sellers of cheap seaman's clothing] to send a Competent number of such necessaries ...[193]

Meanwhile, Pepys, for his part, could be observant. At the Assay Office, he "saw the manner of essaying of gold and Silver, and how silver melted down with gold doth part again, being put into aqua fartis [nitric acid], the silver turning into water [dissolving] and the gold lying whole in the very form it was put in, mixed of gold and silver."[194] The end of this diary entry contains a long description of the manufacture of coins.

Curiosity was recognized at the time as an emotion, as we saw in Table 8.4 and shall see in Chapter 9. But we may see also more obvious sorts of emotions in the writings of these men. Of Mrs. Godolphin, a young woman at court with whom Evelyn had a passionate, if platonic, friendship, he wrote that she is "the person in the world whom I esteemed as my owne life."[195] Less complicated was the affection of Evelyn and Pepys for one another. When Evelyn learned that Pepys had escaped a shipwreck, he wrote, "I have ben both very Long, and very-much concern'd for you, since your Northern Voyage ... and that the dismal Accident was past, which gave me apprehensions for you, and a mixture of Passions, not realy to be Express'd, 'til I was assur'd of your Safty; and I now give God Thankes for it with as much Sincerity, as any Friend you have alive."[196] Pepys, in turn, commissioned a portrait of Evelyn and wrote that he wanted it because of his "Gratitude, Affection and Esteeme."[197]

---

[193] *Ibid.*, 79 (August 27, 1672). [194] *Diary of Pepys*, 4:143 (May 19, 1663).

[195] *Diary of Evelyn*, 4:80 (November 14, 1675). More often Evelyn referred to Mrs. Godolphin as "my dear friend," as, for example, *ibid.*, 4:79 (November 10, 1675). After her premature death, he wrote her biography: John Evelyn, *The Life of Mrs. Godolphin*, ed. Harriet Sampson (Oxford, 1939). On their relationship, see Frances Harris, *Transformations of Love: The Friendship of John Evelyn and Margaret Godolphin* (Oxford, 2002).

[196] *Particular Friends*, 131 (June 5, 1682). It would seem that the valedictory "Your most affectionate and humble servant," which both used at the beginning of their correspondence (for example, Pepys to Evelyn, *Particular Friends*, 92; Evelyn to Pepys, *ibid.*, 55) in fact betokened a more formal relationship. When they had really become friends, the term "affectionate" was rarely used. In 1692, Evelyn called Pepys his "best and worthiest friend," *ibid.*, 233 (August 29, 1692).

[197] *Ibid.*, 205 (August 30, 1689).

Equally important was the affection that Pepys and Evelyn felt for their family members. When Pepys had to leave his wife to go on a journey, he was "very sad in mind to part with my wife tomorrow, but God's will be done."[198] Later he was intensely jealous of her time with her dancing master and also ashamed of feeling that way:

Now, so deadly full of jealousy I am, that my heart and head did so cast about and fret, that I could not do any business possibly, but went out to my office; and anon late home again, and ready to chide at everything; and then suddenly to bed and could hardly sleep, yet durst not say anything ... But it is a deadly folly and plague that I bring upon myself to be so jealous ... But I am ashamed to think what a course I did take by lying to see whether my wife did wear drawers today as she used to do.[199]

When his brother was sick, "it made me weep to see that he should not be able, when I asked him, to say who I was."[200]

Evelyn's pain upon the elopement of his daughter Elizabeth should remind us of the Pastons' feelings when their daughter married their steward: "'tis my hard fate to suffer an irremediless affront ... I ... confesse it harder to me, than had ben her Death."[201] But when Elizabeth died, he likens it to the loss of his oldest daughter, Mary, whose death left him and his wife filled with "unspeakable sorrow and affliction."[202]

Did these men ever get angry? Pepys often spoke of being vexed, though he acted on it only when prudence allowed. Thus, he was willing to scold a servant who told "his mistress that he would not be made a slave of – which vexes me."[203] On the other hand, although "indeed a little vexed," he "said nothing" when he discovered that Edward Shipley, Mountagu's steward, had broken into his study to find a key. When Evelyn's daughter eloped, he spoke of the "disgrace" and wished he might find "the best remedies to allay the passion and Indignation of an injur'd parent and a Man."[204] But, like the Pastons, he restrained himself: "I ... abhorr the meane stratagem, of the betrayers and unworthy Abettors: In my Life was I never addicted to Revenge, (especialy on meane persons)." When he learned from her sister of Mrs. Godolphin's marriage, initially kept secret from him, Evelyn wrote: "Visited Mrs. *Godolphin* [and] expostulated with her about the concealement, & was satisfied, it was not her intention."[205]

---

[198] *Diary of Pepys*, 1.89 (March 16, 1660).   [199] *Ibid.*, 4:140 (May 15, 1663).

[200] *Ibid.*, 5:84 (March 14, 1664).

[201] *Particular Friends*, 149–54 (July 19 – August 3, 1685). For the Pastons in a similar position, see above, Chapter 6 at n. 209.

[202] *Diary of Evelyn*, 4:420 (March 14, 1685).

[203] *Diary of Pepys*, 3:35 (February 24, 1662). For vexation as an emotion, see Table 8.2.

[204] For Pepys' vexation with Shipley, see *Diary of* Pepys 1:71 (February 28, 1660); for Evelyn's reaction to the abduction, see *Particular Friends*, 149-50 (July 29, 1685).

[205] *Diary of Evelyn*, 4:90 (May 3, 1676).

Pepys spoke of pleasure and merriment more than Evelyn; Evelyn was more often sad and sorry than Pepys.[206] Members of emotional communities may have their own personal "takes" on the emotions that they value. But common to both men was undoubtedly an emotional sensibility that privileged delight on the one hand and sorrow on the other.[207]

What sort of theory could make sense of all the diverse emotions of the seventeenth century? What theorist could embrace both melancholy and curiosity under one umbrella term? As we shall see in Chapter 9, Thomas Hobbes' theory did exactly that.

---

[206] Pepys was almost invariably "merry" when dining with others. That this may have been a social rather than emotional norm is suggested by his comment, early in diary, that "we were as merry as I could frame myself to be in that company." *Diary of Evelyn*, 1:29 (January 26, 1660). He got great enjoyment from his musical activities, for example *ibid.*, 1:76 (March 5, 1660): "Early in the morning, Mr. Hill comes to string my theorbo, which we were about 'til past 10 o'clock, with a great deal of pleasure."

[207] See McMahon, *Happiness*, chap. 3, on the twin focus on melancholy and happiness during this period.

9   Hobbes' motions

"7th September. I went to visit Mr. Hobbes, the famous philosopher of Malmesbury, with whom I had long acquaintance. From his windows, we saw the whole equipage and glorious cavalcade of the young French Monarch, Louis XIV, passing to Parliament." So wrote John Evelyn in his diary for the year 1651. He marveled at the splendid parade of officers, nobility, and servants, and "the King himself like a young Apollo."[1]

Thomas Hobbes (1588–1679), born of "obscure parentage" in Malmesbury, England, was educated at Oxford and spent most of his life as tutor and librarian for the Cavendish family, apart from a few other stints, as for example as math tutor to the future Charles II in exile.[2] What Hobbes thought of the procession of Louis XIV we do not know. But he must have had considerably more than Apollonian kings on his mind. Only a few months before, he had published his *Leviathan* in England and in English – even though he had been living in Paris since 1640. The book justified the new Parliamentary authority under Cromwell as much as it justified kings: self-preservation required people to obey whatever regime protected them.

---

[1] *The Diary of Evelyn*, 2:39–41. Hobbes and Evelyn may have met c. 1646 in Paris, where Hobbes was working as tutor in mathematics to the future Charles II in exile. The two men, if not exactly part of the same "set," had many acquaintances in common. See Gillian Darley, *John Evelyn: Living for Ingenuity* (New Haven, 2006), 68, 96, 109, 115. But by the 1680s, Evelyn found Locke's works, which made room for God, more to his taste than Hobbes'; *ibid.*, 280, and in John Evelyn, *Numismata. A discourse of medals, antient and modern. Together with some account of heads and effigies of illustrious and famous persons, in sculps, and taille-douce, of whom we have no medals extant; and of the use to be derived from them. To which is added a digression concerning physiognomy* (London, 1697), 341, he had unflattering things to say about Hobbes' very looks: "a supercilious, Saturnine Opiniatrety [i.e. melancholy obstinacy], pleased with himself." I thank Thomas Dixon for bibliographical help and Francesco Cerrato for reading an earlier draft of this chapter.

[2] For biographical information I rely generally on Noel Malcolm, "Hobbes, Thomas (1588–1679)," DNB (Oxford, 2004); online ed., Sept. 2010, www.oxforddnb.com/view/article/13400, accessed June 19, 2014. The term "obscure parentage" is Hobbes' own, though he does not directly apply it to himself. See Thomas Hobbes, *Leviathan* 10.45, ed. J. C. A. Gaskin (Oxford, 1996) [henceforth *Lev.*], 62.

In Chapter 6 of the *Leviathan*, Hobbes presented a list of "voluntary motions; commonly called the passions."[3] His discussion so early in the book of what he called "motions" – clearly an ancestor of our term "emotions" – suggests that he considered them to constitute an important foundation for his moral and political philosophy. Indeed, he had already talked about the emotions in *The Elements of Law Natural and Politic* (1640), which circulated in manuscript until it was published as two separate books, *Human Nature* and *De corpore politico*, in 1650. These, along with *De cive* (1642), which also had a few things to say about emotions, were no doubt the works that led Evelyn to call Hobbes "the famous philosopher of Malmesbury." Later, in 1655, Hobbes published *De corpore* (part 1 of his *Elements of Philosophy*) with an English translation the following year, and in 1658 his *De homine* appeared, each with further thoughts about the role of the passions in human nature.

Let us first consider Hobbes' theory of voluntary motions. Afterward, we will explore a few of the ways in which it compares with earlier theories of the passions, as well as how it fits into the context of the emotional communities we explored in Chapter 8.

Passionate controversies

"Hobbes generated more hostile literature than any other thinker in the seventeenth century," is the recent lapidary conclusion of G. A. J. Rogers, whose article nevertheless also points out that "Hobbes always had plenty of friends."[4] The controversy continues today even on the issue of Hobbes' theory of the passions. Let us quickly review the sides via the radically different verdicts of Bernard Gert and Francesco Cerrato.

For Gert, Hobbes' theory of the voluntary motions is imperfectly realized, inconsistent, and derivative: "Once Hobbes has the concepts of appetite and aversion, pleasure and pain, his account of the individual passions completely ignores the relation between human behavior and his materialist philosophy. He simply proceeds by way of introspection and experience, along with liberal borrowings from Aristotle's account of the

---

[3] *Ibid.*, 6, pp. 33–42.
[4] G. A. J. Rogers, "Hobbes and His Contemporaries," in *The Cambridge Companion to Hobbes's Leviathan*, ed. Patricia Springborg (Cambridge, 2007), 413–40, quotes at 413 and 432. For more on the reception of Hobbes, see Jeffrey R. Collins, "Silencing Thomas Hobbes: The Presbyterians and *Leviathan*," in *The Cambridge Companion to Hobbes's Leviathan*, 478–500, who makes clear that the chief cause of his suppression were the Presbyterians (who were also responsible for suppressing sectarian groups such as those of Walker's church and those who would soon become the Levellers, as we saw in Chapter 8 at n. 150).

passions."[5] Further, for all of Hobbes' interest in defining his terms, Gert observes that "Hobbes did not take the definitions that he offered in Chapter VI of *Leviathan* very seriously."[6] By way of example, Gert points to Hobbes' definition of diffidence in one place as "constant despair" while in another he uses it as the equivalent of "fear" when talking about "the causes of quarrel."[7] Finally, in Gert's view, Hobbes was not really all that interested in the passions, since "all of the premises about human nature, which Hobbes claims are true of all persons and which he uses in arguing for the necessity of an unlimited sovereign, are in fact statements about the rationally required desires, and not, as most commentators have taken them, statements about the passions."[8]

Cerrato, by contrast, speaks of the "originalità" of Hobbes' approach to the passions.[9] Unlike all other theorists of the time, Hobbes did not imagine that there was a way – via the will or reason or even God's grace – for men to control their own passions. He did not "ignore" the relationship between human behavior and materialism; rather it was the crux of his whole argument. Hobbes assumed that human beings taken individually would have as many passions as they had different bodies, interests, and life experiences.[10] He "did not write a manual on human behavior (*un manuale di comportamento*) because he knew how impossible it was to pursue such an objective given the multitude of affects – so complex, multiform and continually changing."[11] This meant that Hobbes' definitions were provisional: real emotions were always in flux. "Hatred can become anger, which in its turn can be transformed into fear. Fear can change into hope which . . . can turn into joy."[12] Thus, Hobbes' "diffidence" really did include *both* despair and fear. More precisely, for Cerrato, diffidence "is the emotion that is produced as the immediate consequence of a multiplicity of competitive passions. It consists in the fear of another and his ability to cause us harm."[13] Finally, Cerrato argues that Hobbes founded absolute sovereignty not only on "rational desires" but also on certain passions, above all the fear of death, though perhaps that is one of Gert's "rationally required desires."[14] However, the "*necessity* of an unlimited sovereign" is certainly (for

---

[5] Bernard Gert, "Hobbes's Psychology," in *The Cambridge Companion to Hobbes*, ed. Tom Sorell (Oxford, 1996), 157–74 at 160.

[6] *Ibid.*, 162.   [7] *Ibid.*, 161.

[8] *Ibid.*, 164. Gert (164–65) does find Hobbes' discussion of the passions to anticipate some modern findings and debates about emotions.

[9] Francesco Cerrato, *Un secolo di passioni e politica. Hobbes, Descartes, Spinoza* (Rome, 2012), 14.

[10] *Ibid.*, 15.   [11] *Ibid.*, 16.   [12] *Ibid.*, 31.

[13] *Ibid.*, 44, and more generally 39–49 on the desire of human beings to control the future and the anxieties (including diffidence) that that desire provokes.

[14] *Ibid.*, 51.

Cerrato) provided by the passions. Aimed, as they are, at pleasures, particularly future pleasures, they are inevitably frustrated, leading to anxiety and its
progeny: "sorrow, mistrust, and aggression (*dolore, diffidenza e aggressività*),"
the causes of conflict that only the sovereign is able to suppress.[15]

Passions as motions

Let us consider this disputed theory.[16] Like Thomas Aquinas and
Augustine before him, Hobbes began, at least in his earlier work, *Human
Nature*, with the various faculties of man. But for Hobbes this was all so pro
forma that he let his words trail off: "Man's nature is the sum of his natural
faculties and power, as the faculties of nutrition, motion, generation, sense,
reason, &c."[17] Unlike his predecessors, however, Hobbes was not much
interested in reason (we shall soon see why). His focus was the faculty of
sense and how it interacted with things outside of it. For Hobbes, both the
things outside and the things within human beings were in constant
motion. For this, Hobbes adopted Galileo's new theory of inertia. It said
(contrary to Aristotle) that an object in motion would remain in motion at a
constant speed and in the same direction unless acted upon by something
external to itself. An object at rest would remain at rest unless acted upon.
Indeed, an object at rest was moving, as it were, at 0 miles per hour.

Beginning with this idea, Hobbes derived emotions from motions.[18] All of
reality was matter in motion. Hobbes thought of motion in a unit he called a
"conatus," or "endeavor." He defined endeavor as "motion made through
the length of a point, and in an instant or point of time."[19] Thus an endeavor
could not be measured by a number, though that did not mean that it had no
quantity, "for there is no such thing in nature [as being entirely devoid of
quantity]." Therefore, "one endeavor may be compared with another
endeavor, and one may be found to be greater or less than another."[20]

---

[15] *Ibid.*, 46.

[16] For an overview, see Franck Lessay, "Sur le traité des passions de Hobbes: commentaire
du chapitre VI du *Léviathan*," *Études Épistémè* 1 (2002): 21–44.

[17] Thomas Hobbes, *Human Nature* 1.4, in Thomas Hobbes, *The Elements of Law Natural
and Politic*, pt. 1: *Human Nature*, pt. 2: *De Corpore Politico* with *Three Lives*, ed. J.
C. A. Gaskin (Oxford, 1994), 21.

[18] We have already seen that Thomas Aquinas also considered passions to be motions (see
Chapter 5, n. 25 above). But Hobbes, using the non-Aristotelian notion of motion, ended
up with a very different theory of the passions.

[19] Thomas Hobbes, *Elements of Philosophy. The First Section, Concerning Body* 15.2, in *The
Collected [English] Works of Thomas Hobbes*, ed. William Molesworth, 12 vols. (rpt.
Routledge, 1992, orig. pub. 1839–45), 1:206. On the background and uses of the idea
conatus/endeavor, see Jeffrey Barnouw, "Hobbes's Psychology of Thought: Endeavours,
Purpose and Curiosity," *History of European Ideas* 10/5 (1989): 519–45 at 519–25.

[20] Hobbes, *Elements of Philosophy*, 1:206.

One could, then, compare endeavors on the basis of their different velocities, complexities, and intensities.[21] The importance of this will soon become evident.

Motion in the external world, acting in accordance with the laws of inertia, produces internal motion. This happens in sequence: first in the sense organs, then in the brain, and finally in the heart.[22] The senses apprehend not sound or color or image and so on, but rather a motion that is *understood* as color or image and the like. But in truth such attributes are "apparitions" or "conceptions."[23]

The effect of the "object" – really, the movement – on the brain does not stop even when the object is gone. The image remains, though (as other objects impinge on the brain) it does so "more obscurely." That "obscure conception" is imagination.[24] Because imagination holds all the perceptions, it can put them together in new ways that the person did not actually experience. Then "remembrance," like a sort of sixth sense, "takes notice" of the conceptions of the brain, holds on to them, and seeks to put them into some sort of cause and effect order.[25]

Not all experiences are equal. Those that are desired and those that are feared make a stronger impression than the others.[26] This is what constitutes the intensity of the endeavor, which either advances or retreats. Hobbes called the endeavor that advances "appetite" or "desire"; the endeavor that retreats is "aversion."[27] The many varieties of desires and aversions are the passions. They are infinite in number, since different people will have different desires and aversions, and they will be of varying intensity. Nevertheless, Hobbes listed some of them.

No doubt he felt obliged to give a list along with their definitions and subcategories because lists were traditional in theories of emotions, as we have seen. But Hobbes had additional reasons to name some of the passions. He "recognized the extraordinary impact of language on thought": as much as sense perceptions, language itself determined people's conceptions.[28] Only with well-defined words can people engage in the "acquisition of science."[29] Only with words can people think and, above all, string together sequences of cause and effect.

[21] See the remarks in Cerrato, *Un secolo di passioni*, 19.   [22] Hobbes, *Lev.* 1.4, p. 9.

[23] For apparition, Hobbes, *Human Nature* 2.4, p. 23; for conception, *ibid.*, 3.6, p. 29.

[24] *Ibid.*, 3.1, p. 26. Emphasizing the role of imagination in Hobbes' thought as the generator of the passions is Daniela Coli, "Hobbes's Revolution," in *Politics and the Passions, 1500–1850*, ed. Victoria Kahn, Neil Saccamano, and Daniela Coli (Princeton, 2006), 75–92.

[25] Hobbes, *Lev.* 3.5, p. 17.   [26] *Ibid.*, 3.4, p. 16.   [27] *Ibid.*, 6.2, p. 34.

[28] Gert, "Hobbes's Psychology," 158; Hobbes, *Lev.* 4.1, p. 20, speaks of "names or appellations ... whereby men register their thoughts; recall them when they are past; and also declare them one to another." See also *ibid.*, 4.22, p. 26: "... *understanding* being nothing else but conception caused by speech."

[29] *Ibid.*, 4.13, p. 24. Hobbes, *Human Nature* 8.1, p. 46, notes that people have given names to only a few passions. No doubt that fact limited their ability to think about them.

People do not sense "just anything"; they seek what will give them pleasure and avoid what will give them pain. Pleasure and pain are at the core of the Hobbesian theory. Each pertains to both the body and the mind. Bodily, they are sensations of the heart that "either help or hinder that motion which is called vital."[30] When a motion helps, it is "called DELIGHT, contentment or pleasure, which is nothing really but motion about the heart." Similarly when it hinders the vital motion, "it is called pain."[31] Mentally, pleasure and pain are conceptions that arise from the human ability to think not only about the past and present but also the future. Mental pleasure and pain "arise from the expectation, that proceeds from foresight of the end ... [namely] whether those things in the sense please or displease." The pleasure in this case is called joy, the displeasure grief.[32] When the object of desire is present, the term for the motion is love. Similarly when the object of avoidance is present, the motion is called hate.

Hobbes called seven motions – appetite, desire, love, aversion, hate, joy, and grief – the "simple passions."[33] Actually, since appetite and desire are synonyms, there are only six.[34] Compared to earlier lists – the eleven of Thomas Aquinas, the five of Gerson – two obvious passions are missing here: anger and fear. But Hobbes explained that the various other species of emotions are either forms of the simple in various circumstances or are the products of compounds.[35] For example, hope, despair, and fear are derived from simples: "For *appetite* with an opinion of attaining, is called HOPE. The same, without such opinion, DESPAIR. *Aversion*, with opinion of HURT from the object, FEAR."[36] But, jealousy is the result of a compound of love and fear: "*Love* ... with fear that the love is not mutual, [is] JEALOUSY."[37] The one motion that is neither a simple nor a compound is "CONTEMPT [which is] nothing else but an immobility, or contumacy of the heart, in resisting the action of certain things." We have contempt for "those things which we neither desire, nor hate."[38] The motions covered in the *Leviathan* are summed up in Table 9.1.

Only a few of these motions – above all, curiosity and admiration – were true of human beings and not animals. (See Plate 9.1.) Hobbes listed under

---

[30] A "vital motion," as Hobbes made clear in *On the Body* 15.12, p. 131, is the "motion of the blood, perpetually circulating ... in the veins and arteries." Here Hobbes paid explicit homage to William Harvey (d. 1657), whose observations about the circulation of blood were published in 1628.

[31] Hobbes, *Human Nature* 7.1, p. 43.   [32] Hobbes, *Lev.* 6.12, p. 36.

[33] *Ibid.*, 6.13, p. 36.   [34] *Ibid.*, 6.5, p. 34.

[35] As in Timothie Bright's treatise (see Chapter 8 above), the ideas of "simples" and "compounds" came from medieval medical practice.

[36] Hobbes, *Lev.* 6.14–16, p. 36. María L. Lukac de Stier, "Hobbes on the Passions and Imagination: Tradition and Modernity," *Hobbes Studies* 24 (2011): 78–90 at 84, suggests that Hobbes followed Aquinas here: his "simple passions" were Aquinas' concupiscible, while his "derived" were equivalent to Aquinas' irascible.

[37] Hobbes, *Lev.* 6.33, p. 37.   [38] *Ibid.*, 6.5, p. 34.

Table 9.1 *Hobbes' motions in the* Leviathan

Simples, their species, and subspecies:
appetite/desire
  ambition
  benevolence, good will, charity
  covetousness
  curiosity
  despair
    diffidence[a]
  felicity
  good nature
  hope
    confidence
  revengefulness
  will
aversion
  fear
    panic terror
    religion
    superstition
    true religion
  courage
    anger
      indignation
grief
  dejection
  emulation
  envy
  pity, compassion, fellow-feeling
  shame
    blushing
  sudden dejection
    weeping
hate
joy
  admiration
  glorying
    confidence
    laughter
    sudden glory
    vain-glory, pride, self-conceit[b]
love
  kindness
  luxury[c]
  natural lust
  passion of love

Table 9.1 (*cont.*)

Compounds:

desire + fear
    pusillanimity
        parsimony
        wretchedness, miserableness
love + fear
    jealousy

Neither simple nor compound:
contempt
    cruelty
    impudence
    magnanimity
        liberality
        valor, fortitude

[a] This table leaves out the objects with which Hobbes associates
the motions, an omission especially problematic here,
because (for example) Hobbes is talking about "diffidence of
ourselves" when he classifies it under despair.

[b] The synonyms for vainglory are given in Hobbes, *Lev.* 8.18,
p. 49. Hobbes also says here that vainglory is one of two sources
of madness (dejection of mind is the other). Dominique Weber,
Hobbes et le désir des fous. Rationalité, prévision et politique (Paris,
2007), argues that this sort of madness is in fact the key to
Hobbes' view of both this world and the next.

[c] That is, the same as natural lust but "acquired from . . .
imagination of pleasure past."

"*desire*, to know why, and how, CURIOSITY; such as is in no living creature
but *man* . . . which is a lust of the mind, that by a perseverance of delight in
the continual and indefatigable generation of knowledge, exceedeth the
short vehemence of any carnal pleasure."[39] How far this is from
Augustine's and Aelred's condemnation of the "concupiscence of the
eyes," which they equated with curiosity![40] Yet, even while praising
curiosity and its powerful delight, Hobbes also recognized its weaknesses.
Science was "conditional knowledge," based on the past but never fully
certain of the future.[41] Originating in anxiety about the future, its own
limits generated anxiety.[42]

[39] *Ibid.*, p. 37.   [40] For more on this positive view of curiosity, see below at n. 123.
[41] Hobbes, *Lev.* 7.4, p. 43.
[42] *Ibid.*, 12.24, p. 70: "anxiety for the future time, disposeth men to inquire into the causes
of things."

Plate 9.1 *Leviathan* title page, sketch for Charles II

Plate 9.1

This frontispiece sketch was created by Abraham Bosse in collaboration with Hobbes for the presentation copy of the *Leviathan* for Charles II. It shows the bust of a regal figure looming over a landscape, a bishop's crosier in his left hand, a sword in his right. Below the image of a city are three panels: under the crosier are the symbols of the ecclesiastical power and beneath the sword are images of worldly power. The symbols on the right and left panels correspond horizontally: the castle (on the viewer's left) is matched by the church; the crown by the miter; the cannon by the thunderbolt, signifying excommunication;[i] implements of war by "the weapons of logic" shaped to signify the "scholastic techniques of forked argument";[ii] and battle is paired with the ecclesiastical disputation (or inquisition).

The bust presiding over all of this is composed of heads. Without doubt these are the heads of the people who have abandoned their liberty in favor of obeying a common power that will protect them. Hobbes' fifth "law of nature" likened the men who made up the commonwealth to stones used to build an edifice.[iii] First the stones had to be prepared: their rough edges had to be smoothed out, and any that would not fit had to be discarded. So, too, wrote Hobbes, men have rough edges "rising from their diversity of affections." The fifth law of nature is "*that every man strive to accommodate himself to the rest.*" If "for the stubbornness of his passions, [he] cannot be corrected," he is to be "left, or cast out of society."[iv] In Bosse's depiction of the Leviathan, the heads are quite literally the building blocks. "With their excited, sometimes anxious facial expressions," the people within the torso clearly still have passions.[v] At the same time they are thoroughly subordinated to the looming figure. © The British Library Board, MS Egerton 1910 F1.

[i] As Hobbes, *Lev.* 42.31, p. 342, explains. For further references to this association, see Quentin Skinner, *Hobbes and Republican Liberty* (Cambridge, 2008), 193–94 and n. 54.

[ii] *Ibid.*, 194, where nn. 56–57 explains what is written on the forks: on the left Syl/logis/me; on the right Real/Intentional; in the middle (front) Spiritual/Temporal; middle (back and slanting) Directe/Indirecte; on the horns underneath, Di/le/ma. See also Horst Bredekamp, "Thomas Hobbes's Visual Strategies," in *Cambridge Companion to Hobbes's Leviathan*, 29–60 at 32.

[iii] Hobbes, *Lev.* 14.3, defines a law of nature as "a precept, or general rule, found out by reason, by which a man is forbidden to do, that, which is destructive of his life ... and to omit, that, by which he thinketh it may be best preserved." The fifth law comes under the latter heading.

[iv] *Ibid.*, 15.17, pp. 100–1.

[v] Bredekamp, "Hobbes's Visual Strategies," 40.

If only two passions were proper to man alone, why did Hobbes call them all "voluntary" motions? Were they voluntary in animals, as well? Yes, said Hobbes, for the will ("voluntary" coming from the Latin *voluntas*, or "will") is not "in the reason." Rather, the will is simply the last step in "deliberation," the final outcome of both desire and aversion.[43] It is, as Lessay puts it, "desire translated into act."[44]

But even if the will *were* in reason, Hobbes' notion of reason made it a far cry from Augustine's or Aquinas'. For Hobbes, reason was the ability of our minds to put names to thoughts and to manipulate those thoughts for our own purposes.[45] Well, then, perhaps "reason" is the wrong word; perhaps "deliberation" was Hobbes' substitute for reason. There is some truth to this. Hobbes thought the word was derived from "de+liberation." By considering the consequences of "appetites, aversions, hopes and fears, concerning one and the same thing, aris[ing] alternately . . . [deliberation] is a putting an end to the *liberty* we had of doing, or omitting, according to our own appetite, or aversion." In that sense, it could put a break on the passions.[46] But "beasts also deliberate," because they too have "desires, aversion, hopes and fears, [that] continued till the thing be either done, or thought impossible."[47]

So "reason" manipulates words, and "deliberation" and "will" put together and then carry out the sum total of alternating passions as understood by reason.[48] Having put names to its mental images, reason puts them together in two ways: either unguided, as in dreams, or guided

[43] *Ibid.*, 6.53, p. 40: "In *deliberation*, the last appetite, or aversion, immediately adhering to the action, or to the omission thereof, is that we call the WILL . . . The definition of the *will*, given commonly by the Schools, that it is a *rational appetite*, is not good." For Thomas Aquinas' view of the appetitive will, see above, Chapter 5, and for Augustine's notion of the will in controlling emotions, see Chapter 1. But in Hobbes, *Human Nature* 12.5, p. 72, "will to do is appetite, and will to omit fear; the causes of appetite and of fear are the causes also of our will." Here, in this earlier work, "deliberation" is omitted, though "opinion" seems to have a similar function: "our wills follow our opinions, as our actions follow our wills."

[44] Lessay, "Sur le traité des passions," 29. On the development of Hobbes' notion of will and its historical context, see Jürgen Overhoff, *Hobbes's Theory of the Will: Ideological Reasons and Historical Circumstances* (Lanham, 2000).

[45] Hobbes, *Lev.* 5.2, p. 28: "REASON . . . is nothing but reckoning . . . of the consequences of general names agreed upon, for the *marking* and *signifying* of our thoughts."

[46] *Ibid.*, 6.49–50, pp. 39–40. Tilmouth, *Passion's Triumph*, 237–44, sees deliberation as Hobbes' "reason." He emphasizes the role of fear in both, but on 234, looking more at the discussion in *Human Nature* than at the one in the *Leviathan*, he finds deliberation to have been for Hobbes a *generator* of more passions.

[47] Hobbes, *Lev.* 6.51, p. 40.

[48] By this account, Hobbes does not seem to recognize a conflict between reason and passion. Gianni Paganini, "'Passionate Thought': Reason and the Passion of Curiosity in Thomas Hobbes," in *Emotional Minds: The Passions and the Limits of Pure Inquiry in*

by "passionate thought." Here thoughts are "*regulated* by some desire, and design."[49]

But such regulated thought does not tell people what they *should* desire. Good and evil are subjective notions based on a person's experience: "whatsoever is the object of any man's appetite or desire; that is it, which he for his part calleth *good*: and the object of his hate, and aversion, *evil*."[50] This was not so different from the theory of an Aelred or a Thomas Aquinas. Aelred said that love always carefully discerned what it would choose, but its discernment might be wrong.[51] Aquinas knew that the passions might desire the wrong objects, and even the intellective faculty might be mistaken.[52] But then *they* went on to define a real and objective good beyond subjective experience. Hobbes' passions, dependent on the ever-changing outer world for their conceptions, mirrored the world's chaos. "Life itself is but motion," he wrote.[53] While Aquinas had a predictable sequence for the passions (see Figure 5.3 above), Hobbes' passions were in continual flux.

Moreover their pursuit of pleasure had no end. This was not because people had unstoppable desires. It was rather because, in order to satisfy even modest desires, people had to have power, which Hobbes defined as "the present means to obtain some future apparent good."[54] All sorts of things enhanced power: wealth, glory, eloquence, honor. "A man" – and a woman? – was in restless pursuit of power, not because "he cannot be

---

Early Modern Philosophy, ed. Sabrina Ebbersmeyer (Berlin, 2012), 227–56, sees an evolution in Hobbes' thought from the conflict (dualism) of reason and passions to their unity. Arguing for a more general dualism in Hobbes' thought is Arrigo Pacchi, "Hobbes and the Passions," *Topoi* 6 (1987): 111–19, who claims (111) "that the cornerstone of Hobbes' political philosophy is the opposition between reason and the emotions." Arguing the contrary is Giovanni Fiaschi, "'. . . partly in the passions, partly in his reason,'" in *La filosofia politica di Hobbes*, ed. G. M. Chiodi and R. Gatti (Milan, 2009), 81–107, esp. 81–86 and 96–99, who denies Hobbes' dualism while nevertheless acknowledging the sort of opposition Hobbes speaks of in his dedicatory epistle to *The Elements of Law*, 19: "From the two principal parts of our nature, Reason and Passion, have proceeded two kinds of learning, mathematical and dogmatical."

[49] Hobbes, *Lev.* 3.3, p. 16.   [50] *Ibid.*, 6.7, p. 35.   [51] Above, Chapter 4 at n. 37.

[52] Above, Chapter 5 at n. 114. Conversely, even for Hobbes there was on occasion a "real good": Thomas Hobbes, *De homine* 12.1, in *Thomas Hobbes Malmesburiensis opera philosophica quae latine scripsit, omnia in unum corpus nunc primum collecta*, ed. William Molesworth, 5 vols. (London, 1839–45) [henceforth OL], 2:103, says that the affects (*affectus*) "are called perturbations (*perturbationes*) because they often impede right reasoning (*propterea quod officiunt plerumque rectae ratiocinationi*)" about the real good (*bonum verum*) in favor of "the apparent and most immediate good." There is a partial English translation in Thomas Hobbes, *Man and Citizen (De Homine and De Cive)*, trans. Charles T. Wood, T. S. K. Scott-Craig, and Bernard Gert (Indianapolis, 1991), 33–85, here p. 55.

[53] Hobbes, *Lev.* 6.58, p. 41. Lessay, "Sur le traité des passions," 24, points to desire as "la substance même de la vie (the very substance of life)," citing *Lev.* 8.16, p. 48: "For as to have no desire, is to be dead: so to have weak passions, is dullness."

[54] *Ibid.*, 10.1, p. 58.

content with a moderate power: but because he cannot assure the power and means to live well, which he hath at present, without the acquisition of more."[55]

In striving for more and more power, people enter into competition, and this involves "contention, enmity, and war: because the way of one competitor, to the attaining of his desire, is to kill, subdue, supplant or repel the other."[56] Because people recognize this, desire and delight lead straight to the Leviathan! So does fear, the natural response to the dangers of war. And hope, as well, given the potential of the state to create peace and the conditions for "commodious living."[57] In short, the passions themselves unite to create the state: "Desire of ease, and sensual delight, disposeth men to obey a common power: because by such desires, a man doth abandon the protection that might be hoped for from his own industry, and labour. Fear of death, and wounds, disposeth to the same."[58]

Although the Leviathan is a frightful image in the Bible, Hobbes' Leviathan is not so very monstrous.[59] It is a kind of person – a "mortal God," as Hobbes put it – made up of the very people over whom it looms.[60]

---

[55] *Ibid.*, 11.2, p. 66.   [56] *Ibid.*, 11.3, p. 66.

[57] *Ibid.*, 13.14, p. 86. On the importance of hope in Hobbes' theory, see Lessay, "Sur le traité des passions," 33–34. Raffaella Santi, "*Metus* Revealed: Hobbes on Fear," *Agathos* 2 (2011): 67–80, sees fear as Hobbes' key passion. In Hobbes, *Lev.* 28.27, p. 212, Hobbes emphasizes pride as well: "I have set forth the nature of man, (whose pride and other passions have compelled him to submit himself to government)."

[58] *Ibid.*, 11.4, p. 66. Hobbes makes essentially the same point at 13.14, p. 86: "The passions that incline men to peace, are fear of death; desire of such things as are necessary to commodious living; and a hope by their industry to obtain them." He continues the passage by discussing the role of reason, which enters the picture to carry out the inclinations of the passions: "And reason suggesteth convenient articles of peace, upon which men may be drawn to agreement. These articles, are they, which otherwise are called the Laws of Nature." Anna Maria Battista, *Nascita della psicologia politica* (Genoa, 1982), 15–16, and "Hobbes e la nascita della psicologia politica," in *Politica e diritto in Hobbes*, ed. Giuseppe Sorgi (Milan, 1995), 193–224, esp. 201–2, argues that the key to Hobbes' theory is not passion per se but human self-love, which is independent of sense perceptions. She is thinking of, for example, Thomas Hobbes, *De cive* 1.2, corr. ed. (Basel, 1782), 6: "Animi … voluptas omnis, vel gloria est (sive bene opinari de se ipso) vel ad gloriam ultimo refertur (Every pleasure of the soul/mind is either glory [or to think well of oneself] or refers ultimately to glory)." But it is unclear to me why Battista considers that these and similar references do not refer to the passions. For vainglory, pride, and self-conceit, see Table 9.1. Franco Ratto, *Hobbes tra scienza della politica e teoria delle passioni* (New York, 2000), takes up the less-explored topic of the causes (including the passions) that Hobbes thinks lead to the *dissolution* of the state; see *Lev.* 29, 212–21.

[59] The biblical Leviathan is mentioned in a variety of places, for example Isaiah 27:1 and at length in Job 40–41. Hobbes, *Lev.* 28.27, p. 212, quotes Job 41:33–34. See Noel Malcolm, "The Name and Nature of Leviathan: Political Symbolism and Biblical Exegesis," *Intellectual History Review* 17 (2007): 29–58, showing that in some exegetical circles by Hobbes' time the term "Leviathan" could stand for society, "the joining together of many" (32), and a ruler such as a king or prince.

[60] Hobbes, *Lev.* 17.13, p. 114.

The sketch that Hobbes' artist made of the Leviathan for presentation to Charles II (in exile in Paris) shows it as a bust composed of the heads of numerous people looking outward (see Plate 9.1). However, on the frontis-piece of the published book (see Plate 9.2), the bust consists of men (and women?) turned away from the reader as they gaze at the Leviathan's face.

But if the motions create the Leviathan, what does the Leviathan do to the motions in turn? "The desires, and other passions of man, are in themselves no sin. No more are the actions, that proceed from those passions, till they know a law that forbids them; which till laws be made they cannot know: nor can any law be made, till they have agreed upon the person that shall make it."[61] That "person" is the Leviathan. Its laws forbid actions; the actions derive from the passions. In effect, the Leviathan creates an "emotional regime" that keeps individual motions in check.[62] As people live under its laws, their modified passions become habits, and "then it is also that propriety begins."[63] It is at this point that Hobbes speaks about justice – the font of virtue for him, as for Aquinas.[64]

Consistencies and divergences

Hobbes' ideas about the motions, like his motions themselves, changed over time. Gert argues that Hobbes' ideas in *Human Nature* were so different from those in the *Leviathan* that they should not be taken as representing Hobbes' thought. Most commentators use the works of Hobbes as if they complement one another.[65] It seems that a middle position is possible: to

---

[61] *Ibid.*, 13.10, p. 85.   [62] For the term "emotional regime," see the Introduction, n. 35.
[63] Hobbes, *Lev.* 15.3, p. 96.
[64] *Ibid.*, 15.4, p. 96, where Hobbes introduces his discussion of justice by rewriting Ps. 14:1: "The fool hath said in his heart, there is no God," to "The fool hath said in his heart, there is no such thing as justice." On this passage, see Andrew James Corsa, "Thomas Hobbes' Response to the Fool: Justice and Magnanimity," *Philosophy-Dissertations*, Paper 67 (Syracuse University, 2011). For the "development of socially compliant impulses" under the civil authority, see Tilmouth, *Passion's Triumph*, 241–46, and on the ways in which Hobbes reconciled his theory of human egotism with God's original intentions, 250–51.
[65] Gert, "Hobbes's Psychology," 173 n. 2, notes that the role of imagination in *Lev.* is different from that in *Human Nature* and warns against using the latter altogether "to determine Hobbes's views on any subject. That work was an early draft of *De cive* and *Leviathan* and was not intended to be published." Lukac de Stier, "Hobbes on the Passions," 79 n. 4, explicitly disagrees, as does Ioannis D. Evrigenis, "'Not Truth but Image Maketh Passion': Hobbes on Instigation and Appeasing," in *Passions and Subjectivity*, 165–80. But in fact most commentators implicitly assume considerable accord among Hobbes' works, especially the philosophically inclined articles in *Hobbes Studies*, as for example Timo Airaksinen, "Hobbes on the Passions and Powerlessness," *Hobbes Studies* 6 (1993): 80–104. For a survey of some of the scholarship arguing pro and con the issue of Hobbes' evolving thought, as well as his own view that Hobbes simply clarified his thinking over time, see Weber, *Hobbes et le désir*, 58–60. A useful and balanced comparison of the two works is Tilmouth, *Passion's Triumph*, 221–34 *et passim*.

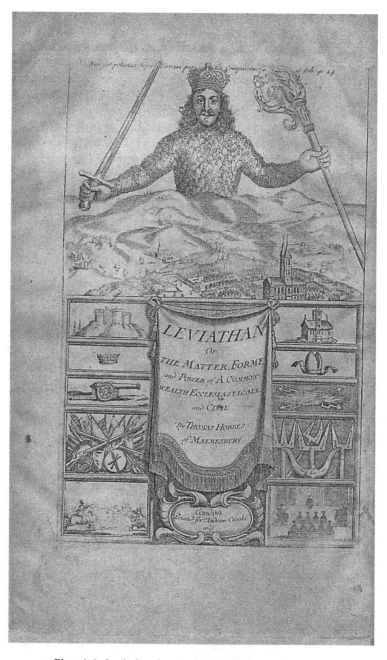

Plate 9.2 *Leviathan* frontispiece (1651)

Plate 9.2

The frontispiece created by Bosse for the first edition of the *Leviathan* seems at first glance not much different from his sketch for Charles II (Plate 9.1). The panels show the same images, and the landscape above them is only slightly modified. But the torso of the Leviathan is here made up of some 300 figures turned *away* from the viewer and made to gaze upward at its head. In this way, the passions of the people are hidden.

Nevertheless, Hobbes' own passions were (subtly) on display. In the decades before writing the *Leviathan*, he had been intensely interested in optics, writing a Latin treatise on the topic in Latin around 1640 and one in English in 1645/6. In Paris he discovered the "perspective glass," which allowed the viewer to merge fragmented images into one. In the *Leviathan* he wrote about the invention, comparing it favorably to the distorted "magnifying lenses" afforded by the passions: "For all men are by nature provided of notable multiplying glasses (that is their passions and self-love) through which, every little payment appeareth a great grievance; but are destitute of those prospective [perspective] glasses (namely moral and civil science) to see afar off the miseries that hang over them, and cannot without such payments [that is, the various petty miseries that people must suffer living under a sovereign] be avoided."[i]

That Hobbes connected this way of seeing with his own passions is suggested in a prefatory note he wrote for William Davenant's poem Gondibert: "I believe (Sir) you have seen a curious kind of perspective, where, he that looks through a short hollow pipe, upon a picture containing diverse figures, sees ... some one person made up of their parts ... I find in my imagination an effect not unlike it from your Poem. The virtues you distribute there amongst so many noble persons, represent (in the reading) the image but of one mans virtue to my fancy, which is your own; and that so deeply imprinted, as to stay for ever there, and govern all the rest of my thoughts and affections."[ii] Thus, according to Hobbes' own theory of motion, the figures of Davenant's poem, read by Hobbes' eye, impinged on his brain, producing conceptions in his imagination that gave him great pleasure and dominated his thoughts and "affections" – that is, his passions.[iii]

In the frontispiece engraving, the people, all with cloaks and hats, provide the reader/viewer with the experience of a perspective glass as they merge into the figure of the sovereign.[iv] Photo Courtesy of The Newberry Library, Chicago, Call # Case, folio JC153 .H65 1651b.

[i] Hobbes, *Lev.* 18.20, p. 122.

[ii] Sir William D'Avenant, *Gondibert: An Heroick Poem* (London, 1651), 64.

[iii] For the equivalence of affections and passions, see for example his "fifth law of nature," quoted in the caption of Plate 9.1.

[iv] For further reading on the images, see Bredekamp, "Hobbes's Visual Strategies," and Noel Malcolm, "The Title Page of *Leviathan*, seen in a Curious Perspective," in Malcolm, *Aspects of Hobbes* (Oxford, 2002), 200–33, who, however, reads the figure of the Leviathan in Plate 9.1 rather than the frontispiece here as influenced by the theory of the perspective glass.

acknowledge that Hobbes' ideas evolved over time, but to claim at the same time that all his ideas should be taken seriously.

Franck Lessay has noted a number of important differences between Hobbes' discussion of the passions in *Human Nature* and in the *Leviathan*.[66] In *Human Nature*, Hobbes said that delight, love, pleasure, appetite, and desire were nearly synonyms: "divers names for divers considerations of the same thing."[67] By implication, he said the same about pain, hatred, aversion, and fear. In this earlier work, fear was aversion in its future form; it was the motion of pain "in respect of the displeasure expected."[68] In the *Leviathan*, by contrast, fear's role was "diluted." Rather than being the future form of aversion, it was one of its derivatives: "*aversion*, with opinion of HURT from the object."[69] Still more significant, in *Human Nature* Hobbes argued that "common peace" was impossible "without the erection of some common power, by the fear whereof [people] may be compelled both to keep the peace amongst themselves, and to join their strengths together, against a common enemy."[70] Here the "common power" – which would become the Leviathan in his later work – engendered fear. But in the *Leviathan* fear and hope together – fear of one's fellows and hope for future peace – created, rather than simply responded to, the sovereign power.[71]

In its emphases, too, Hobbes' discussion of the passions in *Human Nature* was not the same as in the *Leviathan*. In the earlier work, the chapter devoted to the "passions of the mind," offered a twofold classification system based on honor: "In the pleasure men have, or displeasure from the signs of honour or dishonour done unto them, consisteth the nature of the passions in particular."[72] The first passion that Hobbes described here was glory and its variants (false glory, vainglory) and then its contraries (humility, dejection, and shame). Next came courage, "the absence of fear in the presence of any evil whatsoever," and anger, which was "sudden courage."[73] Lessay is quite right to see Hobbes here describing heroic passions.[74] He was interested in the passions of "every man by himself, without relation to others."[75] His scheme was less a taxonomy than a metaphor – life as a race to be foremost.

---

[66] Lessay, "Sur le traité des passions," 32–37.   [67] Hobbes, *Human Nature* 7.2, p. 44.
[68] *Ibid.*   [69] Hobbes, *Lev.* 6.16, p. 36.   [70] Hobbes, *Human Nature* 19.6, p. 106.
[71] See above at n. 57. Arguing that fear's role in creating the Leviathan gives people the illusion of their own sovereignty and thus makes life bearable is Samantha Frost, "Fear and the Illusion of Autonomy," in *New Materialisms: Ontology, Agency, and Politics*, ed. Diana Coole and Samantha Frost (Durham, 2010), 158–75.
[72] Hobbes, *Human Nature* 8.8, p. 50.
[73] For courage, *ibid.*, 9.4, p. 51; for anger, 9.5, p. 52.
[74] Lessay, "Sur le traité des passions," 35.   [75] Hobbes, *Human Nature* 13.1, p. 73.

The comparison of the life of man to a race, though it holdeth not in every point, yet it holdeth so well for this our purpose that we may thereby both see and remember almost all the passions before mentioned. But this race we must suppose to have no other goal, nor no other garland, but being foremost.[76]

In that race: "To endeavour is appetite; To be remiss is sensuality; To consider them behind is glory:" and so on.[77] But it was a race without end. Felicity was the goal, to be sure. But felicity "consisteth not in having prospered, but in prospering." It was, in short, "continual," not final.[78] Table 9.2 summarizes the passions from *Human Nature* in alphabetical order.

Table 9.2 *Hobbes' passions in "life's race to get ahead"*[a]

anger
appetite
charity
courage
despair
die
emulation
envy
felicity
glory
hatred
hope
humility
indignation
laugh (disposition to, seeing another fall)
love
magnanimity
misery
pity
pusillanimity
repentance
sensuality
shame
vainglory
weep (disposition to, when suddenly falling)

[a] Listed in Hobbes, *Human Nature* 9.21, pp. 59–60. Underlined passions were not included in the list in *Leviathan* (see Table 9.1).

[76] *Ibid.*, 9.21, p. 59. For Hobbes' "pursuit of 'felicity' as a competitive race against others [and] against oneself, each man continually aspiring to exceed his previous achievements," see Tilmouth, *Passion's Triumph*, 224 and 228–30.

[77] Hobbes, *Human Nature* 9.21, pp. 59–60.   [78] *Ibid.*, 7.7, p. 45.

By contrast, Hobbes' main concern in the *Leviathan* was to set forth the social effects of the emotions. In that later work, as Cerrato has observed, Hobbes "considered the movements of the passions in relation not to individuals but rather to the collectivity."[79] Thus he began not with glory but with hope; he made courage simply an aversion "with the hope of avoiding ... hurt";[80] and he subordinated glory to joy. Even felicity was slightly softened. It was "continual success in obtaining those things which a man from time to time desireth."[81]

It is therefore perhaps not terribly surprising that over a quarter of the words in Table 9.2 do not appear in Hobbes' *Leviathan*. It seems reasonable to imagine that he had his list from *Human Nature* to hand when working on the later book. But the image of life as a race to get ahead no longer dominated his thinking. Anxiety did. In the *Leviathan* Hobbes' man was not running; he was lashed to a rock, like Prometheus, "so that man, which looks too far before him, in the care of future time, hath his heart all the day long, gnawed on by fear of death, poverty, or other calamity, and has no repose, nor pause of his anxiety, but in sleep."[82] The execution of Charles I (1649) had made its mark.

Old and new

Hobbes takes us into the thick of the English Renaissance.[83] He translated Thucydides; wrote an abbreviated version of Aristotle's *Rhetoric* (a work that treated the passions at length); and was steeped in the ancient Latin rhetorical traditions of Cicero and Quintilian.[84] Of "modern" thinkers, he knew, among others, the works of

---

[79] Cerrato, *Un secolo di passioni*, 16. Tilmouth, *Passion's Triumph*, 230–31, makes the same point.

[80] Hobbes, *Lev.* 6.17, p. 36.   [81] *Ibid.*, 6.58, p. 41.

[82] *Ibid.*, 12.5, p. 72. For the role of anxiety in Hobbes, see Cerrato, *Un secolo di passioni*, 39–49.

[83] On "Hobbes's humanist career," see Quentin Skinner, *Reason and Rhetoric in the Philosophy of Hobbes* (Cambridge, 1996), 215–49. On the precedents to Hobbes' *Leviathan* in classical and contemporary thought, see Catherine Wilson, "Thomas Hobbes' *Leviathan*," in *The Oxford Handbook of British Philosophy in the Seventeenth Century*, ed. Peter R. Anstey (Oxford, 2013), 519–41. Alone in its low opinion of Hobbes' Greek is the editorial intro. to Thomas Hobbes, *Historia Ecclesiastica*, ed. Patricia Springborg, Patricia Stablein, and Paul Wilson (Paris, 2008), 149, which claims that for his translation of Thucydides, Hobbes relied on Lorenzo Valla's Greek to Latin translation "as a Latin crib."

[84] On the importance of Aristotle in Hobbes' theory, see Daniel M. Gross, *The Secret History of Emotion: From Aristotle's* Rhetoric *to Modern Brain Science* (Chicago, 2006), esp. 43–50.

Machiavelli, Paolo Sarpi (a supporter of Galileo and a thinker in his own right), and the humanist philosopher Justus Lipsius.[85] He may have read Montaigne's *Essais* in the translation by John Florio published in London in 1603.[86] Hobbes was in touch with Descartes; their disagreements and dislike of one another are legendary.[87] As tutor to William Cavendish, Hobbes had a major hand in collecting and recording the books in the Cavendish library at Hardwick Hall.[88] We have a book list from this library in Hobbes' own hand, divided into "general" and "ecclesiastical" works. For our purposes, we should note that among the latter were works of Augustine, including the *City of God*, and Thomas Aquinas' *Summa theologiae* – precisely the section on the passions.[89] To be sure, having access to a book does not prove its influence. But at the very least we can say that Hobbes knew about these works.[90]

Hobbes' notion of human nature had some congruence with that of Augustine. Indeed, Herbert Deane, writing about Augustine's views, observes, "This picture of man's restless striving for material satisfactions [that we find in Augustine] reminds us of Hobbes's portrait of natural man, who spends his entire life in the effort to satisfy one desire after another and never attains real repose or enduring satisfaction."[91] But it reminds us of Hobbes because Hobbes derived some of his picture from Augustine! However, Augustine condemned the direction of most desires, dwelling particularly on curiosity (the desire for new knowledge) and the lust for power. Hobbes inverted these judgments.

Similarly, old ideas about the uses of the passions – Evagrius' strategy to drive out one vice with another and the long tradition (which we have traced in our theoretical chapters) of associating feelings with virtues and vices – were gaining new meaning in the writings

---

[85] *Ibid.*, 68. Tilmouth, *Passion's Triumph*, 214–21, argues that Hobbes and others of his persuasion were working within the tradition of Tacitus, assuming, "namely, man's habit of prioritizing self-interest over all other goods."

[86] See Emiliano Ferrari, *Montaigne. Une anthropologie des passions* (Paris, 2014), 153–74, for Montaigne's probable influence on Hobbes.

[87] Susan James, *Passion and Action: The Emotions in Seventeenth-Century Philosophy* (Oxford, 1997), 124–36, outlines some of the differences and also a few points in common in their views of the passions.

[88] James Jay Hamilton, "Hobbes's Study and the Hardwick Library," *Journal of the History of Philosophy* 16/4 (1978): 445–53.

[89] Hobbes, *Historia Ecclesiastica*, Appendix B, 282–92 at 282–83.

[90] Even though Hobbes, *Lev.* 4.13, p. 24, ridicules those who "value [words] by the authority of an Aristotle, a Cicero, or a Thomas," Ioannis D. Evrigenis, *Images of Anarchy: The Rhetoric and Science in Hobbes's State of Nature* (Cambridge, 2014), emphasizes Hobbes' use of lessons from Thucydides, Euclid, and Aristotle's *Rhetoric* in all of his writings.

[91] Deane, *Political and Social*, 46.

of Machiavelli and (closer to home and to Hobbes) Francis Bacon. "This ... is of speciall vse in Morall and Ciuile matters; howe I say to sett affection againste affection, and to Master one by another, even as wee vse to hunt beast with beaste, and flye byrde with birde."[92] That could have been said by Evagrius (it is in fact a quote from Bacon), apart from the reference to "civil matters." But that reference was the important point, for Bacon continued by observing that states used reward and punishment, corresponding to "the predominante affections of *feare* and *hope*."[93]

Certainly Hobbes' theory did not represent so decisive a break from medieval traditions as the theologians of his day seemed to think when they accused him of atheism and heresy. We can see the Stoic prepassions (or "first movements") behind Hobbes' notion of endeavor, which he defined in the *Leviathan* as "small beginnings of motions, within the body of man, before they appear in walking, speaking, striking, and other visible actions."[94] For that matter, as we have seen, Thomas Aquinas, too, saw the passions as motions.[95] And both Hobbes and Aquinas considered the heart's movements to be the inextricable accompaniment of the passions. But Aquinas' notion of motion drew on Aristotelian physics, according to which objects sought their proper end and resting place.[96] Hobbes saw no rest for the passions because he accepted the new (Galilean) theory of inertia, which made movement endless unless stopped by an outside force. This is why he needed a Leviathan.

Both Aquinas and Hobbes thought that passions moved toward the good and away from evil, however defined. Both thought that that movement brought pleasure (or, when frustrated, pain). However, Aquinas thought that there was an objective good, God. From this fact derived the virtue – or the vice – of the emotions. Hobbes did not identify God as the proper object of the emotions; everyone's individual history and circumstances determined what they considered to be good for them, and God per se had nothing to do with that choice.[97] Nevertheless, there were two

---

[92] Francis Bacon, *The Advancement of Learning*, in *The Oxford Francis Bacon*, IV, ed. Michael Kiernan (Oxford, 2000), 150. See further discussion in Albert O. Hirschman, *The Passions and the Interests: Political Arguments for Capitalism before Its Triumph* (Princeton, 1977), 22.

[93] Bacon, *Advancement*, 150.   [94] Hobbes, *Lev.* 6.1, p. 34.

[95] As did Gerson. See Chapter 7 n. 37. That is in part why he could assimilate them to music, which depends on the motion of vibration.

[96] See Chapter 5 at n. 42.

[97] To some degree this must be qualified by the fact that Hobbes did argue for the existence of God as derived from Scripture. See George Wright, *Religion, Politics, and Thomas Hobbes* (Dordrecht, 2006), 14–15, and bibliography cited there.

constants for Hobbes: everyone wanted to avoid death and to pursue pleasure.

Both Aquinas and Hobbes had some notion of "basic emotions." Thomas had eleven; Hobbes, in his *De homine*, named fifteen and in his *Leviathan* seven. As for the rest, even though they offered some terms, both considered it impossible – and useless – to name all the species of emotions. That was largely because, unlike many modern scientists, both Aquinas and Hobbes were less interested in single emotions than in emotional transformations. (That had been Alcuin's interest as well.) For Aquinas, emotional mutations were predictable and sequential: he had an "order" of the passions, starting with love and ending with joy or sorrow. For Hobbes, the mutations were less predictable, though also always striving toward future joy.

Hobbes was engaged in new debates, as well. He dissented from his contemporary French theorist of emotions, Descartes, whose *Passions of the Soul* was published in 1649. Hobbes even wrote a set of "objections" to Descartes' *Meditations*.[98] And yet, as Cerrato shows, both men were grappling with similar issues.[99] Hobbes also debated with the theologians of his time. The entire third and a portion of the fourth part of his *Leviathan* were devoted to "a Christian commonwealth."[100] Moreover, when Hobbes published a Latin version of that work in 1668, it included an appendix on the principles of the Christian religion in the form of a dialogue between a disciple (A) and a teacher (B).[101]

Emotional communities

Hobbes' theory of human nature has always been connected with the violence of the English Civil War. It should also be linked to the general sense of melancholy – so highly valued even as it was bewailed.[102] Burton

[98] Thomas Hobbes, "Objectiones ad Cartesii meditationes," in OL, 5:249–74. For a brief summary of Hobbes' disquiet concerning Descartes, see Noel Malcolm, "A Summary Biography of Hobbes," in Malcolm, *Aspects of Hobbes*, 1–26 at 13–14.

[99] Cerrato, *Un secolo di passioni*, 67–120, takes up Descartes. Battista, *Nascita*, 14, and in greater detail in Battista, "Hobbes e la nascita della psicologia politica," 195–98, argues that only in France did Hobbes discover thinkers dealing with the twinned theme of passions and politics, whereas in England such interest developed later, toward the end of the seventeenth century.

[100] Weber, *Hobbes et le désir*, 7–41, argues that Hobbes never denied religious thought and feeling but, on the contrary, found a new way to consider God and the after-life.

[101] Thomas Hobbes, *Appendix to Leviathan*, ed. and trans. George Wright, in Wright, *Religion, Politics, and Thomas Hobbes*, 36–173.

[102] On this point, see Gianfranco Borrelli, "Prudence, Folly and Melancholy in the Thought of Thomas Hobbes," *Hobbes Studies* 9 (1996): 88–97, who explores images

and Hobbes agreed that mankind was frail and most people were miserable. So did the members of Walker's gathered church, while even the cheerfulness of Spenser's Redcrosse was "solemn sad." All sought ways out of the Slough of Despond, as Bunyan put it. Some found the solution in religion, others in medicine, and Hobbes in autocratic government.[103]

But Hobbes was not himself particularly melancholy. Nor did he express his emotions in dramatic fashion. In a letter to Samuel Sorbière, he wrote of his feelings when learning of the "death of a man who was a very dear friend (*amicissimi*)." He bore it, he said, with sorrow (*aegrè*) but since all were mortal, "we ought not weep long over the death of one person."[104] How far this was from Aelred's passionate outburst about the death of his friend in the twelfth century! But how close it was to Thomas Aquinas' ideas about mitigating the passions by the power of reason.[105] Thus it is wrong to imagine that social control or the civilizing process placed its heavy hand on the seventeenth century. Or, to put the matter differently, those processes were active in all the periods that we have studied, although to greater or lesser degrees depending on the emotional communities.[106]

Hobbes' own emotional community was close to that of Evelyn and Pepys. He derived great pleasure from his studies and his "glory," he was curious about all sorts of scientific matters and inventions (see Plates 9.1 and 9.2), he took pride in his relations with his patrons. We have seen how his theory of the "voluntary motions" justified the emotional norms of men like Pepys and Evelyn, ambitious and curious to the core.

Yet, unlike Evelyn and Pepys, Hobbes was not invited to become a member of the Royal Society (founded in 1660).[107] Why not? As Noel

---

of melancholy in *Lev*, and Mauro Simonazzi, "Thomas Hobbes on Melancholy," *Hobbes Studies* 19 (2006): 31–57, who, however, claiming to follow the usage of the sixteenth and seventeenth centuries, has a very broad definition of melancholy as "any form of mental and nervous disorder" (31 n. 2). Hobbes, *Lev.* 8.20, p. 49, describes melancholy as a madness born of extreme dejection.

[103] Though Borrelli, "Prudence," 96, suggests that "the condition of melancholy man does not favour ... the positive exit from the state of nature."

[104] Thomas Hobbes, *The Correspondence*, ed. Noel Malcolm, 2 vols. (Oxford, 1994), 2:513 (1660).

[105] See above, Chapter 5, n. 89.

[106] On tears in the seventeenth century and the various attitudes of different groups toward weeping, see above, Chapter 8, and Capp, "Jesus Wept."

[107] On the place of Pepys in the Royal Society, see Norman J. W. Thrower, "Samuel Pepys FRS (1633–1703) and the Royal Society," *Notes and Records of the Royal Society of London* 57 (2003): 3–13; on that of Evelyn, see Margaret Denny, "The Early Program of the Royal Society and John Evelyn," *Modern Language Quarterly* 1 (1940): 481–97, and Rhodri Lewis, "John Evelyn, the Early Royal Society, and Artificial Language Projection: A New Source," *Notes and Queries* 51 (2004): 31–34.

Malcolm puts it, "in general intellectual terms, Hobbes was on the same side as these leading scientists – a proponent of the mechanistic 'new science' against the old scholasticism."[108] True, Hobbes trailed a faint whiff of atheism. But, as Quentin Skinner has pointed out, this was not at the time adduced as a reason for exclusion from the Society, and, besides, "there were undoubtedly men of very dubious orthodoxy even among the founding Fellows of the Society."[109] Again, it is true that Hobbes was not known for his experimental science. But many members of the Society also were not, while, on the other hand, some truly experimental scientists did not become members.[110] Skinner introduces evidence to show that Hobbes was "wholly impatient of contradiction," "dogmatical," and "disparaging," and concludes that "personal feelings were allowed to play a considerable part." Hobbes was a "club bore."[111]

"Personal feelings" brings us to emotions. Did Hobbes not fit into the "emotional community" comprised of the members of the Royal Society? To be sure, it is not clear that it *was* an emotional community; Skinner calls it "inchoate."[112] But Michael Hunter points out that it included mainly Londoners and cultivated a "relatively high social tone."[113] And it did have a group of "founders" who, if not entirely in accord – even on the questions of Hobbes' membership – nevertheless managed to get along.[114] I suggest following Malcolm here, who points out that Hobbes was not always a "club bore" – unpleasant, irascible, and hard to get along with. He had friends, and he belonged to "clubby" groups like the "regular gathering of philosophers and scientists in Mersenne's rooms in the convent of Minim friars in Paris."[115] The reason that he was excluded from the Royal Society was not that he was so different – as a scientist, "club member," or person-ality – from its members. Rather it was because Hobbes was "becoming an increasingly disreputable figure, both politically and theologically; and the people who felt that it was most in their interests to blacken his reputation

---

[108] Malcolm, "Hobbes," DNB.

[109] Quentin Skinner, "Thomas Hobbes and the Nature of the Early Royal Society," *The Historical Journal* 12/2 (1969): 217–39.

[110] *Ibid.*, 227–36. Noel Malcolm, "Hobbes and the Royal Society," in *Perspectives on Thomas Hobbes*, ed. G. A. J. Rogers and A. Ryan (Oxford, 1988), 43–66 at 47–48, cites evidence that Hobbes did indeed perform experiments.

[111] Skinner, "Hobbes and the Early Royal Society," 222–23, and 238.   [112] *Ibid.*, 222.

[113] Michael Hunter, *The Royal Society and Its Fellows 1660–1700: The Morphology of an Early Scientific Institution* (Chalfont St Giles, 1982), 6–8. See also Hunter, *Establishing the New Science: The Experience of the Early Royal Society* (Woodbridge, 1989).

[114] Charles Webster, *The Great Instauration: Science, Medicine and Reform, 1626–1660* (New York, 1976), 88–99, discusses the early culture of the Society, with its "active nucleus of twelve" members (91), its "conscious decision . . . to avoid contentious issues" (95), and its gradually adopted goal of "world reformation" (99).

[115] Malcolm, "Hobbes and the Royal Society," 49.

further were the ones who were vulnerable to embarrassing comparisons between his position and their own."[116] He was *too much* like them!

And what were the Royal Society members like from the point of view of their emotional norms? Let me simply suggest that they cultivated two rather contradictory stances. On the one hand the Royal Society was a gentlemen's club that consciously cultivated "civility." One of its founders, William Petty (1623–87), explained: the Royal Society should exclude work that might excite "passion or interest, faction or party."[117] Civility was, as Anne Goldgar has put it, a "mode of social cohesion."[118] On the other hand, its members were happily disputatious, contentious and competitive, as Robert Hooke's attack on the young Isaac Newton and Newton's "insulting" reply suggests.[119]

The Royal Society went through various periods of crisis and renewal well chronicled by Hunter.[120] It was never as professionalized as some wanted it. Nor was it as open as it might have been: Skinner argues that its members were so tied to "gentility" that they came to lose interest in practical results, leaving those to the tradesmen and engineers.[121] But some of the Society's values – emotional and otherwise – came to dominate in the next century. The "birth of a consumer society" meant new "curiosity about the material world," including scientific knowledge. Everyone wanted to attend courses about the wonders revealed by telescopes, and children were given microscopes to play with.[122] If this book had another chapter, it would be about the eighteenth-century "culture of

---

[116] *Ibid.*, 60.

[117] Quoted in Steven Shapin and Simon Schaffer, *Leviathan and the Air-Pump: Hobbes, Boyle, and the Experimental Life* (Princeton, 1985), 303, and, more generally for the "ideal community of the experimenters," which involved limited toleration and assent within certain bounds (rather than enthusiasm for and coercion on behalf of one point of view), 298–310. See also Steven Shapin, *A Social History of Truth: Civility and Science in Seventeenth-Century England* (Chicago, 1994), 122–25.

[118] Anne Goldgar, *Impolite Learning: Conduct and Community in the Republic of Letters, 1680–1750* (New Haven, 1995), 8.

[119] Richard S. Westfall, "Newton, Sir Isaac (1642–1727)," DNB (Oxford, 2004); online ed., Jan. 2009, www.oxforddnb.com/view/article/20059, accessed July 3, 2014.

[120] Hunter, *Royal Society*, 36–37, details "an almost total cessation of recruitment," as well as a decline in meeting attendance in the 1670s. But soon (*ibid.*, 39) it revived as it recruited new members and found some "active enthusiasts." Margaret 'Espinasse, "The Decline and Fall of Restoration Science," *Past and Present* 14 (1958): 71–89, attributes the Society's revival to Newton (elected in 1672, president 1703–27), but Hunter, *Royal Society*, 48–52, disputes this vigorously.

[121] Skinner, "Hobbes and the Early Royal Society," 239.

[122] See Neil McKendrick, John Brewer, and J. H. Plumb, *The Birth of a Consumer Society: The Commercialization of Eighteenth-Century England* (Bloomington, 1982), 316–34, quote on 317. On a "culture of curiosity," see P. Fontes da Costa, "The Culture of Curiosity at the Royal Society in the First Half of the Eighteenth Century," *Notes and Records of the Royal Society of London* 56/2 (2002): 147–66.

curiosity" and its many variants and deviants. Curiosity itself was nothing new – Augustine and Aelred had called it a form of desire, while Thomas Aquinas had seen the kindred emotion of *admiratio* (wonder) as admirable.[123] What was new was curiosity's prestige and greatly enhanced valuation. The history of emotions is not about "old and new" or "lost and found." Nor, on the other hand, is it about hardwiring and universality. It is about repurposing and revaluing – and therefore about transforming felt experience. Yes, emotions are in the DNA: in recombinant DNA.

---

[123] See above Chapter 1, n. 52; Chapter 4, n. 55; and Chapter 5, Table 5.2. On the career of curiosity, see Daston and Park, *Wonders*, 122–25, 273–76, 303–28. Around the same time as Hobbes was writing, Descartes made "admiration" one of his six basic emotions. See Laurence Renault, "Nature humaine et passions selon Thomas d'Aquin et Descartes," in *Les Passions antiques et médiévales*, 249–67, and John Sutton, "Controlling the Passions: Passion, Memory, and the Moral Physiology of Self in Seventeenth-Century Neurophilosophy," in *The Soft Underbelly of Reason: The Passions in the Seventeenth Century*, ed. Stephen Gaukroger (London, 1998), 115–46. Paganini, "Passionate Thought," 246–55, discusses the implications of the fact that Hobbes uses the word "curiosity" to talk about one type of regulated thought – the kind that hunts out all sorts of causes and effects (for which see Hobbes, *Lev.* 3.5, p. 17). See also Barnouw, "Hobbes's Psychology," esp. 532–41.

Conclusion

In each time and place there are multiple emotional communities. They are not usually isolated from one another, though they may function fairly independently. They often know about each other, as John Paston II knew about the court of Burgundy; as in that case, they interact. Sometimes certain "emotional arenas," to borrow Mark Seymour's term, bring an assortment of emotional communities together. Samuel Pepys and his wife found themselves at a "mock-wedding," where one Mrs. Carrick and one Mr. Lucy were freed "to perform as husband and wife." Pepys testily reported on "a great deal of fooling among them that I and my wife did not like."[1]

Pepys' reference to his wife raises two questions touched upon only glancingly in this book. Did women form their own emotional communities? Were women, whether in their own communities or as part of larger groups, expected to feel differently from men – especially to be "more emotional" than men? To the first question, the answer is not yet in. It must be sought in the particular sources of particular women's groups. Perhaps female monasteries in twelfth-century England had very different emotional norms from Aelred's Rievaulx. But what should we say of the women's monasteries that admired and tried to imitate the Cistercian lifestyle? At the present state of our knowledge, we simply do not know.[2]

But we do have an answer to the second question: it varied considerably. The primarily male emotional community of the seventh-century Neustrian courtiers imagined women as histrionic, and to some extent, as we see in the letters of Herchenefreda, mother of Desiderius of Cahors, women *did* express their emotions more volubly than men. But at the court of Toulouse in the twelfth century, women were portrayed as

---

[1] *Diary of Pepys*, 1:27 (Jan. 24, 1660), and n. 2.

[2] Charles-Louis Morand, "Building Power through Disaster: Christine de Pizan, Widowhood and a Community of Women following the Battle of Agincourt," unpublished paper, sees Christine actively trying to build an emotional community of strong widowed women. I thank him for letting me see his paper prior to publication.

314

calculating, indifferent to true love, and generally incapable of love themselves. In Gerson's writings, women were "softer" than men and more
prone to tears, a "fact" of which he disapproved. But at the very time
Gerson was writing, Burgundian chroniclers highly appreciated male
tears and bodily gestures. Across the channel, the Pastons, both women
and men, were temperate in emotional expression. And in Henry
Walker's gathered church in the mid-seventeenth century, both women
and men gave vent to such similar emotions that sometimes it is impossible to know whose testimonials we are reading. Thus, in the end, it is
variety, not any general rule, that must be stressed.

William Reddy has called emotion a "domain of effort."[3] Emotions,
he notes, have always to be tamped down, counteracted, controlled,
opposed, mastered, and managed. Occasionally, they may be subli-
mated. Who has done the tamping down? For Reddy, it is largely
political regimes. Thus, political regimes become "emotional regimes":
they inculcate a "set of normative emotions" and their associated rituals
and practices.[4] This is the context in which Reddy wrote that "emotional control is the real site of the exercise of power: politics is just a
process of determining who must repress as illegitimate, who must
foreground as valuable, the feelings that come up for them in given
contexts and relationships."[5] For Arlie Hochschild, who has looked at
the training of flight attendants – to smile, to feel cheerful – this domain
of effort requires real work and leads her to coin the phrase "emotional
labor."[6]

There is much truth in the notion that emotions are a domain of effort.
Certainly we see it reflected in all the *theories* that we have reviewed here.
Cicero's good emotions were few and were felt for limited objects under
limited circumstances. Augustine called on God's grace to get the will
(and therefore the emotions) in line. Alcuin's lay reader needed a guide to
manage his virtues and vices. Thomas Aquinas – ever the optimist – only
needed love to fix on the right good to get all the other emotions in order.
But that "only" was hardly obvious or easy. Jean Gerson thought people
needed a way to practice the emotions of the heart; that's why he assimilated them to the Guidonian hand. Finally, Hobbes' emotions were so
unruly that only the Leviathan could prevent them from running riot.
These theories suggest why emotions are often used judgmentally. People
who talk loudly and angrily are "popping off"; people who cry a lot are
"crybabies." In our day emotions are not (usually) called virtues

---

[3] Reddy, *Navigation*, 57, and elsewhere.   [4] *Ibid.*, 129.
[5] Reddy, "Against Constructionism," 335.
[6] Hochschild, *The Managed Heart*, with later editions.

and vices, but the words "normal" and "abnormal" function rather similarly.[7]

On the ground, however, emotional communities do not seem to struggle with the effort to control their emotions. Because there are multiple emotional communities at any one time, the effort to conform to one does not bar finding another that is more congenial. If there are indeed emotional regimes, they are not so hegemonic as to preclude numerous variants. Further, emotional communities seem to relish their emotional norms and values. Given the connection of emotions to virtues, vices, and value judgments in general, it is no surprise that emotional communities tend implicitly to see their styles as virtuous (and others as less virtuous). Let us review those we have seen in this book.

In the seventh century Gregory of Tours and Fortunatus welcomed sentimental feelings. Fortunatus made his career out of honeyed words, while Gregory expected even evil people to care about their families – if often seeing through their duplicity. At the Neustrian court a younger generation was distrustful of sentiment and basked in the virtue of their tepid modes of emotional expression. They got satisfaction, too, from laughing at others – women, mainly – who were more demonstrative than they. Later in the century, the elites who wrote and read the lives of martyrs enjoyed dwelling on rancorous emotions.

In the twelfth century, the Cistercian monk Aelred embraced charity, an offspring of love. As charity created the friendships that led to Christ and the various loves that led to the three Sabbaths, numerous other feelings – rejoicing, sorrowing, anxiety, fear – came in its train. Aelred applauded them: strong feelings were part of the human condition. Tears linked you to God. To be sure, Aelred knew the temptations of power and the pains of betrayal. He expended a lot of effort telling his fellow monks about all of these things, and he tried to shape their sensibilities and, certainly, their emotions. Here we have something like an emotional regime within the monastery. But it was ambiguous enough to allow for ire and indignation as well as love and compassion. And it was meant to lead to a pleasure exceeded only in heaven: "Finding no one among them whom I did not love and no one by

---

[7] This is most easily documented by citing scientific studies: for example, Gregory P. Strauss et al., "Emotion Regulation Abnormalities in Schizophrenia: Cognitive Change Strategies Fail to Decrease the Neural Response to Unpleasant Stimuli," *Schizophrenia Bulletin* 39/4 (2014): 872–83; Jee In Kang et al., "Abnormalities of Emotional Awareness and Perception in Patients with Obsessive-Compulsive Disorder," *Journal of Affective Disorders* 141/2–3 (2012): 286–93; Megan L. Willis, "Orbitofrontal Cortex Lesions Result in Abnormal Social Judgements to Emotional Faces," *Neuropsychologia* 48/7 (2010): 2182–87.

whom I was not loved, I was filled with a joy (*gaudio*) that surpassed all the delights of the world."[8]

Just a bit later, at the court of Toulouse, the counts also celebrated love and were worried about betrayals. They announced these feelings in forthright manner. Their charters stated their love and expectations for love in return, but at the same time they anticipated betrayal and therefore threatened loss of love, ire, and rancor. These were the very emotions that had once intrigued the elites of seventh-century Francia and that even Aelred sometimes found it necessary to express. Meanwhile, the counts' troubadours sang of female betrayals, thus turning realistic fears into verse fantasies. The poets expressed – with extraordinary variety, charm, and wit – contrasting feelings of love and anger, hope and bitterness, fidelity and heartache. They had a marvelously large, ambiguous, flexible language with which to do this. Just their one word *ira* telegraphed both sorrow and anger.

Like the court at Toulouse, the fifteenth-century Burgundian court was a place of entertainment. But it fostered pageantry over poetry, visual virtuosity over wordplay. Although using the vernacular, it employed fewer emotion words than the troubadours did, and issues of love and treachery, though not lacking, took a back seat to feelings of sorrow and pity. Burgundian chroniclers celebrated their dukes and nobles by emphasizing their emotional sensitivity. Like the Cistercians, they welcomed tears and highlighted their compassion. They responded to the wars and assassinations of their age with dolor and pity. These feelings, painful as they were, were also pleasurable. Otherwise why would La Marche pay special attention to a "pitiable" and "special" tableau? The feelings emphasized at court expressed the virtue and exquisite sensibilities of the upper classes.

Still in the fifteenth century, the English mystic Margery Kempe cultivated, even more than the Burgundians, a melodramatic emotional style. It was met with scorn on the one hand and admiration on the other. Margery's tears were public and prolonged, her behavior provocative. Her emotional community seems to have been rather dispersed – a cleric here, an admirer there – though, because she valued the derision of others, she may well have exaggerated the number of her detractors. Margery emphasized a variant of sorrow – despair – as well as its opposite, joy and merriment. How different this was from the Pastons, not too far away, who cultivated an understated emotional style! From what we can tell of the one Paston family member who was at the king's court, the emotional regime there was like neither the Paston family norms nor Margery's. Yet

[8] Chapter 4, n. 75.

both found room under that same political regime for their own modes of emotional expression.

With the printing press came more possibilities for the imposition of emotional norms. Yet the contrary seems to have been the case. Numerous regimes – emotional and otherwise – roiled seventeenth-century English political and emotional life. The one emotional "common denominator" of the period – melancholy – was rooted in many different developments: the celebration of melancholy by Renaissance Italian writers; the religious sensibilities of a Margery transposed into a Protestant milieu; the rise of a mode of spiritual autobiography (also a Protestant phenomenon) that stressed rising from "despond" to "joy"; the proliferation of ministers of various brands of Protestantism who wanted to give guidance; the new prestige of medical theories after Harvey's discovery of the circulation of the blood; and probably many other reasons as well. The one thing that cannot explain the emphasis on melancholy is the political regime, since the period saw too many of those: monarchy, the Cromwellian revolution, and the Restoration.

And anyway, not everyone professed melancholy. Pepys and Evelyn did not; Hobbes did not. The testimonials in *Spirituall Experiences* followed emotional sequences that led from despair to hope and comfort. The Levellers put such religious feelings together with civic aspirations. But they did not express melancholy; their focus was on freedom and happiness. These would be gained through the laws of the state, determined by the English people themselves. The Levellers were aware that their program offended the elites; they were up against "the violent passions of Powers and Principalities."[9] But they were very happy – at least they argued that they were: they approved their own emotional community, which brought them "Tranquillity of mind, and peace of Conscience."[10]

But if they are so happy and comfortable with their norms, why do emotional communities change over time? I have suggested some reasons throughout this book. A charismatic personality may enter a community – as Columbanus did in Neustria – and transform notions of both virtue and feeling. Competition among groups may cause one to redefine itself – emotionally and in other ways – against another. Here again the Neustrian court is a good example, given its competition with the Austrasian court of Brunhild. Or consider the Levellers finding their own brand of happiness against the religious sort sought by others in the Puritan movement. The desire to imitate prestigious groups might also initiate change: a whole society does not become "melancholy" without the claim bringing some

[9] See above, Chapter 8, n. 168.   [10] Chapter 8, n. 170.

advantage. Older theories of change certainly have some validity: Peter Stearns is surely right to think that social and economic changes engender emotional adjustments; Jan Plamper is correct in seeing theories as changing the emotions people accept; and William Reddy is certainly on to something when he suggests that "emotional suffering" leads to the search for "emotional liberty."[11] But not everyone is affected by social changes; not everyone believes in the same theory; and emotional suffering may mean that an individual will find his or her own way out of the community that induces suffering to one that provides comfort. The believers in Walker's gathered church were certainly engaged in this process.

And then, to be sure, there is the possibility that an emotional community will not change – that it will remain "stuck" in one mode that goes on for generations. That community may remain under the historian's radar for a very long time unless, for some reason, its particular style comes to the fore – via political or economic power or the vagaries of fad or new prestige.

In an email exchange, Mark Seymour told me that the notion of emotional communities suggested to him "the image of cells dividing viewed through a microscope – I could visualise communities breaking off with different emotions values, even though we know it happened in a very slow way." This is a useful metaphor, especially when considered together with the discovery of genome mosaicism. As James R. Lupski wrote in 2013, "it is becoming increasingly apparent that a human individual is made up of a population of cells, each with its own 'personal' genome."[12] Some of these are the results of "copy number variants": even clones of embryonic stem cells show such variations. Others are due to errors during replication, "genomic rearrangements," and other mutations. Finally, exposure to certain environments – tobacco smoke, for example – may induce new genome configurations in some cells. Such mutations may explain the onset of diseases and the ailments of old age, since they accumulate throughout the body over time. But mutations are also often adaptive. They are, for example, useful in the immune system, where variants help "to combat a wide variety of pathogens and antigens."[13]

I would liken the emotional communities of any given time within any particular society (however defined) to genome mosaicism. They persist over time, but they also mutate. Within the body politic they nurture the

---

[11] For these three theories of change, see Barbara H. Rosenwein, "An Historian in the Amazon," in *Visions of Community: Comparative Approaches to Medieval Forms of Identity in Europe and Asia*, ed. Andre Gingrich and Christina Lutter = *History and Anthropology* (2014), unpaginated.

[12] James R. Lupski, "Genome Mosaicism – One Human, Multiple Genomes," *Science* 341 (2013): 358–59.

[13] *Ibid.*, 359.

possibilities of adaptations to new environments, partly because they are
affected by those environments, and partly because their own internal
changes fit new circumstances – or do not, leading to their marginalization and even, perhaps, their disappearance.

Scientists have not yet observed the precise processes through which
genome mosaicism is created, but they can see the results: different
genomes in large samples of blood and tissues. Most such studies have
hitherto concentrated on blood samples, but Lupski hopes that all sorts of
tissues will eventually be tested. Similarly, *Generations of Feeling* has
provided evidence of *emotional* mosaicism in France and England,
600–1700, but exactly how one gets from, say, the despair of a Margery
Kempe to the very different sort of despair of members of a gathered
church is not clear.[14]

If, as I propose here, new generations take bits and pieces from old
emotional vocabularies, sequences, and styles while combining them in
new ways, then the search for "origins" becomes futile. Compassion, says
Ute Frevert, is a construct of modernity.[15] But already Gregory the Great
c. 600 was making the rector's empathy – his ability to feel the feelings of
others, his *compassio* – a key part of his job.[16] Empathy was generalized to
the feelings among friends and love of neighbor in the thought of Aelred of
Rievaulx.[17] Pity and compassion were at the very center of Gerson's
emotional cross.[18] Or consider romantic love, which, says William
Reddy, was a construct of the troubadours who reacted against the
Gregorian Reform.[19] But romantic love was already part of the emotional
expectations of Gregory of Tours and Fortunatus; recall Cupid hovering
over the marriage of Sigibert and Brunhild.[20] Cheerfulness "arrived" with
the Enlightenment, according to Peter Stearns.[21] But saints (as we saw as
early as the seventh century) were often cheerful.[22] Stearns is nearer to the
mark when he speaks of a "new emphasis" on cheer's "importance." But a
better way to see this is the "democratization" of cheerfulness as saints
descended – and ordinary people gained – in status. Emotions – not
hardwired, but embedded in culture – are reused and redeployed. They
are not "invented."

Further, pointing to the new status of this or that emotion leaves out the
ways in which emotions interact with one another, forming sequences

---

[14] In some instances, texts may provide the intermediaries. The dukes of Burgundy, for
example, adopted some emotional norms from Old French romances; but they put those
into prose – into chronicles of their own history – thus recontextualizing them. See Plate
6.1.
[15] Frevert, *Emotions in History*, 70.   [16] Rosenwein, *Emotional Communities*, chap. 3.
[17] See above, Chapter 4.   [18] Above, Chapter 7.
[19] Reddy, *The Making of Romantic Love*, Part 1.   [20] Above, Chapter 2.
[21] Stearns, "Modern Patterns," 29.   [22] Above, Chapter 2.

that are even more important for emotions history than the story of any individual emotion. Thus we can find tears, abundant tears, highly valued among both men and women, both before and after the Protestant Reformation. But within the larger sequence of religious emotions across the "medieval/modern divide," those tears had different meanings and were therefore *felt* differently: in the first instance, they were signs of grace and accompanied feelings of comfort; in the second, they were signs of sorrow and companions of anguish. Memories, interpretations, and traditions both familial and cultural allow the bits and pieces that constitute human values, words, goals, and feelings to come together and disperse in new ways depending on needs, ideologies, and predilections. This coming together, reshaping, and reworking forms the history of emotions across the generations.

Bibliography

Primary Sources

A Collection of Several Passages concerning his late Highnesse Oliver Cromwell, In the time of his Sickness. London, 1659.

Acosta, José de. *The naturall and morall historie of the East and West Indies Intreating of the remarkable things of heaven, of the elements, mettalls, plants and beasts which are proper to that country: together with the manners, ceremonies, lawes, governments, and warres of the Indians.* Translated by Edward Grimeston. London, 1604.

Aelred of Rievaulx. *Aelred of Rievaulx: The Historical Works.* Translated by Jane Patricia Freeland. Edited, with an Introduction and Annotations, by Marsha L. Dutton. Kalamazoo, 2005.

Aelred of Rievaulx's De institutione inclusarum: Two English Versions. Edited by John Ayto and Alexandra Barratt. London, 1984.

Aelredi Rievallensis. Opera Omnia, 1: Opera ascetica. Edited by Anselme Hoste and Charles H. Talbot. CCCM 1. Turnhout, 1971.

De bello standardii. PL 195, cols. 701–12.

De institutione inclusarum. In OO, 1, pp. 637–82.

De speculo caritatis. In OO, 1, pp. 3–161.

De spiritali amicitia. In OO, 1, pp. 287–350.

Eulogium Davidis regis Scotorum. In *Pinkerton's Lives of the Scottish Saints*, edited by William M. Metcalfe, 2 vols., 2:269–85. Rev. ed. Paisley, 1889.

Genealogia Regis Anglie Henrici iunioris. PL 195, cols. 711–37.

Sermones XLVII-LXXXIV. Edited by Gaetano Raciti. CCCM 2B. Turnhout, 2001.

Sermones LXXXV-CLXXXII. Edited by Gaetano Raciti. CCCM 2C. Turnhout, 2012.

Spiritual Friendship. Translated by Lawrence C. Braceland. Edited and introduction by Marsha L. Dutton. Collegeville, 2010.

The Mirror of Charity. Translated by Elizabeth Connor. Introduction and notes by Charles Dumont. Kalamazoo, 1990.

Aimeric de Belenoi. *Le Poesie.* Edited by Andrea Poli. Florence, 1997.

Alcuin. *De virtutibus et vitiis liber ad Widonem comitem.* PL 101, cols. 613–38.

Disputatio de rhetorica et de virtutibus sapientissimi Regis Caroli et Albini magistri. In *The Rhetoric of Alcuin and Charlemagne: A Translation, with an Introduction, the Latin Text, and Notes*, edited and translated by Wilbur Samuel Howell. Princeton, 1941.

Epistolae. Edited by Ernst Dümmler. MGH Epistolae 4: Epistolae karolini aevi 2. Berlin, 1895. Reprint, 1994.

Ambrose. *Expositio psalmi CXVIII*. Edited by Michael Petschenig. CSEL 62. Vienna, 1913.

An Account of the Last Houres of the late Renowned Oliver Lord Protector. London, 1659.

Antonius. *Vita sancti Simeonis stylitae*. PL 73, cols. 325–34.

Aristotle. *Nicomachean Ethics*. Translated by Harris Rackham. Cambridge, MA, 1932.

On the Soul. In *On the Soul. Parva Naturalia. On Breath*, translated by W. S. Hett, pp. 1–203. Cambridge, MA, 1935.

Physics. Translated by R. P. Hardie and R. K. Gaye. Online at www.logicmuseum.com/authors/aristotle/physics/physics.htm.

Augustine. *Confessions*. Edited and translated by Pierre de Labriolle, 2 vols. Paris, 1969, 1977.

De civitate dei. Edited by Bernard Dombart and Alphonse Kalb. CCSL 47–48. Turnhout, 1955.

De libero arbitrio. In *Il "De Libero Arbitrio" di S. Agostino. Studio introduttivo, testo, traduzione e commento*, edited by Franco De Capitani. Milan, 1987.

De quantitate animae. Edited by Wolfgang Hörmann. CSEL 89, pp. 131–231. Vienna, 1986.

Enarrationes in psalmos. In *Enarrationes in Psalmos 1–50*, edited by Clemens Weidmann. CSEL 93/1A. Vienna, 2003.

Epistula 149. Edited by Alois Goldbacher. CSEL 44, pp. 348–80. Vienna, 1904.

Tractatus. In *Commentaire de la Première Épître de saint Jean*, edited and translated by Paul Agaësse. SC 75. Paris, 1961.

Avitus of Vienne. *Epistularum ad diversos libri tres*. Edited by Rudolf Peiper. MGH AA 6.2, pp. 35–103. Berlin, 1883.

Letters and Selected Prose. Translated with an introduction and notes by Danuta Shanzer and Ian Wood. Liverpool, 2002.

Bacon, Francis. *The Advancement of Learning*. In *The Oxford Francis Bacon*, IV, edited by Michael Kiernan. Oxford, 2000.

Baudonivia. *De vita sanctae Radegundis liber II*. Edited by Bruno Krusch. MGH SRM 2, pp. 377–95. Hannover, 1888. Reprint, 1984.

Bernart de Ventadorn. *Poems*. In *The Songs of Bernart de Ventadorn*, edited and translated by Stephen G. Nichols, Jr., John A. Galm, and A. Bartlett Giamatti, with Roger J. Porter, Seth L. Wolitz, and Claudette M. Charbonneau. Chapel Hill, 1965.

Bobolenus. *Vita Germani abbatis Grandivallensis*. Edited by Bruno Krusch. MGH SRM 5, pp. 33–40. Hannover, 1910. Reprint, 1997.

Boniface of Mainz. *Sermo 7*. PL 89, cols. 856–57.

Bright, Timothie. *A Treatise of Melancholie. Containing the causes thereof, and reasons of the strange effects it worketh in our minds and bodies*. London, 1586.

Bunyan, John. *Pilgrim's Progress*. Edited by Roger Sharrock. London, 1966.

Burton, Robert. *The Anatomy of Melancholy*. Edited by Thomas C. Faulkner, Nicholas K. Kiessling, and Rhonda L. Blair. Commentary by J. B. Bamborough and Martin Dodsworth, 6 vols. Oxford, 1989–2000.

Cadenet. *Poems*. In *Les Poésies du troubadour Cadenet. Edition critique avec introduction, traduction, notes et glossaire*, edited and translated by Josef Zemp. Bern, 1978.

Catalogues raimondins (1112–1229). *Actes des comtes de Toulouse, ducs de Narbonne et marquis de Provence*. Edited by Laurent Macé. Toulouse, 2008.

Calvin. *Institutes of the Christian Religion*. Edited by John T. McNeill. Translated by Ford Lewis Battles, 2 vols. Philadelphia, 1960.

Cassian, John. *De institutis coenobiorum et de octo principalium vitiorum remediis libri XII*. Edited by Michael Petschenig. CSEL 17. Vienna, 1888.

Chanson de la Croisade albigeoise. Edited and translated by Eugène Martin-Chabot, 3 vols. Paris, 1957–61.

Chastelain, Georges. *Chronique*. In *Oeuvres*, vols. 1–6.

   Complainte d'Hector [recte *Les Epitaphes d'Hector*]. In *Oeuvres*, 6:167–202.

   Mystère sur la paix de Péronne. In *Oeuvres*, 7:423–52.

   Oeuvres de Georges Chastellain. Edited by Kervyn de Lettenhove, 8 vols. Brussels, 1863–66.

Chaucer. *The Nun's Priest's Tale*. In *The Riverside Chaucer*, edited by Larry D. Benson, pp. 253–61. 3rd ed. Boston, 1987.

Chronique du religieux de Saint-Denys. Edited and translated by M. L. Bellaguet, 6 vols. Paris, 1839–52.

Church of England. *The Two Books of Homilies Appointed to be Read in Churches*. Oxford, 1859.

Cicero. *De inventione*. In *De inventione. De optimo genere oratorum. Topica*, translated by Harry M. Hubbell, pp. 2–345. Cambridge, MA, 1960.

   Laelius de Amicitia. In *De senectute. De amicitia. De divinatione*, translated by William A. Falconer, pp. 108–211. Cambridge, MA, 1964.

   M. Tulli Ciceronis Tusculanae Disputationes. Edited by Michaelangelus Giusta. Turin, 1984.

Colthrop, Sir Henry. *The Liberties, usages, and customes of the city of London; confirmed by especiall Acts of Parliament . . .* London, 1642.

D'Avenant, William. *Gondibert: An Heroick Poem*. London, 1651.

d'Escouchy, Mathieu. *Chronique*. Edited by G. du Fresne de Beaucourt, 3 vols. Paris, 1863–64.

Defensor of Ligugé. *Liber Scintillarum*. In *Defensor de Ligugé, Livre d'étincelles*, edited by Henri-Marie Rochais, 2 vols., SC 77, 86. Paris, 1961–62.

Desiderius of Cahors. *Epistulae S. Desiderii Cadurcensis*. Edited by Dag Norberg. Stockholm, 1961.

Devotio Moderna: Basic Writings. Translated by John Van Engen. New York, 1988.

Downame, George. *The Christians freedome wherein is fully expressed the doctrine of Christian libertie*. Oxford, 1635.

Dynamius. *Vita sancti Maximi*. PL 80, cols. 31–40.

Epistolae Austrasicae. Edited by Wilhelm Gundlach. MGH Epistolae 3: Epistolae Merowingici et Karolini aevii 1, pp. 110–53. Berlin, 1892. Reprint, 1994.

Evelyn, John. *Numismata. A discourse of medals, antient and modern. Together with some account of heads and effigies of illustrious and famous persons, in sculps, and taille-douce, of whom we have no medals extant; and of the use to be derived from them. To which is added a digression concerning physiognomy*. London, 1697.

   The Diary of John Evelyn. Edited by E. S. de Beer, 6 vols. Oxford, 1955.

The Life of Mrs. Godolphin. Edited by Harriet Sampson. Oxford, 1939.

The Writings of John Evelyn. Edited by Guy de la Bédoyère. Woodbridge, Suffolk, 1995.

Fabri, Félix. *Les errances de Frère Félix, pèlerin en Terre sainte, en Arabie et en Égypte (1480–1483),* vol. 2: *Troisième et quatrième traités.* Edited and translated by Jean Meyers and Nicole Chareyron. Montpellier, 2000.

Ficino, Marsilio. *Three Books on Life.* Edited and translated by Carol V. Kaske and John R. Clark. Binghamton, NY, 1989.

Fortunatus, Venantius. *De vita sanctae Radegundis liber I.* Edited by Bruno Krusch. MGH SRM 2, pp. 364–77. Hannover, 1888. Reprint, 1984.

Liber de virtutibus s. Hilarii. Edited by Bruno Krusch. MGH AA 4.2, pp. 7–11. Berlin, 1885.

Poems. In *Poèmes,* edited and translated by Marc Reydellet, 3 vols. Paris, 2002–4.

Venantius Fortunatus: Personal and Political Poems. Translated by Judith George. Liverpool, 1995.

Venantius Fortunatus: Poems to Friends. Translated by Joseph Pucci. Indianapolis, 2010.

Vita Germani episcopi Parisiaci. Edited by Bruno Krusch. MGH SRM 7, pp. 372–418. Hannover, 1920. Reprint, 1997.

Froissart, Jean. "The Online Froissart: A Digital Edition of the Chronicles of Jean Froissart." Edited by Peter Ainsworth and Godfried Croenen. Online at www.hrionline.ac.uk/onlinefroissart/.

Gaucelm Faidit. *Poems.* In *Les poèmes de Gaucelm Faidit. Troubadour du XIIᵉ siècle,* edited and translated by Jean Mouzat. Paris, 1965.

Gerson, Jean. *Canticordum au pèlerin.* In *La doctrine du chant du Coeur de Jean Gerson.* Edition critique, traduction et commentaire du "Tractatus de canticis" et du "Canticordum au pélerin," edited and translated by Isabelle Fabre, pp. 479–524. Geneva, 2005.

De passionibus animae [long]. In OC, 9:1–25.

De passionibus animae [short]. In OC, 9:155–57.

Enumeratio peccatorum ab Alberto posita. In OC, 9:160–66.

Oeuvres complètes. Edited by Palémon Glorieux, 10 vols. Paris, 1960–73.

Tractatus de canticis. In *La doctrine du chant de Jean Gerson,* pp. 310–376.

Gregory of Tours. *Historiarum libri X.* Edited by Bruno Krusch and Wilhelm Levison. MGH SRM 1.1. Hannover, 1951. Reprint, 1993.

Liber in gloria confessorum. Edited by Bruno Krusch. MGH SRM 1.2, pp. 294–370. Hannover, 1885. Reprint, 1969.

Liber vitae patrum. Edited by Bruno Krusch. MGH SRM 1.2, pp. 211–94. Hannover, 1885. Reprint, 1969.

Gregory the Great. *Moralia in Job.* Edited by Marcus Adriaen. CCSL 143B. Turnhout, 1985.

Pastoral Care. In *Grégoire le Grand, Règle pastorale,* edited by Floribert Rommel, translated by Charles Morel, vol. 2. SC 382. Paris, 1992.

Hakluyt, Richard. *The principal navigations, voyages, traffiques & discoveries of the English nation made by sea or overland to the remote and farthest distant quarters of the earth at any time within the compass of these 1600 years.* Introduction by John Masefield, 8 vols. London, 1927.

Hobbes, Thomas. "Objectiones ad Cartesii meditationes." In OL 5:249–74.
Appendix to Leviathan. Edited and translated by George Wright. In George Wright. *Religion, Politics, and Thomas Hobbes,* pp. 36–173.
De cive. Corr. ed. Basel, 1782.
De homine. In *Thomas Hobbes Malmesburiensis opera philosophica quae latine scripsit, omnia in unum corpus nunc primum collecta,* edited by William Molesworth, 5 vols., 2:1–132. London, 1839–45.
De homine. In *Man and Citizen (De Homine* and *De Cive),* translated by Charles T. Wood, T. S. K. Scott-Craig, and Bernard Gert, pp. 33–85. Indianapolis, 1991.
Elements of Philosophy. The First Section, Concerning Body. In *The Collected [English] Works of Thomas Hobbes,* edited by William Molesworth, 12 vols. Vol. 1. Reprint, Routledge, 1992. Orig. pub., 1839–45.
Historia Ecclesiastica. Edited by Patricia Springborg, Patricia Stablein, and Paul Wilson. Paris, 2008.
Human Nature. In *The Elements of Law Natural and Politic, pt. 1: Human Nature, pt. 2: De Corpore Politico with Three Lives,* edited by J. C. A. Gaskin. Oxford, 1994.
Leviathan. Edited by J. C. A. Gaskin. Oxford, 1996.
The Correspondence. Edited by Noel Malcolm, 2 vols. Oxford, 1994.
Hulsius, Friedrich van. *The character of a Christian as hee is distinguished from all hypocrites and hereticks. With the freedome of the faithfull: as they are proposed by our Saviour, in the words of the Gospell.* London, 1627.
Isaac of Stella. *Sermo 17.* In *Isaac de L'Étoile, Sermons,* edited by Anselm Hoste. SC 130, pp. 311–39. Paris, 1967.
Isidore of Seville. *Sententiae.* Edited by Pierre Cazier. CCSL 111. Turnhout, 1998.
Jacques de Vitry. *The Life of Marie d'Oignies.* Translated by Margot King. In *Medieval Women's Visionary Literature,* edited by Elizabeth Alvilda Petroff, pp. 179–83. New York, 1986.
Jerome. *Libellus de virginitate servanda (Epistula 22).* Edited by Isidor Hilberg. CSEL 54, pp. 143–211. Vienna, 1910.
John of Damascus. *De Fide Orthodoxa: Versions of Burgundio and Cerbanus.* Edited by Eligius M. Buytaert. Louvain, 1955.
Jonas d'Orléans. *Instruction des laïcs.* Edited and translated by Odile Dubreucq, 2 vols. SC 549–50. Paris, 2012.
Jonas. *Vita Johannis abbatis Reomaensis.* Edited by Bruno Krusch. MGH SRM 3, pp. 502–17. Hannover, 1896. Reprint, 1995.
Vitae Columbani abbatis discipulorumque eius libri duo. Edited by Bruno Krusch. MGH SRM 4, pp. 64–152. Hannover, 1902. Reprint, 1997.
La Marche, Olivier de. *Mémoires.* Edited by Henri Beaune and Jean d'Arbaumont, 4 vols. Paris, 1883–88.
Lactantius. *On the Anger of God.* In *Lactance, La colère de dieu,* edited by Christiane Ingremeau. SC 289. Paris, 1982.
Lefèvre, Jean. *Chronique.* Edited by François Morand, 2 vols. Paris, 1876, 1881.
Les Grandes chroniques de France. Edited by Jules Viard, 10 vols. Paris, 1920–53.
Lilburne, John. *A Worke of the Beast or A Relation of a most unchristian Censure, Executed upon Iohn Lilburne, (Now prisoner in the fleet) the 18. of Aprill 1638*

with the heavenly speech uttered by him at the time of his suffering. 1638. Accessed via EEBO.

Englands birth-right justified against all arbitrary usurpation. 1645. Accessed via EEBO.

Londons Liberty in Chains discovered. London, 1646.

and William Walwyn, Thomas Prince, Richard Overton, and others. *A Manifestation*. [April 16] 1649.

and William Walwyn, Thomas Prince, and Richard Overton.] *An agreement of the free people of England* [1 May 1649]. In *The English Levellers*, edited by Andrew Sharp. Cambridge, 1998. Online at www.constitution.org/lev/eng_lev_12.txt.

Milton, John. *The doctrine and discipline of divorce: restor'd to the good of both sexes, from the bondage of Canon Law, and other mistakes, to Christian freedom, guided by the Rule of Charity*. London, 1643.

Missale ad usum Sarum. Edited by Francis H. Dickinson. Burntisland, 1861–83.

Monstrelet, Enguerrand de. *Chronicle*. In *La Chronique d'Enguerran de Monstrelet*, edited by L. Douët-D'Arcq, 6 vols. Paris, 1857–62.

Particular Friends: The Correspondence of Samuel Pepys and John Evelyn. Edited by Guy de la Bédoyère. Woodbridge, 1997.

Passio Leudegarii episcopi et martyris Augustodunensis I. Edited by Bruno Krusch. MGH SRM 5, pp. 282–322. Hannover, 1910. Reprint, 1997.

Paston Letters and Papers of the Fifteenth Century. Parts 1 and 2, edited by Norman Davis, part 3, edited by Richard Beadle and Colin Richmond. Oxford, 2004–5.

Peire Raimon. *Poems*. In *Le Poesie di Peire Raimon de Tolosa. Introduzione, testi, traduzioni, note*, edited and translated by Alfredo Cavaliere. Florence, 1935.

Peire Vidal. *Poems*. In *Les poésies de Peire Vidal*, edited and translated by Joseph Anglade. Paris, 1913.

Poems. In *Poesie*, edited by Silvio Avalle d'Arco, 2 vols. Milan, 1960.

Poems. In *The Songs of Peire Vidal: Translation and Commentary*, edited and translated by Veronica M. Fraser. New York, 2006.

Pepys, Samuel. *The Diary of Samuel Pepys*. Edited by Robert Latham and William Matthews, 11 vols. Berkeley, 1970.

Pseudo-Alcuin. *Confessio fidei*. PL 101, cols. 1027–98.

Pseudo-Augustine. *Sermo 254*. PL 39, cols. 2215–16.

Pseudo-Dionysius. *De divinis nominibus*. In *Dionysiaca. Recueil donnant l'ensemble des traditions latines des ouvrages attribués au Denys de l'Aréopage*, edited by Philippe Chevalier, vol. 1, pp. 3–561. Paris, 1937.

The Divine Names. In *Pseudo-Dionysius: The Complete Works*, translated by Colm Luibheid with Paul Rorem, pp. 47–132. New York, 1987.

Raimon de Miraval. *Poems*. In *Les poésies du troubadour Raimon de Miraval*, edited and translated by L. T. Topsfield. Paris, 1971.

Rogers, Timothy. *A Discourse Concerning Trouble of Mind and the Disease of Melancholly*. London, 1691.

Rolle, Richard. *The Fire of Love*. Translated by Clifton Wolters. New York, 1972.

Seneca. *Ad Lucilium. Epistulae morales*. Edited by L. D. Reynolds, 2 vols. Oxford, 1965. Online at http://www.intratext.com/IXT/LAT0230/#fonte.

Shakespeare, William. *Hamlet*. Edited by Ann Thompson and Neil Taylor. London, 2006.

Shepard, Thomas. *The works of Thomas Shepard: first pastor of the First Church, Cambridge, Mass.: with a memoir of his life and character*, 3 vols. Boston, 1853. Accessed via *Sabin Americana*. Gale, Cengage Learning.

Spenser, Edmund. *The Faerie Queene*. Edited by A. C. Hamilton. Text edited by Hiroshi Yamashita and Toshiyuki Suzuki. 2nd rev. ed. London, 1977.

Spirituall experiences, of sundry beleevers. Held forth by them at severall solemne meetings, and Conferences to that end. With the recommendation of the sound, spiritual, and savoury worth of them, to the sober and spirituall Reader, By Vavasor Powel, Minister of the Gospel. 2d ed. London, 1653. Accessed via EEBO.

Suso, Henry. *The Life of the Servant*. In *Henry Suso: The Exemplar, with Two German Sermons*, edited and translated by Frank Tobin, pp. 61–204. New York, 1989.

The Book of Margery Kempe. Edited by Barry Windeatt. Harlow, 2000.
  Edited by Sanford Brown Meech and Hope Emily Allen. Oxford, 1940.
  Translated by Lynn Staley. New York, 2001.

The Holy Bible ... made from the Latin Vulgate by John Wycliffe and his Followers. Edited by Josiah Forshall and Frederic Madden, 4 vols. Oxford, 1850. Reprint, 1982.

The Lanterne of Liȝt. Edited by Lilan M. Swinburn. London, 1917. Reprint, 1971.

The Rule of Saint Benedict. Edited and translated by Bruce L. Venarde. Cambridge, MA, 2011.

The Towneley Plays. Edited by George England and Alfred W. Pollard. London, 1897. Reprint, 1973.

The Writings of William Walwyn. Edited by Jack R. McMichael and Barbara Taft. Athens, GA, 1989.

Thomas Aquinas. *Commentary on Aristotle's Physics*. Translated by Richard J. Blackwell, Richard J. Spath, and W. Edmund Thirlkel. Introduction by Vernon J. Bourke. London, 1963.
  Corpus Thomisticum. S. Thomae de Aquino Opera Omnia. Edited by Enrique Alarcón. Pamplona, 2000. Online at www.corpusthomisticum.org.
  Le passioni dell'anima. Translated with an introduction by Silvana Vecchio. Florence, 2002.
  Quaestiones disputatae. In *Corpus Thomisticum*.
  Scriptum super Sententiis. In *Corpus Thomisticum*.
  Summa contra Gentiles. In *Corpus Thomisticum*.
  Summa theologiae. In *Corpus Thomisticum*.

To the Right Honourable the Lords and Commons assembled in Parliament, the Humble Petition of [blank]. 1645. Accessed via EEBO.

Visio Baronti Monachi Longoretensis. Edited by Wilhelm Levison. MGH SRM 5, pp. 377–94. Hannover, 1910. Reprint, 1997.

Vita Alcuini. Edited by Wilhelm Arndt. MGH SS 15.1, pp. 182–97. Hannover, 1887.

Vita Desiderii Cadurcae urbis episcopi. Edited by Bruno Krusch. MGH SRM 4, pp. 547–602. Hannover, 1902. Reprint, 1997.

Vita Sanctae [Domnae] Balthildis A. Ed. Bruno Krusch. MGH SRM 2, pp. 482–508. Hannover, 1888. Reprint, 1984.

Vita Sanctae Geretrudis A. Edited by Bruno Krusch. MGH SRM 2, pp. 453–64. Hannover, 1888. Reprint, 1984.

Vita Wandregiseli abbatis Fontanellensis. Edited by Bruno Krusch. MGH SRM 5, pp. 13–24. Hannover, 1910. Reprint, 1997.

Walker, Henry. *A Gad of Steele, wrought and tempered for the Heart to defend it from being battred by Sathans temptation, and to give it a sharpe and lasting edge in heavenly Consolation.* London, 1641.

——— *A Sermon Preached in the Chappel at Somerset-House in the Strand.* London, 1650.

——— *A Sermon, Preached In the Kings Chappell at White-Hall.* N.p., 1649.

——— *An Elogie or Eulogie on the Obits of the Right Honorable Ferdinando Lord Fairefax.* London, 1648.

——— *Perfect Occurrences of Parliament And chief Collections of Letters from The Lord Generall, Sir William Waller, the Lord Fairfaxes quarters, and others concerning Lyme, Derby, York, Oxford, Gloster, and other parts of the Kingdome,* no. 23. May 24, 1644.

——— *The Heavenly Guide to True Peace of Conscience.* London, 1641.

——— *The Sermon of Henry Walker, Ironmoger: Having beene twice Apprehended, for Writitng seditious Pamphlets.* London, 1642.

Walter Daniel. *Centum sententiae.* In Charles H. Talbot. "The *Centum Sententiae* of Walter Daniel." *Sacris Erudiri* 11 (1960): 266–374.

——— *Epistola ad Mauricium.* In *VA*, pp. 66–81.

——— *Lamentatio.* In Charles H. Talbot. "La Lamentation de Walter Daniel sur la mort du bienheureux Aelred." *Collectanea Cisterciensia* 5 (1938): 9–20.

——— *The Life of Aelred of Rievaulx by Walter Daniel.* Translated from the Latin and annotated by Frederick M. Powicke. Introduction by Marsha L. Dutton. Kalamazoo, 1994.

——— *The Life of Ailred of Rievaulx.* Edited and translated by Frederick M. Powicke. Oxford, 1978.

Walwyn, William. *Englands lamentable slaverie.* 1645. Online at bcw-project.org/texts/englands-lamentable-slaverie.

——— *Strong Motives or Loving and Modest advice, unto the Petitions for Presbiterian Government.* In Como, "An Unattributed Pamphlet," 377–82.

Wauquelin, Jean [Jehan]. *Chronique des ducs de Brabant.* Edited by Edmond de Dynter, 3 vols. Brussels, 1854–60.

William of Tocco. *Ystoria sancti Thome de Aquino de Guillaume de Toco (1323).* Edited by Claire le Brun-Gouanvic. Toronto, 1996.

Secondary Sources

A Companion to Aelred of Rievaulx. Edited by Marsha L. Dutton. Brill, forthcoming.

A Companion to Augustine. Edited by Mark Vessey. Chichester, 2012.

A Companion to Jean Gerson. Edited by Brian Patrick McGuire. Leiden, 2006.

A Companion to The Book of Margery Kempe. Edited by John H. Arnold and Katherine J. Lewis. Cambridge, 2004.

Abyzov, Alexej, J. Mariani, D. Palejev, Y. Zhang, M. S. Haney, L. Tomasini, A. F. Ferrandino, L. A. Rosenberg Belmaker, A. Szekely, M. Wilson, A. Kocabas, N. E. Calixto, E. L. Grigorenko, A. Huttner, K. Chawarska, S. Weissman, A. E. Urban, M. Gerstein, and F. M. Vaccarino. "Somatic Copy-Number Mosaicism in Human Skin Revealed by Induced Pluripotent Stem Cells." *Nature* 492/7429 (2012): 438–42.

Adventus. Studien zum herrscherlichen Einzug in die Stadt. Edited by Peter Johanek and Angelika Lampen. Cologne, 2009.

Aers, David, and Nigel Smith. "English Reformations." *Journal of Medieval and Early Modern Studies* 40 (2010): 425–38.

Airaksinen, Timo. "Hobbes on the Passions and Powerlessness." *Hobbes Studies* 6 (1993): 80–104.

Alduc-Le Bagousse, Armelle. "Comportements à l'égard des nouveau-nés et des petits enfants dans les sociétés de la fin de l'Antiquité et du haut Moyen Âge." In *L'enfant, son corps, son histoire*, 81–95.

Alessi, Giorgia. "Discipline. I nuovi orizzonti del disciplinamento sociale." *Storica* 4 (1996): 7–37.

Althoff, Gerd. "Demonstration und Inszenierung: Spielregeln der Kommunikation in mittelalterlicher Öffentlichkeit." *Frühmittelalterliche Studien* 27 (1993): 27–50.

"Empörung, Tränen, Zerknirschung. 'Emotionen' in der öffentlichen Kommunikation des Mittelalters." *Frühmittelalterliche Studien* 30 (1996): 60–79.

"*Ira Regis*: Prolegomena to a History of Royal Anger." In *Anger's Past*, 59–74.

Verwandte, Freunde und Getreue. Zum politischen Stellenwert der Gruppenbildungen im frühen Mittelalter. Darmstadt, 1990.

Amado, Claudie. "Effets de la Croisade albigeoise sur les valeurs nobiliaires méridionales." In *La Croisade albigeoise. Actes du Colloque du Centre d'Etudes Cathares Carcassonne, 4–6 octobre 2002*, edited by Michel Roquebert, 211–17. Carcassonne, 2004.

Anciaux, Paul. "La date de composition de la Somme de Godefroid de Poitiers." *Recherches de Théologie ancienne et médiévale* 16 (1949): 165–66.

Anderson, Wendy Love. "Gerson's Stance on Women." In *A Companion to Jean Gerson*, 293–315.

Andraud, Paul. *La vie et l'oeuvre du troubadour Raimon de Miraval. Étude sur la littérature et la société méridionales à la veille de la guerre des albigeois.* Paris, 1902. Reprint, Marseille, 1973.

Anger's Past: The Social Uses of an Emotion in the Middle Ages. Edited by Barbara H. Rosenwein. Ithaca, NY, 1998.

Aquinas's Moral Theory: Essays in Honor of Norman Kretzmann. Edited by Scott MacDonald and Eleonore Stump. Ithaca, NY, 1999.

Archer, Ian V. "Popular Politics in the Sixteenth and Early Seventeenth Centuries." In *Londinopolis: Essays in the Cultural and Social History of Early Modern London*, edited by Paul Griffiths and Mark S. R. Jenner, 26–46. Manchester, 2000.

Arnold, John H. "Margery's Trials." In *A Companion to* The Book of Margery Kempe, 77–93.

Ashley, Kathleen. "Historicizing Margery: *The Book of Margery Kempe* as Social Text." *Journal of Medieval and Early Modern Studies* 28 (1998): 371–88.

Atkinson, Clarissa W. *Mystic and Pilgrim: The Book and the World of Margery Kempe*. Ithaca, NY, 1983.

Atturo, Valentina. "*Languor carnis*. Echi di memoria salomonica nella fisiologia emozionale dei trovatori." In *Dai pochi ai molti. Studi in onore di Roberto Antonelli*, edited by Paolo Canettieri and Arianna Punzi, 49–78. Rome, 2014.

Augustiniana Traiectina. Edited by Jan den Boeft and Johannes van Oort. Paris, 1987.

Averill, James R. "A Semantic Atlas of Emotional Concepts." *JSAS Catalog of Selected Documents in Psychology* 5/330 (1975) (Ms. No. 1103).

Bader, Günter. *Psalterspiel. Skizze einer Theologie des Psalters*. Tübingen, 2009.

Bagley, C. P. "*Paratge* in the Anonymous *Chanson de la Croisade albigeoise*." *French Studies* 21 (1967): 195–204.

Baker, Philip. "*Londons Liberty in Chains Discovered*: The Levellers, the Civic Past, and Popular Protest in Civil War London." *Huntington Library Quarterly* 76/4 (2013): 559–87.

Baladier, Charles. *Érôs au Moyen Âge. Amour, désir et "delectatio morosa."* Paris, 1999.

Bamborough, J. B. "Burton, Robert (1577–1640)." DNB. Oxford, 2004. Online ed., Oct. 2009, www.oxforddnb.com/view/article/4137.

The Little World of Man. London, 1952.

Barasch, Moshe. *Gestures of Despair in Medieval and Early Renaissance Art*. New York, 1976.

Barber, Richard. *The Pastons: A Family in the Wars of the Roses*. London, 1981.

Barnouw, Jeffrey. "Hobbes's Psychology of Thought: Endeavours, Purpose and Curiosity." *History of European Ideas* 10/5 (1989): 519–45.

Barron, Caroline. "Who were the Pastons?" *Journal of the Society of Archivists* 4 (1972): 530–35.

Baseotto, Paola. "*Disdeining life, desiring leaue to die*": Spenser and the Psychology of Despair. Stuttgart, 2008.

"Godly Sorrow, Damnable Despair, and *Faerie Queene* I.ix." *Cahiers Élisabéthains* 69 (2006): 1–11.

Battista, Anna Maria. "Hobbes e la nascita della psicologia politica." In *Politica e diritto in Hobbes*, edited by Giuseppe Sorgi, 193–224. Milan, 1995.

Nascita della psicologia politica. Genoa, 1982.

Bavel, Tarcisius J. van. "The Influence of Cicero's Ideal of Friendship on Augustine." In *Augustiniana Traiectina*, 59–72.

Bawcutt, N. W. "Puritanism and the Closing of the Theaters in 1642." *Medieval and Renaissance Drama in England* 22 (2009): 179–200.

Bazán, B. Carlos. "The Human Soul: Form and Substance? Thomas Aquinas' Critique of Eclectic Aristotelianism." *Archives d'histoire doctrinale et littéraire du moyen âge* 64 (1997): 95–126.

Berger, Karol. "The Guidonian Hand." In *The Medieval Craft of Memory: An Anthology of Texts and Pictures*, edited by Mary Carruthers and Jan M. Ziolkowski, 71–82. Philadelphia, 2004.

Berman, Constance H. "Were There Twelfth-Century Cistercian Nuns?" *Church History* 68 (1999): 824–64.

Bermon, Emmanuel. "La théorie des passions chez saint Augustin." In *Les Passions antiques et médiévales*, 173–97.

Bhattacharji, Santha. "Tears and Screaming: Weeping in the Spirituality of Margery Kempe." In *Holy Tears: Weeping in the Religious Imagination*, edited by Kimberley Christine Patton, and John Stratton Hawley, 229–41. Princeton, 2005.

Blockmans, Wim, and Walter Prevenier. *The Promised Lands: The Low Countries under Burgundian Rule, 1369–1530*. Translated by Elizabeth Fackelman. Translation revised and edited by Edward Peters. Philadelphia, 1999.

Boccadoro, Brenno. "La musique, les passions, l'âme et le corps." In *Autour de Guillaume d'Auvergne (†1249)*, edited by Franco Morenzoni and Jean-Yves Tilliette, 75–92. Turnhout, 2005.

Boettcher, Susan R. "Confessionalization: Reformation, Religion, Absolutism, and Modernity." *History Compass* 2 (2004): 1–10.

Bonnet, Max. *Le latin de Grégoire de Tours*. Paris, 1890. Reprint, 1968.

Boquet, Damien. "Affectivity in the Spiritual Writings of Aelred of Rievaulx." In *A Companion to Aelred*, chap. 7.

———. *L'ordre de l'affect au Moyen Âge. Autour de l'anthropologie affective d'Aelred de Rievaulx*. Caen, 2005.

Borrelli, Gianfranco. "Prudence, Folly and Melancholy in the Thought of Thomas Hobbes." *Hobbes Studies* 9 (1996): 88–97.

Boucquey, Denis. "Enguerrand de Monstrelet, historien trop longtemps oublié." *Publications du Centre européen d'études bourguignonnes (XIVᵉ–XVIᵉ s.)* 31 (1991): 113–25.

———. "Une conception de l'histoire à la fin du Moyen Âge: la *Chronique* d'Enguerran de Monstrelet." *Mémoire de licence*, Louvain-la-Neuve, 1989.

Boyle, Leonard E. "The Setting of the *Summa theologiae* of Saint Thomas." In *The Gilson Lectures on Thomas Aquinas*, introduction by James P. Reilly, 19–45. Toronto, 2008.

Brady, Thomas A., Jr. "Confessionalization: The Career of a Concept." In *Confessionalization in Europe*, 1–20.

Brann, Noel L. *The Debate over the Origin of Genius during the Italian Renaissance: The Theories of Supernatural Frenzy and Natural Melancholy in Accord and in Conflict on the Threshold of the Scientific Revolution*. Leiden, 2002.

Bredekamp, Horst. "Thomas Hobbes's Visual Strategies." In *The Cambridge Companion to Hobbes's Leviathan*, 29–60.

Brennan, Brian. "The Career of Venantius Fortunatus." *Traditio* 41 (1985): 49–78.

Brett-James, Norman G. *The Growth of Stuart London*. London, 1935.

Brown, Peter. *Augustine of Hippo: A Biography*. Berkeley, 1969.

Brown, Warren C. *Violence in Medieval Europe*. Harlow, UK, 2011.

Bullough, Donald A. "Alcuin and Lay Virtue." In *Predicazione e società nel medioevo: riflessione etica, valori e modelli di comportamento = Preaching and*

Society in the Middle Ages. Ethics, Values and Social Behaviour. Atti/Proceedings of the XII Medieval Sermon Studies Symposium. Padova, 14–18 luglio 2000, edited by Laura Gaffuri and Riccardo Quinto, 71–92. Padova, 2002.

"Alcuin and the Kingdom of Heaven: Liturgy, Theology, and the Carolingian Age." In *Carolingian Renewal: Sources and Heritage,* by Donald Bullough, 161–240. Manchester, 1991.

Alcuin: Achievement and Reputation. Being Part of the Ford Lectures Delivered in Oxford in Hilary Term 1980. Leiden, 2004.

Buridant, Claude. "La phrase des chroniqueurs en moyen français: l'exemple de Monstrelet – Le Fèvre." In *Le moyen français: philologie et linguistique. Approches du texte et du discours,* edited by Bernard Combettes and Simone Monsonégo, 319–38. Paris, 1997.

Burt, Donald X. *Friendship and Society: An Introduction to Augustine's Practical Philosophy.* Grand Rapids, 1999.

Burton, Pierre-André. *Ælred de Rievaulx (1110–1167). De l'homme éclaté à l'être unifié. Essai de biographie existentielle et spirituelle.* Paris, 2010.

Buschmann, Nikolaus. "Zwischen Leidenschaft und Disziplinierung: 'Treue' als gefühlspolitischer Kampfbegriff an der neueren deutschen Geschichte." *Arcadia* 44/1 (2009): 106–20.

Butera, Giuseppe. "On Reason's Control of the Passions in Aquinas's Theory of Temperance." *Mediaeval Studies* 68 (2006): 133–60.

Byers, Sarah C. *Perception, Sensibility, and Moral Motivation in Augustine: A Stoic-Platonic Synthesis.* Cambridge, 2012.

Callus, Daniel A. "The Powers of the Soul: An Early Unpublished Text." *Recherches de Théologie ancienne et médiévale* 19 (1952): 131–70.

Cameron, Euan. *Enchanted Europe: Superstition, Reason and Religion, 1250–1750.* Oxford, 2010.

Campbell, Ted A. *The Religion of the Heart: A Study of European Religious Life in the Seventeenth and Eighteenth Centuries.* Columbia, SC, 1991.

Capp, Bernard. "'Jesus Wept' but Did the Englishman? Masculinity and Emotion in Early Modern England." *Past and Present* 224 (2014): 75–108.

Carlin, Norah. "Leveller Organization in London." *The Historical Journal* 27/4 (1984): 955–60.

Carrera, Elena. "The Spiritual Role of the Emotions in Mechthild of Magdeburg, Angela of Foligno, and Teresa of Avila." In *The Representation of Women's Emotions in Medieval and Early Modern Culture,* edited by Lisa Perfetti, 63–89. Gainesville, 2005.

Carruthers, Mary. *The Craft of Thought: Meditation, Rhetoric, and the Making of Images, 400–1200.* Cambridge, 1998.

Carvalho, M. C., J. M. Santos, G. S. Bassi, and M. L. Brandao. "Participation of NK1 Receptors of the Amygdala on the Processing of Different Types of Fear." *Neurobiology of Learning and Memory* 102 (2013): 20–27.

Casagrande, Carla. "Agostino, i medievali e il buon uso delle passioni." In *Agostino d'Ippona. Presenza e pensiero. La scoperta dell'interiorità,* edited by Alfredo Marini, 65–76. Milan, 2004.

and Silvana Vecchio. "Les théories des passions dans la culture médiévale." In *Le sujet des émotions,* 107–22.

and Silvana Vecchio. *I sette vizi capitali. Storia dei peccati nel Medioevo*. Turin, 2000.

Cazeaux, Isabelle. *French Music in the Fifteenth and Sixteenth Centuries*. New York, 1975.

Cerrato, Francesco. *Un secolo di passioni e politica. Hobbes, Descartes, Spinoza*. Rome, 2012.

Chadwick, Henry. *Augustine of Hippo: A Life*. Oxford, 2009.

Chaytor, Henry John. *Savaric de Mauléon, Baron and Troubadour*. Cambridge, 1939.

Chenu, Marie-Dominique. *Toward Understanding Saint Thomas*. Translated by A.-M. Landry and D. Hughes. Chicago, 1963.

Cheyette, Fredric L. *Ermengard of Narbonne and the World of the Troubadours*. Ithaca, NY, 2001.

Citroni Marchetti, Sandra. "'I Could Not Love Caesar More': Roman Friendship and the Beginning of the Principate." *The Classical Journal* 99 (2004): 281–299.

Clavis patristica pseudepigraphorum medii aevi, 1: *Opera homiletica, pars A (Praefatio) (Ambrosius-Augustinus)*. Edited by John J. Machielsen. Turnhout, 1990.

Clavis scriptorum latinorum medii aevi. Auctores Galliae, 735–987, vol. 2: *Alcuinus*. Edited by Marie-Hélène Jullien and Françoise Perelman. Turnhout, 1999.

Clen, Shauna L., Douglas S. Mennin, and David M. Fresco. "Emotion Regulation Strategies." In *The Wiley Handbook of Cognitive Behavioral Therapy*, edited by Stefan G. Hofmann, David J. A. Dozois, Winfried Rief, and Jasper Smits, 3 vols., 1: 85–105. Oxford, 2014.

Clore, Gerald L., and Andrew Ortony. "The Semantics of the Affective Lexicon." In *Cognitive Science Perspectives on Emotion and Motivation*, edited by Vernon Hamilton, Gordon H. Bower, and Nico H. Frijda, 367–96. Amsterdam, 1988.

Cluny. Les moines et la société au premier âge féodal. Edited by Dominique Iogna-Prat, Michel Lauwers, Florian Mazel, and Isabelle Rosé. Rennes, 2013.

Coates, Simon. "Venantius Fortunatus and the Image of Episcopal Authority in Late Antique and Early Merovingian Gaul." *English Historical Review* 115 (2000): 1109–37.

Cohen, Jeffrey Jerome. *Medieval Identity Machines*. Minneapolis, 2003.

Cole, Andrew. *Literature and Heresy in the Age of Chaucer*. Cambridge, 2008.

Coleman, Joyce. "The Text Recontextualized in Performance: Deschamps' Prelection of Machaut's *Voir Dit* to the Count of Flanders." *Viator* 31 (2000): 233–48.

Coli, Daniela. "Hobbes's Revolution." In *Politics and the Passions, 1500–1850*, edited by Victoria Kahn, Neil Saccamano, and Daniela Coli, 75–92. Princeton, 2006.

Collins, Jeffrey R. "Silencing Thomas Hobbes: The Presbyterians and *Leviathan*." In *The Cambridge Companion to Hobbes's Leviathan*, 478–500.

Como, David R. "An Unattributed Pamphlet by William Walwyn: New Light on the Prehistory of the Leveller Movement." *Huntington Library Quarterly* 59/3 (2006): 353–82.

Confessionalization in Europe, 1555–1700: Essays in Honor and Memory of Bodo Nischan. Edited by John M. Headley, Hans J. Hillerbrand, and Anthony J. Papalas. Aldershot, 2004.

Connolly, Thomas. *Mourning into Joy: Music, Raphael, and Saint Cecilia.* New Haven, 1994.

Connolly, William E. "The Complexity of Intention." *Critical Inquiry* 37 (2011): 791–98.

Consolino, Franca E. "L'eredità dei classici nella poesia del VI secolo." In *Prospettive sul tardoantico. Atti del convegno di Pavia (27–28 novembre 1997),* edited by Giancarlo Mazzoli and Fabio Gasti, 69–90. Como, 1999.

Constantinou, Stavroula. "The Gift of Friendship: Beneficial and Poisonous Friendships in the Byzantine Greek Passion of Sergius and Bacchus." In *Friendship in the Middle Ages and Early Modern Age,* 201–30.

Corbeill, Anthony. *Nature Embodied: Gesture in Ancient Rome.* Princeton, 2004.

Corner, Paul. *Popular Opinion in Totalitarian Regimes: Fascism, Nazism, Communism.* Oxford, 2009.

Corsa, Andrew James. "Thomas Hobbes' Response to the Fool: Justice and Magnanimity." *Philosophy-Dissertations,* Paper 67. Syracuse University, 2011.

Cosmides, Leda, and John Tooby. "Evolutionary Psychology: A Primer." (1997). Online at http://www.cep.ucsb.edu/primer.html.

Court and Civic Society in the Burgundian Low Countries c. 1420–1530. Edited by Andrew Brown and Graeme Small. Manchester, 2007.

Creelman, Valerie. "'Ryght worchepfull mastres': Letters of Request and Servants' Scripting of Margaret Paston's Social Self." *Parergon* 26/1 (2009): 91–114.

Cropp, Glynnis M. *Le vocabulaire courtois des troubadours de l'époque classique.* Geneva, 1975.

Cunningham, Valentine. "The Novel and the Protestant Fix: Between Melancholy and Ecstasy." In *Biblical Religion and the Novel, 1700–2000,* edited by Mark Knight and Thomas Woodman, 39–58. Aldershot, 2006.

Dales, Douglas. *Alcuin: His Life and Legacy.* Cambridge, 2012. *Alcuin: Theology and Thought.* Cambridge, 2013.

Dalrymple, Roger. "Reaction, Consolation and Redress in the Letters of the Paston Women." In *Early Modern Women's Letter Writing in England,* edited by James Daybell, 16–28. New York, 2001.

Darley, Gillian. *John Evelyn: Living for Ingenuity.* New Haven, 2006.

Daston, Lorraine, and Katharine Park. *Wonders and the Order of Nature, 1150–1750.* New York, 2001.

Davidson, Clifford. *Corpus Christi Plays at York: A Context for Religious Drama.* New York, 2013.

Davies, Brian. *Thomas Aquinas's* Summa Theologiae: *A Guide and Commentary.* Oxford, 2014.

Davis, J. C. "The Levellers and Christianity." In *Politics, Religion and the English Civil War,* edited by Brian Manning, 225–50. London, 1973. *Utopia and the Ideal Society: A Study of English Utopian Writing, 1516–1700.* Cambridge, 1981.

Davis, Norman. *The Paston Letters: A Selection in Modern Spelling.* London, 1963.

Dawson, Lesel. *Lovesickness and Gender in Early Modern English Literature.* Oxford, 2008.

"De Libero Arbitrio" di Agostino d'Ippona. Commentary by Goulven Madec, Franco De Capitani, Luca F. Tuninetti, and Ragnar Holte. Palermo, 1990.

Deane, Herbert A. *The Political and Social Ideas of St. Augustine.* New York, 1963.

Débax, Hélène. "Les comtesses de Toulouse. Notices biographiques." *Annales du Midi* 100 (1988): 215–34.

—. "Stratégies matrimoniales des comtes de Toulouse (850–1270)." *Annales du Midi* 100 (1988): 131–51.

Découper le temps. Actualité de la périodisation en histoire = Atala. Cultures et sciences humaines 17 (2014).

Déjean, Jean-Luc. *Quand chevauchaient les Comtes de Toulouse, 1050–1250.* Paris, 1979.

Denny, Margaret. "The Early Program of the Royal Society and John Evelyn." *Modern Language Quarterly* 1 (1940): 481–97.

Deusen, Nancy van. *Theology and Music at the Early University: The Case of Robert Grosseteste and Anonymous IV.* Leiden, 1995.

DeVries, Kirsten. "Episcopal Identity in Merovingian Gaul, 397–700." PhD diss., Loyola University Chicago, 2009.

Dictionnaire des Lettres françaises: Le Moyen Âge. Edited by Geneviève Hasenohr and Michel Zink. Rev. ed. Paris, 1994.

Dictionnaire du Moyen Français (1330–1500). Online at http://atilf.atilf.fr.

Diem, Albrecht. "The Rule of an 'Iro-Egyptian' Monk in Gaul: Jonas' *Vita Iohannis* and the Construction of a Monastic Identity." *Revue Mabillon,* n.s., 19 (2008): 5–50.

Dietz, Elias. "Aelred on the Capital Vices: A Unique Voice among the Cistercians." *Cistercian Studies Quarterly* 43/3 (2008): 271–93.

Dihle, Albrecht. *The Theory of Will in Classical Antiquity.* Berkeley, 1982.

Diller, George T. "The Assassination of Louis d'Orléans: The Overlooked Artistry of Enguerran de Monstrelet." *Fifteenth-Century Studies* 10 (1984): 57–68.

Dillon, Emma. *The Sense of Sound: Musical Meaning in France, 1260–1330.* Oxford, 2012.

Disciplina dell'anima, disciplina del corpo e disciplina della società tra medioevo ed età moderna. Edited by Paolo Prodi. Bologna, 1994.

Dixon, Thomas. *From Passions to Emotions: The Creation of a Secular Psychological Category.* Cambridge, 2003.

Documentary Culture and the Laity in the Early Middle Ages. Edited by Warren C. Brown, Marios Castambeys, Matthew Innes, and Adam J. Kosto. Cambridge, 2013.

Doing Emotions History. Edited by Susan J. Matt and Peter N. Stearns. Urbana, 2014.

Doudet, Estelle. "Mettre en jeu, mettre en écrit. Les Grands Rhétoriqueurs bourguignons face aux textes de théâtre." In *L'écrit et le manuscrit à la fin du Moyen Âge,* edited by Tania Van Hemelryck and Céline Van Hoorebeeck, 99–110. Turnhout, 2006.

"Un dramaturge et son public au XVe siècle: George Chastelain." *European Medieval Drama* 9 (2005): 61–86.

Douglas, Jennifer. "Kepe wysly youre wrytyngs: Margaret Paston's Fifteenth-Century Letters." *Libraries and the Cultural Record* 44/1 (2009): 29–49.

Dror, Otniel E. *Blush, Adrenaline, Excitement: Modernity and the Study of Emotions, 1860–1940.* Chicago, forthcoming.

Drost, Mark P. "Intentionality in Aquinas's Theory of Emotions." *International Philosophical Quarterly* 31/4 (1991): 449–60.

Dubreucq, Alain. "Autour du *De virtutibus et vitiis* d'Alcuin." In *Alcuin, de York à Tours. Écriture, pouvoir et réseaux dans l'Europe du haut Moyen Âge*, edited by Philippe Depreux and Bruno Judic = *Annales de Bretagne et des Pays de l'Ouest* 111–3 (2004): 249–88.

Duffin, Jacalyn. *Lovers and Livers: Disease Concepts in History.* Toronto, 2005.

Duffy, Eamon. *The Stripping of the Altars: Traditional Religion in England c. 1400–c. 1580.* New Haven, 1992.

Dumolyn, Jan, and Elodie Lecuppre-Desjardin. "Propagande et sensibilité. La fibre émotionnelle au cœur des luttes politiques et sociales dans les villes des anciens Pays-Bas bourguignons. L'exemple de la révolte brugeoise de 1436–1438." In *Emotions in the Heart of the City (14th–16th century). Les èmotions au Coeur de la ville (XIVe–XVIe siècle)*, edited by Elodie Lecuppre-Desjardin and Anne-Laure Van Bruaene, 41–62. Turnhout, 2005.

Dumont, Charles. "Pourquoi le 'Miroir de la charité' a-t-il été publié? L'identité cistercienne hier comme aujourd'hui." *Collectanea Cisterciensia* 55 (1993): 14–27.

Durham, William H. *Coevolution: Genes, Culture, and Human Diversity.* Stanford, 1991.

Dutton, Marsha L. "Aelred of Rievaulx: Abbot, Teacher, and Advisor to Kings." In *A Companion to Aelred*, chap. 1.

——— "That Peace Should Guide and Society Unite: Ælred of Rievaulx's Political Philosophy." *Cistercian Studies Quarterly* 47/3 (2012): 279–95.

——— "The Conversion and Vocation of Aelred of Rievaulx: A Historical Hypothesis." In *England in the Twelfth Century: Proceedings of the 1988 Harlaxton Symposium*, edited by Daniel Williams, 31–49. Woodbridge, Suffolk, 1990.

——— "The Sacramentality of Community in Aelred." In *A Companion to Aelred*, chap. 10.

Dzon, Mary. "Margery Kempe's Ravishment into the Childhood of Christ." *Mediaevalia* 27 (2006): 27–57.

Early Modern Autobiography: Theories, Genres, Practices. Edited by Ronald Bedford, Lloyd Davis, and Philippa Kelly. Ann Arbor, 2006.

Ebling, Horst. *Prosopographie der Amtsträger des Merowingerreiches von Chlothar II. (613) bis Karl Martell (741).* Munich, 1974.

Eklogai: Studies in Honour of Thomas Finan and Gerard Watson. Edited by Kieran McGroarty. Maynooth, 2001.

Ekman, Paul, and Wallace V. Friesen. "Constants across Cultures in the Face and Emotion." *Journal of Personality and Social Psychology* 17 (1971): 124–29.

Elias, Norbert. *The Civilizing Process: Sociogenetic and Psychogenetic Investigations.* Translated by Edmund Jephcott. Revised edition by Eric Dunning, Johan Goudsblom, and Stephen Mennell. Oxford, 2000.

Über den Prozess der Zivilisation, 2 vols. Basel, 1939.

Ellis, Deborah S. "Margery Kempe and King's Lynn." In *Margery Kempe: A Book of Essays*, edited by Sandra J. McEntire, 139–63. New York, 1992.

Emerson, Catherine. "Je Doncques: The Voice of the Author in Fifteenth-Century Historical Prologues." In *Auctoritas: Authorship and Authority*, edited by Catherine Emerson, Edward A. O'Brien, and Laurent Semichon, 21–38. Glasgow, 2001.

Olivier de La Marche and the Rhetoric of 15ᵗʰ-Century Historiography. Woodbridge, 2004.

Emotional Styles – Concepts and Challenges. Edited by Benno Gammeri = *Rethinking History: The Journal of Theory and Practice* 16 (2012).

Emotions and Health, 1200–1700. Edited by Elena Carrera. Leiden, 2013.

Epp, Verena. *Amicitia. Zur Geschichte personaler, sozialer, politischer und geistlicher Beziehungen im frühen Mittelalter.* Stuttgart, 1999.

'Espinasse, Margaret. "The Decline and Fall of Restoration Science." *Past and Present* 14 (1958): 71–89.

Eustace, Nicole. "Emotion and Political Change." In *Doing Emotions History*, 163–83.

and Eugenia Lean, Julie Livingston, Jan Plamper, William M. Reddy, and Barbara H. Rosenwein. "*AHR* Conversation: The Historical Study of Emotions." *American Historical Review* 117 (2012): 1487–1531.

Evrigenis, Ioannis D. "'Not Truth but Image Maketh Passion': Hobbes on Instigation and Appeasing," in *Passions and Subjectivity*, 165–80.

Images of Anarchy: The Rhetoric and Science in Hobbes's State of Nature. Cambridge, 2014.

Faes de Mottoni, Barbara. "*Excessus mentis, alienatio mentis*, estasi, *raptus* nel Medioevo." In *Per una storia del concetto di mente*, edited by Eugenio Canone, 167–84. Florence, 2005.

Falvy, Zoltán. "La cour d'Alphonse le Sage et la musique européenne." *Studia Musicologica Academiae Scientiarum Hungaricae* 25/1–4 (1983): 159–70.

Ferrari, Emiliano. *Montaigne. Une anthropologie des passions.* Paris, 2014.

Fiaschi, Giovanni. "'. . . partly in the passions, partly in his reason.'" In *La filosofia politica di Hobbes*, edited by G. M. Chiodi and R. Gatti, 81–107. Milan, 2009.

Fiore, Benjamin. "The Theory and Practice of Friendship in Cicero." In *Greco-Roman Perspectives on Friendship*, 59–76.

Fisher, Jeffrey. "Gerson's Mystical Theology." In *A Companion to Jean Gerson*, 205–48.

Fiske, Adele. "Aelred's of Rievaulx [*sic*] Idea of Friendship and Love." *Cîteaux* 13 (1962): 5–17, 97–132.

Floyd, Shawn D. "Aquinas on Emotion: A Response to some Recent Interpretations." *History of Philosophy Quarterly* 15/2 (1998): 161–74.

Fontes da Costa, P. "The Culture of Curiosity at the Royal Society in the First Half of the Eighteenth Century." *Notes and Records of the Royal Society of London* 56/2 (2002): 147–66.

Foronda, François. *El espanto y el miedo. Golpismo, emociones politicas y constitu-cionalismo en la Edad Media.* Madrid, 2013.

Fouquet, Gerhard. "Fürsten unter sich – Privatheit und Öffentlichkeit, Emotionalität und Zeremoniell im Medium des Briefes." In *Principes: Dynastien und Höfe im späten Mittelalter*, edited by Cordula Nolte and Karl-Heinz Spiess, 171–98. Stuttgart, 2002.

Fouracre, Paul. "Merovingian History and Merovingian Hagiography." *Past and Present* 127 (1990): 3–38.

"The Career of Ebroin, Mayor of the Palace, c. 657–680." PhD diss., University of London, 1981.

and Richard A. Gerberding. *Late Merovingian France: History and Hagiography, 640–720.* Manchester, 1996.

Foxley, Rachel. *The Levellers: Radical Political Thought in the English Revolution.* Manchester, 2013.

France, James. "The Cistercian Community." In *The Cambridge Companion to the Cistercian Order*, 80–86.

Freeman, Elizabeth. *Narratives of a New Order: Cistercian Historical Writing in England, 1150–1220.* Turnhout, 2002.

Frevert, Ute. *Emotions in History – Lost and Found.* Budapest, 2011.

Men of Honour: A Social and Cultural History of the Duel, trans. Anthony Williams. Cambridge, 1995.

Christian Bailey, Pascal Eitler, Benno Gammerl, Bettina Hitzer, Margrit Pernau, Monique Scheer, Anne Schmidt, and Nina Verheyen. *Emotional Lexicons: Continuity and Change in the Vocabulary of Feeling 1700–2000.* Oxford, 2014.

Friedeburg, Robert von. "Sozialdisziplinierung in England? Soziale Beziehungen auf dem Lande zwischen Reformation und 'Great Rebellion, 1550–1642.'" *Zeitschrift für historische Forschung* 17/4 (1990): 385–418.

Friendship in the Middle Ages and Early Modern Age: Explorations of a Fundamental Ethical Discourse. Edited by Albrecht Classen and Marilyn Sandidge. Berlin, 2010.

Friendship: A History. Edited by Barbara Caine. London, 2009.

Frijda, Nico H. "The Psychologists' Point of View." In *Handbook of Emotions*, 68–87.

Frost, Samantha. "Fear and the Illusion of Autonomy." In *New Materialisms: Ontology, Agency, and Politics*, edited by Diana Coole and Samantha Frost, 158–75. Durham, 2010.

Fulton Brown, Rachel. *From Judgment to Passion: Devotion to Christ and the Virgin Mary, 800–1200.* New York, 2002.

Fulton, Helen. "Autobiography & the Discourse of Urban Subjectivity: *The Paston Letters.*" In *Early Modern Autobiography*, 191–216.

Galeazzi, Umberto. "Le passioni secondo Tommaso d'Aquino: *De veritate*, q. 26." *Aquinas. Rivista internazionale di filosofia* 47/3 (2004): 547–70.

Gallagher, David M. "Thomas Aquinas on Self-Love as the Basis for Love of Others." *Acta philosophica* 8/1 (1999): 23–44.

Garnier, Claudia. *Amicus amicis-inimicus inimicis. Politische Freundschaft und fürstliche Netzwerke im 13. Jahrhundert.* Stuttgart, 2000.

Gaunt, Simon. "A Martyr to Love: Sacrificial Desire in the Poetry of Bernart de Ventadorn." *Journal of Medieval and Early Modern Studies* 31/3 (2001): 477–506.

Geary, Patrick J. *Phantoms of Remembrance: Memory and Oblivion at the End of the First Millennium*. Princeton, 1994.

Gellert Lyons, Bridget. *Voices of Melancholy: Studies in Literary Treatments of Melancholy in Renaissance England*. New York, 1971.

Gendron, Maria, Debi Roberson, Jacoba Marietta van der Vyver, and Lisa Feldman Barrett. "Perceptions of Emotion from Facial Expressions are not Culturally Universal: Evidence from a Remote Culture." *Emotion* 14 (2014): 251–62.

Kristen A. Lindquist, Lawrence Barsalou, and Lisa Feldman Barrett. "Emotion Words Shape Emotion Percepts." *Emotion* 12 (2012): 314–25.

Gentles, Ian. "London Levellers in the English Revolution: The Chidleys and Their Circle." *Journal of Ecclesiastical History* 29 (1978): 281–309.

George, Judith W. *Venantius Fortunatus: A Latin Poet in Merovingian Gaul*. Oxford, 1992.

Gert, Bernard. "Hobbes's Psychology." In *The Cambridge Companion to Hobbes*, edited by Tom Sorell, 157–74. Oxford, 1996.

Gertsman, Elina. "The Facial Gesture: (Mis)Reading Emotion in Gothic Art." *Journal of Medieval Religious Cultures* 36/1 (2010): 28–46.

Ghil, Eliza Miruna. *L'Age de Parage. Essai sur le poétique et le politique en Occitanie au XIIIe siècle*. New York, 1989.

Gilsdorf, Sean. *The Favor of Friends: Intercession and Aristocratic Politics in Carolingian and Ottonian Europe*. Leiden, 2014.

Glorieux, Palémon. "La vie et les oeuvres de Gerson. Essai chronologique." *Archives d'Histoire doctrinale et littéraire du Moyen Âge* 25–26 (1950–51): 149–91.

Goldgar, Anne. *Impolite Learning: Conduct and Community in the Republic of Letters, 1680–1750*. New Haven, 1995.

Goodman, Anthony. *Margery Kempe and Her World*. London, 2002.

Gowland, Angus. "Melancholy, Passions and Identity in the Renaissance." In *Passions and Subjectivity*, 75–93.

"The Problem of Early Modern Melancholy." *Past and Present* 191 (2006): 77–120.

Graver, Margaret R. *Cicero on the Emotions: Tusculan Disputations 3 and 4*. Chicago, 2002.

Stoicism and Emotion. Chicago, 2007.

Greco-Roman Perspectives on Friendship. Edited by John T. Fitzgerald. Atlanta, 1997.

Green, Ian. *Print and Protestantism in Early Modern England*. Oxford, 2000.

Greenwood, Jennifer. "Wide Externalism and the Roles of Biology and Culture in Human Emotional Development." *Emotion Review* 4 (2012): 423–31.

Grévy-Pons, Nicole, and Ezio Ornato. "Qui est l'auteur de la chronique latine de Charles VI, dite du Religieux de Saint-Denis?" *Bibliothèque de l'École des Chartes* 134 (1976): 85–102.

Greyerz, Kaspar von. *Vorsehungsglaube und Kosmologie. Studien zu englischen Selbstzeugnissen des 17. Jahrhunderts*. Göttingen, 1990.

Gross, Daniel M. *The Secret History of Emotion: From Aristotle's Rhetoric to Modern Brain Science*. Chicago, 2006.

Guay, Manuel. "Les émotions du couple princier au XVe siècle: entre usages politiques et *affectio conjugalis*." In *Politiques des émotions au Moyen Âge*, 75–92.

Guenée, Bernard. *Un roi et son historien. Vingt études sur le règne de Charles VI et la Chronique du Religieux de Saint-Denis*. Paris, 1999.

Guerreau-Jalabert, Anita. "'Aimer de fin cuer.' Le cœur dans la thématique courtoise." In *Il cuore*, 343–71.

Guida, Saverio. "L'attività poetica di Gui de Cavaillon durante la crociata albigese." *Cultura neolatina* 33 (1973): 235–71.

"L'autore della seconda parte della *Canso de la crotzada*." *Cultura neolatina* 63 (2003): 255–82.

"Per la biografia di Gui de Cavaillon e di Bertran Folco d'Avignon." *Cultura neolatina* 32 (1972): 189–210.

Gumperz, John. "The Speech Community." In *International Encyclopedia of the Social Sciences*, edited by David Sills, 381–86. Macmillan, 1968. Reprinted in *Language and Social Context: Selected Readings*, edited by Pier Paolo Giglioli, 219–31. Harmondsworth, 1972.

Haan, Bertrand, and Christian Kühner. "D'intérêt comme d'émotion. L'amitié, lien social et politique par excellence in France et an Allemagne du XIIe au XIXe siècle." 2013. Online at http://www.perspectivia.net/content/publikationen/discussions/8-2013/haan-kuehner_interet.

Halsall, Guy. "The Preface to Book V of Gregory of Tours' Histories: Its Form, Context and Significance." *English Historical Review* 122 (2007): 297–317.

Hamilton, James Jay. "Hobbes's Study and the Hardwick Library." *Journal of the History of Philosophy* 16/4 (1978): 445–53.

Hamon, Philippe. "Du Moyen Âge aux Temps modernes: une 'charnière' canonique et ses remises en cause." In *Découper le temps*, 133–45.

Handbook of Emotions. Edited by Michael Lewis, Jeannette M. Haviland-Jones, and Lisa Feldman Barrett. 3rd ed. New York, 2008.

Harding, Wendy. "Medieval Women's Unwritten Discourse on Motherhood: A Reading of Two Fifteenth-Century Texts." *Women's Studies* 21 (1992): 197–209.

Harris, Frances. *Transformations of Love: The Friendship of John Evelyn and Margaret Godolphin*. Oxford, 2002.

Haseldine, Julian P. "Monastic Friendship in Theory and in Action in the Twelfth Century." In *Friendship in the Middle Ages and Early Modern Age*, 349–94.

Hasenohr, Geneviève. "Aperçu sur la diffusion et la réception de la littérature de spiritualité en langue française au dernier siècle du Moyen Age." In *Wissensorganisierende und wissensvermittelnde Literatur im Mittelalter*, edited by Norbert R. Wolf, 57–90. Wiesbaden, 1987.

"Religious Reading amongst the Laity in France in the Fifteenth Century." In *Heresy and Literacy, 1000–1530*, edited by Peter Biller and Anne Hudson, 205–21. Cambridge, 1994.

Haskell, Ann S. "The Paston Women on Marriage in Fifteenth-Century England." *Viator* 4 (1973): 459–71.

Heyd, Michael. *"Be Sober and Reasonable": The Critique of Enthusiasm in the Seventeenth and Early Eighteenth Centuries*. Leiden, 1995.

Hill, Carole. *Women and Religion in Late Medieval Norwich*. Woodbridge, 2010.

Hinnebusch, William A. *The History of the Dominican Order*, vol. 1: *Origins and Growth to 1500*. New York, 1965.

Hirschman, Albert O. *The Passions and the Interests: Political Arguments for Capitalism before Its Triumph*. Princeton, 1977.

Historical Catalogue of Printed Editions of the English Bible, 1525–1961. Edited by T. H. Darlow and H. F. Moule, revised by A. S. Herbert. London, 1968.

Histoire de l'Église. Edited by Augustin Fliche and Victor Martin. Vol. 14.2: *L'Église au temps du grand schisme et de la crise conciliaire (1378–1419)*, edited by Etienne Delaruelle, Edmond-René Labande, and Paul Ourliac. Paris, 1962.

Hobbins, Daniel. "Gerson on Lay Devotion." In *A Companion to Jean Gerson*, 41–78.

⸻. *Authorship and Publicity Before Print: Jean Gerson and the Transformation of Late Medieval Learning*. Philadelphia, 2009.

Hochschild, Arlie Russell. *The Managed Heart: Commercialization of Human Feeling*. Berkeley, 1983.

Holte, Ragnar. "St. Augustine on Free Will (De libero arbitrio, III)." In *"De Libero Arbitrio" di Agostino d'Ippona*, 67–84.

Hoppin, Richard H. *Medieval Music*. New York, 1978.

Howard, Donald R. *The Three Temptations: Medieval Man in Search of the World*. Princeton, 1966.

Hudon, William V. "Religion and Society in Early Modern Italy – Old Questions, New Insights." *American Historical Review* 101 (1996): 783–804.

Huizinga, Johan. *Herfsttij der middeleeuwen*. Haarlem, 1919.

⸻. *The Autumn of the Middle Ages*. Translated by Rodney J. Payton and Ulrich Mammitzsch. Chicago, 1996.

Hunter, Michael. *Establishing the New Science: The Experience of the Early Royal Society*. Woodbridge, 1989.

⸻. *The Royal Society and Its Fellows 1660–1700: The Morphology of an Early Scientific Institution*. Chalfont St. Giles, 1982.

Il cuore/The Heart. Florence, 2003 = *Micrologus* 11 (2003).

In the Garden of Evil: The Vices and Culture in the Middle Ages. Edited by Richard Newhauser. Toronto, 2005.

Jablonka, Eva, and Marion J. Lamb. *Evolution in Four Dimensions: Genetic, Epigenetic, Behavioral, and Symbolic Variation in the History of Life*. Cambridge, MA, 2005.

Jackson, Stanley W. *Melancholia and Depression: From Hippocratic Times to Modern Times*. New Haven, 1986.

Jacoby, Joachim. "The Image of Pity in the Later Middle Ages: Images, Prayers and Prayer Instructions." *Studi medievali*, ser. 3ª, 46 (2005): 569–605.

Jaeger, C. Stephen. "Friendship of Mutual Perfecting in Augustine's *Confessions* and the Failure of Classical *amicitia*." In *Friendship in the Middle Ages and Early Modern Age*, 185–200.

⸻. *Ennobling Love: In Search of a Lost Sensibility*. Philadelphia, 1999.

James, Susan. *Passion and Action: The Emotions in Seventeenth-Century Philosophy.* Oxford, 1997.

Jamroziak, Emilia. *Rievaulx Abbey and Its Social Context, 1132–1300: Memory, Locality, and Networks.* Turnhout, 2005.

The Cistercian Order in Medieval Europe, 1090–1500. London, 2013.

Jensen, Frede. "Provençal 'cor' and 'cors': A Flexional Dilemma." *Romance Philology* 28 (1974): 27–31.

Jiménez-Sanchez, Pilar. *Les catharismes: modèles dissidents du christianisme médiéval, XIIe–XIIIe siècles.* Rennes, 2008.

John Evelyn and his Milieu. Edited by Frances Harris and Michael Hunter. London, 2003.

Jong, Mayke de. *The Penitential State: Authority and Atonement in the Age of Louis the Pious, 814–840.* Cambridge, 2009.

Jordan, Mark D. "Aquinas's Construction of a Moral Account of the Passions." *Freiburger Zeitschrift für Philosophie und Theologie* 33 (1986): 71–97.

"Ideals of *Scientia moralis* and the Invention of the *Summa theologiae.*" In *Aquinas's Moral Theory,* 79–97.

Jugie, Sophie. *The Mourners: Tomb Sculptures from the Court of Burgundy.* New Haven, 2010.

Jussen, Bernhard. *Spiritual Kinship as Social Practice: Godparenthood and Adoption in the Early Middle Ages.* Translated by Pamela Selwyn. Newark, 2000.

Kaeuper, Richard. "Vengeance and Mercy in Chivalric *Mentalités.*" In *Peace and Protection in the Middle Ages,* edited by T. B. Lambert and David Rollason, 168–80. Toronto, 2009.

Kang, Jee In, Kee Namkoonga, Sang Woo Yoo, Kyungun Jhunga, and Se Joo Kim. "Abnormalities of Emotional Awareness and Perception in Patients with Obsessive-Compulsive Disorder." *Journal of Affective Disorders* 141/2–3 (2012): 286–93.

Karant-Nunn, Susan C. "'Christians' Mourning and Lament Should not Be Like the Heathens': The Suppression of Religious Emotion in the Reformation." In *Confessionalization in Europe,* 107–29.

The Reformation of Feeling: Shaping the Religious Emotions in Early Modern Germany. Oxford, 2010.

Kardong, Terrence. "Justitia in the Rule of Benedict." *Studia Monastica* 24 (1982): 43–73.

Kaufman, Peter Iver. "Reconstructing the Context for Confessionalization in Late Tudor England: Perceptions of Reception, Then and Now." In *Confessionalization in Europe,* 275–87.

King, Peter. "Aquinas on the Passions." In *Aquinas's Moral Theory,* 101–32.

"Emotions." In *The Oxford Handbook of Aquinas,* edited by Brian Davies and Eleonore Stump, 209–26. Oxford, 2012.

Kleinginna, Paul R., Jr., and Anne M. Kleinginna. "A Categorized List of Emotion Definitions, with Suggestions for a Consensual Definition." *Motivation and Emotion* 5 (1981): 345–79.

Klibansky, Raymond, Erwin Panofsky, and Fritz Saxl. *Saturn and Melancholy: Studies in the History of Natural Philosophy, Religion, and Art.* London, 1964.

Knuuttila, Simo. *Emotions in Ancient and Medieval Philosophy.* Oxford, 2004.

Koebner, Richard. *Venantius Fortunatus. Seine Persönlichkeit und seine Stellung in der geistigen Kultur des Merowingerreiches.* Leipzig, 1915. Reprint, 1973.

Konstan, David. *Friendship in the Classical World.* Cambridge, 1997.

———. *Pity Transformed.* London, 2001.

———. *The Emotions of the Ancient Greeks: Studies in Aristotle and Classical Literature.* Toronto, 2006.

Krieger, Gerhard. "'Theologica perscrutatio labi debet ad inflammationem affectus.' Der Zusammenhang von mystischer Theologie und Philosophie bei Johannes Gerson." In *Scientia und ars im Hoch- und Spätmittelalter,* edited by Ingrid Craemer-Ruegenberg and Andreas Speer, 2:605–19. Berlin – New York, 1994.

Kuhn, Thomas S. *The Copernican Revolution: Planetary Astronomy in the Development of Western Thought.* Cambridge, MA, 1957.

L'enfant, son corps, son histoire. Edited by Luc Buchet. Sophia Antipolis, 1997.

La chair des émotions. Pratiques et représentations corporelles de l'affectivité au Moyen Âge = Médiévales 61 (2011).

La Rocca, Cristina. "Venanzio Fortunato e la società del VI secolo." In *Alto medioevo mediterraneo,* edited by Stefano Gasparri, 145–67. Florence, 2005.

Lahr, John. "Caught in the Act: What Drives Al Pacino?" *New Yorker,* September 15, 2014.

Lake, Peter. "The Historiography of Puritanism." In *The Cambridge Companion to Puritanism,* 346–71.

Landgraf, Artur. "Studien zur Erkenntnis des Übernatürlichen in der Frühscholastik." *Scholastik* 4 (1929): 1–37, 189–220, 352–89.

Larson, Christine L., Arielle R. Baskin-Sommers, Daniel M. Stout, Nicholas L. Balderston, John J. Curtin, Douglas H. Schultz, Kent A. Kiehl, and Joseph P. Newman. "The Interplay of Attention and Emotion: Top-Down Attention Modulates Amygdala Activation in Psychopathy." *Cognitive, Affective, & Behavioral Neuroscience* 13/4 (2013): 757–70.

Lavis, Georges. *L'expression de l'affectivité dans la poésie lyrique française du moyen âge (XIIᵉ–XIIIᵉ s.). Etude sémantique et stylistique du réseau lexical joie-dolor.* Paris, 1972.

Le Jan, Régine. "Le lien social entre Antiquité et haut Moyen Âge: l'amitié dans les collections de lettres gauloises." In *Akkulturation. Probleme einer germanisch-romanischen Kultursynthese in Spätantike und frühem Mittelalter,* edited by Dieter Hägermann, Wolfgang Haubrichs, and Jörg Jarnut, 528–46. Berlin, 2004.

———. "*Quem decet trinam observare regulam, terrorem scilicet et ordinationem atque amorem.* Entre crainte et amour du roi: les émotions politiques à l'époque carolingienne." In *Geschichtsverstellungen. Bilder, Texte und Begriffe aus dem Mittelalter. Festschrift für H.W. Goetz zu 65. Geburtstag,* edited by Steffen Patzold, Anja Rathmann-Lutz, and Volker Scior, 392–411. Cologne, 2012.

Le sujet des émotions au Moyen Âge. Edited by Piroska Nagy and Damien Boquet. Paris, 2008.

Les Passions antiques et médiévales. Théories et critiques des passions 1. Edited by Bernard Besnier, Pierre-François Moreau, and Laurence Renault. Paris, 2003.

Lessay, Franck. "Sur le traité des passions de Hobbes: commentaire du chapitre VI du *Léviathan*." *Etudes Epistémè* 1 (2002): 21–44.

Lethbridge Kingsford, Charles. *English Historical Literature in the Fifteenth Century*. Oxford, 1913.

Levenson, Robert W. "Blood, Sweat, and Fears: The Autonomic Architecture of Emotion." *Annales of the New York Academy of Sciences* 1000 (2003): 348–66.

Levy, Emil. *Petit dictionnaire provençal-français*. Heidelberg, 1909.

Lewis, Rhodri. "John Evelyn, the Early Royal Society, and Artificial Language Projection: A New Source." *Notes and Queries* 51 (2004): 31–34.

Leys, Ruth. "Affect and Intention: A Reply to William E. Connolly." *Critical Inquiry* 37 (2011): 799–805.

———. "How Did Fear Become a Scientific Object and What Kind of Object Is It?" *Representations* 110 (2010): 66–104.

———. "The Turn to Affect: A Critique." *Critical Inquiry* 37/3 (2011): 434–72.

Leyser, Conrad. "'Divine Power Flowed from this Book': Ascetic Language and Episcopal Authority in Gregory of Tours' *Life of the Fathers*." In *The World of Gregory of Tours*, edited by Kathleen Mitchell and Ian Wood, 281–94. Leiden, 2002.

Liliequist, Jonas. *A History of Emotions, 1200–1800*. London, 2012.

Lindley, Keith. *Popular Politics and Religion in Civil War London*. Aldershot, 1997.

Little, Lester K. *Religious Poverty and the Profit Economy in Medieval Europe*. Ithaca, NY, 1978.

Liu, Tai. *Puritan London: A Study of Religion and Society in the City Parishes*. Newark, 1986.

Lochrie, Karma. *Margery Kempe and Translations of the Flesh*. Philadelphia, 1991.

Loeb, Ariane. "Aimer et servir: le vocabulaire féodo-vassalique dans la poésie des troubadours." PhD diss., Université de Toulouse-Le Mirail, 1992.

———. "Les relations entre les troubadours et les comtes de Toulouse (1112–1229)." MA Thesis, Université de Toulouse-Le Mirail, 1982.

———. "Les relations entre les troubadours et les comtes de Toulouse (1112–1229)." *Annales du midi* 95 (1983): 225–59.

Loewen, Peter V. *Music in Early Franciscan Thought*. Leiden, 2013.

Lombardo, Nicholas E. *The Logic of Desire: Aquinas on Emotion*. Washington, DC, 2011.

Lottin, D. Odon. *Psychologie et morale aux XIIᵉ et XIIIᵉ siècles*, vol. 1: *Problèmes de psychologie*. Louvain, 1942.

Love in Africa. Edited by Jennifer Cole and Lynn M. Thomas. Chicago, 2009.

Lucken, Christopher. "*Chantars no pot gaire valer, si d'ins dal cor no mou lo chans*. Subjectivité et *poésie formelle* dans le *grand chant* des troubadours et des trouvères." In *Il cuore*, 373–413.

Lukac de Stier, María L. "Hobbes on the Passions and Imagination: Tradition and Modernity." *Hobbes Studies* 24 (2011): 78–90.

Lupski, James R. "Genome Mosaicism – One Human, Multiple Genomes." *Science* 341 (2013): 358–59.

Lutton, Rob. "Connections between Lollards, Townsfolk and Gentry in Tenterden in the Late Fifteenth and Early Sixteenth Centuries." In

Lollardy and the Gentry in the Later Middle Ages, edited by Margaret Aston and Colin Richmond, 199–228. Stroud, 1997.

Lollardy and Orthodox Religion in Pre-Reformation England: Reconstructing Piety. Woodbridge, 2006.

Lynch, Kathleen. *Protestant Autobiography in the Seventeenth-Century Anglophone World.* Oxford, 2012.

MacDonald, Michael. "Religion, Social Change, and Psychological Healing in England, 1600–1800." In *The Church and Healing*, edited by W. J. Sheils, 101–25. Oxford, 1982.

Mystical Bedlam: Madness, Anxiety, and Healing in Seventeenth-Century England. Cambridge, 1981.

and Terence R. Murphy. *Sleepless Souls: Suicide in Early Modern England.* Oxford, 1990.

Macé, Laurent. "Amour et fidélité: le comte de Toulouse et ses hommes (XIIᵉ– XIIIᵉ siècles)." In *Les sociétés méridionales à l'âge féodal (Espagne, Italie et sud de la France Xᵉ–XIIIᵉ s.). Hommage à Pierre Bonnassie*, edited by Hélène Débax, 299–304. Toulouse, 1999.

"La trahison soluble dans le pardon? Les comtes de Toulouse et la félonie (XIIᵉ–XIIIᵉ siècles)." In *La trahison au Moyen Âge*, edited by Mäité Billoré and Myriam Soria, 369–84. Rennes, 2010.

Les comtes de Toulouse et leur entourage. Rivalités, alliances et jeux de pouvoir, XIIᵉ– XIIIᵉ siècles. Toulouse, 2003.

Maddern, Philippa. "Honour among the Pastons: Gender and Integrity in Fifteenth-Century English Provincial Society." *Journal of Medieval History* 14 (1988): 357–71.

Madec, Goulven. "Unde malum? Le livre I du *De libero arbitrio*." In *"De Libero Arbitrio" di Agostino d'Ippona*, 11–34.

Magill, R. Jay, Jr. *Sincerity.* New York, 2012.

Mahony, Michael. "Presbyterianism in the City of London, 1645–1647." *The Historical Journal* 22/1 (1979): 93–114.

Malcolm, Noel. "Hobbes and the Royal Society." In *Perspectives on Thomas Hobbes*, edited by G. A. J. Rogers and A. Ryan, 43–66. Oxford, 1988.

"Hobbes, Thomas (1588–1679)." DNB. Oxford, 2004. Online ed., Sept. 2010, www.oxforddnb.com/view/article/13400.

"The Name and Nature of Leviathan: Political Symbolism and Biblical Exegesis." *Intellectual History Review* 17 (2007): 29–58.

Aspects of Hobbes. Oxford, 2002.

Mancia, Lauren E. "Affective Devotion and Emotional Reform at the Eleventh-Century Monastery of John of Fécamp." PhD diss., Yale University, 2013.

Mancini, Mario. *Metafora feudale. Per una storia dei trovatori.* Bologna, 1993.

Marenbon, John. *From the Circle of Alcuin to the School of Auxerre: Logic, Theology and Philosophy in the Early Middle Ages.* Cambridge, 1981.

Marix, Jeanne. *Histoire de la musique et des musiciens de la cour de Bourgogne sous le règne de Philippe le Bon (1420–1467).* Strasbourg, 1939.

Marocco Stuardi, Donatella. *Alcuino di York nella tradizione degli "Specula principis."* Milan, 1999.

Marshall, Peter. *Reformation England, 1480–1642.* London, 2003.

Religious Identities in Henry VIII's England. Aldershot, 2006.

Matsumoto, David, Dacher Keltner, Michelle N. Shiota, Maureen O'Sullivan, and Mark Frank. "Facial Expressions of Emotion." In *Handbook of Emotions*, 211–34.

Mayer Brown, Howard. *Music in the French Secular Theater, 1400–1550*. Cambridge, MA, 1963.

Mayeski, Marie Anne. "Secundum naturam: The Inheritance of Virtue in Aelred's *Genealogy of the English Kings*." *Cistercian Studies Quarterly* 37/3 (2002): 221–28.

Mazour-Matusevich, Yelena. "La Position de Jean Gerson (1363–1429) envers les femmes." *Le Moyen Age* 112/2 (2006): 337–53.

McCormick, Michael. *Eternal Victory: Triumphal Rulership in Late Antiquity, Byzantium, and the Early Medieval West*. Cambridge, 1986.

McEvoy, James. "Friendship and Mutual Deception in Book IV of the Confessions of Augustine." In *Eklogai*, 3–19.

"Les *affectus* et la mesure de la raison dans le livre III du *Miroir*." *Collectanea Cisterciensia* 55 (1993): 110–25.

McGinn, Bernard. *Thomas Aquinas's "Summa theologiae": A Biography*. Princeton, 2014.

McGuire, Brian Patrick. "Constitutions and the General Chapter." In *The Cambridge Companion to the Cistercian Order*, 87–99.

"In Search of Jean Gerson: Chronology of His Life and Works." In *A Companion to Jean Gerson*, 1–39.

Jean Gerson and the Last Medieval Reformation. University Park, PA, 2005.

McKendrick, Neil, John Brewer, and J. H. Plumb. *The Birth of a Consumer Society: The Commercialization of Eighteenth-Century England*. Bloomington, 1982.

McKitterick, Rosamond. *The Carolingians and the Written Word*. Cambridge, 1989.

McLaren, Mary-Rose. *The London Chronicles of the Fifteenth Century: A Revolution in English Writing*. Cambridge, 2002.

McLoughlin, Nancy. *Jean Gerson and Gender: Rhetoric and Politics in Fifteenth-Century France*. New York, 2015.

McMahon, Darrin M. *Happiness: A History*. New York, 2006.

and Samuel Moyn. "Ideas Still Have Consequences." *The Chronicle Review* (February 21, 2014), B10–B12.

McNamer, Sarah. *Affective Meditation and the Invention of Medieval Compassion*. Philadelphia, 2010.

Mews, Constant J. "Cicero on Friendship." In *Friendship: A History*, 65–72.

Meyer, Wilhelm. *Der Gelegenheitsdichter Venantius Fortunatus*. Berlin, 1901.

Middle English Dictionary. Online at quod.lib.umich.edu/c/cme/.

Miller, Peter N. "Nazis and Neo-Stoics: Otto Brunner and Gerhard Oestreich before and after the Second World War." *Past and Present* 176 (2002): 144–86.

Milner, Matthew. *The Senses and the English Reformation*. Farnham, 2011.

Miner, Robert. *Thomas Aquinas on the Passions: A Study of* Summa Theologiae, *1a2ae 22–48*. Cambridge, 2009.

Minet-Mahy, Virginie. "L'iconographie du cœur et de la croix dans le *Mortifiement* de René d'Anjou et les *Douze Dames de Rhétorique* de George

Chastelain. Un dialogue avec Jean Gerson." *Le Moyen Age* 113/3–4 (2007): 569–90.

Mitchell, Marea. *The Book of Margery Kempe: Scholarship, Community, and Criticism*. New York, 2005.

Miura, Ayumi. *Middle English Verbs of Emotion and Impersonal Constructions: Verb Meaning and Syntax in Diachrony*. Oxford, 2015.

Molleur, Joseph. "The Notion of the Three Sabbaths in Aelred's *Mirror of Charity*." *Cistercian Studies Quarterly* 33/2 (1998): 211–20.

Monagle, John F. "Friendship in St. Augustine's Biography: Classical Notion of Friendship." *Augustinian Studies* 2 (1971): 81–92.

Moore, Robert I. *The War on Heresy*. Cambridge, MA, 2012.

More, Ellen S. "Congregationalism and the Social Order: John Goodwin's Gathered Church, 1640–60." *Journal of Ecclesiastical History* 38/2 (1987): 210–35.

Morris, Penelope, Francesco Ricatti, and Mark Seymour. *Politica ed emozioni nella storia d'Italia dal 1848 ad oggi*. Rome, 2012.

Moshenska, Joe. "'A Sensible Touching, Feeling and Groping': Metaphor and Sensory Experience in the English Reformation." In *Passions and Subjectivity*, 183–99.

Mulchahey, M. Michèle. *"First the Bow is Bent in Study . . . ": Dominican Education before 1350*. Toronto, 1998.

Müller, Jan-Dirk. "Johan Huizinga (1872–1945) und der Herbst des Mittelalters." In *Kulturwissenschaftler des 20. Jahrhunderts. Ihr Werk im Blick auf das Europa der frühen Neuzeit*, edited by Klaus Garber with Sabine Kleymann, 263–82. Munich, 2002.

Murray, Jacqueline. "Individualism and Consensual Marriage: Some Evidence from Medieval England." In *Women, Marriage, and Family in Medieval Christendom: Essays in Memory of Michael M. Sheehan*, edited by Constance M. Rousseau and Joel T. Rosenthal, 121–51. Kalamazoo, 1998.

Nazzaro, Antonio V. "Intertestualità biblico-patristica e classica in testi poetici di Venanzio Fortunato." In *Venanzio Fortunato tra Italia e Francia*, 99–135.

Newhauser, Richard. "'These Seaven Devils': The Capital Vices on the Way to Modernity." In *Sin in Medieval and Early Modern Culture: The Tradition of the Seven Deadly Sins*, edited by Richard G. Newhauser and Susan J. Ridyard, 157–88. York, 2012.

Newman, Martha G. "Foundation and Twelfth Century." In *The Cambridge Companion to the Cistercian Order*, 25–37.

   The Boundaries of Charity: Cistercian Culture and Ecclesiastical Reform, 1098–1180. Stanford, 1996.

Nicholas, David. "In the Pit of the Burgundian Theater State: Urban Traditions and Princely Ambitions in Ghent, 1360–1420." In *City and Spectacle in Medieval Europe*, edited by Barbara A. Hanawalt and Kathryn L. Reyerson, 271–95. Minneapolis, 1994.

Niedenthal, Paula M. "Emotion Concepts." In *Handbook of Emotions*, 587–600.

Norberg, Dag. *La poésie latine rythmique du haut moyen âge*. Stockholm, 1954.

Nussbaum, Martha C. *The Therapy of Desire: Theory and Practice in Hellenistic Ethics*. Princeton, 1994.

Nuttall, Geoffrey F. *Visible Saints: The Congregational Way, 1640–1660*. Oxford, 1957.

O'Daly, Gerard. *Augustine's Philosophy of Mind*. London, 1987.

O'Donnell, James J. *Augustine: A New Biography*. New York, 2006.

O'Hara, Alexander. "The *Vita Columbani* in Merovingian Gaul." *Early Medieval Europe* 17 (2009): 126–53.

Oakley, Francis. "Gerson as Conciliarist." In *A Companion to Jean Gerson*, 179–204.

Oestreich, Gerhard. "'Police' and Prudentia civilis in the Seventeenth Century." In Oestreich, *Neostoicism*, 155–65.

——— "Strukturprobleme des europäischen Absolutismus." *Vierteljahresschrift für Sozial- und Wirtschaftsgeschichte* 55 (1968): 329–47.

——— "The Structure of the Absolute State." In Oestreich, *Neostoicism*, 258–73.

——— *Neostoicism and the Early Modern State*. Edited by Brigitta Oestreich and H. G. Koenigsberger. Translated by David McLintock. Cambridge, 1982.

Offenstadt, Nicolas. *Faire la paix au moyen âge. Discours et gestes de paix pendant la guerre de Cent Ans*. Paris, 2007.

Orgelfinger, Gail. "The Vows of the Pheasant and Late Chivalric Ritual." In *The Study of Chivalry: Resources and Approaches*, edited by Howell Chickering and Thomas H. Seiler, 611–43. Kalamazoo, 1988.

Os, Henk van. *The Art of Devotion in the Late Middle Ages in Europe, 1300–1500*. Translated by Michael Hoyle. Princeton, 1994.

Oschema, Klaus. *Freundschaft und Nähe im spätmittelalterlichen Burgund. Studien zum Spannungsfeld von Emotion und Institution*. Cologne, 2006.

Otto, Benjamin, Supriya Misra, Aditya Prasad, and Kateri McRae. "Functional Overlap of Top-Down Emotion Regulation and Generation: An fMRI Study Identifying Common Neural Substrates between Cognitive Reappraisal and Cognitively Generated Emotions." *Cognitive, Affective, & Behavioral Neuroscience* 14/3 (2014): 923–38.

Overhoff, Jürgen. *Hobbes's Theory of the Will: Ideological Reasons and Historical Circumstances*. Lanham, 2000.

Pacchi, Arrigo. "Hobbes and the Passions." *Topoi* 6 (1987): 111–19.

Paden, William D. "The Beloved Lady in Medieval Galician-Portuguese and Occitan Lyric Poetry." *La corónica: A Journal of Medieval Hispanic Languages, Literatures, and Cultures* 32/2 (2004): 69–84.

——— *An Introduction to Old Occitan*. New York, 1998.

Paganini, Gianni. "'Passionate Thought': Reason and the Passion of Curiosity in Thomas Hobbes." In *Emotional Minds: The Passions and the Limits of Pure Inquiry in Early Modern Philosophy*, edited by Sabrina Ebbersmeyer, 227–56. Berlin, 2012.

Paravicini, Werner. "The Court of the Dukes of Burgundy: A Model for Europe?" In *Princes, Patronage, and the Nobility: The Court at the Beginning of the Modern Age, c. 1450–1650*, edited by Ronald G. Asch and Adulf M. Birke, 69–102. Oxford, 1991.

Parker, Kate. "Lynn and the Making of a Mystic." In *A Companion to* The Book of Margery Kempe, 55–73.

Passion, Affekt und Leidenschaft in der frühen Neuzeit. Edited by Johann Anselm Steiger, 2 vols. Wiesbaden, 2005.

Passions and Subjectivity in Early Modern Culture. Edited by Brian Cummings and Freya Sierhuis. Burlington, VT, 2013.

Patrick, Peter L. "The Speech Community." In *The Handbook of Language Variation and Change*, edited by J. K. Chambers, Peter Trudgill, and Natalie Schilling-Estes, 573–98. Oxford, 2002.

Paviot, Jacques. "Étude préliminaire." In *Les Chevaliers de l'Ordre de la Toison d'or au XVe siècle. Notices bio-bibliographiques*, edited by Raphaël de Smedt, xv–xxxii. 2d ed. Frankfurt, 2000.

Peters, Edward. "*Vir inconstans*: Moral Theology as Palaeopsychology." In *In the Garden of Evil*, 59–73.

Pezzini, Domenico. "Aelred's Doctrine of Charity and Friendship." In *A Companion to Aelred*, chap. 9.

"Il riposo come categoria della vita spirituale. I tre sabati nello *Specchio della carità* di Aelredo di Rievaulx." *Vita consacrata* 36 (2000): 357–74.

Picoche, Jacqueline. *Le vocabulaire psychologique dans les chroniques de Froissart*, 2 vols. Paris, 1976–84.

Pietri, Luce. "Venance Fortunat, lecteur des Pères latins." In *Chartae caritatis. Études de patristique et d'antiquité tardive en hommage à Yves-Marie Duval*, edited by Benoît Gain and Pierre Jay, 127–41. Paris, 2004.

Pinker, Steven. *The Better Angels of our Nature: The Decline of Violence in History and its Causes*. New York, 2011.

Piolat, Annie, and Rachid Bannour. "Émotions et affects. Contribution de la psychologie cognitive." In *Le sujet des émotions*, 53–84.

Pohl, Nicole. "Utopianism after More: The Renaissance and Enlightenment." In *The Cambridge Companion to Utopian Literature*, edited by Gregory Claeys, 51–78. Cambridge, 2010.

Politiques des èmotions au Moyen Age. Edited by Damien Boquet and Piroska Nagy=Micrologus 34 (2010).

Posthumus Meyjes, G. H. M. *Jean Gerson – Apostle of Unity: His Church Politics and Ecclesiology*. Leiden, 1999.

Powell, Raymond A. "Margery Kempe: An Exemplar of Late Medieval English Piety." *Catholic Historical Review* 89/1 (2003): 1–23.

Pricoco, Salvatore. "Gli scritti agiografici in prosa di Venanzio Fortunato." In *Venanzio Fortunato tra Italia e Francia*, 175–93.

Raguin, Marjolaine. "Propagande politique et religieuse dans la *Chanson de la Croisade albigeoise*, texte de l'Anonyme." PhD diss., Université Montpellier III, 2011. Forthcoming.

Ratto, Franco. *Hobbes tra scienza della politica e teoria delle passioni*. New York, 2000.

Raymond, Joad. "Walker, Henry (*fl.* 1638–1660)," DNB. Oxford, 2004. Online ed. www.oxforddnb.com/view/article/40242, accessed December 6, 2014.

Raynaud, Christiane. "Le courroux et la haine dans les Chroniques de Jean Froissart." *Bulletin du C.R.I.S.I.M.A.* 2 (2001): 113–234.

Réal, Isabelle. *Vies de saints, vie de famille. Représentation et système de la parenté dans le Royaume mérovingien (481–751) d'après les sources hagiographiques*. Turnhout, 2001.

Rebenich, Stefan. "Augustine on Friendship and Orthodoxy." In *A Companion to Augustine*, 365–74.

Reddy, William M. "Against Constructionism: The Historical Ethnography of Emotion." *Current Anthropology* 38 (1997): 327–51.

The Making of Romantic Love: Longing and Sexuality in Europe, South Asia & Japan, 900–1200 CE. Chicago, 2012.

The Navigation of Feeling: A Framework for the History of Emotions. Cambridge, 2001.

Renault, Laurence. "Nature humaine et passions selon Thomas d'Aquin et Descartes." In *Les Passions antiques et médiévales,* 249–67.

Reydellet, Marc. "Tours et Poitiers. Les relations entre Grégoire et Fortunat." In *Grégoire de Tour et l'espace gaulois,* edited by Nancy Gauthier and Henri Galinié, 159–67. Tours, 1997.

"Tradition et nouveauté dans les *Carmina* de Fortunat." In *Venanzio Fortunato tra Italia e Francia,* 81–98.

Richard, Jean. "Le contexte. L'Etat bourguignon." In *Les Chroniques de Hainaut, ou, Les ambitions d'un Prince Bourguignon,* directed by Pierre Cockshaw and edited by Christiane Van den Bergen-Pantens, 9–11. Turnhout, 2000.

Richmond, Colin. "The Pastons Revisited: Marriage and the Family in Fifteenth-century England." *Bulletin of the Institute of Historical Research* 58 (1985): 25–36.

The Paston Family in the Fifteenth Century: Fastolf's Will. Cambridge, 1996.

The Paston Family in the Fifteenth Century: The First Phase. Cambridge, 1990.

Riddy, Felicity. "Text and Self in *The Book of Margery Kempe.*" In *Voices in Dialogue,* 435–53.

Rieger, Angelica. "Alamanda de Castelnau – Une *trobairitz* dans l'entourage des comtes de Toulouse?" In *Les troubadours et l'État toulousain avant la Croisade (1209). Actes du Colloque de Toulouse (9 et 10 décembre 1988),* edited by Arno Krispin, 183–92. Bordeaux, 1994.

Riehle, Wolfgang. *The Secret Within: Hermits, Recluses, and Spiritual Outsiders in Medieval England.* Translated by Charity Scott-Stokes. Ithaca, NY, 2014.

Rivera, Abelardo. "El Amor de Amistad." Extract of PhD diss., University of Navarra, 2003. Online at encuentra.com/revista/wp-content/uploads/2008/07/amistad_el_amor_de_amistad.pdf.

Robertson, D. B. *Religious Foundations of Leveller Democracy.* New York, 1951.

Roccati, G. Matteo. "La production *de canticis* de Jean Gerson: les circonstances de composition et de diffusion. À propos d'un ouvrage récent." *Le Moyen Age* 112/2 (2006): 355–61.

Rogers, G. A. J. "Hobbes and His Contemporaries." In *The Cambridge Companion to Hobbes's Leviathan,* 413–40.

Rohr, Christian. "Hagiographie als historische Quelle: Ereignisgeschichte und Wunderberichte in der Vita Columbani des Ionas von Bobbio." *Mitteilungen des Instituts für Österreichische Geschichtsforschung* 103 (1995): 229–64.

Rohrhofer, Raphaela Sophia. *Familial Discourses in* The Book of Margery Kempe: *"Blyssed be the wombe that the bar and the tetys that yaf the sowkyn."* Frankfurt am Main, 2014.

Rosenthal, Joel T. *Margaret Paston's Piety.* New York, 2010.

Rosenwein, Barbara H. "An Historian in the Amazon." In *Visions of Community: Comparative Approaches to Medieval Forms of Identity in Europe and Asia,* ed. Andre Gingrich and Christina Lutter = *History and Anthropology* 26 (2015): 76–91.

"Les communautés émotionnelles et le corps." *Médiévales* 61 (2011): 55–76.
"Love, Anger, and Empathy at the Court of the Counts of Toulouse c. 1200."
Forthcoming.
"Modernity: A Problematic Category in the History of Emotions." *History and Theory* 53 (2014): 69–78.
"Taking Pleasure in Virtues and Vices: Alcuin's Manual for Count Wido." In *The Medieval Book of Pleasure*, edited by Naama Cohen and Piroska Nagy. Turnhout, forthcoming.
"The Emotions of Exclusion and Inclusion: The Case of Gregory the Great (590–604)." Forthcoming.
"Thinking Historically about Medieval Emotions." *History Compass* 8/8 (2010): 828–42.
"Transmitting Despair by Manuscript and Print." In *Crying in the Middle Ages: Tears of History*, edited by Elina Gertsman, 249–66. Routledge, 2012.
Emotional Communities in the Early Middle Ages. Ithaca, NY, 2006.
Negotiating Space: Power, Restraint, and Privileges of Immunity in Early Medieval Europe. Ithaca, NY, 1999.
Rubin, Julius H. *Religious Melancholy and Protestant Experience in America*. New York, 1994.
Rüdiger, Jan. *Aristokraten und Poeten. Die Grammatik einer Mentalität in tolosanischen Hochmittelalter*. Berlin, 2001.
Runcie, Daniel E., Ralph T. Wiedmann, Elizabeth A. Archie, Jeanne Altmann, Gregory A. Wray, Susan C. Alberts, and Jenny Tung. "Social Environment Influences the Relationship between Genotype and Gene Expression in Wild Baboons." *Philosophical Transactions of the Royal Society B: Biological Sciences* 368/1618 (2013). Online at http://rstb.royalsocietypublishing.org.
Ryrie, Alec. *Being Protestant in Reformation Britain*. Oxford, 2013.
Sánchez Jiménez, Antonio. "Catalan and Occitan Troubadours at the Court of Alfonso VIII." *La corónica: A Journal of Medieval Hispanic Languages, Literatures, and Cultures* 32 (2004): 101–20.
Sanok, Catherine. *Her Life Historical: Exemplarity and Female Saints' Lives in Late Medieval England*. Philadelphia, 2007.
Santi, Raffaella. "*Metus* Revealed: Hobbes on Fear." *Agathos* 2 (2011): 67–80.
Scheel, Johanna. *Das altniederländische Stifterbild. Emotionsstrategien des Sehens und der Selbsterkenntnis*. Berlin, 2014.
Scheer, Monique. "Topographies of Emotion." In Frevert et al., *Emotional Lexicons*, 32–61.
Schilling, Heinz. "Confessionalization: Historical and Scholarly Perspectives of a Comparative and Interdisciplinary Paradigm." In *Confessionalization in Europe*, 21–36.
Schilling, Heinz. "Disziplinierung oder 'Selbstregulierung der Untertanen'? Ein Plädoyer für die Doppelperspektive von Makro- und Mikrohistorie bei der Erforschung der frühmodernen Kirchenzucht." *Historische Zeitschrift* 264 (1997): 675–91.
Schinkel, Andreas. *Freundschaft. Von der gemeinsamen Selbstverwirklichung zum Beziehungsmanagement. Die Verwandlungen einer sozialen Ordnung*. Fribourg-en-Brisgau, 2003.

Schlierf, Wilhelm Josef. *Adventus Domini: Geschichte und Theologie des Advents in Liturgie und Brauchtum der westlichen Kirche.* Mönchengladbach, 1988.

Schmidt, Anne. "Showing Emotions, Reading Emotions." In Frevert et al., *Emotional Lexicons,* 62–90.

Schmidt, Heinrich Richard. "Sozialdisziplinierung? Ein Plädoyer für das Ende des Etatismus in der Konfessionalisierungsforschung." *Historische Zeitschrift* 265 (1997): 639–82.

Schmitt, Jean-Claude. *La raison des gestes dans l'Occident médiéval.* Paris, 1990.

Schulze, Winfried. "Gerhard Oestreichs Begriff 'Sozialdisziplinierung in der frühen Neuzeit.'" *Zeitschrift für historische Forschung* 14 (1987): 265–302.

Schwartz, Daniel. *Aquinas on Friendship.* Oxford, 2007.

Sciuto, Italo. "Le passioni dell'anima nel pensiero di Tommaso d'Aquino." In *Anima e corpo nella cultura medievale,* edited by Carla Casagrande and Silvana Vecchio, 73–93. Florence, 1999.

"Le passioni e la tradizione monastica." *Doctor Seraphicus* 45 (1998): 5–39.

Scott Stokes, Charity. "Margery Kempe: Her Life and the Early History of Her Book." *Mystics Quarterly* 15 (1999): 3–67.

Scrutton, Anastasia. "Emotions in Augustine of Hippo and Thomas Aquinas: A Way Forward for the Im/passibility Debate?" *International Journal of Systematic Theology* 7 (2005): 169–77.

Sedlmeier, Franz. *Die laienparänetischen Schriften der Karolingerzeit. Untersuchungen zu ausgewählten Texten des Paulinus von Aquileia, Alkuins, Jonas' von Orleans, Dhuodas und Hinkmars von Reims.* Neuried, 2000.

Selwood, Dominic. *Knights of the Cloister: Templars and Hospitallers in Central-Southern Occitania c. 1100–c.1300.* Woodbridge, 1999.

Şenocak, Neslihan. *The Poor and the Perfect: The Rise of Learning in the Franciscan Order, 1209–1310.* Ithaca, NY, 2012.

Seymour, Mark. "Emotional Arenas: From Provincial Circus to National Courtroom in Late Nineteenth-Century Italy." In *Emotional Styles,* 177–97.

Shapin, Steven. *A Social History of Truth: Civility and Science in Seventeenth-Century England.* Chicago, 1994.

and Simon Schaffer. *Leviathan and the Air-Pump: Hobbes, Boyle, and the Experimental Life.* Princeton, 1985.

Sharp, Andrew. "Lilburne, John (1615?–1657)," DNB. Oxford, 2004. Online ed., Oct. 2006, www.oxforddnb.com/view/article/16654.

Shaver, Philip, Judith Schwartz, Donald Kirson, and Cary O'Connor. "Emotion Knowledge: Further Exploration of a Prototype Approach." *Journal of Personality and Social Psychology* 52/6 (1987): 1061–86.

Shaw, David Gary. "Social Selves in Medieval England: The Worshipful Ferrour and Kempe." In *Writing Medieval History,* edited by Nancy F. Partner, 3–21. London, 2005.

Sihvola, Juha, and Troels Engberg-Pedersen. *The Emotions in Hellenistic Philosophy.* Dordrecht, 1998.

Simonazzi, Mauro. "Thomas Hobbes on Melancholy." *Hobbes Studies* 19 (2006): 31–57.

Skinner, Quentin. "Thomas Hobbes and the Nature of the Early Royal Society." *The Historical Journal* 12/2 (1969): 217–39.

Hobbes and Republican Liberty. Cambridge, 2008.

Reason and Rhetoric in the Philosophy of Hobbes. Cambridge, 1996.

Skulsky, Harold. "Spenser's Despair Episode and the Theology of Doubt." *Modern Philology* 78 (1981): 227–42.

Slack, Paul. "The Politics of Consumption and England's Happiness in the Later Seventeenth Century." *English Historical Review* 122/497 (2007): 609–31.

Smagghe, Laurent. "*Sur paine d'encourir nostre indignation.* Rhétorique du courroux princier dans les Pays-Bas bourguignons à la fin du Moyen Âge." In *Politiques des émotions au Moyen Âge,* 75–92.

Les Émotions du Prince. Émotion et discours politique dans l'espace bourguignon. Paris, 2012.

Smail, Daniel L. "Neurohistory in Action: Hoarding in Human History." *Isis* 105 (2014): 110–22.

and Andrew Shryock. "History and the 'Pre.'" *American Historical Review* 118 (2013): 709–37.

Small, Graeme. "Chroniqueurs et culture historique au bas Moyen Âge." In *Valenciennes aux XIVᵉ et XVᵉ siècles. Art et Histoire,* edited by Ludovic Nys and Alain Salamagne, 271–96. Valenciennes, 1996.

"When *Indiciaires* meet *Rederijkers*: A Contribution to the History of the Burgundian 'Theatre State.'" In *Stad van koopmanschap en vrede: literatuur in Brugge tussen Middeleeuwen en Rederijkerstijd,* edited by Johan Oosterman, 133–61. Leuven, 2005.

George Chastelain and the Shaping of Valois Burgundy: Political and Historical Culture at Court in the Fifteenth Century. Woodbridge, 1997.

Smith, Julia M. H. *Province and Empire: Brittany and the Carolingians.* Cambridge, 1992.

Smith, Nigel. *Perfection Proclaimed: Language and Literature in English Radical Religion, 1640–1660.* Oxford, 1989.

Snyder, Susan. "The Left Hand of God: Despair in Medieval and Renaissance Tradition." *Studies in the Renaissance* 12 (1965): 18–59.

Somerset, Fiona. "Excitative Speech: Theories of Emotive Response from Richard Fitzralph to Margery Kempe." In *The Vernacular Spirit: Essays on Medieval Religious Literature,* edited by Renate Blumenfeld-Kosinski, Duncan Robertson, and Nancy Bradley Warren, 59–79. New York, 2002.

Feeling Like Saints. Ithaca, NY, 2014.

Sommerfeldt, John R. *Aelred of Rievaulx: On Love and Order in the World and the Church.* New York, 2006.

Aelred of Rievaulx: Pursuing Perfect Happiness. New York, 2005.

Sorabji, Richard. *Emotion and Peace of Mind: From Stoic Agitation to Christian Temptation.* Oxford, 2000.

Sot, Michel. "Concordances et discordances entre culture des élites laïques et culture des élites cléricales à l'époque carolingienne: Jonas d'Orléans et Dhuoda." In *La culture du haut moyen âge. Une question d'élites?,* edited by

François Bougard, Régine Le Jan, and Rosamond McKitterick, 341–61. Turnhout, 2009.

Spiegel, Gabrielle M. "Theory into Practice: Reading Medieval Chronicles." In *The Medieval Chronicle: Proceedings of the 1st International Conference on the Medieval Chronicle, Driebergen/Utrecht, 13–16 July 1996*, edited by Erik Kooper, 1–12. Amsterdam, 1999.

Romancing the Past: The Rise of Vernacular Prose Historiography in Thirteenth-Century France. Berkeley, 1993.

The Chronicle Tradition of Saint-Denis: A Survey. Brookline, MA, 1978.

Spierenburg, Pieter. "Social Control and History: An Introduction." In *Social Control in Europe*, vol. 1: *1500–1800*, edited by Herman Roodenburg and Pieter Spierenburg, 1–22. Columbus, 2004.

Sponsler, Claire. "Drama and Piety: Margery Kempe." In *A Companion to* The Book of Margery Kempe, 129–44.

Spronk, Rachel. "Media and the Therapeutic Ethos of Romantic Love in Middle-Class Nairobi." In *Love in Africa*, 181–203.

Squire, Aelred. *Aelred of Rievaulx: A Study.* London, 1969.

Stancato, Gianmarco. *Le concept de désir dans l'œuvre de Thomas d'Aquin. Analyse lexicographique et conceptuelle du desiderium.* Paris, 2011.

Stearns, Peter N. "Modern Patterns in Emotions History." In *Doing Emotions History*, 17–40.

Stein, Henri. *Étude biographique, littéraire et bibliographique sur Olivier de La Marche.* Brussels, 1888.

Nouveaux documents sur Olivier de La Marche et sa famille. Brussels, 1922.

Stein, Nancy L., Marc W. Hernandez, and Tom Trabasso. "Advances in Modeling Emotion and Thought: The Importance of Developmental, Online, and Multilevel Analyses." In *Handbook of Emotions*, 574–86.

Stewart, Columba. "Evagrius Ponticus and the 'Eight Generic *Logismoi*.'" In *In the Garden of Evil*, 3–34.

Strauss, Gregory P., Emily S. Kappenman, Adam J. Culbreth, Lauren T. Catalano, Bern G. Lee, and James M. Gold. "Emotion Regulation Abnormalities in Schizophrenia: Cognitive Change Strategies Fail to Decrease the Neural Response to Unpleasant Stimuli." *Schizophrenia Bulletin* 39/4 (2014): 872–83.

Straw, Carole. "Gregory, Cassian, and the Cardinal Vices." In *In the Garden of Evil*, 35–58.

Sutton, John. "Controlling the Passions: Passion, Memory, and the Moral Physiology of Self in Seventeenth-Century Neurophilosophy." In *The Soft Underbelly of Reason: The Passions in the Seventeenth Century*, edited by Stephen Gaukroger, 115–46. London, 1998.

Symes, Carol. *A Common Stage: Theater and Public Life in Medieval Arras.* Ithaca, NY, 2007.

Szarmach, Paul E. "A Preliminary Handlist of Manuscripts containing Alcuin's *Liber de virtutibus et vitiis.*" *Manuscripta* 25 (1981): 131–40.

"The Latin Tradition of Alcuin's *Liber de Virtutibus et Vitiis*, cap. xxvii–xxxv, with Special Reference to Vercelli Homily xx." *Mediaevalia* 12 (1989): 13–41.

Taylor, John. "Letters and Letter Collections in England, 1300–1420." *Nottingham Mediaeval Studies* 24 (1980): 57–70.

Testard, M. *Saint Augustin et Cicéron,* vol 1: *Cicéron dans la formation de Saint Augustin.* Paris, 1958, 59–62.

The Cambridge Companion to Hobbes's Leviathan. Edited by Patricia Springborg. Cambridge, 2007.

The Cambridge Companion to Puritanism. Edited by John Coffey and Paul C. H. Lim. Cambridge, 2008.

The Cambridge Companion to the Cistercian Order. Edited by Mette Birkedal Bruun. New York, 2013.

The Psychological Construction of Emotion. Edited by Lisa Feldman Barrett and James A. Russell. New York, 2015.

Thelliez, Cyrille. "Enguerrand de Monstrelet. Prévost de Cambrai, chroniqueur." *Mémoires de la Société d'émulation de Cambrai* 92 (1968): 9–23.

Thrower, Norman J. W. "Samuel Pepys FRS (1633–1703) and the Royal Society." *Notes and Records of the Royal Society of London* 57 (2003): 3–13.

Tilmouth, Christopher. *Passion's Triumph over Reason: A History of the Moral Imagination from Spenser to Rochester.* Oxford, 2007.

Torrell, Jean-Pierre. *Saint Thomas Aquinas,* vol. 1: *The Person and His Work.* Translated by Robert Royal. Rev. ed. Washington, DC, 2005.

Saint Thomas d'Aquin, maître spirituel. Initiation 2. Fribourg-Paris, 1996.

Treffort, Cécile. "La vie et le corps de l'enfant au VIe siècle. Perception, signification et utilisation du thème de l'enfance dans l'oeuvre de Grégoire de Tours." In *L'enfant, son corps, son histoire,* 115–27.

Truax, Jean A. "A Time for Peace: Ælred of Rievaulx and the End of the Anglo-Norman Civil War." *Cistercian Studies Quarterly* 46/2 (2011): 171–87.

Turner, Denys. *Thomas Aquinas: A Portrait.* New Haven, 2013.

Uffenheimer-Lippens, Elisabeth. "Rationalized Passion and Passionate Rationality: Thomas Aquinas on the Relation between Reason and the Passions." *The Review of Metaphysics* 56 (2003): 525–58.

Vande Zande, Daniel L. "Coercive Power and the Demise of the Star Chamber." *American Journal of Legal History* 50/3 (2008–10): 326–49.

Vatteroni, Sergio. "Le corti della Francia meridionale." In *Lo Spazio letterario del Medioevo 2. Il Medioevo volgare,* vol. 1: *La produzione del testo,* pt. 2, 353–98. Rome, 2001.

Vaughan, Richard. *John the Fearless: The Growth of Burgundian Power.* New York, 1966.

Philip the Good: The Apogee of Burgundy. New York, 1970.

Vecchio, Silvana. "Peccatum cordis." In *Il cuore,* 325–42.

Venanzio Fortunato tra Italia e Francia. Atti del Convegno Internazionale di Studi (Valdobbiadene-Treviso 1990). Treviso, 1993.

Vengeance in the Middle Ages: Emotion, Religion and Feud. Edited by Susanna A. Throop and Paul R. Hyams. Farnham, UK, 2010.

Vincent-Buffault, Anne. *Une histoire de l'amitié.* Montrouge, 2010.

Voices in Dialogue: Reading Women in the Middle Ages. Edited by Linda Olson and Kathryn Kerby-Fulton. Notre Dame, 2005.

Wack, Mary Frances. *Lovesickness in the Middle Ages: The Viaticum and Its Commentaries.* Philadelphia, 1990.

Wallace-Hadrill, John M. *The Frankish Church.* Oxford, 1983.

Wallach, Liutpold. *Alcuin and Charlemagne: Studies in Carolingian History and Literature.* Ithaca, NY, 1959.

Watkins, Owen C. *The Puritan Experience: Studies in Spiritual Autobiography.* New York, 1972.

Watson, Nicholas. "The Making of *The Book of Margery Kempe.*" In *Voices in Dialogue,* 395–434.

Weber, Dominique. *Hobbes et le désir des fous. Rationalité, prévision et politique.* Paris, 2007.

Webster, Charles. *The Great Instauration: Science, Medicine and Reform, 1626–1660.* New York, 1976.

Weisheipl, James A. *Friar Thomas d'Aquino: His Life, Thought, and Works, with Corrigenda and Addenda.* Washington, DC, 1983.

Westfall, Richard S. "Newton, Sir Isaac (1642–1727)," DNB. Oxford, 2004. Online ed., Jan. 2009, www.oxforddnb.com/view/article/20059.

Wetzel, James. "Augustine." In *The Oxford Handbook of Religion and Emotion,* edited by John Corrigan, 349–63. Oxford, 2008.

"Augustine on the Will." In *A Companion to Augustine,* 339–52.

Wharff, Jonah. "Ælred of Rievaulx on Envy and Gratitude." *Cistercian Studies Quarterly* 43/1 (2008): 1–15.

White, Carolinne. *Christian Friendship in the Fourth Century.* Cambridge, 1992.

White, Stephen D. "The Politics of Anger." In *Anger's Past,* 127–52.

Wierzbicka, Anna. *Emotions across Languages and Cultures: Diversity and Universals.* Cambridge, 1999.

Williamson, George. "The Restoration Revolt against Enthusiasm." *Studies in Philology* 30 (1933): 571–603.

Willis, Megan L. "Orbitofrontal Cortex Lesions Result in Abnormal Social Judgements to Emotional Faces." *Neuropsychologia* 48/7 (2010): 2182–87.

Wilson, Catherine. "Thomas Hobbes' *Leviathan.*" In *The Oxford Handbook of British Philosophy in the Seventeenth Century,* edited by Peter R. Anstey, 519–41. Oxford, 2013.

Wilson, Janet. "Communities of Dissent: The Secular and Ecclesiastical Communities of Margery Kempe's *Book.*" In *Medieval Women in their Communities,* edited by Diane Watt, 155–85. Toronto, 1997.

Windeatt, Barry. "1412–1534: Texts." In *The Cambridge Companion to Medieval English Mysticism,* edited by Samuel Fanous and Vincent Gillespie, 195–224. Cambridge, 2011.

Wood, Ian. "Deconstructing the Merovingian Family." In *The Construction of Communities in the Early Middle Ages: Texts, Resources and Artifacts,* edited by Richard Corradini, Max Diesenberger, and Helmut Reimitz, 149–72. Leiden, 2002.

"Family and Friendship in the West." In *The Cambridge Ancient History,* vol. 14: *Late Antiquity: Empire and Successors,* AD *425–600,* edited by Averil Cameron, Bryan Ward-Perkins, and Michael Whitby, 416–36. Cambridge, 2001.

"Jonas, the Merovingians, and Pope Honorius: *Diplomata* and the *Vita Columbani.*" In *After Rome's Fall: Narrators and Sources of Early Medieval History: Essays Presented to Walter Goffart,* edited by Alexander Callander Murray, 99–120. Toronto, 1998.

"'The Bloodfeud of the Franks': A Historiographical Legend." *Early Medieval Europe* 14 (2006): 489–504.

The Merovingian Kingdoms, 450–751. London, 1994.

Wootton, David. "Leveller democracy and the Puritan Revolution." In *The Cambridge History of Political Thought, 1450–1700*, edited by J. H. Burns with Mark Goldie, 412–42. Cambridge, 1991.

Wright, George. *Religion, Politics, and Thomas Hobbes*. Dordrecht, 2006.

Yohe, Katherine M. "Adhering to a Friend in the Spirit of Christ." *Cistercian Studies Quarterly* 33/1 (1998): 29–44.

Yule, George. *The Study of Language*. 4th ed. Cambridge, 2010.

Zink, Michel. *Froissart et le temps*. Paris, 1998.

Zuk, Marlene. *Paleofantasy: What Evolution Really Tells Us about Sex, Diet, and How We Live*. New York, 2013.

Index

acedia, 69, 230, 232n
Aclom, John, 199
Ado, 50
Ælberht, archbishop, 68
Aelred of Rievaulx, abbot, 8, 12–13, 90,
    119, 128, 141–144, 149, 151, 157,
    162, 164, 168, 193, 195, 202,
    246–247, 258, 278–279, 295, 299,
    310, 313–314, 316–317, 320
    Battle of the Standard, 113
    definition of *affectus*, 97
    Eulogy for King David of Scotland, 98, 108
    Formation of Anchoresses, 102
    Genealogy of the Kings of England,
        111–112
    life, 91–93
    On Spiritual Friendship, 94, 104–109, 160
    On the Mirror of Charity, 94, 98,
        102, 106
    three Sabbaths, 100–103, 108, 110,
        160, 316
    view on friendship, 104–108, 112–113
    view on love, 94–97, 99
    view on lust to dominate, 111–112
Aelredus. *See* Aelred of Rievaulx, abbot: *On
    Spiritual Friendship*
Æthelwulf, king, 111
affection, 18, 21, 39, 41–43, 47–48, 52, 65,
    74, 106, 113, 160, 162, 272–273, 279,
    285–286, 308; *see also* love
    expressions of, 220
affliction, 99, 259, 277, 286
Agen, 127, 128
Agnes, abbess, 41–44
Aimeric de Belenoi, 118, 137–138
    Aissi co·l pres que s'en cuia fugir, 138
    Nulls hom non pot complir adreizamen, 138
    Per Crist, s'ieu crezes Amor, 138
Albert the Great, 145
Albigensian Crusade, 115, 139, 193
Alcuin, 12–13, 66, 70, 88, 111, 119, 168,
    309, 315

emotions in writings of, 73–87, 90,
    165, 248
life and works, 67–69
On Rhetoric, 73–75
On the Virtues and Vices, 68, 71–73, 75–77
perturbationes/perturbations, 75
sequence of emotions, 168
Aldebert, archbishop, 116
Alfred the Great, king, 88, 109
Amandus, bishop, 51
Ambrose, bishop, 25, 86
Amiens, 184
anger, topic of, 69–70, 75–76, 79–80,
    129–130, 132, 149–154, 168, 234,
    317; *see also* fury, rancor
anguish, 175, 230, 259, 321; *see also* anxiety
Annegray, monastery of, 49
anxiety, 22, 28, 107–108, 230, 291, 295,
    306, 316; *see also* anguish
Aquinas, Thomas. *See* Thomas Aquinas.
Aregund, 46, 47
Aristotle, 9, 24, 144, 146, 147, 149,
    150–151, 157, 168, 178n, 232, 289,
    291, 307n
    De Anima, 147
    fourteen *pathé*, 150n
    Physics, 150
    Rhetoric, 306, 307n
    view on friendship, 21, 159
Armagnacs and Burgundians, 179, 228, 246
Arn of Salzburg, archbishop, 74
Ashley, Kathleen, 225
Aspasia, abbess, 55, 56
Athanagild, 44
Aubrac, hospital of, 128–129
Augustine, saint, 13, 16, 25, 27, 35, 37, 55,
    62, 64, 65, 70, 75, 107, 111, 151, 158,
    161, 164, 168, 260, 291, 313, 315
    City of God, 25–32, 181, 307
    Confessions, 24, 29, 99
    emotions in writings of, 25–32, 95–97,
        295–298, 307

Augustine, saint (cont.)
    On Free Will, 25–28
    On the Magnitude of the Soul, 86
    Tractatus, 29
    view on friendship, 24–25
    view on lust to dominate, 111
Austrasia, 36, 45, 46, 48–49, 57, 59
    emotional community of, 35, 45, 56, 318
Autun, 58, 62, 64–65
avarice, 69, 70, 107, 260
Avitus, bishop, 54
avoidance, 153, 233, 234, 293; see also
    desire

Bacchus, saint, 27, 106
Bacon, Francis, 308
Balthild, queen, 51, 57–58, 60–61, 65
Barontus, 61–63
Barron, Caroline, 220
Baudoald, bishop, 42–43
Baudonivia, 44
Benedict, saint, 89, 109
benevolence, 18, 21–22, 105
Bernard of Clairvaux, abbot, 89,
    94–96
Bernart de Ventadorn, 117, 119,
    130–134
    Be m'an perdut lai enves Ventadorn, 130
    Conortz, era sai, 130
Berney, John, 217, 218
Berny-Rivière, 46–47
Best, Roger, 222
Beverley, 201
Bishop's Lynn, 194, 201–202, 206, 210
Bobbio, monastery of, 49–51
Bologna, University of, 144
Bonnecombe, monastery of, 128, 142
Boquet, Damien, 98
Bosse, Abraham, 297, 303
Bourges, 177
Boyle, Robert, 285
brethele, 222
Bridget of Sweden, saint, 247
Bright, Timothie, 257–260, 271
    A Treatise of Melancholie, 257
Bruges, 170n
    church of Saint Donatian, 228
Brunham, John, 194
Brunhild, queen, 41, 43–44, 49–51, 53,
    57–58, 318, 320
Bullough, Donald, 72–73
Bunyan, John, 254, 256–257, 261, 310
    Pilgrim's Progress, 256
Burgundians. See Armagnacs and
    Burgundians

Burgundy, Duchy of, 170, 175
    as a theater state, 170
    chroniclers, 170–193, 224–225, 246,
        248, 315, 317
    court and courtiers of, 172, 317
    emotional community of, 3, 14, 168, 174,
        187–189, 193, 206, 210, 246, 248,
        314, 317
Burgundy, Merovingian kingdom, 49, 59, 64
    court of, 49
Burton, Robert, 254, 259–261, 284, 309
    The Anatomy of Melancholy, 248,
        259, 261

Cadenet, 118, 136–137
    No sai qual cosselh mi prenda, 137
    Oimais m'auretz avinen, 137
    S'ieu pogues ma voluntat, 136
Caesarius of Arles, bishop, 71
Caister, 211, 218–219, 221, 224
Calle, Richard, 215, 219–221
Calvin, 249
Cambrai, 173
Candeil, monastery of, 129, 142
Canterbury, 197
Carruthers, Mary, 242
Cassian, John, 70, 71, 76, 243
Cavendish (family), 288
Cavendish (library), 307
Cavendish, William, 307
Cerrato, Francesco, 289–291, 306, 309
Chalon, 43
Champol, monastery of, 189
Chanson de la Croisade albigeoise, 115, 118,
    139–141, 143
Charibert I, king, 35, 46
charity, topic of, 83, 89, 94–97, 99–104,
    142; see also love
Charlemagne, king and emperor, 13,
    67–68, 74, 88
Charles Martel, mayor of the palace, 67
Charles the Bold, duke, 191, 225n
Charles I of Bourbon, duke, 184
Charles I, king, 253, 275, 281, 306
Charles II, king, 282, 288, 297, 301, 303
Charles VI, king, 177, 178, 182, 183
Charter of Charity, 90, 94
Chastelain, George, 174–175, 210,
    225, 246
    Chronicle, 174
    Douze Dames de Rhétorique, 246
    emotional palette in his writings,
        187–192
    Les Epitaphes d'Hector, 191–192
    Mystère sur la paix de Péronne, 191

cheerfulness, 18, 78, 277, 310, 320; *see also* happiness, joy, merriment
Childebert I, king, 46
Childebert II, king, 43, 49
Childeric II, king, 57–58
Childley, Katherine, 274
Chilperic I, king, 35, 38, 46–47, 49
Chramnesind. *See* Sichar and Chramnesind
Christina Mirabilis, 169
Cicero, 7, 13, 16–24, 35, 37, 65, 74–75, 94–95, 113, 119n, 155, 164, 168, 173, 185, 229, 275, 306, 307n
    aegritudines/distresses, 19–20, 22, 32, 37, 60, 73, 193
    constantiae/good emotions, 18, 23, 56, 73, 315
    Laelius on Friendship, 16–17, 21, 23, 24, 27
    list of desires, 56
    On [Rhetorical] Invention, 74, 79
    perturbationes/perturbations, 17, 19, 24, 28, 75, 85, 257, 278
    Tusculan Disputations, 16–18, 20, 23–24, 32, 69, 74
    view on love and friendship, 21–22, 97, 104–105
Cîteaux, monastery of, 89
Clermont, 37
Clore, Gerald, 6–7
Clothar I, king, 35, 38, 46–47
Clothar II, king, 48–51, 54, 57
Clothar III, king, 51, 57, 60–61
Clothild, queen, 38
Clovis (pretender to throne), 58
Clovis I, king, 35, 46
Clovis II, king, 49
Cluny, monastery of, 89
Cnut, king, 111
Cologne, 145
Colthrop, Henry
    The liberties, usages, and customes of the city of London, 280
Columbanus, saint, 49, 52–53, 59, 65, 318
comfort, topic of, 261–273
compassion, 55, 79, 98, 101–102, 110, 113, 143, 199, 200–201, 207–210, 225, 230, 238–242, 246, 249, 257, 316, 317, 320; *see also* pity
    and modernity, 320
concupiscence, 152, 160, 165, 260; *see also* desire
    of the eyes, 29–30, 295

of the flesh, 29
Constance, 198
    Council of, 228
Constantinople, 44, 193
contempt, 293
Cosmides, Leda, 1
Cromwell, Oliver, 253, 270, 271, 273, 288
cupidity, 23, 95–97, 99–100, 105, 113, 128, 142, 164–165, 243, 278
curiosity, 8, 14, 30, 99, 272, 282, 285, 287, 293–295, 307, 312–313

Dado, bishop, 48, 50–51, 53–55
Dagobert I, king, 48–51, 59
Dalrymple, Roger, 215
Daubeney, John, 218
David I, king, 91–93, 98, 102–104, 108–109, 111–113, 142
Davis, Norman, 215
De imagine dei, 75
Deane, Herbert, 307
deceit, 128–130, 132–136, 138–139, 142, 201, 206, 272;
    see also treachery
de Montfort, Guy. *See* Guy de Montfort.
de Montfort, Jehan. *See* Jehan de Montfort.
de Montfort, Simon. *See* Simon de Montfort.
Denys, Agnes, 218
Denys, Thomas, 217–218
Descartes, René, 307
    Meditations, 309
    Passions of the Soul, 309
Desiderius, bishop, 48, 54, 57, 59
    emotional community of, 48
    emotions in letters from and to, 51, 53–56, 65, 314
desire, topic of, 17, 28–32, 153–154, 159–162, 293–301;
    see also curiosity
    of the eyes, 8
    to dominate, 28, 111
despair, topic of, 14, 80, 83–85, 153–154, 165, 204–206, 247–249, 254–259, 261, 265, 290, 293, 320; *see also* melancholy
Deurechildis, 52–53
Dijon, 170
distress, 17, 19–20, 69, 73–74, 193, 263; *see also* Cicero:*aegritudines*/distresses
Dixon, Thomas, 2

Doat Alaman, bailiff, 128
Drayton, 221
Duffy, Eamon, 251
Dundrennan, monastery of, 104
Durham, 91
Dynamius, *rector provinciae*, 44–45, 48
    Life of Saint Maximus, 45

Eadbert, king, 68
East Anglia, 213n, 215
Ebroin, mayor of the palace, 57–61,
    64–65
ecstasy, 102; *see also* Thomas Aquinas:
    ecstasy in
Edmund I, king, 112
Edmund II Ironside, king, 111–112
Edward IV, king, 218, 223
Egbert, archbishop, 68
Eleonor of Aragon, countess, 114, 118,
    136–138, 141
Elias, Norbert, 11–12, 249
Eligius, bishop, 48, 51, 54
Elizabeth, saint, 207
Ellis, Deborah, 201
emotional communities, 6, 8, 12–14, 16,
    34–35, 56, 64–65, 87, 90, 140, 169,
    193, 195, 220, 224, 226, 248, 258,
    287, 289, 310, 318; *see also entries for
    particular emotional communities*
    defined, 3–4, 9, 60, 314, 316
    likened to genome mosaicism, 15,
        319–321
    overlapping, 247
emotional expressions, 4, 13, 34, 53, 59,
    139, 168, 191, 203, 224, 249, 275,
    315–316, 318; *see also* tears
    and rhetoric, 9
    and vernacular, 91
    bodily, 1, 18, 98, 147–149, 158, 164,
        170, 209, 232, 293
    facial, 5
    in gestures, 4–5, 8, 100, 169, 183, 232,
        258, 315
    tamped down by Church and
        State, 250
emotional norms, 6, 44, 46, 49, 90, 117,
    143, 199–201, 210, 214, 220, 225,
    310, 312, 314, 316, 318
    for women and men, 56
emotional regimes, 11, 249, 301,
    315–317
emotional suffering, 319
emotions, 164–165; *see also entries for indi-
    vidual emotion terms and topics,*
    pre-passions, virtues and vices

affectiones, 28, 74, 97, 146
affectus, 28, 32, 97, 110
    and boilerplate, 9, 43, 72
boulésis, 31
    communicative functions of, 5
    concupiscible, 149–154, 230, 233, 260
    defined, 1–3
    irascible, 149–151, 153–154, 160, 165,
        230, 234, 260
motus, 28–32, 150–151
    of demons and devil, 30, 58–62, 64,
        69, 79
passiones, 17, 28, 70, 97, 99, 146, 234
pathé, 17, 70
    performance of, 5, 142
perturbationes, 7, 17, 24, 28, 75, 85, 97,
    299n
    political uses of, 10–11, 65, 109, 184,
        276, 315
    real vs. expressed, 5
    seat of, 23, 29, 74, 78, 98, 119n, 258
    sequences of, 8–9, 14, 270, 318,
        320–321
    theories of, 7, 13–14, 16–17, 68–71, 78,
        86, 95, 119, 146, 148, 227, 289, 292,
        309, 315
emotives, Reddy's notion of, 4
England, 4, 12, 14–15, 67–68, 88, 90, 93,
    178, 194, 200, 247–249, 251–253,
    259, 261, 271, 275, 278–279, 281,
    288, 314, 320
    Church of, 254
English civil wars
    (1135–1154), 90, 93, 111
    (1642–1651), 253, 270, 276
envy, 35, 63, 70, 79, 101, 108, 109, 128,
    142, 175, 230, 257, 260, 278
    of the devil, 61
eupatheiai, 18, 23, 31, 69; *see also* Cicero:
    constantiae/good emotions
Evagrius, 69, 307–308
    eight thoughts as pre-passions, 69–70, 167
Evelyn, Elizabeth, 286
Evelyn, John, 14, 282–283, 288–289, 310,
    318
    emotional palette in his diary,
        283–287
Evelyn, Mary, 286

Fairfax, Ferdinando, 271
Fairfax, Thomas, 273
faith, 23, 128, 130–131, 133, 139–140,
    279; *see also* fidelity
family feeling, 37, 47, 51–52, 65, 184
Fastolf, John, 211

fear, topic of, 1, 17, 32, 81–83, 151, 165, 204–207, 215–218, 237–243, 267–268, 290, 293, 304
Felix of Nola, saint, 27
Ficino, Marsilio, 248
fidelity, 88, 106, 113, 127–129, 131, 140, 144, 317; *see also* faith
first movements. *See* pre-passions
Flanders, 170
Florio, John, 307
Fortunatus, Venantius, 43–48, 52–53, 56, 59, 105, 193; *see also* Gregory of Tours, bishop
    emotions in writings of, 37–43, 97, 114, 316, 320
    life, 36–37
Fouracre, Paul, 58
Framlingham, 219
France, 4, 12–15, 67, 88, 90, 178, 183, 226, 320
    Kingdom of, 140, 179
Francia, 13, 56, 58–59, 67–68, 88
    emotional community of, 35, 317
Francis, saint, 169
Fredegund, queen, 46–47
Frederick II, emperor, 144
freedom, 101, 279–281, 318; *see also* liberty
    of choice, 31
Freeman, Elizabeth, 93
Frévent, castle of, 173
Frevert, Ute, 2, 12n, 249, 320
friendship, topic of, 13–14, 21–22, 24–25, 38–39, 42–43, 104–110, 112–113, 128, 130–132, 140–142, 159–162
Froissart, Jean, 174, 177–178
    Chroniques, 174
Fulcrand, bishop, 116
Fulton Brown, Rachel, 102
fury, 61, 64, 76, 79, 102–104; *see also* anger, rancor

Galilei, Galileo, 291, 307
Gaucelm Faidit, 117, 133–134
    D'un dotç bell plaser, 133–134
    Oimais taing que fassa parer, 133
Gaul, 35, 40, 43, 45, 48–51; *see also* Francia
Geoffrey of Poitiers, 159
George, Judith, 43
Germanus, saint, 40n, 60, 62
Germany, 11
Gerson, Jean, 14, 226, 246–248, 278–279, 293, 315, 320
    Canticordum au pélerin, 228, 240, 243
    compared to Thomas Aquinas, 229–234

Enumeratio peccatorum ab Alberto posita, 229
    life and works, 227–229
    music of the heart (*Canticordum*), 236–246
    On the Passions of the Soul, 229, 232
    theory of the emotions, 229–236
    Tractatus de canticis, 228, 238, 243
Gerson, Jean, Celestine prior (brother of Jean Gerson), 228
Gerson-lès-Barby, 227
Gert, Bernard, 289–290, 301
Gertrude, saint, 64
gluttony, 69–70, 78, 81
Godolphin, Margaret, 285–286
Gogo, 42, 45n
Goldgar, Anne, 312
Gowland, Angus, 249
Grandes Chroniques de France, 173
Grandval, monastery of, 60
Gratian. *See* Aelred of Rievaulx, abbot: *On Spiritual Friendship*
Gregory of Tours, bishop, 56, 114, 184, 193; *see also* Fortunatus, Venantius
    emotions in writings of, 37–43, 45–48, 52–53, 56, 65, 151, 316, 320
    life, 36–37
Gregory the Great, pope, 70, 76, 86, 101–102, 320
    emotions as *cogitationes*, 70
    Pastoral Care, 73
Gregory VII, pope, 89
Gresham, 211
grief, 20, 32, 42, 55, 98, 107, 120, 137–138, 139, 163, 179, 248, 255–256, 267–269, 279, 281, 293; *see also* pain, sorrow
Guido d'Arezzo, 237
Guilhem Arnaud, seneschal, 128
Guntram, king, 35, 38, 43, 46
Guy de Montfort, 139

habit, 79, 159, 164–167, 259, 301
    cognitive, 4n
happiness, 14, 38, 44, 78, 81, 83, 97, 133, 182–183, 234, 243, 280–282, 318; *see also* cheerfulness, joy, merriment
    false, 28
    familial, 100
Hardwick Hall, 307
Harvey, William, 293n, 318
hate, 83, 152–153, 157, 237, 257, 265, 293
Hellesdon, 221
Henry I, king, 111
Henry II, king, 93, 111
Henry V, king, 184

Henry VIII, king, 253
Herchenefreda, 55, 314
Hexham, 91–93
Hilary, saint, 38
Hitler, Adolf, 11
Hobbes, Thomas, 14, 153, 287, 306–309, 315, 318
  compared to Augustine, 295–298, 307
  compared to Thomas Aquinas, 298–299, 301, 308–310
  De homine, 289, 309
  emotional community of, 309–312
  endeavor in, 292, 305, 308
  Human Nature, 289, 291, 301–306
  inertia in, 153, 291–292, 308
  Leviathan, 14, 288–290, 293, 297, 301–304, 306
  life and works, 288–289
  simple, compound, and other passions, 292–295
  social effects of the emotions, 299–301
  theory of the voluntary motions, 289–292, 298–299
Hochschild, Arlie, 6, 315
  emotional labor, 315
Holy Cross, convent, 37, 41, 44
Holy Land, 131, 201
Honorius III, pope, 145
Hooke, Robert, 312
hope, topic of, 151–154, 166, 237, 293, 300, 304, 308
Hugh of Saint Victor, 233
Huizinga, Johan, 169, 181, 187, 213n, 224
human nature, 25–28, 109, 157, 159, 166, 177, 289–290, 307, 309
Hundred Years' War, 172, 174, 177, 178
Hunter, Michael, 311, 312

Illidius, saint, 38–39, 59
Indie, half sister of Raimond VI, 118n, 137
Ingund, daughter of Brunhild, 44
Ingund, queen of Clothar I, 46–47, 65
Injuriosus, 41
Innocent III, pope, 115, 145
  in the *Chanson de la Croisade albigeoise*, 139–141
Innocent V, pope, 145
Isidore of Seville, bishop, 71
  Sententiae, 78n, 81n
Italy, 42, 49, 67–68, 145, 248
Ivo. See Aelred of Rievaulx, abbot: *On Spiritual Friendship*

Jacqueline of Bavaria, countess, 183
Jacques de Guise, 181

Jaeger, C. Stephen, 43, 74
Jaques de Bourbon, king, 182, 185
Jaques de Harcourt, 184
Jean de la Huerta, 189
Jehan de Luxembourg, 173, 174
Jehan de Montfort, duke, 184
Jehan of Brabant, duke, 183
Jerusalem, 62, 198, 207
John V, duke of Brittany, 184
John Lackland, king, 280
John of Damascus, 150–151
  On the Orthodox Faith, 150
John of Réomé, 52; see also Jonas of Bobbio
John the Fearless, duke, 170, 174, 176, 178–179, 187, 189, 191n
John, duke of Bedford, 184
Jonas d'Orléans, 69n
Jonas of Bobbio, 51–53, 56, 59
  Life of Columbanus, 51
  Life of John of Réomé, 51
joy, topic of, 45–46, 53–54, 99, 100–101, 132–134, 136–137, 152–153, 181–182, 237–243, 257–258, 293, 309, 317–318; see also cheerfulness, happiness, merriment
Julian of Norwich, 201
Julius Caesar, 16, 22n
Justinian, emperor, 27

Karant-Nunn, Susan, 251
Kela, Thomas, 214
Kempe, John, 194
Kempe, Margery, 14, 168, 170, 209–210, 215–217, 223, 224–226, 246–247, 248, 258, 273, 320
  accused of Lollardy, 194, 197–198, 201
  Book of Margery Kempe, 194–195, 213
  emotional communities and norms in the *Book*, 195–202, 210, 317–318
  emotional sequences in the *Book*, 203–210, 255, 268–270
  life, 193–194
Kendale, John, 199
King, Peter, 163
King's Lynn, 194
kisses, 42, 53, 74, 98, 103, 106, 109, 128, 131–132, 135, 202

La Marche, Olivier de, 174–175, 187, 191, 225, 317
  emotional palette in his *Mémoires*, 192–193
  Mémoires, 175
La Rouquette, fortification of, 129
Laelius. See Cicero: *Laelius on Friendship*
Lancelot of Naples, king, 184

Laud, William, archbishop, 253
Le Jan, Régine, 49
Le Mans, 178
Lefèvre, Jean de Saint-Rémy, 174, 192, 225
    Chronique, 174
    emotional palette in his *Chronique*, 187–190
Lefevre, Sylvie, 191
Lérins, monastery of, 45, 52
Lessay, Franck, 298, 304
Leudegar, bishop, 58, 60–62, 64–65, 67
    Martyrdom of, 60–62, 64
Levellers, 14, 274–276, 278, 281, 318
    emotional community of, 275
Leviathan, biblical monster, 300–301;
    see also Hobbes, Thomas: *Leviathan*
liberty, 279–281; see also freedom
    emotional, 319
    of choice, 298
    of faith, 277
Life of Desiderius, 52n, 54–55; see also
    Desiderius, bishop
Life of Germanus, 60; see also Germanus,
    saint
Life of Saint Gertrude, 61, 64
Life of Simeon Stylites, 53
Life of Wandregisel, 61, 63–64; see also
    Wandregisel, saint
Lilburne, John, 274–277, 279–281
    A Worke of the Beast, 277
    Englands Birth-right Justified, 276
Lille, 170, 192–193
Lincoln, 206
Lipsius, Justus, 307
Loeb, Ariane, 117
London, 14, 198, 206, 223, 263, 266, 274,
    277, 280, 282, 307
    Exeter House, 283
    Somerset House, 273
    Tower of, 281
    Whitehall, 272
Louis of Orléans, duke, 176, 178–179, 187,
    228
Louis XIV, king, 288
love, topic of, 13–14, 20–22, 29, 32, 41–48,
    52–54, 62–64, 74–78, 89–90, 94–101,
    103–104, 107, 113–114, 127–138,
    141–143, 153–155, 157–162, 168,
    183–185, 202–210, 218–220,
    233–234, 237–239, 246, 257,
    267–268, 293, 314–317, 320
Low Countries, 172
Lupski, James R., 319–320
Lupus, 42
lust, 69–70, 95, 107, 204, 260, 295
    to dominate, 30, 100, 111–112

Luxeuil, monastery of, 49, 58, 62, 64–65
Lyon, 228, 236
    Celestine monastery at, 228

Macé, Laurent, 116, 127–128
Machiavelli, Niccolò, 306–308
Maddern, Philippa, 220
Malcolm, Noel, 310–311
Malcolm IV, king, 104
Malmesbury, 288–289
Margaret of Bavaria, duchess, 189
Marie d'Oignies, 169, 202
Marseilles, 54
Martin, saint, 38
    monastery of, 68, 77
Maximus, bishop, 45
McGuire, Brian, 227
McNamer, Sarah, 102
Meaux-en-Brie, 177
melancholy, topic of, 248–249, 253–261,
    284, 309, 318–319; see also despair
memory, 75, 81, 95; see also remembrance
merriment, 197n, 257, 269, 277,
    287, 317; see also cheerfulness,
    happiness, joy
Mersenne, Marin, 311
Metz, 36n, 43, 113
Milan, 25
Minet-Mahy, Virginie, 246
Monstrelet, Enguerrand de, 173–174,
    193, 246
    Chronicle, 173–174
    emotional palette in his *Chronicle*, 175–183
    view on love, 183–187
Montaigne, Michel Eyquem de
    Essais, 307
Monte Cassino, monastery of, 144
Montereau, 187–189
Montpellier, University of, 144
Mountagu, Edward, earl, 282, 286
Muret, Battle of (1213), 115

Na Vierna, 120n, 131, 132n
Naples, 144–145, 185
    University of, 144
Neustria, 48–49, 57, 59, 65, 67
    emotional community of, 35, 43, 48–51,
    53, 56, 226, 314, 316, 318
New Devout, 169
Newcastle, 200
Newton, Isaac, 312
Nicetius, bishop, 37
Norfolk, 194, 211
    bishop of, 221
    dukes of, 211, 218

Northumbria, Kingdom of, 68
Norwich, 209

Olivier de Penthièvre, count, 184
Ortony, Andrew, 6–7
Overton, Richard, 274–277, 281
Oxford, 288
　Christ Church, 254
　University of, 144

Pacino, Al, 5
pain, topic of, 17–20, 32, 136–139,
　230–233, 246, 293; see also distress,
　grief, sorrow
Pampyng, John, 217
Paris, 46, 154–155, 161, 179–182,
　227–229, 282, 288, 301
　College of Navarre, 227
　convent of Minim friars, 311
　Notre Dame cathedral, 228
　Saint-Jacques, convent of, 145
　University of, 144–146, 228
　Vanves, 282
Paston, Agnes (née Berry), 222, 223
Paston, Clement, 210–211
Paston, Clement II, 223
Paston, Elizabeth, 223
Paston, John I, 211, 214–215, 217–219,
　223
Paston, John II, 3, 218–221,
　223–225, 314
Paston, John III, 214, 219, 220–221
Paston, Margaret (née Mautby), 217–223
Paston, Margery, 219, 221–223
Paston, Margery (née Brews), 213–214,
　219–220
Paston, William I, 211
Pastons (family), 14, 168, 193, 252, 269,
　283, 315, 317
　emotional community of, 210–226, 247
Paulinus of Nola, 27
Pedro of Aragon, 140
Peire Vidal, 117, 119, 120, 125, 131–134
　Ajostar e lassar, 131
　Son ben apoderatz, 132
　Tant ai lonjamen sercat, 132
　Tant me platz, 131
penance, 73, 80, 83–85
Pepys, Samuel, 14, 282–283, 310, 314, 318
　emotional palette in his diary, 283–287
　Memoires Relating to the State of the Royal
　　Navy, 283
Péronne, Treaty of (1468), 191
Peters, Edward, 70
　palaeopsychology, 71, 90

Petty, William, 312
Philip the Bold, duke, 170, 228
Philip the Good, duke, 170–174, 179, 181,
　183–184, 189–190, 191n, 192, 210
　Order of the Golden Fleece
　　(Toison d'Or), 172, 174
Picardy, 173
Picoche, Jacqueline, 178
Pierre d'Ailly, 227
Pintoin, Michel
　Chronique du religieux de Saint-Denys, 173
Pippin II, mayor of the palace, 59, 67
Pippin III, king, 67
Pisa, Council of, 228–229
pity, 132, 139–140, 168, 178, 181, 185,
　190, 193, 207–210, 218, 232, 237,
　243–246, 248, 257, 317, 320; see also
　compassion
Plamper, Jan, 319
Plato, 149
pleasure, topic of, 17, 153–155, 293
Poitiers, 37
Powell, Vavasor, 263
pre-passions, 18, 32, 69–70, 148, 308
pride, 28, 61, 69–70, 111–112, 130,
　136, 265
　of life, 29–30, 99
Prince, Thomas, 274–275, 281
Probianus, 38–39
Prometheus, 306
propathé. See pre-passions
Prudentius, 70
　Psychomachia, 70
Pseudo-Augustine, 72
Pseudo-Dionysius, 161, 229, 233–234

Quintilian, 306

Radegund, saint, 41, 44, 46
Rado, 50
Raguin, Marjolaine, 139
Raimon de Miraval, 118, 134–136
　Be m'agrada, 135
　Chansoneta farai, Vencut, 134
　Dels quatre mestiers valens, 135
　Enquer non a guaire, 135
　S'a dreg fos chantars grazitz, 135
Raimond Aerradus, 129
Raimond de Mauguio, 129
Raimond de Roquefeuil, 140
Raimond Roger, count, 139–140
Raimond V, count, 114–116, 128n, 130,
　132–134
Raimond VI, count, 114–115, 127–129,
　134, 136–137, 139, 145

Raimond VII, count, 114, 115, 118, 139–140, 144
Raimondet. *See* Raimond VII, count
rancor, 13, 80, 83, 104, 175, 317; *see also* anger, fury
Ravenna, 36
reason, topic of, 29, 74, 97–99, 109–110, 162–164, 166–167, 290–291, 298–299
seat of, 74, 164
Reddy, William, 4, 10, 129n, 141n, 249, 315, 319–320
Reims, 36n, 227
remembrance, 292; *see also* memory
Repingdon, Philip, bishop, 206
revenge, 76, 104, 110, 129n, 151, 168, 257, 286
Revesby, monastery of, 93
Reydellet, Marc, 37
Richmond, Colin, 215
Rievaulx, monastery of, 12, 90–94, 103–104, 109–110, 113–114, 141–142, 183, 275, 314
Robert de Bruce, 113
Robert of Molesme, abbot, 89
Roccasecca, castle of, 144
Roger Bernard II, count, 118n, 139
Rogers, G. A. J., 289
Rogers, Timothy
    A Discourse Concerning Trouble of Mind and the Disease of Melancholly, 261
Rokewode, William, 217
Rome, 17, 25, 35, 132, 144, 200, 253
Church of, 265
Sack of, 25
Royal Society, 283
emotional community of, 310–312
Rusticus, 54–56
Ruston, 218
Ryrie, Alec, 251

sadness, 63, 70, 79–80, 83–85, 101, 108, 125, 168, 175–177, 230, 232, 258, 271, 286
Saint Catherine, monastery, 27
Saint-Denis, monastery of, 58
Salerno, University of, 144
Sallustius, bishop, 55
Sarpi, Paolo, 307
Schilling, Heinz, 250
Sergius saint, 27, 106
Seymour, Mark, 319
emotional arenas, 4, 314
Shakespeare, William, 211, 254
shame, 132, 175, 198, 201, 202–205, 215, 220–221, 257, 277, 304

Shaw, John, 284
Shipley, Edward, 286
Sichar and Chramnesind, 38–39, 42, 65
Sicily, Kingdom of, 144
Sigibert I, king, 35–38, 41, 43, 46, 320
Sigibert III, king, 49
Simeon, saint, 53
Simon de Montfort, 115, 139
Simon, Aelred's monastic friend, 98, 107
sin, 28, 30, 70, 80, 165, 204, 246, 256, 264–265, 272, 301
original, 28, 95, 163, 167
sincerity, 6, 65, 80, 85–86, 281, 285
Skinner, Quentin, 311–312
Sorbière, Samuel, 310
sorrow, topic of, 54–56, 63–64, 155, 176–177, 189–190, 193, 230, 232, 237–239, 243, 248–249, 258–259, 286–287, 317; *see also* distress, grief, pain
Sot, Michel, 69
speech communities, 3
Spenser, Edmund, 254, 310
emotional sequence in his oeuvre, 255
The Faerie Queene, 254–255
Spiegel, Gabrielle, 172
Spirituall Experiences, 262–270, 274, 277, 318; *see also* Walker, Henry
spontaneity, 97–98, 283
Sporle, 220
Stearns, Peter, 319–320
Stephen of Blois, king, 111
Suffolk, 211
Suso, Henry, 202
sweetness, 42, 43n, 83, 95, 97, 101, 107, 109–110, 112, 200
Syagrius, 54, 56
Symes, Carol, 193, 245

tears, topic of, 39–42, 55–56, 63, 98–99, 155, 200–201, 207, 246–247, 258, 271, 315–317, 321; *see also* emotional expressions
Theudebert II, king, 49, 57
Theuderic II, king, 49
Theuderic III, king, 57–58, 61
Thomas Aquinas, 7, 13–14, 143, 167–169, 185, 193, 227, 229–234, 260, 291, 293, 298–299, 301, 307n, 308–310, 313, 315
affections, 146, 149, 151, 161
ecstasy in, 160–162
indwelling in, 160–161
life and works, 144–146

Thomas Aquinas (cont.)
  passions of the soul, 146–152
  sequence of the passions, 152–155
  Summa theologiae, 146, 159, 307
  union in, 160–161
  view on friendship, 159–160
  view on love, 157–162, 183–184
  virtues and vices, 162–167
Thucydides, 306, 307n
Tooby, John, 1
Toulouse, 117, 139, 183
  court and courtiers of, 13, 113–114, 125,
    130, 132, 141–142, 155, 185–187,
    193, 278, 314, 317
  Raimondin counts of, 13, 90, 114,
    116–117, 130, 142, 168
Tournai, 183
tranquility, 14, 69, 100, 281, 318
treachery, 14, 108, 112–113, 130, 135, 141,
    317; *see also* deceit
troubadours, 13, 114, 116–117, 139,
    141–142, 155, 168, 185, 187, 317,
    320; *see also single entries for troubadours*
  emotions in poems of, 119–125
Tyl-Labory, Gillette, 191

Ultrogotha, queen, 46

vainglory (or vanity), 69, 70, 83, 167
Valenciennes, 177
Vilicus, bishop, 45
virtues and vices, 13–14, 66, 68–70, 74, 76,
    83, 86, 90, 96, 307, 315, 316; *see also*
    emotions
Vision of Barontus, 61, 64; *see also* Barontus

Waléran of Saint-Pol, count, 177
Walker, Henry, 263, 270–275, 276, 281,
    310, 315, 319; *see also Spirituall*
    Experiences

Perfect Occurrences (newspaper), 270
Walsham, Jane, 218
Walter Daniel, 91, 94, 98–99, 102–104,
    108–111, 113, 141–143
  as interlocutor in Aelred's *On Spiritual*
    Friendship, 94, 105, 107–108
  Centum sententiae, 99n
  Lamentatio, 98
  Letter to Maurice, 103, 110n
  Life of Aelred, 99, 103
Walter Espec, 91, 142
Walwyn, William, 274–281
  Englands Lamentable Slaverie, 276, 278
  Strong Motives, 276
Wandregisel, saint, 61, 63, 98n
Wars of the Roses, 193, 211, 252
Watkins, Owen C., 263
Wauquelin, Jehan, *Chronicles of Hainaut*,
    181
Wetzel, James, 31
Wido, count, 68, 69, 71, 72–75, 83–86, 88,
    168
will, topic of, 31–32, 70, 95, 158, 162–164,
    167, 298
William of Normandy, duke, 88
William of Tudela, 118n, 139; *see also*
    Chanson de la Croisade albigeoise
Willis, Thomas
  Two Discourse Concerning the Soul of
    Brutes, 261
Wood, Ian, 57
Wykes, John, 218

York, 68, 199
  cathedral of, 68
Yorkshire, 91, 199

Zemp, Josef, 136
Zink, Michel, 177
Zuk, Marlene, 2